On Biblical Poetry

ON BIBLICAL POETRY

F. W. DOBBS-ALLSOPP

OXFORD

UNIVERSITY PRESS

OXFORD

UNIVERSITY PRESS

Oxford University Press is a department of the
University of Oxford. It furthers the University's objective
of excellence in research, scholarship, and education
by publishing worldwide.

Oxford   New York

Auckland   Cape Town   Dar es Salaam   Hong Kong   Karachi
Kuala Lumpur   Madrid   Melbourne   Mexico City   Nairobi
New Delhi   Shanghai   Taipei   Toronto

With offices in

Argentina   Austria   Brazil   Chile   Czech Republic   France   Greece
Guatemala   Hungary   Italy   Japan   Poland   Portugal   Singapore
South Korea   Switzerland   Thailand   Turkey   Ukraine   Vietnam

Oxford is a registered trade mark of Oxford University Press
in the UK and certain other countries.

Published in the United States of America by
Oxford University Press
198 Madison Avenue, New York, NY 10016

© Oxford University Press 2015

Library of Congress Cataloging-in-Publication Data
Dobbs-Allsopp, F. W., 1962- author.
On biblical poetry / F. W. Dobbs-Allsopp.
pages   cm
Includes bibliographical references and index.
ISBN 978-0-19-976690-1 (cloth : alk. paper)
1. Hebrew poetry, Biblical—History and criticism.   2. Bible. Old Testament—
Language, style.   3. Bible. Old Testament—Criticism, interpretation, etc.   I. Title.
BS1405.52.D63   2015
221.6'6—dc23   2014041658

3 5 7 9 8 6 4 2
Printed in the United States of America
on acid-free paper

for Les, Will, and Henry

*the Hebrew Poems are written
in Verse, properly so called*
—ROBERT LOWTH,
Isaiah. A New Translation (1778)

Contents

Acknowledgments

THIS BOOK HAS evolved over a prolonged period of time and has benefited immensely from the shared insights of many, many colleagues. I do not dare try to list them all here, yet I do salute them all. I am grateful for the contributions and the book as a whole is a far better piece of scholarship because of them. I want to acknowledge my debt to faculty and student colleagues at Princeton Seminary (my home institution now for fifteen years), who have patiently (and cheerfully) indulged my long-term preoccupation with biblical poetry and to the Seminary more generally for providing me with a most congenial environment to pursue my teaching and research. The Northeast Corridor (from D.C., Baltimore, and Philly to New Haven) now boasts a wealth of talented Hebrew Bible scholars, and one of my great joys over the years has been participating in this region's larger scholarly discourse, fostered above all by the annual meetings of the MARSBL and especially by the monthly gatherings of the Columbia Hebrew Bible seminar and of Princeton's own burgeoning Old Testament Research Colloquium. This is a wonderfully vibrant place to study the Hebrew Bible these days. It has also been my privilege to have some very loyal and close conversation partners on this project in particular whose contributions I gladly recognize. These include Simi Chavel, Alan Cooper, Blake Couey, Ed Greenstein, Elaine James, Tod Linafelt, Paul Kurtz, Michael O'Connor (whose loss I continue to mourn), Dan Pioske, Seth Sanders, Leong Seow, and Sarah Zhang. My thanks to each of these individuals, for the intelligence and keenness of their insight and advice, for the generosity with which they have shared their ideas and knowledge, and for the camaraderie and friendships that have grown out of our collaborations. A special thanks, as well, to Marilyn Lundberg and Bruce Zuckerman for their help with images (as usual)—indeed, for teaching me the value of the image in the first place. Thanks also to Cynthia Read and her team at Oxford University Press (including especially Alyssa Bender, Gwen Colvin, Glenn Ramirez, and Martha Ramsey, who expertly copyedited the manuscript, improving it immensely) for turning my ungainly manuscript into a very smart and beautiful book. A shout-out to the "Poker Group" for keeping me sane all these years and to my Spinnaker Point neighbors for giving me and Les (and sometimes the boys, too) a home during the summer and for watching out over our Oriental, N.C., home (and the *Bouchon!*) during the rest of the year. And lastly, thanks and love to my best friend and my life's partner, Leslie, and my two sons, Will and Henry. Happily, I've spent most of my adult life in the company of these three wonderful people. I can't imagine life without them.

Some material from my "The Poetry of the Psalms," in *The Oxford Handbook of the Psalms* (ed. W. Brown; Oxford: Oxford University Press, 2014) gets sprinkled throughout, especially in chapters 1 and 4. Portions of these same two chapters represent slightly reworked sections from "Space, Line, and the Written Biblical Poem in Texts from the Judean Desert," in *Puzzling Out the Past: Studies in Northwest Semitic Languages and Literatures in Honor of Bruce Zuckerman* (ed. M. Lundberg et al.; Leiden: Brill, 2012), 19–61. At several points I draw on material initially published as "Acrostic," in *The Encyclopedia of the Bible and Its Reception* (ed. H.-J. Klauck et al.; Berlin: de Gruyter, 2009). Chapter 5 represents a somewhat longer and refocused version of "Psalm 133: A (Close) Reading," *Journal of Hebrew Scriptures* 8 (2008) (http://www.jhsonline .org/jhs-article.html, article_97.pdf). And chapter 3 draws on, significantly reworks, and broadens the scope of "The Psalms and Lyric Verse," in *The Evolution of Rationality: Interdisciplinary Essays in Honor of J. Wentzel van Huyssteen* (ed. F. L. Shults; Grand Rapids: Eerdmans. 2006), 346–79. Many of the ideas elaborated here were first aired in presentations, lectures, seminars, and colloquium discussions through the years at: SBL, MARSBL, the Columbia Hebrew Bible seminar, the Old Testament Research Colloquium at Princeton Theological Seminary, the Biblical Colloquium, Emory University, and the University of Chicago. I am grateful to all the rights holders for granting me the necessary permissions to reuse these materials and for the various entities and organizations that supported my initial thinking on topics treated in this volume.

F. W. D.-A.
March 2015

Abbreviations

Abbreviations are according to *The SBL Handbook of Style: For Biblical Studies and Related Disciplines* (2d ed.; ed. B. J. Collins et al.; Atlanta: SBL Press, 2014) and/or *The Assyrian Dictionary* (Chicago: University of Chicago Press, 1956–), unless otherwise noted. Abbreviations for extrabiblical Hebrew inscriptions follow F. W. Dobbs-Allsopp et al., eds., *Hebrew Inscriptions: Texts from the Biblical Period of the Monarchy with Concordance* (New Haven: Yale University Press, 2005).

√	root
LBH	late biblical Hebrew
N	noun
NP	noun phrase
NPEPP	Alex Preminger and T. V. F. Brogan, eds. *The New Princeton Encyclopedia of Poetry and Poetics.* Princeton: Princeton University Press, 1993.
O	object
P	preposition
PEPP	Stephen Cushman, et al., eds. *The Princeton Encyclopedia of Poetry and Poetics.* Princeton: Princeton University Press, 2012. (Kindle ed.)
PP	prepositional phrase
S	subject
SBH	standard biblical Hebrew (sometimes also referenced as classical bible Hebrew)
V	verb
VP	verb phrase

List of Figures

On Biblical Poetry

Introduction

BIBLICAL POETRY BEYOND PARALLELISM

there are other indications of Verse in the
Poetical and Prophetical parts of the
Hebrew Scriptures
—R. LOWTH, *Isaiah. A New Translation* (1778)

SIR ROBERT LOWTH is remembered among biblicists best for his diagnosis of
what he called *parallelismus membrorum*—"the poetical conformation of the
sentences consists chiefly in a certain equality, resemblance, or parallelism
between the members of each period; so that in two lines (or members of the
same period), things for the most part shall answer to things, and words to
words, as if fitted to each by a kind of rule or measure"—in that now famous
Lecture XIX from his *De Sacra Poesi Hebraeorum Praelectiones Academicae
Oxonii Habitae*, which he delivered as Professor of Poetry at Oxford between
1741 and 1751.[1] Indeed, parallelism remains to this day the best known and
best understood feature of biblical Hebrew verse. However, biblical poetry is
not reducible to its best known feature, and this even on Lowth's own analysis.
The topic is treated belatedly and substantively in only a single lecture (XIX)
in Lowth's original statement—the *Praelectiones* (thirty-four lectures in total),
which surveys all facets of biblical poetry as understood by Lowth. And the
mature Lowth, though very much taken with his own analysis of parallelism
("I the more readily embrace the present opportunity of resuming this subject, as what I have formerly written upon it seems to have met with the appro-
bation of the learned"),[2] was well aware, nonetheless, of the surpassing nature
of biblical Hebrew poetry beyond "the correspondence of one Verse, or Line,
with another," which he called "Parallelism," as he remarks in the *Preliminary
Dissertation*: "there are other indications of Verse in the Poetical and Prophetical parts of the Hebrew Scriptures."[3]

Biblical Hebrew poetry, in many respects, is a construction of Lowth, his lectures, and their reception over the last two and half centuries. This book is self-consciously fashioned as an exercise in the literary criticism Lowth inaugurated and, in particular, means to reclaim the broader purview of the Lowthian pose, to conceive biblical poetry again beyond the idea of a defining parallelism. This is pursued piecemeal and thus gesturally through a series of five essays on selected facets of biblical verse other than parallelism (though the latter comes in for comment throughout). My temperament, unlike Lowth's, hews decidedly more toward focused, deep soundings of singular topics. The general approach of the book is guided, moreover, by two central Lowthian dispositions: on the one hand to think of biblical poetry as just another verse tradition, and thus to read and interpret biblical poems like other poems, with the same critical tools and the same kinds of guiding assumptions in place; and on the other hand to recognize that what distinguishes the verse of the Bible is its historicity and cultural specificity, those peculiar encrustations and encumbrances that typify all human artifacts. Lowth was a decidedly literary man. His appointment was as Professor of Poetry at Oxford. He wrote his own poetry, was foundational for the birth of Romanticism, and published one of the first modern grammars of the English language.[4] For Lowth and his eighteenth-century compatriots, the poetry of the Bible was thought to be the oldest known corpus of poetry in the world and thus a natural topic to be investigated by the Professor of Poetry at Oxford. His literary sensibilities and orientation have long been recognized—and continue to wear well. Less appreciated has been Lowth's insistence on the necessity of the historical imagination and his call to historicize: "we must see all things with their eyes, estimate all things by their opinions; we must endeavour as much as possible to read Hebrew as the Hebrews would have read it."[5] To be sure, there were precursors to Lowth who shared this historicist bent, not the least his father, William Lowth, whose words here he borrows.[6] Still, his efforts to elaborate and inculcate such a thoroughgoing historically (and philologically) oriented kind of criticism, especially apparent in the late *Isaiah. A New Translation; with a Preliminary Dissertation,*[7] are noteworthy. Lowth was not only the father of an explicit kind of literary criticism of the Bible, he was also among the early practitioners (certainly in England) of a bourgeoning historical criticism.[8] The strict dichotomy between literary and historical approaches to the Bible that so many in the field today insist on is shown in Lowth already by the middle of the eighteenth century to be something of a false dichotomy.[9] There is even a case to be made that Lowth articulated new standards for literary criticism that were "evolved from the Bible itself"[10]—yet another part of the Lowthian pose I mean to reclaim.

An important consequence of my own hypersensitivity to historicity is an awareness (not so apparent to Lowth) that the poetry of the Bible emerged out of a traditional and predominantly oral culture, and thus the kind of "high" literary (and highly literate) criticism practiced by Lowth (and most biblical critics since), which has proved so revealing and informative of biblical poetry generally, now needs to be ready to temper or reframe its governing assumptions and preferred technologies of criticism in light of the requirements of a potentially very different kind of literacy and textuality forged at the interface of a deeply informing orality. If the literary and the historical, then, are in view throughout this volume, so, too, is the oral and aural, especially as it chastens my own fully literary assumptions and orientation.

Lastly, there is a strong comparative orientation to much of the thinking in this volume. This, too, may be rooted in Lowth's originary work. R. Wellek, in fact, recognizes Lowth as an early pioneer of a distinctly comparative method of literary study.[11] This propensity for comparison, "the capacity to see first sameness in difference, then difference in sameness,"[12] is most evident in the analogical shape of so much of Lowth's way of thinking (see chapter 1 for examples) and permits him both to know his subject matter for what it is— "verse, properly so called"—and to appreciate its distinctiveness; so most famously his recognition of the place of parallelism in the biblical tradition. Lowth's chief standards of measure, the classical poetic traditions and their neoclassical heirs, were mostly inherited by him from his eighteenth-century cultural milieu. A benefit of J. D. Michaelis's otherwise peculiar re-presentation of the *Praelectiones* was to enmesh Lowth's work (through his various annotations) within a more sophisticated and richer understanding of known cognate languages and literature (at the time, especially Syriac and Arabic).[13] And to this day comparative work on biblical literature tends to privilege (as it should) the languages and literatures of the ancient Near East.[14] Yet comparisons made from farther afield are always potentially just as revealing—the insights won by Lowth because of his neoclassical assumptions provide sufficient (local) warrant on this score. So while my own work habitually sights biblical poetry within its broader ancient Levantine milieu, I also profit from knowledge of other, often geographically and/or chronologically disparate and noncontiguous poetic traditions. Indeed, the latter are crucial for much of the argumentation that follows. Mine is an emphatically inclusive comparative project.

I have two principal audiences in view throughout, students of the Bible and students of comparative literature. My chief subject matter is biblical Hebrew poetry, and it is toward a richer understanding of this verse tradition that these essays (individually and collectively) and the thinking that they

evolve are angled in the first place. That is, I am intent on taking a large swipe
at articulating what biblical poetry is all about and exemplifying one (albeit
heterogeneous) way of approaching it. The large ambition of the whole, then,
is nothing less than to evolve a way of thinking about poetry and poetics that
can enable a more perspicuous accounting of biblical Hebrew poetry and
open onto ever richer and more pleasurable readings of biblical poems. Specific contributions are of two kinds. First, each of the first four essays addresses a specific aspect of biblical poetry—line, rhythm, lyric, orality/
textuality—that in my judgment is crucial to any substantive understanding of
this poetry and that generally has been underappreciated by scholarship to
date. In this sense, each is importantly programmatic. The final essay elaborates a close reading of Psalm 133, both to model the art of close reading itself,
something I believe we need more of in the field, and as a means of cashing
out my efforts to think through aspects of biblical prosody and poetics in the
earlier chapters—such construals are only as compelling as the readings they
enable. In a real way, then, the reading on offer in the final chapter enacts the
final movement to the set of arguments mounted throughout the book—this
is especially true for chapters 1 and 2, where the logic of my explication of the
line and of rhythm requires holistic staging. The second kind of contribution
envisioned comes in how questions are posed, in what spirit and from what
angle. This is admittedly a far more nebulous aspiration but not the less crucial for that. My pose means to be gracious and generous at every turn—
before the texts I interpret and with colleagues whose ideas and opinions I
engage—without (I hope) sacrificing rigor and sharpness of insight. I do not
come to these topics innocently but by way of insights of those who have la-
bored before and beside me. Mine is a distinctly dialogic or conversational
means of writing and thinking. One of the great privileges of scholarship for
me has been the opportunity to interact with other thinkers, scholars, writers.
Indeed, I seem only to find my own voice through such interaction. My debt
to others is made abundantly clear throughout. And like many recent con-
tributors,[15] my efforts to understand biblical poetry are thoroughly embedded
within the study of poetry, poetics, and prosody more generally. In fact, all of
the various subfields and disciplines that make up biblical studies are indisputably a part of the larger humanities. As such there is nothing particularly
special about how biblical scholars approach the business of criticism, or at
least nothing methodologically or theoretically that would distinguish biblical
studies (in all of its many facets) from any other area-oriented studies in the
humanities (e.g., American studies, French, East Asian studies). What sets
this field apart from others is the distinctiveness of its object(s) of study—in
this case, the poetry of the Hebrew Bible. This poetry stems from a particular

time and place, the Levant during the first millennium BCE, comes enmeshed in local practice and custom, and eventually gets written down in a specific script and language, Hebrew. Biblical scholars are always unavoidably accountable to the historical, cultural, and linguistic peculiarities of their subject matter, and so, too, must they be responsible to the wider discussion of the theories and methods that frame and authorize their every act of criticism, no matter that this wider discussion will often span the breadth of the humanities, inevitably and untidily transgressing discipline boundaries. Gone are the days when disciplines in the humanities could remain confined to a narrowly parochial form of intellectual discourse. My choice of interlocutors throughout the book from fields beyond my own, then, is most intentional and means, among other things, to make a bid to break open the all too frequently insular nature of our scholarly discourse in biblical studies and to implicate my own work (at any rate) *as a biblical scholar* in a much broader discussion about poetry and poetics.

With respect to the nonbiblicist, the contributions I seek to make are also of two kinds. The first is to place before students of literature more generally an accounting of biblical poetry that is knowledgeable of its subject matter and that also proves by dint of the questions posed, and also the manner of their posing and in whose name, to be familiar and accessible to them, and thus readable by them. Biblical poetry stands as one of the fountainheads of the Western poetic canon (as Lowth, for example, well understood) and not surprisingly, then, literary scholars of every stripe seem ever eager to draw the Bible into their critical discourse. Unfortunately, too often this engagement with the Bible is pursued naively and at times even in ignorance. The historical and linguistic knowledge required to tackle this material with any kind of authenticity and rigor is substantial. Therefore, one way biblical scholarship may serve the larger literary guild is by mediating access to this particular body of literature, yet this can only happen if it is pitched such that it can win a hearing from literary-minded colleagues across the humanities. My aim throughout has been to pitch these essays in just such a manner, each consciously pursued as an exercise in a kind of literary criticism that will be familiar to a broad spectrum of scholars. There are always potential gains to be had from engaging a different or new or other poetic corpus, and thus insofar as this book facilitates such an engagement for those with specialties in textual corpora beyond the Bible it makes an important contribution. Beyond conveying information and such about biblical poetry per se, I also mean to speak more broadly about the several issues addressed in these essays, namely lineation, lyric verse, free verse prosody, orality, and close reading. For example, my discussion of the nature and role of the verse line in biblical

Hebrew poetry in chapter 1 addresses a critical prosodic issue in the biblical corpus, but means to do so in a way that is informative at any number of points about the phenomenon of lineation more generally. Like H. Dubrow,[16] I maintain that literary analyses with a particular historical inflection (e.g., my focus on biblical poetry), insofar as the issues explored have broader occurrence in other historical eras and traditions, may rightly aspire to have a genuine transhistorical reach and significance, to implicate themselves beyond the necessary confines of their originating motivation and focus. There are also occasions (as in the discussion of the Hebrew lyric in chapter 3) where I believe the encounter with the biblical corpus is fundamental, adding something unique or vital to the larger conversation about a given issue, phenomenon, or practice. In other words, the aim in these essays is always at least twofold: to convey positive knowledge about a certain aspect of biblical poetry or poetics and to advance or otherwise enrich the broader scholarly discussion of the particular matters of prosody or practice that are being scrutinized.

Chapter 1, as noted, focalizes the issue of the poetic line in biblical poetry. The question of what counts as poetry is at heart always a historical question. Poems as language art come necessarily mired in cultural, historical, linguistic peculiarities. Therefore, there can be no question of identifying in any meaningful way essential, transcendent, unexceptional characteristics that are everywhere definitive of poetry. Cultural artifacts simply do not behave in such a manner. Rather, at best what is manageable is to isolate from a comparative perspective (itself always staged theoretically and with prejudice) those features that prototypically show up time and again in poems cross-culturally and transhistorically. One such feature is a unit of rhythm, audition, and syntax the segmentation of which periodically interrupts or breaks the otherwise continuous flow of language.[17] This is the (verse) "line." Empirically, there is a vast amount of extant written poetry throughout the world that is specially formatted in ways that graphically isolate the verse line and thus provides eloquent testimony to the widespread facticity of this poetic phenomenon.[18] The very concept of a "line" as "a row of written or printed letters" (*OED*), however, is itself belated and hyperliterate, emerging out of a chirographic world (Hellenistic Greece) with specific conventions in place for how to spatialize the technology of writing. But the phenomenon that the term "line" has come to name in the (English) vernacular of Western literary criticism subsumes whatever culturally specific conventions (if any at all) are in place for spatializing it.[19] In fact, much (if not all) traditional oral verbal art, insofar as it depends primarily on human cognition for reception, consists of such periodically segmented discourse.[20]

Surprisingly, however, the question of the biblical Hebrew poetic line (variously called colon, verset, half-line, stich, or hemistich) though everywhere assumed, has nowhere been substantively scrutinized (aside, perhaps, from the issue of syntax and how syntax interfaces with and is staged by the line).[21] This is no small desideratum. To a large extent, the very sensibility of referring to portions of the Hebrew Bible as *poetic* rests with the ability to successfully articulate the presence and nature of the biblical Hebrew poetic line. The overarching ambition of chapter 1, then, is to suggest why I, for one, think there are lines of verse in the Bible, and therefore, why I continue to think it appropriate to speak about *biblical Hebrew poetry*.[22] To this end, the greatest amount of my attention is dedicated to issues of discernment—what evidence positively shows the existence and importance of segmentation in biblical verse (e.g., special formatting in manuscripts) and more particularly in what does this segmented line consist, what are its leading characteristics (e.g., concision, simple clause structure, parataxis). I also offer some initial observations of a prosodic nature, on how the line factors in a poem's various structures of meaning. As it turns out, not only is the line crucial to the very sensibility of biblical poetry, it is also important prosodically, since so much of what goes on in biblical poems does so at the level of the line.[23] The topic of line grouping also comes in for discussion, both as a means for triangulating on the line as a structural singularity and because biblical poetry is dominantly distichic, its lines come mostly grouped in pairs, as couplets, with the triplet (a gathering of three poetic lines) otherwise being the most common complementing alternative grouping scheme attested in the biblical corpus.

The question of meter in biblical poetry, by contrast, is an old one, dating at least as far back as the Greco-Roman period (Philo and Josephus). Lowth himself asserted quite trenchantly the existence of (biblical) Hebrew meter— in the eighteenth century verse was all but inconceivable outside of a metrical framework—though he did have the good sense to admit that the specifics (namely quantity, rhythm, etc.) were "altogether" unknowable.[24] Others since have not always been so prudent. Until quite recently, in fact, the search for Hebrew meter has been a constant preoccupation of scholars. However, the simple fact is that biblical verse is not metrical—at least not in any way that the term "meter," which "is an organizing principle which turns the general tendency toward regularity in rhythm into a strictly patterned regularity that can be counted and named,"[25] retains any recognizable sense. Rather, biblical verse is nonmetrical, and thus its prosody consists in "rhythmical organization by other than numerical modes";[26] it is, as the comparatist B. Hrushovski [Harshav] has seen best, a kind of free verse, or what he calls free rhythm.[27] Though a consensus about the absence of meter in biblical verse now exists, no one to date has tried to work out Hrushovski's ideas in a thoroughgoing way, or to read biblical Hebrew poetry against the backdrop of the free verse tradition more broadly.[28] In chapter 2 I propose to do just that, albeit in an initially circuitous but hopefully provocative way. In 1933 G. W. Allen published his seminal essay "Biblical Analogies for Walt Whitman's Prosody," in which he contends that Whitman's prosody owes much to biblical models (as mediated through the King James Bible; Whitman did not know Hebrew).[29] Though "free verse" may be approached in various ways, in most genealogies Whitman looms large. The English phrase "free verse" itself most transparently connotes freedom from metrical constraints, and no doubt there was some consciousness of this sort on Whitman's part (and in other early modern practitioners of free verse). Still, it nevertheless is clear, as Allen's essay shows, that there is more to the underlying prosody of Whitman (and other writers of free verse) than a mere revolt against metrical norms. In fact, many of the prosodic features characteristic of free verse are typical of the oral and written poetries from ancient Mesopotamia (Sumerian, Akkadian), Egypt, and the Levant (biblical Hebrew, Ugaritic).[30]

My aim in viewing biblical verse (initially) through a Whitmanesque looking glass is to underscore the fact that this verse is itself a variety of nonmetrical or free verse, and therefore it is to free verse that biblical scholars should look if they want to fully appreciate the nature and dynamics of biblical poetry. I elaborate an understanding of biblical poetry as a variety of a free rhythmic system of verse, building on Hrushovski's seminal insights and expanding them in light of contemporary work on free verse prosody.[31]

Lyric is the topic I take up in chapter 3. As a practical matter, R. Alter notices that biblical verse is used for all manner of things except telling stories,[32] which invariably in the Hebrew Bible is rendered in prose. This is not a given. Epic narrative verse is well known from the period and region (e.g., Gilgamesh, Kirta), so biblical poets could well have chosen to tell stories in verse had they so desired—and no doubt their oral storytelling colleagues and forebears did. To be sure, there are individual poems that incorporate narrative runs and sometimes even develop characters, but for the most part these forms are restricted in scale and put mainly to nonnarrative ends (e.g., Exod 15, Prov 7). Alter has also identified varieties of what he calls "incipient narrativity" in certain Hebrew poems (e.g., 2 Sam 22).[33] But mainly poetry is not a medium used in the Bible for sustained narrative purposes. S. R. Driver, who much earlier also recognized the Bible's lack of epic verse,[34] divided the nonnarrative poetry of the Bible into two broad types, *lyric* and *gnomic*. Though surely reductive, leaving many verse forms in the Bible unaccounted for (e.g., much prophetic verse), the two types are indeed pervasive. I specifically focus on the lyric given the general primordiality of this verse kind and because the genre is foundational for any more surpassing understanding of biblical poetics—and it is also pragmatically beneficial for understanding other kinds of verse in the Bible, such as gnomic or didactic verse, which as Driver notices is not always so easily distinguished from lyric proper.[35] Drawing on a range of theorists,[36] I locate a specifically lyric kind of verse in the Bible by situating it with respect to lyric's chief properties and leading sensibilities as prototypically known from other lyric corpora. What emerges, in the end, is a tradition of lyric verse that is as ancient as (if not more ancient than) that of the Greeks and that through some of its common features (e.g., prominence of a communal voice, dialogic profile, notable rituality) may well open up new possibilities for understanding the capacity and nature of lyric discourse more generally. Among the myriad of important implications to which the lyricism of so much biblical verse gives rise, none is more important than the demand for reading strategies specially attuned to the discourse's key features and practices. Narrative approaches, which still dominate the literary study of the Bible, will only illuminate this kind of poetry to a limited degree. I also consider the possibility of lyric discourse beyond its typical conciseness and how an understanding of the poetics of lyric may advantage a richer understanding of biblical poetry more broadly.

To state that the roots of biblical poetry are oral in nature will elicit little surprise. After all, it has now been over a century since H. Gunkel started articulating his program of form criticism, at the heart of which stood the firm conviction that the poems and stories of ancient Israel and Judah emerged initially as oral productions.[37] And the recent spate of monographs in the field on the broad topic of orality and literacy has underscored the overwhelming and thoroughgoing orality of ancient Israelite and Judahite culture in general.[38] Indeed, as M. O'Connor maintains, much biblical poetry appears "comparably close to the oral poetic situation,"[39] and most (though not all), however originally composed and transmitted, was likely intended for oral performance of one kind or another (e.g., 1 Chron 16:7, 36; cf. Deut 31:30; 32:44–46; 2 Sam 1:17–18; Jer 36:4–8). The central aim of chapter 4 is to elaborate O'Connor's idea and to flesh out the nature and kind of orality that informs so much of this poetic tradition. Orality is not of just one kind or inevitably pure. Rather it is stubbornly pluralistic. Moreover, biblical verse, however indebted its poetics to oral performance, nonetheless has only come down to us in writing, and thus by its very medium of inscription is indubitably marked by textuality and literacy.[40] Indeed, orality and literacy are not monolithic descriptors, at least not in reference to ancient Israel and Judah, where the art of writing would have been well rccognized (writing emerges in the ancient Near East during the middle of the fourth millennium BCE) and begins to intersect and interface with orality from a relatively early period (Iron IIB). "Orality and literacy," in the southern Levant during the Iron Age, then, as in medieval England, "are parts of a subtle, complex, lengthy process of change," and thus "do not occupy discrete and conflicting cognitive spheres."[41] And just because oral poems begin to be written down and copied or composition itself begins to take place in writing does not entail the immediate loss of all (or even most) informing oral sensibilities, for the simple reason that these very sensibilities are the only idioms known for articulating poetry.[42] Even narrative prose—a specifically written genre—as it first emerges, everywhere after the writing down of poetry, bears the telltale signs of an originary oral poetics.[43] There-fore, the picture I begin to paint of biblical poetry's informing orality (and much remains yet to be done on this topic) in this chapter is ultimately a com-plex one, mindful of cultural specifics, orality's operative pluralities, and how textuality in this context impinges on and stages orality on the one hand and on the other how textuality is itself enabled and shaped by this same orality. Indeed, the last part of the chapter is given over to an exploration of emergent textuality in ancient Israel and Judah as it interfaces specifically with the poetic tradition.

To recognize the informing orality of much biblical verse is an impor-tant historical datum. It will also crucially constrain how contemporary readers engage these poems, if only as a reminder that their textuality is complicated, and many will not have originated in writing, as specifically writerly compositions.

The book's first four chapters, then, are given over wholly to "thick" de-scriptions of specific elements crucial to any fully surpassing account of the prosody and poetics of biblical poetry. Each chapter incorporates here and there brief readings of poems or (more often) parts of poems as a means of gesturing toward what I believe is the ultimate raison d'être for all prosodic analysis—reading. My lone, extended effort in this vein comes in the final chapter, in a reading of Psalm 133. In service to the larger book, it provides the kind of in-depth and close reading of a single poem that some of my argumen-tation in the earlier chapters requires, namely, to sight the poetic line, for ex-ample, not only abstracted and hypostasized (through the fixity inputed by writing) but as it resolves itself as such in the very process of enacting the poem it helps to compose. It also means to gesture toward what is consequen-tial about prosodic analysis of the kind I undertake in the first place, a prac-tical cashing out of why do it. In the end, however, the essay, like the others in the book, stands on its own and means beyond the logic of the larger whole of which it is a part. For me, poetry is always finally about reading and about the production of readings. And therefore the celebration of reading (and read-ings) is also very much at the heart of my reading of Psalm 133. It is a long, luxuriating look at this singularly delicious psalm. It is expressly literary in orientation and pointedly philological in manner—philology is the principal disciplinary means at our disposal for fixing and thus accessing poems through their words and worlds,[44] and thus it is, as Nietzsche well appreciated, the ultimate method of close, or as he prefers, "slow" reading: "it teaches to read well...to read slowly, deeply, looking cautiously before and aft, with reservations, with doors left open, with delicate eyes and fingers."[45] There is, of course, no one right way of reading, no tidy, preset template or calculus guaranteed to generate meaningful construals, sure and compelling readings. Reading is a practice, with many modes and an inestimable number of different and competing aims and outcomes. Mine, with a distinct affinity for literary theory and a strong taste for philology, is but one example of what is possible, what is imaginable, what is readable.

The book with its component studies falls well short of any kind of comprehensive statement on the nature and art of biblical poetry. There remain still many topics beyond parallelism (to again recall the wider frame of Lowth's original *Lectures*) that require (renewed) attention. To continue to have work to do is no bad thing. And yet I also am confident that for any who work their way through the whole of this book a basic and substantial orientation to biblical Hebrew poetry, even beyond the immediate focus of the individual chapters, will be had.

"*Verse, Properly So Called*"

THE LINE IN BIBLICAL POETRY

in the Hebrew poetry the line was the unit
—J. H. GARDINER, *The Bible as Literature* (1906)

AFTER SEVERAL INTRODUCTORY lectures focused on poetry generally, R. Lowth begins to address biblical poetry specifically in the third of his field-founding *Lectures on the Sacred Poetry of the Hebrews*.[1] His topic here is meter. The discussion for Lowth is both foundational and an embarrassment. It is foundational because as an English scholar writing and speaking in the middle of the eighteenth century Lowth was unable to conceptualize poetry in the absence of meter:

> But since it appears essential to every species of poetry, that it be confined to numbers, and consist of some kind of verse, (for indeed wanting this, it would not only want its most agreeable attributes, but would scarcely deserve the name of poetry) in treating of the poetry of the Hebrews, it appears absolutely necessary to demonstrate, that those parts at least of the Hebrew writings which we term poetic, are in a metrical form, and to inquire whether anything be certainly known concerning the nature and principles of this versification or not.[2]

For Lowth biblical Hebrew poetry had to be metrical. Indeed, so foundational is meter to Lowth's way of thinking that the lecture by itself constitutes the first part of his study—all else logically and structurally follows from Lowth's initial positing of Hebrew meter. The embarrassment arises in the fact that "as to the real quantity, the rhythm, or modulation, these from the present state of the language [i.e., Hebrew] seem to be altogether unknown, and even to admit of no investigation by human art or industry."[3] Only the merest vestiges remain discernible—Lowth put little stock in the vocalization traditions preserved by the Masoretes, else, as he notes, "we must be under the necessity of confessing, not only, what we at present experience, that the Hebrew poetry possesses no remains of sweetness or harmony, but that it never was possessed of any."[4] The surest evidence of meter—verse "confined to numbers"—lies in the alphabetic acrostics: "in these examples the verses are so exactly marked and defined, that it is impossible to mistake them for prose."[5] Lowth was more specific in his later "preliminary dissertation" to the *New Translation* of Isaiah, his most mature expression (and in his own English) of his conception of biblical Hebrew verse structure.[6] There, isolating the "perfectly Alphabetical" acrostics "in which every Line is marked by its Initial Letter" (i.e., Psalms 111–12),[7] he writes that "we may safely conclude" of these poems that they "consist of Verses properly so called; of Verses regulated by some observation of harmony or cadence; of measure, numbers, or rhythm."[8] Lowth goes on to reason, by way of analogy, that the other acrostics, where the initial letters determine the beginning of stanzas and not lines, must be presumed to be "of the same kind of composition" and to "equally consist of Verses"; and so, too, "in regard to the rest of the Poems of the Hebrews, bearing evidently the same marks and characteristics of composition with the Alphabetical Poems in other respects, and falling into regular lines . . .; that these likewise consist of Verse."[9] As it turns out, Lowth was dead wrong about meter. It is not that the loss of the "true pronunciation of Hebrew" makes the pursuit of Hebrew meter and its enabling principles "vain,"[10] but that biblical Hebrew verse is simply not metrical. This Lowth could not have seen, but it is a finding fully compatible with his own analysis, and now, two and a half centuries later, it is a finding that commands wide consensus in the field (see chapter 2).

Two aspects of Lowth's thoughts on meter retain broad value. First, his strong desire to ground his estimation of the poetic in the poems themselves (and the poetic phenomena they exhibit)—as opposed, say, to the versions of the poems as preserved in particular manuscripts—is laudable. That is, here I see Lowth reaching after those sure signs by which he may know his topic to be what he assumes it to be, seeking to answer the "uncommonly difficult and obscure" question "concerning the nature of the Hebrew verse."[11] Literary scholars continue to debate to this day the distinguishing differentia of poetry. There still is no wide agreement on this issue, with much depending on one's theoretical disposition. D. Attridge sums the current status of the question well:

> Is poetry a definable distinctive type of literature? Much ink has been spilled on this question, and it is evident that if what is implied are intrinsic markers or clear-cut boundaries the answer is no. Just as the borderline between the literary and non-literary is shifting and porous,

so is the borderline between what is called "poetry" and what is not. Several different variables map onto this distinction, and isolating one will always be a somewhat artificial act. And even if we simplify the issue by focusing on one variable, it will be more helpful to think in terms of the degree to which any literary work is poetic, or invites the kind of response we normally accord to poetry, rather than imagining that we can distinguish absolutely between poems and non-poems.[12]

Still, saying what we can say about what distinguishes biblical Hebrew poems, being ever mindful of how we say it (in what language, for example, and with what theoretical commitments) and that the saying is itself always provisional and never fail-safe, is a desirable ambition. Second, just as poetry qua poetry for Lowth had to be metrical, it also had to be arranged in lines. This assumption, too, Lowth owed to his larger cultural milieu, as most of the written poetry known to him was arranged in literal lines.[13] Lowth himself from an early age read classical Greek and Latin poetry and composed his own verse—all lineated. The topic of the line does not receive sustained treatment by Lowth. He does notice it (briefly) as one of the observable manifestations of the metrical norm that he presumes governs biblical verse generally and the most "perfectly Alphabetical" poems in particular. So every single line in Psalms 111 and 112, Lowth says, "is distinguished by its Initial Letter."[14] Moreover, in these poems, he observes, the "Pauses of the Sentences coincide with the Pauses of the Lines."[15] And at one point, as he launches into his discussion of parallelism in his "preliminary dissertation," Lowth explicitly glosses "Verse" with "Line."[16] The lengthiest, and perhaps most explicit, characterization of the line comes in Lowth's assessment of the nonalphabetical poems of the Bible, which he contends "likewise consist of Verse":

> of Verse distinguished from Prose, not only by the style, the figures, the diction; by a loftiness of thought, and richness of imagery; *but by being divided into Lines*, and sometimes into Systems of Lines; which Lines, having an apparent equality, similitude, or proportion, one to another, were in some sort measured by the ear, and regulated according to some general laws of metre, rhythm, harmony, or cadence.[17]

Still more pervasive and far more telling than these few comments is Lowth's unfailing practice in the *Praelectiones* of arranging the Hebrew text of his examples in lines (fig. 1a–b).[18] In fact, he sets the Hebrew (and accompanying Latin translation) one verse line per manuscript line, a practice mostly nonexistent in the Masoretic manuscripts to which he would have had access but normative for the classical verse (Latin and Greek) Lowth knew so well, and now attested in Hebrew manuscripts of the Bible from Qumran.[19] Indeed, 4QPs[b] preserves a few verses from Psalm 112 (vv. 4–5), lineated as Lowth describes,[20] according to the acrostic (see fig. 2):[21]

זרח בחש אור לישרים
חנון ורחום וצדי[ק]
טוב אי[ש חנון ומלוה]

Lowth's practice of lineation underscores the (however literally understated) centrality of the line in his notion of verse and, by extension, his estimate of its role in biblical verse more specifically. Unfortunately, G. Gregory's translation of the *Praelectiones* into English (on which all English editions of Lowth's *Lectures* are based) does not include the Hebrew text of the examples Lowth originally cited throughout, and thus this visual aspect of his argumentation is accessible to only those who consult the Latin original.

My interest in this chapter lies precisely with that topic that Lowth (and apparently everyone else since) felt did not warrant, presuming its primordiality, extended discussion: "Verse, properly so called."[22] My use of this phrase aims both to honor Lowth's insight and to elaborate it, to work out from it ("elaboration" in Gramsci's sense, i.e., *e-laborate*) a sense of verse more properly so called. What Lowth meant by *verse* is closely in line with what the *OED* gives as the primary gloss for the English term: "A succession of words arranged according to natural or recognized rules of prosody and forming a complete metrical line; one of the lines of a poem or piece of versification." Apparent in both Lowth (as I have tried to show briefly, namely, "Verse distinguished...by being divided into Lines") and the *OED* ("one of the lines of a poem"), however, is a slightly narrower sense of the term as poetry arranged in lines. In this sense, the English verse approaches more closely its Latin etymon, *versus*, "a line or row, spec[ifically] a line of writing (so named from turning to begin another line), verse" (*OED*)—not surprisingly, Lowth uses *versus*, and also *versiculus* (lit. "a short line of writing," *OLD*), throughout his *Praelectiones*. It is in the latter sense of the term—an isolate of a structural modality, namely, being arranged in lines—that I take "verse" (here following the Lowth of the *Praelectiones*, especially, quite literally), "properly so called." As such, its chief terminological and categorical correlate, strictly speaking, is the term *prose*, and it is the line that differentiates the two: *verse* is set in lines, *prose* is not.[23]

The term *poetry*, which is often taken (by laypeople and scholars alike) as a rough synonym for verse (a practice I will continue) and which the *OED* glosses as "imaginative or creative literature in general," is more wide-ranging in English, less amenable to a narrow and precise definition. Most would likely give assent to T. V. F. Brogan's notion that at its core poetry (habitually) involves a heightening of discourse—though admittedly, like the *OED*'s gloss, this brings us only so far. Yet to go much further, to become more specific and explicit, would entangle us in large theoretical and historical considerations. For my purposes, several further but still relatively general observations will suffice. First, to reiterate, poetry is used frequently to mean an instance of verbal art set in lines, and thus a synonym for verse. Second, this common usage notwithstanding, there are good reasons to underscore the categorical distinction between verse and prose on the one hand, which are correlate structural modes (of which the line is the differentia), and poetry on the other hand, which, for the lack of a better word, as Brogan notes, is something more like a genre—in this respect it is (somewhat) akin to *drama* and *fiction*.[24] The point here is that poetry, like these other similarly broad overarching genres, may be realized "in either of the modes or any mixture thereof."[25] The reverse cannot be said. The same asymmetry is pointed up by M. Perloff. She notes that if lineation may be rightly said to distinguish prose and verse, it does not so distinguish prose and poetry. Perloff, mindful of the need to account for nonlineated kinds of poetry (such as the modern "prose poem"), goes on to argue that what counts as poetry is always a configuration of historical, cultural, and ideological factors. This leads to a third and final observation. Almost all premodern (prior to ca. 1850 CE) poetry consists of language periodically interrupted, which most frequently was represented in writing as verse, that is, in lines (following the ancient Greek practice for writing out stichic verse).[26] And thus, in addition to common English usage, I find in this strong empirical warrant for my own habit of using verse and poetry interchangeably as synonyms. More significantly, the observation reveals more precisely the chief issue at stake in this chapter: to a large extent, the very sensibility of referring to portions of the Hebrew Bible as *poetic* rests with our ability to successfully articulate the presence and nature of the biblical poetic line. Any minimally compelling definition of biblical Hebrew poetry will need to specify features or characteristics beyond or other than the line,[27] but if there are no lines, then there is no verse (at least as current literary theory understands this term), and our notion of biblical Hebrew poetry will require radical rethinking—"line is what distinguishes our experience of poetry as poetry."[28] What follows in the body of this chapter will suggest, in fact, that there are lines of verse in the Bible, and therefore, it is most appropriate to speak specifically about *biblical Hebrew poetry*.

Behind the "proper" of Lowth's "properly so called" stands an entire theoretical machinery, however tacitly assumed, a specific take on what poetry is and why the poetry of the Hebrew Bible qualifies as such. This theory, as I have tried to indicate in an abbreviated way, is not without certain blind spots—the presumption of meter, from our vantage point, being chief among them. But even so it is a powerfully enabling theory as well, one that allowed Lowth to see so much and to see it so well. In many respects, biblical Hebrew poetry is itself the invention of Lowth and his *Lectures*. This is not to deny that Lowth himself was taking part in and greatly enabled by a larger conversation, involving others whose insights were crucial, too;[29] nor to imply that there is no "there" there, in this case, some primordial textuality that Lowth could in fact call poetry. Rather, by underscoring Lowth's inventiveness I mean to recognize the act of criticism required of Lowth, as M. O'Connor notes, "to observe the crucial phenomena *and* conceive a vocabulary with which to describe them."[30] Someone had to construe what we have since come to call biblical Hebrew poetry as poetry in some initial way in order for such a construal to have any sensibility. And if such a construal is itself not made up out of whole cloth and by necessity considers that which it did not invent, the thoroughgoing nature of its constructedness remains nonetheless. And whatever ongoing sensibility we want to attribute to biblical poetry will itself result from similar acts of construal, feats of criticism, interpretation. These will be judged "proper" (or "improper") based on a whole range of considerations, including the nature of the theories espoused and how they comport with the textual entities being considered. My own championing of the line as the leading differentia of verse, however widely shared and inclusive of both theoretical and empirical considerations, is itself, in the end, an active act of judgment, as in fact is the discernment of every poetic line in the biblical corpus. Therefore, my chief ambition for my different sense of the properness of what I call verse is that however ultimately judged, whether in fact it is finally found to be "proper," it might, like Lowth's "Verse, properly so called," help us to see further and to see better, to eventuate a more perspicuous accounting of biblical verse, and ultimately to open onto ever richer and more pleasurable readings of this poetry.

The discussion that follows, substantial and ambitious, has as its principal focus the line, which, according to B. H. Smith, is "the fundamental unit of poetic form"[31] and, according to many others, is the one widely-agreed-on feature that is distinctive of poetry (verse)—prose has no line structure, poems (most) often do.[32] And yet, aside from the issue of syntax and how syntax interfaces with and is staged by the line (a not unimportant issue),[33] the topic of line structure in biblical Hebrew poetry has not been routinely or closely considered.[34] This is no small desideratum, and my chief ambition here is to begin to address this lack. In particular, attention is dedicated, one, to issues of discernment—what are the kinds of evidences that positively show the existence and importance of the line in biblical Hebrew verse—and two, to scrutiny of the nature and character of the line so revealed: in what does this line consist.[35] In my judgment, the line is both the prosodic motor and the defining feature of biblical verse, and thus the major foci of this chapter are intended to give substance to these claims. In the end, however, the most compelling witness to the presence and importance of the line in biblical poetry comes in read- ings of those individual poems that are alive to the possibilities that line struc- ture puts into play. (See chapter 5 for one extended effort at such a reading.)

Terminology

Some prefatory remarks on terminology are in order before embarking in ear- nest on my topic, both for the sake of clarity and for theoretical purposes. The central phenomenon I am considering here—the *line*—in fact nowhere gets named as such in the Bible. This is not surprising given the absence of any early, indigenous metadiscourse about biblical verse and the overwhelming orality of the biblical world (the two are not unrelated). The concept of a line— "a row of written or printed letters" (*OED*)—is itself a product of writing, of a chirographic world. In Greek, for example, *stichos* emerges out of a context in which the practice was to represent the verse line on its own corresponding line of writing (i.e., the columnar line), and Latin *versus* is so named from the turning (from Lat. *vertere* "to turn") to begin a new line of writing. When some (still mostly spare) comment does arise in the Talmud (e.g., *b. Meg.* 16b; *j. Meg.* 3:7), it is with respect to the special formatting for the two lists in Joshua 12:9–24 and Esther 9:7–9 and a number of the festival songs embedded in prose texts (specifically Exod 15, Deut 32, Judg 5, and 2 Sam 22). The observa- tions are highly literate and pertain to what is literally seen on the manuscript page, that is, the nature of the special formatting used in these texts. The key terms employed, *ʾārîaḥ* and *lĕbēnâ*, "small brick" and "brick" (i.e., the normal, larger brick), respectively, describe a block of writing ("small brick") on a co- lumnar line circumscribed by intervening spans of uninscribed text ("large brick").[36] Two dominant patterns prevail. Deuteronomy 32, and 2 Samuel 22 and Qoheleth 3:2–8 in some manuscripts, is written with two blocks of writing per columnar line with a large intervening span of uninscribed space (i.e., "white space"). In all succeeding lines (as one moves down the folio page) in- scribed and uninscribed spaces are aligned with one another so that the basic perception of the page is of "two rows of writing separated by a row of blank spaces" (see fig. 3).[37] The rabbis called this kind of layout "small brick over small brick, large over large" and prescribed it specifically for Deuteronomy 32 (*b. Meg.* 16b; *Sof.* 1.11; 12:8–12; 13:1) and for the two lists in Joshua 12:9–24 and Esther 9:6–9 (*b. Meg.* 16b; *j. Meg.* 3:7). A second kind of layout, what the rabbis called "small brick over large brick, large over small" (the governing image is that of "the interlocking construction usual with bricks and ashlar masonry"),[38] is stipulated for the poems in Exodus 15 and Judges 5 (see *b. Meg.* 16b; *j. Meg.* 3:7; *b. Menaḥ* 31b; *Sof.* 12:8–12). These are written in a single column of text the width of the folio page (leaving room for margins) with columnar lines composed of either (portions of) three blocks of writing ("small bricks") divided by two large spans of space ("large bricks") or (portions of) two blocks of writing separated by one large span of space. The two columnar line types then alternate as they run down a page (fig. 4).

As J. Kugel suggests, the motivation for these Talmudic prescriptions likely lies in the unusual nature of the layout of these poems.[39] When poems are specially formatted in MT (and they are not always so formatted), as in the three poetic books of Job, Proverbs, and Psalms (אמ"ת), the usual practice is to lay out the writing in two wide columns (per page) instead of the three narrower columns that are otherwise used throughout Masoretic manuscripts of the Hebrew Bible, with the columnar line composed (prototypically) of two blocks of writing separated (where appropriate or possible) by space (of varying lengths, see figs. 5–6).[40] With some exceptions (e.g., Ps 119), the blocks of writing with intervening spacing follow in a running manner across and then down the column. The dominant resulting visual effect is to have columns of text with lines consisting of blocks of writing typically punctuated or broken by a (variable) span of space.[41] Amid the differences in layout, observe that both this *usual* Masoretic practice for formatting poems in the "אמ"ת books," which is not commented on, and the explicitly prescribed *unusual* practice for writing out the several festival songs agree in their presentation of columnar lines consisting of blocks (or bricks) of writing (i.e., the *ārîḥîn*) segmented by spans of space—a graphic strategy of representation that matches well P. Zumthor's explicitly nonchirographic characterization of the structural equivalent of the written verse line in oral poetry as "an autonomous unit between what comes before and what after."[42] This segmented block of writing is the focus of the special formatting of poetic texts in MT that otherwise remains graphically undifferentiated in the columnar line of MT's prevailing running format.

Modern scholarship (i.e., since Lowth) has mostly failed to evolve a consistent and transparent manner of referencing this segmented block of writing and its perceived phenomenological equivalent in nonspecially formatted (portions of) manuscripts (following Lowth), what I have so far (mostly naively) referenced as the line. There are multiple reasons for this, but two stand out for me: one, the lack, already mentioned, of an indigenous vocabulary for the phenomenon, and two, the general failure of scholars to approach the study of biblical poetry from within an explicitly articulated theory of poetry. In the final analysis, my own preference for the term *line* as a means of designating this entity, though admitting a long-standing scholarly tradition of use within biblical studies and having linguistic currency in English usage, is a choice made in deference to the discipline of Western literary criticism and its enabling vocabulary and theoretical machinery. The larger project, of which this chapter is a piece, is undertaken as a specifically literary endeavor, and thus, not surprisingly, my terminology and the informing theory on which I draw are reflective of this broader orientation. More significantly, a chief benefit of speaking specifically about *lines* of biblical verse comes precisely in bringing the phenomenal entity that the term *line* itself denotes into critical view, allowing it to be theorized and thus available to the discourse of criticism. Terminology is not neutral. It already disposes one to a particular orientation—in this case, to seeing lines and in seeing them to be positioned to probe their rhythmic, semantic, and structural significance. The lack of attention to date paid by scholars to this (lineal) entity within biblical poetry has everything to do with its critical invisibility. Theory—whatever its nature—matters because it provides the necessary framework for such entities to take on meaning, to be conceptualized as something worthy of our cognitive attention. Part of my insistence on reading biblical poems *as poems*, as all other poems are read across the world, within a specifically theorized literary paradigm is to leverage the insight and knowledge enabled by the theoretical machinery of literary criticism that, among other things, gives us the very concept of a line of verse.

This lack of indigenous terminology and general disinterest in theory has meant that commentators over the centuries have tended to use whatever terms seemed convenient to hand, and as a consequence, a bewildering and sometimes confusing array of terms for the segmented block of writing called an *'arîah* by the Masoretes appears in the literature on biblical Hebrew verse. In fact, if some of the more idiosyncratic terms are bracketed out (e.g., Sievers's *Reihe* "row"), almost all the most common terms in current use derive from ancient Greek or Latin words for the verse line. I want to briefly survey these terms, in the first place to get straight what and how they reference, and second, to provide a basis from which to judge their fit for talking about biblical verse.

Stichos. There is a whole set of terms (*stich, stichos, hemistich; mono-/di-/tristich; stichometry, stichographic*) that features (etymologically) the Greek nominal *stichos*, most literally a term for a row or line of objects (soldiers, numbers; a course of masonry) and, when applied to writing, signifying a line of verse (prototypically) or prose.[43] In the latter sense, the significance of the Greek term in any given context depends on the nature of the writing in view, whether it is prose or poetry, and if the latter, how the line is divided, metrically or by sense. By convention Greek prose is written out continuously in narrow,

squared-off columns of writing, separated by uniform intercolumns of uninscribed space (fig. 7). The individual lines of writing are relatively short (e.g.,
often only fifteen to twenty-five letters for well-written texts of history, oratory,
or philosophy) and have no inherent structural significance, that is, line-ends
fall where they may depending on the predetermined width of the column. By
contrast, for Greek (stichic) verse, which is metrical, the line of writing is
meaningful, and its length, except in very early papyri (e.g., Timotheos, see fig.
8), which are copied in continuous lines like prose, is determined usually by
the meter; that is, it is normally the length of the complete metrical verse (e.g.,
hexameter, iambic trimeter). Each (metrical) line of verse, then, is written out
on a corresponding (columnar) line of writing, and the resulting columns of
writing tend to be wider than corresponding columns of prose, in order to accommodate the natural lengths of the meters (e.g., hexameter verse has the
longest lines, consisting of sixteen syllables and thirty-four to thirty-eight letters), and have ragged right-hand margins (fig. 9).[44] An alternative method of
line division, at least for lyric verse and the lyric components of drama (i.e., the
choral passages), develops in the Hellenistic period with Aristophanes of Byzantium (ca. 258–180 BCE). He initiates the practice of measuring the length of
the verse line by sense-divisions known as *kōla*—the prosodic subparts of a
particular meter (e.g., the Greek hexameter is often composed of four such
kōla)—and of allotting to each *kōlon* a separate line (or *stichos*) of writing.[45] But
whether divided by meter or colometry, the distinguishing feature of written
Greek verse from the Hellenistic and Roman eras is its stichic layout, that is,
the stich. The Greek *stichos* was used to reference the biblical verse line at least
as early as Origen (ca. third century CE), who uses the term in a Scholion on
Psalm 119:1.[46] Its English derivative, *stich* (or *stichos*), continued in prominence
as the usual term for a "line of verse" into the early 1960s in biblical scholarship;[47] it still can be found in the literature today.

Kōlon. Perhaps the most widely used term today for the verse line in biblical scholarship is *colon* (pl. *cola*; also *bi-/tricolon*).[48] S. Mowinckel, writing in
the early 1960s, credits the rise of the term to the ambiguity caused by the use
of both "stichos" and "hemistichos" (lit. a "half-line" and "half-verse"; from
Gk. *hēmistichion*)[49] to designate a "line of verse."[50] And certainly one of its key
virtues is the clarity of reference that it provides with respect to biblical verse—
there is no question as to the entity so designated, or as to the grouping of two
or three such entities (bicolons and tricolons, respectively). Nonetheless, the
term harbors within itself its own potential for ambiguity.[51] Like *stich* (and the
like), *colon* is of Greek derivation (*kōlon* "limb, member").[52] The Greek term
most concretely designates a literal limb or member of a body (especially a
leg) but gets extended early on in Greek rhetoric (e.g., Aristotle) to designate a

clause (member!) of a *periodos* and then as a subpart—a single prosodic component—of a particular meter.[53] Certain kinds of cola are even "capable of
being used as verses (short periods)" in their own right,[54] and with Aristophanes of Byzantium, as noted, the practice of lineating lyric poetry according
to the shorter metrical cola begins. Sometime prior to Jerome (ca. 347–420 CE)
the latter writing practice was applied to the prose works of rhetoricians, such
as Demosthenes and Cicero,[55] and then Jerome used this "new style of writing"
in his translation of Isaiah (and also of Ezekiel) as an aid for reading—though
he made sure to annotate his writing practice lest there be confusion as to the
(posited) underlying medium of Isaiah:

> Let no one who has seen the Prophets written down in stichs (Lat. *versi-
> bus*) judge them to be in verse (Lat. *metro*) among the Hebrews and at all
> similar to Psalms or the works of Solomon. But, because it is customary
> to write Demosthenes and Cicero *per cola et commata* (even though both
> of them wrote prose and not verse [Lat. *versibus*, lit. "in verses, stichs"]),
> we too (out of concern for a usable text for readers) have used the new
> style of writing to make divisions in the new translation.[56]

Subsequently (esp. from the fifth through ninth centuries CE),[57] other scribes
would emulate this "new style," extending its manner of layout to other books
of the Bible. Hesychius of Jerusalem (ca. 433 CE) is a good example. He treats
the Greek text of the Book of the Twelve in this way, writing them out *per cola
et commata*.[58] And M. B. Parkes exemplifies the practice with a folio page from
the eighth-century Latin Codex Amiatinus in which the Psalms have been
copied (*per cola et commata*) like a prose text: "Here the Psalms are laid out *per
cola et commata*: each new verse, and each of its constituent parts, begins on a
new line close up to the margin. When the unit of sense is too long to be accommodated in a single line the remainder is inset on the next line and the
insetting is continued until the end of the unit."[59] Jerome distinguishes his
new practice of copying from the stichic layout of verse in the Bible (e.g.,
Psalms), and Hesychius of Jerusalem, too, knew of manuscripts in which
some poetic books of the Bible (e.g., Psalms, Job, Song of Songs) were divided
into *stichoi* (*outō meristhenta tois stichois*).[60] The lengths of the verse lines in the
poetical books in Sinaiticus and Vaticanus, for example, are such that the
scribe could only manage two columns of writing instead of the usual three or
four (see fig. 17).[61]

Versus. There are a host of words used by biblical scholars for *verse* that
derive from Latin *versus* (or its congeners, e.g., *verse, versicle, verset, half-verse*),
which, as is evident in J. Treat's foregoing translation of Jerome, is simply the

comparable Latin word for Greek *stichos*.[62] And as noted, both Latin *versus* and *versiculus* feature prominently in Lowth's *Praelectiones*, and Gregory mainly translates both of them literally as "verse(s)" but occasionally as "line(s)" as well (e.g., "the initial letters of each line [*versus* in the original Latin] or stanza following the order of the alphabet").[63]

Membrum. The English term *member* (from Lat. *membrum*) in its now rare sense signifying "a division or clause of a sentence" (*OED*) retains a peculiar currency in biblical studies due entirely to the enormous influence of Lowth's conceptualization of *parallelismus membrorum* ("parallelism between the members") in Lecture XIX of the *Praelectiones*. As A. Baker observes, Lowth's use of *membrum* with this sense "is straight from the usage of classical rhetoricians like Cicero."[64] In fact, Lowth's initial diagnosis of parallelism in the *Praelectiones* is offered chiefly in rhetorical and grammatical terms. This is not surprising since for Lowth "the sententious style" was "the primary characteristic of the Hebrew poetry,"[65] by which he means that "perpetual splendour of the sentences, and the accurate recurrence of the clauses" that "seem absolutely necessary to distinguish the verse."[66] Indeed, there is, writes Lowth, "so strict an analogy between the structure of the sentences and the versification, that when the former chances to be confused or obscured, it is scarcely possible to form a conjecture concerning the division of the lines or verses, which is almost the only part of the Hebrew versification that remains."[67] So when in Lecture XIX Lowth turns to his celebrated analysis of parallelism, the accent is on the "conformation[68] of the sentences," which, Lowth says, "consists chiefly in a certain equality, resemblance, or parallelism between the members of each period; so that in two lines (or members of the same period), things for the most part shall answer to things, and words to words, as if fitted to each by a kind of rule or measure."[69] This way of phrasing his analysis gives Lowth a vocabulary (member, clause, period, proposition) for elaborating the rich play of parallelism in biblical poetry that if always staged by the verse line nonetheless routinely focuses and features subparts of the line: elements—words, phrases, and clauses—that are not necessarily coterminous with the line. The confusing factor comes in the "sententious style" of this poetry, the tendency, as Lowth notes well, for "the close of the verse generally" to fall "where the members of the sentences are divided,"[70] that is, where "every member constitutes an entire verse," and for "periods," too, to divide "into verses, most commonly couplets, though frequently of greater length."[71] Gregory already blurs the distinction between member and line by his occasional glossing of Lowth's *membrum* with an added "line" in translation, as in "frequently one *line* or member (the Latin only has *unum membrum*) contains two sentiments."[72] In this, Gregory is likely influenced by Lowth's later (and more mature) articulation

of his understanding of parallelism in the *Preliminary Dissertation*, which
Gregory actually cites.[73] There more attention is given expressly to the framing
function of the line—"the correspondence of one Verse, or Line, with another,
I call Parallelism."[74] Still, nowhere in either the *Praelectiones* or the later *Isaiah*,
as far as I can discern, is there any confusion on Lowth's part in his use of
member/*membrum* and verse/line/*versus*/*versiculus*.

In a way the situation with respect to the terminology just reviewed is well
understood. Most handbooks dutifully register (and lament) the terminological
diversity and confusion and seek to define and chart the various terms in use
and to get straight the phenomenon in view. The latter is no small accomplishment and should be noted, emphasized, and appreciated. Despite the wide
array of terms and the competing, mostly tacit, theoretical orientations to understanding verse, there is no real confusion as to the underlying phenomenon
that is the focus, namely, what Origen calls a *stichos* and the rabbis (however
restrictively) an *'ārîaḥ* or "small brick." No matter the terminology, then, this
segmented block of language and its recurrent patterns of grouping in biblical
poetry are both well in view. What is presented in the body of the essay consciously builds on this wide-ranging consensus understanding of the field.
I intend to name and to flesh out this understanding, to probe it, elaborate it,
enfold it within and think it through from a particular theoretical perspective,
but the phenomenon itself—the periodic and recurring interruption or checking
of the flow of sense, sound, and rhythm and its resultant segmentation in language that the Masoretes, for example, sometimes wrote out in small bricks (or
chunks) of writing circumscribed by spans of spacing—is well known.

The chief problem with all of these terms is obsolescence. *Member* may be
the most glaring example in the lot. If in Lowth's day it was entirely intelligible
as a designation for a sentential clause, today that sense is all but lost,[75] and
with it the ability to fully appreciate the original discriminating force of
Lowth's terminology. As a result, *member* becomes simply, and mistakenly, a
rough equivalent for *line*, *stich*, *verse*, and *colon*.[76] *Colon*, too, in the sense of a
lineal unit, only rarely occurs outside of a few narrow fields of academic
study—and even there, as in biblical studies, it is not always apparent that
scholars totally appreciate the significance of the term, a situation that provides part of the punch to R. Alter's lampoon of the term as "inadvertently
calling up associations of intestinal organs or soft drinks."[77] To varying degrees similar kinds of obsolescences, in fact, infect the rest of the terms as
well. None of them in current English usage naturally, idiomatically denomi-
nates a line of verse. For that, as Brogan and R. J. Getty note in their treatment
of "stichos" in *The New Princeton Encyclopedia of Poetry and Poetics*,[78] "the noun
form now used is 'line.'"

Also problematic for many of these terms, as Alter notices,[79] is the misleading links they have with classical, and especially Greek, versification. So, for example, the distinctions between *stichos*, *kōlon*, and *komma* (a shorter colon or even a division of a colon),[80] when confined to Greek and Latin works, whether prose or verse, are plain enough. Each involves writing in lines, literally in *stichoi*. The difference is in whether the lines are intentionally divided (as they are not in prose) and if so how they are measured, whether according to meter (the default mode for writing out stichic verse) or sense (as *per cola et commata*). But when these terms are transposed, first, into a discussion of how biblical verse is written out in Greek (and Latin) translation, and then, applied directly to biblical Hebrew poetry itself, the potential for confusion and ambiguity is great. Since biblical Hebrew verse is nonmetrical, there is no meaningful distinction between *stichos* and *kōlon*, as the two become synonymous designations for writing in lines (as opposed to the continuous writing of prose in a running format);[81] nor is there much to differentiate graphically the practice of writing verse in lines because it is verse from the practice of writing prose *per cola et commata* (as in Jerome) as an aid for reading (out loud)— the formatting looks alike in both, hence Jerome's notice in his *Preface to Isaiah* (though obviously other means beyond formatting persisted for distinguishing verse from prose, at least for Jerome). There is also the seemingly ever-present ghost of meter that gets smuggled in under cover of this terminology and that never has been entirely banished from the field's collective imagination. And in the case of a term like *colon*, used in literary discussions from the earliest Greek grammarians and layered with a variety of distinctive if overlapping connotations, a lack of precision accompanies its general usage in reference to biblical poetry.[82]

In the end, the only term in English with currency both in common usage and in the vernacular of literary critical discourse is *line*. As it happens, it is also a term with a pedigree in English-language discussions of biblical verse, at least dating back as far as the Lowth of the *Preliminary Dissertation* and *Isaiah*.[83] Indeed, the terminological shift from the Latin of the *Praelectiones* (*versus, versiculus*) to Lowth's native English in *Isaiah* (verse *and* line) is striking. In a very literal way, then, "Verses properly so called," for the Lowth of *Isaiah*, are most specifically "laid out according to a scale of division" and thus fall "into regular Lines."[84] *Line* is the preferred English gloss for and terminological heir to the Greek *stichos*, as Brogan and Getty indicate, and also for most of the other terms I have reviewed here, including the Latin *versus* and the Greek *kōlon*. And it is, on my accounting, the Hebrew (and West Semitic even) phenomenological equivalent to the Greek *stichos* (following Origen) and the like that are in view here. What is potentially most discomfiting about employing the term *line* in descriptions of biblical poetry is the transparency with which the term foregrounds its etymological origins in a culturally specific manner of writing out verse, *in lines*, a manner that, at the same time, mostly fails to align closely with the normal conventions for formatting biblical verse in the received manuscript traditions (MT). The classically derived terms (e.g., *stich, colon, verse*), with the one exception (*member*), similarly emerge out of chirographic contexts and name practices of writing. In fact, as they are all ultimately rooted in the Greek tradition, they, like the English line, refract the same basic convention for writing out verse, in lines. The vocabulary of the Talmud—ʾārîaḥ and lĕbēnâ—is just one more example of this pattern of denomination. It, too, is thoroughly chirographic in etymology, differing from that of the classical sources, for example, only by dint of the underlying formatting practices that give rise to this specific way of naming—Masoretic conventions foregrounding blocks of writing set amid intermittent spans of uninscribed space, as opposed to the stichic formats of ancient Greek practice. Language, of course, always comes clothed in cultural and historical specifics. It cannot be otherwise. Therefore, we should not become overly distracted by the English term's (or its classical forebears') etymological privileging of one kind of (culturally specific) writing practice. That the interrupting segmentation so characteristic of verse eventually, belatedly gets named for the way it comes to be written out, always in light of culturally specific practices, is a fact (or accident) of history and not terribly surprising or remarkable.

J. Longenbach opens his wonderfully stimulating *The Art of the Poetic Line* by defining poetry as "the sound of language organized in lines" and then says of the line, "More than meter, more than rhyme, more than images or alliteration or figurative language, *line* is what distinguishes our experience of poetry *as poetry*."[85] Longenbach's focus here is not on terminology per se but on the phenomenal reality his chosen terminology ("line") makes visible, namely the shapes, cadences, sounds, and even pulses of thought that the line gives expression to and organizes. I, too, am ultimately interested in this underlying phenomenal reality in biblical verse, by whatever name it may be called. But in calling it specifically a line, in talking about lines as opposed to colons or stichs, for example, we are ushered unmistakably into a world of poems and into a way of talking about poems. This is not insignificant. If what is at stake in the (phenomenal) line is the very sensibility of biblical poetry, then it is the term *line* itself that today in English most readily reveals that fact, that disposes us to encounters with the likes of Longenbach (and Lowth) where lines matter and get theorized. Terminology, as I have said, is never neutral. The English term *line*, with its history of usage by biblicists and its currency in the spoken language as well as in the specialized vernacular of literary criticism, I judge, offers the best chance for coming to know what is at stake in the discussion that follows and for evolving a meaningful and even illuminating way of talking about it, indeed, of having that discussion. The line, phenomenologically and terminologically, is what finally distinguishes our experience of biblical poetry *as poetry*.

Manuscript Evidence for the Line

The question of the line's existence arises, in the first place, because of the lack both of original autographs for ancient biblical poems (only copies of copies have survived) and of a vibrant and contemporary indigenous commentary tradition (like that of fifth-century Athens) that could inform us explicitly about such things as literary norms and conventions, and because the manuscript evidence that has survived does not uniformly deploy metascript conventions for marking poetic line structure. Thus, it must be admitted from the outset that the line in biblical verse will forever be contestable and in need of arguing. Nonetheless, when considered broadly and cumulatively, there is much that points positively and empirically to the existence of the verse line in biblical Hebrew poetry.

I begin by considering the manuscript evidence that does exist. Historically, the visual representation of verse through distinctive page layouts was the leading indicator that something like biblical Hebrew poetry even existed. O'Connor rightly stresses that the breakthrough by Lowth and his eighteenth-century contemporaries came about chiefly because they were "*looking* and not listening."[86] That is, they took their cues *visually* from the manuscript evidence available to them, mainly as embodied in the medieval Masoretic manuscripts.[87] I have already described both the usual pattern of verse formatting that prevails in the three "אמ״ת books" and the unusual patterns commented on explicitly by the rabbis in reference to the various festival songs. In addition, the Masoretes also employ a different accentual system (*t'mym*) in the three books of Job, Proverbs, and Psalms. In actual practice, the scope of what gets specially formatted by the Masoretes is larger still, as Kugel elaborates: "Throughout the Middle Ages, it was common practice for Jewish scribes to use some sort of special spacing at least for the "poetic" books of Psalms, Proverbs, and Job...moreover, isolated songs like the Song of Asaph (1 Chron. 16:8–36), and occasionally Lamentations...as well as lists such as Eccles. 3:2–8, 1 Sam 6:17, Ezra 2:3ff., 1 Chron. 24:7ff., 25:9–14, etc. received special spacing."[88] To summarize, then, the medieval Masoretic manuscripts, through a variety of spatial, columnar, and even lineal formats and a distinctive system of accents, often graphically distinguish a not insubstantial portion of the biblical Hebrew poetic corpus, *though normally the Masoretes wrote out verse in the same manner as prose, in a running format* (e.g., the Latter Prophets).

Special spacing and layout also appear in many copies of the poetic texts of the Bible recovered from the Judean Desert and surrounding environs, some of these predating the earliest medieval Masoretic manuscripts by almost a millennium (e.g., 4QDeut^b, ca. 150–100 BCE; 4QpaleoJob^c, ca. 225–150 BCE). E. Tov, in his recent survey of this material,[89] isolates some thirty scrolls[90] in total that exhibit some form of special layout for poetic texts (4QRP^c [Exod 15]; 1QDeut^b, 4QDeut^b, 4QDeut^c, 4QDeut^q, and 4QpaleoDeut^r [all only Deut 32; if other chapters are preserved, they are in a running format]; 1QPs^a [only Ps 119]; 4QPs^b;[91] 4QPs^c; 4QPs^d (parts of Ps 104); 4QPs^g; 4QPs^h; 4QPs^l; 4QPs^w; 5QPs; 8QPs; 11QPs^a and 11QPs^b [only Ps 119]; 5/6HevPs; MasPs^a; MasPs^b; 4QJob^a; 4QpaleoJob^c; 4QProv^a; 4QProv^b; 3QLam; 5QLam^b; 2QSir; MasSir; 4QMessianic Apocalypse).[92] As he observes, in every instance but one (4QMessianic Apocalypse), stichographic format in the scrolls from Qumran is reserved for biblical texts only (including Ben Sira).[93] The range of poetic texts specially formatted is roughly consistent with what is found in the later Masoretic manuscripts, though at Qumran the formats utilized are more variable and an equal number[94] of manuscripts exists of (often the same) poetic compositions that are set in a running format (4QExod^c and 4QExod^d [with respect to Exod 15]; 4QDeut^j XII [Deut 32]; 1QPs^a [except Ps 119]; 1QPs^b; 1QPs^c; 4QPs^a; 4QPs^c; 4QPs^d [col. III.5 onward]; 4QPs^e; 4QPs^f; 4QPs^j; 4QPs^k; 4QPs^m; 4QPs^n; 4QPs^o; 4QPs^p; 4QPs^q; 4QPs^r; 4QPs^s; 4QPs^u; 4QPs89; 4QPs122; 6QpapPs [?]; 11QPs^a and 11QPs^b [except Ps 119]; 11QPs^c; 11QPs^d; 2QJob; 4QJob^b; 4QLam^a; 4QCant^{a-c}; 5QLam^a; 6QCant; 11QapocrPs)[95]—that is, special formatting for poetic texts apparently was not required at Qumran.[96] Tov describes three principal systems for formatting poetic texts at Qumran. The first utilizes the line of writing as a means for framing the verse line, either with one verse line per columnar line (e.g., 4QDeut^c; 4QPs^b; 4QPs^l; cf. Deut 32 in the Greek P.Fouad inv. 266; 4QDeut^q [contains a combination of one and two lines per columnar line]; see fig. 2)[97] or two (e.g., 4QDeut^b; 4QPs^b (cols. 34–35); 4QPs^g; 4QPs^h; 11QPs^a [only Ps 119]; 4QJob^a; 4QpaleoJob^c; 4QMessianic Apocalypse). Both varieties lack (perceptible) line-internal spacing.[98] The second system recognized by Tov entails two verse lines written on one line of writing, with a space (of uninscribed text) separating the two verse lines and roughly centered in the middle of the columnar line; the first line starts from a straight right margin (e.g., 4QpaleoDeut^r [only Deut 32]; 1QPs^a [only Ps 119]; 4QPs^c;[99] 5QPs; 8QPs; 5/6HevPs; MasPs^a; 4QProv^a; 3QLam; 2QSir; MasSir; see fig. 11). These tend to give the appearance of the "bi-columnar arrangement" typical of Deuteronomy 32 in the Masoretic tradition.[100] In the third system, space is inserted between the individual verse lines (as in the second system) but is not centered on the line of writing, that is, it may occur at different points along the columnar line (e.g., 4QProv[b]; MasPs[b]; see fig. 12). This system resembles (to greater and lesser degrees) the variable Masoretic spacings in the "אמ"ת books."

In general, the specially formatted poetic texts at Qumran do not show any further distinction in their columnar arrangement. All literary compositions, whether verse or prose, from the Judean Desert are organized in columns of writing of more or less uniform dimensions.[101] This follows the general practice evident in both Egyptian papyrus rolls and cuneiform clay tablets—in neither instance does the columnar arrangement vary with regard to the nature of the discourse being copied (figs. 13–14).[102] By contrast, for example, it (eventually) becomes conventional in Greek papyrus rolls from the Hellenistic and Roman eras to display prose in narrower, squared-off columns of writing, separated by uniform intercolumns of uninscribed space (fig. 7), and poetry in wider columns of writing to accommodate the natural lengths of the (metrical) verse lines, which are almost always longer than lines of prose (the hexameter line—sixteen syllables, thirty-four to thirty-eight letters—is the longest verse line), with ragged right-hand margins (fig. 9).[103] The major variation of note in the specially formatted manuscripts from the Judean Desert comes in copies in which the columnar line frames a single verse line. These columns are (comparatively) very narrow (ca. 3.7–4.5 cm; cf. 4QPs[b]; fig. 2).[104]

Two brief observations may be offered with respect to the "special layout" of poetic texts at Qumran. First, it exists—poetic texts are formatted as verse (in a variety of ways)[105] already almost a millennium before the earliest Masoretic manuscripts. Second, not all verse compositions at Qumran receive special formatting. Why this is so, as Tov observes, is not entirely clear.[106] However, such variation does effectively demonstrate that verse (qua verse) at Qumran is ultimately separable from the technological formatting it receives in writing at Qumran, that is, specific psalms, for example, retain a recognizable (though variable) compositional identity whether or not they also happen to be arranged in writing with a special layout. Two examples may be offered by way of illustration. Psalm 102:18–29 is formatted with one verse line per column line in 4QPs[b] (fig. 2) and as a running text in 11QPs[a] (see fig. 15a and b). And in B19a (i.e., the Leningrad or St. Petersburg Codex, fig. 16) space (of varying dimensions) is used to delimit the several verse lines in a columnar line. A similar kind of formatting diversity is exhibited with regard to Psalm 18:39–41, which is set as a running text in 11QPs[d] and with two verse lines per columnar line with intervening medial space in 4QPs[c]; and two still different formats are attested in the Masoretic tradition, depending on where the psalm appears, as a part of the Psalms or as a part of Samuel. In both instances, the words and phrases of the psalms remain relatively stable, and the poetic works they enact are identifiably the same.

There are several other early manuscript traditions in which the verse line is graphically displayed. The Samaritan Pentateuch exhibits certain idiosyncrasies in page format but also shares broad similarities with both the medieval Masoretic and Qumran traditions in laying out the poems in Deuteronomy 32 and Exodus 15.[107] Significantly, in the Samaritan Pentateuch the latter conventions are extended to include the list of blessings in Leviticus 26:3–13 and the poems in Numbers 23–24 (23:7–10, 18–24; 24:3–10, 15–24). Septuagint manuscripts (including some of the oldest uncials, such as Vaticanus, Sinaiticus, and Alexandrinus) and papyrus fragments frequently arrange portions of the biblical poetic corpus *per cola et commata*.[108] These regularly include the same poetic texts that receive special formatting in the Hebrew manuscript traditions (especially Psalms, Job, and Proverbs but also a part of Deuteronomy 32 in P.Fouad 266b). However, in several instances, the Greek manuscripts provide our earliest examples of special formatting for several biblical poetic collections, including most spectacularly that of the Song of Songs (see fig. 17).[109] Both Jerome and Hesychius of Jerusalem, as noted, explicitly state their awareness of verse formatting for Psalms, Proverbs, Qoheleth, Job, and Song of Songs. Treat cites the much earlier commentary on the Song by Hippolytus of Rome (ca. second century CE) in which the stichometry of the Song is tallied.[110] He goes on to remark, "examination of the manuscripts at our disposal [Vaticanus, Sinaiticus, and Alexandrinus, among others] gives some comfort to the notion that the Song of Songs was arranged *per cola et commata* from a very early period."[111] The general practice answers well to Parkes's description of the layout of the Psalms in Codex Amiatinus: each line of verse is written on a corresponding manuscript line, and should the verse line need to be carried over to a second manuscript line, the latter is indented.[112] What is especially significant about the stichographic layout of the Song in the various Septuagint manuscripts—and it should be stressed that Septuagint manuscripts without line divisions of the Song are also preserved (e.g., 952, Venetus)—is that while the lineation generally (though not always by any means) follows the sense divisions suggested by the Masoretic tradition of accentuation,[113] the Masoretes do not themselves distinguish line structure in the Song visually through special page layout. And thus, the Greek tradition substantially expands the graphic evidence for verse formatting of this poetic collection from the Bible.

The later Greek and Latin manuscript traditions also preserve evidence for the stichographic arrangement of some poetic portions of the Hebrew Bible. But after Jerome, of course, the simple fact of a text laid out in lines according to sense cannot be taken on its face as evidence of verse. Jerome himself makes this clear in his insistence on the prosaic nature of Isaiah despite his choice of layout schemes. Still, one might choose to dispute this contention, for example, as most contemporary scholars now do (following Lowth), in which case, given the "sententious style" of biblical verse, one may—and in fact should—choose to consult Jerome's sense-based lineation when attempting to discern the shape and form of individual lines of verse in any of the Isaianic traditions. In other words, even post-Jerome *per cola et commata* layouts, regardless of their originating motivations, ultimately are not irrelevant for understanding and appreciating biblical Hebrew poetic line structure.

In sum, it may be fairly (empirically) stated that the several manuscript traditions I have reviewed here—Masoretic, Qumran, Samaritan Pentateuch, and the various Septuagint manuscripts and papyri fragments—display through columnar and stichographic formats a substantial portion of what contemporary scholars, post-Lowth, recognize as verse in the Bible— a small bit of Third Isaiah (Isa 61:10–62:9) in 1QIsaᵃ (a manuscript otherwise formatted as a running text) containing extra spacing that displays the poetry's line structure (fig. 18)[114] shows that even verse from the Latter Prophets, at least on this one occasion, could receive special formatting in antiquity. Moreover, in terms of coverage (i.e., what gets formatted; compare especially the Qumran and Masoretic traditions), of the nature, content, and extent of the verse line itself, and even of the techniques of formatting (i.e., the use of spacing and the line of writing—obviously leaving aside the Greek and Latin manuscripts in this instance as they reflect entirely different cultural conventions for writing out verse), these traditions exhibit "within large bounds" noticeable similarities and a rough consistency.[115] O'Connor's estimation that these traditions of writing biblical "verse as line units" are the "greatest source" for our knowledge of biblical Hebrew verse[116] and, more specifically, of the verse line itself is surely right, and, if anything, deserves underscoring. Indeed, we in the West are so accustomed to seeing lineated verse in writing that it is easy to forget that neither the graphic display of verse in writing nor the specific convention of *lineation* ("division into lines," *OED*) are themselves inevitable or ubiquitous. Special formatting for verse in writing, whatever its nature, is a "metascript" convention of the kind that is "always incorporated into a writing system."[117] Such conventions, though peripheral to a writing system's main visual component, the grapheme, nonetheless, provide readers with important, supplementary information like direction of writing, word division, punctuation, paragraphing, and so on that is "essential to the writing system."[118] The material particulars of any "metascript" convention, when and if they eventually occur, whether they are deliberately designed or arise incidentally, will vary with time, place, and script tradition. That is, "metascript" conventions, like the script traditions and writing systems of which they

are a part, are themselves artifactual in nature. They are technologies,[119] practices (of writing) that arise and take on meaning only locally, in culturally and
historically specific environments. Therefore, whether or not verse structure, for
example, is given explicit, graphic representation in any particular writing system
is not a given but falls out (if it falls out) as a matter of local practice.

The usual practice of displaying verse in writing (or print) by setting individual verses on a line of their own most familiar to those of us in the West is
a case in point. It has a specifiable genealogy. The convention may be traced
back through the various European vernacular traditions (e.g., Old English,
Old French) to Medieval Latin models, which in turn were themselves borrowed and adapted from Greek forerunners.[120] In fact, the practice of writing
hexameter verse with each verse on a line of its own appears to date as far back
as the eighth century BCE (e.g., "Nestor's cup," see fig. 19).[121] However, there is
no reason to think that this manner of representation is the only way to display
verse in writing. To the contrary, even the most cursory of surveys reveals not
only a bewildering array of spaces, points, wedges, lines, and other forms of
punctuation (individually or in combination) used to display verse in known
writing systems but also writing systems in which verse is *not* distinguished
(graphically) from prose. Three examples may be offered by way of illustration.
Consider, initially, one of the earliest writing traditions, Mesopotamian cuneiform, where special formatting conventions for verse were in place from an
early period and predate the advent of any written Greek conventions by millennia (see fig. 14). B. R. Foster describes the typical means for representing
Akkadian verse: "each line tends to be divided into halves, sometimes indicated, especially in later manuscripts, by a blank space in the middle of the
[columnar] line."[122] Also a "colon," consisting of either a diagonal or vertical
wedge, or even two vertical wedges, could be used to separate the two poetic
lines on a columnar line. Other times, one line per column line was used, with
additional spacing between signs when the number of words was insufficient
to fill up the line completely.[123] Here, then, there is a use of lineation for formatting verse, but it has an entirely different profile from the Greek one-verse-
line-per-column-line convention and is often combined with a use of spacing
and/or extra cuneiform wedges. The presence of the latter (cuneiform wedges)
further makes apparent the always informing imprint of local custom and culture on the practices of writing, including layout. It is the materiality of the
writing surface (on clay) and the manner of impression (with a reed stylus)
that leads to the employment of cuneiform wedges as verse dividers.

Medieval Latin verse conventions offer another telling example. Here it is the
variability and plurality of the conventions that are of note, especially since their
defining feature, the one verse per line format, is so obviously indebted to Greek

forerunners.[124] Parkes identifies three basic layouts for medieval Latin poetry, in each the individual verse was copied on a line of its own: hexameter verse was aligned against the left margin, with one verse following another without any formal grouping; in elegiac couplets, the first line of the couplet (hexameter) was aligned against the margin, and the second (pentameter) was indented; in lyric stanzas, the first line was set against the margin, and all remaining lines were indented.[125] Variations on these basic layouts abound, and all may get overlaid with multiple forms of punctuation (e.g., points marking the end of verses, braces joining rhyme words, a *littera notabilior* heading individual verses or stanzas (fig. 20)—Latin hymns, for example, were often written continuously across the manuscript line with only points separating the individual verses.[126]

A final example by way of illustration is the customary Egyptian practice of writing everything (including verse) continuously across the writing space.[127] Sometimes Egyptian verse compositions are graphically distinguished. For example, there is a Third Intermediate Period copy of the *Teaching of Amenenope* in which "each line of verse was written on a separate line," and red "verse points" would be used (often inconsistently) in some verse compositions (beginning already in the Middle Kingdom but becoming widespread only in the New Kingdom) to mark the ends of lines[128]—the latter practice even influenced the writing down of two Akkadian compositions in Egypt.[129] But in Egyptian "texts were generally written continuously."[130] And this is normative—"stichic writing is extremely rare."[131] The "tendency *not* to distinguish verse from prose in writing," as R. Parkinson and S. Quirke observe, "is far from unique" (see fig. 13).[132] Old English verse as a rule "is copied in long lines across the writing space" (fig. 21), with no consistent scribal distinctions for marking verse (at least until very late, when some line-end pointing is evidenced, e.g., Oxford, Bodleian Library, Junius 11). The use of nonlinguistic spatial and graphic conventions as aids for decoding and reading in Old English manuscripts develops only gradually over time.[133] The same is true of the ancient Levant. Verse compositions were not initially set out with any kind of special formatting, at least as far as we can tell. Admittedly, there are only two major corpora of verse currently extant, the Ugaritic mythological texts (ca. thirteenth century BCE; fig. 22) and the collection of Aramaic proverbs attached to the figure of Ahiqar (Elephantine, ca. fifth century BCE; fig. 23). There are also several display inscriptions (ink on plaster), those from Deir ʿAlla (*KAI* 312; 800–750 BCE; fig. 24) and one from Kuntillet Ajrud (*KA* 4.2; ca. 800 BCE; fig. 25), whose patently high literary registers (which contrast noticeably with the workaday register of West Semitic epigraphs) are suggestive of West Semitic and biblical poetry more generally.[134] Neither, however, manipulates space or the like systematically for the specific purpose of displaying line format. In the case of Ugaritic, although the normal practice is to write verse, like prose, continuously across the column, there are some notable exceptions, such as CAT 1.10 and, to a lesser extent, CAT 1.23 (cf. CAT 1.96, 161), where the verse line corresponds to the columnar line on the tablet.[135] Otherwise only in the so-called Carpentras stele (*KAI* 269; fig. 26), an Aramaic funerary inscription of the fifth or fourth century BCE, do we have a kind of graphic display of line format in West Semitic prior to Qumran. Even in Greek papyrus rolls, early finds, such as the Timotheos papyrus (ca. fourth century BCE; fig. 8),[136] suggest that Greek verse was not always written out in the one-verse-per-line format that eventually became the norm for Greek stichic verse and ultimately was taken over by the European vernacular traditions during the Middle Ages and Renaissance.[137]

The large point to be made in light of these several examples is that there is no zero-sum, universally applicable standard for the presentation of verse forms in writing. It simply does not follow that verse will inevitably be distinguished in writing, let alone lined out, for example, in the fashion of Greek metrical verse. This suggests that any notation of line structure in the biblical manuscript traditions is noteworthy. The manuscript traditions' major blind spot—the Latter Prophets—remains somewhat obscure, though it is probably not inconsequential that prophetic verse is treated all but uniformly—recall the small bit of Third Isaiah (Isa 61:10–62:9) that is specially formatted in 1QIsaᵃ. And on all current evidence, it appears that poetic texts (verse) from the biblical period, like their prosaic counterparts, were written normatively in a running format—that Egyptian practice was the principal model for writing on papyrus and leather at this time and in this region cannot be overemphasized.[138] Moreover, that the lack of visual distinctiveness in the writing down of verse (vis-a-vis prose, for example) is no impermeable barrier to the ultimate apprehension and appreciation of the underlying medium also needs underscoring. The addition of spatial and graphic cues, such as the special layout schemes in evidence for poetic texts from the Judean Desert or in the various Masoretic manuscripts, surely assisted readers in decoding by providing additional interpretive information.[139] But just as surely written poetic texts are readable as "verse" even in the absence of such spatial cues. As Brogan, for example, emphasizes, line structure in verse is not only or even primarily a graphic entity, something which must always be made manifest in writing, on the page. To the contrary, the poetic line has rhythmic, sonic, and even syntactic structure such that its shape is ultimately apprehensible no matter the manner of presentation.[140] Furthermore, allowances are also to be made for the different kinds of demands that different kinds of formatting require of readers. What is required in those cases in which verse compositions are not laid out with any special format is a different kind of readerly contribution, one that involves bringing a great deal of predictive knowledge and expertise to the reading process.[141] So ancient readers (mostly scribes) of biblical poems, who still would have been profoundly shaped by a predominantly oral world and thus their reading practices mediated (to a large extent) by voice,[142] would not have come to these kinds of texts de novo, but would have encountered them within a context of expectations, knowing, for example, the (general) content and relevant poetic conventions,[143] and thus the presence of parallelism, a relative terseness or concision of phrasing, uniformity and simplicity of clause structure, and other (nongraphic) indicators of biblical verse, like the presence of rhyme in some medieval Latin lyrics written in a running format, would have been sufficient "to arouse a reader's expectations of a poetic text."[144]

Spacing as a means for graphically distinguishing line units, as at Qumran and in the later Masoretic tradition, only begins to evolve during or just before the Hellenistic period, out of specifically (later) Aramaic scribal practices.[145] Therefore, that large portions of the poetic materials from the period—especially the poems (or parts of poems) that eventually get embedded in the Former Prophets or amassed in the various collections of the Latter Prophets—should continue to be found in a running format is perhaps unremarkable.[146] Even at Qumran not only are there versions of biblical verse in running format but nonbiblical verse is copied as a rule in a running format (e.g., 4QH[a–f]; 4QShirShabb[a–f]; the one exception is 4QMessianic Apocalypse, written with two verse lines per columnar line). Moreover, it seems likely that Kugel is correct in his assumption that at some point the rabbinic discussion interfered with and eventually blocked the evolution and possible expansion of the special formatting traditions to biblical Hebrew verse more generally.[147] One notices here and there in the various manuscript traditions signs of analogical extension of the practice(s) of spacing and lineation (e.g., Ben Sira at Qumran and Masada, Lamentations in B19a [Leningrad Codex], Num 23–24 in the Samaritan Pentateuch, the Song in OG), but ultimately the scribal convention as to what of biblical verse gets specially marked (for whatever reason) becomes more or less fixed as described above. Finally, however important is page layout for our scholarly ability to discern the facticity of biblical verse—and it is absolutely crucial—the belatedness (quite literally so with respect to all extant manuscripts of biblical poems) of these practices, their "epiphenomenality,"[148] requires underscoring. What Parkes says of classical antiquity, that "there is little evidence before the sixth century [CE] that...punctuation...originated with the author,"[149] would surely apply as well to the scribal cultures of the ancient Near East. That is, even were archaeologists to uncover, say, a seventh-century manuscript containing biblical poems, not only would it likely have been written in a running format, given the prevailing scribal conventions of the day (e.g., *KA* 4.2), but even were there to be some graphic indications of verse (e.g., the use of the columnar line to frame a parallel couplet, as in the Carpentras stele or the display of several of the proverbs from the Ahiqar collection) those would still not likely go back to a presumptive "author."[150] The widespread assumption on the part of many biblical scholars that the graphic display of the verse line in writing is inevitable, somehow inherent to the very nature of verse itself, is more naive than anything else, reflective, I suspect, of the strong (and mostly unexamined) literate bias of contemporary Western scholarship, but at any rate running counter to all expectations based on current understandings of ancient scribal and authorial practices.

* * *

TO CONCLUDE THIS section's survey of manuscript evidence for the verse line, I want to return to Lowth, for importantly this eighteenth-century divine did not share the rabbis' convention-bound inhibitions as to what of the biblical text could and could not be specially formatted.[151] As O'Connor recognizes, one of Lowth's truly remarkable achievements comes precisely in expanding what is to be considered verse in the Bible.[152] The magnitude of this accomplishment is not to be missed. O'Connor emphasizes the latter by observing on the one hand the "unusual selection of verse" that is "presented in lineation" in the manuscript traditions known to Lowth and on the other hand the lack of even a "hint" that "the poetic character of the rest of Hebrew verse was recognized."[153] And yet Lowth, in what remains a mostly compelling way, manages "to observe the crucial phenomena *and* conceive a vocabulary with which to describe them."[154] The logic that undergirds Lowth's project of expansion is analogy. He reasons that "whatever plain signs or indications there yet remain of metre, or rhythm, or whatever else it was, that constituted Hebrew Verse"[155] in the so-called poetic books (Psalms, Proverbs, Job)[156] similarly should be construed as signs of verse in other parts of the Hebrew canon. This logic is verbalized explicitly in a number of places, and is especially elaborated and exemplified in the *Preliminary Dissertation*.[157] Here, however, I want to return to the visual component of Lowth's argumentation remarked on briefly earlier, a dimension that has not always received adequate attention. One of the distinctive features of Lowth's three Latin editions of the *Praelectiones* (1753, 1763, 1775) is the inclusion in them of the Hebrew text of the biblical passages he cites throughout.[158] The following exemplifies his practice (see fig. 1a–b):

מקולות מים רבים

אדירים משברי ים

אדיר במרום יהוה:

(Ps 93:4)[159]

יאבד יום אולד בו
והלילה אמר חרה גבר:
(Job 3:3)[160]

כמים הפנים לפנים
כן לב האדם לאדם:
(Prov 27:19)[161]

יערף כמטר לקחי
תזל כטל אמרתי:
כשערים עלי דשא
וכרביבים עלי עשב:
(Deut 32:2)[162]

In each case, the Hebrew is unvocalized and right adjusted, and each verse line is set on a single line on the page—the latter convention, no doubt, inspired by the formatting of the Greek and Latin poets Lowth had read and studied since his school days at Winchester College and by the English verse conventions of his own day. (Lowth after all was a poet himself.)[163] These examples come from the three poetical books and Deuteronomy 32, and the line breaks in them match the spacing typically used to divide lines in the Masoretic manuscripts of these books, as may be judged by comparing, for example, the appropriate folios in the Aleppo Codex and B19a.[164]

This is Lowth's practice throughout the *Praelectiones*, even—and this is the significant bit—in those cases where the Masoretes did not use any special kind of spacing or stichographic format. That is, Lowth extends his line format to passages that he establishes on other grounds (e.g., from the presence of parallelism) as poetic. So, for example, his first cited poetic text (coming in Lecture IV) is Genesis 4:23–24, which he sets in lines contrary to what he would have seen in any of the Masoretic manuscripts to which he had access or even in Michaelis's printed edition (see fig. 27):[165]

עדה וצלה שמען קולי
נשי למך האזנה אמרתי:
כי איש הרגתי לפצעי
וילד לחברתי:
כי שבעתים יקם קין
ולמך שבעים ושבעה:

In this manner, Lowth extends the graphic presentation of biblical Hebrew verse beyond anything known at that time. It would still take roughly another century and a half before Lowth's practice was "canonized" in R. Kittel's first edition of *Biblia Hebraica*,[166] published in 1905–6 and printed with almost all of biblical verse set off in lines, and another half century more before his Latin and English verse translations were emulated, as in the 1952 Revised Standard Version, the very influential modern English-language translation of the Bible.[167]

There are now a handful of places where manuscript evidence has emerged since Lowth in which the logic and sense of his judgment may be gauged *graphically*. The small bit of Third Isaiah (Isa 61:10–62:9) in 1QIsa[a] wherein extra spacing displays the poetry's line structure in a manuscript otherwise formatted as a running text provides a stunning example (fig. 18). The spacing in this small portion of 1QIsa[a] broadly reflects the accentuation in MT, and in 62:5 it mirrors exactly the lineation displayed in Lowth's *Praelectiones* (figs. 28–29),[168] which he arranges one verse line per manuscript line in the following manner:

כי יבעל בחור בתולת

יבעלוך בניך

ומשוש חתן על כלה

ישיש עליך אלהיך

Here, then, the special layout of this part of 1QIsa[a] mirrors the verse layout generated by Lowth's logic of analogy, that is, by his reasoning that "whatever plain signs or indications there yet remain of metre, or rhythm, or whatever else it was, that constituted Hebrew Verse" in the three poetic books similarly should be construed as signs of verse in other parts of the Hebrew canon.[169]

The other example of note is Ben Sira. With only Greek translations available to him, Lowth nonetheless was able to discern the poetic nature of the presumed Hebrew original. Here he is comparing Ben Sira explicitly to Proverbs:

> There is great similarity in the matter, the sentiments, and the diction; the complexion of the style, and the construction of the periods, are quite the same; so that I cannot entertain a doubt, that the author actually adopted the same mode of versification, whatever it was, if we can admit that any knowledge of the Hebrew metres was extant at the time when he was supposed to have written.[170]

So confident was Lowth that he offered a "Hebrew translation" of Ben Sira 24 to close his lecture on didactic poetry (XXIV). This he dutifully lined out as was his custom in the *Praelectiones* more generally, that is, one verse line per manuscript line (fig. 30).[171] One of the great text finds of the nineteenth century was the recovery of a great many manuscripts from the Cairo Geniza, among which were found Hebrew fragments of Ben Sira.[172] Several of the

Geniza Ben Sira manuscripts (esp. B, see fig. 31; but also E and F)[173] were in fact specially formatted: two poetic lines (a couplet) are written on each manuscript line, with a large intervening intercolumn of space separating the two poetic lines. And then in 1964 a similarly formatted papyrus scroll of Ben Sira was recovered from Masada.[174] Unfortunately, neither the Masada scroll nor any of the (lineated) Geniza manuscripts preserve material from Ben Sira 24, so we do not have the kind of very precise graphic confirmation of Lowth's lineation that the version of Isaiah 62:5 found in 1QIsa[a] furnishes. Still, the lineated Geniza manuscripts and the Masada scroll do offer visual testimony (through their formatting) to the poetic nature of Ben Sira more generally (i.e., it can be set as verse). Moreover, the blocks of writing separated by spacing in these manuscripts conform generally to the special layout conventions that prevail in the Masoretic manuscripts and throughout the Dead Sea Scrolls and are more or less equivalent to the poetic line that Lowth routinely sets on its own throughout the *Praelectiones*, and especially here in his version of Ben Sira 24.

I have lingered over Lowth's graphic display of the Hebrew verse line for a variety of reasons. First, it represents a level of argumentation in the *Praelectiones* that is easily missed because it is not explicitly narrativized, conveyed discursively in propositional content. Instead, it is argued graphically, given to the eyes (almost alone) for an unabashedly literate audience. More particularly, it illustrates, quite stunningly and graphically, one way Lowth extrapolates from insights gleaned from the received tradition about biblical verse (namely, that which was embodied in the Masoretic manuscripts). Further, Lowth's graphic presentation shows (again literally) the critical importance of the line to his own conception of poetry (verse) and, as crucial, his perception of the centrality of the line to biblical Hebrew verse structure, as O'Connor, again, well notices.[175] Indeed, this perception itself, especially in those places where it moves out beyond the graphic displays of the Masoretic tradition, in turn, becomes an important resource for considering biblical Hebrew line structure. Lowth's lineation is always open to question, of course, as are others', including the graphic formatting traditions canonized in the Masoretic tradition.[176] In fact, it was Lowth's perception of variability in that tradition[177] that gave him warrant not only to question the line formats of MT (these are themselves but somebody's construals, however privileged they may be) but to perceive the presence of verse even in those places where the Masoretes had failed to lineate. Thus, Lowth models the only way by which contemporary critics can ultimately get at biblical Hebrew line structure, namely: through interpretation, that is, by actively construing them as *lines*. Finally, in juxtaposing Lowth's line formats with those of MT (and other textual traditions, namely Qumran, Samaritan Pentateuch, Septuagint, Vulgate, etc.), especially (again) in those places where Lowth moves beyond MT, it begins to become apparent that the major difference between these is a matter of technology, that is, a matter of how biblical verse is displayed *in writing*. As I continue to stress hereafter, there is no reason to assume that graphic display is at all *necessarily* integral to the notion of biblical Hebrew verse. There is no denying its "great importance" to the field's recovery of biblical verse (for which Lowth and his contemporaries deserve much credit), but that it is itself definitional of biblical verse can hardly be sustained.

The "Verse Line" in Oral Poetry

In this next section, I frame the discussion from the perspective of oral poetry. There is no doubt that any historical assessment of biblical literature (poetic or otherwise) ultimately will need to be ready, as R. Thomas urges with respect to ancient Greek literature, "to countenance literacy and orality together."[178] My emphasis here on orality is heuristic and pragmatic, to focus on the possibility of articulating line structure without visual or graphic cues. Thus, it is enough to stipulate the overwhelming orality of the biblical world, the oral roots of biblical verse as an art form, and the likelihood that much (though not all) of biblical verse, however originally composed and finally transmitted, was intended to be vocalized in some kind of oral performance (for details, see chapter 4).

Historically, the graphic display of the verse line on the page of a manuscript is epiphenomenal.[179] It is a byproduct of writing and the scribal conventions that grow up around this particular technology and not, at least initially, inherent to the notion of which the line itself is but a literate conceptualization. The presence or absence of the visual display of the verse line of the same poetic works at Qumran captures quite effectively something of this epiphenomenality—but the same point could be made (to different degrees) by considering several other of the poetic corpora mentioned above, namely the mythological texts from Ugarit, Ahiqar, and so on. The chief upshot here, well articulated by Brogan (among others), is that "the distinction between v[erse] and pr[ose] is not one between media and essences, precisely, but between structures and effects" and the latter, though surely associated with lineation, in fact inhere in the linguistic sequences themselves and their segmentation "regardless of presentational mode" and "would be left intact" even without the graphic representation of writing.[180] R. Tsur underscores this point with reference to the role of "intonation patterns" in poetry reading:

> Just as the graphic arrangement on the page presents the lines as perceptual units to the eye, the intonation contours heard in the reading of

poetry present the lines as perceptual units to the ear. *In fact, the main function of the graphic arrangement on the page is to give the reader instructions concerning the intonation contours appropriate to the lines*; whereas the intonation contours appropriate to the syntactic units are determined by our linguistic competence.[181]

Once the technology of writing is invented, and specific metascript conventions for displaying verse structure (such as *stichic* lineation in ancient Greek scribal practice) are elaborated, then they, too, become available for exploiting prosodically. Various forms of contemporary free verse depend most explicitly on a visual prosody in order to indicate the shape of the line.[182] Of course, as J. Hollander shows, examples of poems written as much for the eye as for the ear predate the advent of modern free verse by centuries.[183] Indeed, Akkadian and Hebrew acrostic poems, insofar as they are predicated on an explicitly graphic conceit,[184] are among the world's earliest poems composed for the eye. But even in these cases to think that the line can function without the resources of sound and rhythm is to succumb to what Perloff describes as the "linear fallacy."[185] And Perloff is not alone among critics and poets who stress the underlying and always informing auditory reality of verse.[186] It is the latter that is necessarily paramount in orally performed poetry of all varieties. As J. M. Foley notices with reference to the (then) Yugoslav *guslari* studied by M. Parry and A. B. Lord, "the minimal 'atom' in their compositional idiom was the poetic line."[187] Line structure, if it is to exist in an oral poem,[188] if it is to be perceived in performance, must be articulated in the absence of the (now) usual visual aids (e.g., lineation, white space) that we in the West have grown accustomed to in writing. Without the graphic signals enabled by writing, oral verse forms must use other means for marking line-ends, as well as other junctures in a poem's macrostructure. Some of these—pitch, tone, loudness, facial and hand gestures, melody—will be encoded only in the most intentional and self-conscious written transcripts of an oral poem,[189] and almost never in written versions of poems (however orally inflected) from antiquity. Others, however, impact the language itself or its content in ways that may still be discerned in writing. Four of these means are especially relevant for considering line marking in biblical Hebrew poems.

Silence and Pausal Lengthening

The outstanding means for signaling line-end in orally performed verse is silence, a breaking off of the language material: lines in oral verse are "usually marked at both ends by short or long pauses."[190] One of the chief functions of pauses in rhythmic structure more generally is to delimit and individualize. Energy is either being conserved or released—"Line breaks define energy."[191] At the moment of reversal between the two there is "an interval, a pause, a rest, by which the interaction of opposed energies is defined and rendered perceptible."[192] In fact, our brains require pauses every several seconds in order to assess and assimilate the percepts of observation. Rhythm enhances this capacity. Though silence cannot be literally translated in writing, it can be represented (e.g., by oblique strokes, space) and not infrequently is associated with observable phonological shifts and the like, such as pausal lengthening.[193] Pausal lengthening is common in Tiberian Hebrew.[194] And while the phenomenon itself does not differentiate prose and verse (both were read out loud), other considerations, such as the percentage of pausal forms with the *'atnāḥ* (higher in the nonpoetic books),[195] the appearance of pausal forms with the *'ôleh wĕyôrēd* (only in the poetic books),[196] and the generally more regular units demarcated by pausal forms in poetic compositions,[197] do. The facticity of pause, then, and the phonological lengthening that it triggers are both positive indicators of line-end in biblical verse. Both are, as well, primordially aural phenomena, of which any graphic representations are, as a matter of course, belated, secondary.

Sentence Logic

Calculating the pause, figuring when it is to come, is often a matter of numbers—meter.[198] After the designated number of stresses, syllables, words, or whatever,[199] is reached, the line ends and there is a pause, silence. But not all oral poetry is metrical.[200] And in nonmetrical varieties of oral verse other means or reasons for ending a line are (of necessity) exploited. Sentence logic is one such other reason to end a line.[201] It is very common in much oral verse—and also in much (if not most) conventional metrical written verse—for lines to be made up of syntactic wholes, complete sentences, clauses, and phrases; line-end and syntactic juncture coincide. In large part this is in deference to the needs of the perceiving human brain. "To hold longer stretches in mind, you need to make an effort to remember the *meanings* of short phrases rather than the *sounds* of individual words, thereby building larger observations."[202] So cutting up the flow of speech into *meaningful* chunks—phrases, clauses, and the like—is crucial to the comprehension and enjoyment of larger wholes in oral verbal art. Indeed, "the most natural way to a pause," writes M. Kinzie, "is to come to the end of a phrase, clause, or sentence."[203] As the experience of this coincidence is repeated and ultimately conventionalized, clausal or phrasal boundaries themselves become effective signals of line-end. Biblical verse, as often noted,[204] is of this kind, that is, it is prominently end-stopped; line-boundary normally converges with the end of discrete syntactic units. This is precisely what Lowth means by his notion of "sententious style," that tendency for period and pause to coincide at line-end.[205] Indeed, the characteristically closed and recursive shape of biblical Hebrew poetic rhythm is itself chiefly a product of end-stopping and parallelism. A clausal or sentential whole (frame) is articulated and then reiterated once or twice over, producing (optimally) a halting or pulsing series of progressions—one step forward, iteration, and then another step forward, reiteration, and sometimes twice over (in the case of triplets), and so on. The recursion of parallelism redoubles the syntactic frame, and in the process reinforces the projection of wholeness and the felt fullness of the stop at line-end.

This end-stopping (sententious) style is the hallmark of oral art forms because it facilitates the easy consumption of whole ideas and "because of the paratactic ordering and linear progression of thought" that it allows, and thus perhaps one of the surest signs of biblical poetry's deep rootage in and enduring debt to oral performance.[206] End-pauses punctuate and thus circumscribe these syntactic wholes.[207] The opposite of end-stopping is enjambment, "the linked continuation of phrase or clause across the line boundary, creating a certain 'tugging' effect."[208] It is the counterpointing of syntax against the line that creates the sense of "tugging" (and other effects).[209] The effectiveness of this tug—whether it is perceived as strong or weak—depends on a variety of features, but in particular is isomorphic to the plasticity of line marking. In print cultures, where the line is presented visually, the counterpointing effect of enjambment can probably have its strongest and most varied effects. Since readers can assess line boundaries visually,[210] the poet (if she wishes) can devote all her linguistic and poetic efforts to the play in other dimensions. Slowed-down, written modes of expression also facilitate the processing of more complex (and linear) syntactic structures as well,[211] meaning that the most violent forms of enjambment are rare in oral-based poetic traditions. Still, run-on sentences are possible, and indeed not uncommon, in oral and oral-derived verse. So, for example, in Homer's *Iliad* enjambment is not at all uncommon, amounting to some 51.2 percent of the lines.[212] Homer's verse is metrical, and the line, to a large degree, is itself articulated by the numerical counting that constitutes the meter, and as a consequence other linguistic features (e.g., syntax) or poetic tropes (e.g., anaphora) are not (as) required for end-fixing and thus are freer to be used as vehicles for counterpointing. But even in nonmetrical varieties of oral (and oral-derived) verse, run-on sentences occur, in roughly the same percentages and roughly of the same character. When the coincidence of line boundary and major syntactic juncture (sentence, clause, phrase) is maintained, the cuts are mostly mild in effect and usually result in an additive (or supplementary) kind of syntax, that is, where main clauses are expanded in typical ways. The result is a "parsing" kind of line in which the line, though not end-stopped, nonetheless generally follows "the normative turns of the syntax, breaking it at predictable points rather than cutting against it."[213] A. Woodbury cites an example from Central Alaskan Yupik Eskimo:

> "Aa ^tua:=i=w' tangentril[ngua] ^camek!"
> "Aling aren piyagaat=llu=ggem amllelartut;
> lagiyagaat=llu,
> mat'um nalliini."
>
> "Oh ^well.but I.didn't.see ^anything!"
> "Dear me! My! but.baby.ons.after.all they.are.abundant;
> and.baby.geese,
> of.this at.its.time."[214]

The last two lines supplement or modify the otherwise syntactically complete main clause in the second line. More noticeable effects can be achieved, even while maintaining phrasal integrity, either by stacking clauses in a single line or staging word order in nonnormative ways. The former may be illustrated by another Central Alaskan Yupik Eskimo example taken from Woodbury's discussion:

> Tutgara'urluqelriigneg ilaluteng. Tutgara'urlurlua ^im',
> tan'ga'urlull'rauluni angutnguluni=w'
>
> and.two.in.grandchild.relationship they.included. Her.poor.grandchild ^that
> he.was.a.por.little.boy he.being.a.male.though.[215]

The sense of closure at line-end pause is substantially eroded by the continuation of the syntax.

In biblical Hebrew verse two broad types of run-on lines are in evidence. In the first, parallelism continues to frame the component lines of a couplet or triplet, but various kinds of syntactic dependencies are formed between succeeding couplets and/or triplets.[216] Psalm 106:47 is a good example:

hôšî'ēnû yhwh 'ĕlōhênû	Deliver us, O LORD our God,
wĕqabbĕṣēnû min-haggôyim	and gather us from among the nations,

> *lĕhōdôt lĕšēm qodšekā*   to acclaim Your holy name,
> *lĕhištabbēaḥ bithillātekā*   to glory in Your praise (NJV)

The infinitive constructs of the last two lines in this example are dependent on the main clauses in the first, while the lines within each couplet parallel one another. More commonly (making up as much as a third of the biblical poetic corpus),[217] the couplet or triplet's internal parallelism is dropped and the sense and syntax of the first line spills over into the succeeding lines. In almost all instances, there remains a strong coincidence between line and major constituent boundaries (i.e., syntactic cuts are made mostly at phrase and clause boundaries, only occasionally at word boundaries, and never at domains below the word level) and a full stop usually occurs at the end of the couplet or triplet. Most result in normal kinds of syntactic expansions, for example, through the addition of prepositional or appositional phrases, dependent nominals, and so on.[218] The following examples illustrate:

> *māgēn 'im-yē'āreh wārōmaḥ*   Was shield or spear to be seen
> *bĕ'arbā'îm 'elep bĕyiśrā'ēl*   among forty thousand in Israel?
>   (Judg 5:8, NRSV)

> *yārōnnû wĕyiśmĕḥû*   Let those who desire my vindication
> *ḥăpēṣê ṣidqî*   shout for joy and be glad
>   (Ps 35:27, NRSV)

> *wattēḥāšeb lô liṣdāqâ*   And that had been reckoned to
>   him as righteousness
> *lĕdōr wādōr 'ad-'ôlam*   from generation to generation forever
>   (Ps 106:31, NRSV)

In each case, the first line, containing the main clause, is syntactically complete, and thus the syntactic tug that accompanies the expansion in the second line is mild and belated, almost like an afterthought. Occasionally, disrupted word order will enhance the syntactic tug at line-end. In Ps 5:8, for example, the verb is only given in the second line:

> *wa'ănî bĕrōb ḥasdĕkā*   As for me, in your abundant steadfast love,
> *'ābô' bêtekā*   I will enter your house (cf. ASV)

This flouting of normal (biblical Hebrew) VSO word order (here it is SPP/V) draws the auditor on in search of the requisite verb (*'ābô'*), which only comes in the second line. And yet, somewhat counterintuitively, it also gives emphasis

to the performed pause between the lines—insofar as the pause is not coterminous with a complete or full syntactic stop. Thus, the recognition of abnormal
word order, however belated, itself can become a signal of line-end, especially
when habituated, as, for example, in Lamentations 1–4.[219]

The typical enjambed lines of biblical verse are broadly in keeping with what
is found more generally in oral and oral-derived poetries,[220] and for them sentence logic is also a factor in articulating line structure. The coincidence of
line-end and syntactic stop that routinely accompanies parallelism provides the
very conventional environment enabling the kinds of syntactic cuts that characterize enjambment. As E. Kafalenos observes, "if the demand for a pause at the
end of every line is accepted, there is no need for the syntactical pause to be
positioned at the end of a line. The more complex rhythm produced by placing
syntactical pauses in other positions, in a series of adjacent lines, is often desirable."[221] But even assuming the conventional enabling force of parallelism and
end-stopping, other local strategies, such as nonstandard word order, will be
required to help secure the perception of line-end in enjambed lines.[222]

O'Connor notices that the most salient fact about formulas described in all
oral verbal art is that "they are sentences or phrases of definable grammatical
shape"—that is, syntax is a dominant driving force behind formulas.[223] The
question of formularity in biblical poetry and its nature remains understudied,
with R. C. Culley's dissertation on "oral formulaic language" in the Psalms
being the only substantial study of its kind so far attempted.[224] Much in this
work needs rethinking forty-plus years on, not the least is its strong dependence on the Parry-Lord model of oral formulaic composition,[225] but Culley
successfully reveals, nevertheless, evidence of convential or formulaic phrasing in psalmic verse, which may be plausibly associated with an informing
orality (see chapter 4). What is most striking about the repeated phrasing that
Culley surveys in the Psalms is how much of it is coextensive with the verse
line. These formulaic phrases more often than not prove to be good indicators
of biblical poetic line structure, and thus help to reveal the reality of that structure. Indeed, the formulas themselves may very well have been precisely in
service of performing the poetic line.

Length

Length is also a means for line-fixing insofar as line length in oral verse is
strictly constrained by the limited capacity and duration of working (or short-
term) memory. In his now classic paper from 1956 "The Magical Number
Seven, Plus or Minus Two,"[226] G. A. Miller estimates the capacity of working
memory at roughly seven plus-or-minus two items. Researchers since have

revealed the actual reliable capacity to be somewhat smaller, only around three to five chunks of information, and "the span is shorter for list items that are phonemically lengthy rather than phonemically short, that is, it's shorter for lists of polysyllabic words rather than lists of monosyllabic words, since longer words take longer to say and consequently fewer can be maintained."[227] The time span of working memory is limited to roughly two seconds (e.g., a little longer than the time in which one can remember a telephone number without rehearsal),[228] otherwise without constant rehearsal the information stored decays in three to twenty seconds.[229] During this (two-second) period, Tsur stresses, working memory acts as an "echo box": "In order to render a verse line perceptible as a rhythmic whole, the reciter must manipulate his vocal resources in such a way that the verse line can be completed before its beginning fades out in short-term memory."[230] There is, then, a hard limit on the cognitive capacity and duration of working memory, our online, "temporary storage buffer" in use in all language functions. The upper limit on line length beyond which the line as an auditory phenomenon ceases to be perceptible as a rhythmical whole appears to be around sixteen syllables, with the decasyllabic line as the prototypical length in much verse cross-culturally.[231] In actuality, the perceptual present routinely varies. It can be stretched to accommodate slow-arriving percepts or shrunk for more rapid-fire events. Still, there are limits. It can be only so long or so short.[232]

Students of oral poetry are aware of performance constraints on line lengths, though they tend to conceptualize (often tacitly) the matter from the perspective of the lungs and the pulmonary tract, and thus speak about the "breath-group" or "pause phrasing."[233] Foley is typical: "As with so many poetries outside the narrow confines of the Latin-based Western languages, the line is a breath-group rather than a syllabic abstraction."[234] And B. Antomarini makes explicit the connection between the oral "breath-group" and the written line: "The hemistich is the fossil of that short breath specific to poetry."[235] Whatever the explanation,[236] it is at least clear that the human performer of an oral poem and her audience implicate (bodily, cognitively) constraints on line length, that is, it cannot be too short or too long.[237]

"There is no reason to believe," says S. J. Willett, "that Greek choral lyric was exempt from the limitations of working memory, which governs all perception and production of language."[238] The same may be said of biblical poetry. Being nonmetrical, actual line lengths in biblical poems are never consistently (numerically) the same for long stretches (with the closest symmetries being achieved within couplets and triplets) but vary within specifiable, measurable limits (i.e., ultrashort and ultralong lines do not generally appear). This is not unlike the variability of the perceptual present. Not too long. Not too short. As a result, biblical Hebrew poetic lines exhibit a general (though variable) symmetry in length that contrasts, as S. Geller observes,[239] noticeably with the *randomness* of clause and sentence length in biblical Hebrew prose. The longer length, on average, of clauses and sentences in biblical Hebrew prose also points up (in a gross way) the overall concision of the biblical verse line,[240] a concision that is achieved (from a postprose perspective)[241] principally through various forms of ellipses, for example, verb gapping, double-duty prepositions, reduced usage of the so-called prose particles (definite article, relative particle, *nota accusativi*). This concise but variable line normally[242] consists of five to twelve syllables,[243] three to five words,[244] and two to four stresses,[245] and thus can be sung or recited comfortably within the nominal two-second capacity of working memory.[246] And as significant, the combination of two, and especially of three, such lines, on average, most often would be too large, containing too many discrete chunks of data, to be perceptible as a singular rhythmic whole;[247] which is to say that the block of verse isolated through spacing in the special layouts of the various Hebrew manuscript traditions (e.g., Masoretic, Qumran) has a perceptual saliency that any combination of blocks cannot claim. And not accidentally, perhaps, the (proto)typical length of the biblical Hebrew poetic line—"eight or nine syllables (or so)"—corresponds roughly to a single "syntactical" unit, and thus (perception-based) length constraints and syntax become mutually reinforcing of line structure.[248] Indeed, R. Jourdain reminds us that the "perceptual present"—another way of referring to the temporal slice perceivable by short-term memory—"is more a biteful of conception than a biteful of time."[249] That is, the meaningfulness of these bite-size chunks is all important.

As with the syntactic framing of lines discussed above, line length in biblical verse is not predictive in nature, that is, specific lines cannot be generated ahead of time. Indeed, this lack of prescriptive generation is the hallmark of this poetry's prosody and free rhythm—it is *nonmetrical*. But the lack of precise predictability in any given instance does not mean that line-length constraints do not play a role in signaling the end of lines. Geller's estimation of the process (framed from a readerly perspective) is cogent:

> It is reasonable to suppose that passages with such symmetry form an expectation in the reader's mind that after a certain number of words [or syllables or stresses] a caesura or line break will occur. The specific phonetic, and therefore prosodic, aspect is the silence, real or imagined, awaited at the limit of expectation, which usually corresponds to clause closure. The unit so delimited is the line.[250]

The force of these constraints may be appreciated, as well, by comparing the line shapes in both metrical and free verse varieties of postbiblical Hebrew poetry. The length of the line in the former is routinely much more even and precise, even calculable, as it is determined numerically (stress and syllable pattern, word count, rhyme scheme), and in the latter more random, sometimes with especially violent swings in extremes, with some really short lines and also some extremely long lines, so long, in fact, that one could never imagine them emerging aboriginally in a primary oral context. The Bible's generally concise though variable line, however achieved, stands out noticeably against this wider background of Hebrew line types.

Parallelism and Other Means of Line-Fixing

In addition to silence, sentence logic, and line length, oral poets use a range of linguistic devices and rhetorical tropes to signal the beginnings and ends of lines, for example, complexes of initial and final words, particles, and affixes, rhyme schemes of various sorts or other strategies of sound repetition, and so on.[251] In biblical Hebrew verse the beginning of a line is not normally so obviously and systematically set apart. Anaphora is sometimes used to set off the beginnings of a run of consecutive lines,[252] as in Psalm 13:2–3,

'ad-'ānâ yhwh tiškāḥēnî neṣaḥ	**How long**, O LORD? Will you forget me forever?
'ad-'ānâ tastîr 'et-pāneykā mimmennî	**How long** will you hide your face from me?
'ad-'ānâ 'āšît 'ēṣôt běnapšî	**How long** must I bear pain in my soul,
yāgôn bilbābî yômām	and have sorrow in my heart all day long?
'ad-'ānâ yārûm 'ōyěbî 'ālāy	**How long** shall my enemy be exalted over me? (NRSV)

or Psalm 74:13–15:

'attâ pôrartā bě'ozzěkā yām	**You** divided the sea by your might;
šibbartā ro'šê tannînîm 'al-hammāyim	you broke the heads of the dragons in the waters.
'attâ riṣṣaṣtā ro'šê liwyātān	**You** crushed the heads of Leviathan;
tittěnennû ma'ăkāl lě'ām lěṣiyyîm	you gave him as food for the creatures of the wilderness.
'attâ bāqa'tā ma'yān wānāḥal	**You** cut openings for springs and torrents;

'attâ hôšabtā nahărôt 'êtān   **you** dried up ever-flowing streams.
lĕkā yôm 'ap-lĕkā lāylâ   Yours is the day, yours also the night;
'attâ hăkînôtā mā'ôd wāšāmeš   **you** established the luminaries and the sun.
'attâ hiṣṣabtā kol-gĕbûlôt 'āreṣ   **You** have fixed all the bounds of the earth;
qayiṣ wāḥōrep 'attâ yĕṣartām   you made summer and winter. (NRSV)

But the span of repetition is not usually very great. Even less systematically, semantic emphasis, such as the fronting of the topics in each of the four sections
of Psalm 19 (*haššāmayim*, v. 2; *laššemeš*, v. 5; *tôrat yhwh*, v. 8; *gam-'abdĕkā*, v. 12),
and other rhetorical figures (e.g., the repetition of the root *d-r-k* a the beginning
and end of the couplet in Ps 25:8), always in the service of other ends as well,
may be used to isolate or emphasize line-beginnings.[253] Yet it is the end of the
line that receives the biblical poet's greater attention, and the main device used
for fixing the line-end is parallelism, itself a very common oral technique for
end-fixing.[254] Since Lowth, Western scholarship has been mostly accustomed
to "seeing" parallelism on the "silent" page of a biblical manuscript. But parallelism itself is engineered for efficient aural uptake and remembrance. It is the
voiced (spoken, sung) word and groups of voiced words that are acoustically
shaped into iterative patterns by parallelism.[255] Like the silence of a pause, parallelism marks the end of a line only belatedly, retrospectively.[256] The cues
come after the line actually ends in the auditor's recognition of iteration, the
engine of parallelism and the sign that a new line is under way. The unit iterated is the line, its shape emerging as the matching syntactic frames of the
adjacent lines are set in equivalence.[257] Isaiah 11:3 is a typical example:

> *wĕlō'-lĕmar'ê 'ênāyw yišpôṭ*
> *wĕlō'-lĕmišma' 'oznāyw yôkîaḥ*
> Conj-Neg-PP + V
> Conj-Neg-PP + V
> and-not-according-to-the-vision-of-his-eyes will he judge
> and-not-according-to-the-hearing-of-his-ears will he decide

The matching syntactic frames here are most exact. The onset of the frame
(Conj-Neg-PP), repeated from the initial line, in *wĕlō'-lĕmišma' 'oznāyw* of the
second line throws the ending of that first line after *yišpôṭ* into relief. And concomitantly, recognition of the reiterated frame as a whole enhances the closural force that accompanies *yôkîaḥ* in the second line, which itself mimes the
line-ending *yišpôṭ* of the first line.

The full effectiveness of this kind of strategy for line marking depends to a
large degree on habituation and convention, a preexisting familiarity with the

techniques to be put into play—biblical poetry is a thoroughgoingly traditional form of verbal art. For the uninitiated, appreciation of how parallelism signals line-ends will not always be immediately perceptible from individual local examples. But as the device is repeated, say over the course of a poem, acoustic perception and its accompanied force increases.[258] Consider Isaiah 11:3 together with verses 4–5:

wĕlō'-lĕmar'ê 'ênāyw yišpōṭ	He shall not judge by what his eyes see,
wĕlō'-lĕmišma' 'oznāyw yôkîaḥ	or decide by what his ears hear;
wĕšāpaṭ bĕṣedeq dallîm	but with righteousness he will judge the poor,
wĕhôkîaḥ bĕmîšôr lĕ'anwê-'āreṣ	and decide with equity for the meek of the earth;
wĕhikkâ-'ereṣ bĕšēbeṭ pîw	he shall strike the earth with the rod of his mouth,
ûbĕrûaḥ šĕpātāyw yāmît rāšā'	and with the breath of his lips he shall kill the wicked.
wĕhāyâ ṣedeq 'ēzôr motnāyw	Righteousness shall be the belt around his waist,
wĕhā'ĕmûnâ 'ēzôr ḥălāṣāyw	and faithfulness the belt around his loins. (NRSV)

Here the auditor is exposed four times over in a succession of eight lines to the use of parallelism as a means for fixing local line-ends.

The mechanism itself is quite flexible and open, potentially allowing for a strongly additive and successive kind of line marking. Consider the opening to *The Wedding Mustajbey's Son Bećirbey*, a South Slavic epic song:

> Oj! Djerdelez Alija arose early,
> Ej! Alija, the tsar's hero,
> Near Visoko above Sarajevo,
> Before dawn and the white day—
> Even two full hours before dawn,
> When daybreaks and the sun rises
> And the morning star shows its face.[259]

Foley calls attention to the "additive, granular organization" of these lines, and then says: "One line-unit follows the next, one name or time designation parallel to another, with each verse structurally independent from those that flank it. The lines work together in this passage, of course, but each one can and does exist in combination with other decasyllables elsewhere in the poetic tradition"—that is, the "whole lines" have an integrity of their own, "increments that...are parallel, but themselves discrete."[260] Compare the following passage from the Ugaritic Kirta epic (CAT 1.14.III.38–49):

pd. in. bbty. ttn	And what is not in my house you shall give
tn. ly. mṭt. ḥry	Give to me Lady Ḥuraya
nʿmt. šph. bkrk	The Fair One, your firstborn child
dk. nʿm. ʿnt. nʿmh	Who's as fair as Anat
km. tsm. ʿṭtrt. tsmh	Who's as beautiful as Astarte
dqh. ib. iqni.	Whose pupils are pure lapis lazuli,
ʿpʿ[p]h sp. ṭrml.	Whose eyelids are alabaster bowls
thgrn. [u]dm[261]	They are girded with rubies
ašlw. bṣp. ʿnh	That I might repose in the gaze of her eyes
dbḥlmy. il. ytn	Whom in my dream El gave
bḍrty. ab. adm	In my vision, the father of mankind
wld. šph. lkrt	That she might bear an heir for Kirta
wġlm. lʿbd. il	A lad for the servant of El

Here, too, one notices the "additive, granular organization" of the whole and the obvious prominence of parallelism. But the West Semitic poetic tradition is dominantly di- and tristichic, not stichic like the South Slavic poem just cited, and therefore the parallelism prevails within couplet and triplet boundaries, where the integrity of the individual line is also most pronounced. The couplets and triplets themselves remain open, uncoiling in their parsing narrative logic, additively, phrase by bite-size phrase.

The poetry preserved in the Bible is different still. Being mostly nonnarrative in nature (see chapter 3) it does not often uncoil with the same kind of narrative ("granular") logic as exhibited in either of the two previous examples taken from epic traditions—though there are runs of what Alter calls "incipient narrativity" (e.g., Ps 106:19–23). But the line-marking force of parallelism persists, nonetheless, and is exercised (as in Ugaritic narrative poetry) chiefly within the couplets and triplets that constitute the basic texture of biblical Hebrew line grouping. Consequently, as a practical matter, line structure is most visible at the local level. And, in fact, it is parallelism that has most enabled scholars (following Lowth) to perceive the verse line even in those compositions (as in the

Latter Prophets) for which we are lacking specially (graphically) formatted manuscripts. Further, given the pattern of deploying parallelism (chiefly) within
couplet and triplet boundaries—and thus effecting, as many have noticed, a
principal means for linking lines into larger groupings, initial and medial line-
endings are more strongly marked than the endings in final lines. That is, since
the iterated (syntactic) frames mark line-endings only belatedly, the lack of recursion after the second line of a couplet or the third line in a triplet means that
the perception of closure in these lines will be less pronounced—at least, locally. This weakened closural force can be, and often is, compensated for contextually. So, for example, in Isaiah 11:3–5, the change in syntactic frame after
every couplet is itself a means for bringing those second lines and their ends
into sharper relief. Further, depending on the design of a given poem, other ad
hoc features (e.g., logical or temporal connectors, thematic development, semantic emphasis), usually in combination with other considerations, may serve
to underscore the beginnings and endings of lines.[262] Notice in Isaiah 11:3–5 the
use of the conjunctive *waw* to head every line, serving as a kind of line-marking
anaphora. But the conjunctive *waw*s are especially important after the second
lines of the four couplets, as they help—in combination with changes in syntactic frame, the instances of pause indicated by the disjunctive accents in MT
(accompanied by pausal lengthening where possible, e.g., *'āreṣ*, v. 4)—to secure
the integrity of those lines, again retrospectively. And when you add in the noticeable symmetry of line length (especially within each couplet) and the clausal
or sentential (end-stopped) nature of the lines themselves, the line structure of
Isaiah 11:3–5 is rather impressively, if heterogeneously, indicated. Indeed, one
might even hazard that the delimitation of lines in this short passage, in the
end, is unproblematic, perhaps even obvious.

   This last example illustrates an important characteristic of line-fixing in
many oral traditions, especially nonmetrical ones, namely: the tendency to fix
lines in a combinatory and heterogeneous manner. Line marking in Kuna oral
discourse is not untypical, as J. Sherzer explains:

> These lines are marked by a set of distinct devices. Not all of the de-
> vices are operative in every case. In addition, the devices have other
> functions besides marking lines. As a result there is not always congru-
> ence among them. In fact, a most interesting aspect of the various line-
> marking devices in Kuna is the ways in which speakers play them off
> against each other, creating contrasts and tensions among them.[263]

One need not ramify this pattern of line marking. There are many varieties of
oral or oral-derived verse where numerical quantification of various sorts fixes

the line (Homer's *Iliad* and *Odyssey* being the best known examples). Contemporary students of oral poetry stress the rich diversity of oral forms and practices. What the Kuna example (and others like it) shows is that line marking can be conceptualized and enacted in ways different from and beyond the norms of quantification inherited in the West from classical antiquity.

Biblical scholars have never succeeded in identifying a consistent quantification mechanism (meter) by which biblical Hebrew line structure is generated. In my opinion, this is because none exists (see chapter 2 for details). Rather, line structure in a given poem emerges holistically and heterogeneously. Potentially, a myriad of features (formal, semantic, linguistic, graphic) may be involved. They combine, overlap, and sometimes even conflict with one another. Whether this manner of line-fixing is inherited from biblical poetry's oral roots or falls out as a matter of its nonmetrical nature—or, as likely, even a combination of the two—is hard to say with any specificity. That it has this character, nonetheless, seems clear. And thus what is called for is a patient working back and forth between various levels and phenomena, through the poem as a whole, considering the contribution, say, of pausal forms alongside and in combination with other features, until, as D. Hymes notes, "gradually you arrive at an analysis that seems best *at that stage of your knowledge.*"[264]

A final word about parallelism before concluding. It is in the function of end-fixing and its various entailments (e.g., the linking of lines into larger groups) that parallelism distinguishes biblical Hebrew verse. This point should be underscored. Parallelism qua parallelism is unremarkable. In literature the world over, written as well as oral, it is a common stylistic trope and has no significance as such for defining biblical Hebrew verse—aside, perhaps, from noting its wide pervasiveness, its rich tropological use, and its ultimate origins in oral culture. In fact, as many scholars have noted, as a trope parallelism is also to be found (though much less frequently) throughout biblical narrative prose.[265] As it turns out, then, parallelism is not quite the sine qua non of biblical verse that it has so often been made out to be. After all, a substantial portion (perhaps as much as a third) of the biblical poetic corpus consists of nonparallelistic lines.[266] Rather, what is so distinctive about parallelism in biblical Hebrew verse is its prominent (though not ubiquitous) role in end-fixing and in joining adjacent lines and the peculiar rhythm of recursion that its play of matching helps to effect, neither of which applies to the use of parallelism in the prose portions of the Bible.

* * *

IN THE END, only the first of the four practices discussed here—end-of-the-line pause and the phonological lengthening that it often triggers—can be counted with full confidence as arising out of a performative context, and thus oral in origin. But demonstrating the origin of these practices of line-fixing is not my chief concern. The fact that all four—pause, sentence logic, line length, and parallelism—are both evident in the biblical Hebrew poetic corpus and commonly found (to lesser and to greater degrees) across a spectrum of oral (and oral-derived) poetries is sufficient, one, to demonstrate that line structure can indeed be articulated without recourse to explicitly graphic cues, and, two, to adduce yet further evidence for the biblical verse line, evidence that is consistent with and supportive of the manuscript evidence reviewed above and at the same time more expansive than the manuscript evidence.

The Line from the Other's Perspective

As remarked at the outset, no early, indigenous metadiscourse about biblical verse exists, let alone even the most oblique of references to the verse line. Such emerges only with the "sharpened analysis" and "increasingly articulate introspectivity" enabled by writing.[267] The very concept of a "line" as "a row of written or printed letters" (*OED*) itself emerges out of a chirographic world with specific conventions in place for how to spatialize the technology of writing. There is a tantalizing reference in the Masada Ben Sira manuscript (MasSir vii 11 = Sir 44:5) to "those who compose psalms" (*ḥqry mzmwr*) *'l qw*, which some take to reference "line" or "verse" in a technical sense (cf. 1QHod i 28–29),[268] but most gloss as "measure" or "rule" in light of the variant in Sirach 44B:5, *'l ḥwq*.[269] But even in the absence of a fully certain reference to the verse line itself, the Ben Sira passage does exemplify the typical kind of references about poetic compositions found in the Bible, oblique, situational, and via practical or performative (genre-like) designations (here *mzmwr* "psalm" and *mšl* "proverb"; cf. the gloss in LXX, NRSV), which themselves are not ever overly well defined. The designation *mizmôr*, for example, occurs only in the superscriptions of psalms in the Bible (some fifty-seven times, e.g., Ps 13:1; 19:1; 23:1; 29:1; 48:1; 88:1; 98:1), and thus the best indicators of the term's meaning are the compositions it designates. These tend to share leading characteristics of what critics for most of the history of literary criticism in the West have called "lyric verse," a category of verse that in its broadest, most phenomenological sense, distinguishes the various nonrepresentational, nondramatic, nonnarrative types of poetry (see chapter 3).[270] That is, they exhibit a palpable tropological density, a ready dependence on "pure verbal resources" (e.g., alliteration, wordplay, repetitions, grammatical twists);[271] they are routinely small in scale and highly paratactic in structure (i.e., nonsequential, fragmentary, disjunctive), and regularly feature voice(s) instead of character; and many manifest a sung quality that, as in ancient Greece, suggests rootedness in a tradition of song and music. In fact, the very semantics of the noun *mizmôr*—etymologically derived from the root *z-m-r* "to sing"—implies some kind of originary concern for music. The verb *zmr* "to sing" is frequent as well in many of these psalms (e.g., Ps 9:3, 12; 21:14; 30:5, 13; 47:7,8; 66:2, 4; 98:4, 5) and occurs some forty-one times in total in the Psalms. And not infrequently it is precisely in these *mizmôr*-designated psalms where some of the most explicit references to musical instruments occur (e.g., Ps 47:6; 49:1–5; 92:4; 98:6).²⁷² In biblical usage *mizmôr* designates only these ritual or cultic poems. For Ben Sira, however, the term appears to have a broader semantic range (cf. 49:1), more akin to what gets termed *šîr* (or *šîrâ*) in the Bible, "the most widely used word, and possibly the generic term for 'song' or 'poem'" in the Bible (cf. modern Hebrew *šîr*).²⁷³ The latter, while by no means precisely equivalent to the Greek-derived "lyric," does designate a rather large variety of verse in the Hebrew Bible, including celebratory songs (e.g., Exod 15:1; Jud 5; 2 Sam 22:1; cf. 1 Sam 18:6), love songs (e.g., Ezek 33:32; Ps 45:1; Song 1:1), prophetic oracles of various kinds (e.g., Isa 5:1; 23:15; 42:10).

There is slightly more information to be inferred about *māšāl*, often glossed as "proverb," the other designation employed in our passage from Ben Sira. Originally, it appears to have been an oral-performative genre (e.g., Num 23:18; 1 Kgs 5:12; Ps 49:5; 78:2; Prov 26:9), though proverbs eventually came to be written down and gathered in collections (Qoh 12:9; Sir 44:5; implicit in the biblical book of Proverbs). One typically "lifts up" (*nāśāʾ*) a proverb (e.g., Num 23:7; Isa 14:4; Mic 2:4; Job 27:1; 29:1), just as one "lifts up" a *qînâ* "dirge, lament" (e.g., Jer 7:29; Ezek 26:17; 27:2; Amos 5:1), presumably referring to an (originally) oral undertaking (esp. Num 23:18). Yet as with *mizmôr* the best indication of what a *māšāl* entails is denoted by the kind of compositions it designates (Num 23:7, 18; 24:3, 15, 20, 21, 23; Prov 1:1; 10:1; 25:1). Most often *māšāl* refers to a short (typically framed in a couplet), pithy (wisdom) saying, though on occasion (especially in the Prophets) more expansive verse forms are isolated by the term (e.g., Num 23:7; 24:3; Isa 14:4; Ezek 24:3). In many respects the basic medium of such verse is not unlike that of the *mizmôr* or the *šîr* just described,²⁷⁴ except that music and song are not centrally associated with the *māšāl*.²⁷⁵ Emblematic of the latter is the fact that in biblical usage *mĕšālîm* (like *qînôt*) are never literally sung (i.e., never occur with verbs for singing such as *zmr* or *šyr*).

This manner of reference—especially in the cases of *šîr*, *māšāl*, and *qînâ*—is strongly reminiscent in several key respects (e.g., nonabstraction, lack of definition) of the "situational logic" that otherwise characterizes dominantly oral cultures. I note this not so much to insist on a precise characterization of ancient Israelite or Judahite culture, but to problematize our own often tacit expectation of finding in the historical record explicitly articulated and theorized concepts.

Such an expectation is itself long habituated in the practices of reflection enabled by writing. Furthermore, even such spare and oblique reference implies a world of practical but very real knowledge. In this case, the knowledge is of art forms whose distinctiveness is sufficient enough to warrant (on occasion) being called by different names and part of what distinguishes these sometimes differently named art forms, at least as viewed from our much belated perspective, is their segmentation into poetic lines. That the references contained in the Masada scroll of Ben Sira themselves come apportioned in columnar lines composed of couplets is, of course, quite irrelevant to the facticity of the mentioning of verse forms there. But it is very much worth recalling that such special formatting itself provides eloquent if silent witness to the same world of practical knowledge—the large point made in the earlier discussion of the manuscript evidence for poetic line structure. That a concept does not get explicitly named or theorized does not make the concept any less real or useful.

In addition to the deictically discriminating function of terms like *mizmôr* and *māšāl* (however unpremeditated), there are also a few poems that incorporate self-designating first person forms that implicate a conscious intent to compose or perform the bit of verse in which they are embedded. The prose frame introducing the poem in Exodus 15 clarifies the nature of the self-reference in the poem's opening line, "I sing of/to/for Yahweh" (*ʾāšîrâ l-yhwh*, v. 1): "Then Moses and the Israelites sang this song of/to/for Yahweh [*yāšîr... ʾet-haššîrâ hazzōʾt l-yhwh*], saying..." (v. 1). The use of the same verbal phrase for singing (*šyr* + *l-*), the explicit (deictic) reference to the song itself (*haššîrâ hazzōʾt*), and the quotative frame (*wayyōʾmĕrû lēʾmōr* lit. "and they said, saying") all implicate the very act of singing that is this poem as the principal referent of the speaker's notice (see Judg 5:1, 3; Isa 5:1; Ps 108:1–2). Indeed, the editorial framing of songs itself (especially within blocks of prose narrative), though belated, nonetheless shows consciousness on the part of the scribes who copied these poems, especially when the poems receive some overt naming as in Exodus 15 (e.g., Num 23:7, 18; 24:3, 15; Judg 5:1; 2 Sam 1:17–18; 2 Sam 22: 1).[276] Psalm 45 contains a different but still fairly transparent kind of self-designating reference. The poem is labeled a "love song" (*šîr yĕdîdōt*), and the opening triplet embeds the psalmist's explicit mention of his own act of composition:

> My heart overflows with a goodly theme [*dābār ṭôb*];
> I address [*ʾōmēr ʾānî*] my verses [*maʿăśay*] to the king;
> my tongue is like the pen of a ready scribe. (NRSV)

The reference to "my verses" (*maʿăśay* lit. "my works") is unique, but there can be little doubt that the "work" referred to is the work of composing (and singing) that is this poem (*poesy*).[277]

In a similar vein Alter notices a "convention" for beginning poems in the Bible "in which the poet/speaker calls attention to his own utterance and invokes an audience—or more often a witness—for his utterance."[278] As an example he cites Genesis 4:23: *ādâ wĕṣillâ šĕma'an qôlî / nĕšê lemek ha'zēnâ 'imrātî* "Adah and Zillah, hear my voice. / wives of Lamech, listen to my word." Deuteronomy 32:1–3 may well be the best known example of this kind (cf. Judg 5:3), and the prophets are especially fond of explicitly naming witnesses and audiences (e.g., Isa 1:2; 28:23; 51:4; Mic 1:2; Joel 1:2) and the cries of the Psalmist are often similarly self-implicating (e.g., Ps 5:2; 17:1; 55:2; 78:1; 141:1; cf. Job 33:1; 34:2). So we get in the Bible not only the occasional special labeling of verse forms but also some indication that the ancient poets/singers (and scribes/editors) themselves were aware of the difference(s) of verse. Neither are maximally explicit, and ultimately we must infer from the examples before us (e.g., Exod 15, Ps 45) more precisely what these art forms are, whether or not, for example, they measure up to our notion of poetry or verse; or whether so glossing them in this way is at all pragmatically or heuristically helpful.

Early Jewish and Patristic Commentators

More explicit comment on biblical poetry comes only after the biblical period. I have already discussed one stream of postbiblical commentary, namely, that of the rabbis as embedded in the Talmud. Another stream comes from Jewish and Christian writers of the Hellenistic and Roman eras. Like the first, this second stream of commentary tradition today is generally well known, and therefore I do not need to elaborate every detail.[279] The earliest and most significant commentators include Philo of Alexandria (ca. 15 BCE–45 CE), Josephus (37–100 CE), Origen (184–254 CE), Eusebius (264–340 CE), and Jerome (331–420 CE). In every instance, each writer, whether in Greek or Latin, references a body of biblical poetry that is distinguished from Hebrew prose (esp. Jerome)[280] on the one hand and thought analogous to either Greek or Latin verse on the other hand. Both are quite extraordinary, the significance of which has not been always or fully appreciated by biblical scholars. It is clear, given the terminology (e.g., hexameter, trimeter, pentameter), that these early Jewish and patristic commentators were looking at biblical verse through Greco-Roman eyes, and this has mostly deflected the scholarly conversation to a discussion of (a putative) Hebrew meter. However, the imputation of meter to biblical verse is not the only or even most obvious implication of this discussion. Eissfeldt is adamant on this point:

> When Josephus...says [these things about the poems of Moses] he is simply applying to Hebrew poetry the concepts of classical metre, in

order to make plain to his Hellenistically educated readers a literature which otherwise would be unintelligible to them, just as Philo does in his *Vita Contemplativa*....These and similar judgments by Josephus and others are insufficient to prove that these poems or Hebrew poetry as such was constructed on the basis of metrical laws.[281]

The implied methodology is thoroughgoingly comparative in nature.[282] That these writers should choose to couch their assessments in a particular theoretical language (in this case making plain to "Hellenistically educated readers") is no different from what every comparatist does to this day; indeed, what anyone must do if they choose to compare artifacts (literary, art historical, or whatever) from different cultures.[283] Furthermore, we have no right to expect anyone to see except through the always particular categories provided by their specific cultures, which, in this instance, presumed a strong correspondence of poetry and meter. "Whether," as Gray remarks, these commentators as a matter of fact "point to any discernment of the real principles of that [i.e., biblical Hebrew] poetry, and whether they do not betray at once misconceptions and lack of perception, is another question."[284] And yet however flawed these (mis)perceptions they nonetheless enabled the apprehension of a corpus of poetic verse in the Bible. This should not be lost sight of, and it, too, should count, it seems to me, in our consideration of a biblical verse tradition.

No doubt that a variety of features will have contributed to this assessment by early Jewish and patristic thinkers, but there is good reason to think that a perception of poetic line structure, probably as inferred through manuscript layout, was chief among them. For one, Origen, as noted, explicitly mentions the presence of *stichoi* in his scholion on Psalm 119—a psalm that because of the presence of the acrostic always gets specially formatted, even in manuscripts that are otherwise copied as a running text (e.g., 11QPs^a). The presence of actual *stichoi* in manuscripts of poetic works such as the Psalms, Proverbs, and the Song of Songs known to him is implied by Jerome in his comments on writing *per cola et commata* in his *Preface to Isaiah* cited earlier. It was precisely the resulting similarity in appearance in writing (i.e., both are written out in lines, in *stichoi*) that prompted Jerome's clarifying comment. Finally, the fact that all of these comments are directed to poetic works in the Bible for which we know specially formatted manuscripts did exist—Job, Proverbs, and Psalms; the several festival songs (e.g., Exod 15, Judg 5); Lamentations and Song of Songs (in Greek)—is surely not accidental. That is, I suspect that this early commentary on biblical poetry was provoked as much by what these writers literally saw—verse specially laid out—as by anything else.[285] But at any rate that they are calling attention to art forms that remind them of classical traditions of verse is patent. And thus, this body of commentary from (later) antiquity, however spare and even if finally flawed in certain ways, does recognize (in the categories at hand) a verse tradition within the Bible and thereby stands as our earliest articulate discussion of biblical verse.

Biblical Poetry through Medieval Jewish Eyes

Talk of biblical poetry does not end here. Two additional moments in the history of the reception of biblical verse in the runup to Lowth may be briefly considered. Medieval Jewish scholars were keenly aware that the Bible contained poetry.[286] In fact, a presumption of a specifically biblical kind of poetry was very much indebted to the special formatting and system of accents used for the poetic books in Masoretic manuscripts of the Bible, the discussion of these formats in the Talmud, and the biblical terminology (e.g., šîr) that was sometimes used of biblical poems.[287] But Jewish scholars from the twelfth through the seventeenth centuries would refine and elaborate this traditional knowledge and test it against their own contemporary understandings of verse. The obvious lack of rhyme and quantitative meter in the biblical poetic corpus was one of the leading issues discussed, since the cultural models of verse for these writers were provided by Arabic and medieval Hebrew poetry, metrical and rhymed traditions of verse. As with Lowth after them, it was difficult for these thinkers to conceptualize verse outside the normative categories of verse known to them. And yet, as Berlin makes clear, "no one could make a case for sustained meter or rhyme throughout a large section of biblical poetry, and quantitative meter, even within a verse, was impossible to find (except for the simplest of metrical patterns)."[288] Indeed, had modern biblical scholarship been better read in this body of literature, it is hard to imagine that it would have spent the several centuries that it did (post-Lowth) pursuing the chimera of meter in biblical verse. The outstanding importance of the postbiblical Hebrew verse traditions, from a comparative perspective, is to make plain the nonmetrical nature of biblical verse (see chapter 2).[289] Three other observations bear more directly, though still somewhat obliquely, on the question at issue here. First, the persistence to insist on a verse tradition in the Bible, even in the absence of meter and however chauvinistically motivated,[290] preserves an implicit (if embryonic) awareness of a likeness shared with other verse traditions that is significant. Second, the lack of meter forced these writers to begin to articulate and describe biblical verse through other than metrical categories (e.g., rhetorical figures and tropes, music and rhythm, style, imagery), an endeavor that continues to require critical attention. Finally, though the verse line only rarely comes in for specific comment, that it sparks any comment at all is telling. Berlin, in fact, identifies three authors (Moshe ibn Tibbon, Joseph ibn Kaspi, Immanuel Frances) who point to the line (and its binariness) as a significant formal marker of verse.[291] Moshe ibn Tibbon is of special interest because he makes explicit the comparative nature of his insight. He writes that Proverbs, Job, and Psalms (reacting to the special formatting of these books in medieval Hebrew manuscripts) are poetry because "they have divided verses [*pesuqim*], like verses [in medieval poetry; *batim*], although the parts are not equal."[292] Here, then, there is a keen awareness of the facticity of biblical verse and even the beginnings of a critical metadiscourse about it.

The English Renaissance

The second (and last) moment in the reception history of biblical verse that I want to consider is that of the so-called English Renaissance of the sixteenth and seventeenth centuries. Here, too, one finds a well-articulated awareness of a verse tradition within the Bible. Philip Sidney is emblematic:

> The chief both in antiquitie and in excellencie were they that did imitate the inconceiuable excellencies of God. Such were *Dauid* in his Psalmes, *Salomon* in his song of Songs, in his Ecclesiastes, and Prouerbs, *Moses* and *Debora* in theyr Hymnes, and the writer of Iob, which, beside other, the learned *Emanuell Tremelius* and *Franciscus Iunius* doe entitle the poeticall part of Scripture.[293]

That Sidney would use biblical poetry as a part of his defense of poetry more generally is quite telling in its own right, but he was by no means alone during this period in recognizing the facticity of biblical verse.[294] In fact, as B. K. Lewalski contends, "the articulation and practice of a fully-developed theory of biblical aesthetics is...a Renaissance/seventeenth-century phenomenon,"[295] and part and parcel of this theory was the knowledge that the Hebrew Bible contained much poetry, especially of the lyric variety.[296] The foundational knowledge about biblical poetry was again mostly inherited—chiefly through the patristic sources (e.g., Jerome), but also apparent from the manuscript tradition[297] and predicated on Jewish scholarship of the day.[298] And again the question of meter was an issue of chief interest. As E. R. Curtius observes, for Greek and Roman antiquity, as for the European Middle Ages, poetry simply was "metrical discourse," and therefore the poetry of the Bible must, by definition, be metrical. Most assumed its prosody to be quantitative in nature, like Latin and Greek poetry, and following the general line of thought handed down through Hellenistic and patristic sources.[299] But there was also an awareness

that the classical quantitative norms did not always suit biblical verse so precisely. Sidney gives initial voice to this worry when in affirming the metrical
nature of biblical verse he avers, "although the rules be not fully found."[300]
George Wither (1588–1667 CE), poet and literary critic, is among those who go
farthest in questioning the assumption of quantitative meter in the Bible:

> The *Hebrews* are full of variety in their *Numbers*, and take great liberty
> in their *Verses*. For as *Marianus Viclorius* reports, they are not alwaies
> measured out by the same Number or quality of Syllables, as the *Greeke*
> or *Latine Verses* are; but sometime lengthened and sometime ab-
> breuiated in the pronountiation by accents of time, according to the
> manner of the *Italian Measures*, and that liberty which it seemeth our
> *English* vsed in their *Poems*, about foure hundred yeeres agoe: for to vs
> now (though I am perswaded, they are as they were at first intended to
> bee) there appeares sometime to be a want, and sometime an *Ouerplus*,
> in the Syllables of many of their *Verses*.[301]

And Baroway even roots the later accentual-based conception of biblical
prosody (championed most famously by J. Ley) in the Renaissance, and specifically in the thought of Augustinus Steuchus (1496–1549 CE), J. J. Scaliger
(1540–1609 CE), and Johann Vossiius (1577–1649 CE).[302]
    Beyond this mass of metacritical commentary (whether by scholar or lay-
person; in biblical commentaries, prefaces of all sorts, rhetorical manuals, ser-
mons, or academic dissertations), an informed appreciation of biblical verse as
verse is just as apparent (if less discursively oriented) in the avalanche of metrical translations and paraphrases of biblical poetic works through the sixteenth
and seventeenth centuries (and even into the eighteenth century)[303] and in the
seventeenth-century flowering of the English devotional lyric (e.g., Donne,
Herbert, Vaughan, Traherne, Taylor).[304] In both instances biblical verse is the
chief model and inspiration, and as such these verse translations and devotional
lyrics refract in their own right an important recognition of poetry in the Bible.
Such refraction is perhaps most easily glimpsed in the metrical translations or
paraphrases. That biblical Hebrew verse was metrical, as noted, was widely assumed, and therefore a chief motivation for the myriad of verse translations of
the poetic portions of the Bible during the period was to offer comparable renditions in English, namely: in verse and employing English meters (and rhyme
schemes) in place of the putative Hebrew original.[305] The driving motivation is
imitation.[306] The publication of the King James Bible, a prose translation, called
yet more attention to the difference in medium between the verse original and its
rendering into English prose (however spectacularly) and, if anything, intensified

interest in poetic paraphrases of biblical poetry.³⁰⁷ This mania for metrical paraphrases of biblical poetry continued into the eighteenth century and did not
begin to subside until after Lowth's *Praelectiones* (1753), with its explication of
parallelism and the latter's role in biblical Hebrew prosody, and especially after
the *New Translation* of Isaiah (1878), where, making explicit the theory of translation implicit in his earlier study, for the first time Lowth modeled a kind of
nonmetrical yet rhythmic verse translation in English of a biblical poetic corpus.
The importance of the change in the principle of biblical verse translation that
Lowth's work ushers in, Roston says, "can scarcely be overemphasized."³⁰⁸

Not surprisingly, the line almost never comes in for any kind of explicit explica-
tion.³⁰⁹ And yet, as with the later Lowth, it is tacitly assumed throughout, and most
assuredly in the metrical translations and the emergent devotional lyric tradition.
Wither provides several stunning examples in his *A Preparation to the Psalter*
where the mostly submerged assumptions about line structure briefly breach the
surface. In a chapter dedicated to the discussion of biblical prosody he cites Psalm
102:9–10, both in Hebrew (à la Lowth) and in transliteration, "to shew...what
affinity the Ancient *Hebrew Verses* have with" the English poems of his day:³¹⁰

כל-היום חרפוני איבי
מהוללי בי נשבעו
כי-אפר כלחם אכלתי
ושקוי בבכי מסכתי

    Col-hayom hherephuni oyebai
    Meholalai bi nishbaü:
    Chi eper callehhem acalthi,
    Veshikkuvai bi bhchi masachthi.

As with Lowth, it is the visual display of the Hebrew and accompanying transliteration that communicates Wither's understanding of the lineation. Such
lineation, while abiding by the spacing and accents evidenced in the Aleppo
Codex, for example, is nonetheless contrary to the line structure of that manuscript (in which two verse lines are contained on a single manuscript line)
and of any other known medieval Hebrew manuscript. And yet here, too,
Qumran furnishes manuscript evidence where the actual lineation matches
Wither's manner of transcription—4QPsᵇ (col. XX, 1–2) preserves Psalm 102:10
precisely as Wither lines it out (fig. 2).³¹¹ Wither, then, offers two translations
of Psalm 102:9–10. In the first,

    All day, my foes reuile me; And who were
    Mad at me, against me sweare.

> For, Ashes I, as bread, deuour'd;
> And teares among my drinke I pour'd.

he translates in the "vnequall *Measures*" "according to the fashion of the *Hebrew Verse.*" The second, containing "equall *Numbers*" and "making all the Staues of one length, in this, or some such like Stanza":

> All day, my foes reproches I haue borne,
> Who, mad against me, haue against me sworne.
> I therefore feed on Ashes, as on bread:
> And teares, immingled with my drinke, I shed.

—as "if I should turne them sutably to the *Measures* most vsuall in our Times."[312] Here, then, we witness firsthand both the modeling and metrical rendering by which we may perceive "that there is *Verse* in the Holy Scripture."[313]

* * *

THERE ARE OTHER moments in the history of the reception of biblical poetry between Jerome and Lowth that deserve attention, but these suffice for my purposes insofar as they show that Lowth did not come to his topic and insights innocently and they witness the testing of the poeticality of biblical verse from divergent cultural contexts and perspectives. The latter may be elaborated. From the earliest moment recorded, through Lowth, and continuing to this day, readers of the Bible consistently have found in the Bible what appears to them to be poetry, verse. To be sure, none of these readers comes to his or her readings naively, bereft of ideological commitments, and the categories used often seem from our current perspective ill suited and even badly mistaken (as with the ever tenacious metrical hypothesis). Still, this record of reading remains impressive and not easily dismissed. The sponsoring historical epochs and cultural contexts are both diverse and many, and yet in each sufficient similarities in theme, structure, genres, and even underlying media are recognized to warrant distinguishing some parts of the Bible as poetry, however named (or not) and however context dependent are the individual criteria marshaled. And on occasion even the matter of the verse line in the Bible comes in for observation and illumination.

To worry over the imposition of categories and concepts foreign to any particular database is endemic to good comparative methodology. The history of reading and commentary briefly charted here is that of outsiders who come equipped with ideas and concepts derived from outside the biblical world. Indeed, that some such imposition of the etic is unavoidable in any comparative enterprise is a given. And yet this need not vitiate the knowledge generated—in this instance, the very perception of biblical poetry. But the only practicable check on the worry of disabling imposition is continued comparisons that run the risk ever anew of imposition. One of the outstanding achievements of nineteenth- and twentieth-century archaeology in the Middle East was the recovery of an immense corpus of literature from Mesopotamia, Egypt, and the Levant contemporary to that of the traditional literature eventually collected in the Hebrew Bible. Throughout this corpus there is much that compares most favorably to what in the Bible our readers have called "poetry." In fact, Wither already in 1619 is able to "glympse" this "likelinesse" and uses the insight as a comparative check—in this case, on his worry over the attribution of quantitative meter to biblical verse based on a too facile comparison with "the two learned Tongues of *Europe, Greeke* and *Latine*." By contrast, the more telling comparison with respect to prosodic matters ("the manner of their *Verse*"), Wither argues, is to "her neighbours and kindred"—"in the tongues of the Easterne parts; *Arabiscke, Chaldean*, or the olde *Punicke*, which was a Dialect of the *Hebrew*; and more anciently called the *Phoenician* tongue." What is revealed in this yet further act of comparison is a similar kind of verse to that found in the Bible, one that admits a "freedome in their Composures" and a "Staffe" varied "at their pleasure, making it now longer, now shorter, as they listed, or best fitted the matter." This is, Wither says, "I doubt not but I may ghesse as neere the manner of their *Verse*, as those who have sought for it by the *Greeke* or *Latine* rules."[314]

Kugel, though not entirely happy with the concept of "poetry" as applied to the Bible,[315] nonetheless concedes that there is a case to be made for it, citing in particular "the centuries-old tradition" affirming the notion.[316] Even on the basis of the small selection of this tradition on view above, it is apparent that these perceptions of biblical poetry were sometimes (though not always) closely and carefully considered. This and the tenacious persistence of the affirmation from varied and multiple perspectives over such a long period of time offer powerful warrants indeed for the conception of a biblical kind of poetry, and even more specifically, of verse composed of lines, of "verse, properly so called."

Internal Evidence for the Line

My final set of considerations focuses on phenomena that both reveal the line as a structural modality and fall out in some way from various aspects of the language art (of poetry) itself. This is a diverse lot. The idea is to transfix on the line obliquely, indirectly; to consider phenomena that implicate for one reason or another its facticity.

The Acrostic

Lowth employs essentially the same logic in his explication of meter in the alphabetic acrostic reviewed earlier. The acrostic by its nature does not offer articulate or direct testimony about meter in biblical verse. Rather, meter is an implication that Lowth discerns in the acrostics, since, as he says, "in these examples the verses are so exactly marked and defined, that it is impossible to mistake them for prose."[317] The posited implication in this instance is predicated almost wholly on a faulty presumption, the imputation (by definition) of meter to all verse, and thus is infelicitously made. But the manner of discernment is sound, and if the biblical acrostics do not implicate meter, they do reveal the structural reality of the line—"it is impossible to mistake them for prose." The basic formal conceit of the acrostic is that the initial letters or signs of a specified structural domain (e.g., line, couplet, stanza), when read in succession, spell out a name, sentence, alphabet, or alphabetic pattern. In the Bible, all of the acrostics are alphabetical in nature. That is, they (mostly) spell out the Hebrew alphabet in one or the other of its two traditional orders. The smallest domain at which the acrostic is operative in biblical verse occurs in those most "perfectly Alphabetical" acrostics of Lowth, Psalms 111 and 112, "in which every Line is marked by its Initial Letter."[318] In these two instances, then, the structural facticity of the line is laid bare most tellingly, marked linguistically,[319] and visibly, by the placement of successive letters of the alphabet at the head of each line in the psalms. A striking graphic analog is provided by the use of *littera notabilior* ("more noticeable letters") to head a line of verse in medieval Latin copies of poems, as in this selection from a ninth-century (CE) copy of the *Aeneid* (8.592–96; cf. fig. 20):

> S tant pauide muris matres oculisque secuntur
> P uluercam nubem et fulgentis aere cateruas
> O lli per dumos qua proxima meta uiarum
> A rmati tendunt it clamor et agmine facto
> Q uadrupedante putrem sonitu quatitungula campum[320]

End-rhyme in other poetic traditions implicates line structure in a similar fashion, except that it affects the end and not the beginning of lines and is an aural and not a visual trope.[321]

Parallelism

In a similar but much more pervasive way, parallelism also exposes the line as a structural entity.[322] I have already called attention to the end-fixing function of parallelism. Here I want to consider the implications of its logic, how parallelism works and what this reveals about line structure in biblical verse.[323] Phenomenologically, and at its broadest, parallelism is centrally concerned with correspondence, "the quality or character of being parallel or analogous" (*OED*),[324] and its principal mode of manifestation (especially in the verbal arts) is through iteration or recurrence, a pattern of matching.[325] O'Connor glosses parallelism in its prototypical biblical guise as "the repetition of identical or similar syntactic patterns in adjacent phrases, clauses, or sentences."[326] Since Alter's quite keen analysis of the possibilities for aesthetic and even narrative development through the device of parallelism,[327] biblical scholars have tended to emphasize what is not alike in the parallel lines, what differences the play of matching points up. And this is not wrong, of course. Alter is surely correct to note that biblical poets were very much alive to the chances for dynamic interplay between parallel lines, in which, for example, "feelings get stronger, images sharper, actions more powerful or more extreme."[328] And yet we should not lose sight of the recurrence and redundancy, the matching that is the motor of this parallelistic play that can also open onto difference and newness. The primacy of recurrence is rooted deeply in oral culture and the cognitive needs of oral discourse, which without benefit of mind-external backlooping technology (e.g., writing) tends to "move ahead more slowly, keeping close to the focus of attention much of what it has already dealt with. Redundancy, repetition of the just-said, keeps both speaker and hearer surely on the track."[329] The logic governing parallelism is, at heart, a logic of repetition, or, as Lowth put it, of "correspondence," "where things for the most part shall answer to things, and words to words, as if fitted to each other."[330] That which is repeated—"subjoined to it, or drawn under it, equivalent, or contrasted with it"[331]—is singular, its very iterability constituting an identity.[332] And while parallelism in biblical poetry is not solely a line-level trope, given the propensity in biblical verse for there to be "a certain relation between the composition of the Verses and the composition of the Sentences," it is not surprising that the prototypical entity of singularity (or identity) that parallelism picks out is the line: "The correspondence of one Verse, or Line, with another," says Lowth, "I call Parallelism."[333] Biblical parallelism is often conceptualized the other way around, that is, from the perspective of the couplet, which is the most common frame for parallelism encountered in biblical poems. But this is mistaken insofar as it misjudges or obscures the central force of the iteration of the singular that is made manifest, as Lowth knew well, in the fact that parallelism occurs not only in pairs but also in threes, fours, and fives.[334] Indeed, the higher reaches of iteration's additive horizon are mostly left unrealized in biblical forms of poetic parallelism. Though there may well be a preference for bilateral parallelism in oral art forms,[335] there are corpora of oral (or oral derived) verse, ancient and modern, however, that more fully exploit this potential and in the process reveal more plainly the focus of the singular or identical that is constitutive of this phenomenon.[336]

Furthermore, the biblical poets themselves on occasion, as both R. Gordis and M. Gruber notice,[337] show that they, too, conceived of parallelism as consisting of two entities. In a number of examples (1 Sam 2:8; Isa 49:15; Ezek 18:26; 33:18, 19; Zeph 2:6–7; Job 13:20–21; 22:21), as Gordis explains, "Biblical Hebrew uses a plural pronoun to refer to a single object or action if it is expressed by two distinct terms in parallelism."[338] 1 Samuel 2:8 is a case in point:

> He raises the poor [$dāl$] from the dust,
> from the ash heap he lifts the needy [$'ebyôn$],
> to make (them) sit with nobles
> and a seat of honor to cause them to inherit [$yanḥîlēm$].

The plural pronominal suffix on the final verb (-$ēm$) referring back to the conjoined "poor" ($dāl$) and "needy" ($'ebyôn$), which otherwise are both singular nominals.[339] Of Job 13:21 ("withdraw your hand far from me, / and do not let the dread of you terrify me," NRSV) Gordis writes: "Here God's removing the hand and his desisting from frightening Job are obviously identical, yet the poet refers to them [in v. 20] as $štym$, two acts!"[340] In these examples (cf. Isa 49:15; Zeph 2:6–7; Job 22:21), the parallelistic phrasing that the poets single out and then quantify is distributed lineally as well. That is, the single line is distinguished. Indeed, as Gruber emphasizes,[341] this ancient construal, which he renders algebraically as "A + B = 2," jibes well with the insights of modern scholars like Alter and Kugel whose exploitation of difference in the play of parallelism assumes the very singularity of the entities played on or picked out, the A and B terms, for example, in Kugel's "A, and what's more, B" formulation of biblical parallelism.[342]

Sound Play

The line is more than syntax, semantics, and beat, and more even than a graphic entity. It has an auditory reality as heard, too.[343] It is, as Longenbach says, "ultimately a sonic…element of the poem."[344] The aural line historically predates the visual line, as noted earlier,[345] and in fact the graphemes of any writing system ultimately point readers back to the spoken language, which they only imperfectly transcribe.[346] And even in an age when poetry is written as much for the eye as for the ear,[347] poets still inevitably underscore the importance of sound to their craft. D. Levertov is emblematic when she writes that the "primary impulse" for her "was always to make a structure out of words,

words that *sounded* right."[348] And thus the sounds of a line are integral to what makes the line, what shapes it and gives it coherence and identity. Not surprisingly, then, in biblical verse sound patterns and repetitions often seem orchestrated in ways that reveal the line itself as a structural entity.[349] A few examples by way of illustration. In Lamentations 3:52 the initial line of the opening couplet in the ṣade stanza is itself defined by the alliterating consonance of the ṣade:

ṣôd ṣādûnî kaṣṣippôr	They hunt me (tirelessly) like a bird,
ʾōyĕbay ḥinnām	my enemies without cause.

The intentionality of the play is suggested on the one hand by the constraint of the acrostic, which demands at this point in this poem that the head word (at a minimum) in each of the three couplets of the this stanza begin with a ṣade (cf. ṣāmĕtû and ṣāpû at the heads of the succeeding couplets; also see esp. ṣādû ṣĕʿādēnû (MT), the opening line of the ṣade couplet in Lam 4:18). On the other hand the alliteration as it constrains the line here also effectively mimes the trapping that is the outcome of the bird-hunt alluded to in the couplet—birds in antiquity were commonly hunted with traps and lures (esp. Amos 3:5; Ps 124:7; Prov 7:23; Qoh 9:12). Here the line and sound play separate the enemy hunters from the trapped speaker in a way not dissimilar to the representation of fowling on one of the tombs of Beni Hasan in Egypt, in which the trap is manipulated by the hunters from a blind.[350] Such line framing alliteration occurs outside of acrostic poems as well, as in Exodus 15:9:

ʾāmar ʾôyēb ʾerdōp ʾaśśîg	The enemy said, "I will pursue, I will overtake,
ʾăhallēq šālāl timlāʾēmô napšî	I will divide the spoil, my desire will be satisfied upon them,
ʾārîq ḥarbî tôrîšēmô yādî	I will draw my sword, my hand will destroy them."

The initial line of the triplet is set off by the alliteration of *aleph*s (*ʾāmar ʾôyēb ʾerdōp ʾaśśîg*), which is then echoed in each of the chiming head words of the two succeeding lines (*ʾăhallēq* and *ʾārîq*). And end-rhyme joins the last two lines (*timlāʾēmô napšî // tôrîšēmô yādî*). So sound in several interlocking ways is integral to the shaping of all three lines in this example. Job 15:29 offers another telling example:

lōʾ-yeʿšar wĕlōʾ-yāqûm ḥêlô	he will not be rich and his wealth will not endure
wĕlōʾ-yiṭṭeh lāʾāreṣ minlām[351]	and he will not stretch possessions to the underworld

The thrice repeated /lō/ enfolds and defines the first line of the couplet, and its echo in the alliterated *lamed*s nicely scripts the second line as well. The assonating repetition of /u/ and /a/ sounds, together with the consonance of *nun*s and gutturals, give the first line in the couplet in Isaiah 53:4 a distinguishing sonic shape:

> *wa'ănaḥnû ḥăšabnûhû nāgûa'*   But we accounted him stricken,
> *mukkeh 'ĕlōhîm ûmĕ'unneh*   struck by God and afflicted.

And the second line, too, is shaped sonically, through the chiming of like sounds at the beginning and ending of the line (*mukkeh // ûmĕ'unneh*). Note the striking acrostic-like anaphora with word-initial *sin*s and *shin*s (*śa'rēk, šeggālĕšû, šinnayik, šě'ālû, šekkullām, wĕšakkulâ*) that bind the first half of the middle section (vv. 1b–2) of the *wasf*-like description poem in Song 4:1–7.[352] The rhyming of different roots in the second, shorter line of the qinah-shaped couplet in Lamentations 2:5c (*ta'ăniyyâ wa'ăniyyâ* "moaning and groaning") sharpens the formal integrity of this line.[353] In fact, the Lamentations poet frequently uses sound play of various sorts to fine point the shape of either the first (Lam 1:3c, 18c, 21c, 22b; 2:10a, 11c, 13a, 16a, 21b, 22c; 3:1, 4, 23, 42, 46, 51, 63; 4:4b, 5a, 15b, 17c, 18a, b, 21a) or second (Lam 1:12a, 17b; 2:13b, 16b, c, 18a; 3:24, 28, 54; 4:15a, 21b) lines of a couplet. The internal rhymes in the couplet at the end of Isaiah's "Song of the Vineyard" (*mišpāṭ // miśpāḥ, ṣĕdāqâ // ṣĕ'āqâ*, Isa 5:7) both distinguish the constituent lines and provide the needed punch (in this instance wonderfully enhanced by the repeating play of parallelism) required by the "gotcha" logic of the poem:

> *wayqaw lĕmišpāṭ wĕhinnê miśpāḥ*   He hoped for justice, but instead there
>   was oppression,
> *liṣdāqâ wĕhinnê ṣĕ'āqâ*   for righteousness, but instead there
>   was outcry!

And sometimes the play spills over the line boundary, exploiting that boundary, such that our awareness of the sonic shape of both lines is enhanced while also strengthening the formal cohesiveness of the whole. Lamentations 4:4b offers a good example of the latter:

> *'ôlālîm šā'ălû leḥem*   Children beg for bread,
> *pōrēš 'ên lāḥem*   but there is no provider for them.

The initial line is marked by the consonantal play of *aleph*s, *ayin*s, *lamed*s, and *mem*s, which in forming a backdrop for the end-rhyme (*leḥem* "bread" // *lāḥem* "for them") makes the rhyme (esp. in the Tiberian vocalization) stand out all the more (cf. Lam 1:1b, 2b–c; 2:22c; 3:18, 40, 42). The repeated, mostly word-final /i/ sounds in Song 5:2 bind the two couplets forming the boy's whispered entreaties to be let into his lover's house, while at the same time mimicking the light (and eager) tapping (*qôl dôdî dôpēq* "Hark! My love is knocking") that accompanied them:

piṯḥî-lî ʾăḥōtî raʿyātî	Open to me my sister, my love,
yônātî tammātî	my dove, my perfect one.
šerrōʾšî nimlāʾ-ṭāl	My head is damp with dew,
qĕwuṣṣôtay rĕsîsê lāylâ	my hair with the wet of the night.

The lone word internal chime (*rĕsîsê*) in the final line perhaps sonically foreshadows the boy's departure (cf. v. 6), the faint echo of the knocking fading as the girl dithers (vv. 3–5).

This kind of play with sounds at the level of the line is never exploited in the biblical poetic corpus systematically (such as with the alliterative patterning in Anglo-Saxon poetry). But it is sufficiently prevalent, even on the basis of the small sampling offered here, to make clear a myriad of ways in which sound helps shape and thus articulate line structure in biblical verse, and as a consequence provides a further means of fixing on the reality of the verse line in biblical poetry.

Syntax

If the line is always irredeemably sonic, it also "exists because it has a relationship to syntax."[354] "Syntax," writes Kinzie, "is one necessary defining principle of the poetic line."[355] A crucial part of any verse prosody turns on the relation of line and syntax—how the syntax of a poem's sentences moves and plays across its lines, how line and syntax converge to shape thought and shade meanings, what happens to the syntax at the ends of lines. Bringing the verse line in biblical Hebrew poetry into critical view opens all such matters to the scrutiny of criticism. Of more consequence for the current question—what evidence of the line?—is that the line, given this integral relationship to syntax, is always amenable to syntactic description. In fact, O'Connor in his *Hebrew Verse Structure* demonstrates that a consistent and cogent syntactic description of the biblical poetic line as known, at base, from the manuscript tradition is achievable. In general, he shows that the biblical poetic line consistently falls within specifiable parameters that are amenable to syntactic analysis and characterization.[356] That such a characterization can be cogently and consistently mounted means that there is something there in the first place to be so characterized, described, defined—the line. Clause and sentence profiles in standard biblical prose, whatever the overlap with the biblical verse tradition—and there is necessarily a great deal that is shared since all verse traditions are rooted in natural languages and everyday discourse, and conversely, since written prose narrative in ancient Israel and Judah will have evolved, in part, from oral poetic narrative—never exhibits the kind of uniformity (however variable) that is enforced by the lineal constraints of the biblical verse tradition. And were the spacing reflected in the Masoretic and Qumran manuscript traditions, for example, wholly ornamental, syntactic chaos, not consistency, would surely be the norm revealed by any investigation.[357] In short, the facticity of syntactic describability itself offers yet another means of isolating the poetic line in biblical verse, largely distinct, as O'Connor stresses, from (the logic and end-fixing function of) parallelism,[358] but also from the various other means already surveyed in the body of this essay.

Grouping and the Prevailing Binarism of Biblical Poetry

Lastly, I want to consider the logic of line grouping and what it may reveal about the status of the line in biblical verse. Verse is often described as either stichic, that which is written in a continuous run of lines, or stanzaic (or strophic), wherein lines are grouped together by formal or thematic structures into integral units.[359] Examples of stichic verse include the dactylic hexameter of ancient Greek epic, blank verse, and much contemporary free verse, while stanzaic forms (e.g., ballad stanza, ottava rima, rhyme royal, terza rima, sonnet, cinquain) are at the heart of much of the traditional metrical verse that emerged (initially) in the various vernacular traditions in imitation of classical lyric forms. But these are by no means monolithic descriptors, and neither traditions nor individual verse forms necessarily fall out purely as one or the other (i.e., mixture and the like is not uncommon). Ancient Greek verse, for example, famously contains both stichic (e.g., dactylic hexameter, iambic trimeter) and stanzaic (e.g., lyric) forms, including the popular elegiac distich (or couplet; a hexameter followed by a pentameter).[360]

Biblical verse does not normally feature regular and repeated stanza forms. The major exception is the acrostic poem, several of which (e.g., Lam 1–3, Ps 119) exhibit conspicuous stanzaic structures formed by the repeating and succeeding run of the alphabet. This does not mean that biblical poetry is completely devoid of stanzaic structure, however. Stanzas, at least in the most basic sense of the term as a grouping of lines,[361] do commonly occur. They just tend to be irregular and heterogenous in nature, very much akin to the sections or so-called verse paragraphs so typical of contemporary free verse.

Sometimes refrains (of a sort) even occur, dividing poems into discrete sections (Isa 9:7–20 and 5:25–30). And while single lines of verse do appear in
the Bible, a point to which I return momentarily, no biblical poems, however
brief, consist wholly of a run of such singular lines. Biblical verse is not stichic
in the ancient Greek sense (*kata stichon*). Rather, it is dominantly distichic;
that is, it consists mostly of runs of couplets, with triplets (tristichs), especially, helping to vary things, often appearing at structurally or thematically
pertinent places—though triplets do also occasionally form the basic grouping
scheme in sections of a poem and even in whole poems (e.g., Ps 93; Job 3:3–10).[362]
Larger groupings of lines do occasionally occur as well, but as often as not in
the form of combinations involving couplets and triplets. Not surprisingly,
then, when quotations or citations of poems are encountered in the Bible,
they most often come in groupings—or "snatches" as E. L. Greenstein calls
them, after the Arabic term for such poetic fragments (Ar. *qiṭʿa*)[363]—of two
lines or more. So the parade example is the quotation of the couplet in Exodus
15:21: *šîrû l-yhwh kî-gāʾōh gāʾâ / sûs wĕrōkĕbô rāmâ bayyām* "Sing to Yahweh for
he has triumphed gloriously, / horse and rider he cast into the sea." In this
instance, we have the larger poem from which the citation is made, Exodus
15:1–18. The poetic fragment in Joshua 10:12–13 about the sun and moon also
is shaped distichicly and is clearly a citation, as the source is specifically noted
(the scroll of Jashar, v. 13)—whether the fragment is a quote from a larger composition or itself constitutes a whole is by its nature less certain. More often
such certainty about the facticity of the quotation is not possible, since the
putative source is not preserved (e.g., Gen 4:23; Num 17–18; 1 Sam 18:7; 21:11).
What is extant, then, may simply be little ditties, complete on their own. But
in (almost) every case, whether quotation or whole poem, these snatches inevitably come grouped in twos and threes. The dearth (see immediately below)
of citations of singular lines does not mean that the line itself has no structural reality. Rather, it reveals in stunning fashion the dominantly distichic
nature of the biblical poetic tradition.

This preference for grouping lines is apparently related to the consistently
compressed length of the typical biblical Hebrew poetic line, often containing
only two or three stresses and from seven to nine syllables. "Being essentially
a single unit," writes Hrushovski, such abbreviated lengths "cannot create a
line balanced inwardly and are only a part of greater groupings."[364] In biblical
Hebrew poems, groupings of two and three such short lines dominate. The
commonality with which specially formatted manuscripts of biblical poems
from Qumran to the Masoretes group two lines (or parts thereof) of verse, with
or without intervening spans of space, on a single columnar line gives eloquent
visual expression to this distichic character. No doubt various factors (e.g.,

aesthetic, economic) will have informed the scribal preference for this style of formatting, but it is surely very telling that the typical column widths more readily fit the distich and not the tristich (see esp. the Masada scroll of Ben Sira). The prevailing "binarism"[365] of biblical verse has not been fully appreciated, as most fold it into their understanding of parallelism. It may well be that the "bilateral" shaping of parallelism in oral and oral-derived poetic traditions is not completely unmotivated (so Jousse). Still, not all such traditions exhibit dominantly binary forms of parallelism, and even the biblical tradition itself features triplets prominently enough—parallelism qua parallelism need not only or mostly come in twos. Moreover, nonparallelistic lines in the Bible also come grouped in twos and threes, and thus the dominantly distichic character of the tradition persists even in the absence of parallelism. Maintaining a distinction between the two phenomena—parallelism and a preference for binary sets of lines—is not only descriptively perspicuous (i.e., the two are not fully overlapping or self-identical) but prosodically meaningful as well. As Brogan and W. B. Piper remark, the couplet, by virtue of "standing midway between stichic verse and strophic," "permits the fluidity of the former while also taking advantage of some of the effects of the latter."[366] That is, there is something very much at stake interpretively in getting the description right.[367]

The Couplet

The couplet, "two contiguous lines of verse which function as a ... unit,"[368] gains its integrity as a perceptual whole from factors such as similarity, proximity, strength of closure, and the like,[369] though which specific grouping effects are drawn on and how will vary depending on the couplet(s) under review (e.g., language, nature of prosody). Sometimes broad generalizations obtain. So Smith observes that rhymed couplets generally acquire their perceptual unity from both the contiguity (proximity) of the couplet's component lines and the repetition of the same sounds (similarity) at the ends of these lines.[370] The ancient Greek elegiac couplet, which West says "enjoyed more popularity and diffusion" than all the rest of the strophic forms "put together,"[371] also depends for its sense of coherence on the proximity of its component lines, though these lines normally exhibit no obvious or strong similarities to each other. Rather, the force of similarity, in this instance, obtains in the repeated pattern of grouping a hexameter line of verse with an immediately following pentameter line of verse, a pattern that can only be known conventionally[372] or retrospectively after an auditor has experienced a sufficiently long run of such couplets,[373] as, for example, in the first ten lines of fragment 10 from Tyrtaeus:

τεθνάμεναι γὰρ καλὸν ἐνὶ προμάχοισι πεσόντα
   ἄνδρ' ἀγαθὸν περὶ ἧ πατπίδι μαρνάμενον,
τὴν δ' αὐτοῦ προλιπόντα πόλιν καὶ πίονας ἀγροὺς
   πτωχεύειν πάντων ἔστ' ἀνιηρότατον,
πλαζόμενον σὺν μητρὶ φίλῃ καὶ πατρὶ γέροντι
   παισί τε σὺν μικποῖς κουριδίῃ τ' ἀλόχῳ.
ἐχθρὸς μὲν γὰρ τοῖσι μετέσσεται οὕς κεν ἵκηται,
   ξπρησμοσύνῃ τ' εἴκων καὶ στυγερῇ πενίῃ,
αἰσχύνει τε γένος, κατὰ δ' ἀγλαὸν εἶδος ἐλέγχει,
   πᾶσα δ ἀτιμίη καὶ κακότης ἔπεται.[374]

For it is fine to die in the front line,
   a brave man fighting for his fatherland,
and the most painful fate's to leave one's town
   and fertile farmlands for a beggar's life,
roaming with a mother dear and aged father,
   with little children and with wedded wife.
He'll not be welcome anywhere he goes,
   bowing to need and horrid poverty,
his line disgraced, his handsome face belied;
   every humiliation dogs his steps.[375]

While no unifying force obtains from any of these distichs when taken individually, as experienced repeatedly and successively the wholeness of the elegiac couplet begins to emerge as a perceptual reality.

Often additional unifying forces are revealed when individual couplets are scrutinized. Consider the couplet addressed "To the Reader" that opens Ben Jonson's volume of *Epigrammes*:

Pray thee, take care, that tak't my booke in hand,
To read it well: that is, to understand.[376]

Again the proximity of the lines and the sameness of sound in the end-rhymes unify this couplet, as is true of rhymed couplets more generally. The cohesive force of the whole is strengthened additionally by the similarity of meter and rhythm, use of line-initial capitalization, thematic integrity, and syntactic closure.[377]

In biblical poetry, the parallelistic couplet is the commonest form of line grouping.[378] It provides the figural ground or basic texture for most biblical poems. In general, its unity is effected through the contiguity of its component

lines and the similarity manifested in the matching play of parallelism and in
the rough equivalence of line lengths that often falls out as a result of this play.
Additional grouping factors (e.g., anaphora, sound play, semantic emphasis),
usually in the ad hoc manner exemplified in Jonson's epigram, may also occur,
binding the distich "even more closely as a single perceptual form."[379] So parallelism, at least in this one respect, functions analogously (as a force of similarity) to end-rhyme in rhymed couplets—what is different is how the similarity
is achieved. Further, in contradistinction to the isometric pattern of much traditional English verse, for example, in which successive runs of rhymed couplets generally exhibit a larger pattern of uniformity between the individual
couplets (i.e., each couplet strongly resembling the next), intercouplet similarity generally does not obtain in runs of biblical parallelistic couplets beyond
the fact of the parallelism itself. These lines from Lamentations 5 (vv. 1–3,
11–13) are typical:

zĕkōr yhwh meh-hāyâ lānû	Remember, O Yahweh, what has happened to us,
habbêṭ (K) *ûrĕʾê ʾet-ḥerpātēnû*	look and see our reproach!
naḥălātēnû nehepkâ lĕzārîm	Our inheritance has been turned over to strangers,
bāttênû lĕnokrîm	our houses to foreigners.
yĕtômîm hāyînû ʾên ʾāb	We have become orphans, without a father,
ʾimmōtênû kĕʾāmānôt	our mothers like widows.
...	
nāšîm bĕṣiyyôn ʿinnû	Women in Zion are raped,
bĕtûlōt bĕʿārê yĕhûdâ	girls in the towns of Judah.
śārîm bĕyādām nitlû	Princes are hung by their hands,
pĕnê zĕqēnîm lōʾ nehdārû	the elders are not respected.
baḥûrîm ṭĕḥôn nāśāʾû	Young men bear the grind
ûnĕʿārîm bāʿēṣ kāšālû	and boys stagger under loads of wood.

Line lengths are variable (albeit within limits), as are the varieties of parallelism called on—no obvious formal mechanisms carry over from one couplet
to the next. Such isomorphism, of course, is achievable in biblical Hebrew
poetry. Psalm 19:8–10 offers a stunning biblical example:

tôrat yhwh tĕmîmâ	The law of the LORD is perfect,
mĕšîbat nāpeš	reviving the soul;
ʿēdût yhwh neʾĕmānâ	the decrees of the LORD are sure,
maḥkîmat petî	making wise the simple;
piqqûdê yhwh yĕšārîm	the precepts of the lord are right,

mĕśammĕḥê-lēb	rejoicing the heart;
miṣwat yhwh bārâ	the commandment of the LORD is clear,
mĕʾîrat ʿênāyim	enlightening the eyes;
yirʾat yhwh ṭĕhôrâ	the fear of the LORD is pure,
ʿômedet lāʿad	enduring forever;
mišpĕṭê yhwh ʾemet	the ordinances of the LORD are true,
ṣādĕqû yaḥdāw	and righteous altogether. (NRSV)

Each of the six couplets consists of a three-word line followed by a two-word line (the unbalanced long-short pattern of the so-called qinah meter, discussed later), and the lines are parallel to one another—the noun phrase "N + Yahweh" is elided in the second lines. And—here is the isomorphism—the couplets themselves are parallel to one another. They all exhibit the following pattern:

> Construct phrase (law synonym + Yahweh) + N/Adj
> Participle + N

Only the final couplet breaks the pattern (its second line contains a finite verb (*ṣādĕqû*) instead of an adjective) and thus gestures toward the close of the stanza that comes in the next set of couplets (v. 11). And many more examples could be added especially from the postbiblical traditions of Hebrew poetry. The different profile that prevails in so much biblical poetry (wherein, for example, intercouplet likenesses are normally not pronounced) is chiefly a consequence of the tradition's overarching nonmetrical prosody.[380]

   The unity of nonparallelistic or enjambed couplets in biblical poems is effected somewhat differently. Here, too, proximity (the "form of grouping is most natural [and strongest] which involves the smallest interval") is a unifying factor, which is enhanced and strengthened through syntactic closure. That is, these couplets tend to be closed syntactically—syntax only rarely runs over couplet (or triplet) boundaries in biblical poetry[381]—and thus are perceived as syntactic wholes.

gālĕtâ yĕhûdâ mēʿōnî	Judah has gone into exile with suffering
ûmērob ʿăbōdâ	and hard servitude;
hîʾ yăšĕbâ baggôyīm	she lives now among the nations,
lōʾ māṣĕʾâ mānôaḥ	and finds no resting place;
kol-rōdĕpeyhā hiśśîgûhā	her pursuers have all overtaken her
bên hammĕṣārîm	in the midst of her distress. (Lam 1:3, NRSV)

lĕsūsātî bĕrikbê parʿōh	To a mare among the chariots of Pharaoh
dimmîtîk raʿyātî	I compare you, my love. (Song 1:9)

bĕšeṣep qeṣep histartî	In overflowing wrath I hid
pānay regaʿ mimmēk	my face momentarily from you. (Isa 54:8)

Note that in contrast to the typical parallelistic couplets the component lines of these enjambed couplets do not stand out as obvious singular entities. Of course sound or other features may be deployed to highlight or backlight one line or the other, as the chiming *taʾăniyyâ waʾăniyyâ* in *wayyereb bĕbat-yĕhûdâ / taʾăniyyâ waʾăniyyâ* "and he multiplied in Daughter Judah / moaning and groaning" (Lam 2:5c), which sets off and thus identifies the second line of the couplet. But in general the unity of these enjambed couplets *as couplets* is much more pronounced than the identity of their component lines.[382]

A third couplet type commonly encountered in the biblical corpus acquires its sense of unity in a yet different manner. The qinah meter (not a meter at all!) is a couplet form that prototypically consists of a longer line of verse followed by a shorter line of verse, though the pattern is also sometimes reversed (shorter followed by longer). Such couplets tend to be mostly enjambed (e.g., Lam 1:3), though as seen from Psalm 19:8–10 parallelistic versions also occur. In this respect, part of the unity of these couplets is projected in the same way(s) as other enjambed or parallelistic couplets. And whether known from convention or through the experience of repeated runs of such qinah shaped couplets, the routinized pattern of couplets made up of unbalanced (long-short, short-long) lines itself, as with the elegiac couplet from Greece, becomes an additional affective unifying force.[383]

The Triplet

What I have said in general terms about the unifying forces of parallelistic and enjambed couplets holds true as well for triplets, and, indeed, for larger groupings of lines (e.g., the quatrain). That is, parallelistic or enjambed triplets, for example, generally have the same kind of unifying forces evident in couplets, as illustrated in Judges 5:10 and Psalm 133:3:

rōkĕbê ʾătōnôt ṣĕḥōrôt	O you who ride on white donkeys,
yōšĕbê ʿal-middîn	you who sit on rich carpets,
wĕhōlĕkê ʿal-derek śîḥû	and you who walk on a path, tell of it!
	(Judg 5:10; cf. NRSV)

kî šām ṣiwwâ	There Yahweh
yhwh ʾet-habběrākâ	commands the blessing—
ḥayyîm ʿad-hāʿôlām	life always! (Ps 133:3)

However, the additional line in a triplet also offers an opportunity to complicate matters. Consider these examples from Exodus 15:

mî-kāmōkâ bāʾēlīm yhwh	Who is like you, O LORD, among the gods?
mî kāmōkâ neʾdār baqqōdeš	Who is like you, majestic in holiness,
nôrāʾ těhillōt ʿōśê peleʾ	awesome in splendor, doing wonders?
	(v. 11; NRSV)

ʾāz nibhălû ʾallûpê ʾědôm	Then the chiefs of Edom were dismayed;
ʾêlê môʾāb yōʾḥăzěmô rāʿad	trembling seized the leaders of Moab;
nāmōgû kōl yōšěbê kěnāʿan	all the inhabitants of Caanan melted away.
	(v. 15; NRSV)

těbîʾēmô wětiṭṭāʾēmô běhar nahălātěkā	You brought and planted them on the mountain of your possession,
mākôn lěšibtěkā pāʿaltā yhwh	the place that you made for your abode, O LORD,
miqqědāš ʾădōnāy kôněnû yādeykā	the sanctuary, O Adonai, that your hands established. (v. 17; cf. NRSV)

In contrast to Judges 5:10, which exemplifies a rather straightforward kind of
parallelistic triplet, the three triplets from Exodus 15 vary one of the lines, thus
allowing for the added wrinkle of complexity. Proximity remains a chief force
of unity, its pull especially noticeable in these examples as the two more alike
lines attract and help hold the added line in place. In verses 11 and 17, in which
either the third or the first lines are altered, one effect is to build more expressed syntactic continuation into the triplet. As a consequence, one feels
both the parallelistic play of matching and the onward tug of modestly enjambed lines. Furthermore, both evidence what is often described in the literature as "staircase parallelism," a form of parallelism in which each succeeding
line both assumes information provided in the preceding line(s) and adds
new information. The chief mechanism that makes such play possible is ellipsis or gapping.[384] In verse 15, where the change-up comes in the middle
line, the predominant feel of three parallelistic lines remains—the different
word order and subject of the second line offering a slightly different way of
framing what is essentially the same underlying propositional content.[385]

Larger Groupings

In larger groupings of lines the unifying forces most commonly in play are variations on or extensions of the forces already illustrated with respect to couplets and triplets. This is not surprising since these larger groupings are often built up out of combinations of couplets and triplets:

šĕlōšâ hēmmâ niplĕʾû mimmennî	Three things are too wonderful for me;
wĕʾarbaʿ lōʾ yĕdaʿtîm	four I do not understand:
derek hannešer baššāmayim	the way of an eagle in the sky,
derek nāḥāš ʿălê-ṣûr	the way of a snake on a rock,
derek-ʾŏniyyâ bĕleb-yām	the way of a ship on the high seas,
wĕderek geber bĕʿalmâ	and the way of a man with a girl.
	(Prov 30:18–19; NRSV)

kî-tēšēb lilḥôm ʾet-môšēl	When you sit down to eat with a ruler,
bîn tābîn ʾet-ʾăšer lĕpāneykā	observe carefully what is before you,
wĕśamtā śakkîn bĕlōʿekā	and put a knife to your throat
ʾim-baʿal nepeš ʾāttâ	if you have a big appetite.
	(Prov 23:1–2; NRSV)

ʾal-tithar bammĕrēʿîm	Do not fret because of evildoers.
ʾal-tĕqannēʾ bāršāʿîm	Do not envy the wicked;
kî lōʾ-tihyeh ʾaḥărît lārāʿ	for the evil have no future;
nēr rĕšāʿîm yidʿāk	the lamp of the wicked will go out.
	(Prov 24:19–20; NRSV)

hāgô sîgîm mikkāsep	Take away the dross from the silver,
wayyēṣēʾ laṣṣōrēp kĕlî	and the smith has material for a vessel;
hāgô rāšā lipnê-melek	take away the wicked from the presence of the king,
wĕyikkôn baṣṣedeq kisʾô	and his throne will be established in righteousness. (Prov 25:4–5; NRSV)

ḥesed weʾĕmet ʾāl-yaʿazbūkā	Do not let loyalty and faithfulness for sake you;
qošrēm ʿal-gargĕrôteykā	bind them around your neck,
kotbēm ʿal-lûaḥ libbekā	write them on the tablet of your heart.
ûmĕṣāʾ-ḥēn wĕśēkel-ṭôb	So you will find favor and good repute
bĕʿênê ʾĕlōhîm wĕʾādām	in the sight of God and of people.
	(Prov 3:3–4; NRSV)

'al-tilḥam 'et-leḥem ra' 'āyin	Do not eat the bread of the stingy;
wĕ'al-tit'āyw [Q] *lĕmaṭ'ammōtāyw*	do not desire their delicacies;
kî kĕmô-šā'ar bĕnapšô ken-hû'	for like a hair in the throat, so are they.
'ĕkōl ûšĕtê yō'mar lāk	"Eat and drink!" they say to you;
wĕlibbô bal-'immāk	but they do not mean it.
pittĕkā 'ākaltā tĕqî'ennâ	You will vomit up the little you have eaten,
wĕšiḥattā dĕbāreykā hannĕ'îmîm	and you will waste your pleasant words. (Prov 23:6–7; NRSV)

Runs of multiple parallel lines, as in Proverbs 30:18–19, where the four ways (*derek* + N) not understood are listed in four separate lines (cf. vv. 21–23, 29–31), and even loosely conjoined run-on lines (Prov 23:1–2) are always possible. As such the basic trajectory of expansion and ever more complex possibilities for realizing intragroup coherence seen in the triplet continues. However, ordinarily these larger groupings break down into combinations of couplets and triplets, for example, Proverbs 25:4–5 (quatrain: couplet + couplet), Proverbs 3:3–4 (five lines: triplet + couplet), Proverbs 23:6–7 (seven lines: couplet + triplet + couplet). Therefore, in addition to the kinds of unifying forces that bind individual couplets and triplets together there are forces that work in and among the grouping's component couplets and triplets. Here, too, the central mechanisms of unity are parallelism and syntactic dependency, often in combination. Proverbs 24:19–20, for example, consists of two synonymously (e.g., Prov 4:14; 14:19) parallelistic couplets whose separate unities come off as result of the forces of proximity and general likeness (semantics, syntax, word order—the couplet in verse 19 is especially tight). The two couplets themselves are joined, then, into a larger whole by contiguity, syntactic dependency (esp. *kî* "for, because" at the head of v. 20), and the interweaving iteration of like (*rĕšā'îm*, v. 19b // *rĕšā'îm*, v. 20b) or closely related (*mĕrē'îm*, v. 19a // *rā'*, v. 20a) terms. The holism of Proverbs 25:4–5, another four-line group (or quatrain), is managed a little differently. Here intracouplet unity is effected chiefly through syntactic dependency: statement of an action (removal of dross or the wicked) and its consequence (creation of a silver vessel or a righteous reign). Intercouplet unity on the other hand results from the immediate contiguity of two couplets that parallel one another (esp. word order!) very closely—the repetition of the same couplet initial verb (*hāgô* "take away") helps ensure that this otherwise nonnormative kind of parallel play does not go unnoticed:

> *hāgô* (impv.) + O (*sîgîm*) + PP (*mikkāsep*) / conj. + V (*wayyēṣē'*) + PP (*laṣṣōrēp*) + S (*kĕlî*)

hāgô (impv.) + O (*rāšă*) + PP (*lipnê-melek*) / conj. + V (*wĕyikkôn*) +
PP (*baṣṣedeq*) + S (*kisʾô*)

While the specifics of how any given larger grouping of biblical verse lines
secures group unity and to what degree will vary, the general pattern, as
evidenced in the two quatrains from Proverbs just reviewed, is clear enough.
In such groupings, made up of couplets, triplets, and even the occasional
quatrain (e.g., Prov 30:18–19, a six-line group made up of a couplet, v. 18, and
a following quatrain, v. 19), forces for unity normally get enacted at the level
both of the individual component couplets, triplets, or quatrains and of these
components as they interrelate with one another as a larger whole.[386]

Isolated Lines

The very existence of the verse line in biblical poetry is questioned in no small
part because of the dominantly distichic character of this verse tradition—one
simply does not see too many unattached singular lines in biblical poems.
Rather, they mostly come grouped in twos and threes, and occasionally even in
larger denominations, as illustrated. And the capacities of these groupings to
achieve perceptible forms of unity has allowed what are complex, nonidentical,
nonundifferentiated wholes, to be mistaken for self-identical, homogeneous
wholes, that is, singularities. This is never closely argued, but the informing
conception is implicit, for example, in the language of hemistichs, half lines and
half verses, versets, two- and three-part lines, and the like.[387] The total absence of
unaffiliated single lines in strictly stanzaic forms or traditions, of course, does
not imply the inconsequentiality of the line as a structural entity,[388] let alone its
nonexistence, that is, stanzas (like couplets) are complex poetic entities built up
out of smaller wholes, lines. And one aim of the immediately foregoing discussion is to indicate that wholeness, unity, may be predicated of both singular (e.g.,
lines) and complex (e.g., groups of lines) lineal phenomena. But in point of fact
almost every scholar who has attended to the issue agrees that single, unaffiliated lines do occur in biblical poems. Watson, for example, is most emphatic on
this point: "it is meaningless to deny that monocola [i.e., single lines] exist."[389] By
all accounts there are not many such lines and almost every one identified is
contestable owing to the tradition's strong preference to group lines, especially
in couplets. For example, longer lines, such as Exodus 15:12, *nāṭîtā yĕmînĕkā
tiblāʿēmô ʾāreṣ* "You stretch out your right hand, the earth swallows them," is
amenable to being analyzed as a couplet made up of two short lines:

nāṭîtā yĕmînĕkā   You stretch out your right hand,
tiblāʿēmô ʾāreṣ   the earth swallows them. (so *BHS*, NRSV)

Or through the banding force of proximity single lines can always be perceived as a part of immediately adjacent groups or stanzas, especially if the
adjacent group is a couplet or triplet, given the relative commonality of triplets
and quatrains in the tradition. Exodus 15:18 provides a good illustration:

yhwh yimlōk lĕʿōlām wāʿed   "Yahweh will reign forever and ever"

Taken as a single line,[390] Exodus 15:18 offers a strong closural gesture as it
departs at poem's end from the pattern of line grouping (mostly couplets and
triplets) that otherwise permeates the poem.[391] But the rarity of singular lines
means that the inclination to join the line to the preceding triplet in verse 17
(NRSV)—aided by the palpable attraction of immediate proximity to a larger
whole—or divide it into a couplet (*BHS*) is powerful.

   As noted, normally snatches of quoted verse in the Bible come chiefly
grouped as couplets or triplets (or larger combinations of the same). The first
line of Jeremiah 17:8, *wĕhāyâ kĕʿēṣ šāṭûl ʿal-mayim* "and he will be like a tree
planted beside water," may offer a notable exception to this practice (perhaps
because it comes in the context of a larger poetic saying, Jer 17:5–8). It is a close
version of a line also found in Psalm 1:3, *wĕhāyâ kĕʿēṣ šāṭûl ʿal-palgê māyim* "and
he will be like a tree planted beside streams of water." The latter, slightly longer
version is open to alternative construal, for example, breaking it into a couplet
as suggested in *BHS*. But the Aleppo Codex clearly construes the psalmic line
as a singular whole,[392] and such a construal of the Jeremianic version is consistent with the line patterning in the larger poetic saying of which it is a part,
Jeremiah 17:5–8.[393] The putative direction of influence has long been debated,
but nothing in either text requires priority, and neither seems to allude intentionally to the other.[394] In fact, the two poems are demonstrably different, that
is, in their structures, poetics, language, even in the staging of the contrasting
similes at the heart of both. It may simply be that Jeremiah 17:8 and Psalm 1:3,
however originally composed, feature a striking remembered line, whatever
may be determined about that line's origin.[395] In any event, such a recollection
of a singular line (perhaps twice over) provides impressive evidence for the
facticity of the poetic line in biblical verse.

   A number of other possible isolated lines stand out in psalms. So the
closing *šālôm ʿal-yiśrāʾēl* "Peace upon Israel" in Psalm 128:6 mostly falls outside the structural scaffolding of the larger psalm, and thus is an effective

closing gesture.³⁹⁶ The final line in Psalm 2, ʾašrê kōl-ḥôsê bô "How commend-able are all who take refuge in him!" (v. 11), again falls outside that psalm's larger pattern of lineation, and of course many think the line is intentionally added to form a closing envelope structure with the opening ʾašrê of Psalm 1 (v. 1). The closing of Psalm 13, ʾāšîrâ l-yhwh kî gāmal ʿālāy (v. 6), may be con-strued as a couplet (Aleppo) or as a singular whole (B19a). And whether au-thorially or editorially hălĕlû yāh is frequently staged as an independent line (e.g., Ps 111:1; 146:10).

M. Fox identifies a "monostich" in Proverbs 30:15a (la ʿălûqâ šĕtê bānôt hab hab "The leech has two daughters: 'Give' 'Give'"), which "differs sharply from the didactic couplets and epigrams of proverbs"—"it serves here as a pivot verse between two epigrams."³⁹⁷ Aleppo clearly presents the line spatially as a single entity.³⁹⁸

Also there are isolated lines in the Song of Songs. Least disputable is Song 2:10: ʿānâ dôdi wĕ·ʾāmar lî lit. "My love answers and says to me." The line intro-duces the section (vv. 10–13) of the poem (Song 2:8–17) containing the Song's famous ode to spring. The boy beckons the girl to join him on one of their nighttime trysts, enticing her (so it seems) through a beautifully evocative depiction of the awakening of spring, that perennial time of love the world over. The section proper consists of four couplets and a triplet and is framed by an inclusio: qûmî lāk raʿyātî yāpātî / ûlĕkî lāk "Arise, my darling, my beauty, / and come away" (vv. 10, 13). The uniqueness of this quotative frame in the Song³⁹⁹—direct speech otherwise is never formally introduced—and the exact mirroring nature of the inclusion makes it unlikely that we are to fold the line into the first rendition of the inclusio, turning the latter into a triplet.⁴⁰⁰ Besides, lines embedding quotative frames are one of the more common species of isolated lines to appear in both the Bible (e.g., Isa 45:14; 49:8, 25; 50:1; 66:1; Jer 6:9, 16; 25:32; 30:18; 31:16; Amos 1:3, 6, 9, etc.)⁴⁰¹ and especially in Ugaritic narrative poetry (e.g., CAT 1.4.II.21; 14.III.21).⁴⁰² Jere-miah 6:16 may be quoted in full as it contains both a singular quotative frame paralleling the quotative frame in Song 2:10 and an additional isolated line to close the unit:

kōh ʾāmar yhwh	Thus says the LORD:
ʿimdû ʿal-dĕrākîm ûrĕʾû	Stand at the crossroads, and look,
wĕšaʾălû lintîbōt ʿôlām	and ask for the ancient paths,
ʾê-zeh derek haṭṭôb ûlĕkû bāh	where the good way lies; and walk in it,
ûmiṣʾû margôaʿ lĕnapšĕkem	and find rest for your souls.
wayyōʾmĕrû lōʾ nēlēk	But they said, "We will not walk in it." (NRSV)

The messenger formula here introduces Yahweh's command, which is set as a quatrain composed of syntactically dependent and paralleling couplets (ABA'B') and featuring imperatives. The response is given in a line of its own.

There are several other possible isolated lines in the Song, though none are beyond question. The likeliest is the final rendition of the mutuality pledge in Song 7:11,[403] which famously plays on and overturns the curse leveled against Eve in Genesis 3:16:

> *'ănî lĕdôdî wĕ'ālay tĕšûqātô*   I am my lover's and upon me is his desire.

The line, of course can be broken into a couplet (so *BHS*),[404] which would imitate the rhythmic feel of the curse, but the resulting lines would be short (though not impossibly short). By contrast the other versions of the mutuality pledge in the Song, on which the line trades as well (esp. 6:3), strongly suggest the lineal singularity of 7:11:

> *dôdî lî wa'ănî lô*   My lover is mine and I am his (Song 2:16)
> *'ănî lĕdôdî wĕdôdî lî*   I am my lover's and my lover is mine (Song 6:3)

A little further on in the same poem, the girl invites her lover to join her in the garden, reprising and replaying language of the boy's earlier invitation (2:10–13). After two triplets' worth of invitation, featuring a cluster of first person plural verb forms ("let *us* go forth...let *us* see...") and clauses dependent on them,[405] the girl breaks off most abruptly:

> *šām 'ettēn 'et-dôday lāk*   There I will give my love to you (7:13)

The presence of the adverbial *šām* and lone first person singular verb (*'ettēn*) underscores the change-up. The line of course can always be folded into the preceding triplet,[406] but the warrant for doing so would seem to be chiefly the tendency for lines to come grouped in biblical verse. Yet even in such construals the singularity of the line stands out, and thus taking it as a genuine single line may at least boast of abiding by the larger contours and sensibilities of the poem.[407]

A final possibility of a single line from the Song may be considered. It comes in the immediately preceding poem (7:1–7), the last *wasf*-like poem in the sequence. The line dedicated to admiring the girl's neck (*sawwā'rēk kĕmigdal haššēn* "your neck is like a tower of ivory," 7:5) stands alone, without any further embellishment. Noting the uniqueness of this lack of elaboration in such similes in the Song—"the other descriptions are either couplets or triplets"—many commentators suppose that a line (at least) has dropped out.[408] Such warrant is not to be lightly dismissed. And yet it is worth noting that in a number of these couplets and triplets no actual embellishment of the initial body part admired appears. Instead, there is extension (if that is what it is) by paralleling with a simile involving a closely related *but different* part of the body. So in 5:11 and 7:6 admiration of the head is joined within the couplet extolling the hair. In 4:3 similes for the girl's lips and mouth are joined as a couplet—contrast the treatment of the boy's lips in 5:13 with proper elaboration. And in 5:16 the boy's sweet-tasting mouth is matched—not extended or embellished—with mention of the desirability of the boy's whole body (*kullô*). In other words, lines very much of the same kind as 7:5 appear in the poems and could also conceivably be taken as singular entities (esp. the "head" lines, 5:11; 7:6).[409]

As noted, none of these last examples from the Song can be posited as un-attached, individual lines of verse with absolute certainty. But it is sufficient for my purposes to recognize that they all could be so posited and that the chief reason for resisting such a supposition is the overwhelming binary (and ternary) nature of line grouping in biblical Hebrew verse.

In sum, then, there is no real question about the existence of unattached single lines of verse in biblical poetry. Their relative rarity and the ambiguities that permeate our attempts at confidently isolating specific examples are chiefly a consequence of the dominantly distichic character of biblical verse. And that both single lines and triplets are nonetheless present and even well attested (especially in the case of the triplet) in the tradition, alongside the more common couplet, makes it most apparent that the line (by whatever name, e.g., colon, etc.) is both a distinguishable entity and the entity of the lowest degree of complexity relevant for stanza formation. This even holds for those who would continue to insist that the couplet is the base lineal unit of biblical verse, as the only way to generate a single line from a couplet is by dissolving (halving) the latter into a yet simpler entity. The fact that the result-ing simpler entity, the line, then occurs in isolation and is required for the formation of triplets (as well as other larger groupings of lines)[410] shows that even had the line originated as the subpart of a more complex entity, the couplet, it is the simpler line that is practically pertinent for stanza formation in biblical verse as we currently know it. Of course, I find no compelling war-rant for assuming the originating singularity of the couplet in biblical poetry. As already indicated, though both parallelism and the pervasive binarism of the tradition may give way to such a perception, that perception ultimately is a *mis*perception. There is no reason for parallelism qua parallelism to be restricted in scope to correspondences between two and only two entities. Besides, even the biblical poets themselves on several occasion make it clear that they understood parallel couplets to be composed of two (lineal) entities, $A + B = 2$.[411] And the distichic character of so much biblical poetry is a convention of line grouping that is well known cross-culturally and to be set alongside other means for organizing lines in poems (e.g., stichic and stanzaic verse). More straightforward (Occam's proverbial razor) is the assumption that the isolated line is the base unit with larger magnitudes (or collections) formed through successive aggregation or adjunction—a "multiplicity measurable by the one" (Aristotle, *Metaphysics*, 1057, a).[412] That such additive logic is congenial and isomorphic to, if not generative of, stanza structure in biblical poetry is indicated by examples like Proverbs 30:18–19 cited above, which turn on counting and the additive logic that counting presumes.[413]

The Logic of Counting

Counting, no simple cognitive ability, "requires that the whole numbers be arranged in a sequence in which each number, after 1, is obtained by adding 1 to the number before it."[414] And thus a group or collection is counted by assigning to every member one of the whole numbers "in *ordered succession* until the collection is exhausted." The number "assigned to the last member is called the *ordinal number* of the collection," which is, of course, precisely equivalent to the number of members in the collection.[415] The parallelism in Proverbs 30:18 with respect to the numerical sequence "three . . . / and four . . ." is not that of synonymous word-pairs, as so often supposed since Lowth.[416] Such numbers "are clearly not synonymous."[417] Rather, the logic trades on knowledge of counting. The last number—here "four"—is the "ordinal number" of that which is being counted, the precise number of "ways" that are not comprehended, which are then related successively in four lines in the following verse. The counting up of the four "ways" in the four lines, in other words, is no accident. The additive logic itself is plain to see and replicated elsewhere in Proverbs 30 (vv. 15b–16, 24–28, 29–31), for example, though the summing itself can be grouped differently and carried out over fewer or greater numbers of lines. That the counting trope in these examples is a sequence of only two numbers is a factor primarily of the distichic structure of biblical verse and the abbreviation it requires in this instance. As G. Ifrah stresses, "any natural integer presupposes its preceding numbers as the cause of its existence"; "it subsumes all preceding numbers in the sequence."[418] In other words, rehearsal of the entire counting sequence is not needed in order for the additive force of the counting to be implicated, that is, the sequence of three and four (in this instance) is sufficient to signify the ordinal number of the collection, the sum of its contents.

Extended longer literal counts, though not common in the preserved corpus of biblical verse (e.g., Isa 17:6), are well attested in both Akkadian and Ugaritic narrative verse.[419] There are several instances, however, of the brief but holistic numerical sequence "one // two" (Ps 62:12; Job 33:14), which is precisely fitted to the Bible's preferred distichic manner of grouping lines. In Psalm 62:12–13a that which is counted is a couplet of divine speech, a summing of one line of verse added to a second:

'aḥat dibber 'ĕlōhîm	One (line of verse)[420] God has spoken,
šĕtayyim-zû šāmā'tî	two which I have heard:
kî 'ōz lē'lōhîm	that strength belongs to God
ûlĕkā-'ădōnāy ḥāsed	and to you, O Lord, steadfast love.

This still does not quite add up to an explicit explication of the additive logic that I presume informs line grouping in biblical verse. But it is likely as close as we can hope to come. The frame couplet apportions the counting trope lineally ("one.../ two..."), with the second and last number ("two") providing the ordinal number of the group, the sum of the count. The second couplet then mimes the implicit additive logic by listing precisely the two counted "words," again apportioned lineally, one word ("that strength belongs to God") constituting the first line of the couplet and the second word ("and to you, O Lord, steadfast love") the second line.[421] The sequence is complete; it isolates the distich, that quintessential form of line grouping in biblical poetry, and even shows off the ability to count discrete chunks of language—here the verse lines that are revealed, for example, through the spacing in the Aleppo Codex (though very faint in places; cf. B19a).

* * *

IN SUMMARY, THE principal ends in view of the foregoing discussion have been, one, to gather an assortment of considerations that positively and empirically show the existence and importance of the line in biblical verse, and two, to reveal in what that line consists, its character, scope, pattern of appearance, and so forth. Evidence of the punctuating segmentation so integral to verse generally—what I have called throughout (after contemporary literary parlance) the *line*—in the (posited) corpus of biblical poetry is overwhelming; indeed, it is both substantial and wide-ranging. The facticity of the line may be glimpsed variously—graphically, sonically, rhythmically, syntactically; it falls out from consideration of sundry phenomena—parallelism, human cognitive capacities, sound play, line grouping; and it has been attested to throughout history by a myriad of readers. That there is no single resource that shows indisputably every line of biblical verse, or that scholars cannot always settle on their line construals with maximum confidence, is quite beside the point. Like every feat of historical reconstruction, deciding on lines in biblical verse is fraught with problems of evidence, uncertainty, and contestation at every turn. But this is the very stuff of historical research.

The finding that there are lines (by whatever name) in biblical poetry is not altogether surprising or unanticipated. In my discussion of terminology I emphasized that despite the range of terms used (and the confusion such diversity has often caused) and the utter lack of any but the most tacit theorization, "the periodic and recurring interruption or checking of the flow of sense, sound and rhythm and its resultant segmentation in language that the Masoretes, for example, sometimes wrote out in small bricks (or chunks) of writing circumscribed by spans of spacing" is actually quite well known in the field, a place of consensus on which I knowingly build. What I have endeavored to do in the preceding discussion is to give this kind of field-specific knowledge precision and perspicuity and to evolve my description of the phenomenon more intentionally and theoretically such that the knowledge generated can then be the more readily assessed and put to work constructively on behalf of criticism—a good deal of Lowth's success and wide appeal comes from the fact of his evolving a way of talking about biblical poetry (the very invention of a new literary criticism), precise and detailed, to be sure, but also composed with "elegance" and "infectious" in its admiration of the subject matter.[422] The outstanding significance of the facticity of lines in biblical poetry is the very sensibility itself of the idea of biblical poetry. If there are lines then there is very good reason to think that there is also in fact verse, since almost all verse prior to the mid-nineteenth century, whether oral or written, is characterized by periodic pulsations of interrupting segmentation, that is, arranged (in the explicitly literate vernacular) lineally. O'Connor calls this a "fact of generality": "poetry is generally written in units [i.e., lines] of characterizable extent."[423] So much talk in recent years of a putative "prose/poetry continuum" in the Bible is mostly a chimera of chirography. This is not to rule out of hand the possibility of genre-bending works—though the so-called prose poem is pointedly a modern, post-Gutenberg phenomenon. Nor do I doubt that continuities in trope, style, and figures (e.g., parallelism in its non-line-fixing capacity) pervade the poetry and the prose of the Bible, but such continuities are unremarkable and are found in almost every literary tradition. Rather, what seems patent to me is that the supposition of a great swath of biblical literature that appears not to readily resolve itself either as poetry or as prose arises and finds such current assent chiefly through a trick of chirographically acculturated eyes. That so much of the post-Lowthian corpus of biblical poetry does not come down to us in specially formatted manuscripts appears only to confirm the supposition, that is, if it were truly poetry it would *look* like poetry, be set in lines. Hopefully, enough has been said here about the epiphenomenal and variable nature of the graphic display of verse in writing throughout world literature to show the perception for the *mis*perception that it is. Verse as a matter of historical fact was not always written out in the southern Levant, and when it was written out it was not always distinguished graphically from written prose. The question of the verse line in biblical Hebrew poetry, as in many other premodern verse traditions, does not hang on its graphic display, though such display is itself crucial and informative and once in place and conventionalized can become relevant prosodically. Moreover, that biblical verse, in part, does also receive special formatting in antiquity provides graphic evidence of the verse line. But the biblical verse line may also be sighted and triangulated on from a multitude of other perspectives and considerations. That there are lines of biblical verse means that at the level of medium there is no such thing as a "prose/poetry continuum" because it is the line itself that is the chief feature that distinguishes the two. Poems are unequivocally more than the sum of their lines, and therefore any sufficiently encompassing description of biblical verse, for example, will need to consider and adduce additional matters and elements (e.g., patterned syntax, diction, rhythmic movement) that help constitute biblical poetry as poetry. Line structure is only one element, albeit unparalleled in importance. As Longenbach says, "lines make poetry."[424] That biblical poetry is made of lines is quite beyond question, a point, nevertheless, very much worth underscoring.

What constitutes the base lineal unit in this verse tradition is from a purely evidentiary standpoint a more equivocal matter. On my account the structural entity that most contemporary biblical scholars know of as the colon is that base unit, and hence my preference for the English term *line*. If the line's (or colon's) phenomenality falls out, in smaller and larger ways, as a consequence of all of the considerations reviewed above, several of those considerations point more directly to the presumption of the line as the base of the lineal system. Perhaps the strongest warrant in support of this supposition is the limited capacity and duration of working memory and the brute constraints this imposes on the length of the verse line in oral poems. Lengths of individual lines (cola) of biblical verse are variable but almost never exceed the limits imposed by working memory; whereas couplets and triplets (bicola and tricola) routinely violate these limits. It is difficult to imagine a prosody that originated in an overwhelmingly oral environment having at its foundation a lineal entity that was so contrary to human performative capacities unaided by writing. Also telling is the logic of several of the phenomena treated above that features singularities that are prototypically satisfied by the line. Parallelism, as I describe it, is a trope of correspondence or repetition, and as such always acts on some singularity as the fulcrum of its play. Prototypically, the line (colon) serves as this fulcrum of singularity in biblical poems, especially in parallelism's central line-fixing function—a fact crucial to Lowth's ability to discern (non–specially formatted) verse in the Former and Latter Prophets. Parallelism, of course, operates on both smaller and larger scales in biblical verse, but it is the single line that is most often at the heart of this corresponding phenomenon, a fact that did not go entirely unnoticed by the biblical poets themselves.[425] The logic of line grouping (stanza formation) is pertinent here as well. The simplest entity relevant to line grouping in biblical verse is again the single line (colon). While larger groups can be (and often are) formed by combinations of couplets and triplets, sometimes it is quite apparent that these larger groupings are made up of single lines alone or, more usually, single lines in combination with couplets and/or triplets. This together with the fact of single isolated lines (however small in number) and triplets, neither of which are straightforwardly (though not impossibly) derivable from couplets alone, show the identity of the simplest singularity relevant for this phenomenon. The dominantly distichic character of biblical verse—that strong tendency for lines to appear in poems mainly grouped in twos—is entirely consistent with the supposition of a more basic, simpler lineal unit. Indeed, the couplet is one of the most common forms of line grouping in poetry cross-culturally.[426]

The strong tendency for sound play and sentence structure to be coterminous with what these other considerations pick out as a line of biblical verse is surely not accidental. Nor that the line as I understand it admits independent syntactic description, or is isolated consistently in Hebrew manuscripts by spacing, that most characteristic feature of special formatting in these manuscript traditions, or that almost without exception the entity in focus by readers down through the ages when commenting on biblical poetry is again the line or colon, and not the couplet or bicolon. The several other phenomena and considerations reviewed above are consistent with such a construal though they do not require or point toward it in quite the same strong way as those just tallied. At bottom my brief for the line as the base lineal unit of biblical poetry is but one construal of the data. It privileges a general literary theoretical perspective and an implicit comparative methodology and will be found compelling, in large measure, to the degree that these informing perspectives are judged appropriate for and congenial to the subject matter in all of its diversity and substance.

Throughout I have spoken of lines of verse mostly in the abstract, as if they were a kind of phenomenon that could be picked out and scrutinized independently. And while, especially for analytical purposes, the line is an immanently isolatable phenomenon, it also is a phenomenon that never arises outside the context of a realized poem. Longenbach is most emphatic on this point:

> These three ways of thinking about the line—metered verse, syllabic verse, free verse—have different effects, but in any case the line exists not because it has a certain pattern of stresses, a certain number of syllables, or an irregular number of stresses and syllables: the line exists because it has a relationship to syntax. You might say that a one line poem doesn't really have anything we can discuss as a line, except inasmuch as we feel its relationship to lines in other poems. We need at least two lines to begin to hear how the line is functioning.[427]

That is, lines only resolve themselves as lines in the process of constituting the very poems of which they are a part and apart from which they cannot exist. They do not come preordained—not even in metrical verse!—but are actualized only in the realization of actual poems (whether in oral or written performance). Individual lines always (potentially) admit of quotation, and thus recontextualization, as evidenced above all by my many quotations of biblical verse lines on offer above.[428] But quotation by its nature assumes the authorization of a preceding performative (oral or written) context for the quote—in this case, actual poems. And with respect to biblical poems, for which autographs are wholly lacking, the dynamic nature of line resolution, as a practical matter, never becomes completely stable, is never fully resolved. If anything, lines of biblical poems are felt to be even more primordially in the process of construction and resolution since the poems that they help constitute are themselves forever needing to be construed, resolved, interpreted, recomposed, read, and reread. They have no otherwise settled identity, and in fact very well may not have had such even in their originary textualizations (see chapters 3 and 4).[429] The reading of Psalm 133 in the final chapter of this book offers (among other things) a sustained look at the poetic line in its native environment, so to speak, in the context of an actual poem. The reading of poems affords a means of both ramifying the idea that lines are not self-evident or self-identical entities and of illustrating one of the abiding benefits of the kind of critical scrutiny I have engaged in for most of this chapter, the prospects of reading individual poems alive to the possibilities that line structure puts into play, which in turn provides yet another means of measuring the presence and importance of the line in biblical poetry.

The Free Rhythms of
Biblical Hebrew Poetry

in ancient Hebrew poetry, though there was always
rhythm, there was (so far as has yet
been discovered) no metre
—S. R. DRIVER, *An Introduction to the Literature*
of the Old Testament (1892)

Through Whitman's Eyes

That Walt Whitman's mature style, especially as manifested in *Leaves of Grass*, owed a great debt to the English Bible has become a standard part of Whitman scholarly lore and is widely stipulated.[1] Its earliest appearance in print dates at least as far back as 1860, to an unsigned review in the Boston *Cosmopolite* that remarks, "In respect of plain speaking, and in most respects, *Leaves* more resemble the Hebrew Scriptures than do any other modern writings."[2] But the classic statement on the topic occurred in a pair of articles from the early 1930s by G. W. Allen, "Biblical Analogies for Walt Whitman's Prosody" (1933) and "Biblical Echoes in Whitman's Works" (1934).[3] Allen well articulates the overall ambition of his line of inquiry: "But unmistakably a detailed comparison of *Leaves of Grass* and biblical poetry is greatly needed, first to determine exactly why the rhythms of Whitman have suggested those of the Bible...and second to see what light such an investigation throws on Whitman's sources."[4] Of these two large aims, Allen regarded the first "as more important because it should reveal the underlying laws of the poet's technique."[5] The second aim, what can be said positively of Whitman's use of the Bible as a resource, which Allen tackles most forthrightly in "Biblical Echoes," serves chiefly to provide warrant for Allen's recourse to biblical analogies as a means of elucidating Whitman's free verse prosody.[6] In that analysis parallelism as understood primarily through R. Lowth's biblical paradigm figures prominently—the "first rhythmic principle" of both Whitman and the poetry of the Bible.[7] Recall that

at the time literary scholars were still casting around for ways to make sense
of nonmetrical verse, a mostly new phenomenon (in the middle of the nineteenth century) in a poetic canon otherwise dominated since classical antiquity by meter. Allen sees in the analogy of biblical prosody the revelation of
"specific principles" that enable a more perspicuous analysis and explanation
of "Walt Whitman's poetic technique."[8] The analysis, though not without
problems,[9] successfully establishes (among other things) the presence and
significance of parallelism in Whitman, especially as it bears on his underlying prosody, and the likelihood that the Bible is an important source of
Whitman's knowledge of parallelism. It also is important as an early effort at
articulating a prosody that means to accommodate the differences of nonmetrical verse.

  However, it is one of Allen's more understated observations that I want to
spotlight initially in my own efforts to elucidate the prosody[10] of biblical verse.
In his slightly later (1935) treatment of Whitman in *American Prosody*, Allen
observes with regard to the putative newness of Whitman's "free" rhythms
(i.e., his free verse) that "the truth of the matter" is that these rhythms "are not
new, since they are, to go no farther back, at least as old as Hebrew poetry."[11]
This is not an insignificant point for the history of free verse,[12] but it is absolutely crucial, I believe, for any minimally compelling assessment, explication,
and appreciation of the prosody of biblical poetry. Here, early in the modern
era,[13] a scholar notices the nonmetrical nature of biblical verse. To be sure, this
is in no way Allen's chief interest. And yet anyone who comes to Whitman
from a fresh encounter with biblical poetry, whether in (English) translation
or in the original Hebrew, cannot help but sense the broad prosodic and
rhythmic kinship that joins the one to the other. Whitman's belatedly dubbed
"American Bible" has far more in common with King James's more originary
English Bible than just the chapter and verse numbers added for the 1860
edition of *Leaves*.[14]

  Historically, of course, the countervailing supposition that biblical verse
is metrical has dominated critical discussion. What Allen's perception of
"biblical analogies" to Whitman points up is the crucial importance of the
standard of measure. From the very beginning of recorded commentary on
biblical poetry the standard of comparison has been of a metrical kind of
verse, whether the Greek and Latin varieties of classical antiquity or the Arabic
and Hebrew meters so familiar to medieval Jewish scholars.[15] The givenness
of the metered nature of all verse was still broadly assumed through most of
the eighteenth century. Lowth himself asserts the view quite trenchantly. The
short third lecture ("The Hebrew Poetry is Metrical") of his *Lectures on the
Sacred Poetry of the Hebrews* is dedicated to the issue.[16] The lecture by itself

constitutes the first part of Lowth's larger study and in his view is foundational for everything that follows on it. At that time Lowth could no more envision a nonmetrical kind of verse than imagine the Earth to be older than what could be calculated based on the biblical accounts of creation. It was simply not an easy possibility given the world he inhabited. Meter, according to Lowth, "appears essential to every species of verse."[17] What will forever redound to Lowth's credit, however, is the decision (perhaps born out of futility) not to let the (then) current inability to recover the presumed meter of biblical verse ("altogether unknown, and even to admit of no investigation by human art or industry")[18] deflect Lowth from inquiring into other aspects of biblical versification (e.g., parallelism). In these efforts Lowth would lay the foundation for future critical work on nonmetrical prosodies. Such prosodies, as Allen well understood, are not really "free," but consist in "rhythmical organization by other than numerical modes."[19] Therefore, the kind of close attention Lowth paid to other aspects of biblical verse could eventually be exploited toward more specifically prosodic ends. Allen's appropriation of Lowth's understanding of parallelism[20] by which "to analyze and explain Walt Whitman's poetic technique" is a case in point. And Lowth himself eventually came to foreground the role of parallelism in his understanding of biblical prosody.[21]

Furthermore, Lowth's own efforts at offering nonmetrical translations of biblical verse, especially in the *New Translation* of Isaiah (1778), would turn out to be highly influential, both with respect to English translations of biblical poetry and to the creation of original poetry. One practical consequence of the long-standing assumption of biblical poetry's metrical base was of a compensatory nature, a keen interest in offering renditions of biblical poems in translation employing meters (and rhyme schemes) in place of the lost putative Hebrew original. With roots already in the fifteenth century metrical translations or paraphrases of the Bible in English flourished especially during the sixteenth and seventeenth centuries and would linger into the eighteenth century.[22] This mania for metrical paraphrases of biblical poetry did not begin to subside until after Lowth's *Praelectiones* (1753), with its explication of parallelism and the latter's role in biblical Hebrew prosody, and especially after the *New Translation*, where, making explicit the theory of translation implicit in his earlier study, for the first time Lowth models a kind of nonmetrical yet rhythmic verse translation in English of a biblical poetic corpus. The importance of the change in the principle of biblical verse translation that Lowth's work ushers in, M. Roston says, "can scarcely be overemphasized."[23]

Lowth's work also inspired active poets, including perhaps most (in)famously James Macpherson, the writer responsible for the English "translations" of the Ossian poems. In 1760 Macpherson announced he had discovered an epic about Fingal written by one Ossian (putatively stemming from the third century CE). Over the next several years he published what he represented as his own English prose translations of Ossian's corpus, eventually collected in *The Works of Ossian* (1765).[24] Debate over the authenticity of this corpus seems to have erupted almost immediately and continues to this day.[25] While it now appears that Macpherson did draw on genuine Gaelic manuscript and oral traditions,[26] his so-called translations turn out to be "freely creative" adaptations of these traditions.[27] The affinities with the English Bible are patent, and there is good reason to think that Macpherson, who was a divinity student at King's College Aberdeen when Lowth's *Praelectiones* (1753) were first published, was familiar with Lowth's work and especially his theory of parallelism.[28]

I cite this rather peculiar case of Lowth's influence here because Ossian is one of the poetic influences, alongside the Bible, that Whitman explicitly acknowledges. So, for example, in "A Backward Glance o'er Travel'd Roads," where Whitman notes his early reading of the Bible—"I went over thoroughly the Old and New Testaments"—he also remarks on his reading of Ossian (alongside other works of literature)—"and absorb'd ... Shakspere, Ossian, the best translated versions I could get of Homer, Eschylus, Sophocles, the old German Nibelungen, the ancient Hindoo poems, and one or two other masterpieces, Dante's among them."[29] Other frequently posited precursors to Whitman, such as Christopher Smart and William Blake, interestingly also have connections to Lowth.[30] And the poet with whom Whitman's contemporaries most often associated him, Martin Farquhar Tupper, was himself plainly influenced by the King James Bible.[31] Whitman, then, whether through his own reading (and rereading) of the Bible or through the likes of a Macpherson or a Tupper, or perhaps even simply caught up in the spirit of his time— or as likely some mixture of them all, was significantly affected by the rhythms of biblical poetry. When looked at from the perspective of an interest in the question of biblical prosody, Whitman and the nonmetrical tradition of verse that he epitomizes provide in their combined poetic output eloquent if indirect testimony to the nonmetrical nature of biblical verse. That is, these poets do not hear in the English cadences of the King James Bible or Lowth's own rendition of Isaiah, for example, the numerical counting of meter but the ebb and flow of a distinctly nonmetrical, freer rhythm. My aim in sighting biblical verse here initially through a Whitmanesque looking glass is to underscore the fact that the verse of the Hebrew Bible is itself a variety of nonmetrical verse; it is, as Allen intimates and as B. Hrushovski in fact has best seen, a kind of free verse.[32] And therefore it is to free verse (exemplified here by the "barbaric yawp" of Walt Whitman) that biblical scholars should look—and not to the metrical varieties of poetry from classical antiquity or their imitators in the various national vernacular traditions of the West so favored by nineteenth- and twentieth-century biblical critics—if they want to fully appreciate the nature and dynamics of biblical poetry. Though a consensus about the absence of meter in biblical verse now exists,[33] no one to date has tried to work out Hrushovski's ideas in a thoroughgoing way,[34] or to read biblical Hebrew poetry against the backdrop of the free verse tradition more broadly. In this chapter I propose to do just that. I elaborate an understanding of biblical poetry as a variety of free verse, building on Hrushovski's seminal insights and expanding them in light of contemporary work on free verse prosody.[35]

Biblical Hebrew Poetry Is Not Metrical

I begin with working definitions of "rhythm" and "meter." D. Attridge defines rhythm as "a patterning of energy simultaneously produced and perceived; a series of alternations of build-up and release, movement and counter-movement, tending toward regularity but complicated by constant variations and local inflections."[36] By contrast, "meter is an organizing principle which turns the general tendency toward regularity in rhythm into a strictly-patterned regularity, that can be counted and named."[37] Keeping the two concepts distinct, says Hrushovski, is crucial, for "we save, on the one hand, the concept of meter from destruction by exact measurement and avoid, on the other hand, confusing the systemization of meters...with an understanding of the contributions of rhythmical effects to the whole poem as a work of art."[38] All natural languages have distinctive rhythms, ways—often through the manipulation of syllables, stress (or accent), and syntax—of marshaling and economizing on the expenditure of energy through time.[39] Poetic rhythm is a heightening and exploitation through a myriad of means—manipulation of sounds, form, phrasing, syntax, and the like—of the tendencies toward regularity inherent in a language's natural speech rhythms. Such poetic rhythms are not organized into longer, sustained, repeated units. As Attridge remarks, "they begin, project themselves forward, peter out, change, or stop, but they don't fall into regular patterns made up of groups of rhythmic pulses."[40] Once such regular patterns appear, units are repeated and become countable, and the numbers become significant, then we are in the realm of meter. That no such countable units get repeated for long stretches—never more than a couplet or two or three or even slightly more (see discussion below)—in biblical poetry is the telling and simple argument against the notion that this poetry is in any way metrical. It is not. No matter what phenomenon is isolated—individual words, syllables, stresses, syntactic frames—no "strictly-patterned regularity" that can be counted and thus scanned ever emerges to any sustained degree and certainly never over the course of an entire poem, no matter how short. Biblical Hebrew poetry is not metrical.[41]

There is now an enormous amount of secondary literature, from the nineteenth and twentieth centuries in particular, in which scholars from various perspectives and with myriads of ends in view provide counts of all kinds (but especially of syllables and stresses) with respect to biblical poems,[42] and the one consistent and persistent finding is that those counts, no matter their kind, never add up, are never sustained for long stretches of a poem, and can only be shown to subsist through the most excessive of emendatory processes—if enough material is whittled away then regularity may eventually be created.[43] Hrushovski sums matters with respect to stress (though his comments apply more broadly) this way:

> For many generations scholars have argued over the "stress" of biblical prosody; there have been attempts to correct or rewrite the text so that it might conform with pseudoclassical regularized "feet," equalized hemistichs, or stanzas of recurring numbers of lines. Such attempts seem pointless today since no exact regularity of any kind has been found and since rhythm need not be based on strict numerical regularity.[44]

Biblical Hebrew poetry is not metrical.

In lieu of any kind of sustained analysis, whether of scholarship or of a large swath of textual material, I offer brief consideration of a counterpointing set of examples by way of pointing up the lack of meter in biblical poetry. Lowth in his third lecture points to the acrostic poems of the Bible (Ps 25, 34, 37, 111, 112, 119, 145; Prov 31:10–31; Lam 1–4) as "Hebrew writings" that are "in some degree confined to numbers"—"in general so regularly accommodated, that word answers to word, and almost syllable to syllable."[45] The first stanza of Psalm 119 (vv. 1–8) is emblematic:

ʾašrê tĕmîmê-dārek / hăhōlĕkîm bĕtôrat yhwh
ʾašrê nōṣĕrê ʿēdōtāyw / bĕkol-lēb yidrĕšûhû
ʾap lōʾ-paʿălû ʿawlâ / bidrākāyw hālākû
ʾattâ ṣiwwîtâ piqqūdeykā / lišmōr mĕʾōd
ʾahălay yikkōnû dĕrākāy / lišmōr ḥuqqeykā
ʾāz lōʾ-ʾēbôš / bĕhabbîṭî ʾel-kol-miṣwōteykā
ʾôdĕkā bĕyōšer lēbāb / bĕlomdî mišpĕṭê ṣidqekā
ʾet-ḥuqqeykā ʾešmōr / ʾal-taʿazbēnî ʿad-mĕʾōd

The first word of each of the eight couplets that make up the stanza starts with an *'aleph*, the first letter of the Hebrew alphabet. The counts of words, major stresses, and syllables per line are remarkably, even tantalizingly, close, but the "same pattern of nonconformity to a specific pattern," concludes D. N. Freedman, holds throughout the stanza and the entire psalm.[46] The counts simply never add up. It is the miss, the failure to add up repeatedly, that stubbornly persists even here in this most regular of biblical Hebrew poems—indeed that comes into stark relief precisely because of the counterpointing regularity of the alphabetic conceit—and finally always defeats all scansions. These verses are simply not countable, they are not metrical.

A section of Psalm 19 (vv. 8–10) offers another telling example. This time the psalm is not an acrostic, though its focus on Torah in this section exhibits a strong kinship with the thematic preoccupation of Psalm 119. No one treating the psalm has ever been tempted to see any kind of regularity of numbers that carries through the poem as a whole. But there can be no mistaking the psalmist's desire to tighten up the formal controls in verses 8–10:

tôrat yhwh tĕmîmâ	The law of the LORD is perfect,
mĕšîbat nāpeš	reviving the soul;
'ēdût yhwh ne'ĕmānâ	the decrees of the LORD are sure,
maḥkîmat petî	making wise the simple;
piqqûdê yhwh yĕšārîm	the precepts of the LORD are right,
mĕśammĕḥê-lēb	rejoicing the heart;
miṣwat yhwh bārâ	the commandment of the LORD is clear,
mĕ'îrat 'ênāyim	enlightening the eyes;
yir'at yhwh ṭĕhôrâ	the fear of the LORD is pure,
'ômedet lā'ad	enduring forever;
mišpĕṭê yhwh 'emet	the ordinances of the LORD are true,
ṣādĕqû yaḥdāw	and righteous altogether. (NRSV)

Here, though the syllable counts do not add up consistently, the number of stresses and words do. These verses are made up of unbalanced qinah couplets, all made up of an initial long line consisting of three words with three stresses and a short line (formed through ellipsis or gapping) with two words and two main stresses—so H.-J. Kraus, for example, advises that these verses are "to be read ... in the 3 + 2 meter."[47] Two observations. One, even in biblical Hebrew poetry, as these lines plainly show, a strict numerical (and thus metrical) accounting is possible. Two, and equally remarkable, such numerical accountings almost never occur in the Bible, and when they do, as in these verses from Psalm 19, their compass is always relatively brief—here sustained for only six couplets. Conclusion: biblical verse is not metrical.

Lest it be thought that Psalm 19:8–10 is some kind of fluke and that Hebrew for some reason is a language uniquely allergic to meter, a brief look at the larger, postbiblical Hebrew poetic corpus is in order. For here one discovers a rich abundance of metered verse. Much biblical scholarship, content with an inward-looking disciplinary focus, has not often thought to consider biblical Hebrew poetry in light of the larger Hebrew poetic corpus. M. O'Connor was an exception. In the "Afterword" to his second edition of *Hebrew Verse Structure*, he gestures quite insightfully to this larger view. He observes:

> A major tool published in the last quarter-century for the study of biblical poetry is *The Penguin Book of Hebrew Verse*, edited by the Israeli poet T. Carmi (1981). This volume affords a full survey of verse in Hebrew, from the Bible to the poets of Carmi's own, post-war generation, and provides insights and information on every page to a reader of the Bible; the diversity of the literature in the various forms of Hebrew is an important and largely neglected lesson.[48]

So precisely to O'Connor's point, Carmi's survey includes a generous sampling of metrical verse in Hebrew. Two short examples may suffice. The first is the initial stanza of an anonymously authored poem (an early *piytim*) about the Akeda, 'ētān limmad da'at:

> 'ētān limmad da'at
> bĕṭerem yĕdā'ăkā kōl
> gillâ lĕkol yāṣûr
> derek lĕhithallek-bāh[49]

Each line in the stanza, and throughout the poem, is headed by the appropriate letter of the alphabet and contains exactly three words. The second example, the *avoda* of Yosi ben Yosi (fourth/fifth centuries CE), is made up of lines with four major stresses:

> 'azkîr gĕbûrôt 'ēlôah ne'dārû bakkōaḥ
> yāḥîd wĕ'ên 'ôd 'epes wĕ'ên sēnî[50]

As Hrushovski remarks, the basic tendency of postbiblical Hebrew poetry was to "regularize" the rhythmic traditions of the Bible, whether through a "permanent number of words" per line, or a "regular number of major stresses";

or whether of a quantitative measure, as in Spain from the tenth through the fifteenth centuries, or the accentual-syllabic meters of the modern period.[51] One lesson to be learned from this larger diversity of Hebrew poetry is that metrical poetry is eminently achievable in Hebrew, and we have lots of specific examples of what it does and does not look like. And what it does not look like most specifically is biblical verse.[52] Even the most cursory reading of Carmi's collection alone points up the spuriousness of the now millennia-long metrical hypothesis about biblical poetry. The simple fact is that biblical poetry is not metrical, at least not in any way that the term "meter" retains any recognizable sense and not in any way that resembles any of the multitudinous corpus of actually attested metrical verse in Hebrew. The postbiblical corpus of Hebrew verse offers quite a confirming counterpoint to Whitman's biblically inflected verse and provides yet further warrant for the nonmetrical nature of biblical poetry.[53]

The Shape of Poetic Rhythm

The scholar who has seen the nonmetrical nature of biblical verse and its free rhythmic prosody most perceptively is Hrushovski, and his one-page sketch of biblical prosody in his 1960 "On Free Rhythms in Modern Poetry"[54] provides the foundation for my own assessment of biblical poetic prosody. That brief original sketch is embedded in Hrushovski's larger efforts to get a critical grip on the rhythm of modern free verse: "If we cannot afford simply to dismiss important parts of modern poetry (as well as of Goethe, Heine, Hölderlin, the Bible, and so forth)," we will need "to revise thoroughly our old notions on poetic rhythm...and then to come back to a structural and meaningful description of free rhythmic phenomena."[55] At the heart of his suggested revision is a principled distinction between meter and rhythm, not to ramify an absolute dichotomy, as there remains much poetry where "meter is the constant organizing factor" in the poem's total rhythmic expression, but rather to make space for a more perspicuous appreciation of poems whose rhythmic organization is, in C. O. Hartman's words, "by other than numerical modes."[56] The holism evident in Hrushovski here anticipates much current thinking about the need for prosodic analyses of verse rhythm to handle both metered and unmetered verse, and indeed, to be articulated in light of a theory of rhythm generally and thus potentially applicable to poetic rhythms of whatever nature (free or traditional) but also to the rhythms of prose and speech and of other media, too.[57] Meter here is a specialized (or marked) component of the larger (unmarked) phenomenon known as rhythm.[58] Where there is no evidence of meter—"of course, there are poetic rhythms without any meter, as there are poems without any metaphor"[59]—then recourse must be made to other aspects of the poem's language material for realization of a poem's rhythmic sensibilities. That is, viewed from the perspective of meter, the rhythms of nonmetrical verse may be understood heuristically, suggests D. Wesling, "as versions that subtract certain sorts of possible beauty [namely, meter!], in order to emphasize other sorts and phases."[60]

Poetry, as an art of language, is rooted in speech and aboriginally (at least) in oral performance. The sources of poetic rhythm, then, are at least twofold. One is physiological and exploits, as Attridge stresses, the fact that "spoken language *moves*" (through time) and "is *in* sound" and thus is naturally rhythmic, a "continuous motion that pushes language forward, in more or less regular waves, as the musculature of the speech organs tightens and re-laxes, as energy pulsates through the words we speak and hear, as the brain marshals multiple stimuli into ordered patterns."[61] "Sound," W. J. Ong re-minds us, "exists only when it is going out of existence"—"it is sensed as eva-nescent."[62] The restriction of words to sound in oral culture means that knowledge, ideas, stories, songs, if they are not simply to disappear in their soundings, if they are to be recalled, reused, without the aid of writing, must be memorable, must above all, capitalizing on the spoken word's natural rhythmicity,

> come into being in heavily rhythmic, balanced patterns, in repetitions or antitheses, in alliterations and assonances, in epithetic and other formulary expressions, in standard thematic settings…in proverbs which are constantly heard by everyone so that they come to mind readily and which themselves are patterned for retention and ready recall, or in other mnemonic form.[63]

As M. Jousse emphasizes, in oral art rhythm, "muscular movement made easier," is above all "a mnemonic expression of thought," that which enhances and renders more precise "the revivification of, and memory for, propositional gestures."[64] Language, even once it gets written down, can never truly escape its natural habitat, the world of sound and the rhythmicity (currents, contours, shapes of energy pulsating through time) that attends to its every sounding. At base, writing (with any attendant metascript conventions, e.g., page layout) is but a conventionalized notation system designed ultimately to point us back to the spoken word. No script tradition, including alphabetic writing, is fully isomorphic with the spoken language it records. It is always ultimately defec-tive.[65] The "old Hebrew" script (like the linear alphabetic script traditions from the southern Levant more generally), for example, is consonantal and therefore only imperfectly capable of signifying a word's full vocality. Readerly knowledge of the language itself is required in order to fully vocalize the written Hebrew word. The written text of a poem, then, certainly in the "old Hebrew" script but also in every other script tradition, is best understood, as Smith commends, as "analogous to the score of a piece of music."[66] Its "printed words," she says, "are not so much the symbolic representation of sounds as a conventionalized system of directions for making them."[67] And in a related vein, S. Stewart emphasizes that "the poem itself is an utterance, an expression of a person that we apprehend in turn as the expression of a person," bringing to bear on the written poetic text (whether in a vocalized, subvocalized, or even unvocalized manner) "our memories of speech experience, including what we may know of the intended speaker's speech experience."[68] But here we have tumbled into the second source of rhythmicity in language arts: reception.

Every moment of human cognition has temporality and rhythm as its basic modality. "The slightest sensation," writes Jousse, "gives us an...invisible jolt" and sparks a nervous current of energy that, as soon as it enters the nervous system,

> spreads all over it, activating the organs and viscera which lie at the endpoints of the system. And since even the tiniest parts of the organism are linked by the nerves to the central nervous system, one can boldly assert that every stimulus tends—within limits that cannot be precisely defined—to set in motion the whole organism.[69]

This is as true of ocular reception as it is of audition (and indeed of all psycho-physiological modalities of perception),[70] and thus even silent reading excites currents of energy (however subtle or externally imperceptible) that then course rhythmically through human consciousness. R. D. Cureton is the most insistent among contemporary prosodists that "rhythmic structures" in poetry be considered as "cognitive representations of the flow of energy in the stream of our experience,"[71] though many others are also appreciative of the informing role of human perception in the felt-rhythmicity of poems.[72] And there is no denying the centrality of perception to aesthetic experience. As J. Dewey emphasizes, "the work of art...is *perception*."[73] But Cureton's unrelenting insistence on "perceived rhythm," though strictly speaking correct in reference to poetic rhythm, since poems as arts of language can only be encountered by humans through the mediation of the body and mind, risks obscuring the fact that, aside from our own spontaneous poetic compositions, poems come into our consciousnesses as givens, exterior to our bodily selves, from others who will have had some role in exciting the rhythmicity of the poems we encounter, however we encounter them. So Stewart says "poems compel attention to aspects of rhythm" and reminds us, as just noted, that they are in fact utterances, expressions of a person.[74] And Dewey, too, underscores the need to remain mindful not only of perceived rhythmic effect but also of the mode of rhythm's effectuation, the fact that the art object (in this case), as a consequence of human creativity and intentionality, operates "to pull together energies" and "to give them that particular rhythmic organization."[75] Jourdain notes that in the very act of our second-by-second perception of music it is ("more correctly") the music that "moves on to us."[76] Rhythm in poems is actively orchestrated, coerced, produced, as well as perceived.

More problematic, Cureton, who aspires to articulate a theory of poetic rhythm that is intelligible within a more general theory of rhythm, seems to have forgotten that rhythm, however cognitively dependent human beings are for its perception, is not solely a human phenomenon. Dewey writes matter-of-factly, "the first characteristic of the environing world...is rhythm."[77] And S. K. Langer, whose thought helped shape Cureton's early ideas about rhythm,[78] notes that "rhythm is the basis for life," echoing Dewey, "but not limited to life."[79] She cites as examples the swing of a pendulum, a bouncing ball, and the breaking of waves ("the most impressive example of rhythm known to most people"). Langer observes that the swing of a pendulum "is rhythmic, without our organizing interpretation (which is what makes a mere succession of sounds—all we perceive in listening to a watch, for instance—rhythmic for us)."[80] The latter observations are intended to remind us that rhythm, though necessarily always rhythm *for us* and thus "perceived rhythm," in language is a complex affair, potentially with multiple sources. The marks on the page are not in themselves rhythmic—"meter, for example, is certainly not a property of the text itself, but only of its performance"[81]—but cues that compel our readerly/performative attention to rhythm. Hence, Attridge's phrasing, rhythm as "a patterning of energy simultaneously *produced and perceived*," nicely captures the bilateral sourcing of rhythm in poetry.[82]

Rhythm in the broadest sense of the term refers "to patterns of temporal distribution of events, objects, symbols, or signs in general," and as such, says M. H. Thaut, "every work of art possesses rhythm"—and certainly the so-called arts of time: music, poetry, drama, and dance.[83] The characteristic shape of rhythm is well described by Jourdain:

> Rhythm lacks the repetitive, evenly paced accentuations of measured
> rhythm [meter!]. In music it is built up by a succession of irregular

sonic shapes that combine in various ways like the parts of a painting, sometimes hanging in exquisite balance, sometimes joining forces to gyrate or plunge or swirl.[84]

Jourdain's comments here pertain to the rhythm of music, but such rhythm is the same as that in organic movement more generally, that of "the runner and the pole vaulter,"[85] "cascading water," a "howling wind," "the soaring swallow and the leaping tiger." "It is also," Jourdain stresses, "the rhythm of speech."[86] This rhythm of music—which he calls *phrasing*[87]—is vocal in character because "it naturally arises from song."[88] In poems, as in other language art, the stuff of rhythm, the building blocks out of which rhythm's pulsating patterns of energy are formed and organized into discernible temporal structures, is language itself. Therefore the rhythm of poems is always potentially multidimensional and hierarchical. Language is a naturally hierarchical system, made up of elements that nest recursively within ever higher levels of organization, and all aspects of the language material—grammar, sound, syntax, meaning, rhetoric, conventions and tropes, even script, punctuation, and page layout in written poems—are available for rhythmic deployment and organization. Selected elements, individually or in (often ad hoc) combinations, are shaped into patterns (through grouping, repetition, variation) that meander through or crosscut a poem like so many eddies in a stream or breaking waves in a steady surf. Such rhythmic movement has four cardinal tendencies: (1) toward some point that lies ahead; (2) away from some point already passed; (3) as part of a relatively static moment; and (4) as part of an arrival toward which the previous movement of language has been building.[89] These movements begin and end, come to a peak, then subside. The patterns may be simple or complex. Some will have only a short duration, others will be maintained over the course of an entire poem. When a pattern becomes regularized sufficiently then meter may emerge (especially at lower levels of linguistic structure, e.g., stress, syllables). However, in much nonmetrical verse, the patterns of rhythm must establish themselves independently, without the aid of convention or meter's strict regularity. The movement and intensity of the separate rhythmic cadences can overlap, reinforce, or counter one another. Sometimes they work together, achieving coherence; other times they clash and crash and fragment the whole, counterpointing and contrasting one cadence with another. They can heighten language, project forward movement, elaborate a sense of design and control, underscore closure, effect memorability and mimetic and emotional suggestiveness.[90] But in all events rhythm is a matter of whole poems and therefore steadfastly organic. No two poems will ever manifest the exact same rhythmic profile.

As a means of elaborating and thickening this caricature of poetic rhythm, a brief survey of leading features characteristically associated with rhythmic experiences may be offered.[91] The resulting taxonomy is neither comprehensive nor prescriptive but more heuristic and pragmatic both in nature and intent, a means of circumscribing and underscoring the complexity and multidimensionality of rhythmic phenomena. Rhythms are complex and "inherently hierarchical and interactional," says Cureton; "their expressive power derives from the intersecting perceptual forms that they present on *many* levels of structure within the expressive medium."[92]

Continuance (Prolongation)

For Langer, the heart of rhythm's wave-like action is "the preparation of a new event by the ending of a previous one."[93] She explains: "Rhythm is the setting-up of new tensions by the resolution of former ones. They need not be of equal duration at all; but the situation that begets the new crisis must be inherent in the denouement of its forerunner."[94] In addition to the way new waves are shaped by the back flow of previous waves, Langer uses breathing, the heartbeat, and perhaps most illuminating human motion to exemplify this central aspect of rhythmic experience. Of the latter she writes, "A person who moves rhythmically need not repeat a single motion exactly. His movement, however, must be complete gestures, so that one can sense a beginning, intent, and consummation, and see in the last stage of one the condition and indeed the rise of another."[95] This experience of continuance is crucial to rhythm's overall shape. "Again," R. Wallaschek writes, "rhythm of itself incites to a continuance of rhythmical movement."[96]

Anticipation (Expectation)

Rhythm creates anticipation, "a demand for something to come."[97] It is an initiating force. Wallaschek explicates the creation of this force with the example of someone walking down a road, tapping every lamp-post or fence post.

If for any reason we are obliged to leave out one of the series, or to desist from want of the object in question, a slight blank is felt, which is very faintly unpleasant. The nervous system has put itself into a position of expectancy, and is ready for the appropriate discharge at the right moment. If the opportunity for the discharge is wanting, the gathered energy has to dissipate itself by other channels, which involves a certain amount of conflict and waste.[98]

Hence arises the craving for a rhythmical succession. The perception of energy shapes consisting of "a beginning, intent, and consummation" is crucial to this sense of anticipation or expectation, an awareness of a teleological trajectory to rhythmic movement.[99] T. V. F. Brogan, for whom "expectation turns out to be a more powerful force in perception than actual stimulus," explicates the phenomenon in terms of regularity, a characteristic often used to describe rhythm.[100] But as Smith shows, much in line with Langer's thinking, strict regularity or repetition is not absolutely crucial for eliciting expectation. The poetic structure of anticipation she describes in this way:

> The experience of patterns and principles of generation is dynamic and continuous. Poetic structure is, in a sense, an inference which we draw from the evidence of a series of events. As we read the poem, it is a hypothesis whose probability is tested as we move from line to line and adjusted in response to what we find there.[101]

No doubt patterns of regularity (so Brogan), and certainly repetition, can give rise to rhythmic expectation,[102] whether to satisfying or frustrating ends, but so, too, can other perceptible but not strictly regular or iterative shapes or frames of energy—hence Langer's example of a person moving rhythmically. As G. B. Cooper observes, "'rhythm-creating elements' could be anything that sets up, in a hearer or reader, an expectation that can be satisfied or frustrated."[103] Indeed, "everything that prepares a future," states Langer, "creates rhythm."[104]

Repetition (Recurrence, Iteration)

"Repetition," following Smith, "is the fundamental phenomenon of poetic form,"[105] and thus not surprisingly is "deeply involved" in the generation and perception of rhythm.[106] L. Windsor and P. Desain note that rhythm refers to the succession of events in time specifically "where the events occur with some repetitive structure."[107] The repeating of rhythm is not in Smith's term an instantiation of a "systematic repetition," but is a repetition riven (as perhaps is all iteration) by variation and equivalence, ultimately stopping short of strict regularity. Such repetition is "occasional," may be "separated by other material," and may "involve formal or thematic elements, or both."[108] The "tending toward regularity" distinctive of rhythmic recurrence requires that phenomena need only be "equivalent" and "patterned"—"oftentimes a fairly free variant of what came before, a mere analogy, and only logically a repetition."[109] Recurrence, says Cureton, "multiplies opportunities for both structural anticipation and the rise and fall of...saliences."[110] When the repetition turns regular or systematic, especially at lower structural levels, then the metrical domain of rhythmic structure may be realized—meter is regular and predictable.

Variation

Uniform runs of repeated elements or actions are not inherently rhythmic, at least not without variation. Hence, variation features prominently in Dewey's short definition of rhythm: "ordered variation of changes."[111] There is no rhythm without change and no rhythm unless that change is placed—not only comes but belongs, has a "definite place in a larger whole." In "differentiating the part within a whole," explains Dewey, variation exposes "the force of what went before while creating a suspense that is a demand for something to come."[112] If the hallmark of meter is the presentation of a regularly recurring sequence of beats, then one of the characteristics of rhythm that makes it such a radically different phenomenon is its constant variation.[113]

Regularity (Periodicity)

Regularity, however fuzzy a notion, is the mark of meter, which figures prominently in the overall rhythm of many poems. As Cureton observes, "one of the best ways of generating energy is to vary repeating units across a rigid frame."[114] That is, the pulse of meter is an unceasing beat that rhythmic patterns (may) overlay. "Idealized," says Jourdain, "pulse exists as the steady recurrence of contraction and relaxation, tension and release, every beat a renewal of experience."[115] Regularity of beat or pulse is cognitively necessary because "just a few seconds' lapse and the listener can become lost."[116] In contrast, rhythm per se is characterized by the lack of strict regularity, a tending toward regularity that finally falters, an irregular regularity that if no longer mathematical is yet vital.[117] Musicologists define free rhythm in music as "the rhythm of music without perceived periodic organization."[118]

Salience (Prominence)

"Central to rhythmic form is the perception of peaks of salience/energy."[119] Such peaks often coincide with moments of critical interest in poems. Saliences appear as a consequence of patterns of repetition and variation (from grouping) when viewed against some larger grounds (or competing and contrasting groundings). As Dewey notices, "recurring *relationships* serve to define and delimit parts, giving them individuality of their own," and thus prominence.[120]

Points of prominence may be picked out at multiple levels (e.g., sound, line structure, meaning) and as often as not in ametrical rhythms are relative.

Grouping (Chunking)

As Hrushovski notices, "the organization of perceptibly similar elements into groups, similar groups into higher groups, and so forth, is a major tendency of human perception."[121] Without the ability to cut up information flow or observational data into consumable bite-size chunks, the human brain would be quickly overwhelmed. The brain is a natural chunking machine, and one of the chief functions of rhythm is to aid the brain in this task. Not surprisingly, then, grouping or chunking may well be "the primary psychological given in rhythmic perception."[122] Rhythmic markers give cues to beginnings and endings; isolate figures, ideas, images of one sort or another; and create patterns and patterns of patterns. Saliences are perceived only "relative to non-saliencies in 'chunks' of one to seven" items—plus or minus two, as per G. A. Miller's seminal essay on the capacity of short-term memory.[123] Grouping in language (and music) often operates hierarchically, as Hrushovski infers. The smallest chunks are digested instantly in short-term memory and then grouped into ever larger chunks until more capacious segments are absorbed with the aid of (longer term) memory.[124] "Comprehension," writes Jourdain, "remains tentative until suddenly everything snaps into place."[125] Cureton offers an elegant description of this dimension of rhythm:

> Grouping extracts more irregular shapes from structures (more) inherent in the medium, looks both backwards and forwards from some point of structural culmination, and orders the shapes into hierarchical structures in a continuous layering from the most local levels to the level of the rhythmic structure as a whole.[126]

Grouping or chunking is the central mechanism by which the specific patterns or shapes of energy—those runs of recurrence riven by difference and variation—that are themselves constitutive of rhythm get patterned and shaped, always emerging, taking place, as clusters of equivalencies in and against some larger informing whole.

Temporality

"Rhythm organizes time."[127] And therefore as with the other so-called arts of time, rhythm is crucial to the organization and appreciation of poetry, especially lyric poetry, whose temporal medium has been well emphasized, for example, by both Smith and Hartman.[128] So Smith exposes the temporality of (lyric) poetry in her understanding of a poem as a "representation of an utterance," in which the very form of this particular language art trades (and is even parasitic) on the rhythmicity of the utterance it mimes. As it takes place in time it takes time, producing "experiences which occur over a period of time and are continuously modified by successive events."[129] This is an especially helpful image for considering biblical poetry since its originary poetics was that of an expressly uttered, performed, and thus oral poetry, whether narrative (epic) or lyric (most of what has been preserved) in nature. Rhythm is that which divides up the flow of time in such poems into discrete and recurring events and in the process draws on both real-time processing of short-term memory and simulated time of longer term, analytic memory (i.e., that memory that enables the retrospective perception in Smith's idea of "retrospective patterning").[130] Or with Cureton, who, drawing on the ideas of P. Fraisse, emphasizes three different temporal sensibilities: relatively objective time, typically projective in action; structural time, considerably broader and prototypically involving grouping or patterning to effect design (irregular shapes), control, and the like; and subjective time, prospective in orientation and more dependent on the perceiver than the medium itself.[131]

Hierarchy

Language is naturally hierarchical, namely, morphemes are constituents of words, words constituents of phrases, phrases of clauses, and so on, and poetic rhythm naturally organizes itself along these hierarchical lines. Brogan explains: "Patterns on lower levels of rhythmic series are frequently repeated across wider spans on higher levels, melding the whole together to yield 'a complex action so integrated that it is perceived as simple.'"[132] Rhythmic hierarchies not only are vertically continuous (like language and music) but are also leveled, horizontally continuous, and recursively defined. And the entire system is highly relational. A disturbance at one level impacts all other levels.[133] Hierarchies are one of the most effective ways of generating complexity from simple units. Indeed, Cureton stresses that poetic rhythm, whether metrical or not, is far more complex than scholars often recognize. If the information flow at any one hierarchical level begins to exceed the brain's capacity to process it, perception can shift to larger levels of organization.[134] Interestingly, one of the outstanding features of much non-Western so-called free rhythm music (i.e., music in which the rhythm is not organized metrically, periodically) is precisely its complexity, which can often confound even the best-trained Western musician.[135]

Organicism

"The essence of all composition" (musical as well as poetic), according to Langer, "is the semblance of *organic* movement, the illusion of an indivisible whole," and "the characteristic principle of [such] vital activity is rhythm."[136] And in a similar vein, Dewey writes, "the first characteristic of the environing world that makes possible the existence of artistic form is rhythm."[137] For both thinkers rhythm is vital, processual, organic in Coleridge's sense of the term: "it shapes, as it develops itself from within"—arising "out of the properties of the material" (language in the case of poetry); "and the fullness of its development is one and the same with the perfection of its outward form"—it evolves as a holistic unity.[138] Its overall shape is that of "forked lightening" or "the whorls of sepals and petals" or the "changing shadows of clouds on a meadow." It ebbs and flows, pulses, comes in waves. Its constituent energies emerge and come to visibility, identity, prominence in resisting each other. "Each gains intensity for a certain period, but thereby compresses some opposed energy until the latter can overcome the other which has been relaxing itself as it extends. Then after a pause the operation is reversed and another wave of energy is set in motion."[139] This organic shape of rhythm—"it has a life of its own"[140]—is as true of rhythm in metered as in unmetered poetry. One of Cureton's more telling critiques of traditional prosodic analysis of metrical verse is the way the positing of abstract metrical schemes (e.g., iambic pentameter) and conventional, given forms (e.g., sonnet) occludes and short-circuits any appreciation of the richer rhythmic contours that typify even the most hyper-metrical poem.[141] Consequently, it has been critics seeking to articulate the prosodies of nonmetrical or free verse, verse that renounces, as it were, the support of abstract and conventional schemes, who have (almost by necessity) best appreciated rhythm's innate organicism and the ways of reading that it requires.[142] For example, in characterizing the rhythmicity of James Wright's habitual use of syllables, stress, and sound, especially as they veer away from the "strictly-patterned regularity" of meter, Cooper provides, in brief, a good sense of a typical kind of organicistic shape that rhythm takes in much non-metrical poetry: "Complex, ad hoc patterns are frequently repeated and varied within a given poem, but these patterns must establish themselves independently, without aid of the well-worn and inviting iambic groove for the reader to fall into."[143]

* * *

TOWARD THE END of his *Rhythms of English Poetry*, Attridge offers a stunning summary of the global effects of rhythmic form in poems, and in the process references many of the features just surveyed. This long quote from Attridge will serve to bring my wave-like characterization of the shape of poetic rhythm to a close—one last comber breaking on my shore of exposition.

> Rhythm contributes to the sense of momentum not just on its own, but also in the interplay between the rhythmic sequence and the other sequential features of the poem; the continuous confirming or contradicting of metrical expectations overlaps with other patterns of expectation and satisfaction to impel the verse forward and to delay a sense of closure. Metrical relaxation may occur at a point when the syntactic pressure for continuation is high (the obvious example is enjambment), or vice versa (the syntactic pause within the line); rhythmic parallelism may be accompanied by syntactic variation, or syntactic repetition by metrical changes; a stanza may end with a structural resolution but leave strong semantic expectations; iambic openings and masculine endings may encourage a rising rhythm while the contours of words and phrases encourage a falling one. All such effects may contribute to the meaning of the poem, whether through imitation, affective embodiment, emphasis, or connection; but they also have an important non-semantic function, creating a form that is experienced not as a static object but as a sequential progression, alternately disturbing and satisfying, challenging and calming, and usually ending with a sense, however momentary, of conflict resolved. Music offers a close analogy: a composer can draw on a common stock of melodic, harmonic, and rhythmic material to create a series of expectations at several levels, whose simultaneous fulfillment is postponed until the end of the work. The satisfaction experienced at the close of a heroic couplet, for instance, is not merely the sum of the separate satisfactions provided by the completion of patterns in meaning, syntax, metre, and rhyme, but the experience, on reaching the final word of the couplet, of *simultaneous* completion of all these levels. And a poem as a whole may achieve completeness by setting up a series of expectations, whether emotional, narrative, syntactic, logical, rhetorical, or formal, which are only completely and simultaneously fulfilled at the end.[144]

Orality, Song, and Music

Thus far my chief ambition has been to evolve in successive waves (to build on Langer's favorite image for rhythm) an ever richer and thicker description of poetic rhythm, first, to get straight what precisely rhythm is, and second, to enable some preliminary assessment of Allen's thesis about the continuity between the free rhythms of Whitman's verse and those of biblical poetry—that Whitman's free rhythms in fact are not new at all, "since they are, to go no farther back, at least as old as Hebrew poetry"—with all that this implies, namely, that biblical poetry is as Hrushovski claims a natural free rhythmic system of verse. The latter part of the chapter is given over entirely to a description and explication of rhythm in biblical poetry, elaborated in light of the foregoing "thick description" of poetic rhythm, and thus constitutes (cumulatively) the strongest statement of the chapter's guiding thesis, that is, that biblical poetry is nonmetrical and naturally free rhythmic.

Less explicitly, I have pointed to potential motivations (or partial motivations) for the naturalness of rhythm, warrants for why we might more readily look to rhythm when trying to understand the governing prosody of biblical poetry. Here I want to make this line of thinking more explicit, recouping and elaborating on observations already made, as well as adding some new ones. The presumption of meter in biblical poetry is almost entirely an accident of history, a consequence of the fact that Western (literary) scholarship is the heir of a tradition in which meter was normative. By initially coming to my topic somewhat obliquely through the poetry of Walt Whitman, my intent is to alter the perspective from which biblical poetry is approached, to decenter the givenness of meter in the collective imaginations of biblical scholars. In one sense, this is a quintessential postmodern move, to change up the conversation, the questions asked, so that new perspectives, sometimes even on very old topics, may be achieved. Here the cachet of modern free verse (iconized in the poetry of Whitman) serves in part as a heuristic to leverage a new look at biblical prosody, one in which rhythm, and not meter, plays a central, even normative role. The implication: there are ways of thinking poetic prosody through beyond meter. Furthermore, in ramifying Allen's thought about the potential age of such free verse prosodies, dating at least as far back as the Bible,[145] I intend a subtle deconstruction of the authority that habitually gets projected onto Greek antiquity. Priorities, firsts, origins have no inherent superiority or claims to preference. In this case, however, the possibility that free verse has a more ancient genealogy than the canonical accounts of its origins typically allow for—the idea that phenomenologically free verse was not only the product of some modernist revolt against metrical norms—provides compelling historical warrant for entertaining the existence of nonmetrical prosodies before the modern era and subtly deflects the presumption of meter's priority—the cultures of the ancient Near East, for example, are just as old as that of Greece, with a record of written remains that is considerably older.[146]

There is no givenness to meter. It is a cultural construct like all such phenomena, including all free rhythms.

In fact, it is precisely historical and cultural considerations, a priori and aside from any actual analysis of the texts themselves, that warrant close attention to rhythm in biblical poetry. Both the informing orality of the Bible's poetic tradition and the likely nature of its music strongly implicate rhythm, whether or not aspects of that rhythm (e.g., its beats) also become regularized, and thus metrical. Oral poetry is necessarily rhythmic, to be sure, as a product of the human voice, but also most significantly because rhythm is "an aid to memory." Before writing "everything had to be preserved by memory alone," and rhythm is a natural boon to human memory, both short- and long-term varieties. "Any rhythmic schema," says Jousse, "that makes a propositional gesture 'dance' on the laryngo-buccal muscles of an improviser or reciter, acquires, by that very fact, the tendency to 'dance' again"—both on the tongue of the oral performer and in the ears and minds of her audience. At the heart of oral style, then, is a rather loose and fairly free rhythm.[147] And already in 1925 Jousse was convinced of the overwhelming oral sensibility of (much) biblical verse, in no small part because of the "rather free" rhythm (and "fairly loose" parallelism) that pervades so much of that poetry, as he makes clear in a comment (via a quotation of A. Condamin):

> Oral style is a living thing in which, as in all series of human gestures, "the parallelism is fairly loose, and the rhythm rather free. [And] if it is sometimes asserted or believed [as *our* bookish poetic training leads us to do, in spite of ourselves] that [such or such a reciter, for example] Jeremiah [composed orally, prior to putting them into] writing, only rhythmic schemas with a strict and rigorous parallelism, with a very regularly balanced [*metrical*] rhythm [running through each recitation], with an [according to *our* rules] accomplished craftsmanship, this is an *a priori* conception, for which it is impossible to furnish proof or even any probable ground" (CONDAMIN: B, 238), and which contradicts, in the most glaring fashion, the traditional texts and the *living* ethnological facts.[148]

E. A. Havelock, for whom "rhythm as a principle of composition is more extensive than meter"—"it is the genus of which meter is a species," echoes Jousse both in the belief that rhythm is essential to oral art and in the identity of some of this ametrical rhythm's leading components. With respect to the latter, Havelock writes: "At the acoustic level it can be set up by assonance, alliteration and the like, and at the level of meaning it can be generated by parallelism, antithesis and the simpler figures of speech like chiasmus."[149] Havelock even goes on to illustrate the typical (nonmetrical) rhythm of an oral "saying" through a reading and commentary on Proverbs 1:8–9:

> My son hear the instruction of thy father
> and forsake not the law of thy mother
> for they shall be a chaplet of grace unto thy head
> and chains about thy neck.[150]

I cite Havelock's exposition in whole because it affirms Jousse's own strong impressions about rhythm and the informing orality of the larger biblical corpus and it offers a brief glimpse at some of the key ingredients to the Bible's poetic rhythm:

> The rhythmic devices which at the acoustic level contribute to the memorisation of the statement, and hence to its survival value, can be properly observed only in the original. But even the English translation brings out the system of balances, parallelisms and contrasts which at the thematic level contribute to the total rhythm of the saying. The sentiments are arranged in pairs: the first couplet lists two directives referring to two parallel figures, father and mother, while at the same time exploiting the antithesis between father and son, and the correspondence between instruction and law. The second couplet lists two parallel statements which are linked to the two preceding directives as a commentary upon them and are put together with the aid of similar parallelism and antithesis.... This saying provides an example of particular appropriateness in the context of my present argument, for it happens to identify that cultural procedure which guarantees the life of the saying itself. It is indeed like a chain placed round the neck, for the child, in order to acquire the cultural tradition, has to respond to adult instruction. The convenient adult, chosen by most if not all cultures for this purpose, is the parent. There is no other way in which the identity of the tradition can be preserved, for being wholly oral it is carried solely in the personal memories of individuals in the succeeding generation as they memorise it.[151]

Therefore, the (here mostly posited by way of Jousse and Havelock) informing orality of so much biblical poetry—what S. Niditch calls an "oral register"— strongly suggests the likelihood (all things being equal) of a free rhythmic schema at the heart of this poetry's prosody. This is not to say that meter cannot emerge out of such free rhythms. It can and has. The Greek example is enough to make this possibility plain to see. The point is that rhythm (and not meter) is the default mode of oral verbal art, and therefore where the numbers do not add up, as they do not in the Bible, meter cannot be. The supposition of a metered biblical poetry was mistaken almost from the first. Its tenacious hold on the Western scholarly imagination was not because of the evidence, which, as even Jousse was aware, "contradicts, in the most glaring fashion, the traditional texts," but because of the accident and prejudice of the Western scholarly tradition itself (Jousse: "*our* bookish poetic training"), a tradition rooted in classical antiquity and thereby blinded to other realities.

Considerations of ethnomusicologists point in the same direction. They have long noted the anomaly of Western tonal music and, by contrast, that much non-Western, traditional music, which only began being collected in earnest during the twentieth century, is not metrical but consists of often very complex free rhythms. Free rhythm, in its musical sensibility, may be defined as the rhythm of music "without perceived periodic organization,"[152] an ametrical rhythm that is not organized within a "pulse-based temporal framework."[153] Thaut elaborates: "Free rhythms consist of extended or brief groups of rhythmic events that are characterized and distinguished from each other by changes in contour, timing, intervals, durations of sequences, tempo changes, or accent patterns. As such, they utilize structural organization in temporal distribution of elements to build patterns."[154] There may well be an underlying pulse, but if so it will not have temporal equality or be organized periodically.[155] The overall organization is not accidental or random and will often involve far more rhythmic complexity than is typically encountered in Western music.[156] Here is C. Sachs's illuminating if somewhat romantic description:

> Rhythmical freedom must therefore not be looked upon as lawbreaking with a judge's contemptuous eye. It is neither inferior or rudimentary, but just dissimilar. Far from being chaotic or defective, the rhapsodic strains of a shepherd lonely on the hills can have the wild, exciting beauty of horses, unbridled and panting, that gallop across the savanna. And again they have the soothing, tender, often melancholy charm of a streamlet rippling forth in dreamy monotone. Indeed, they might not even suggest that much motion; wide-spun and often with long fermatas and rests, they seem to defy the lapse of time and to hover motionless in the air. Nor could you or would you lift your baton to the song of a lark, although you sense its perfect, lawful orderliness, irrational as it may be. Indeed, you feel that any "normalcy" of song and motion would kill their charm in an unnatural mechanization.[157]

Such free rhythms are common throughout the world, and most notably, for my purpose, J. Frigyesi isolates in particular "the territory between North Africa and East Asia" as "a continuous, loosely related cultural zone" where free rhythm "is an essential, genre-related characteristic" of music.[158] Moreover, free rhythm forms are typical of ancient music—Sachs calls free rhythm "a precious heirloom from our animal ancestry," "doubtless the earliest quality"[159] of music in traditional cultures (e.g., "improvised folk music from illiterate cultures"),[160] and of received liturgies in many religious traditions, and of the vocal genres utilizing free rhythms, the influence of speech rhythm is palpable.[161]

Frigyesi is rightly cautious about tying the free-flowing rhythm of the Jewish "Nusah" (one genre of specific interest to her) historically to the known free rhythm music of the Middle East: "It is not unlikely that there is a relationship between modern European Jewish and the modern musics of the Middle East, but this conclusion is usually too hastily made. The modern situation cannot be projected back to previous historical periods."[162] Very prudent. Still, whether or not Jewish liturgical rhythms can be rooted confidently and historically in more ancient forebears, it would not be surprising to discover that the music of ancient Israel was of a free rhythmic kind, given the culture's overwhelming orality, its geographical location (square in the center of one of the prominent free rhythm music zones in the contemporary non-West), and the (presumed) antiquity of the style itself. And Frigyesi is quite wrong, I believe, in asserting the lack of evidence for the antiquity of free rhythms. To be sure, we do not have commentary or widespread notation systems from the ancient Near East, for example, but we do have an abundance of song texts themselves, literally "the words" of songs (cf. *dibrê haššîrâ hazzōʾt*, Deut 31:30, with reference to the following song in Deut 32). The major burden of the second part of this chapter is to spell out in some detail more precisely what the free rhythms of biblical song entail. But, again, even in advance of such (necessary) positive and empirical argumentation, our initial expectations, all things being equal, should be to find rhythms free and flowing, in the first instance, and then if there is positive evidence for meter, so much the better. But musicologically it is rhythm that is of the first order and not meter.

Finally, human physiology and cognition offers still further warrant for attending to poetic rhythm that is not necessarily metrical. Biologically, we are rhythmic creatures, our minds and bodies are built for rhythm. It is no surprise, on reflection, that the work product of these very minds and bodies— here the making of songs, of poems—should exploit biological predispositions. This is not to doubt the organism's capacity to work against such dispositions or to harness them differently—say, for example, to regularize them. But if poems are found to have rhythm, though the numbers (whatever is being counted) never seem to quite add up, then it may simply be that rhythm is all there is, a rhythm that is conducive to the movements of our bodies and the oscillations of our minds. Looked at biologically, it is again rhythm and not meter that is natural, given. Rhythm is the unmarked category, which when regularized becomes marked and metrical.

I belabor the point. But the metrical hypothesis about biblical poetry has maintained a stranglehold on the scholarly imagination, even when there is now a consensus that biblical poetry is not metrical. So overstatement has its uses, here to bludgeon open our collective eyes to other nonmetrical rhythmic possibilities. Each of the considerations just reviewed, on my view, makes it very likely that biblical poetry should be of a free rhythmical kind of song. The surprise, in fact, would be to find meter. But no amount of counting and re-counting of syllables, stresses, words, or whatnot has been able to uncover that meter. The rhythms of biblical Hebrew poetry are not metrical but free and flowing. They are free rhythms.

The Free Rhythms of Biblical Poetry

For Hrushovski, "the poetry of the Hebrew Bible" is "a 'natural' free-rhythmic system."[163] By "free rhythms," he means "poems which (1) have no consistent metrical scheme, that is, in tonic syllabic poetry have a freedom from the prev-alent, predetermined arrangement of stressed and unstressed syllables; but (2) do have a poetic language organized so as to create impressions and fulfill functions of poetic rhythm."[164] Hrushovski here is not thinking of the musico-logical notion of free rhythms just discussed, though that phenomenon, in fact, is one and the same, especially when speaking of the songs of ancient Israel, an overwhelmingly oral culture in which music was dominated by voice.[165] Rather, for his terminology he is drawing on the German *freie Rhyth-men* "free rhythms," which he prefers to the more negatively marked French *vers libre* or its English counterpart, "free verse."[166] The implication is that such free rhythms are positively *free*, to play and form in a variety of ways, making use of all manner of linguistic material, and are not just *freed* from some metrical norm—the corresponding musical notion of free rhythms helps accentuate the positive sensibility of this way of phrasing matters. The German term itself, a relatively late coinage (late nineteenth century), desig-nates "unrhymed, metrically irregular, nonstrophic verse lines of varying length,"[167] which, as K. M. Kohl stresses, "in all essentials...coincides with what is elsewhere called 'vers libre' or 'free verse.'"[168] The earliest exemplars of *freie Rhythmen*, however, date to the 1750s, five poems ("hymns") by the German poet Friedrich Gottlieb Klopstock. They have "no rhyme, no regular organization of syllables, no regular line lengths, and no regular groups of lines."[169] A most tantalizing aspect of Klopstock's innovative rhythm is the explicit debt it owes to the Bible, especially the Psalms. Indeed it is intriguing to think that free verse in America (predominantly through Whitman) and *freie Rhythmen* in Germany (through Klopstock) both emerge under the impress of biblical poetic rhythm—at the very least the Bible deserves more attention than it habitually receives in genealogies of modern free verse.[170] More immediately relevant here, Klopstock and German *freie Rhythmen* provide yet further warrant for crediting Hrushovski's thesis about the free rhythms of biblical poetry.

Such free rhythm is multidimensional, a rhythm "based on a cluster of changing principles."[171] In fact, as previously noted, one of the deleterious consequences of (Western) literary criticism's preoccupation with meter and metrical scheme is the obscuring of the complexity and the multifaceted nature of poetic rhythm, even in metrical poems.[172] Hrushovski's conception of free rhythms is one that applies to whole poems—"we have to deal with a whole aspect and not with merely a certain a priori known element of it"—and involves a plethora of "rhythmic factors": "practically everything in the written poem can contribute to the shaping of the rhythm."[173] The basis of the Bible's free rhythms is "semantic-syntactic-accentual" (to use Hrushovski's phrase), which may be taken metonymically as an indication of the larger informing multidimensionality that typifies rhythm generally. In the survey that follows I isolate the most common elements out of which a biblical poem's rhythm is made, illustrating, along the way, typical conventions and patterns of deployment, always mindful that in the end to most adequately describe a poem's rhythm is to look at the poem as a whole. The specific components isolated are broadly typical of poetic rhythm in general, and include linguistic elements (e.g., syllables, morphemes, words, phrases, meaning), tropes (esp. parallelism), and conventions (e.g., the line)—the latter two involve what Cureton calls the "presentation of phenomena by the perceptual medium"[174]— here the perceptual medium is poetry. This decomposition[175] into constituent elements is pragmatic, a means for facilitating identification and interrogation. Ultimately a move back to the whole is required, a tracking of how rhythm's manifold components interact in singular poems. Poetic rhythm— especially when free flowing and multidimensional—is best and most fully appreciated, as Hrushovski recommends, "by going within" a poem and "moving in a hermeneutic circle from the whole to the parts, and vice versa."[176] Here I mostly move out from the parts, with only occasional glances given to more holistic considerations—my reading of Psalm 133 in chapter 5 offers the one fully worked example in this book where a biblical poem's rhythm is appreciated more directly in the circular manner Hrushovski advocates.

Syllables and Stress

Every language has its natural cadences, a rhythm whose job is to economize on the energy expended in speaking. The syllable is at the core of biblical Hebrew's natural (prose)[177] rhythm. Each syllable, as in other languages (e.g., English), is "a little articulation of energy produced by the muscles that expel air out of the mouth, shaped by the vocal cords and the organs of the mouth."[178] Biblical Hebrew is a stress-timed language, as stress is phonemic;[179] therefore stress figures prominently in the rhythmic drive of the language, which naturally pulsates through its words and phrases, pushing ever forward "with a certain evenness and predictability."[180] Usually the final syllable of a biblical Hebrew word (in the Tiberian vocalization of MT) receives the additional emphasis. It is accented or stressed expiratorily, "by contracting the muscles of the rib cage and thereby pushing more air out of the lungs."[181] In biblical prose the number of unstressed syllables between every stressed syllable varies (usually anywhere from one to four or five syllables). Word choice, phrasing, and syntax can all be used to shape the language's natural rhythmic contour further.

As Attridge emphasizes, "poems are made out of spoken language."[182] Biblical Hebrew poetry is no exception. It is simply "erroneous," concurs O'Connor, to suppose that biblical poetic language is "a phenomenon entirely apart from ordinary language."[183] Biblical poetry takes over the syllable and stress structure natural to biblical Hebrew and heightens and exploits it.[184] The heightening is effected in any manner of means, including word choice, phrasing, and syntax, as in biblical prose, though usually to a greater degree. Also repetitions of all sorts (phonological, morphological, lexical), semantics, and rhetorical tropes are habitually manipulated to support and fine point the rhythmic cadences of the syllables. But in biblical Hebrew poetry it is the line and the constraints it enforces that most dramatically (re)shapes biblical Hebrew's natural rhythm, distinguishing it from the spoken register of the everyday vernacular and even from the Bible's typical prose rhythms.[185] The natural grouping enforced by phrasing and sentence structure are here heightened even further by the constrained length of biblical poetic lines. The number of stresses per lineal unit remains free and variable, but they are restricted; the lines "almost never consist of one or of more than four stresses." And the number of syllables between stresses, though also free, "are made to be within a limited range" (e.g., by mostly "excluding two adjacent stresses" and by "providing secondary stresses for long words").[186] So Sachs: "now one, now two, three, or exceptionally four unaccented syllables" are placed "before the packed energy whipped down in an accent."[187] The net result, as Hrushovski notes, is that the lineal groups, though free and variable, "can be felt as similar, simple, correlated units"[188]— an impression reinforced when the numbers, especially within couplets and triplets, are made to be equal or nearly equal. In stress-timed languages, lines with roughly equivalent numbers of stresses tend to be similar in time; and when both syllables and stresses are brought into alignment in lines, the resulting equivalencies are made even closer, both in actual timing and perceived timing.[189] It is this shapelier rhythmic profile of so many biblical poems, in contrast to the looser rhythms of biblical prose, I suspect, that has helped to seduce so many over the centuries into thinking of biblical poetry as metrical.[190] There is of course a perceptible pulse to biblical poetry. The "packed energy" of word accent, made stronger by the compactness of the biblical poetic line—in bringing the accents closer together and limiting their number they become more conspicuous.[191] In fact much non-Western free rhythmic music also has a perceptible pulse. A definite beat. But, all importantly, it is a pulse that is not "organized periodically."[192] No "formal, regular patterns of meter or stress" ultimately prevail.[193] Biblical poetry is, as Sachs says, "the classical example of a free accentual rhythm."[194] As in other free rhythmic systems, the beats or pulses finally never admit predictability. They are not organized metrically. Yet their persistent if irregular thump, though not quite the "rigid frame" of meter, nonetheless effectively pushes the poetry ever forward in its pulsating ebb and flow and in the process creates coherence and a basic ground against which other more complex rhythmic clusters or contours may play, vary, and be synchronized.

Line

"When rhythm renounces the support of abstract or independent systems— meter or isochrony—the basic principle of the line emerges and takes absolute control."[195] Hartman here is thinking primarily of written, modern free verse, but his claim holds for all nonmetrical verse, including traditional and oral (or oral-derived) varieties, as long as whatever visual or spatial contributions that might arise from the fact of writing are bracketed out. In fact, if anything, in oral poetry the line—by whatever name—may be even more significant as it is the principal means for punctuating poetic discourse in the absence of actual punctuation marks (commas, periods, and the like). "Each line can and must make it own rhythmic statement."[196] The line figures into a biblical poem's rhythm in two major ways: (1) as the chief bit of structural scaffolding by which the poem's language material—sound, grammar, syntax, meaning—is simultaneously staged and shaped into consumable perceptual unities, and (2) as a perceptual unit (e.g., set off in oral performance by pauses) that is itself amenable to rhythmic manipulation, especially through variations in length and through grouping patterns. The former, though easily overlooked, is fundamental. The basic rhythmic substructure of every biblical poem consists of language periodically segmented, punctuated. So at the level of the syllables and stresses (just discussed), what distinguishes biblical poetic rhythm is not the fact of word stress or its linguistic manipulation, a phenomenon and capabilities (albeit sometimes exercised differently) common to both biblical prose and biblical poetry, but that the syllables and stresses come periodically interrupted and not in an endless stream. After every two, three, or sometimes four stressed syllables, with any accompanying intervening unstressed syllables, there is a pause, and then another two, three, or four stresses and another pause, and so on. This amounts to an extra layer of textual organization that even in the midst of much freedom and variation gives to the resulting rhythm a distinctive shape and movement that can be palpably felt. Phrasing submitted to the strictures of biblical lineal conventions tends to result in a noticeably more evenly paced cadence, punctuated by more pauses, with shapelier, even symmetrical clauses (especially within couplets and triplets), which may be contrasted (albeit grossly), as S. Geller notices, with the randomness of clause structure and length and the less interrupted flow of language that tends to characterize most biblical prose— the phrasing in prose answering to other rhetorical ends (e.g., descriptive or dialogic verisimilitude).[197] So in 1 Chronicles 16 one hardly needs a specially formatted Psalms manuscript (e.g., 4QPs[b]) to eventually (retrospectively) recognize the transition to verse that occurs at verse 8 and then the transition back to prose at verse 37.[198]

Staying with the line and for the moment bracketing out (somewhat artificially) the language material of which the line is composed,[199] the standard rhythmic flow of periodically segmented syllables and stresses in biblical poems may receive still further molding, sometimes by varying the length of the line, and more often by manipulating the patterns of line grouping. The biblical Hebrew poetic line is concise and ultimately constrained, though variable, ranging in length on average from five to twelve syllables,[200] three to five words,[201] and two to four stresses.[202] Even though these concise but varying lines are not strictly, predictively patterned, the "limit of variability" is sufficient to create rhythmic expectations. Smith explains with reference to a poem by William Carlos Williams ("Sunflowers"), in which "the number of syllables in each line varies between four and eight, and the number of major stresses between two and four":

> These limits are confined enough to establish a principle that corresponds to the metrical "norm" of a conventional poem: it is experienced as an iambic norm would be, as a probability of occurrence that creates a rhythm and controls the reader's expectations. What the reader expects here, from line to line, is not a fixed number of syllables or pattern of stresses, but that certain limits of variability will not be exceeded.[203]

One mark of the rhythmic effectiveness of such "a limit of variability" with respect to the typical biblical poetic line is precisely the tenacity with which scholars (over centuries) have sought recourse to the idea of a metrical norm as a means of making sense of their felt readerly experiences of these poems' rhythms.

The "limit of variability" for line length in most biblical poems normally operates within a fairly narrow range, averaging, for example, seven or eight syllables.[204] Occasionally, outliers on the length continuum will be used to signal special points of rhythmic interest. So the major rhythmic contours of Isaiah 5:1–7 get marked (among other ways) by variation in line length.[205] The opening description of the lover's vineyard is conducted in short lines, mostly consisting of six or seven syllables—the succession of *wayʿazzĕqēhû waysaqqĕlēhû* in verse 2 at ten syllables being the only overly long line in the section.[206] The call for judgment (vv. 3–4) begins with a couplet composed of two noticeably longer lines, containing fourteen and nine syllables, respectively—the contrast making the longer lines all the more striking. The next juncture, the announcement of judgment beginning at verse 5 (which like v. 3 is headed by *wĕʿattâ* "and now"), also opens with long lines (syllables: nine, nine, twelve, eleven). And the poem's final movement (v. 7), where the meaning of the little allegory is revealed, is composed in longer lines (syllables: eleven, ten, ten, nine). Here, too, the contrast with an immediately preceding run of shorter lines (v. 6) stages and thus underscores the final shift to longer lines. The lines in Isaiah 5:1–7, then, vary in length throughout, though like all biblical poetry the variability is ultimately constrained. Still, there is enough range within this variability to allow for relative contrasts in length, which then may be exploited to rhythmic (and other) ends. In this case, the local contrasts point up peak moments in the poem's rhythmic structure. These distinctions in length are both a matter of degree—either longer or shorter than normal—

and relative to the local poetic context, that is, what counts as long or short depends on the standards established by the surrounding lines.[207]

Psalm 1 provides a more limited example. The psalm itself is fairly brief and not overly complicated. It is a celebration of the way of the righteous and pursues its theme in good wisdom fashion by comparing and contrasting the righteous with the wicked. At the heart of the poem are two similes, that of the lush, well-watered tree (v. 3) and that of chaff (v. 4). The former is positive, and the image symbolizes the righteous. It is elaborated in four or five lines (depending on the division) of mostly standard length (i.e., six to eight syllables). The second simile, the image of chaff, is negative and associated with the wicked. It is elaborated in three of the shortest lines of the poem (syllables: five, four, six). The contrast is intentional. The short run of short lines mimes the ephemerality of chaff that once tossed into the air disappears and is no more—such is the way of the wicked! And as the only run of short lines in the psalm, especially coming immediately after the contrasting positive image of the tree elaborated in normal-length lines, a momentary shift in the poetry's movement is effected and with it a certain climax is achieved, albeit one that is negatively charged.

Such change-ups in line length are commonly found in free verse poetry and often exploited to various ends, including rhythmic ones.[208] In fact, the predominance of one end of the length continuum or the other has come to characterize two of the more prominent genres of modern free verse: long-line (e.g., Whitman) and short-line (e.g., Williams) free verse.[209] The long-line, Whitmanesque variety of free verse is a product of chirography, and even the printing press, and therefore it does not factor into the biblical corpus. However a specifically short-line variety of the Bible's already fairly concise poetic line, of the kind already met with in Psalm 1, has long been recognized by biblical scholars and is featured often enough in stanzas (Ps 1:3) or sections (Ps 19:8–11) of poems and even in whole poems (Ps 142).[210] As G. Fohrer well emphasizes, "the short verse is not the basic poetic and stylistic unit" of biblical poetry but mostly "a dependent and auxiliary member" of poems, whether singly or in groups, frequently signaling (through contrast with the longer more normative poetic line) critical structural or rhetorical or rhythmic junctures, such as the onset of a poem's ending. Some poems are, of course, entirely made up of short lines. They tend to be fairly small in overall compass, mirroring their component lines. In other poems long and short lines appear to mix freely.[211] The outstanding feature of this poetry is the relative shortness of the line, which, again, varies in length but consistently remains at the short end of the length continuum, rarely exceeding eight syllables or so. The shortened length impinges directly on what can take place in the scope of the line. That is, only so much can be said in biblical Hebrew in six to eight syllables.[212] A typical syntactic profile of what is possible in such a short line is well evidenced by Psalm 142, in which most lines are composed of a verb, nominal, and prepositional phrase (e.g., *'espōk lĕpānāyw śîḥî* "I pour out before him my complaint," v. 3). Of course other typological profiles prevail, but the resulting clauses nonetheless are always short and constrained. In modern short-line verse, such as that of Williams, enjambment (and often with very severe cuts) is utilized to enlarge sentential scope and to relieve the potential monotony and syntactic restrictedness of a poem full of lines composed of simple, short sentences.[213] And while biblical short-line verse sometimes relies on enjambment, the cuts are mostly mild, tending to follow the syntactic contours of normal biblical Hebrew phrasing. Consequently, more discursively ambitious gestures, such as the closing lines that cinch the little allegory in Isaiah 5:1–7 (*wayqaw lĕmišpāṭ wĕhinnê miśpāḥ / liṣdāqâ wĕhinnê ṣĕ'āqâ*), usually require more space to spin out their logic or argument than can be accommodated by a shorter line. Line-internal troping is also more easily handled in larger spans of discursive space. Line-internal parallelism, for example, because it involves matched or mirrored phrasing, most often requires the larger palette of the Bible's standard or longer line.[214]

So manipulation of the length of the line is one way the basic underlying rhythmic profile of (most) biblical poems—runs of lines consisting of from two to four stresses (on average) with intervening unstressed syllables—may be more finely shaped to one end or another. The limited range of variation ultimately constrains what is achievable through such manipulation, mostly affecting local shifts, though sometimes more sustained patterning (often of shorter than average lines) may result. A more muscular and thus more robust means of molding and sculpting a biblical poem's rhythmic structure—still thinking of the line devoid of its linguistic content—is through line grouping. That is, if the alternation of stressed and unstressed syllables as segmented into fairly concise lines provides every biblical poem with its basic rhythmic substructure, it is how the lines are grouped and the patterns the grouping effects that give each individual poem a unique rhythmic shape at the macro level. Biblical poetry is dominantly distichic, a yet further distinguishing feature of its typical rhythmic profile—contrast, for example, the stichic traditions of ancient Greek poetry or of so much contemporary free verse. Couplets provide the base-level grouping scheme for most biblical poems, with single lines and, more commonly, triplets used to figure, shape, and fine point the rhythmic structure.[215] For example, Psalm 114 is made up entirely of couplets, as are the acrostics in Lamentations 1–4. Couplets also dominate in the short-line acrostics in Psalms 111 and 112, but in both instances closure is signaled by (among other things) changing the grouping pattern at the end of these poems: each closes with two triplets (Ps 111:9–10; Ps 112:9–10). The very compact Psalm 133 has a similar macrostructure, consisting of four couplets and a closing triplet. In the *wasf*-like Song 4:1–7, the body of that poem (vv.1–5) is given over to the boy's admiring description of the girl's upper torso (from head to breasts). The main section breaks into two symmetrical halves, each featuring three similes (e.g., "your hair is like a flock of goats") rendered in four couplets—the third simile in each half is elaborated with an additional couplet. The description is brought to a close in verse 5 with the notice of the girl's breasts, which is effected in a triplet, underscoring the intentionality of the stopping place (other of the Song's *wasf*-like poems are more holistic, for example, Song 5:2–6:3; 7:1–7).

Psalm 19 offers a more complex example in which line length and line grouping join to shape the major contours of the poem's rhythm. The first half of the poem (vv. 2–7), which focuses on creation in highly mythological terms, features the longest lines in the poem (some as long as ten or eleven syllables) and a mix of couplets and triplets. In fact, the two triplets (vv. 5c–7) distinguish the stanza dedicated to the sun—the first stanza being elaborated wholly in couplets. The second half of the poem (vv. 8–15), which is also composed of two stanzas (vv. 8–11, 12–14), is characterized by short lines (there are none of ten or more syllables) grouped almost entirely as couplets. The only triplet comes, appropriately, at the poem's conclusion (v. 15), the change in grouping pattern helping to secure closure. In addition, the Torah stanza (vv. 8–11) features eight qinah-shaped couplets, the first six of which contain some of the most closely matched lines in all of the Hebrew Bible: line length, syntax, word order, and even semantics are all closely aligned and mirror one another. Closure at the end of the stanza (v. 11) is signaled not by a change of grouping pattern but by a relaxing of the strict lineal alignments that characterize the earlier couplets: the two couplets continue the qinah pattern, and the lines remain relatively short, but they do not mirror the length, syntax, word order or semantics of the earlier lines. The example is quite stunning as it illustrates what is manageable even within fairly constrained parameters. Indeed, Psalm 19 as a whole is a parade example of the rhythmic subtleties that may be achieved through the manipulation of line length and line grouping alone.

In Job 3 the first section of the poem (vv. 3–10) is demarcated by an enveloping inclusio made up of two couplets: (*yōʾbad yôm ʾiwwāled bô / wĕhallaylâ ʾāmar hōrâ gāber*, v.3; *kî lōʾ sāgar daltê biṭnî / wayyastēr ʿāmāl mēʿênāy*, v. 10). In between, Job's verbal bid to undo creation is enacted mostly in triplets, which stand out rhythmically, since the remainder of the poem (v. 11–26) is rendered exclusively in fairly well-balanced couplets.[216] The contrast lends the opening section a chaotic feel and flow that mimes the return to chaos, un-creation, that Job desires. Triplets, of course, may also be interspersed amid the Bible's dominating distich to less rhetorically focused ends. The older poems of Exodus 15 and Judges 5 are good examples, where the interspersed triplets seem to mainly vary or trouble the rhythmic substructure of couplets. The general pattern with respect to line grouping in these examples is more or less typical of most (if not all) biblical poetry. The couplet or distich is the base-level norm for line grouping and provides the rhythmic ground of every biblical poem. This ground is frequently varied by the triplet, often to distinct rhetorical or semantic ends, but also to no such obvious ends (i.e., in free variation). What is perhaps most remarkable is the rhythmic variability with this one parameter (line grouping) and two variables (couplet and triplet). The only biblical poems in which line grouping effects a roughly similar rhythmic profile are several of the acrostics (e.g., Lam 1–3; Ps 111–12), and in each case rhythmic distinctiveness is eventually built in by other means, for example, variation in line length, use of parallelism or enjambment, semantics. Larger groupings of lines also occur from time to time, as do single, isolated lines. But these are much rarer than the triplet. When they do occur they may vary the rhythm in many of the same ways that the triplet does and further complicate the rhythm by adding additional layers of patterning.

So far I have considered the line abstractly, artificially, bracketing out all reference to the linguistic material of which the line is composed as a means of focusing on the rhythmic effects that fall out because of the line's perceptual unity and the patterns that unity forms through variation in length and grouping. In reality, the line has no tractable, actual existence except when bound up simultaneously with specific elements of language—lines of verse, like sentences, are made up of sound, words, and phrases—and thus these elements, to the extent that they can be iterated, varied, counterpointed, become yet more material out of which a poem's rhythm is constructed, fine-tuned, even reshaped. It is in this linguistic content—sounds, morphemes, syntax, meaning—as marshaled into patterns that the multidimensionality touted so much by recent theorists of poetic rhythm (e.g., Cureton, Attridge) comes into view. Many of the finer rhythmic contours that crosscut and complicate the basic pulse of the syllables and stresses in biblical poems, like them, are framed and staged initially and primordially by the line, at line level—given the biblical Hebrew poetic line's general coincidence with a consumable slice of the perceptual present. The line proves crucial to the consideration of all rhythmic contributions made by a poem's disparate and hierarchically organized language material, a point that will become apparent in the discussion that follows.[217]

Syntax

Perhaps the place in biblical poetry where the line's entanglement with the language material it sponsors has the most obvious rhythmic consequences is syntax, a dimension of language that is sometimes excluded from rhythmic calculations.[218] But syntax—in traditional grammars a property of sentences— can be patterned to rhythmic ends just as significantly (or not) as any other linguistic element. That is, there is nothing inherently rhythmic about syntax. Rather, as Smith stresses, a syntactic unit is experienced as rhythmic "only insofar as it participates in a pattern of similar units."[219] This holds for all manner of poetry.[220] But as a practical matter the import of syntax to poetic rhythm often gets magnified in nonmetrical verse precisely in compensation (so to speak) for meter's absence. That is, in the absence of meter, syntax is one of those other linguistic elements that must bear more of the poetic burden.

Chunking is a normal brain function, crucial to human intelligence and memory. We normally process information in bite-size chunks. With respect to language, syntax performs this essential work. It both separates and joins linguistic elements (words, phrases, clauses) into ever larger meaningful groupings, with different degrees of strength, and in this way syntax "contributes crucially to our experience of language as movement."[221] Comprehension is suspended "as a phrase arrives, then pausing to gulp the whole thing down."[222] Sentences are formed (in large varieties) from core structures and build outward by adding related elements. In biblical Hebrew, like many languages, that core structure, a clause, consists of a subject or topic, usually a nominal of some kind, and a predicate that comments on the subject, which may be verbal or verbless in character.[223] In verbal predications, which are dominant (as in all Semitic languages), the minimal meaningful clause consists of a verb with optional nominal arguments (subject, object)—biblical Hebrew is a null subject language.[224] Every verb is marked morphologically for subject (person, gender, number), and objects may be optionally indicated through affixing suffixes. Of course, a verb's nominal arguments may also be realized explicitly in the surface structure of the sentence. Typical word-order patterns in biblical Hebrew depend on various factors, including clause type (main, subordinate, narrative, dialogue), presence of nominal arguments in surface structure, and pragmatic (focus, topic shift) and stylistic (troping and the like) considerations. Historically, biblical Hebrew featured VS (and VO) word order, and this word order persists in many clausal environments (e.g., subordinate clauses, narration with *wayyiqtol* forms). But an important shift to SV word order in main clauses eventually takes place and is plainly detectable in the corpus.[225] Adjuncts of various sorts (e.g., prepositional phrases, adverbials) may always be added, providing yet further material for rhythmic patterning. Verbless clauses always require at least two elements, subject and predicate, with the unmarked (basic level) subject-predicate order mirroring the evolved SV order of main clauses in verbal predications. Other adjuncts are optional in verbless clauses as well. A sentence may be coextensive with a single clause (subject and predicate), or it may consist of two or more clauses. The brain processes language as it arrives. It is habituated from a young age to search out a language's core syntactic structures, what E. B. Voigt calls the "fundament."[226] It will suspend comprehension until the fundament comes. Once the fundament arrives, the brain then interprets both the already processed (but suspended) language material and any related language material yet to come in light of the fundament. Fundament-first constructions make for easier cognitive processing, though the inflectional morphology of biblical Hebrew verbs provides built-in aids for tracking syntactic relations and makes for more flexibility in clause structure. Still, there are also a number of prototypical constructions (e.g., circumstantial clauses) that also signal non-fundament-first constructions, effectively telling the brain to suspend comprehension.

Biblical Hebrew syntax mostly unwinds additively in what are known as branching patterns. In such patterns, as Voigt describes (for English), "modification follows in close proximity to what is modified" so that listeners are not overly taxed in remembering or anticipating referents.[227] This branching pattern in part compensates for the erosion of the case system on nouns that happened in proto-Hebrew. Without cases to explicitly indicate grammatical function, biblical Hebrew makes use of function words, word order, and proximity to help map syntactic relations.

Clauses in natural languages tend to be related to each other in two large ways, either through hypotaxis, which involves complex subordinating structures where interclause relations are explicitly indicated, or through parataxis, in which clauses follow one another with no or only very minimal linking devices. Biblical Hebrew exhibits both structures, though parataxis is broadly dominant. Its character varies depending on medium and style. Biblical narrative prose, for example, is marked by sequences of clauses and sentences joined principally by a prefixed conjunction, *wĕ-* "and"—the form of the verb used to carry the main narrative line, the so-called *wayyiqtol* form, comes with the conjunctive *waw* directly attached. English readers of the Bible will be familiar with the strongly paratactic nature of biblical narrative, since the early translators of the Bible into English (beginning with William Tyndale) commonly and consistently rendered the Hebrew conjunction with the simple "and" in English; hence the long sequences of sentences in the KJB that begin with "and." Biblical poetry similarly favors parataxis but differently. As most of the poetry of the Bible is nonnarrative in nature, the *wayyiqtol* form is far less prominent, especially in later verse traditions when the form is dying out altogether. There are still plenty of conjunctive *waw*s, of course, but not nearly so many as in the Bible's standard prose style. Equally often, clauses and sentences simply follow one after another with no overt marker of connection. Of course, larger spans of discourse will frequently deploy some indicators (syntactic, pragmatic) of connectivity, even in the most nonnarrative of genres. So hypotaxis is met with on smaller and larger scales, but it tends to be ultimately constricted. The same basic profile is shared by oral performative art in less chirographically developed cultures. Memory, both long and short term (the two work in tandem when listening to a poem or song, for example), is likely responsible for such patterning. The mind's ability to track strings of hierarchical, hypotactic relations unaided is ultimately limited. Writing, of course, turns out to be our most significant aid to memory as it allows for literal rereading and thus reprocessing in order to isolate and identify all relevant dependencies. Once biblical Hebrew compositions begin to originate in writing (as opposed to the writing down of orally composed compositions), clauses elongate, and syntactic dependencies can become more complicated.[228] Performative art, too, has means to deploy in support of syntactic mapping (e.g., rhythm, sound play, parallelism, gesture), but in general in these art forms' syntactic structures hew more closely to the limiting constraints of short-term memory and prefer the simpler linking structures of parataxis. Any slice of Ugaritic narrative verse will illustrate this general profile. Consider again (see chapter 1) the example taken from the Ugaritic Kirta Epic, which tells the story of Kirta's quest to obtain an heir to the throne (CAT 1.14.III.38–49):

pd. in. bbty. ttn	And what is not in my house you shall give.
tn. ly. mṭt. ḥry	Give to me Lady Ḫuraya,
n'mt. šph. bkrk	the Fair One, your firstborn child,
dk. n'm. 'nt. n'mh	whose fairness is like the fairness of Anat,
km. tsm. 'ttrt. tsmh	like the beauty of Astarte is her beauty,
dqh. ib. iqni.	whose pupils are pure lapis lazuli,
'p['p]h sp. ṯrml.	her eyelids are alabaster bowls.
thgrn. [u]dm[229]	They are girded with rubies.

ašlw. bṣp. ʿnh	I will repose in the gaze of her eyes,
dbḥlmy. il. Ytn	whom in my dream El gave,
bḏrty. ab. Adm	in my vision, the father of humankind,
wld. špḥ. Lkrt	and she will bear an heir for Kirta
wġlm. lʿbd. Il	and a lad for the servant of El.

Here the lines measure out the narrative in integral, holistic chunks—every line is a complete thought, semantically and syntactically. All of the couplets and triplets are highly parallelistic—the iteration underscoring the narrative description and aiding the mind's comprehension of that description and the assimilation of new information. The opening triplet is typical. Movement from line to line is aided by repetition of material. The second line begins with a form of the same verb with which the first line ends (*ttn / tn*). The mention of Lady Ḥuraya in the second line explicitly identifies "what is not" in Kirta's house (*pd. in. bbty.*)—a wife. The third line names her two more times, *nʿmt. špḥ. bkrk* "the Fair One, your firstborn child." The connection between the two lines is facilitated both by iteration—the further naming of Ḥuraya—and syntax—the additional names are linked appositionally. The couplets and triplets that follow elaborate the narrative description with a strongly additive logic. Story logic and character—here a protracted description of Ḥuraya—tremendously aid the mind's comprehension of the scene. There is some minimal marking of syntactic connectivity in further support of narrative coherence. So lines 41–42 and 43–45 are connected to what precedes them by the subordinating relative particle *d-* ("who"), and lines 48–49 are headed by a conjunctive *w-* ("and"). The highly parallelistic and iterative nature of these couplets and triplets builds in the redundancy, rhythm, and time that facilitates assimilation of this larger connectivity, especially in a performative context. And making the joins at the heads of lines allows lineation to provide yet additional support for auditory tracking of syntax at these higher levels of discourse.

The rhythmic upshot of syntax is predominantly a factor of how it is staged and intersected by the line, "whether," as Voigt observes, "a line will be primarily consonant with the syntax, parsing it, or dissonant, in counterpoint."[230] So in the Kirta example line and syntax are strongly consonant. And so, too, in much biblical verse. Indeed, perhaps the most salient feature of biblical poetry, as Kinzie notes, is that it "consists of lines that close at the ends of phrases."[231] Biblical Hebrew poetry is predominantly end-stopped, with lines usually composed of syntactically discrete units, that is, phrases, clauses, sentences. Even when the syntax runs over line-ends, as it does roughly a third of the time,[232] the resulting *enjambed* syntax is still highly rounded, following the

normal turns of biblical Hebrew syntax and thus evidencing what Longenbach describes as a "parsing line."[233] The end-stopped and markedly rounded
nature of the Bible's poetic syntax is likely attributable to the tradition's roots
in oral culture.[234] Highly complicating, subordinating syntax, as observed, is
in large measure a product of writing and not easily consumable by the human
mind in an oral, performative context. The constraints of short-term memory
strictly limit what can be tracked linearly and sequentially. In oral poetry, the
line, as circumscribed by pauses and/or by other means (e.g., gesture), is the
principal mechanism for performing the work of punctuation or emphasis.[235]
Actual punctuation marks (e.g., periods, commas, and the like), of course, are
the products of the invention of writing and do not exist (as such) in oral art.
Indeed, they are only incipiently present in some of the early manuscripts
of written biblical poems from Qumran, where spacing, for example, is used
to distinguish lineal units.[236] This manner of formatting is actually quite
telling, as it visually underscores the punctuating function of poetic lines in
the Bible's orally derived poetry.

Lest the force of the line in this capacity be lost on a highly literate Western
reading public accustomed to the visual cues provided by punctuation marks
of various sorts, consider a section from W. S. Merwin's "The Estuary":[237]

> By day we pace the many decks
> of the stone boat
> and at night we are turned out in its high windows
> like stars of another side
> taste our mouths we are the salt of the earth
> salt is memory
> in storm and cloud
> we sleep in fine rigging like riding birds
> taste our fingers
> each with its own commandment
> day or night it is harder to know than we know
> but longer
> we are asleep over charts at running windows
> we are asleep with compasses in our hands
> and at the bow of the stone boat
> the wave from the ends of the earth keeps breaking

Halfway through his 1963 volume *The Moving Target* Merwin drops the use
of punctuation altogether, in part, he says, to emphasize the spoken-ness of
poetry. The movement of the words as staged by the line do the punctuating.[238]

Merwin, of course, still writes for a highly literate audience, but his practice illuminates the effectiveness of lineation alone (though inclusive of the language material out of which it is constructed)[239] as a means of punctuation, of scripting the syntactic flow of language. In "The Estuary" Merwin shapes his lines according to the natural contours of English syntax. His line is a parsing line, eschewing the sharp, often ungrammatical cuts, say, of many of Williams's poems.[240] By manipulating the lengths of his lines (e.g., compare especially the staging of the "like" clauses in ll. 4 and 8, or the lines headed by "taste" in ll. 5 and 9), Merwin effectively mimes the rhythmic ebb and flow of the "wave" in the final line of the poem that "keeps breaking" ("from the ends of the earth").

This manner of measuring out lines of verse in discrete, integral syntactic chunks effects a rhythmic evenness, a roundedness, that typifies all biblical poems. Biblical poems unfold line by line in syntactically meaningful strings of language. Allen characterizes the rhythm that typifies both the poetry of the Bible and that of Walt Whitman as "a rhythm of thought."[241] As a comprehensive descriptor this notion misses much that is relevant to the overall rhythm of biblical verse, yet it does nicely underscore the overwhelmingly end-stopped profile of most biblical poetic lines. Indeed, if the traditional notion of a sentence as "a complete thought expressed in words" is no longer linguistically perspicuous,[242] that idea nonetheless fits well the sentential profile of the biblical poetic line.[243]

If anything, this highly sentential and even rhythm is magnified all the more by the constrained nature of the biblical poetic line and the resulting simpler and more symmetrical clause structure (vis-a-vis biblical Hebrew prose) that obtains. Line after line of biblical verse unfolds in meaningfully coherent and discrete syntactic phrases, clauses, and sentences, and these chunks come in roughly the same sizes (with some meaningful variation, see discussion of the line in the preceding section). In much (contemporary) free rhythmic verse, how the line tends to crosscut syntax and to what rhythmic effects often depends on whether the line is typically long or typically short. As noted, long-line verse allows for more line-internal syntactic play since the line's length is usually longer than most individual units of syntax, while most short-line free verse can accommodate only the smaller grammatical units, requiring that larger scale phrasing and sentence structure most often will spill over line-ends. The constrained length of the Bible's characteristic poetic line and the highly rounded-off nature of its poetic syntax mean that recourse to these standard ways of orchestrating and fine tuning rhythm at the line/ syntax interface are only minimally effective in biblical poetry. Yet even if the degree of syntactic variation at line level is not so great—the basic phrasal and

clausal contours of biblical Hebrew syntax are almost always observed—
rhythmic nuances are nonetheless manageable and, indeed, noticeable. There
is a norm. Syntax and line structure in biblical poetry tend to be consonant
with one another. That is, the poetic lines are dominantly end-stopped. A chief
effect of the highly parallelistic nature of a majority of biblical poetic couplets
(and triplets, etc.), in fact, is to reinforce and dramatically enhance the perception of this consonance. So consider Psalm 37:30:

> *pî-ṣaddîq yegeh ḥokmâ*
> *ûlĕšônô tĕdabbēr mišpāṭ*
> the-mouth-of-the-righteous (S) + utters (V) + wisdom (O)
> and-his-tongue (S) + speaks (V) + justice (O)

Here the lines are composed of independent clauses—line and syntax are consonant, and thus mutually reinforcing. In addition, the iterative play at the
heart of parallelism in this instance manifests itself in the repeated word-
order frames (S + V + O // S + V + O), which in turn emphasize how the syntax
does not carry across line-ends. By contrast, consider Lamentations 1:3c:

> *kol-rōdĕpeyhā hiśśîgûhā*
> *bên hammĕṣārîm*
> all-of-her-pursuers (S) + overtake-her (VP = V + O) +
> between-the-narrow-places (PP)

Here the syntax is still rounded off but nonetheless clearly carries across that
initial line-end—the second line consisting of a prepositional phrase (*bên
hammĕṣārîm*) that is syntactically dependent on the clause in the first line.
And that initial clause is itself self-contained, a syntactic whole, requiring no
further elaboration: "All of her pursuers overtake her." As much as a third of
the biblical poetic corpus contains enjambed lines like these. Violent syntactic
cuts are not at all common, though syntax does occasionally overflow couplet
and triplet boundaries, especially as an aid to building coherence into the
larger poetic discourse above the levels of clauses and sentences (e.g., Lam
3:28–36; Job 3:13–15; Ps 7:4–6; Prov 7:4–5, 8–9; cf. the foregoing discussion of
CAT 14.III.38–40).[244] The latter is worth underscoring as it is another indicator of the nonstichic nature of biblical verse. That is, that enjambment is
mostly confined to within couplet and triplet boundaries is consonant with
the distichic and tristichic nature of biblical verse.[245]

Biblical poems manipulate these two basic patterns, namely, end-stopping
and enjambment, to discernible rhythmic ends. Sometimes extremes prevail.

For example, the short Psalm 114 is composed entirely of couplets consisting of end-stopped lines (e.g., "the sea looked and fled, / the Jordan turned back," v. 3). The couplets themselves are all end-stopped, except perhaps for the last one, in which *hahōpĕkî* at the head of the first line of verse 8 may be construed appositionally,[246] further characterizing *'ādôn* "Lord" / *'ĕlôah yaʿăqōb* "God of Jacob" of verse 7, namely "who turns..." Of course the definite participle that heads verse 8 can also always be taken more straightforwardly as an independent clause, namely "The one who turns..." But in either case the consistently end-stopped nature of the lines provides the poem with a pronounced rhythmic integrity, perhaps with the slightest interruption at poem's end, with the onward tug of the syntax pulling the audience to (and thus underscoring) the psalm's close. Lamentations 1–4 illustrates the other extreme. Conservatively estimated, some 166–177 of these poems' 244 couplets involve some form of enjambment.[247] This more than doubles the likely percentage (perhaps 30 percent or so) of nonparallelistic, enjambed lines in the entire biblical corpus. The chief rhythmic effect, as with the end-stopped lines of Psalm 114, is to create an even and consistent texture (albeit different in character from that in Psalm 114) that helps to hold these poems together.[248]

Another of the characteristic rhythmic features of the enjambing line in Lamentations is that the tug of forward movement that the enjambment provokes is quickly checked by a major pause at the end of the couplet, as syntax and semantics are routinely brought to a full stop. The effect of this pause is underscored and strengthened formally by the habitual shortening of the second line in the qinah-shaped couplet that dominates these poems. Thus, the coincidence of this foreshortening (a form of catalexis)[249] and a syntactic stop strongly underscores the closed nature of the couplet in Lamentations.[250] The momentum created by enjambment is only rarely allowed to continue building beyond the couplet, and then only for a short span. As a result, bursts of onward thrust alternate with moments of stasis. This herky-jerky, go-and-stop movement complements the limping movement established by Lamentations' dominant unbalanced line, the qinah. Both couplet-shape and enjambment counterpoint the regularity and evenness constructed by the uniformity of stanzaic form and the (graphic) march of the alphabetic acrostic and of the closed couplets in Lamentations. The former play off and against the background established by the latter. This is one way that the poet is able to promote a sense of movement and control the pace of this verse without relying on emplotment or even strong characterization.[251]

Not all enjambment results in this kind of rhythmic profile, of course. The texture and movement promoted by enjambment in Lamentations may be usefully contrasted, for example, with the use of enjambment in Psalm 106,[252]

especially as a means of undergirding narrative connectivity.²⁵³ The psalm
recounts the history of Yahweh's great deeds on behalf of Israel. One of the
major dilemmas for a predominantly parallelistic poetry is overcoming the
stasis that inheres in any trope of repetition and projecting the sense of coherence, movement, and sequentiality that is vital to narrative. The poet of Psalm
106 is able to accomplish the latter by employing alongside predominantly
parallel and balanced lines a variety of strategies, including specific attention
to thematic development, a liberal use of the *wayyiqtol* form (or *waw* consecutive)—the narrative form par excellence in biblical Hebrew prose!—and frequent recourse to enjambment.²⁵⁴ The self-contained section in verses 19–23
recounting the incident of the golden calf provides a representative example:

* yaʿăśû-ʿēgel bĕḥōrēb*	They made a calf in Horeb
wayyištaḥăwû lĕmassēkâ	And worshiped a molten image.
wayyāmîrû ʾet-kĕbôdām	They exchanged their glory
bĕtabnît šôr ʾōkēl ʿēśeb	For the image of an ox eating grass.
šākĕḥû ʾēl môšîʿām	They forgot El, who saved them,
ʿōśeh gĕdōlôt bĕmiṣrāyim	Who did great things in Egypt,
niplāʾôt bĕʾereṣ ḥām	Wondrous works in the land of Ham,
nôrāʾôt ʿal-yam-sûp	Terrible deeds at the Red Sea.
wayyōʾmer lĕhašmîdām	And therefore he said to destroy them,
lûlê mōšeh bĕḥîrô	Except Moses, his chosen one,
ʿāmad bapperes lĕpānāyw	Stood in the breach before him
lĕhāšîb ḥămātô mēhašḥît	To turn his anger away from destroying.

The opening lines (v. 19a–b) are balanced and parallel; however, the use of
the *wayyiqtol* form (*wayyištaḥăwû*) and the sequential development implied
thematically in the two verbs—one has to make (*ʿśh*) the calf before it can be
worshiped (*šḥh*)—already builds in Alter's notion of incipient narrativity. This
sense of sequentiality is maintained in verse 20 through adjunct enjambment²⁵⁵
and in verses 21–22 through an extended example of appositional enjamb-
ment.²⁵⁶ Note how the latter maintains the feel of parallelism while effecting
(through addition) the sense of forward movement required by narrative. The
episode is concluded with an extended quotative frame. These lines from Psalm
106 differ dramatically from the kind found in Lamentations: a sense of parallelism is effectively maintained—aided tremendously by the balanced line
lengths; there is an obvious presence of thematic development; and enjambment carries over the couplet boundary on two occasions—the presence of
wayyiqtol forms at the heads of two couplets (vv. 20, 23) also helps to overcome
the sense of closure that regularly accompanies closed couplets. Thus, the

noticeable flow exhibited in these lines contrasts markedly with the herky-jerky and episodic movement so characteristic of the poetry in Lamentations, yet both make recourse to the same basic phenomenon of enjambment.

In fact, the mixture of syntactic frames apparent in Psalm 106 obtains more broadly in biblical poetry in general—that is, the more purified extremes of one kind (excessively end-stopped) or the other (excessively enjambed) are rarer. However narrow the ultimate range between the end-stopped and enjambed versions of the typical biblical poetic line, enough variety prevails to ensure that the overall syntactic profile and its accompanying rhythmic upshot is never quite replicated in any two biblical poems. A few more examples will underscore the point. Psalm 13, a classic individual lament, is made up of still prominently end-stopped lines, the "rhythm of thought" doled out in discrete bite-size chunks, easily consumable. Repetition of phrasing (e.g., ʿad-ʾānâ "how long?" repeated at the head of four of the poem's first five lines, vv. 2–3) and parallelism (e.g., "and as for me in your faithfulness I trust" // "my heart rejoices in your salvation" [ABC // C'B'], v. 6a–b) measure out these chunks. But there are nonetheless perceptible lineaments of discursive logic linking aspects of the psalm together. In the middle section of the poem (the two couplets making up vv. 4–5), the barest marker of syntactic linkage is indicated at the beginning of verse 5 through the repetition of *pen-* "lest" from the complex sentence that makes up the second line of verse 4:

> pay attention answer me O Yahweh my God
> give light to my eyes lest [*pen*] I sleep the (sleep of) death
> lest [*pen*] my enemy says, I overcome him
> my foes rejoice because I totter (vv. 4–5)

All four lines are composed of complex sentential structures that are self-contained, end-stopped. What links the four (within the frame of their parallelistic couplets) is first the gapping of the divine name in verse 4b and then the repetition of *pen-* in verse 5a. As a result the initial vocative governs the whole set of lines and verse 5 is linked appositionally according to the line-internal syntax of verse 4b. The *wa ʾănî*, literally "and I," that heads the psalm's closing triplet signals (however minimally) the logical dependence of this concluding thought on what has come before, albeit still within the frame of sententially integral lines:

> and as for me in your faithfulness I trust
> my heart rejoices in your salvation
> I sing to Yahweh because he does right by me

The psalm hangs together and emits an evenly measured rhythm with only minimally explicit indicators of syntactic linkage. The poem is brief, and the logic of its argument is neither complex nor semantically thick.

More ambitious poems, with richer semantic elaborations, often entail a broader array of explicit syntactic markers, both inside and outside of couplet and triplet boundaries. Consider Proverbs 1:20–33, still a fairly brief poem but with an argument to make. Personified Wisdom is imagined at a street corner (vv. 20–21) calling out to passersby, informing them that their continued failure to mind her wise words will end in disaster. The first two couplets (v. 20–21) are parallelistic and made up of sententially integral lines. These turn out to introduce the content of Wisdom's speech (ʾămāreyhā tōʾmēr "her words she speaks," v. 22)—but the prevailing parallelism, tārōnnâ, tittēn, tiqrāʾ, keeps the phrase from seeming overorchestrated (e.g., as with the use of lēʾmōr). The increased syntactic connectedness of the poem may be measured initially simply by the dramatic increase in syntactic connectors at heads of lines: conjunctive waws (eleven times), hinnê (v. 23c), yaʿan (v. 24a), gam (v. 26a), bĕbōʾ (v. 27a, c—miming the line-internal dependency realized in v. 26b), ʾāz (v. 28a), taḥat kî (v. 29a), and kî (v. 32a). Most of these are clause-external markers, logically connecting couplets and triplets to one another. The strength of the logical dependencies realized varies. The most pronounced ones come in verses 24–27 and 29–31. Only the conjunctive waw (vv. 22b, c, 25b, 27b, 29b, 31b, 32b, 33b), the one hinnê (v. 23b), and the third repetition of bĕbōʾ (v. 27c) coordinate lines within couplets or triplets. Overall parallelism and clausal integrity dominate. The enjambment that exists is mild, coordinating, but sufficient to thicken the rhythm of the poem. If we hear the basic rhythm as being elaborated in integral syntactic chunks grouped in couplets and triplets, as also in Psalm 13, the density has increased. The couplets and triplets because of the explicit coordination feel tighter, and they, too, are more tightly bound one to another. This is felt purely at the syntactic level. The slight narrative frame (vv. 20–21) and the consistency of voice (all the reported words of personified Wisdom), along with the semantics of the speech—what it literally says—further enhance the feel of coherence and rhythmic tightness of the whole.

One last example, this time from the first oracle in the book of Micah, 1:2–7.[257] As with personified Wisdom's speech, prophetic oracles are often keen to make explicit arguments. Indeed, one way much prophetic poetry characteristically differs from the core of the Bible's lyric corpus (e.g., Psalms, Song of Songs) is precisely in the higher incidence of syntactic connectivity. Micah 1:2–7 is composed of couplets, with but a single triplet, which comes in verse 7 right before a concluding couplet—the change in grouping strategy helping to signal the oracle's impending conclusion. With only two exceptions (the first two couplets in

v. 5), each couplet and the single triplet that follow the opening address ("Hear, all you peoples…") are explicitly linked through syntax to what precedes them: *wîhî* "and he was" (v. 2c), *kî-hinnê yhwh* "for Yahweh…" (v. 3a), *wĕnāmassû* "and they will melt" (v. 4a), *kaddônag* "like wax" (v. 4c), *ûmî* "and who is…" (v. 5e), *wĕśamtî* "and I will set" (v. 6a), *wĕhiggartî* "and I will roll" (v. 6c), *wĕkol-pĕsîleyhā* "and all her images" (v. 7a), and *kî* "for" (v. 7d). The first two couplets in v. 5 are also linked to what immediately precedes them, but lexically instead of syntactically. In the first line of v. 5 (*bĕpešaʿ yaʿăqōb kol-zōʾt*), the *kol-zōʾt* finds its immediate antecedent in Yahweh's theophanic activity (esp. vv. 3–4), and it is the repetition of *pešaʿ* "crime, rebellion" that joins the couplets in verses 5a–b and c–d. In contrast, the individual lines themselves are prominently end-stopped, with seven conjunctive *waws* joining sets of lines (vv. 3b, 4b, 5b, 6d, 7b, c, e). The strongest bit of enjambment comes in the appositional comparative clauses that make up verse 4c–d: *kaddônag nipnê hāʾēš / kĕmayim muggārîm bĕmôrād* "like wax before fire, / like water being poured down a slope." There is a rhythmic evenness by which line moves onto line within the couplet or triplet. The phrases and clauses (with few exceptions, e.g., v. 4c-d) are wholes and have integrity, and only sometimes (esp. toward the end of the poem) is this harsh parataxis relieved ever so slightly by the addition of a conjunctive *waw*. Coherence and connectivity are built in more explicitly above the level of the line, at couplet and triplet boundary. The touch remains light, but sufficient to tighten up the whole noticeably. There can be little doubt, even in advance of a review of the oracle's semantic content, that the rousing of Yahweh and the deity's impending judgment is to be directly tied to Samaria's and Jerusalem's "crime, rebellion."

If the nature of how syntax interfaces with the line and with groups of lines offers one important dimension by which syntax may effect a biblical poem's rhythm, other patterns may also prevail. The nature of the clauses in a poem, for example, may be patterned to rhythmic ends. Biblical Hebrew, like other Semitic languages, is dominantly verbal. That is, the verb plays the central role in predication.[258] Normally, then, the basic syntactic texture of a biblical poem is one that features verbal predication. Isaiah 5:1–7 (discussed earlier) is a typical example. Most of the poem's clauses consist of verbal predicators— and these mostly involve finite verb forms. There is a change-up, however, at poem's end in verse 7. Here the identity of the players in the allegory are revealed in a longer-line couplet consisting of verbless clauses:

kî kerem yhwh ṣĕbāʾôt bêt yiśrāʾēl	For the vineyard of Yahweh Sabaoth is the house of Israel
wĕʾîš yĕhûdâ nĕṭaʿ šaʿăšûʿāyw	and the people of Judah are the planting of his delight.

The actional flow of verbal clauses momentarily stops in the stasis created by the two verbless clauses for the allegory's unveiling. The final couplet, as well, though set up verbally (*wayqaw* "and he hoped"), derives its punch through the contrasting verbless clauses at the ends of both lines (*wĕhinnê miśpāḥ...wĕhinnê ṣĕʿāqâ*). Here the stasis underscores the damning disappointment and contrary reality and quite literally stops the poem. In Psalm 19 the Torah section of the poem (vv. 8–11) stands out from the surrounding sections dominated by verbal predication precisely in its sixfold sequence of main verbless clauses (e.g., "the Torah of Yahweh is perfect"). It is as if the temporal movement of the poem pauses for the audience's consideration of Torah, with the sixfold repetition of these mirroring verbless structures extending the pause, prolonging auditors' time for contemplation. Verbless clauses in both of these examples vary the normal rhythm of verbal predication to specific ends, like the way that triplets frequently interrupt (often meaningfully) the Bible's dominantly distichic rhythm. Of course, verbless clauses will just as frequently pepper a poem, and thus trouble the flow of verbal clauses, with no obvious larger ends in view.

Extremes of one variety or the other are sometimes met with. In Lamentations 2:1–8, for instance, clause after clause, line after line, is relentlessly verbal. In this opening section of the poem, the poet depicts Yahweh's destruction of Jerusalem. These twenty-four couplets feature thirty-three finite verbs, thirty of which are third person masculine singular forms, mostly of an active-transitive nature, featuring the violent activity of Yahweh (the explicit or implicit subject of these verbs). There are no verbless clauses. The resulting rhythm has a highly muscular feel to it, making clear the futility of all efforts to resist the onward march of such divine power and leaving no doubt who is responsible for Jerusalem's destruction. By contrast, Song 4:1–7 in its portraiture of the beloved girl offers (in part) a poetic rendition of a commonplace Canaanite motif in two- and three-dimensional representational art, the "woman in the window."[259] Befitting the plasticity of the art form that the poem means to mime, the body of the poem (vv. 1–5) features almost all verbless clauses—the only two finite verbal clauses appear as dependent clauses. Rhythmically, the use of verbless clauses lends itself to the suggested spatiality of the verbalized portrait, while providing again the semblance of a temporal pause to facilitate our auditory/readerly assimilation and appreciation of the boy's admiring (and loving) gaze.[260]

How the line stages syntax (in consonance or dissonance) and the nature of clausal predication are but two ways syntax may be harnessed rhythmically in biblical poems. Surely other syntactic features (e.g., word order) are similarly exploited. The two just isolated here will suffice to illustrate the kinds of contributions syntax can make to a biblical poem's overall rhythm.

Parallelism

"The human brain is avid for pattern, by which to register, store, and retrieve information," writes Voigt, and "parallelism" is one of the more common means of pattern making available to language, with syntax as its core.[261] Jousse well understood parallelism's deep-rootedness in human psycho-physiology and hence its centrality to oral performative art: "Parallelism is but the consequence and transposition of the bilateral structure of the human body onto the oral mechanism."[262] Parallelism, of course, since Lowth's celebrated analysis in the middle of the eighteenth century,[263] is also the best known characteristic of (much)[264] biblical poetry, and indeed, since the early 1990s, parallelism is now also the best understood feature of biblical poetry. Its many varieties and common tendencies, its basic mechanisms and informing structures, have been well researched, catalogued, and exemplified. If parallelism per se cannot be constitutive of biblical poetry, since there is a substantial amount of nonparallelistic, enjambed lines in the biblical Hebrew poetic corpus—there is no denying its significance when present—the keenness of Lowth's original insight continues to redound to this day. Of those aspects of parallelism that are most distinctive of biblical verse, it is the trope's contribution to rhythm that I focus here. Jousse himself underscores the rhythmic import of parallelism with his preferred gloss of the concept of "rhythmic schema."[265] Like the sheer quantity of parallelism in biblical poems and its prominent use in end-fixing, the exploitation of parallelism to rhythmic ends is a quintessential orally derived phenomenon. This is not to say that parallelism in written verse cannot have rhythmic consequences. It can and it does—there is no better example of the latter than Whitman's poetry. But Jousse's diagnosis of "the deep-seated laws of the 'human compound' of flesh and spirit" that "dictate that each improvised utterance has a curious tendency to trigger, in the phonatory system of the speaking subject, one or more utterances of parallel construction and of similar or opposed meaning" is surely on target.[266] Parallelism is common to oral performative art because it is homologous with and emerges out of human biology. Or Jousse again: "The improvisation and rememorization of rhythmic oral compositions are greatly facilitated by this linguistic phenomenon, which is found in all communities, employing the oral style."[267]

Parallelism may contribute to the rhythm of a biblical poem in at least two broad ways: through patterns formed by the play of parallelism (qua parallelism) itself and through patterns formed by the different structures of matching sponsored by individual parallel frames. The former is the broader of the two and results in perhaps the most pronounced rhythmic effect of biblical verse. In poems composed predominantly of parallelistic couplets and triplets, the forward movement of the rhythm is periodically, routinely even, checked by moments of felt-stasis as the balancing and repetition at the heart of parallelism—one propositional gesture instinctively triggering another of like form and meaning[268]—enact their bilateral pulse. Such poems have a deliberative, ambling pace as their basic rhythmic ground: one step forward, iteration; another step and another iteration, and sometimes two (in triplets); a further step accompanied by a further iteration; and so on.[269] There may be no better description and illustration of this rhythm than that provided by J. Hollander in his delightful imitation of it in English translation:

> The verse of the Hebrew Bible is strange;
> the meter of Psalms and Proverbs perplexes.
> It is not a matter of number,
> no counting of beats or syllables.
> Its song is a music of matching,
> its rhythm a kind of paralleling.
> One half-line makes an assertion;
> the other part paraphrases it;
> sometimes a third part will vary it.[270]

Not only does this effectively catch the rhythmic feel of so much biblical verse, Hollander's emphasizing of the *rhythmic* consequences of parallelism makes its own critical contribution to the understanding of biblical verse—rhythm does not figure prominently in most accounts of parallelism in biblical poetry.

Psalm 105 offers an extended example of this basic rhythmic profile in its narrative recital of Israel's Egyptian captivity (esp. vv. 16–43). In these twenty-seven couplets (no triplets in this psalm), fully twenty-three (vv. 16, 18–20, 22–27, 29, 31–36, 39–43) exhibit some form of parallelism. The bilateral statement and restatement pacing of the psalm's telling is made all the more apparent given the broadly sequential nature of the (presumably) well-known events recounted. This is especially clear in the sequence featuring the plagues (vv. 26–36). Generally, each plague is accommodated by a single couplet (e.g., "he turned their waters to blood, / and he killed their fish," v. 29; "and he struck down every firstborn in their land, / the first of all their strength," v. 36). Sometimes the plague is elaborated beyond the couplet: "he said and the locust came, / and grasshoppers without number, / and they ate every green thing in their land, / and they ate the fruit of their soil" (vv. 34–35). Once a couplet contains two plagues, though they are figured parallelistically like most of the others: "he said and the gnats came, / flies in all of their country" (v. 31, cf. v. 34). Even when strict parallelism may be missing (v. 28, 30), or when the incipient narrativity of some couplets (e.g., the changing of the waters to blood sequentially leads to the killing of the fish), for example, dissolves some of the parallelism's iterative force, nonetheless the rhythmic pattern enforced by the parallelistic norm subsists in the psalm's auditory experience. Even the most relentlessly metrical verse varies itself periodically. What is crucial is to establish the norm and maintain it sufficiently to ensure its ongoing perception.[271] In this psalm the two-step pace of its overwhelmingly parallelistic idiom is never allowed to stray too long or too far.

Curiously, even though parallelism is itself a dominant trope quantitatively in biblical poetry, there are not many individual poems that are as resolutely parallelistic as Psalm 105. Often the rhythmic feel of biblical parallelism's habitual bilateral movement (statement and restatement, one step forward, iteration, then another step forward and another iteration) persists precisely because enough is done to set up this rhythmic norm and maintain it, all the while varying it in potentially significant ways. Proverbs 7 is a case in point. In this poem the didactic frames circumscribing the poem's narrative body (vv. 1–5, 24–27) are rendered entirely in parallelistic couplets, and parallelism appears frequently in the main body of the poem (e.g., vv. 6–9, 14, 15, 18, 20). So the sense of recursion and balancing projected by the prominence of the parallelism is easily felt, especially as supported by the dominance of the couplet—the only triplet is used to introduce the foolish boy (v. 7)—and of the nearly symmetrical nature of the pairs of lines making up the individual couplets. And yet parallelism is let go of almost entirely in several places, and perhaps not accidentally. The biggest chunk comes in verses 10–13, where the "strange woman" (*'iššâ zārâ*, cf. v. 5) enters the narrative. Until this point, the only major deviation from the poem's parallelistic idiom occurs in the final line of the triplet in verse 7, underscoring the introduction of the boy:

> and I saw among the simple ones
> I noticed among the boys
> a lad lacking of heart (i.e., sense)

The break from the parallelism in verse 10, then, echoes this earlier deviation, highlighting the appearance of the little narrative's second main character, the woman:

> And now a woman to meet him
> harlot-garbed guarded of heart (i.e., cunning, devious)

This commences a brief run of nonparallelistic couplets (vv. 10–12). Verses 11–12 offer an aside, providing a narratorial characterization of this woman:

hōmiyyâ hî' wĕsōrāret	she is loud and wayward
bĕbêtāh lō'-yiškĕnû ragleyhā	in her house her feet do not stay
pa'am baḥûṣ pa'am bārĕḥōbôt	one in the street, another in the squares
wĕ'ēṣel kol-pinnâ te'ĕrōb	and beside every corner she lies in wait

There is absolutely no parallelism here (except line-internally, *pa'am baḥûṣ //* *pa'am bārĕḥōbôt*). Indeed, its lack—especially given the run of parallelistic couplets to this point—rhythmically mimes the woman's unruly (from the father's disapproving perspective) behavior, that is, her feet, unfettered, roam here and there about the town. After this point in the narrative, parallelism fades in and out. Occasionally, it is most pronounced, as in the unbalanced couplet in verse 18: "Come, let us have our fill of love till the morning, / let us delight in lovemaking." Other times it is completely absent (e.g., "I have perfumed my bed with myrrh, / aloes and cinnamon," v. 17). And still other times the parallelism is not all pervasive—for example, in verse 13 each line contains two verbal clauses, but their syntactic frames only partially align (*wĕheḥĕzîqâ bô // hē'ēzâ pāneyhā, wĕnāšĕqâ-llô // wattō'mar lô*)—and we notice the misses— and the semantics almost totally diverge, that is, are nonsynonymous (seized, kissed // hardened, said). Still, there is enough parallelism throughout to ensure its rhythmic contribution is felt, especially given the emphatic and unfailing parallelistic shaping of the poem's concluding didactic frame (vv. 24–27). Yet the divergences subtly alter the poem's overall rhythmic profile as well. Dominantly parallelistic, yes, but not relentlessly so. The subtle change-up in rhythm in the lines dedicated to the depiction of the other woman, in which parallelism never seems to regain its strong footing, underscores the didactic worry of the whole.

Isaiah 1:2–20 is another dominantly parallelistic poem, though how it is parallelistic turns out to make a great deal of difference in the poem's felt rhythm. Many of the lines within couplets and triplets are also related syntactically (e.g., vv. 6a–b, 7c–d, 8a–b, 11a–b, 12a–b, 15a–b, c–d, 18a–b). This is especially the case at important seams or transition points in the poem. For example, the oracle begins and ends with nonparallelistic sets of lines:

šim'û šāmayim wĕha'ăzînî 'ereṣ	Hear, O heavens, and give ear, O earth,
kî yhwh dibbēr	for Yahweh has spoken (v. 2)....
wĕ'im-tĕmā'ănû ûmĕrîtem	and if you refuse and rebel
ḥereb tĕ'ukkĕlû	then by a sword you will be devoured
kî pî yhwh dibbēr	for the mouth of Yahweh has spoken (v. 20)

Something similar happens midway through the poem at verses 9–10. The first three lines in verse 9 are joined syntactically ("If the Lord of hosts / had not left us a few survivors, / we would have been like Sodom," NRSV), as are the two couplets in verse 10:

> Hear the word of Yahweh,
> O rulers of Sodom.
> Give ear to the teaching of our god,
> O people of Gomorrah.

Thus variation from a rhythmic norm is used to figure (and thus support, highlight) some other poetic dimension—the figure standing out against some ground. In this instance, what is figured are elements of the poem's macro structure.

There is a subtlety and complexity here, too. The feel of parallelism remains strong even amid such obvious deviation, because parallelism yet prevails at other levels. It is there line-internally in v. 2 ("hear, O heavens" // "give ear, O earth"), between the couplets in verses 18–20—the "if.../then...." couplet pattern is repeated four times over, and at a distance between the closing lines in the first couplet and the last triplet (*kî yhwh dibbēr // kî pî yhwh dibbēr*). Similarly in verses 9–10 parallelism prevails line-internally ("we would have been like Sodom, / and become like Gomorrah," v. 9), lexically (hear/give ear, vv. 2, 10; Sodom/Gomorrah, vv. 9, 10), and between couplets ("Hear the word of Yahweh, / O rulers of Sodom" // "Give ear to the teaching of our god, / O people of Gomorrah," v. 10). The parallelism at these other levels compensates, in a fashion, for the lack of strict interlinear parallelism, and thus auditors easily assimilate these deviations from the parallelistic norm, almost unknowingly. Something more than just compensation happens here rhythmically, however. The parallelistic rhythm that prevails in Isaiah 1:2–20, though reminiscent of that of poems such as Proverbs 7 or Psalm 105, is also noticeably different. For one thing, the variation in interlinear linking keeps the poem from succumbing to an overnumbing monotony. And the not infrequent use of enjambment also builds in increments of connectivity (through the syntactic joins) that help stitch the larger poem together. As a result there is a palpable tightness to the poem that belies its informing nonnarrativity—strikingly different from the other two poems discussed, both of which depend (to varying degrees) specifically on elements of story. And by extending the play of parallelism beyond the line to other levels (both below and above the line) the poem's rhythm gains a richness and complexity not present in the other poems—all the while keeping to the kinds of rhythmic gestures so congenial to an oral performative context.

These three poems will suffice to illustrate both the common bilateral pulse that accompanies the parallelistic rhythm of so much biblical verse and the always distinctive manner in which this rhythm is realized in individual poems. Much rhythmic variability is permitted by the manipulation of just two basic parameters, parallelism and enjambment. Another way parallelism may contribute to a biblical poem's overall rhythm is through a finer scripting of the specific structural patterns of matching that parallelism forms from couplet to couplet and triplet to triplet. Here I am not concerned with parallelism qua parallelism in all of is rich diversity but with the specific dispositions of given incidences of parallelism. Parallelism may occur at various levels—grammar, meaning, sound—and in different patterns, all of which are always potentially available for rhythmic manipulation.[272] The short Psalm 114 offers a striking example of how strictly parallelism—in this instance at several levels—may be brought into alignment:

bĕśēʾt yiśrāʾēl mimmiṣrāyim	VP + NP + PP	When Israel went out from Egypt
bêt yaʿăqōb mēʿam lōʿēz	__ + NP + PP	the house of Jacob from a people of strange language
hāyĕtâ yĕhûdâ lĕqodšô	VP + NP + PP	Judah became his holy (one/place)
yiśrāʾēl mamšĕlôtāyw	__ + NP + NP	Israel his dominion
hayyām rāʾâ wayyānōs	NP + VP + VP	the sea looked and fled
hayyardēn yissōb lĕʾăḥôr	NP + __ + VP + PP	the river turned back
hehārîm rāqĕdû kĕʾēlîm	NP + VP + PP	the mountains skipped like rams
gĕbāʿôt kibnê-ṣōʾn	NP + __ + PP	the hills like sheep
mah-llĕkā hayyām kî tānûs	Intrg + NP + prt + VP	what is it to you, O sea, that you flee
hayyardēn tissōb lĕʾăḥôr	__ + NP + __ + VP	O river, that you turn back
hehārîm tirqĕdû kĕʾēlîm	__ + NP + __ + VP + PP	O mountains, that you skip like lambs
gĕbāʿôt kibnê-ṣōʾn	__ + NP + __ + (__) + PP	O hills, like sheep
millipnê ʾādôn ḥûlî ʾāreṣ	PP + VP + NP	from before the Lord writhe, O earth
millipnê ʾĕlôah yaʿăqōb	PP + __ + NP	from before the God of Jacob
hahōpĕkî haṣṣûr ʾăgam-māyim	VP + NP + NP	the one who turned the rock into a pool of water
hallāmîš lĕmaʿyĕnô-māyim	__ + NP + PP	the flinty rock into a spring

Each of the psalm's eight couplets are parallelistic. Both word order and semantics are tightly aligned, with gapping (__) in every second line. Such strict
patterning over the course of a whole poem turns out to be rare in biblical
verse—the psalm's brief compass is likely the chief facilitating factor in this
instance (cf. Num 23:7–10, 18–24; 24:3–9, 15–19). Sometimes specific sections
of a poem will be made to stand out by aligning the lines into mirroring parallelistic shapes, as in the Torah section of Psalm 19 (vv. 8–10). In the small-
scale oracles of Balaam in Num 23:7–10 and 18–24, for example, the lines are
mostly grouped into couplets and triplets through parallelistic frames involving matching word order schemes. The only chiasms appear in the initial
couplet of Numbers 23:7–10 ("**from-Aram** + did-he-bring-me + *Balak,* / *the-
king-of-Moab* + **from-the-eastern-mountains**," v. 7) and the final couplet of
Num 23:18–24 ("he-will-not-lie-down + until + **he-eats** + *the-prey* / *and-the-
blood-of-the-slain* + **he-drinks**," v. 24), setting apart the beginning and ending,
respectively, of these oracles. But the norm is for prominently parallelistic
poems to be composed of sets of lines exhibiting variable parallel patterns,
often at a diversity of levels. The variation counterpoints the repeated use of a
singular trope. The change-up in patterns occasionally point up rhythmic
high points in a poem. For example, the two wonderful vignettes at the end of
Judges 5, the one with Jael (vv. 24–27), the other with Sisera's mother (vv.
28–30), both start out with splashes of chiasm to grab the audience's attention
(vv. 24, 28). But mostly the patterns seem to be in free variation. Yet the net
effect, especially when joined with the fact that most prominently parallelistic
poems always involve a number of enjambed couplets or triplets, is to vary
the rhythmic feel. There is an overwhelming sense of family resemblance
in each biblical poem, as the iterative bilateral thump of parallelism pulses
ever forward. Yet the mixing in of different matching patterns (sometimes
at different levels) and the frequent interweaving of nonparallelistic lines
persistently varies this rhythmic pulse, leavens it just enough, gives it spice
and difference.

Sounds

The segments of meaningful sound that make up a language, called phonemes, are relatively few, and though individually meaningless they are
almost always deployed in language to meaningful ends, to produce morphemes, words, phrases, sentences, and so on. Aside from the odd onomat-
opoetic formation or the result of sound change (e.g., assimilation, vowel
harmony), speech sounds as a rule do not normally or naturally fall into
patterns of repeated sonic effects. This is not to say, of course, that sound, like
the other elements of a language, cannot be organized to sonic ends. It can,

certainly. Sound in language can even be exploited rhythmically.[273] Alliteration—the repetition of word-initial consonantal sounds—plays a significant role in the rhythmic organization of Anglo-Saxon verse. Prototypically there are three alliterations on strongly stressed word-initial syllables per line, two in the first hemistich and one in the second:

Oft **Sc**yld **Sc**ēfing   scea**þ**ena **þ**rēatum,
monegum **m**ǣge**þ**um   **m**eodo-setla oftēah;
There was Shield Sheafson, scourge of many tribes,
a wrecker of mead-benches, rampaging among many foes. (*Beowulf*, ll. 4–5)[274]

The omnipresence of such patterned alliterations establishes a rhythmic base line for many Old English poems, building in continuity and coherence, even amid the constant variation of different alliterating sounds and the not infrequent failures to fully realize the pattern. And end-rhyme, too, may be exploited rhythmically, as in the Hebrew verse of Immanuel of Rome (ca. 1261–1332 CE). The opening stanza of "My breasts are firm" is typical:

šāday nĕkônîm, śa'ărî ṣimmēaḥ,   My breasts are firm and my hair is long,
wā'ēšbâ 'ērōm wĕ'eryâ bōšet.   yet I still sit in nakedness and shame.
dôdîm lĕ'onyî yārĕ'û miggešet,   My poverty has frightened away all of the
wā'ēšbâ bārō'š bĕbêt marzēaḥ.   suitors, and I sit [as if] at the head of
                                         the table in a house of mourning.[275]

The *abba* rhyme scheme provides obvious rhythmic shape for these lines. The scheme is repeated in the second stanza of the sonnet—Immanuel of Rome introduces the sonnet form into Hebrew (and at a very early period!)[276]—and thus helps to gather the *octave* as a structured temporal grouping. The expectation of end-rhyme that this creates in the process is then momentarily frustrated in the first triplet of the sonnet's concluding *sestet*, as none of the line-ending words rhyme with one another or with any of the previous end-rhymes—*cde*. But the concluding triplet eventually satisfies the delayed expectation, providing rhymes (*cde*) to echo the initial triplet's line-ends and creating a happy stasis to the movement of language at the poem's end.

Biblical Hebrew poetry is rife with all kinds of sound plays—alliteration, consonance, assonance, various types of rhyme. Indeed, the play of sound remains an underappreciated dimension of biblical poetics.[277] Still, sound is almost never exploited systematically in the poetry of the Bible. The sonic profile of much biblical poetry, like biblical prose, is the mostly unscripted burble of sound natural to the language itself. When patterns of sound do emerge, even if only briefly, they are often orchestrated to specific ends, including rhythmic ones. Most typically, short runs of repeated sounds punctuate (in deviating from) the otherwise normal cacophonous mixture of sounds in the language. So in the fragment-like poem Song 1:5–8, the *qinah*-shaped couplet in 1:6 is bound together through consonance involving *shin*s, *resh*es, and repeated instances of the first person morpheme *-nî*:

'al-tir'ûnî še'ănî šĕḥarḥōret	Do not gaze at me because I am dark,
šeššĕzāpatnî haššāmeš	because the sun has gazed on me. (NRSV)

Exodus 15 is punctuated three times over by alliterating runs of *aleph*s (vv. 2, 9, 15). A spectacular example of (conscious) alliteration occurs in Eliphaz's speech in Job 5:8, where every word in the couplet, save one, begins with an *aleph*, which Job, then, mimics in Job 13:3.[278] Sometimes these sonic interruptions serve to support rhythmic contours that are articulated at other levels of organization. In Psalm 9–10, for example, the basic rhythmic contour of the poem is indicated graphically through the alphabetic acrostic (see later in this chapter), and the repeated word-initial *aleph* at the head of each of the four lines in the *aleph* stanza provides an extra bit of emphasis isolating the start of the poem—the requisite grapheme (letter) appears only once at the head of all other stanzas. In the *waṣf*-like Song 4:1–7, the first part of the main body of the poem (vv. 1b–2) is distinguished rhythmically chiefly through line grouping (four couplets), word order (fronting of the body part), figures (featuring similes), and semantics (featuring domesticated animals), all of which is supported and underscored by beginning six of the section's eight lines with either a *shin* or *sin*. The opening couplet and closing triplet of Psalm 133 are linked through a threefold repetition of sounds:

/-ām/: the /-ām/ of *šām* "there" and *'ôlām* "forever" in v. 3 echoing the /-am/ of *gam* "also, aloud" in v. 1
/-ā/: the final /-ā/ in *ṣiwwâ* and *habbĕrākâ* (v. 3) echoing the doubled *mah* of v. 1
/-îm/: the /-îm/ of the plural morpheme in *ḥayyîm* (v. 3) resounding in *nā'îm* and *'aḥîm* (v. 1)

Even such slight sound repetition, given the poem's small scale and the enveloping shape achieved, is enough to undergird the poem's sense of unity and signal closure.

Perhaps the Bible's most celebrated bit of rhyming helps to cinch and thus close the poem in Isaiah 5:1–7:

wayqaw lĕmišpāṭ wĕhinnê miśpāḥ	He hoped for justice but instead there was bloodshed,
liṣdāqâ wĕhinnê ṣĕʿāqâ (Isa 5:7)	for righteousness but instead there was outrage.

Here the missed expectations are mimed sonically in the consonantal mismatches in the pairs *mišpāṭ // miśpāḥ* and *ṣĕdāqâ // ṣĕʿāqâ*—the rhyming holds the pairs together so that we can hear the mismatch. Isaiah 5:1–7, like almost all other biblical poems, does not systematically orchestrate one kind of sound effect to any specific end, rhythmic or otherwise. However, in its wide use of various kinds of sound patterns, it comes closer than many other biblical poems to using sound to effect a rhythmic norm (i.e., beyond the semantically directed mishmash of sounds natural to the language): the sixfold repetition of -*î* in the opening couplet and the threefold repetition of segohlates (in the Tiberian tradition) in the second couplet (v. 1); verse 2 opens with three *wayyitol* forms from two different binyanim, which nonetheless are manipulated to effect a repeated cadence (*wayʿazzĕqēhû waysaqqĕlēhû / wayyiṭṭāʿēhû*), while the component lines of the succeeding two couplets are joined through end-rhyme (-*ô*, -*îm*); a splutter of consonance involving *aleph*s and *ayin*s resounds through the opening couplet in verse 5; and line-internal rhyming and chiming punctuates verses 5–7 (e.g., *lōʾ yizzāmēr wĕlōʾ yēʿādēr*, v. 6). This is by no means regularized, but the periodicity of some kind of sound play is sufficient to rival the rhythmic norm of unscripted sounds and to create the anticipation (however nonpredictive) of yet further sonic flourishes. So when the rhyming does come in the poem's final couplet auditors are not at all surprised. Indeed, a great deal of felt satisfaction accompanies such a closing, as if the poem was heading to this way of ending all along, even though we could not have known that ahead of time and even though other means of closing the poem equally satisfactorily are imaginable. The glut of these varied sonic effects also increases the felt density of the language, which, when combined with the semantic opacity of this prophetic oracle (e.g., who is speaking? who owns the vineyard? why is it trampled? why the love theme?), effectively ensures a slower, more measured pace to the poem.

Morphology

How morphology is exploited rhythmically (or otherwise) depends on the nature of the language. For example, inflectional morphology in modern English is spare and minimal (having been eroded over time) and therefore offers little material capable of being grouped and patterned formally. By contrast biblical

Hebrew is a more richly inflected language (evidencing only minor erosions, such as to the original case system on nouns), and its morphology, then, proves a fruitful resource for prosodic manipulation of all sorts, including rhythmic. Most often morphology in biblical poems figures as a part of punctuating or counterpointing rhythmic clusters. Consider the opening couplets of Psalm 142:

qôlî ʾel-yhwh ʾezʿāq	With my voice I cry to the LORD,
qôlî ʾel-yhwh ʾethannān	With my voice I make supplication to the LORD.
ʾešpōk lĕpānāyw śîḥî	I pour out my complaint before him,
ṣārātî lĕpānāyw ʾaggîd	I tell my trouble before him. (NRSV)

The basic rhythmic profile of this lament is established by the syllables and stresses as they are shaped into consistently short lines, averaging seven to nine syllables, three stresses, and three words each. These lines are grouped uniformly into couplets, with but one exception, the triplet of verse 6. The finer rhythmic contours of the poem are figured against this basic ground. Verses 2–3 are a case in point. These lines form the psalm's initial plea. The two couplets are highly troped, making use of parallelism, mirroring and chiastic word orders, word repetition, and morphological patterning. The latter in particular gives these sets of lines their unique rhythmic signature. The first person singular imperfect verb form is used four times in these four lines: *ʾezʿāq*, *ʾethannān*, *ʾešpōk*, and *ʾaggîd*. The first two appear at the end of the lines in a highly parallelistic couplet—verbatim word repetition, except for the verbs and perfectly matching word order. The second couplet is also parallelistic in nature, but here the play of matching is figured chiasticly. So the first line of the couplet is headed by the first person verb form, while the second line concludes with the matching verb, returning to the verb-final word order of the first couplet. There are only three other imperfects in the psalm. The first (*ʾăhallēk*, v. 4) has no obvious rhythmic significance. The second and third occur in the lament's closing couplet (v. 8) and would appear to intentionally echo the poem's opening couplet as a gesture of closure:

bî yaktîrû ṣaddîqîm	The righteous will surround me,
kî tigmōl ʿālāy	for you will deal bountifully with me. (NRSV)

The slightly weakened morphological connection (because of the mismatch in person) is bolstered by the sonic echo in *bî* ("in me") and *kî* ("for, because") of the first person morpheme *-î* that is given structural prominence four times over in the opening couplets—the kind of rhyming that is facilitated by the repetition of the same morpheme is common in inflected languages.

Another example in which repeated verb forms help to shape one of the rhythmic subcontours in a poem comes in Lamentations 2:1–8. The rhythmic baseline of this poem is set by the acrostic and the limping cadence of the *qinah* shaped couplets that are grouped by threes into stanzas. The first section of the poem (vv. 1–8) portrays Yahweh as the Divine Warrior destroying Jerusalem and Judah. Of the thirty-three finite verb forms in this section, thirty are third person masculine singular forms with Yahweh as the subject or implied subject—they are almost all verbs of destruction! And of those thirty, twenty-five are perfects. Nowhere else in the poem is there such a uniform run of verb forms.[279] On a smaller scale is the sevenfold parade of participles in the opening stanza (vv. 8–9) of the poem in Song 2:8–17 used to render the boy's twilight appearance in the guise of a gazelle or deer. The dynamism and durativity implicated by the morphology are crucial to the verisimilitude of the scene. The participles wonderfully map the stop-and-start movements (e.g., *mĕdallēg* "leaping," *mĕqappēṣ* "bounding") so typical of these shy and skittery creatures. There is a palpable dynamism even to the poem's presentation of the gazelle-like boy's coming to a stop outside the wall (*hinnê-zeh ʿōmēd* "then there he is standing"), which when applied to the boy's subsequent staring in at the girl (*mašgîaḥ, mēṣîṣ*) is transformed into a capacious intensity. The actional rhythm pervading this stanza due to the repeated participles is then held in abeyance in the next section of the poem (vv. 10–13) as the girl relates her lover's entreaties chiefly in perfective verb forms. The participle makes a brief reprise in verse 15 in the apostrophe imploring the capture of the scavenging foxes (*Vulpes vulpes*), or, as likely, jackals (*Canis aureus*), as they "are ruining" (*mĕḥabbĕlîm*) the vineyards, and not only the vineyards but the gazelle and dove, too, as they are just the right sort of prey for these opportunistic omnivores. The brief flash of participial energy reaches back rhythmically to the poem's opening stanza.

Lamentations 1, another poem featuring *qinah* couplets grouped into stanzas organized by the alphabetic acrostic, shows that other morphological aspects may be wielded to rhythmic ends as well. Structurally, this poem divides into two halves. In the first half (vv. 1–11) personified Zion's sorry state is described, while Zion herself laments this state in the second half (vv. 12–22). The two halves are distinguished rhythmically by their respective pronominal profiles. The first half is peppered by the serial repetition of third person feminine pronouns (*hîʾ*) and pronominal affixes on nouns (*-āh, -hā*) and verbs (*t-, -â*), while the second half of the poem is characterized by an equal density of first person singular forms (e.g., *ʾănî, -î, -ay, -nî, -tî*).

Similarly, though on a smaller scale, the ninefold use of the first common plural suffix (*-nû*) rhythmically binds together the opening section of Psalm 137 (vv. 1–3). Psalm 142 exhibits an analogous use of pronominal inflection. In this instance, it is not simply the overwhelming use of first person singular forms but the prominence of the /-î/ sound itself in the three separate first person morphemes -î, -nî, and -tî that is noticeable. It appears twenty times in this fairly short poem. Here the rhythmic function is not to articulate a specific contour against a larger ground but to undergird the ground itself. That is, the repeated -îs themselves shore up the cohesion of the whole.

Words

At the lowest syntactic level words group syllables, phonemes, and morphemes into singularities that can be manipulated rhythmically in various ways.[280] Like other discrete syntactic entities (e.g., phrases, clauses, sentences), and especially like the verse line, words may sponsor rhythmic effects both as frames for staging lower level phenomena and as perceptual unities in their own right. The potential for the former has been illustrated already in the foregoing discussion, as stress, rhyme, and the like necessarily enter language, as it were, on the backs of words. The prominence in biblical Hebrew of word-final stress and bisyllabic noun formations gives a general iambic bent to the flow of the language, which potentially could be orchestrated to one rhythmic end or another but mostly is not.[281] So I focus my comments here on the kinds of rhythmic contributions that word repetition can make in biblical poems.[282] M. Buber famously coined the term *Leitwort* ("leading word") to call attention to one common stylistic feature found throughout biblical literature. "By *Leitwort*," Buber writes, "I understand a word or word root that is meaningfully repeated within a text or sequence of texts or complex of texts."[283] The semantic importance of *Leitwörter*—in attending to such repetitions one "will find a meaning of the text revealed or clarified, or at any rate made more emphatic"—generally is now well appreciated in the field and factors prominently in readings of biblical texts. But repeated *Leitwörter* cash out stylistically in a multiplicity of ways beyond bare meaning, as Buber's notice "or at any rate made more emphatic," an attributed rhetorical effect, already hints at.[284] He specifically highlights aesthetics—especially sonic effects—as one dimension of textual meaning to which the repeated *Leitwort* may be marshaled. Rhythm is another. In underscoring the idea that the *Leitwort* in a Semitic language like biblical Hebrew may consist in a "diversity of forms" related by root, Buber remarks that such "diversity of forms" itself "often strengthens the overall dynamic effect."[285] He then continues:

> I say "dynamic" because what takes place between the verbal configurations thus related is in a way a *movement*; readers to whom the whole is

present feel the waves beating back and forth. Such measured repetition, corresponding to the inner rhythm of the text—or rather issuing from it—is probably the strongest of all techniques for making a meaning available without articulating it explicitly.[286]

So from the start Buber is well attuned to the rhythmic possibilities of the *Leitwort*, which in the compressed textual space of a poem become even more pronounced than in the large expanse of prose narrative, the principal focus of Buber's early statements.

A parade example is the use of *qôl* "voice, sound" in Psalm 29. It appears seven times in this relatively short poem—always line-initially and as a part of the larger phrase *qôl yhwh*. The psalm extols Yahweh as the quintessential god of the storm, a metaphorization of the deity that was especially popular in the southern Levant, a region of the world where agriculture depends critically on rain:

qôl yhwh ʿal-hammāyim	The *qôl* of Yahweh over the waters,
ʾēl-hakkābôd hirʿîm	the God of Glory thunders,
yhwh ʿal-mayim rabbîm	Yahweh over mighty waters. (v. 3)

Here the *qôl* is the growl of thunder as it comes off the Mediterranean and approaches the Levantine shoreline, a well-trod storm track. Then an angry outburst of three quick claps of thunder as the storm comes close by, *qôl yhwh* heading the next three lines in succession (vv. 4–5a). This is followed by a slight but eerie lull as one awaits the next peals of thunder to roll through. They come in verse 7, in a sequence of three successive thunderclaps. But this time, the storm at its height, the claps themselves are more sustained—the lines containing *qôl yhwh* lengthen out, as does the intervening space between the last two iterations—and more intense, the rumbles now shaking the ground (v. 8) and the accompanying lightning splitting trees (v. 9; cf. v. 5). The psalm began with a call to laud Yahweh (vv. 1–2) in anticipation of the approaching storm that would make manifest the majestic fury of this god of the storm. The storm itself as it moves across the topography of the poem, uneven in pace (note the punctuating force of the two triplets, vv. 3 and 9, and the lone isolated line, v. 7)[287] but steadily progressing and growing ever more intense, eventually escorting the auditor through to the poem's end, where awestruck the poem's voice beseeches the storm god for the blessing of well-being (*šālôm*) that the rain will bring (v. 11). The pair of closing couplets (vv. 10–11) answers the opening pair (vv. 1–2), the two sets giving voice, adding their voices, however unthematized, to the "voice" (*qôl*) of the storm at the center of this psalm. The poverty of the English lexicon, lacking a single word that means "voice-sound-thunder," saps the psalm in English translation of the bit of its felt movement that depends on the semantics of the *Leitwort*. English readers can appreciate the repetition itself and therefore that part of the rhythm that comes off as a consequence of the sheer force of iteration. But the foregrounding of personification ("the *voice* of Yahweh") of most English translations mutes the storm imagery and the rhythmic contribution that experientially based knowledge of rainstorms makes to the psalm.

Buber distinguished between central and peripheral *Leitwörter*, and even recognized that some repetitions were entirely incidental, and therefore not *Leitwörter* at all.[288] The centrality of *qôl* to Psalm 29 and its import for the psalm's informing rhythm is patent. The psalm opens with the threefold repetition of *hăbû* "give," one each coming at the head of first three lines (vv. 1–2). A peripheral *Leitwort*. Yet this initial threefold succession anticipates the two succeeding runs of threes to come, and thus in its own way jump-starts the stormy movement of the poem, the panicked calls to laud and honor the god of the storm anticipating the impending onslaught of the storm itself.

As a second extended example I consider Song 2:8–17, which features two central Buberian *Leitwörter*, *qôl* and *dôdî*, and a twofold (near) repetition of a set of lines. I begin with the latter because it shows well why Buber emphasized the importance of the meaningfulness of the repetition ("meaningfully repeated" / "in a highly significant manner")[289] and not just its sheer quantity. Up to this point in the Song, the poems gathered have a pronounced sense of fragmentation about them. They are experienced more as bits and pieces than as wholes. Only with the ode-like celebration of springtime love in Song 2:8–17 do more perceptibly articulated poems begin to be encountered. Though fragmentation and disjunction remain dominant sensibilities in Song 2:8–17, too, the staging of the beloved boy's coming and going as a gazelle at the beginning and the end effectively frames the poem as a poem, as a whole. The sets of lines that effect the frame are not exact matches but close enough:

dômeh dôdî liṣbî	My love is like a gazelle,
'ô lĕʿōper hāʾayyālîm	or a young stag (v. 9)
sōb dĕmê-lĕkā dôdî liṣbî	Turn, be like a gazelle, my love,
'ô lĕʿōper hāʾayyālîm	or a young stag (v. 17)

These lines are not placed at the structural extremities of the poem, yet their high significance is palpable and therefore sufficient to register rhythmically. The first set of lines comes in the poem's first stanza and reveals the identity of that which has been bounding and leaping at twilight over the hills, the girl's gazelle-like lover (i.e., her lover imagined as a gazelle). The second set of lines is equally notable, for it reprises the language of the first set—the repetition alone calling attention to itself—and bids the gazelle-boy to flee back into the hills whence he came as the morning breezes gently stir and the night's shadows start to recede—lovers the world over not wishing to be discovered in their tryst.

Considered by themselves, these repeated sets of lines' rhythmic consequences are minimal and mostly structural, effecting an enveloping frame to contain the poem and thus to underline ever so lightly its unity as an integrated movement, a whole—cohesion being another of those multipurposes of Buberian *Leitwörter*.[290] Yet as free rhythm poems tend to effect a complex rhythmic profile made up of multiple and varied elements, it will not come as a surprise that this one rhythmic contour in Song 2:8–17 becomes ever more enriched as it gets stitched into the broader rhythmic fabric of the poem. Now for the central *Leitwörter*, *qôl* and *dôdî*, which (not accidentally) announce themselves immediately as they make up the poem's first line: *qôl dôdî*. *Dôdî* "my love(er)" is the girl's chief pet name for the boy in the Song and is repeated five times over in this poem (vv. 8, 9, 10, 16, 17), occurring in three of the poem's five (vv. 8–9, 10–13, 14, 15, 16–17) stanzas. While lacking the closely packed density of the repeated *qôls* in Psalm 29, still the periodic thump of *dôdî* in this poem, however stretched out, remains palpable, perceptible. Its unevenly spaced fivefold sounding effects a slow, irregularly measured beat that effectively joins one stanza to another, and thereby helping to stitch the body of the poem together, joining it to the opening and closing frames, and to guide and shape temporal experience at the surface of the poem. The two distinct rhythmic contours complement one another and combine to achieve a more complex rhythmic whole.

The rhythmic contribution of *qôl* in this poem is more diffuse and parasitic in nature and difficult to quantify. The term's four repetitions are not really staged to signify consistently throughout the poem, at least not actionally or physically in the manner of the subsisting thump of *dôdî*, for example. Rather, what is foregrounded is ambiguity and density and retrospective patterning, one net rhythmic effect of which is to slow down the pace of the poem. The first mention of *qôl* comes as the poem's first word, and its sense is steadfastly obscured. Neither "sound" nor "voice," the prototypical meanings of the term, are obviously elicited (at least as initially encountered). The appearance at the head of the immediately following line of *hinnê*, chiefly a presentative particle though often rendered in English translations as "Behold! Lo!," suggests that initially *qôl* functions similarly, only at the auditory level, and thus has something like the sense of "Hark!" (cf. Gen 4:10; Isa 52:8; Jer 3:21; Mic 6:9; Zeph

1:14)—so "Hark! My lover!" It eventually becomes clear in verse 9 that it is the "sound" (and then the "sight") of the deer-lover that has caught the speaker's—who we know must be the girl (from her use of *dôdî*)—attention. By metaphorizing the boy as a gazelle the poem's auditors can readily fill in from their experiential knowledge base the kind of scene required, for example, one where the snap of a twig or the rustle of the brush would alert one to a deer's presence. But what is crucial to see with respect to the poem's overall rhythmic sensibility is how this initial staging of this single instance of *qôl*, layering how it means, already retards, slows down, counterpoints the otherwise natural temporal thrust of the language—the diffuseness of the semantics clogging cognitive uptake.

In verse 10 the girl then recollects what the boy says to her ("my love answered and said to me"), presumably while standing outside her wall and window (cf. v. 9). Here, then, the poem's initial word takes on its other main meaning, "voice," and again it does so retrospectively. That is, the poem's auditors hear the girl relaying what the boy said to her. She ventriloquizes his voice, and thus there is a kind of ghosting of *qôl* here that though not literal is still palpable. The play of *qôl*, even in the absence of literal iteration, slows the poem's (perceptual) pace so as to enable the cognitive processing necessary to its understanding.

The first literal iteration of *qôl* occurs in verse 12, where the boy (as revocalized by the girl) reports the reemergence of birdsong (lit. "the sound/voice [*qôl*] of the turtledove") with the onset of spring. So *qôl* again finds itself attached to the animal world. This holds as well for the final two renditions of the term in the short stanza making up verse 14. Here the imagery changes. Now the girl is addressed by the boy as "my dove" (*yônātî*), a favored pet name of the boy for his lover (5:2; 6:9) and thus imagined as a "dove" (nesting safely high in the craggy cliffs). The boy continues speaking (as restaged by the girl) and begs of her, "Let me hear your voice [*qôlēk*] / for your voice [*qôlēk*] is sweet." Here, then, the girl's dove-like voice formally and semantically recoups and reiterates the earlier mention of the "voice of the (turtle)dove [*tôr*]" in verse 12. This voiced (and revoiced) animal desire, as it were, calls forth the girl's own voice, heard first in the apostrophe in verse 15 and then in the closing extolling of her love and her bid for him to flee (vv. 16–17). This nonanimally figured voicing of the girl, like that attributed earlier to the boy (v. 10), also goes unmarked at the surface of the poem, and thus adds to the poem's rhythmic density. Moreover, this rendered resumption of the girl's voice provokes an awareness that the entire poem is voiced by her, suffused in her voice, and thus achieves a kind of vocal unity. As it turns out no part of the poem is untouched by voice, literal (*qôl*) or figured. The girl's "voicing" that is the poem may be heard at once as a response in kind to the "sound" (v. 8) and then "voice" (vv. 10–13) of her lover and as the very "voice" that the boy so desires to hear (v. 14). And these "voicings," then, join in with the other "voices"/"sounds" of spring (v. 12) to form a virtual chorus.

A final, brief worked example may be given in order to illustrate Buber's awareness that words (e.g., nouns and verbs) in biblical Hebrew (and Semitic languages generally) have in the bare root ("the sequence of consonants that stay constant in a set of verbs and nouns with meanings in some semantic field") a "direct formal derivational source" beyond the specific lexeme that potentially may be exploited poetically and rhythmically.[291] Psalm 111 is a hymn shaped formally as an alphabetic acrostic—in this instance each succeeding line of the psalm is headed by the appropriate successive letter of the Hebrew alphabet, starting with *aleph*, the first letter of the Hebrew alphabet, and proceeding letter by letter and line by line through to the final letter, *taw*. In this way the line is defined (just as effectively as by anaphora or end-rhyme) and the psalm's overarching (lineal) rhythmic pace established. After an introductory couplet of praise (v. 1), the psalm divides into two halves: the first (vv. 2–7a) is made up of a couplet and three succeeding triplets, while the second (vv. 7b–10c) consists of a triplet and three couplets. The sixfold repetition of the root *ʿ-ś-h* "to do, make" helps to fine point this structural grouping. The first stanza is circumscribed by a chiasm involving *maʿăśê* (*maʿăśê yhwh*, v. 2a // *maʿăśê yādāyw*, v. 7a), with two additional repetitions of the root coming in between (*ʿāśâ*, v. 4a; *maʿăśāyw*, v. 6a). All reference Yahweh's doing or deeds. The opening triplet (vv. 7b–8) and closing couplet (vv. 10b–c) of the second stanza similarly feature the root *ʿ-ś-h*, though this time the reference is to Israel's practical response to these divine deeds/doings (*ʿăśûyīm*, v. 8b; *ʿōśêhem*, v. 10b).[292] In other words, the psalm's basic alphabetic pace is punctuated repeatedly by words derived from the root *ʿ-ś-h* such that the basic stanzaic structure of the poem is given additional rhythmic expression.[293]

Meaning

Allen says that the parallelism of biblical poetry (and by extension of Whitman) "may be called a rhythm of thought."[294] In a way this is misleading,[295] as it places the emphasis wrongly on semantics, something that Lowth's own exposition and the exigencies of translation can encourage. And yet it also gets right something very crucial about the rhythm of nonmetrical verse: namely, that meaning is always one of the linguistic elements potentially relevant to a poem's fully expressed rhythm. As R. G. Moulton (one of Allen's sources of knowledge about biblical verse) stresses, "thought may be rhythmic as well as language, and the full meaning and force of Scripture is not grasped by one who does not feel how thoughts can be emphasized by being differently re-stated, as in the simplest couplet; or how a general thought may reiterate itself to enclose its particulars, as in the envelope figure."[296] In fact, human physiology requires the rhythmicity of thought, as Jousse well understood: "The *earliest [rhythmic schema] was, then, not [an expression] of feeling, but above all, [a mnemonic expression] of thought.*"[297] If Jousse emphasizes the role of rhythm in the creation and preservation of ideas, Hrushovski stresses how meaning—semantics—is part of the language material available to the shaping of rhythm in poetry: "Inasmuch as elements of meaning…take part in the shaping of the rhythm, we have to describe them as real structural elements existing in the written poem."[298] In a sense, of course, there can be no question of bracketing out meaning from language art, as Smith well emphasizes from the very beginning of her study. Part of what makes the "temporal and dynamic qualities" of poetry more complex than music is the double-sided nature of language, the fact that a language's formal elements always come enshrouded with meaning.[299]

One ready way to feel the potential rhythmic contribution of meaning is to recall how the manipulation of plot can speed up or slow down the pace of a story, interrupt it, or build to a satisfying ending. An example from Ugaritic narrative verse by way of illustration. One convention used to give verisimilitude to the passing of time is the count of seven days, as in the instructions given for Kirta's journey:

lk. ym. wṯn.	March a day, and a second.
ṯlṯ. rbʿ ym	A third, a fourth day.
ḥmš. ṯdṯ. ym.	A fifth, a sixth day.
mk. špšm bšbʿ.	Then at sunrise on the seventh…(CAT 1.14.III.2–4)

The bare count itself mimics, economically, the passage of seven days, and time's arrow—ever moving forward—provides the sequence with its implicit direction. But when it comes to the report of Kirta's actual journey, the march is interrupted after day three so that Kirta may make a vow to Asherah of Tyre:

tlkn ym. wṯn.	They marched a day, and a second.
aḥr špšm. bṯlṯ	After sunrise on the third…(CAT 1.14.IV.31–33)

Only after giving details about the vow (ll. 34–43) does the sequential conceit resume, and Kirta finally arrives at his destination after another four days:

ylk ym. wtn.	He marched a day, and a second.
tlt. rbʿ. ym.	A third, a fourth day.
aḫr. špšm. brbʿ	After sunrise on the fourth … (CAT 1.14.IV.44–46)

The implied directionality of the story's movement continues to project a for-ward thrust. The pace of the story (and its telling) in being interrupted, how-ever, is slowed, allowing for the conveyance of information that will prove crucial to the story's plot. The sequential movement stalls momentarily. The contrast in the two sequences is all the more telling as most of the narrative report is itself almost a verbatim repetition of the instructions given to Kirta in his dream—the major difference being the shift in the verbs from impera-tives to finite forms.

Narrative verse is mostly missing from the Bible, though there are smaller runs of narrative here and there and they, too, manipulate meaning and the-matic structure to rhythmic ends. Proverbs 7 contains one such narrative run (vv. 6–23), briefly described earlier. The poem itself is didactic in orientation, framed by sets of lines (vv. 1–5, 24–27) urging the adolescent boys who are the poem's intended audience to beware of the seduction of the other woman—the woman, that is, who is not their wife. That is, the inset narrative is not there ultimately to serve its own narrative ends but as a parade example as to why the boys should not let their "hearts turn aside to her ways" (v. 25). Still, the narrative evolves its own rhythm in its telling and meaning plays its part in a number of different ways. The lineal pace is established by the didactic frame as the couplet—the line grouping pattern that characterizes Proverbs more generally. That is, the narrative unfolds couplet by couplet, with but a single triplet, verse 7.[300] The slight retardation that accompanies the added line of the triplet here is reinforced semantically in that the foolish boy who serves as the poem's negative example is introduced in this added line: "a lad lacking in heart." Meaning here is crucial to pace. Progress stops briefly while the boy enters the narrative. Indeed, this is a good example of where rhythmic prominence gets registered at various levels, and thus thickened and under-scored—the meaningful unveiling of the boy coinciding with the break in the heretofore repeated run of parallelistic couplets. The next change in rhythm comes with the introduction in verse 10 of the other woman, who is said to be "wily of heart" in contrast to the boy's "lacking of heart." And as if to under-score this point her initial characterization (vv. 10–12) is rendered in lines packed with content words, usually two (nouns, participles, infinitives, finite verbs) per line. This contrasts with the far simpler (lines mostly of single clauses or phrases) depiction of the simple (senseless) boy at the outset of the narrative. This overcrowding with meaning words creates density and intensity.

So the depiction of the woman in verses 11–12 as "bustling and restive" (NJV), who cannot keep her feet planted at home, but is "now in the street, now in the square, / and beside every corner she lies in wait," takes on a rollicking rhythm that mimes the content. Here again meaning shades the same basic rhythmic contour effected through the poem's deployment of parallelism (see earlier discussion in this chapter). The perceived rhythm changes from the leisurely amble of the boy wandering the streets to the hustle and bustle of a woman up to no good. The uptick in pace and frenzy reaches a crescendo of sorts in verse 13, which has the only couplet in the poem containing two finite verbs in each of its component lines. The characterization of the woman has impeded all actual narrative progression—basically we have been told that the woman went out to meet the boy (v. 10). Then all of a sudden the action leaps forward, compelled quite literally by the woman's habitual frantic activity. Note that her lying in wait at every corner (v. 12) picks up on and replays the language used earlier of the boy, who, not accidentally, was "passing through the street beside her corner" (v. 8). The two must meet, and they do:

> She seizes him and kisses him,
>   and with impudent face she says to him … (v. 13)

Again it is meaning that is key. Two finite action verbs charge the narrative with activity. This jolt forward is almost immediately checked with the introduction of the woman's speech (vv. 14–20)—although this speech is the heart of the seduction that the wise teacher has warned about (v. 5; cf. v. 21): a turning over of sorts of the "persuasion to love" that provides the basic logic of many love poems (e.g., Song 2:10–13).[301] Still, literal narrative action pauses for the woman's "smooth speech." After she finishes, the close of the narrative comes quickly. The heavy-handed, didactic narrator, making sure his adolescent audience does not miss the point, informs us that the seduction succeeds (v. 21). So we are not surprised to learn in the next couplet (v. 22) that the boy follows after her, ultimately risking his own life. This woman, we learn in her seduction, is married, but her husband is away. The penalty for adultery (sex with a married woman) can be death for both paramours. The similes at the tale's end (vv. 22–23)—"like an ox to the slaughter," "like a stag toward the trap," "like a bird into a snare"—underscore the senselessness of the risk and slow the story so that its stopping may be savored.

In this way the temporal sequencing of the story logic itself has rhythmic implications. Its ebb and flow, bursts of energy and sudden pauses, shapes the very movement of the tale, places emphasis, engineers mimetic effects, and implicates closure—the woman who sets out at the beginning of the story to seduce the boy with her "smooth lips" (v. 21)—both literally, in her kissing of him (v. 13), and figuratively, in the content of her speaking (vv. 14–20)—by the end succeeds, with the boy going along after her to her house and perfumed bed (v. 22; cf. vv. 16–17). In the end, Proverbs 7 as a poem is more than this little story. At verse 24 the poem breaks out of the narrative mode, and the voice of the wise teacher returns to reiterate the moral of the tale: "Do not let your heart turn aside to her ways, / do not stray onto her paths" (v. 25). The framing redoubles the story's sense of closure. And Proverbs 7 as a whole also has its own felt-sense of closure, of wholeness. The enveloping didactic frames inscribe this formally, but there is also a thematic logic to the poem's argument.[302] The logic is not that of a formal syllogism involving chains of reasoning but a more informal logic of traditional wisdom. The authoritative voice of tradition commands attention and assent (vv. 1, 24): beware of the other woman who is not your wife (cf. Exod 20:17; Deut 5:21; Ezek 22:11; Prov 6:24, 29). The little tale is there to make the moral stick in the adolescent male mind. At poem's end, then, this traditional wisdom logic projects wholeness and closure no less satisfying than the temporal logic that undergirds the telling of the tale at the center of the poem.

The dialogues of Job (Job 3–41) are rife with the logic of argument. It is not an overly formal logic or philosophical in the Greek mode. Rather it answers more obviously to the less formal kind of argument that Smith identifies as typical in much lyric verse: "If we are engaged in supporting a point, making a case, or persuading an audience to do or believe something, our argument is likely to develop informally and irregularly through analogies, examples, and inferences, and to be interrupted by digressions or elaborations."[303] Smith's special focus in her monograph is on how poems end, so what she finds most interesting about logical sequence in poems, even of this less formal variety, is how it is most pointedly "directed toward a *conclusion*."[304] This directedness—that the words must mean one thing and not another, for example, or must be sequenced in one way and not another—will have rhythmic consequences readily apparent even without close analysis. To reveal the specific rhythmic contribution that the logical sequencing of any one of Job's speeches, or that of his friends, or of Elihu, or of the voice from the storm-wind, of course, does require exposition. But the fact of meaning's rhythmicity in such logically argumentative poetry seems plain enough (e.g., evident in the summative, moral closings of some Joban poems, such as Job 18:21, 20:29, and 28:28). And in a similar vein, to the extent that much prophetic verse is meant to persuade to one end or another, meaning there, too, may be safely assumed to be organized and thus potentially important to a specific poetic oracle's overall achieved rhythm. Amos's famous counting oracle ("For three transgressions.../ and for four...") in 1:3–2:16 is not atypical. Each of the subsections of the oracle focuses on a local polity (e.g., Damascus, Tyre, Ammon). The prophet announces Yahweh's judgment: because (*'al*) of that polity's crimes, which are spelled out, Yahweh sends some kind of disaster (e.g., fire) by way of punishment. The logic is always sequential. The punishment is triggered by the crime. The phrasal movement of the specified punishment is always at first a moving away from (as a consequence of) the stipulated crime, but also an arrival of sorts, as the logic is such that the punishment fits the crime. This arrival is then underscored in the larger poem by the bit of stasis incurred by the transition to a new polity, with the repetition of the counting trope, namely "for three transgressions.../ and for four..." The same basic sequential logic and phrasal movement obtains in each of the individual subsections. The logic of the larger whole is more paratactic than sequential. The ordering of the polities treated is not crucial, except for Israel, the ultimate focus of the oracle, which must come last. There must be a sufficient number of other polities in order to build up familiarity with the basic pattern (counting trope, crimes, punishments) and thus create a forward-projecting expectation in anticipation of the next iteration of the pattern— variation on a theme is one of the more common forms of paratactic structure. The identity of the polities is important. For an Israelite audience they must all be non-Israelite. That is, the prophet is playing on a bit of ethnocentrism, an "us versus them" logic. The polities are all Levantine, and an Israelite audience would have appreciated that regional competitors are to come in for a bit of misfortune. In fact, the prophet was surely counting on his audience's easy assent as he moved through his parade of polities—what polities, with what meaning, definitely matter. The gotcha comes in the oracle's last and longest subsection (2:6–16), as Israel comes under the same scrutiny and judgment. One of the fundamental problems for paratactic structure is closure. There is no inherent means within paratactic structure to determine a concluding point. One common mechanism is to alter the basic pattern at the end, and in that way communicate the onset of closure, what Smith calls "terminal modification."[305] In this instance, the formal pattern remains in place, though it is elongated, which supports the closural force of this subsection. But the principal change, what stops the poem dead, is the shift in focus to Israel rather than another non-Israelite polity—the subsection dedicated to Judah (if original) immediately preceding the Israel subsection (2:4–5) telegraphs something of the oracle's ultimate telos. Everything else remains the same. The Israelite audience has by now bought into the logic that crimes (social or political) logically require redress and punishment. The same holds true even when the focus is Israel itself.

Meaning, thus, is crucial to the rhythmic flow of the oracle throughout. It provides the basic direction of the phrasal rhythm within each of the oracle's subsections. These thrusts of movement are checked briefly as the transitions are made to succeeding subsections. This basic sequential logic and movement of the subsections is layered over with the repetitive movement of the larger whole. As the patterns get repeated time and again, the ever forward movement of parataxis begins to be felt. But the whole is brought to a stunning halt by a single word, Israel: "For three transgressions of *Israel*, / and for four, I will not revoke the punishment" (Amos 2:6). A paradigm example of how lexical meaning can impact rhythmic movement in a poem. Or after Cureton, how a certain kind of rhythmic prominence (in this case a breaking of forward movement) is established by semantic or informational prominence.[306] Another name and the beat goes on. The beat and oracles do go on, for another bunch of verses, in fact. But the momentum of the poetry has changed dramatically, effectively stopping all forward progress as attention has shifted to the in-group. There is no possibility that the poem might continue on after this to tally another nation.

If meaning's contribution to the rhythm of narrative, didactic, and even many prophetic poems, given the sequential structures endemic to such poems, is easily specified and conceptualized, this is no less true of more paratactically or associatively organized poems, though the logic is different enough. My brief look at Amos 1:3–2:16 has already illustrated some of how parataxis projects rhythmic movement. Here I consider a final example by way of underscoring and elaborating on the rhythmic possibilities in paratactic and associative thematic structures, since a goodly portion of biblical verse exhibits these kinds of structures. The key point is that meaning still matters, even if sequential logic is not paramount. My example is the individual lament of the Psalms; the distinguishing features of this genre of psalm are almost all thematic in nature, namely address, complaint, petition, motivations, and expression of confidence,[307] and are structured paratactically, though the form the structure takes is indebted ultimately to the "list," another common kind of parataxis and well-known ancient Near Eastern genre.[308] The use of literal lists, with their paratactic logic, is well evidenced in biblical poetry, whether in the summing trope of Proverbs 30:18–19 ("Three things are too wonderful for me; / four I do not understand: / the way of an eagle.../ snake.../ ship.../ man with a girl") or Isaiah's judgment of the "daughters of Zion" featuring a list of finery that Yahweh will take away (Isa 3:16–26). In each of the latter cases the paratactic logic of the list is supplemented and shaped by theme, and with the proverb, also by a mathematical logic—recall that all paratactic structure requires something additional (to the generating principle of parataxis) to conclude it or change it in any way. The informing paratactic structure of the individual lament is list-like. It is no conventional list. What gets listed are precisely those thematic elements that constitute a lament, that is, address, complaint, and the like. We know the basic stock of elements that get listed because the individual lament is one of the best attested psalmic genres. What has bedeviled scholarship is the underlying paratactic logic of this kind of poem. Tacitly scholars have wanted to discover a sequential logic that would make sense out of these poems, that would ensure that we know when they begin and end and why. This likely reflects readerly experience with much contemporary poetry (or what Smith glosses as more "sophisticated poems") in which lines and stanzas "usually 'follow' from one another, either logically, temporally, or in accord with some principle of serial generation."[309] Smith elaborates the distinction between paratactic and nonparatactic thematic structure in this way:

> In a nonparatactic structure (where, for example, the principle of generation is logical or temporal), the dislocation or omission of any element will tend to make the sequence as a whole incomprehensible, or will radically change its effect. In paratactic structure, however, (where the principle of generation does not cause any one element to "follow" from another), thematic units can be omitted, added, or exchanged without destroying the coherence or effect of the poem's thematic structure.[310]

Individual laments are of the latter, paratactic nature. As a rule, no sequential logic prevails, and (most) individual elements can be omitted, added, exchanged, or reordered without destroying the essential identity of the psalm type itself—the sense that a lament is well achieved and does what laments do, lament, complain.

All of this eventually bears on the kind of rhythmic experiences that can be projected semantically by an individual lament. The most noticeable rhythmic effect is the pronounced disjointedness and fragmentation that typify the lament as a whole. With only minimal or no (logical, temporal, figurative) connections among constituent elements, the rhythm tends to pulse, being brightest and strongest within the individual elements themselves, and then abruptly dissipates and fragments as a new, (mostly) unmotivated element is encountered with its own distinct rhythmic pulse. The resulting bumpiness and disjuncture become part of the rhythmic signature of such a poem. It is only weakly directed, if at all, and whatever final sense of coherence or stability a given lament achieves from its thematic content is achieved mainly retrospectively, at the end of the psalm. Only then can an auditor assess fully whether what has been experienced contains enough constituent elements to give the lament identity as a lament.[311]

Of course, form and content work together in all poems. So even in laments rhythm will have other resources than what is offered thematically. Consider Psalm 13, already treated some earlier, as a first example. It is brief (only twelve lines) but otherwise a typical psalmic lament. The psalm breaks into three stanzas, verses 2–3, 4–6, and 6. The lament opens with a threefold complaint (about Yahweh, the suffering, and the enemy) measured out in five fairly long lines (seven to twelve syllables, mostly containing four content words—there is a single short line that forms the second, shorter line in the qinah-shaped couplet in v. 3), four of which are headed by ʿad-ʾānâ "How long?" The anaphora provides these opening lines with its basic rhythmic punch, supporting the repeated complaint. The succeeding stanza (vv. 4–5) is composed of two parallelistic couplets that petition the deity ("Look! Answer me!") with motivations mixed in ("Lest I die, lest my foes rejoice!"). There is no overt thematic reason for the petition to come where it comes in this lament—in Psalm 3 it comes at the end (vv. 8–9); in Psalm 7 at the beginning and again in the middle (vv. 2–3, 10); and in Psalm 25 the entire beginning (vv. 1–7) and end (vv. 16–22) of the lament are shaped as petitions. So there is a juncture to be negotiated, and then a new slightly different rhythmic contour starts up. The lines are a little shorter (ten syllables, four words per line in the first couplet; eight syllables, three words per line in the second couplet). This has something of a tapering-down effect, which is supported by the reduction in number of lines from five to four. The pattern continues in the final stanza, which is composed of three slightly shorter (on average) lines (nine syllables, three words in two of the three lines), the chief effect of which is to give the movement of language in this lament some minimal sense of directionality—a narrowing down to the end.[312] The repetitive rhythm of the iterated ʿad-ʾānâs takes on a more pronounced binarism in these verses as both couplets are shaped parallelistically, with the repeated syntagm pen + VP joining the two together (syntactically and through the repetition itself) and in the process reprising a short burst of the iterative rhythm from the first stanza. The transition to the closing triplet (v. 6), in which the lamenter confides trust in Yahweh and the promise of song, again is turbulent. Expressions of trust and convictions of being heard are common in laments, helping to imprint the prototypical comic shape that biblical laments tend to have. And although such expressions are found at the ends of laments (e.g., Ps 7:18; 17:15; 27:13–14; 35:28; 54:8–9), there is nothing semantically to signal that the lament's abrupt end is at hand. Perhaps the strongest signal of closure is belated, the silence that would follow an oral performance or the extra bit of spacing in a manuscript (e.g., as in the Aleppo Codex) that separates this psalm from the one that follows. Then, on reflection, the slightly tapered shape of the psalm, the fact that the final triplet begins with the poem's lone conjunctive *waw*, and the lack of any consistent rhythm in the final three lines—a kind of letting go or unwinding—will add some satisfaction to the poem's closing. An awareness that Yahweh is named once in each stanza—in the first lines of the first two stanzas and in the final line of the last stanza—and that ics forms (nineteen in total) clutter the whole, build in yet more layers (however thin) of constancy and coherence. And there are also enough of those list-like elements that typify a lament (address, complaint, petition, expression of trust) to make clear the psalm's identity as a lament, but again mostly appreciated retrospectively. There is no question that Psalm 13 has a distinctive and crafted rhythm, but it is pocked by juncture and disturbance, lacking in any strong sense of semantic predictability.

Like all convention-based knowledge, habituation brings the possibility of richer appreciation. But even then endless possibilities remain for modulating the rhythm of any single lament. Length alone is an obvious catalyst. Psalm 13's bumpy and fragmented rhythm is quite abbreviated when compared to a much longer lament, such as Psalm 22 (thirty-two verses) or Psalm 35 (twenty-eight verses). Thematic additions, repetitions, and omissions will inevitably impact the placement of rhythmic prominence. Psalm 88 is a striking example. Aside from the opening petition to Yahweh (vv. 2–3: "Let my prayer come before you!"), the entire lament (vv. 4–18) consists of complaint, much of which is directed pointedly at Yahweh. There is no missing what is thematically prominent here. The omission of all other elements, including most especially any sentiment of trust or confidence of being heard, gives this lament a distinctly tragic trajectory. And far from the interruptive rhythm of most biblical laments, here the unrelenting repetition of one complaint after another has a suffocating feel about it. The repeated complaints pound and suffuse the auditor in the way the speaker of the lament is assaulted and surrounded, day and night, by terrible suffering.

Visual and Spatial Matters

Once poems begin to be written down in ancient Israel and Judah, script and metascript conventions of writing (e.g., spacing, page layout) become available to be organized rhythmically. An early and persistent worry about (modern) free verse is that its identity as verse is all courtesy and typography—that is, "convention and lineation." Aside from the fact that what counts as poetry (and prose) is always unavoidably a matter of cultural convention, Smith reasonably responds,

> We should recognize that there is nothing illegitimate in the free-verse poet's exploitation of courtesy and typography...to help define the formal structure of his poem and control the reader's perception of its rhythm....While it is evident that certain [modern] varieties of free verse could not flourish in a culture without printing or at least writing, it is just as evident that not all free verse depends upon typography for its form or or the determination of its lines.[313]

The latter part of Smith's comment is even more "evident" when speaking about free rhythmic verse that emerges out of traditional, (dominantly) oral cultures where the spatialization of verse is either unknown or belated and then restricted to a small class of elites. Poems in oral cultures must evolve their prosodies in the absence of writing and the conventions of writing. Certainly there was no book culture during the time of Israel and Judah's historical existence. Any readers were generally restricted to the professional class of scribes and some small number of elites. One of the large arguments of this book is that poetic art is immanently achievable outside highly literate contexts. Once poems begin to be written down, the earlier part of Smith's comment is just as evident: why indeed should not those (ever evolving) conventions of writing become potentially exploitable rhythmically, even if for only a relatively small group of elites (and as cues for vocal performance)?

Appreciation of biblical poetry has been persistently blunted by a cultural myopia consisting on the one hand of the thought that conventions for spatializing verse are of one kind and universally available (namely, the one-verse-line-per-columnar-line format inherited in the West from ancient Greek custom) and on the other hand of the seemingly allied notion that verse qua verse comes spatialized and distinguished from other forms of writing (especially prose). Neither assumption can withstand cultural or historical scrutiny with any depth or breadth. Biblical poems do eventually get written down, and the conventions of this writing down begin to play a role in a poem's overall rhythm. The most obvious example where the conventions of writing implicate themselves rhythmically is the alphabetic acrostic.[314] The basic conceit of an acrostic is that the initial letters or signs of each line, couplet, or stanza, when read in succession, spell out a name, sentence, alphabet, or alphabetic pattern. In the Bible, the fifteen partial or complete acrostics (Nah 1:2–9; Pss 9–10, 25, 34, 37, 111, 112, 119, 145; Prov 31:10–31; Lam 1–4; Sir 51:13–30), as well as the three acrostics from Qumran (11QPsᵃSirach = Sir 51:13–30; 11QPsᵃZion;

11QPsª155),[315] are all alphabetic in nature. That is, they (mostly) spell out the Hebrew alphabet, in one or the other of its two traditional orders, with the initial letter of each line, couplet, or stanza. So, for example, in Psalm 111, the first word (*'ôdeh* "I give thanks") of the first line of the psalm begins with *aleph* (the first letter of the Hebrew alphabet), the first word (lit. a preposition + a word, *bĕsôd* "in the company") of the second line begins with the next letter in the Hebrew alphabet, *bet*, and so on, proceeding successively letter by letter through the alphabet with each new line, until reaching *taw*, the last letter of the Hebrew alphabet (cf. Ps 112). Other patterns are attested as well. In Psalm 145 and Proverbs 31:10–31, the acrostic shapes the initial line of every couplet, instead of every line; while in Psalm 37 and Lamentations 1, 2, and 4, only the initial line of each stanza is constrained by the alphabetic pattern. Lamentations 3 and Psalm 119 evidence the two most complex usages of the acrostic: in both, every couplet in each of the multicouplet stanzas (Lam 3 has three couplets per stanza; Ps 119 has eight couplets per stanza) is made to follow the appropriate alphabetic sequence. Further, in several psalms (Pss 9–10, 25, 34), a letter or two is missing—whether through intention or accident is not always apparent; the half acrostic (*aleph* throughout *kaph*) in Nahum 1:2–9 appears to be deployed with some intention (cf. 11QPsª155). Another variation on this form is exhibited in Psalms 25 and 34. Both omit the *waw* couplet and add an additional *pe* couplet at the end (cf. 11QPsªSirach), and as a result the initial letters of the first, middle, and final couplets in the poems may be read to spell out *'lp*, the name of the first letter of the Hebrew alphabet.[316] Finally, several of the poems (Ps 9–10; Lam 2, 3, and 4; LXX of Prov 31:10–31) exhibit a variant ordering of the alphabet, wherein *pe* precedes *ayin* instead of the more normative *ayin* before *pe* sequence.

I say the acrostic is the most obvious example of a kind of poem where writing impinges on rhythm because it is a trope of writing and explicitly visual in orientation—that is, it needs to be seen in order to work. This is most readily apparent in the acrostics from Mesopotamia, Greece, and even the postbiblical Hebrew poetic corpus that spell out names or sentences (e.g., "I, Saggilkinamubbib, am adorant of god and king," from the *Babylonian Theodicy*)[317]—they literally can only be read, not heard. But this is also evident in poems such as Lamentations 1 and 2, where the alphabetic frame (occurring only once every six lines) would hardly be recognizable if it were only a matter of aurality[318]—repetition, as in Lamentations 3 or Psalm 119, or a very brief compass and relatively straightforward content would be required to hear (without the aid of vision) the patterned sequence of alphabetic sounds. Indeed, the acrostic may well be among the earliest unequivocal visual tropes in literary history.[319] That the alphabetic acrostic is itself a trope of writing is suggested above all by the fact that its likely inspiration was a very common kind of scribal school text, the abecedary. Abecedaries are exercise texts in which students (scribes) practice writing the letter forms of the alphabet, usually in a standard order. The earliest extant West Semitic abecedaries come from Ugarit (ca. thirteenth century BCE), where, in the alphabetic cuneiform syllabary created to write the local Northwest Semitic dialect, more than a dozen tablets have so far been recovered from the ongoing excavations at Ras Shamra (the main tell of ancient Ugarit) and its environs that contain abecedaries (CAT 5.4, 5, 6, 8, 9.I.le.e., r.e., 12, 13, 16, 17, 19, 20, 21, 24, 25; RS 88.2215; see fig. 32).[320] The earliest abecedary written in the early linear alphabetic script comes from Izbet Sarta and dates to around 1200 BCE (fig. 33).[321] The fifth line of this ostracon contains a complete abecedary written horizontally from left to right. And significantly the order of the signs in this line is the *pe-ayin* sequence reflected in some of the biblical acrostics. Ancient Hebrew abecedaries are attested from Kuntillet Ajrud (*KA* 3.11–14; ca. 800 BCE; fig. 34), a caravan site in the Sinai,[322] and now also there is the Tell Zayit stone, on which an abecedary (with several pairs of letters in variant orders, e.g., *waw-he*) is carved (ca. mid-tenth century BCE).[323]

What links the biblical acrostics to the abecedary is that both evidence the same two (dominant) traditions for sequentially ordering the alphabet and especially that the alphabetic conceit as attested in the acrostics is itself shaped by the number of graphemes (i.e., the letter signs themselves) of the Hebrew alphabet (twenty-two), and not the number of phonemes (ultimately twenty-three). By way of confirmation of the latter, note in particular the variation in the *šin/śin* lines, couplets, and so on in the biblical acrostics. That poems can use words beginning with either *šin* (e.g., Ps 25:20; 34:21; 112:10) or *śin* (e.g., Ps 111:10; Lam 4:21), or even *šin* and *śin* in multiline stanzas (e.g., Ps 119:161–68; Lam 3:61–63), but no poems have disparate *šin* and *śin* segments (i.e., in Ps 119 there is not an eight-couplet *śin* stanza followed by an eight-couplet *šin* stanza, but only the one *šin/śin* stanza with the variation noted) shows that the conceit is graphemic in origin—*šin* and *śin* share the same grapheme (sign) in the Hebrew script (ש), though they are distinct phonemes.[324]

Literarily, the alphabetic acrostic is polyvalent, with rhythm featuring among the variety of ways it signifies. The alphabetic frame paces these poems, measuring out a more or less regular beat with the succession of letter forms; builds in coherence and signals closure, as the acrostic quite literally holds the poems together, like a container; and through its long-standing, conventional sequence of letter forms (i.e., *aleph, bet, gimel*, etc.) guides the reader from beginning to end.

In the aftermath of writing—and certainly post-Gutenberg—readers of poems must always be prepared to reckon with the possibility of poems appealing (even if only ambiguously) to both ear and eye. As for those contemporary free verse poems that "do rely on typographical lineation for clues to formal structure," says Smith, "we might as well concede that they exist"— William Carlos Williams being the parade modernist example.[325] For a stunning example of how the acrostic in an ancient poem may contribute visually to that poem's rhythm, consider Psalm 119 again, but now as it is presented in 11QPs[a] (fig. 35). The longest surviving Psalms scroll from Qumran (measuring almost five meters), 11QPs[a] appears to be nearly complete and contains most of the psalms known from Books IV and V of the MT-150 Psalter (i.e., parts of psalms from Ps 93–150), albeit often in different sequences and with differences in content, including an additional ten or eleven psalms not contained in MT. The psalms collected in this scroll are written in a running format, with spacing and indentation used to distinguish individual psalms as the only graphic representation of larger poetic structure. The one exception is Psalm 119 (fig. 35). Here the acrostic is given special visibility. Every couplet in the eight-couplet stanzas is headed by the appropriate letter of the acrostic scheme and written on its own columnar line, with extra spacing used to separate the individual stanzas. These special formatting features set Psalm 119 apart in this scroll and in the process strengthen visually the psalm's sense of cohesion and closure. And the framing of the couplets on a single columnar line, in support of the alphabetic acrostic, enhances the felt rhythm of the couplets as they counterpoint the more irregularly shaped rhythm of the individual lines. The heightening effect of the visual display may be judged by contrasting it with this scroll's version of Psalm 145, also an acrostic in which the alphabetic scheme frames each couplet (fig. 36). But because the alphabetic scheme is not supported visually—this psalm is written in a running format like all the other psalms in this scroll—the counterpointing play of lineal and couplet rhythms lacking visual support is not nearly as pronounced.

The contrast in formatting of these two acrostics in 11QPs[a] shows that once biblical poems start to be written down, how they are written down can have rhythmic implications for their readers. Writing unleashes the possibility for additional (supporting or conflicting) rhythmic patterns to get layered over and thus crosscut the rhythms established through the manipulation of purely linguistic material. And when they do so they complicate what is already a complex rhythmic phenomena. One last example. As elaborated earlier (chapter 1), the premiere metascript convention that evolves (first at Qumran, then again during the medieval period) for writing out biblical poems is the use of spacing to distinguish individual poetic lines, to mark line breaks. The rhythmic implication of this spacing, when it occurs (it was not required and never systematized), is not dissimilar to that of literal "lineation," which Smith says "tells [the reader] how to pace his performance so as best to perceive the rhythm *designed* to emerge from it." She continues with a specific example:

> Certainly we hear a different structure of sounds in Williams' "Sun-flowers" when we read it not as prose but following the instructions implied by the lineation: slowly enough to permit the physical qualities of the words to reveal themselves, pausing at the ends of lines, stress-ing certain stresses—all in such a way as to make as prominent as pos-sible the potential rhythmic parallelism of successive lines.[326]

Lineation is one kind of metascript convention and like all metascript conven-tions arises as an aid to readers. Ancient readers (mainly scribes), especially early on, had to bring lots of preknowledge to the reading process. The diffi-culty that the Greek *scriptio continua* convention caused readers is well docu-mented. The presence of lineation in Greek manuscripts (at least from the fourth century on, see fig. 9) told readers (by convention) that they were read-ing poetry. That is, it gave visual expression to the interrupted nature of poetic discourse and in the process also gave minimal instructions about how to navigate this kind of discourse ("pausing at the ends of lines"). The nonlin-eated fourth-century BCE manuscript of Timotheos (fig. 8) does not mean that the poetry contained in this manuscript is any less poetic than if it were written out stichicly, in lines. It is just that the reading cues provided by line-ation are absent and that any visual effects accompanying (graphic) lineation are necessarily left unrealized.

Spacing, though a different kind of metascript convention, is still a metas-cript convention, and when present in Levantine manuscripts (from the Hel-lenistic and medieval periods, see figs. 2–4, 6, 16) informs readers that they are reading poetry and eases the reading process, facilitating readier compre-hension of line units and their more dexterous oral performance. The extra intratextual space acts as a kind of guide for eye fixation, which enables max-imum parafoveal and peripheral visual acuity and a broader span of language (and paralanguage) material (words, phrases, verse lines) that can be decoded (however finely or grossly) before having to be pronounced (the "eye-voice span").[327] Indeed, one of the oldest explanations of the presence of line spac-ing in Qumran poetic manuscripts was that it served as an aid for liturgical performance. And this may not be wrong. But the real benefit to the ancient reader/performer of such poetically spaced texts should not be overstressed. As P. Saenger reminds us, the contexts for reading and writing in antiquity and the habits they provoked were very different from our own. Ease and speed of reading (e.g., to consult reference materials, facilitate the sight-reading of multiple and complex genres, effect a greater diffusion of literacy) were not necessarily seen as desirable or advantageous by ancient readers.[328] Poetic texts in a running format (i.e., absent specific spatial cues for line boundary, e.g., fig. 15a–b) are still eminently performable as poems, especially by trained professionals aided by prereading (*praelectio*), memorization, and vocalization. Indeed, the presence of word separation (a standard practice of West Semitic scribal tradition, see fig. 37), as Saenger's study shows in detail, is already a great boon to the neurophysiology of reading. So from a gross functional perspective, that the biblical Hebrew manuscript tradition exhibits a variety of formats and page layouts for poetic texts is not overly remarkable. The professional readers of the day (the scribes) would have been able to negotiate any of the formats, yet from a purely informational perspective, the comparison of a single psalm written in one manuscript with added lineal spacing and in another without it (figs. 2, 15b, 16) makes the added visual information in the former plain to *see*! And the information conveyed through this visual dimension of the text, that is, spatial cues as to line boundary, tells readers, just as surely as does lineation in ancient Greek poetry manuscripts or modern print versions (such as with Williams's poems), how to pace their "performance so as best to perceive the rhythm *designed* to emerge" from the poem.[329]

* * *

OTHER ELEMENTS OF language, style, convention, and presentation remain that can factor into the rhythm of a biblical poem. The foregoing survey is by no means comprehensive. The chief aim has been to isolate many of the major components and illustrate some of the typical ways they get deployed and to what rhythmic ends. The rhythmic baseline for every biblical poem is composed of (mostly) alternating stressed and unstressed syllables as staged by the verse line: after every two or three and sometimes even four stressed syllables, with any accompanying intervening unstressed syllables, there is a pause—a lineal interruption, and then another two, three, or four stresses and another pause, and so on. Even in the midst of much freedom and variation, the constraints in place are sufficient to give to the resulting rhythm a distinctive shape and movement that contrasts palpably, for example, with metered and unmetered verse from the postbiblical Hebrew poetic canon on the one hand and with biblical narrative prose on the other. There is enough variability with these elements alone to ensure that no two biblical poems enact exactly the same kind of rhythm. The beat of the stressed syllables as cut up and orchestrated by line units is always ultimately pulsating through every poem differently. Aside perhaps from meaning (all language comes enfleshed with meaning), the remaining features surveyed, no matter how prominent, do not always figure into a biblical poem's rhythm—they are all ultimately optional. When present they add layers of complexity onto a biblical poem's rhythmic base. The resulting "rhythmic gestalt" is "a complex product of the interaction of recurrent groupings" on multiple "levels of structure."[330] These interactions occur within and among the distinct rhythmic levels or units. "Articulation at one point in a rhythmic structure can disturb the whole structure. All units are related to all other units."[331] Points of rhythmic prominence at one level may be contested or reemphasized at other levels. Not all levels will necessarily overlap, and not infrequently two or more levels or elements will join together to figure the whole. And the temporal nature of the art form means that these various and variable interactions evolve in a continuous shaping as the poem moves via manipulation of the language material from beginning to end. Grouping is the central mechanism in biblical poems by which the specific patterns or shapes of energy that are themselves constitutive of rhythm get patterned and shaped. The emphasis above was placed on singular rhythmic contours with only some probatory glances at how these contours mesh with or counter other contours or how they join to effect a larger rhythmic whole. The latter, of course, is every bit as crucial for a fully fathomed appreciation of the free rhythms of biblical poetry, and is given the kind of sustained attention required in the reading of Psalm 133 that closes this book (chapter 5).

In coming initially to the question of rhythm in biblical verse through the poetry of Walt Whitman I wanted to leverage Whitman's ready identity as poet and iconic association with American free verse. Poetry can be conceptualized beyond the category of meter, and in fact it is Whitman's nonmetrical variety of poetry, a poetry of free-flowing rhythms, that still dominates the current Anglo-American poetic landscape. That this would become so, of course, was not obvious at the time to Whitman or his contemporaries. Poetry in the middle of the nineteenth century in the West was still dominantly thought of as involving meter (and rhyme). In fact, almost all of Whitman's own pre-*Leaves* poetry was metrical—only the three poems published in the summer of 1850—"Blood-Money,"[332] "The House of Friends,"[333] and especially "Resurgemus"[334]—begin to anticipate the ametrical rhythms of the poet's mature free verse. The self-conscious nature of Whitman's decision to elaborate a rhythmical style free of "arbitrary and rhyming meter" is manifest in all his post-1850 poetry—the break with his own earlier metrical practice simply underscores this fact. And yet Whitman, aware that "rhyme" and the "measurements" of meter continued "to furnish the medium" for much poetry of his day, argued repeatedly and explicitly throughout his life on behalf of his own unrhymed and unmeasured "new American poetry." This begins already in his early notebooks ("a perfectly transparent plate-glassy style, artless, with no ornaments")[335] and is present in the 1855 Preface ("poetic quality is not marshaled in rhyme or uniformity or abstract addresses to things")[336] and its later poeticized versions (e.g., "Rhymes and rhymers pass away"),[337] for example. One of Whitman's most explicit statements on the topic comes in *Two Rivulets* (1876): "the truest and greatest poetry, (while subtly and necessarily always rhythmic, and distinguishable easily enough,) can never again, in the English language, be expressed in arbitrary and rhyming meter, any more than the greatest eloquence, or the truest power and passion."[338] The page layout in *Two Rivulets* features poems on the top half of the page and prose on the bottom half, the two being separated by a wavy horizontal line. In this instance the two poems, "Wandering at Morn" and "An Old Man's Thought of School" (presented on the top halves of pp. 28 and 29), exemplify the kind of "always rhythmic" but nonmetrical verse that Whitman is advocating. And then in his late essay "The Bible as Poetry" (1883), he leverages the Bible, much in the same spirit as I have leveraged Whitman, to authorize his own unmetered and unrhymed verse. He references a "discourse on 'Hebrew Poets'" by F. de Sola Mendes, a New York rabbi, and then he quotes "Dr. Mendes" on the topic of rhyme and meter in the Bible: "rhyming was not a characteristic of Hebrew poetry at all. Metre was not a necessary mark of poetry. Great poets discarded it; the early Jewish poets knew it not."[339] The fact of quotation itself—which Whitman in the poetic theory he started evolving in the early 1850s had resolved to do without ("In writing, give no second hand articles— no quotations—no authorities")[340]—is not insignificant. But it is the content of the quotation that I wish to emphasize. For here, some fifty years in advance of Allen's essays, Whitman, too (through the observation of de Sola Mendes), recognizes the absence of meter in biblical poetry—"the early Jewish poets knew it not." Biblical poetry is not metrical and though the countervailing (metrical) supposition still holds ready appeal, there have been many down through the ages like Whitman (e.g., Moses ibn Ezra, Wither, Stuart, Driver, Allen, Sachs, Hrushovski) who have recognized this fact. The driving ambition of the foregoing discussion has been to recollect (some of) these voices and to say more substantively of what these unmetered, free rhythms of biblical verse consist. We can perhaps ask for no more congenial guide to how to read and appreciate them than the "barbaric yawp" of Walt Whitman.

3

The Idea of Lyric Poetry in the Bible

we can say that biblical literature contains an abundance of lyric
poetry and that it contains no epic poems and no drama
—L. ALONSO SCHÖKEL, *A Manual of Hebrew Poetics* (1988)

THE IDEA OF lyric poetry in the Bible is not new, as the quotation from L. Alonso Schökel in the epigraph, for example, makes clear,[1] yet sustained treatments of the topic in the field remain few.[2] In the largest part of what follows I offer a phenomenological analysis of the lyric, a thick description of leading characteristics and practices associated with lyric verse generally (and generically), both for definitional purposes—to make available a robust and substantive working understanding of this kind of discourse—and as a means for transfixing (in an initial way) what of the biblical poetic corpus most felicitously may be described as lyric and how such poetry works (prosodically). In my view, the manner of discourse underlying a good many biblical poems (though by no means all) may be usefully and accurately described as lyric (e.g., Psalms, Song of Songs, Exod 15, Judg 5, 2 Sam 1:19–27, Isa 5:1–7). To fully substantiate such a judgment will require a more sustained effort than can be accomplished here. For the moment, then, it will suffice to (re)introduce the notion of "lyric" as a critical idiom and along the way point to some of the potential payoffs that its use holds for criticism and interpretation of biblical poetry. After this initial discussion of the lyric's constitutive elements and tendencies relevant to the biblical version(s) of this genre, I turn in a more abbreviated fashion to consider, first, the possibility of lyric discourse on an expanded scale (through a consideration of the Song of Songs), and second, how the idea of lyric poetry may benefit a richer understanding of biblical poetry more broadly.

The Hebrew Lyric

What is lyric? The term itself (Gk. *lurikos*) comes down to us from ancient Greece (as does the impetus for the kind of criticism I am herein enacting), though the basic sense with which I deploy the term—that which is more or less implicit in the threefold genre distinction between lyric, epic, and drama that has been at the heart of literary criticism in the West for much of its history[3]—does not receive more concrete expression until the Alexandrian era.[4] That is, importantly, "lyric" as an idiom of criticism even in its first use in its native Greece is belated and anachronistic. Neither Plato nor Aristotle, for example, knew or used the term—lyric as a nonmimetic kind of verse is apparently nowhere in view in the Poetics[5]—and the archaic poets (e.g., Sappho, Alcaeus, Pindar) the Alexandrians referenced in their use of the term called their own poetry by various other names, including most especially, *melos*. Still, the broad phenomenological distinction between narrative and nonnarrative kinds of (poetic) discourse was certainly relevant prior to the archaic period in Greece and more broadly, too (in the ancient Near East and elsewhere), whether it was indigenously named as such or not. G. Nagy makes precisely this point with respect to Greek lyric, which he says "is just as old as epic, which clearly predates the archaic period," and like epic was "rooted in oral poetry."[6] Indeed, lyric may well be the most widely attested genre of all oral verbal art.[7] "It is reasonable to suppose," moreover, as J. W. Johnson observes, "that the first 'lyrical' poems came into existence when human beings discovered the pleasure that arises from combining words in a coherent, meaningful sequence with the almost physical process of uttering rhythmical and tonal sounds to convey feelings."[8] And there is an extraordinary breadth of historically known lyric traditions preserved in writing—from the ancient Near East, Greece, Persia, the Arab Middle East, the vernacular European traditions, Russia and Eastern Europe, Africa, India, China, Japan, and so on.[9] The lyric, then, though mainly theorized and scrutinized with a pronounced Western bias and inevitably (with rare exceptions) rooted specifically in the ancient Greek tradition,[10] is a genre broader and older than its most revered instantiation from ancient Greece.[11]

This is not to insist on lyric as an essentialized or universal category. There are no such things.[12] Whatever features are isolated, as D. Lindley well notes, are "profoundly affected by fluctuation in systems of classification and poetic practice through history"[13]—and, I might add, from tradition to tradition. So, in discussing archaic Greek lyric (or better melic) poetry, for example, to accentuate the sung quality of most of this verse makes good sense in light of scholars' knowledge about the composition of these poems—to be accompanied by the lyre, *aulos*, or other instruments—and the kinds of contexts in which they were routinely performed. In contrast, for a poet like Horace, who never sang his verse, the *literal* use of music ceases to be a meaningful genre criteria. And in much contemporary theoretical and critical discussion, to cite another kind of example, the term *lyric* has become more or less synonymous with the term *poetry*—or, perhaps more accurately, it is taken as the prototype of a poem.[14] An awareness of such historical variation has two consequences worth underscoring. First, whatever the extent of lyric verse in the Bible, it will inevitably be shaped and marked by the particularity of its time, place, and language and the larger literary tradition of which it is a part—its singers were "historically bonded to the physical material" of culturally specific "words."[15] That is, I have no investment in (and see no benefit to) uncovering specific kinds of lyric verse in the Bible, whether they be Romantic, modernist, or even early Greek. Other bodies and traditions of lyric verse are, of course, crucial to the kind of study I am conducting here, but principally as a means for gauging the possibilities and varieties of lyric discourse as a backdrop for a better appreciation of the kind of lyric found in the Bible. So J. Culler: "A broad conception of lyric as genre is helpful for thinking about short, non-narrative poetry and, particularly, how its relation to the historical tradition and to a broad range of possibilities for lyric in many periods and languages can help prevent a certain narrowing of conception of lyric."[16] To press my point, consider the symposium, one of the primary contexts in which Greek monody was performed. This is an especially Greek cultural institution with nothing quite like it in ancient Israel or Judah, and thus on this basis alone one can expect both qualitative and quantitve differences in the kind of lyric verse realized in the two cultures.

Second, what ultimately is counted as lyric depends on the specific criteria that are privileged. Is there any hope, then, "of defining 'lyric' as a generic label?" asks Lindley. His answer is that it "must be tentative." He elaborates:

> It must be accepted that a wide variety of determinants may properly be felt as significant in allocating a poem to a lyric category. While a "personal" poem in stanza form about the pains of love and intended to be set to music would universally be accepted as a "lyric," it is in no sense an authoritative model. For throughout literary history there has been not only a wide range of possible subject matter, but considerable divergence in the criteria that have been felt as paramount..., so that all decisions about a work's generic status must be conditioned by an awareness of that history. It is also inevitable that many poems might hover on the edges, and to pretend to a certainty that can judge infallibly between a lyrical narrative or a narrative lyric [for example]... would be to misunderstand the way readers actually use (or are used by) their generic awareness and the way poets play with and upon generic expectations.[17]

The group of features highlighted below, though idiosyncratic and eclectic to be sure, nonetheless reflect insights taken from a fairly broad spectrum of criticism and lyric traditions (oral and written) and has the chief merit of pointing up what is most *distinctive phenomenologically* about lyric discourse, and thus offers a concrete set of measures for identifying and characterizing lyric discourse in the Bible. My aim here is not to be reductionist or to reify classificatory schemes for their own sake. There will be more and less lyrical poems in the Bible, and poems that are not lyrical at all.[18] As C. Guillén rightly observes, "there are no pure forms,"[19] and in any case the lyric's "differences from other literary products are not radical," as S. Langer writes, "and there is no device characteristic of lyric composition that may not also be met in other forms."[20] M. K. Blasing stresses "the variety of lyric modes"—"song, supplication, pronouncement, prayer, and so forth," which has the advantage of decentering the thought that lyric is just one kind of song or poem.[21] The chief outcome, then, sought in the review of these several lyric practices and tendencies is finally to make an initial brief for the facticity of the Hebrew lyric (in its various modes) and to sharpen and extend our understanding of the inner workings of this kind of biblical poetry. I pursue this particular line of inquiry pragmatically and heuristically, which is to say, in full awareness that the attraction of my thesis lies ultimately in its usefulness for reading these poems and for making sense of their prosody.

A Sung Word

What is perhaps most distinctive about lyric verse generally is its originary and ongoing indebtedness to music and song—musicality is the very way of naming this particular poetic art: "lyric poetry is a genre of song."[22] Lyric originates in traditional cultures as a performative and oral art form: "Lyric poetry, in the general sense of a (relatively) short non-narrative poem that is sung, is of extremely wide occurrence; it can probably be regarded as universal in human culture."[23] And certainly during the effluence of Greek lyric from the seventh to the mid-fifth centuries BCE many of the solo (monody) lyrics were composed to be sung at symposia to the accompaniment of the *aulos* (an oboe-like wind instrument) or lyre, while choral songs were mostly performed at festivals (such as the great Panhellenic festivals) or on other special occasions. Greek lyric shares this use of music with "many other bodies of high lyric poetry" (e.g., Chinese, Provençal), among which W. R. Johnson counts Hebrew.[24] Since H. Gunkel, students of the Hebrew Bible have appreciated the oral heritage of much biblical literature. For example, Gunkel famously conjectures that an old "poetic form" underlies many of the prose "legends" in Genesis (e.g., the Eden story). It was "strictly rhythmical" and must "have been sung."[25] That much of the poetry actually preserved in the Bible—almost all of it nonnarrative in kind (see discussion in the immediately following section, "Nonnarrative Poetry")—was also a specifically "sung" kind of word can be stipulated from a variety of considerations. First, certainly lyric forms (e.g., the hymn) obtained throughout the wider ancient Near East. They commonly embed references to singing ("Sing of the goddess," *RA* 22 170: I; "May the name of ʿAttartu be sung," *RIH* 98/02.1)[26] and sometimes more explicit information about performance is provided as well, as in *RA* 35 3 iii 14: "one of the *kalû*-singers stands up...and sings an e r š e m m a-song to Enlil to the accompaniment of the *ḫalḫallatu*-drum" (*CAD* Z, 37a).[27] Second, although there is no extant body of criticism from ancient Israel and Judah commenting on the musicality of biblical verse, there are nonetheless aspects of the texts themselves that are indicative of the presence of music. Several stand out. To begin with, there is the terminology used for this kind of verse, which in several instances refers explicitly to "song" and "singing." The most generic term is *šîr*/*šîrâ* "song" (e.g., Exod 15:1; Num 21:17; Deut 31:22, 30; Isa 5:1; Song 1:1; Ps 18:1).[28] As R. Lowth writes: "These compositions which were intended for music, whether vocal alone, or accompanied with instruments, obtained among the Hebrews the appellation of *Shir*."[29] The verb *š-y-r* "to sing" is equally widespread (e.g., *ʾāšîrâ l-yhwh* "I will sing to Yahweh," Ps 13:6). The other common root in biblical Hebrew for song and singing is *z-m-r* (e.g., Judg 5:3; 2 Sam 22:50 = Ps 18:50; 1 Ps 98:5; 1 Chron 16:9)—*mizmôr* "psalm, song" appears fifty-seven times as a designation for a psalm, all in psalm titles (e.g., Ps 13:1; 19:1; 23:1; 29:1; 48:1; 88:1; 98:1). Both roots by their semantics alone imply an originary concern for music and song for the compositions so designated or characterized. Moreover, references to musical instruments are common in psalms in particular (e.g., Ps 33:1–3; 47:6; 49:1–5; 81:3, 4; 92:4; 98:6; 144:9; 147:7; 150:3–5; 2 Chron 5:13; cf. Amos 6:23)[30] and also in other poems that are sung or described as songs (e.g., Exod 15:20–21; 1 Sam 18:6–7; Isa 23:16; cf. Amos 6:5; Ezek 26:13); and most scholars assume that some of the obscure technical terms in the superscriptions to individual psalms (e.g., *ʿal haššĕmînît*, Ps 6:1; 12:1; cf. 1 Chron 15:21) likely refer to instruments or to melodic or rhythmic patterns and tones.[31] Also there are textual indications of the existence of a professional group of singers and musicians (e.g., Gen 4:21; Ps 68:26; 1 Chron 15:16–24; 16:4–6)—"male and female musicians" are listed among the tribute sent by Hezekiah to Sennacherib in 701 BCE (according to the latter's annals, *ANET*, 288), and among those deported to Babylon by Nebuchadrezzar and receiving oil rations was the "director of singers from Ashkelon."[32]

A third consideration consistent with the sung quality of biblical Hebrew lyrics is the plethora of material remains from the Levant and surrounding areas attesting to the cultivation of music. Remains of musical instruments have been recovered, as well as numerous iconographic representations of instruments and musicians and singers (playing and singing, see figs. 38–39), and even a complete hymn (in Hurrian) with instructions for performance.[33] Finally, from an ethnomusicological perspective "in the earliest cultures words and music are closely associated," while solo instrumental music is clearly a secondary development.[34] That is, most "primitive" music is vocal (or partly vocal)—"music produced by the human voice."[35] In other words, where we have cultivation of music in antiquity—as we do in ancient Israel and Judah and the Near East more generally—we can expect most of that activity to be concerned with voice—*qôl zimrâ* "the voice of song" (Isa 51:3), and therefore, though we mostly lack indications of melody,[36] tune, and the like from antiquity, the "words" that are preserved in writing (and consistently isolated through word division, e.g., fig. 37) are in fact a most decisive indicator of ancient song; the nonnarrative poems themselves attest to the reality of ancient music and song.[37] And from the written words other aspects of lyric's pervasive musicality may be discerned, especially in "those elements which [lyric] shares with the musical forms"[38]—rhythm, meter, a pervasive heightening of sonority through alliteration, assonance, and the like.[39] And though all language art may use such musical resources, it is "the frequency and importance" of such musical practices, "rather than their exclusive use," wherein lies their lyric distinctiveness.[40]

In sum, it may be confidently concluded that, as in ancient Greece,[41] and in fact as in many traditional and primarily oral cultures throughout history, much lyric verse of the Bible evolved literally as song and was frequently accompanied by instrumental music. That is, it consisted of "sung words," verse where the music exists for the sake of words, where melody, rhythm, voice, dance, and the lyre all conspire "to reinforce and emphasize separate syllables and to augment the clarity of the sung words."[42] And if, as with ancient Greek lyrics, we have no idea about the details of the Hebrew lyric's music—beyond the facticity of its existence—since it too is irredeemably lost to us, the thump of its rhythm at times still can be felt and the sweet sounds of its song even occasionally heard,[43] and thus Hebrew lyric, as with almost all lyric poetry, modern or ancient, never really escapes or forgets its origin in music and performance.[44] Indeed, not a few of the lyric's leading discriminators (e.g., prominence of voice, its adding style, brevity of scope) find their origin in the genre's aboriginal orality, as I will note.

Musical expression in antiquity also will have likely included chanting and recitation to musical accompaniment and rhythms (A. Welsh identifies "three roots of the melopoeia of lyric poetry"),[45] though tracking such muted modes of musicality, without the benefit of express linguistic traces, is difficult. Consider the *qînâ* "dirge," which in the Hebrew Bible is usually "raised or lifted up" (*n-ś-ʾ*; cf. Jer 7:29; 9:9; Ezek 19:1; 26:17; 27:2, 32; 28:12; 32:2; Amos 5:1) or (etymologically) "keened" (*q-y-n*; cf. Ezek 27:32; 32:16; 2 Chron 35:25) but never literally "sung" (*š-y-r*). Indeed, laments and dirges were often thought of as the antithesis of song (e.g., Amos 8:10; Ps 137:1–4; Lam 5:14–15; cf. Prov 25:20). Nevertheless, ethnographic studies of funeral dirges clearly show that if dirges were not sung as were songs on more festive occasions, they were still chanted in song-like fashion.[46] In 2 Chronicles 35:25 "male and female singers" (*haššārîm wĕhaššārôt*) are said to have been responsible for lamenting (*wayqônēn*) Josiah's death. Even the Mesopotamian city laments, which are themselves deeply indebted to the funeral dirge, represent themselves as "songs" (š i r; e.g., LN 54, 56; *balag* 4:b + 260) that were chanted normally to the beat of the *balag*-drum and/or other percussion instruments (e.g., CA 200–201)—Lamentations, the Bible's best example of a lamentation for a destroyed city, itself mostly lacks explicit references to song or music (cf. Lam 5:15: *nehpak lĕʾēbel mĕḥōlēnû* "our dancing has turned to mourning"). And there are many psalmic laments whose musicality is sometimes otherwise suggested (e.g., Ps 6:1; 12:1; 60:1; 80:1). All this by way of reminder that there may well have been shades of musicality in performance beyond that of the full-throated singing of song. For the *qînâ*, the ghost of such musicality is still faintly but distinctly perceivable in the rhythm of its words and especially the limp of its often unbalanced sets of lines, that is, the so-called qinah meter.

The rise of textuality in Israel and Judah, beginning in earnest no later than the early eighth century BCE (Iron IIB), means that writing becomes a potential factor in the staging and experience of Hebrew lyric. Writing does not immediately change matters, especially the reception of poems, which remains vocal certainly through the Persian period.[47] Yet writing in the long run dramatically shifts lyric verse historically from a "sung" and thus "heard" word to a word that for most of literary history now (especially in the West) has been dominantly "seen" on the page (e.g., Horace never sang his verse).[48] This wider historical perspective raises the possibility of unsung and unchanted lyrics in the Bible (especially after the advent of writing, e.g., Job 3), a topic I return to (in a manner) at the end of the chapter.

Nonnarrative Poetry

One way to gain a firmer fix on the lyric is, following the lead of N. Frye,[49] to say what it is not: the lyric is not a narrative; or better, it is *chiefly*, as I have already said, a nonnarrative, nondramatic, nonrepresentational kind of poetry.[50] In fact, beyond the pervasive imprint left by the lyric's originary entanglement with music, what so distinguishes the medium of lyric verse and shapes the basic contours of its discourse is the noncentrality, and indeed frequent absence, of features and practices (plot, character, and the like) that are otherwise definitive of more discursive modes of discourse (e.g., narrative, drama). As Culler succinctly states, "narrative poems recount an event; lyrics...strive to be an event."[51] The outstanding characteristic of biblical poetry, of course, is its fundamental *nonnarrativity*. R. Alter puts his finger on precisely this "peculiarity": "The Hebrew writers used verse for celebratory song, dirge, oracle, oratory, prophecy, reflective and didactic argument, liturgy, and often as a heightening or summarizing inset in the prose narratives—but only marginally or minimally to tell a tale."[52] Epic verse (narrative) is well exemplified from the various surrounding cultures of the ancient Near East, but in the preserved literature of the Bible, narrative becomes predominantly the preserve of prose, so much so in fact, that the two extremes on the (ideal) discourse continuum represented by lyric and narrative are often synonymous in the Bible with the distinction between poetry (verse) and prose. Indeed, triangulating from the various uses of verse, for example, in ancient Syria, Mesopotamia, and even Greece on the one hand and from the (mostly perceptible) poetry/prose divide in biblical literature on the other brings the nonnarrative, nonrepresentational nature of much biblical Hebrew verse sharply into view. So much so in fact, that this aspiration toward something other than narrative may well be the most tractable lyric characteristic of biblical verse more generally.

Alter dedicates his second chapter ("From Line to Story") in *The Art of Biblical Poetry* to illustrating the various ways biblical Hebrew poems, though "fundamentally nonnarrative" in nature, do manifest at times a noticeable narrative impulse (e.g., incipient narrativity, episodic narratives). Among the poems he considers in more detail are 2 Samuel 22 (= Ps 18), Job 16:9–14, Joel 2, Judges 5, Exodus 15, and Proverbs 7. Two aspects of his treatment are worth underscoring here. One, the fact that modal and genre boundaries are easily (and even commonly) transgressed,[53] and two, that in every instance the particular impulses toward narrative on display ultimately serve larger, nonnarrative ends, for example, to hymn Yahweh, to celebrate a victory, to convey moral instruction.

In the following paragraphs I take the opposite tack from Alter. Instead of charting how biblical poems may move toward narrative, and as a consequence gaining a better angle from which to appreciate these poems' defining nonnarrativity, I come at the latter by considering the swerve away from narrative in Psalm 114. Psalm 114, a somewhat unusual psalmic composition, invites the narrative comparison in two broad ways. First, it explicitly uses story—the exodus from Egypt—to frame its discourse. This is accomplished immediately in the poem's opening line: *běṣē't yiśrā'ēl mimmiṣrāyim* "When Israel went forth from Egypt" (Ps 114:1). Psalms do not generally begin in this way, and in fact the grammar itself—"the infinitive construction with concomitant subordination of the second poetic line"—is common in narrative (esp. Exod 13:8).[54] Second, almost every line reflects an awareness of Israel's larger narrative traditions: verses 3 and 5 recall the events at the Red Sea (Exod 14–15) and the crossing of the Jordan (Josh 3:1–5:1)—though in both cases as refracted mythopoetically (e.g., Isa 51:9–11; Ps 74: 12–17; Job 38:8–11; 40:25–32; cf. Josh 4:23); the image of mountains and hills "skipping" (*rāqědû*) like rams and lambs (cf. esp. Ps 29:6) in verses 4 and 6 is taken from the old hymns recounting the march of the Divine Warrior from the southland (cf. Deut 33:2; Judg 5:4–5; Hab 3:3–6; Ps 68:8–9; also *KA* 4.2); and verse 8 draws on the the wilderness traditions (Exod 17:1–7; Num 20:2–13). And yet there is no narrative here. The poem does not go on to narrate the story of the exodus, or any of these other traditions. H.-J. Kraus's observation about the narrative episodes in Psalm 106 is applicable here as well: they "are generally presumed to be familiar and therefore taken up only allusively."[55] Indeed, the poem does not appear to make good sense discursively at all. If anything, it flouts good discursive logic. For example, who or what is the poem about? The topicalized entities in the first three clauses are all differently named—Israel, Jacob, Judah.[56] The clauses of the second couplet (v. 2), which are grammatically subordinated to those in the opening couplet, do not appear to follow any kind of story logic, or even to make literal sense: how is it that *Israel's* coming out from Egypt (literally) established *Judah* as "his sanctuary"? And who is the grammatical antecedent for the possessive suffix here and in the next line? The poem never *explicitly* says. And then there is the hodgepodge collection of traditions reflected in the poem.[57] These are not sequenced or otherwise developed logically. And though the *Chaoskampf* imagery has attracted the attention of scholars (e.g., Kraus entitles his comments on the poem "Miracles of Subduing the Sea"),[58] the poem's climax in verse 7 (*millipnê 'ādôn ḥûlî 'āreṣ* "Before (the) Lord, writhe, O land!") depends most explicitly on the old theophany traditions—the "land/earth" (*'ereṣ*) "shakes" (*rā'āšâ*) "from before Yahweh" (*mippěnê yhwh*) in Judges 5:4–5 and is shaken (lit. *waymōded*) by Yahweh in Habakkuk 3:6, and the whole concludes (curiously) by recalling Israel's wanderings before entering the land. Finally, the *wayyiqtol* form, the paradigm grammatical trope of Hebrew narrative, is used only once (*wayyānōs*, v. 3), and that for local effect.[59]

My point (exaggerated to be sure) is that this poem does not seem very interested in telling a story (which story?), developing characters (indeed, that which most commentators take to be the poem's chief subject, Yahweh, is never explicitly topicalized!), or even in constructing an argument. Such a presentation, as Kraus rightly notes, cannot be called "a real narration or description."[60] That is, its basic dynamics and chief practices are other than what we routinely associate with narrative; they are, I submit, expressly lyrical in orientation. To offer a fully persuasive lyric reading of this psalm would presume much of the discussion that is to follow. Still, several considerations— beyond the absence of narrative and narrativizing devices—may be offered as preliminary indicators of the psalm's lyricism. First, there is its hymnic nature, stipulated to by most commentators (even if uneasily so).[61] The hymn is a quintessential specimen of lyric discourse (by any definition).[62] As Lowth observes, the hymn (or "ode") is "sufficiently expressive" of its origin and abiding nature, "the offspring of the most vivid and the most agreeable passions of the mind—of love, joy, and admiration."[63] It enacts "an effusion of praise" to the deity, "accompanied with suitable energy and an exultation of voice."[64] The hymn of praise in the psalms is sometimes rendered self-reflexively and declaratively, as in Psalm 146:2 ("I will praise [*ăhalĕlâ*] Yahweh as long as I live!"), but more often it is composed of a call to praise followed by a *kî* clause giving the reason for the praise (e.g., Ps 117), with the expression of praise itself more a consequence of pragmatic implicature than conventional semantics.[65] But the main point, captured well by Lowth, is that the content of such hymns (what they are all about, what they do) is neither argument nor description but the "effusion of praise" itself, the expressed consciousness "of the goodness, majesty, and power of God." Psalm 114, if a hymn, is a darker kind of hymn, as epitomized by the climatic call in verse 7 for the "land/earth" to "writhe (in agony)" before Yahweh.[66] The precise language used here, *ḥûlî 'āreṣ*, though surely intended to play off (and on) the more normative calls to praise (e.g., *halĕlû yāh*) that typify Israelite hymns and echo throughout the Hallel sequence in particular (e.g., Ps 111:1; 112:1; 113:1, 9; 115:18; 116:19; 117:2; cf. 69:35; 148:7),[67] is drawn from the poetic commonplace depicting the reaction to bad news (Isa 13:8; Jer 4:19; Hab 3:10; cf. Isa 21:3; Jer 6:24; 50:43)[68] and thus evokes sensations of fear, dread, and anguish at the prospects of the warrior deity's immanent theophany—very much akin to the darkness that is hymned in Psalm 29.[69]

The poem, as I have already noticed, is highly fragmented, made up of bits and pieces of various traditions, and its discourse develops mostly associatively, as is typical of lyric discourse more generally (see discussion "Rhythm of Association" later in this chapter). The initial reference to the exodus from

Egypt (v. 1) calls to mind the mythopoetic representation of that event as Yahweh's battle over the chaos power, Sea (v. 3; cf. Exod 15). The similar personification of the Jordan (unique to this psalm) in the following line is a consequence of the tradition's explicit interpretation of the crossing of the Jordan in terms of the Re(e)d Sea events (Josh 4:23; cf. Ps 66:6).[70] The reaction of Sea and River then suggests the analogous reaction of the Mountains and Hills prevalent in the march of the Divine Warrior traditions,[71] with the latter then giving way to the poem's climatic call to "writhe!" Without plot and character the lyric, as Langer notes, "must depend most directly on pure verbal resources,"[72] and thus lyric discourse is often highly troped. Wordplay (*ḥûlî/halĕlû*, v. 7), personification (vv. 3–5, 5–6[73]), "bold apostrophe" (v. 7),[74] and the like must bear more of the meaning-making burden.[75] Continuity and coherence are built in through lineation and rhythm—the poem is constructed out of parallelistic couplets, all of which involve gapping (ellipsis), and the foreshortened second lines that result from the gapping create a rocking rhythm that mimes the writhing and skipping that the poem imagines.[76]

And finally, it is often the case in lyric discourse that as much goes on behind the scenes (or under the poem's surface), as it were, as specifically in the text. As D. Levertov observes, lyric poetry's "way of constructing" discourse depends as much on "silences" as on the selection of specific "words."[77] Kraus explains the purpose of Psalm 114 as proclaiming "the powerful appearance of the God of Israel."[78] Such an explanation is on the right track but ultimately goes astray by failing to appreciate the poem's figured "silences"—that which is left unstated, the represented absences. The presence of the deity that is hymned here is that which is otherwise not manifestly apparent, that which is literally absent. Nowhere in the poem is Yahweh specifically topicalized—the direct antithesis of the old hymns to the Divine Warrior in which we witness the deity marching (as it were) across the surface of the poem. No antecedents for the pronominal suffixes in verse 2 are ever explicitly identified, though the referent is obvious to all. And even in the poem's "great dénouement" the deity only appears obliquely (*millipnê 'ādôn . . . millipnê 'ĕlôah*),[79] as if we somehow just missed the appearance itself. And this figuring of Yahweh's presence amid apparent absence seems to be at the core of much of the poem. For example, the hearer knows only too well that it is Yahweh whom personified Sea sees and recoils from in verse 3. But by withholding the explicit mention of the deity, Yahweh's presence is marked by literal—here linguistic—absence. And similarly in verses 5–6. The questions put to Sea and company are not really intended to taunt or ridicule,[80] but again to linguistically figure the deity's presence amid apparent absence. With this in mind, the poem's otherwise enigmatic concluding couplet (v. 8) comes into clearer focus. It alludes to the incident at Massah and Meribah where, according to the tradition in Exodus (17:1–7, esp. v. 7), the Israelites "quarreled and tested the LORD, saying, 'Is the LORD among us or not?'" (NRSV). The issue there as well, then, is the presence of Yahweh, whose physical manifestation was apparently in question.[81] The allusion to the episode in Psalm 114:8 would thus appear to remove Yahweh one step further from the poem's literal surface, yet the point is to (re)affirm that even at those times where the deity's absence is most palpable Yahweh is present. And thus if I were to commit the cardinal sin of New Criticism and offer a (brief) paraphrase of this psalm, it would go something like this: "Writhe in anguish, O Jacob, for Yahweh is present even in the midst of the most tangible signs of his absence."

Whether one agrees with every aspect of my own (abbreviated) reading of Psalm 114, that the poem is fundamentally nonnarrative in its basic structure and orientation I hope is plain to see. Narrative, though clearly present, is subsidiary, as is common in lyric discourse. As W. R. Johnson observes, "behind every lyric, sometimes vaguely sketched, sometimes clearly defined, is a story that explains the present moment of discourse and accounts for the singer's present moods and for his need or choice to sing. But in lyric poems…the story exists for the song, and what gives the poem its form, its resonance, and its texture" is a specifically lyric kind of sensibility that is made manifest in the "selection of language, sound, and image."[82] Psalm 114 is made of the stuff of narrative—quite explicitly so—but these narrative elements are molded and deployed lyrically.[83]

The Most Obviously Linguistic Creation

Lyric's typical eschewal of narrative and its attendant devices, as summarily shown in the foregoing reading of Psalm 114, entails important consequences for the kind of verbal discourse that it enacts. The first such consequence, and in many ways the most basic as well, is that the fundamental resource of lyric proper, "its plastic medium," is, by default, language itself—"its material dimension."[84] Since lyric poetry (habitually) makes no recourse to plot or character, it must depend, as Langer explains, "most directly on pure verbal resources—the sound and evocative power of words, meter, alliteration, rhyme, and other rhythmic devices, associated images, repetitions, archaisms and grammatical twists. It is the most obviously linguistic creation, and therefore the readiest instance of poesy."[85] That is to say, "there is a tendency," as M. Kinzie notes, "for words" (and other linguistic elements, too) "in the specialized fabric of the poetic line to take on more than their usual significance."[86] It is precisely such linguistic ornamentation (e.g., rhythm, sound patterning, and the like) that

enable aural input to stick in the mind (minus plot and such) and that differentiates the lyric from narrative and mimetic modes generally.[87] This is the
"babble"—those nonsemantic features of language such as sound, rhythm,
puns and the like—of Frye's famed twin constituents of lyric, "babble and
doodle,"[88] and it is most why the lyric, according to Frye, shows so clearly the
"hypothetical core of literature, narrative and meaning in their literal aspects as
word-order and word-pattern."[89] One may gain an impression of the "babbledness" of biblical song, for example, by perusing the (sometimes mechanical)
listings of figures and tropes in the late nineteenth-century compendia of I. M.
Casanowicz and E. König, or in the richly evocative work of more recent literary
scholars, such as A. Berlin, E. Greenstein, and D. Grossberg.[90] Here, however, I
accentuate, first, the superabundance of meaning that sometmes accompanies
a poet's choice of diction, and then I exemplify the foregrounding of the nonsemantic features of language in the lyric poetry of the Bible by considering the
(general) nature of formal structure and the use of metaphor as (or in lieu of)
argument. These are intended to serve as stand-ins for the other kinds of tropes
(wordplay, sound play, and the like) that typify much poetic discourse in the
Bible and mark it as specifically lyric in nature—these would need to be surveyed in a more thoroughgoing statement of this particular lyric quality.

The poet's choice of diction often activates connotations over and above a
given statement's more narrowly denotative meaning.[91] I illustrate with several examples from Lamentations. In Lamentations 2:20b the specter of cannibalism is raised. The language is quite evocative. The NRSV, "should women
eat their offspring," sanitizes the imagery in its overtly denotative rendering.
The term for "offspring," *pĕrî*, more literally means "fruit," and while it is true
that this term is frequently used figuratively for offspring (see Gen 30:2; Deut
7:32; Ps 21:11), as indeed it is here, nevertheless the poet means through this
choice of diction to color the mother's act of cannibalism with the lush enjoyment and everyday occurrence of eating fruit: "Should women have to eat
their children as if they were eating fruit?" The resulting contrast of images is
jarring and very effective. The utterly abhorrent thought that a mother would
be compelled to cannibalize her own children as a means of survival is made
even more heinous by the sensuality and commonality implicit in the fruit
imagery. This tainting of the inhumane, the bestial with sensuous (even
erotic) delight continues through the end of the couplet, as the *hapax lego-
menon* *ṭippuḥîm* "to be reared" (NRSV: "borne") puns on the erotically charged
tappûaḥ (pl. *tappûḥîm*; esp. Song 2:3, 5; 7:9), a word typically (though uncer-
tainly) glossed as "apple."[92]

Another good example of how diction can provide an oversurplus of
meaning is Lamentations 1:10. Here the enemy are portrayed as stretching

their hands over Zion's "precious things" (*maḥămaddeyhā*) and as "entering" (*bāʾû*) her sanctuary. As D. R. Hillers, for one, rightly stresses,[93] the imagery surely intends to depict the looting of the temple treasures by the Babylonians (cf. 2 Kgs 25:13–17). And yet the prominence of the personification of Zion as a woman in this poem freights the key terms in this verse with double meaning. Both of the terms for "precious things" (Song 5:16) and "entering" (Gen 6:4; 16:2; 19:31; 38:9; Judg 16:1; 2 Sam 16:21; Ezek 23:44; Prov 6:29) are used elsewhere to connote sexual intercourse. And thus A. Mintz is right to see in this verse a metaphorical image of sexual violation, which he explains as being "founded on the correspondence body // Temple and genitals // Inner Sanctuary." "So far have things gone," Mintz continues, "that even in the secret place of intimacy to which only the single sacred partner may be admitted, the enemy has thrust himself and 'spread his hands over everything dear to her (1:10).'"[94] It is the metaphorical surplus that suffuses the depiction of the enemy's spoliation of the Jerusalem temple that most pointedly registers the Lamentations poet's feelings of shame, shock, and deep hurt—feelings that are not activated at the purely denotative level of meaning.[95]

One of the elemental functions of plot in narrative is to shape a story, to give it a beginning, middle, and end, and thus to provide a sense of coherence and continuity.[96] Plot is, as P. Brooks states, "the principle of interconnectedness...which we cannot do without in moving through the discrete elements—incidents, episodes, actions—of a narrative" and "that allow[s] us to construct a whole."[97] Without plot per se lyric must find alternative means for organizing its discourse, for demarcating boundaries, for guiding auditors through to a satisfying denouement. At one extreme, lyric verse routinely employs purely (or principally) formal means for articulating structure, such as with the given (conventional) forms well known from the metrical tradition of English verse (e.g., sonnet, villanelle, and the like). In biblical verse the most manifestly formal structuring device used is the alphabetic acrostic (e.g., Ps 9–10, 25, 34, 37, 111, 112, 119, 145; Lam 1–4). The acrostic, unfortunately, has not always been appreciated by biblical exegetes, many of whom routinely decry its patent artificiality. But, of course, such artificiality, or better, artifactuality, is one of the chief marks of poesy, that making out of language that is at the center of all language art.[98] And, more to the point, it is in forms like the acrostic that the lyric's dependence on the double-sided (tropological) use of linguistic signs—Kinzie's notion of taking "on more than their usual significance"—is so plainly on display: the appropriate letter of the alphabet functions both at the word level (i.e., as a part of the spelling of a specific lexeme) and at the composition level (i.e., as a part of the formal conceit by which the larger whole is articulated).[99] Other more or less formal means for articulating holistic structure in the Psalms, for example, include large-scale envelope structures, such as inclusios (e.g., *yhwh 'dnynw / mh-'dyr šmk / bkl-h'rṣ*, Ps 8:2, 10; *bny 'dm*, Ps 12:2, 9; *hwdw lyhwh ky-ṭwb / ky l'wlm ḥsdw*, Ps 118:1, 29; *halĕlû yāh*, Ps 147:1, 20)[100] and chiasms (e.g., *'lhym lnw mḥsh w'z // mśgb-lnw 'lhy y'qb*, Ps 46:2a, 12b), and the occasional use of refrains (e.g., *mh-tštwḥḥy npšy*, Ps 42:6, 12; 43:5; *ky l'wlm ḥsdw*, Ps 136:1–26). And we should probably not discount the possibility that the conventional forms identified by form criticism (beginning with Gunkel) could themselves appeal "as form" (though here thematic elements begin to come into play as well).[101] For example, the bifold structure of the (imperative) hymn of praise—call to praise (with an imperative) followed by a causal clause (usually beginning with *kî*) giving the reason for praise[102]—can be used to structure whole poems (e.g., Ps 100, 117) or sections of poems (e.g., Ps 96:1–6; 98: 1–3; 135:1–4).[103]

Far more common, however, the containing form of a biblical Hebrew lyric poem is "organic," to use a term from Coleridge: "it shapes, as it develops, itself from within," arising "out of the properties of the material."[104] That is, as is the case more generally with nonmetrical verse (or free verse poems), the patterned repetition that generates formal structure,[105] in lieu of a strong tradition of conventional stanzaic structure, rhyme schemes, and the like, will routinely involve a host of diverse linguistic elements (e.g., lineation, sound play, parallelism, word repetition) distributed in a variety of overlapping and mutually informing and delimiting ways (see chapter 2).[106] I have already noted (in passing) a simple example of such "discovered form" in the discussion of Psalm 114. There the psalm's gross structure is articulated formally by the uniform use of parallelistic couplets (eight of them), each involving gapping and composed of slightly unbalanced lines—as B. H. Smith notes, our recognition of such formal patterning is properly "retrospective," that is, we cannot be sure of it until it is concluded (or "announced as concluded").[107] The finer points of that psalm's structure are then "figured" against this "ground" of uniform parallelism. The poem divides into three main sections (or stanzas).[108] The middle section (vv. 3–6) is the longest and is characterized above all by word- and phrase-level repetition (involving Sea, Jordan, Mountains, and Hills—only *rā'â*, *mah-llĕkā*, and *kî* are not repeated). The opening (vv. 1–2) and closing (vv. 7–8) sections are distinguished by the presence of tighter intercouplet syntactic dependencies (i.e., both involve subordinating constructions—infinitival in vv. 1–2 and appositonal in vv. 7–8), and thus form an enveloping structure that (formally) rounds off the poem.

Song 4:1–7 finds its way from beginning to end still differently, though no less nonnarratively. The poem, sung in the boy's voice, declaims the beauty of the girl the boy loves. The opening and closing couplets (vv. 1a, 7), which form an inclusio, plainly express the poem's sole preoccupation: "Wow! You are so beautiful, my love, / Wow! You are so beautiful!" (v. 1a). The structure of the poem is very intentional. Its main body is divided into two symmetrical halves (vv. 1b-2, 3–4), each containing four couplets and featuring three similes, the last of which in each half is more elaborate than the other two (having an additional couplet). This structure is further articulated through syntax and the kind of metaphors employed in each section. In the first section, the part of the body in focus is fronted syntactically at the head of each couplet—"your eyes," "your hair," "your teeth." Each of the metaphors is drawn from the animal world, and more specifically, they feature domesticated animals: "doves," "goats," and "sheep." In the second section, the vehicle of the metaphor is fronted syntactically with the preposition *kĕ-* "like or as": "like a scarlet thread," "like a slit of pomegranate," and "like the tower of David." The metaphors in this half no longer feature domesticated animals but the products of human culture—textiles, fruits, architecture. The descriptive aspect of this *wasf*-like poem is brought to a conclusion in verse 5 with the boy's appreciation of his lover's breasts. The intentionality of the stopping place is patent, even though other similar poems of description in the Song are more (physiologically) inclusive (i.e., head to foot). All of the formal patterns of repetition employed to structure the main body of the description—line structure, syntax, deployment of metaphors—are here exploded, and with this change of pattern the description's closing movement is effectively announced. The simile is given in a triplet and not the couplet that otherwise pervades the whole of this poem. Both of the fronting patterns just noted are upset by the insertion of a number, "two," at the head of the triplet. And the metaphor, though returning to the animal world, features not a domesticated animal but the wild "gazelle." The whole offers another poetic rendition of the "woman in the window" motif (cf. 2:9)[109]—the upper torso of the girl is presented to the mind's eye of the auditor, framed window-fashion, just as in an ivory figurine, by the poem's opening and closing inclusio. After registering the boy's resolve to join his lover (v. 6), the poem concludes by replaying the boy's opening exclamation of the girl's beauty with enough change to close the poem intentionally and with satisfaction: "The whole of you is beautiful, my love, / and there is no flaw in you" (v. 7).

A final, and more complex, example is Psalm 19. The poem divides into two main parts, verses 2–7 and 8–15.[110] Lineation is the chief formal indicator of this poem's structure (though form and content are mutually reinforcing throughout). The lines in the first section of the poem are generally longer, with several triplets thrown in amid the couplets. In the second half, the poem is characterized by couplets with short lines in which the first line tends to be longer than the second—the so-called qinah meter.[111] The only triplet in this section comes at the very end (v. 15), thus effectively signaling the poem's concluding movement. These main sections are composed of two stanzas apiece (vv. 2–5b, 5c–7; 8–11, 12–14), and the theme of each stanza is topicalized in the initial word—"heavens" (v. 2), "sun" (v. 5c), "Torah" (v. 8), "your servant" (v. 12). In the first section, the "sun" stanza is further distinguished by its constituent triplets,[112] while the "Torah" stanza is differentiated in the second part by the especially tight (syntactic, grammatical, and semantic) parallelism that is manifested among its constituent couplets.

In sum, form (sometimes by itself but more frequently in tandem with thematic elements) in the lyric verse of the Bible shoulders a great deal of the continuity and sequencing functions that in narrative more generally fall to the domain of plot, and thus does a great deal more than simply ornamenting the poem's otherwise paraphrasable meaning(s). In a similar way, instead of argument—though, of course, there is no reason why particular lyric poems should not engage in more discursive forms of discourse, for example, as in some prophetic and didactic verse—one finds a variety of stand-ins, including, most interestingly, metaphor.[113] Metaphor epitomizes the coming "to mean twice" that typifies the tropologically dense discourse of lyric verse.[114] So in Psalm 133 the poem's central invocation, "How good and how pleasant it is / that brothers dwell together" (NJV), is never argued or even exemplified. (Gerstenberger: "these metaphors [in vv. 2–3] cannot very well explain the peaceful coexistence of 'brothers.'")[115] Rather, it is more a matter, as Kraus says, of being "accompanied...by friendly sentiments."[116] That is, the exclamation is supported by two images of superabundance and refreshment—that of oil and that of dew—and we are won over to its point of view largely by the "extravagance" of these similes. In Psalm 1 simile (metaphor) is equally crucial to the poem's success. Here, too, we chiefly have to do with "a joyous exclamation,"[117] "Happy is the man...!" and its main appeal is secured, positively (v. 3) and negatively (v. 4), through similes. The inherent attractiveness of the tree metaphor, plus its elaboration in the poem, is one of the chief ways the poet presses this point. By contrast, the image of chaff that is blown by the wind is inherently negative (note that the negative particles in the poem, vv. 1, 4, 5, always characterize the activity of the wicked) and very brief—the chaff, once blown away, is no more. Such doubleness in the usage of metaphor—both as an image event in its own right and as (or in lieu of) argument—is analogous to the superabundance of meaning that can attach itself to a poet's diction or the doubleness of form illustrated here, and each exemplifies the tropological density (the taking on of "more than their usual sense") that customarily (necessarily) attends lyric discourse.[118]

Utterance of a Voice

In characterizing the lyric, Culler highlights the genre's typical vocality: it "seems to be an utterance...the utterance of a voice."[119] Culler, like many commentators on modern lyric, sublimates the originating orality that births lyric in the first place. This "seemingness" of modern lyric is the bequest of a once living performative tradition whose only medium was the uttered human voice. As P. Zumthor remarks, "'orality' is the historical authenticity of a voice."[120] This vocality has (at least) two distinguishing properties. The first is physical. R. Pinsky gets at this physicality in his notion of lyric poetry as "a vocal, which is to say a bodily, art."[121] He continues: "The medium of poetry is the human body: the column of air inside the chest, shaped into signifying sounds in the larynx and mouth."[122] To focus as Pinsky does on the physical operation of the voice and its production of sound is to recall the lyric's debt to music (which after all was synonymous with singing and song in antiquity) and orality,[123] to stress its sonic qualities, to appreciate that it is an art form that is/was intended to be heard. Rhythm, melody, and euphony (sound play) are all important features of biblical verse, even if our own perception of them through the preserved textual medium(s) is muffled and dim. The rhythmic cadences of biblical Hebrew verse are the most tractable of these musical elements today. So, for example, the mostly balanced cadences of Psalms 33, 111, and 112 contrast noticeably with the unbalanced limp of Psalms 114 and 19:8–11. And though sound play in biblical poetry generally is nonsystematic, its presence and even occasional scripting for larger effect (such as in the chiming *-ah // -â, -am // -ām*, and *-îm // -îm* that frame Ps 133, or the rhyming that punctuates the close of Isa 5:1–7, namely *mišpāṭ // mišpāḥ, ṣĕdāqâ // ṣĕʿāqâ*) is beyond doubt. One of the scandals of lyric poetry, writes Culler, is precisely that these "contingent features of sound and rhythm systematically infect and affect thought."[124]

Moreover, to focus the uttered-ness of the lyric is to recall as well its reutterability—the lyric is quintessentially that medium of discourse that is intended to be reuttered.[125] Again to quote Pinsky: "when I say myself a poem...the artist's medium is my breath. The reader's breath and hearing embody the poet's words. This makes the art physical, intimate, vocal, and individual."[126] And it is through its capacity to be reuttered that lyric verse effects the superposition of "the subjectivity of the scripted speaker on the reader."[127] Or as R. Greene writes, the hearer or reader of the lyric "might be said to shed his or her all-too-specific person, and to take on the speaking self of the poem."[128] In other words, he or she entertains the statements made by the poem's speaker, tries them on, and reexperiences them from the inside, as it were.[129]

Such reutterability is literally true of traditional lyric; that is, what (in part) makes traditional lyric traditional is its familiarity to everyone "as of old"— "what our ancestors have told us" (Ps 78:3),[130] and thus its consummate reutterability. And as E. L. Greenstein observes, "Biblical verse is virtually all direct discourse."[131] This accounts for the openness of psalmic discourse, for example, which P. D. Miller calls attention to in his comments on the identity of the enemies in the laments: "The enemies are in fact whoever the enemies are for the singers of the psalms.... The laments become appropriate for persons who cry out to God in all kinds of situations."[132] E. A. Howe observes that there is "precisely" an appropriate "vagueness" about the voice of the speaking/ singing lyric-I that is all important, that allows the audience to equate it with the poet/singer or identify with it themselves or "see it as a universal 'I' belonging to no-one and to everyone."[133] Such reutterability is strikingly confirmed by the many times psalms are historicized and embedded in biblical narrative—literally placed into the mouths of characters who (re)utter them (e.g., 1 Sam 2:1–10; 2 Sam 18; Isa 38:10–20; Jer 11:18–12:6; 1 Chron 16:8–36). Both Deuteronomy 32 (cf. Deut 31:19) and 2 Samuel 1:19–27 (cf. v. 18) are poems whose narrative stagings presume future reutterings by those who are to be taught the songs. Exodus 15 gets reperformed by Miriam and "all the women" (vv. 20–21). And though we only get snatches, there is an implied reutterability (reiterative-ness) inherent to group singing (e.g., Num 21:17–18; 1 Sam 18:6–7).

A second property of lyric vocality is its figuredness as "incantation, rather than the presentation of telling or ritual."[134] So this is in part why Culler privileges the "apostrophe" ("a turning aside...to address to a someone or something that is not an ordinary empirical listener") as the master trope of lyric—it "foregrounds the act of address"; it is "a troping on the circuit of communication or situation of address."[135] Here one notices most the absence of developed (fictional) characters, which more often than not appear to have mutated into disembodied or orphaned voice in the lyric (and if named are only equivocally or inferentially named)[136]—viewing matters from the perspective of narrative, which is a heuristic felicity in deference to modern literary proclivities; no such mutation was strictly necessary as lyric is every bit as old as narrative (epic).[137] And as a result of this incantatory shaping of vocality—that "it is, precisely, *invoked*"[138]—the lyric takes on what W. R. Johnson describes as its *typical*[139] pronominal form. He identifies three principal patterns in which pronominal forms are deployed in lyric verse.[140] The prototypical pronominal pattern is the I-You form,[141] which primordially gains its shape from "the presence of the singer before his audience."[142] Ancient lyric in particular, as G. N. Shuster notices, "was addressed to somebody, primarily because it was either sung or read and the traditions of song and recitation required that there be a recipient."¹⁴³ Though narrative representations of such performative contexts are not many in the Bible and never as richly detailed as we might want, they do occur (e.g., Exod 15:1, 20–21; Num 21:16–18; Judg 5:1; 2 Sam 1:17–18).¹⁴⁴ A more thoroughgoing indicator that much of the Bible's lyrics were shaped primordially in live performance is the pluralized "you" and "we" encountered so commonly (e.g., communal hymns and laments of the Psalms)—their deictic values explicitly index the communal coefficient of these utterances.¹⁴⁵ The lyric-I of the singer of songs would have been every bit as prominent in ancient Israel and Judah as the dominantly focalized (by scholarship) "singer of tales" (see chapter 4). There were specialists, like the cultic singer (and perhaps writer) of psalms supposed by S. Mowinckel,¹⁴⁶ but songs (whether whole or in snatches) are routinely put in the mouths of nonspecialists in biblical narrative as well (e.g., Exod 15: 20–21; Num 21:17; Judg 5:3; 1 Sam 2:1–10). Such songs express all manner of things (e.g., praise, complaint, victory, love),¹⁴⁷ and the live audience, when present, may be presumed to have been an active coefficient in the performance as a whole—and sometimes is even addressed overtly (e.g., Isa 5:5; Ps 78:1). Most often such songs explicitly address an unidentified and frequently absent lyric-you—many times in the religious lyrics of the Bible this is Yahweh, of course (e.g., in the Psalms),¹⁴⁸ but others may be focalized in this manner as well, the lovers in the Song of Songs,¹⁴⁹ for example, not to mention more obvious apostrophes (e.g., "Give ear, O heavens, and I will speak," Deut 32:1). One effect of this second person address is to accentuate the presentness that seems to enfold the act of lyric speech.¹⁵⁰ Oral performance could also be enacted privately (e.g., Hannah's song, 1 Sam 2:1–10). The second variation identified by W. R. Johnson is more impersonal, more meditative, as if the poet is speaking to himself or herself or to no one in particular, or even sometimes to apostrophized, inanimate objects (e.g., Song 4:16). The last variety is more dialogic in nature. The lyric-I either recedes fully into the background, giving way to a interchange of voices, or takes part as one of the voices in a larger dialogue (e.g., Song of Songs). Of these "ideal" types, the first and third dominate in the traditional lyric of the Bible, as the presence of a real or imagined interlocutor is crucial to "sustained thought" in prominently oral cultures—"it is hard to talk to yourself hours on end."¹⁵¹ This is not to rule out the possibility of more meditative moments in oral or oral-derived lyric verse, but it is a modality that is most naturally nurtured in the isolation of writing. Job 3, not prototypically lyric (e.g., it was likely not a sung piece), is one of the more meditative poems in the Bible. Strictly speaking, it falls outside the dialogic framework by which the poetry of Job is staged. And yet even here, the poem and its meditation are sustained with help from the apostrophized "day" and "night" that are cursed.¹⁵²

The prominence of first person voice in Greek lyric has often been reified (especially during the Romantic period)[153] as *the* defining feature of lyric verse (see the *OED*'s definition of "lyric"). The problematic nature of such an identification is, as Lindley notes, obvious: "Though it is one of the devices that poets may employ, it is by no means self-evident that all poetry using this mode of speech is 'lyric,' nor that poetry which does not should be excluded from the lyric category."[154] In fact, it is not only on conceptual grounds that such an identification fails but on empirical grounds as well. To judge only by W. R. Johnson's own (rough) statistical sampling of the distribution of his pronominal types in various lyric poets from the Greeks forward, the lyric-I, though at times absolutely dominant (as in ancient Greece), is by no means omnipresent.[155] And in contemporary Anglo-American lyric verse it is the diversity of voice that is the norm and not a foreordained lyric-I.[156] Yet even to highlight the mode of discourse, first person or otherwise, tells us nothing in particular about the persona of that voice. Even in Greek lyric, as E. Bowie stresses, one cannot naively assume the identity of poet and the speaking I of the poem.[157] The voice of biblical lyric, like other traditions rooted in oral performance, certainly favors the first person singular (and plural) of a singer of songs in live performance. But such singers, like their better studied cousins, the singers of tales, are adept at modulating from one voice to another. And thus that a certain multivocality is achievable in biblical lyric is no surprise, though it does not finally approach the kind of hypervariability of so much contemporary lyric verse.

Smallness of Scale

The question of scale, though not insignificant, requires little comment. A certain smallness of scale (as exhibited by most biblical poems) is generally associated with the lyric.[158] As Frye belatedly observes, "a lyric is anything you can reasonably get uncut into an anthology."[159] Such brevity results from the lyric's general eschewal of devices (e.g., plot, argument, temporal sequence, consistency of setting) that would enable more encompassing discourse in performance and means, as a purely practical matter, that lyric poems will be limited in the scope of their subject matter. And with only language itself as its chief medium of discourse it is difficult for lyric poems to sustain themselves over long stretches of time and space. Writing, of course, becomes the principal means for extending lyric's reach. The singular achievement of writing is the spatialization (and thus fixing) of language, which, among other things, unshackles comprehension from the lifeworld of performance and the strict limits of human memory, and, in the case of lyric poetry, makes possible a dramatic expansion in scale. But some enlargement of the lyric's native brevity is manageable even in the absence of writing. One strategy is to engage more explicitly in narrative or utilize the various devices of narrative poetry, such as is in evidence, for example, in Psalms 78, 105, and 106. Another means for increasing the lyric's otherwise confining amplitude is to successively link a number of individual lyric poems and mold them into a greater, organic whole. What gets enacted in such a process, then, is a sequence of lyric poems or movements whose nature and dynamic, holistically considered, is essentially that of a lyric poem writ large. As literary critics are discovering, the latter approach is a compositional strategy that translates well into writing and turns out to be quite common and knows very few chronological or geographical boundaries.[160] Such verse sequences, in fact, are best known from written traditions, and yet the technology is not restricted to the written medium. In oral performance, it is the singer who bodily navigates and guides the audience from one song to the next,[161] a process I will explore in more detail with respect to the Song of Songs.

Rhythm of Association

Smith identifies two principal means for generating thematic structure in poems, parataxis and sequence.[162] Of the two the latter will be well known, as sequence (of some sort) usually lies at the heart of story and plot. And while there are biblical poems in which the sequential order of thematic elements is generated primarily from some "extraliterary principle of succession,"[163] such as the tradition-historical rehearsal of Yahweh's "glorious deeds" in Psalm 78 (cf. Exod 15; Judg 5), more often biblical lyrics hew closer to the paratactic end of the structuring continuum. And indeed parataxis is prototypical of lyric discourse, no doubt, as Smith suggests, reflecting the lyric's origin in oral song.[164] "When repetition is the fundamental principle of thematic generation," as so often in traditional or naive song styles, "the resulting structure will tend to be paratactic"[165] and associative in nature—what Frye aptly labels "the rhythm of association."[166] The "oral" logic of this "adding style" is well explained by J. A. Notopoulos:

> The spoken word, unlike the written word, must be winged, impelled ever onward by the spontaneity and urgency of verbalization in oral poetry. Creation by means of the spoken word leaves the poet little time to pause and appraise the lines he is shaping in terms of the larger pattern.... This technique inevitably results in the λέξις εἰρομένη, the strung-along and adding style, and in the paratactic handling of his material.[167]

In other words, oral verbal art "necessarily follows a temporal sequence."[168] In such instances, the lyric's centers of "emotionally and sensuously charged awareness," according to M. L. Rosenthal and S. M. Gall, radiate out and relate to one another associatively, through "felt relationship." The resulting play of tonal depths and shadings and shiftings is achieved through "strategic juxtaposition of separate...passages without a superimposed logical or fictional continuity."[169] And thus, the dislocation or omission of individual thematic units, unlike in sequentially structured discourse, will not render the whole unintelligible or make it incoherent. To the contrary, one of the hallmarks of paratactic structure is that thematic elements may be added, omitted, or exchanged quite happily. Junctures or gaps between a lyric's component elements without explicit scripting become a prominent part of the discursive fabric that is to be negotiated, and as a consequence fragmentation and disjunction—a susceptibility to disintegration[170]—become central to the founding fiction of the paratactically structured lyric poem, especially once written down and divorced from an informing performance context.[171] Any reading of such a lyric "must accommodate discontinuity as well as continuity, allow for the spatial dimension of lyric temporality, and offer a means of getting into and over" the junctures between elements "without brutally closing them."[172] Whatever fiction, whatever stratagem of discourse is manifested, therefore, necessarily partakes in and celebrates or otherwise gives prominence to fragmentation.[173]

On my reading, it is the nonsequentuality of parataxis that governs the thematic structure in Psalm 114. There it is not a matter of temporal or logical sequence but of association and juxtaposition—the events of the Red Sea calling to mind the crossing of the Jordan, nature's similar reactions to Yahweh's variously traditioned theophany attracting one another. Smith identifies the "list" as one of the most obvious forms manifesting paratactic structure.[174] Lists are especially prominent, for example, in Mesopotamian hymnody, but they are recognizable as well in various aspects of Israelite psalmody, as in the typical use of the so-called hymnic participle or in the listing of Yahweh's various qualities.[175] But no doubt the paradigm of paratactic structure in the Psalms comes in the conventional (given) forms isolated by the form-critical study of the Psalms. Here, as Gunkel saw better than most, it is chiefly a matter of thematic (as opposed to strictly formal) structure that is most definitive of the various verse forms. And, what is more relevant here, only rarely are these forms thematically sequenced. The psalms of lament are a case in point. These poems, communal and individual alike, have a recognizable set of family resemblances (consisting of common elements such as addresses, petitions, complaints or laments, motivational clauses, affirmations of trust).

But as is well known, "they are rarely precisely alike, though repeated formulas are not uncommon...; and they may vary significantly in their length and the degree of elaboration of their component parts. Some are very succinct while others are extended in one or more of their basic elements. Some do not contain all of the elements that other [laments] do."[176] What Miller describes here is the epitome of paratactic structure.

Moreover, the play of parataxis effects a dynamic interaction among different (and sometimes conflicting and competing) perspectives that is not unlike the montage effect in film, which Alter describes in a different context.[177] Alter quotes the following description of montage offered by S. Eisenstein:

> The juxtaposition of two separate shots by splicing them together resembles not so much a simple sum of one shot plus one shot—as it does a *creation*. It resembles a creation—rather than a sum of its parts—from the circumstance that in every such juxtaposition *the result is qualitatively* distinguishable from each component element viewed separately.... Each particular montage piece exists no longer as something unrelated, but as a given *particular representation* of the general theme.[178]

Of course, the analogy is not exact. The seams that result from the paratactic splicing of different perspectives or images in language are much more noticeable than in (some) photography and film, in part, at least in orally rooted biblical lyrics, because the borders of a song's component movements (stanzas) tend to be overtly marked through gesture, sound, and sense and thus literally call attention to the shift in structural shape.[179] This can result in a more complex image. Not only does one have the "particular representation" created by the montage but the component elements also signify on their own. As but one example of the montage effect of parataxis consider Psalm 74:12–17.[180] The passage, as J. Levenson notes, "is the *locus classicus* of the idea that the God of Israel...defeated the Sea and its monsters...and then created the familiar world." Levenson then continues:

> Surely no text would seem more imbued with [Y.] Kaufmann's "basic idea of Israelite religion," that "there is no realm above or beside YHWH to limit his absolute sovereignty."[181] But the context of these verses [vv. 10–11, 18–20] belies the unqualified note of triumphalism in this theology. For the context of vv. 12–17 in Psalm 74 shows that the celebratory language of victory is invoked here precisely when conditions have rendered belief in God's majesty most difficult.[182]

The upshot of this (paratactic) juxtaposition, according to Levenson, is that the psalmist in Psalm 74 "acknowledges the reality of militant, triumphant, and persistent evil, but he steadfastly and resolutely refuses to accept this reality as final and absolute."[183] Such a stance is manifestly the result of the montage-like juxtaposition of two different moods or movements, whose seams are readily apparent, and indeed it may well be, as Levenson contends, that "the continuity between v. 11 and v. 18 strongly suggests that the hymn in vv. 12–17 has been interpolated."[184]

What is crucial to see in all of these examples is the centrality of fragmentation and discontinuity to the type of discourse enacted and that any minimally adequate reading of them, as the foregoing quote from Greene makes clear, must accommodate the discontinuity that is so definitive of paratactic structure and offer ways of getting into and over the resulting gaps and junctures. Such a way of reading, of course, is in many respects the very antithesis of how we habitually read narratives.

Fit for Ritual

"The earliest recorded evidence of l[yric] poetry," writes J. W. Johnson, "suggests that such compositions emerged from ritual activity accompanying religious ceremonies."[185] Certainly much biblical and ancient Near Eastern lyric poetry (e.g., hymns, laments) was originally (and quite literally) "fit...for 'ritual.'"[186] While both "ritual and fictional phenomena," as "correlative modes of apprehension," are theoretically available in every specimen of lyric discourse—and indeed, "even to privilege one is usually a matter not of ignoring the other," as Greene rightly maintains,[187] it is lyric's ritual values that prototypically "define the phenomenology of the single lyric."[188] This state of affairs is somewhat ironic, as it is also the case that the dominant strain of lyric verse in the Western poetic tradition, from ancient Greece through the twenty-first century, has been the fictional.[189] By "fictional" Greene means "represented speech"—"that the speaking, addressing, expressing, and alluding are themselves fictive verbal acts."[190] Here I probe the more "open" and performative end of the lyric continuum, the ritual lyric, since it is a dominant mode of the Bible's lyric verse and the mode of lyric generally least familiar to contemporary sensibilities.

Lyric's ritual dimension is what M. C. Nussbaum refers to when she talks about lyric's engendering capacity: "The lyrics both show us and engender in us a process of reflection and (self)-discovery that works through a persistent attention to and (re)-interpretation of concrete words, images, incidents."[191] This dimension has been described more generally by Greene as a poem's performative aspect; its office as a set of directions for performance, a script, a score compounded of sounds, rhythm, and form and the patterns that organize these in the audience's immediate experience (here and now).[192] The chief aim of ritually oriented lyrics is to effect through a type of transitivity an experience of communitas or collectivity, a synchronous, performative unity into which all actors are induced. Blasing recognizes this communitarian shaping of lyric discourse in this way:

> The lyric "I" makes the communal personality of a people audible. It both resounds individuating histories and formally transmits public traditions of how a linguistic community has patterned and remembered the material in excess of referential functions. It does not exist apart from these constitutive histories; it articulates them as what articulate it. Communities cohere around linguistic experience, and poetry is the ritualized confirmation of that coherence—explicitly so in preliterate languages. The communal being is audible in the materials of language, not in what a poem says.[193]

This ritual agenda is manifested in and enacted by a poem's rhythm and other prosodic features—especially such large-scale structuring devices as calendars, acrostics, and numerologies—but including rhetorical, semantic, and symbolic features as well.[194]

The Psalms are the Bible's largest and perhaps most obvious collection of ritually oriented lyrics—after all many will have been engineered expressly for ritual and liturgy, and, indeed, cast intentionally in broad and generic terms so as to be readily assimilable to a range of occasions and circumstances—as witnessed by how individual psalms are put into the mouths of characters in biblical narrative (e.g., Hannah, 1 Sam 2:1–10; Jonah, Jon 2:3–10).[195] Greene characterizes the Psalms' rituality more specifically:

> Taken singly, the psalms generally belong at the most "open" or performative end of the spectrum that runs from ritual to fiction, for they allow, or better, require the reading voice to assume the identity of their represented speaker; in a certain sense a psalm scarcely represents a speaker at all, but is the script for sacred ritual cast in lyric discourse.[196]

Greene here is commenting explicitly on Sir Philip Sidney's sixteenth-century incomplete translation of the Psalms. Still, even viewed at arm's length and specifically through the lens of a metrical translation into English, Greene reveals (in a preliminary fashion) many of the leading aspects of the Psalter's

pronounced rituality. For my own exposition of the ritual dimensions of the
biblical lyric, I turn to Lamentations. If the poetry of Lamentations in its probable un-sung-ness is not prototypically lyrical, it nonetheless shares many of
the lyric's leading practices.[197] The advantage of using Lamentations as a
worked example here is that the rituality of this poetry is so palpable. As Hillers well observes: "Both the poetic forms found in the book and the organization of the poems fit Lamentations for 'ritual' in the broad sense, in which
many a poem is an abstraction from experience that invites contemplation,
repetition, and the participation of others besides the author."[198]

Lamentations' ritual dimension is activated primarily through form and
rhythm. The alphabetic acrostic formally shapes in one way or another all of
the poems. In the first four poems each stanza begins with the appropriate
letter of the Hebrew alphabet, starting with *aleph* and moving successively
through the alphabet, ending with *taw*. Each poem contains twenty-two stanzas in all, the total number of letters in the Hebrew alphabet. Although the
fifth poem does not employ the acrostic (not insignificant in its own right), it
does contain exactly twenty-two couplets. Each stanza of these poems contains either one, two, or three couplets, with the number remaining consistent
throughout the individual poems.[199] The couplets themselves are normally
closed, that is, they end with a significant syntactic pause, and in the first four
poems are composed of pairs of predominantly unbalanced and variously enjambed lines. That is, the first line of the couplet is usually longer than the
second, and its syntax frequently carries over into the second. In contrast, the
couplets in the fifth poem, reflecting the more common rhythm of biblical
Hebrew verse, contain pairs of more or less balanced and parallel lines.

These dominant patterns of repetition project an experience of materiality
as shape and feel. The acrostic gives body and reach to each poem and provides a palpable sense of measured regularity and a unifying frame that en-
capsulates the otherwise chaotic play of Lamentations' dominant parataxis.
Poetic rhythm, whatever its nature, emanates in bursts of pulsating energy
from the muscular workings of the speech organs and is felt physically by
auditors as much as it is heard or processed cognitively.[200] In Lamentations
the dominant texture of unbalanced lines effects a hypnotic limping beat (pe-
culiarly appropriate for a dirge-like composition), while their propensity for
enjambment effects a distinct feeling of forward movement as the syntax of
the sentence carries over from one line to the next.[201] Of course this tug of
forward movement is almost immediately checked by the major pause at the
end of the predominantly closed couplets. What results, then, are bursts of
onward thrust alternating with moments of stasis. This stuttering movement
complements the limping rhythm established by the unbalanced lines, and

together both counterpoint the regularity and evenness constructed by the stanzaic march of the acrostic and the sequence of closed couplets. Both the acrostic and the qinah meter constrain poet/scribe and audience alike, and yet these constraints, if yielded to, produce, somewhat paradoxically, a self-liberating and almost trance-like state conducive to audience participation and the promotion of experiential immediacy. That is, through materiality, be it formal shape or rhythmic feel, the ritually orientated (nonnarrative) poem becomes accessible, open, in a way analogous to liturgies and other structures of devotion and achieves a kind of transitivity whereby the poem can be a coercive and potentially powerful vehicle for promoting political or ideological or even theological agendas.[202]

Sound, of course, is another important means for accessing and initiating the ritual dimension of lyric poetry. As Greene observes, commenting specifically on the ritual force of glossolalia, that token of pure sound, it "always exerts a strongly ritual pull on its auditors. They repeat it attentively and lovingly, fully aware that they participate in something of much greater import than noise."[203] And it seems clear that sound was ritually significant for Lamentations, though this can only be imperfectly perceived at the distance of two thousand–plus years. But there are some telltale signs. For example, the *'êkâ* ("Alas! Ah! Oh!") that begins three of the poems (Lam 1:1a; 2:1a; 4:1a) is principally a token of glossolalia, an ejaculation that voices or expresses in a pre- or postreferential kind of language the complex set of emotions death and loss trigger in human beings, emotions that in a very real sense can never be fully articulated. Moreover, one can still perceive the traces of various kinds of consonance and assonance that would have engendered (and occasionally still do) an infectious musicality. Note, as an example where the traces are still perceptible to the contemporary reader, Lamentations 1:2. *Lamed* is given prominence in the first couplet (and is more noticeable because of this throughout the whole stanza as well), as are *bet* and *kap* in the first line. The final words (*ballaylâ, lehĕyāh*) in both lines end with /ā/, as does the first word in the second line (*dim'ātāh*). Assonance plays out in the remainder of the stanza as well, as for example in *mikkol-'ōhăbeyhā* and *kol-rē'eyhā* in lines 4 and 5 and *bāgĕdû bāh* and *hāyû lāh* in lines 5 and 6. Another obvious example of assonance appears in Lamentations 2:5c, *ta'ăniyyâ wa'ăniyyâ*. Notice the chiming and rhyming engendered by the poet's use of suffixes in Lamentations 1:14 (/ī/ at the end of lines 3 and 4, and chiming with *nĕtānanî* in line 5; /ay/ at the ends of lines 1 and 5; and the chiming of *bĕyādô* and *'ullô*) and in 1:15 (/ay/ in *'abbîray . . . 'ădōnāy . . . 'ālay . . . bahûrāy . . . 'ădōnāy*). And as a final example, Lamentations 1:10 is remarkable for its internal rhyming: *yādô // yābō'û; mahămaddeyhā // miqdāšāh; rā'ātâ* (3 f. sg.) *// siwwîtâ* (2 m. sg.); *bā'û* (pf. 3 m. pl.) //

yābōʾû (impf. 3 m. pl.) (The formal differences among all these pairs suggest that the rhyming is not accidental.)

Therefore, sound joins form and rhythm as the principal means for activating Lamentations' ritual transitivity, that specific property of lyric verse (in particular) that effects the superposition of "the subjectivity of the scripted speaker on the reader."[204] Lyric is uniquely reutterable. Or as Greene writes, the hearer or reader of the lyric "might be said to shed his or her all-too-specific person, and to take on the speaking self of the poem."[205] In other words, he or she entertains the statements made by the poem's speaker, tries them on, and reexperiences them from the inside, as it were.[206] "After meeting in the society of the text and submitting to its revalorizations—of what we bring to it, and of its own sounds and meanings—we take those everyday selves back, restructured or reanimated."[207] In this manner the ritual lyric promotes a transcendence that can begin to envision alternative realities. Such reutterability contrasts with the dominant fictional mode of the lyric, which represents alternative worlds that participants must enter—the world of the poem is no longer coextensive with the poem's performance or the world of its readers/auditors.[208]

This kind of transitivity is implicit in much of Lamentations, and intuitively felt as the audience find themselves fully identifying with the sentiments expressed, for example, by personified Zion in either of the first two poems. However, this transitive agenda is also at times explicitly scripted in the text itself. The most obvious instance occurs in Lamentations 3. The poem opens with the memorable words "I am the man [*haggeber*] who has seen affliction / Under the rod of his anger." The first section of the poem (Lam 3:1–18) proceeds to articulate and detail in the stereotypical language well known from the Psalms how "the man" has suffered at the hands of Yahweh. These reflections are cast very specifically in terms of what has happened to the speaker. The sequence of first person forms is readily apparent. Then in the next sections (vv. 19–24, 25–39) "the man" reflects on a series of wisdom teachings that counsel patience and long suffering in the belief that Yahweh will eventually help those who wait for Yahweh's salvation and bear their suffering. These wisdom-inspired reflections are cast more broadly, as is typical of their genre, to reflect human experience in general. To this end, the scribe presents the reflections using third person forms (instead of the first person forms of vv. 1–18) and employs a succession of terms for "man" or "human being": *geber* (vv. 27, 35, 39), *bĕnê-ʾîš* (v. 33), and *ʾādām* (vv. 36, 39). The net effect of both strategies is to significantly broaden the poem's perspective to include humanity in general, of which, of course, the poem's audience (readerly or aurally) is a part. The explicit use of the term *geber*, both at the beginning and the end of this section, intentionally links the section with the poem's opening line (a Buberian *Leit-wort*). Auditors experience, then, the litany of suffering in verses 1–18 retro-spectively, not only as the experience of a particular individual but also as the experience of a "man" who is more broadly representative of "Everyman," to use Hillers's term.[209] The clinching movement whereby the audience is written explicitly into the text comes in verses 40–47, where the speaker all of a sudden shifts into the first person plural voice—the communal voice of tradition par excellence: "Let *us* test and examine *our* ways! / Let *us* return to Yahweh!" (v. 40). The "man's" experience, his sufferings as well as his hopes and longings, are *our* experience, that is, the experience of the larger community (of the text); his voice is *our/communal* voice. The merger between individual and commu-nity is complete. Beginning in verse 48 the poet returns to the first person singular and maintains this voice for the duration of the poem. Some com-mentators have noticed a perceptible difference between the "I" of verses 1–18 and the "I" of verses 48–66.[210] However, one need not suppose that the distinc-tion results (only) because of different sources or different speakers. Rather, at the outset of the poem the individuality of the speaking "I" is foregrounded. Whereas by the poem's end the speaking "I" has become all-inclusive, resem-bling in many respects the all-embracing voice Whitman achieves in much of his *Leaves of Grass*.[211] Through such a strategy transitivity is scripted explicitly into the text. Individual auditors are encouraged to try on this voice and what it says because they have been explicitly included in that voice—this poem "is a site where 'our' 'coinciding' looks [to] form a community."[212]

The precise content of what gets transacted through transitivity in Lamen-tations requires a fully detailed and engaged reading of these poems, which cannot be undertaken here.[213] Suffice it here to accentuate the communal ori-entation of this poetry, manifested most objectively in the communal nature of the speaking voices. The several speeches rendered in the first person plural form ("we") are de facto manifestations of the communal voice (Lam 3:40–47; 4:17–20; 5:1–22). And, while the "man" (*haggeber*) of Lamentations 3 and personified Zion (esp. in Lam 1 and 2) clearly speak from their own spa-tial levels, and therefore require being treated as individuated voices in their own right, they both are nevertheless ultimately to be identified as representa-tives or ventriloquisms of the community.[214] Such communally oriented poetry, like ritual poetry more generally and especially the choral lyrics of the Psalms or ancient Greece,[215] functions to imagine "those emotions which lead us to want to understand both the possibility of our communion with each other and the possibility of our communion with the world" and to persuade us that our hopes of goodness and our fears of social and moral dangers are genuine, and thereby "encourage the necessary marshaling of energies and strengthening of wills and of faith."[216] Indeed, it is precisely for their prizing of communitas that choral poems like these from antiquity deserve a fresh hearing from contemporary audiences.[217]

Finally, the ritual mode impinges as well on the temporality of the lyric. It does so in two ways. First, it is in the lyric's ritual dimension "where the lyric appears to remain more contemporary to its audience than other kinds of literary discourse."[218] There is a certain immediacy and urgency to lyric discourse, an all-pervasive "nowness."[219] As Greene says, "lyric often sees that *here* and *now* burst into the discourse spontaneously, abruptly."[220] Second, ritual fosters a kind of temporal continuity between present and past in the service of the future. In religious festivals and ceremonies it is through ritual reenactment that participants gain access to sacred time, the mythical past. Ritual encourages "the conception of the sacred past as bound up in process with the present." It replays the "past over our own lives—having lived in both times, we remember them as temporally parallel and mutually accessible"—and refashions "an explicit continuum between *then* and *now*."[221] Lamentations exhibits both aspects of this ritual temporality. In biblical Hebrew, temporal location is established contextually and is not indexed morphologically on the verb form. The poetry in Lamentations is almost totally devoid of any markers of temporal location, and therefore, as in lyric discourse more generally, there is no deictic program, no hierarchy of event and utterance that can be mapped and tracked—like the lyrics of so many psalms, these are among the "least temporally plotted."[222] As a consequence past and present are never carefully differentiated. They bump into one another, commingle, and at times even metamorphose each into another and back again, depending on the audience's perspective. A good example of the latter, where in the blink of an eye past and present phase in and out like a mirage, is the account of Yahweh's battle against Jerusalem in Lamentations 2:1–8. It can be read as an account of a past event or as the simultaneous reporting of an event that is still ongoing. The latter is suggested by the use of the imperfective prefix form (*yāʿîb*) to open the passage—and the only such form in the passage. Imperfective forms view events without their end points and thus stress the event's ongoing and dynamic nature. Or perhaps both perspectives are intended. That is, Yahweh's past attack is conjured anew and reexperienced in the telling of it. Past and present are ritually wedded; Yahweh's past attack is bound in process with the present of the poem's reading/hearing—a temporality that is still manifested for readers at a remove of some two thousand years!

And as in many ritually oriented lyrics the present often seems to erupt abruptly through the surface of the poetry in Lamentations. This effect is accomplished not primarily with deictics but through direct discourse[223] and the selective use of the imperfective viewpoint. Both play off the dominant texture of the poems that is established through perfective verb forms (suffix and *wayyiqtol* forms). The perfective viewpoint views events holistically, with both end points in place. While such a perspective need not entail a past temporal location, perfective forms frequently become the typical narrative forms in many languages, as they do in biblical Hebrew prose (esp. in the use of *wayyiqtol* forms). When direct discourse or imperfective viewpoints are used against the predominant background of perfective forms, the net effect is to foreground a sense of dynamicity, vigor, and presence. As one example, take Lamentations 4:14–15. In verse 14, blind people are described as wandering in the streets so defiled in blood that none could touch them. The main action is carried by perfective forms. But then in verse 15 voices out of nowhere cry out: "Away! Unclean!" "Get away! Get away! Do not touch!" This interruption of speech bursts abruptly into the poem, bringing with it a very real sense of immediacy and presence. All of a sudden we are there in the streets and are warding off these blind beggars. A similar effect is achieved by the use of direct speech in Lamentations 2:11. After the recounting of Yahweh's attack in 2:1–8, which, with the exception of the initial verb, is rendered completely with perfective forms, a voice responds:

> My eyes are consumed with tears
> My stomach churns
> My guts spill out on the ground
> Because of the destruction of the Daughter of my people
> Because children and babies faint
> In the streets of the city

The effect of this burst of speech is to turn that possibly past event into a living reality. The immediacy and sense of presence created initially by the imperfective *yāʾîb* (2:1a) returns anew with this direct discourse. Such a move cannot but color how auditors retrospectively evaluate and understand Lamentations 2:1–8.

If these poems intentionally and effectively eschew or otherwise manipulate the notion of temporal consistency, they nevertheless manifest a kind of temporal centeredness, as they are all always situated against the horizon of Jerusalem's destruction. When the destruction is thought to have taken place shifts depending on context, and regardless it is never explicitly stated, but more often simply implied or evoked. The opening stanza of Lamentations 1 well exemplifies the poetry's characteristic evocation of temporality. In the first stanza, we read how the city that was once full of people now sits alone and is abandoned and how the once queenly Jerusalem now resembles a widow or a slave. The past against which the poem is written falls somewhere between these two points, the glorious past and the dismal present. But precisely when the catastrophe occurred is never stated as such. In fact, most of the discourse in Lamentations would seem to take place between the hazily figured past and a future when Yahweh's voice will be heard again.

The figuration of Lamentations 2:1–8 as another march of the Divine Warrior does tap into that mythic paradigm, but in a not uncomplicated way. More classic expressions of the ritual lyric's capacity to give access to sacred time, the mythical past, occur outside Lamentations. Psalm 114 (discussed earlier) is paradigmatic. In the poem itself the crossing of the Jordan (vv. 3–6) is imbued with the mythology of the Reed Sea event (esp. vv. 1–2)—the opening infinitive construct *běṣēʾt* "when (Israel) went forth..." literally stages the former in light of, emerging out of, that earlier halcyon time of Yahweh's mythic battle with the Egyptians. And then the apostrophe to *ʾāreṣ* "O land, earth" (v. 7), a stand-in for the contemporary audience, enfolds that audience into the mythic temporality of both events, allowing those events to be replayed as a part of their lives, and thus that "sacred past" becomes "bound up in process with the present."

I elaborate on this informing rituality in part because nowadays so much lyric verse hews decidedly toward the genre's fictive foundation that we can easily forget this other founding capacity, not to mention the many modern poets whose prosodies are thoroughly ritualistic and even informed (directly or indirectly) by biblical poetry (e.g., Walt Whitman, Edward Taylor); and in part because this means that contemporary readers of Psalms, Lamentations, and other dominantly ritualistic biblical poetry in addition to having to recalibrate their tacit readerly pose toward literature from narrative to nonnarrative will also need to adjust their notions of lyric so as to include an appetite for ritual.

A Feeling through Language

The "emotional element in a lyric poem" has often been "considered its chief identifying trait"—so, according to L. Ryken, "it is above all an utterance of intense emotion."[224] But such prizing of emotion, if typical of the lyric (especially in its Romantic and post-Romantic guise), is not phenomenologically distinctive in the same way as the other elements so far discussed. As Langer remarks, the content of the lyric poem, what it creates, "the occurrence of a living thought, the sweep of an emotion, the intense experience of a mood," is variable.[225] It may in fact be about anything—a shirt, an urn, a lover, death— and at its best engages in critical thinking and aims at doing moral work, but its object remains open. Rather, if there is criterial importance to be attached to the commonality with which lyric discourse engages the passions, it is of a conventional kind, having emerged out of habit and tradition, by dint of lyric's strong propensity throughout the ages to traffic in the emotions.[226]

The lyric has become one place where emotions and feelings are routinely (if not necessarily) valorized, for their own intrinsic worth as well as for the motivational, action-guiding, and cognitive roles they play in human excellence. It is a place where passions are celebrated, explored, and even interrogated. It is a feeling through language; "a projection...of specific qualities and intensities of emotionally and sensuously charged awareness."[227] The aim of such projections is not primarily to reflect or represent, though of course this may and often does happen, but to present, evoke, contemplate. Or as W. R. Johnson writes, lyrical discourse is "the process by means of which the lyric poet describes (and so evokes) an emotion or complex cluster of emotions while simultaneously submitting that evocative description to dialectical scrutiny, to deliberation, to argumentation."[228]

That emotion and passion—whether in the agonizing (and angry) cry of radical suffering ("My God, my god, why have you abandoned me!" Ps 22:2), the expressed ecstasy of sublime devotion ("I am glad and exult in you! / I sing your name, O Most High!," Ps 9:3), the full-throated chauvinism of martial victory ("I will sing to Yahweh, for he has triumphed gloriously; / horse and rider he has thrown into the sea," Exod 15:1), or the ebullient delights of young love ("Let him kiss me with the kisses of his mouth!" Song 1:2)—figure prominently and frequently in the lyric poetry of the Bible, though perhaps widely assumed, is not without importance. T. Linafelt stresses precisely the "willingness to give access to the inner lives of its speakers" as a central distinguishing feature of lyric verse in the Bible, especially compared to the typical opaqueness of characterization in biblical narrative.[229] Psalms and Song of Songs, "where the expression of passion, whether despairing or joyful, is common,"[230] are paradigmatic examples of this privileged use of lyric in the Bible. And as Linafelt also points out, there are plenty of narrative contexts in which "briefer poetic insets...serve to express or intensify emotion" (e.g., Gen 37:33), and "the book of Job serves as an example on a much larger scale," where the poetic dialogues contain (as the narrative frame does not and cannot) "Job's impassioned defense of his integrity."[231]

A consequence of such lyric prizing of emotion is the tacit validation of the emotional, affirmation that the passions are part and parcel of a human being's (bodily) makeup. Indeed, as ancient (and contemporary) readers/hearers were (are) forced to engage such poetry at an emotional level, the emotions themselves are made visible as topics for critical discourse and thinking. And conversely, one of the truths that emotionally charged and evocative verse spurs auditors toward is the recognition of just how impoverished thinking and reasoning would be were it unaccompanied by feeling and emotion. Philosophers and scientists alike are now beginning to (re)appreciate just how crucial the emotions are for the health and well-being of the human creature,[232] and therefore, to have a place—a kind of discourse—so routinely charged with emotion, where engagement with the passions is easy and comfortable, as with so many moments in the Psalms, for example, is perhaps not as insubstantial or ephemeral as has sometimes been thought. The biblical lyric's ready emotiveness, if not (necessarily) definitional of the larger genre, nonetheless stakes out one trajectory for lyric discourse that is not only well-attested (historically) but is now also beginning to be better *thought* of.

The Extravagance of Lyric

A final means of distinguishing lyric discourse is by what Culler calls its "extravagance"—the predilection for "hyperbolic accents."[233] "Exaggeration is the name of the game here," writes Culler; "the tiger is not just orange but 'burning'; the wind is the very 'breath of autumn's being.'"[234] That the Bible's lyric discourse is also accented throughout with hyperbole is (again) perhaps obvious, as the rhetoric of exaggeration punctuates almost every psalm, for example—"How utterly good and lovely...!" (*hinnê mah-ṭṭôb ûmah-nnāʿîm*, Ps 133:1) or "Who is like Yahweh our god!" (*mî k-yhwh ʾĕlōhênû*, Ps 113:5). The Song of Songs begins immediately with such extravagance—"Let him kiss me with the kisses of his mouth!" (NRSV; *yiššāqēnî minnĕšîqôt pîhû*, Song 1:2)—and almost never relents—"Flee, my love!" (*bĕraḥ dôdî*, Song 8:14). And it is extravagance that lies at the core of Alter's "structures of intensification."[235] Alter captures well the hyperbole that is critical to the culminating moment in Psalm 13 (vv. 4–5). The speaker, writes Alter, imagines his own death as

> sleeping the sleep of death, where God's gaze will never be able to light up his eyes—*and as a dramatic scene*—going down for the last time, with his enemies crowing in triumph. *This is the white hot point to which the magnifying glass of the structure of intensification has concentrated the assertions of desperate need.*[236]

Not only is the psalm's rhetoric laced with exaggeration and intensification, but so is Alter's!

The motivating factors for such extravagance are at least twofold. Culler singles out lyric's aspiration to the "sublime," its reach for transcendence: "a relation to what exceeds human capabilities of understanding, provokes awe or passionate intensity, gives the speaker a sense of something beyond the human."[237] It is this pointing beyond that accounts for the prominence in lyric of such rhetorical figures as apostrophe, personification, and prosopopoeia—indeed, Yahweh, tropologically speaking, is the very embodiment of these several figures in the religious lyric of the Bible.[238] A second contributing factor to lyric's penchant for the hyperbolic is its quintessential *occasionalness*, its tendency to give expression to one particular mood or idea at a time and to do so with verve and excitement. As R. Wilbur notes, while such a single sounding "may not represent the whole self of the poet, it can (like the love song, hymn, or curse) give free expression to some one compelling mood or attitude." And, he adds, sometimes we need to "yield utterly to a feeling or idea," however partially it mirrors the complete worldview and thought processes of the poet.[239] Such "utter yielding"—another way of talking about lyric extravagance—has sometimes (especially in reference to biblical psalmody) been misread (reified) as static, monolithic proclamations that are somehow (magically) forever valid. Nothing, of course, could be farther from the enlivening spirit of this poetry. If many of us can and do identify with the cry of abandonment at the beginning of Psalm 22 (and in Ps 88; cf. Lamentations) and are, indeed, grateful that someone has provided us with a language that so precisely matches our own feelings and experiences, this should not mislead us into thinking of such as some unexceptional, eternal statement of truth. Truth it may be, but if so it is a truth that by the dictates of its very medium requires reuttering to have any ongoing or contemporary validity. Moreover, it is but a momentary truth, *one* alongside *many* other truths. If the depictions of Yahweh as "enemy" in Lamentations (2:4–5) and as "mad beast" in Job (16:9–10) somehow seem appropriate and just to the particular moment in these poems, it is surely not the only way these poems imagine the deity—or indeed even the central way they do so. In other words, the extravagance—lyric's habitual over-the-top-ness[240]—is part and parcel to the getting at or evoking or yielding to an often very particular and even momentary matter.

* * *

IN SUM, I have isolated a number of the lyric's more typical ways of achieving meaning while at the same time attending to the task of uncovering the prominence of lyric discourse in the Bible. More could obviously be accomplished along these lines. Still, even from this abbreviated discussion I think the overriding and informing lyricism of parts of the Bible's poetic corpus (e.g., Song of Songs, many psalms, songs like Exodus 15 embedded in biblical prose) is recognizable. The cluster of features just reviewed, from an aboriginal musicality that stages so much of this poetry to its tropological density, pervasive parataxis, typical brevity, and the like, especially in cumulation, unmistakably distinguishes this verse as lyric. What is more, these features are not simply present intermittently but they themselves are central to and defining of the poetic experience achieved in many biblical poems. Indeed the recognition of the lyric as a chief mode of discourse of many biblical poems casts them in a strikingly different light. The lack of story and character, the fondness for repetition and emotion, the prominence of form, and the disjunctive feel of the whole, instead of constituting some of the more enigmatic aspects of such poems, suddenly make good sense and seem all so natural. It is as if we had been looking at many of the Psalms and the Song, for example, all along through the bottom end of a Coke bottle, distorting and obscuring our vision. Once we see them through the corrected lenses of lyric verse, all comes into focus, and our field of vision seemingly expands and gains in acuity, and our picture of such poems clarifies and crystallizes but also explodes with new colors and previously unperceived dimensions and details of texture.

To recognize the overwhelming lyricism of so many biblical poems is to achieve a more perspicuous description of these poems and thereby to sharpen and to extend the critical understanding of them, of their prosody. Narrative approaches, which still dominate (even if only tacitly) the literary study of biblical poetry, will only illuminate its lyric varieties to a limited degree. Lyric verse requires reading strategies properly attuned to the discourse's leading features and central practices. There is historical significance to this recognition as well. Discussions of lyric verse more generally, as noted earlier, often privilege Greek lyric as the main historical source for this kind of discourse. But in the lyric poetry of the Bible and their Near Eastern congeners we have a preserved tradition of lyric verse that is more ancient than that of the Greeks and that through some of its common features (e.g., prominence of a communal voice, a more dialogic profile) may well open up new possibilities for appreciating the capacity and nature of lyric discourse more generally. That is, not only does the comparative perspective help in recognizing and appreciating the possibility of lyric poetry in the Bible but also the peculiarity (historical, cultural, linguistic) of this lyric tradition may have something to offer to a larger understanding of the capacity of lyric discourse—biblical lyric's pronounced rituality is a case in point.

Lyric in extenso: _Probing (Some) Possibilities in the Song_

Lyric, as I have said, is typically short, enacted on a small scale. Only so much can be accomplished in a language art that routinely foregoes the use of cohesion-aiding devices, such as plot, argument, or consistency of character, and thus depends so largely on the naked properties of language itself as its chief medium of discourse. It is difficult for such discourse to sustain itself over long stretches of time and space. Eventually a limit is reached beyond which a lyric poem simply self-implodes. This is especially the case with orally performed lyrics. The question arises, then, was there any possibility in biblical antiquity for achieving surpassing encompassment and largeness of scale in the lyric mode? I have already indicated in brief that writing and oral performance offer two such possibilities. As a practical convenience (and ultimately to mainly heuristic ends), I probe this question in more detail here with the Song of Songs principally in view. The Song, like Psalms, is a corpus of biblical poetry that scholars would most readily assent to calling "lyric."[241] One of the issues perennially debated in Song scholarship is whether the Song is one or many songs, a matter that might be thought to turn precisely on the question of lyric *in extenso*. That is, what the Song is, holistically considered, will have much to do with what is possible given the nature of the Song's underlying poetic medium.

Those who presume there are many "songs" often emphasize "the abrupt shifts of scene, speaker, subject matter...and sometime of mood, and the lack of any apparent structural organization or narrative development."[242] On the other hand those who prefer thinking of the Song as just one "song" underscore the strong sense of unity that pervades this work, that it "exhibits cohesiveness, homogeneity, consistency of character portrayal, and a distinctive vision of love."[243] That the Song in fact has both disjunctive (centrifugal) and cohering (centripetal) sensibilities seems to be the case,[244] and therefore any maximally encompassing account of the Song as a larger whole will want to accommodate these opposing tendencies and forces. The very framing of the debate in terms of opposing the one to the many, even without detailed exposition, seems questionable in a number of respects. For starters, what warrant is there for supposing the possibility of a long, nonnarrative poem from the pre-Hellenistic Near East (absent the support of writing)? By most accounts the long poem, which I presume must supply the principal (if tacit) warrant for conceiving the Song as a single poem, is a distinctly modernist phenomenon, with Walt Whitman's "Song of Myself" (1855) as one of the genre's earliest instantiations.[245] Such a poem, which aspires "to achieve epic breadth by relying on structural principles inherent in lyric,"[246] can only happen in writing. Writing, with the capacity of retrospective processing that it enables (i.e., an ability to reread when necessary)[247], proves to be the ultimate facilitator of lyric discourse on an expanded scale. What ultimately must implode if allowed to go on too long, once fixed and spatialized in writing, may be

countered and absorbed through *reading*. There is no need to discount out of
hand the possibility of (perhaps even very early) premodern precursors to the
(modern) long poem, especially given the myopia that seems to regularly re-
strict the visual field of Western literary criticism.[248] Still, such precursors
require identifying and scrutiny, especially for periods and cultures that are
more oral than literate and where textuality, even if on the rise, never approaches the kind of fully literary textuality we take for granted today and
would ultimately be in support of vocal performance (if any kind of wider
publication were in view). For the Bible, Deuteronomy 32 provides a kind of
rough guide as to the outer limits in length of a typical nonnarrative, orally
performed poem—the narrative presents Moses as performing the poem
(Deut 31:30) and as using the written text of the poem as an aid for helping
"the Israelites" to memorize it (Deut 31:19, 22). In contrast, Psalm 119 achieves
its extreme length (though still shorter than the Song) through form (the alphabetic acrostic) and writing—the acrostic is itself a trope of writing. There
are singular Egyptian love songs, as M. Fox in particular details (e.g., P. Harris
500, group C),[249] but they do not approach anything like the scale of the Song
as a whole; indeed, they can be written on an ostracon (e.g., O. Gardiner 304)
and most are enacted very much on the same scale as is the Bible's nonnarrative verse more generally, including what scholars have posited as independent poems in the Song (e.g., 2:8–17; 3:1–5; 4:1–7; 5:2–6:3). Similarly, much of
the Sumero-Akkadian tradition of "erotic-lyric" poetry also is enacted on a
mostly smaller scale. "The outstanding feature" of the Sumerian balbale-
songs, for example, which make up a prominent portion of the preserved
Dumuzi-Inanna love songs, writes Y. Sefati, "is their brevity," with most not
exceeding "30–40 lines on the average."[250] Not surprisingly, these same bal-
bale-songs mostly lack an orienting narrative framework to provide "background details of the poem" or "opening formulae of the direct speeches."[251]
And the small corpus of Akkadian love poetry, now being studied in detail by
M. Nissinen,[252] seems again to contain mainly relatively short poems as well.
So, for example, even the Neo-Assyrian "Love Lyrics of Nabû and Tašmetu"
(IM 3233 = TIM 9 54 = SAA 3 14), whose cultic setting is not in doubt, still only
comprises the obverse and reverse of a single tablet, some fifty-six lines in
total.[253] In short, it would behoove those who would press for the Song as literally a singular poem to be aware of the prevailing technological capabilities
and to marshal appropriate models and exemplars. Fox's thought that the
Song "is a love song of a new sort" holds much appeal,[254] though further
clarity is necessary as to what "sort" and how it is "new."

Collecting, by contrast, is an old and venerable scribal practice with abundant exemplars from the pre-Hellenistic Near East—indeed, the biblical books
of Psalms and Proverbs present themselves quite explicitly *as* collections (and

subcollections) of psalms and proverbs, respectively.[255] Here, too, writing is paramount. The chief means of accomplishing lyric *in extenso* before the advent of the long poem is to gather individual lyrics into larger wholes—collections, anthologies, songbooks, sequences.[256] The nature of these wholes varies depending on function. In the dichotomous discussions about the Song, only one kind of collocation is primarily in view, namely, the anthology or collection of distinct and unrelated poems gathered for referential purposes. The several Neo-Assyrian prophecy collections inscribed on large, multicolumned tablets are paradigmatic. They gather short reports of prophetic activity from a plurality of prophets, presumably for royal archival purposes.[257] Even more relevant to the Song are the several Egyptian collections of love poetry (e.g. P. Harris 500, groups A and B; P. Chester Beatty 1, group C). As Fox (and others) argue, the individual component poems in these collections are "manifestly independent and autonomous" with "only occasional thematic ties" to join them.[258] The autonomous nature of Mesopotamian love poems is also emphasized. They have been preserved mostly in "manuscripts" (tablets) of singular works, and even when there is more than one composition on a tablet, as on the obverse and reverse of LKA 15, the singularity of the love poem preserved is still plain to see (obv. 1–10, "Ištar and Tammuz"). Portions of at least one four-column library tablet that originally contained "four *irtum* songs" according to the colophon (MAH 16051 iv 18) are extant. There are also catalogues that list the incipits (first lines) of a number of Akkadian love songs (e.g., *KAR* 158, ASJ 10). And some of the preserved colophons of the individual songs indicate belonging to larger series. BM 47507 ("Come in, shepherd") is a good example of the latter. The song is identified in the colophon as belonging to the series *māruma rā'imni* "O darling loving me" (l. 42). It also cites the catch-line to a succeeding composition (l. 40: *ur-ša-nam re-e-a a-za-am-mur-ma* "I shall sing on the heroic shepherd"). Both incipits appear sequentially in the catalogue *KAR* 158:

> [*er-ba-a]m-ma rē'u* (^{lú}SIPA) *ḫar-mi* ° ^{d}*Iš$_8$-tár-ma*
> [*ur?-ša?-a]n*-na rē'a* (^{lú}SIPA) ° *az-za-am-mu-ur-ma* (i 6'-7')

All of these—collection on a singular (multicolumn) tablet, catalogue, thematic organization by series—give expression to that chief modality of Mesopotamian scribal knowledge, *Listenwissenschaft*, in which aggregation serves primarily archival and intellectual ends.[259]

But other kinds of collocations are also known, even from antiquity. In the West, Greek integrated collections are known from a relatively early period, especially those of the Alexandrians. Callimachus (third century BCE) is usually credited as the first Western poet to explicitly call attention to the shape of his sequences (*Iambs* and *Aetia*).²⁶⁰ He and other Alexandrian poets collected and arranged their poems in book-rolls²⁶¹ that contain explicit prologues and epilogues and exhibit structural symmetries and thematic resonances among the individual poems. However, it is very likely that even earlier Greek poets, such as Mimnermus (seventh to sixth centuries BCE), Theognis (sixth to fifth centuries BCE), and Sappho (620–550 BCE), collected their poems in anthologies or connected series as well, though the evidence is sketchy.²⁶² In the ancient Near East, there is the outstanding example of the collection of forty-two Sumerian temple hymns that may date as early as the late twenty-fourth or early twenty-third century BCE.²⁶³ Here we have an obvious collection of individual lyric compositions that have been purposively composed and arranged as a larger whole. The first forty-one hymns share the same basic form²⁶⁴ and are ordered geographically in a general south/southeast to north/northwest orientation as one moves through the sequence.²⁶⁵ The final hymn deviates noticeably from the formal pattern that shapes the other hymns,²⁶⁶ effectively signalling the collection's impending conclusion. And En△eduanna, En-Priestess and daughter of Sargon of Akkad, even explicitly articulates her authorial intent as she identifies herself as the "compiler of the tablet" that "no one has created (before)" (ll. 544–45).²⁶⁷

While scholars are beginning to scrutinize more carefully the possibility of the editorial shaping of the Psalms, for example,²⁶⁸ the most obviously integrative poetic collections in the Bible are some of the prophetic collections (e.g., Amos, Isaiah of Jerusalem, Jeremiah). I say most obvious because of the frequent use of the new technology of written prose narrative as a means for staging (however inelegantly at times) the individual oracles, visions, and the like of a given prophet. Here there are (more and less successful) attempts to situate prophetic utterance in light of a (remembered) prophetic biography.²⁶⁹ In a related vein, the fifth-century collection of Aramaic proverbs from Elephantine gathered in the name of Ahiqar is prefaced by a prose narrative that tells the story of this legendary scribe and wise man (*TAD* C1.1–5). The Joban composition is undoubtedly the high-water mark in the Bible of this strategy for integrating, organizing, and unifying a collection of nonnarrative poems. Written narrative prose frames the entire work (Job 1–2, 42:7–16), setting the scene and story-world for the written poetic dialogues that are gathered and linked by thin prosaic threads introducing new speakers (e.g., "And Eliphaz the Temanite answered and said," Job 4:1).²⁷⁰ Narrative—as specifically involving a description of the sacred marriage rite—also factors in extending the reach of some singular Sumerian love songs (e.g., "Inanna the watered field, who will plow her?" DI P),²⁷¹ as Sefati notices: "for such a description would require significantly greater length."²⁷² And on R. C. Steiner's reading, it is precisely this kind of liturgical description of a New Year's festival that gives the (mostly) poetic miscellany in the first seventeen columns of the enigmatic P. Amherst 63 its coherence—culminating in the sacred marriage ceremony (col. 17.6–19).[273]

These several examples show that the practice of collecting nonnarrative poetry in the ancient eastern Mediterranean is a well-attested scribal act and one that may be disposed toward a myriad of ends and with varying degrees of integration. Hence, on evidentiary grounds, it is plausible to suppose (if only hypothetically) that a collection of love poems might form around the single figure of an anonymous singer and exhibit a plethora of unifying (integrative) sensibilities of the kinds that many commentators of the Song have identified. One could even think of the Song's "newness" (à la Fox) as a kind of pre-Petrarchian sequence or collection of love lyrics. The lyric sequence—a collocation of lyric poems in which the individual "poetic integer" holds "its autonomy as it participates in a larger unity"[274]—is generally thought to have received its Western vernacular identity in the practice of Francis Petrarch (1304–74 CE) and his seminal amatory sequence, *Canzoniere*, which was composed over a period of forty years and contained in its final version a total of 366 lyrics (317 sonnets; 4 madrigali; 7 ballate; 29 canzoni). *Canzoniere* is Petrarch's continuous attempt to realize, sing, encompass, surmount his love for the lady Laura. Petrarch's sequence was a lifetime project. It began with one hundred poems and was not completed until his death. Petrarch spent his life composing new poems, revising old ones, and editing and reorganizing the sequence as a whole, continuously adding and eliminating poems.[275] Amid the disjunctions that naturally inhere in the lyric and the collocation of multiple lyric poems, Petrarch "exceeds the unities of earlier lyric collections."[276] Petrarch's known precursors include Dante's *Vita nuova* (ca. 1292–1300), the thirteenth-century songbooks of the Occitan troubadours, the Augustan poetry books that were published in long papyrus rolls (e.g., Virgil, *Eclogues* and the four *Georgics*; Ovid, *Metamorphoses*; Horace, *Odes*),[277] and the biblical book of Psalms.

After Petrarch, lyric sequences, especially sonnet sequences, became popular in all Western vernacular traditions. In English some of the more notable sequences include Spenser's *Ruins of Rome* (1591), Herbert's *The Temple* (pub. 1633), and Donne's *Holy Sonnets* (1633). Already in the time of Sydney sonnet sequences were being parodied (*Astrophil and Stella*, pub. 1591). And Shakespeare, as suggested by J. Fineman, wrote his sonnet sequence (*Sonnets* ca. 1593–99) after the time of their popularity.[278] The modern rebirth of the lyric sequence is usually associated with Whitman's *Leaves of Grass* (1855).[279] Modern exemplars of the lyric sequence in English are numerous and would include such works as Yeats's civil war sequences, Eliot's *Waste Land*, Pound's *Pisan Cantos*, Williams's *Paterson*, Stevens's "Auroras of Autumn," and Lowell's *Life Studies*. Non-Western lyric sequences have also been identified and are starting to be studied. E. Miner, for example, has called attention to sequences extant from China already in the fifth century BCE (*Shih Ching*, ca. 450) and from Japan beginning in the tenth century CE (*Kokinshū*, ca. tenth century; *Shinkokinshū*, ca. thirteenth century CE).[280]

Such sequences have two counterposing characteristics: on the one hand they are composite works, consisting of multiple discrete and autonomous poetic integers, and thus project a strong sense of fragmentation; on the other hand they exhibit varying manifestations of coherence, whether through large-scale repetition, such as calendrical or numerological patterns, or through smaller scale and less formal means, such as lexical and key word repetition. Yet however fragmented or coherent, the sequence's overarching structure(s) is explicitly lyrical in nature and design, marked by a conspicuous sense of organicism that ultimately defies reduction to thematic, narratological, or logical explication or paraphrase. On the face of it, this seems an apt description of the counterposing forces that typify the Song as a larger whole.[281] Specifically with regard to the debate about the many or the one in Song criticism, the hypothesis of a more integrated poetic collection identifies a technology for writing lyric verse *in extenso* that is every bit as capable of realizing the kinds of unities prized by those who favor the conception of the Song as a singular long poem. Perhaps it is not irrelevant to point out, as Greene does, that in the modern period, after the advent of the long nonnarrative poem, certain challenges arise "in attempting to distinguish between long poem and lyric sequence."[282] "A lyric poem," writes R. von Hallberg, "is a thing of parts,"[283] and an integrated sequence or collection of lyric poems resembles nothing more closely than just such a part-filled lyric poem writ large.[284] Greene writes that the descriptor "lyric sequence"

> is most accurately applied to works that maintain a sense of tension between the unity or the interrelation of the whole and the independent workings of each part. The term is particularly apt when individual integers in a sequence demonstrate some level of engagement with the lyric, be this understood as subject position, level of musicality, or aim toward brevity.[285]

Greene's comments helpfully return us to the point at dispute in the debate about the Song, is it a simple or complex singularity? If all sides agree that there is much interrelating going on throughout the Song, the question is what is the nature of the component parts, the "individual integers" that are doing the interrelating? Are these distinct enough to be called "poems," or are they better described as "parts" of a larger, longer poem? As a historical datum, deciding the issue remains of interest. But even in advance of that, some clarity on a number of matters will have been gained from this exercise, namely, that writing offers the prime technological means for overcoming the sharp conciseness inherent to lyric discourse and that the collection, a paradigmatic artifact of ancient scribal productivity, may be disposed toward more and less unifying ends—that unities may be manifested by complex as well as simple singularities.

It is not uncommon in the debate about the Song (and its songs) for passing reference to be made to the absence of superscriptions or other editorial indicators of separate, isolatable songs in the extant manuscript traditions. The implication of unity is usually thought to be self-evident, namely "the burden of proof lies primarily on those who wish to assert *disunity*."[286] Here I want to probe the Song's textuality more patiently in order to consider the possibility of both a textuality that is not yet fully literary and lyric discourse on an expanded scale that can thrive in the absence of writing. The assumption that "poems," if they exist, must be written out in some special way (e.g., in lines, with lots of white space) is not sustainable on empirical grounds (see chapter 1). Writing as it spatializes language fixes it in materiality, and thus gives it substance that may be touched, pointed to and returned to, conceptualized. The very notion of "poem" as a whole and stable entity, distinct from other similar entities ("fixed, boxed-off, isolated"),[287] is only conceivable once the linguistic verbiage of which it is (in part) composed is transcribed into writing. The "oral poem," in contrast, is not "poem" in this way but more a spectral intimation of the "poem" that textuality eventually makes possible. Though both make use of "a language that is fundamentally the same,"[288] the oral poem is "essentially ephemeral,"[289] marked by immediacy and fragmentation, precisely the absence of unity where the concept of finished-ness or finalizable-ness can hardly come to mind—so long as a poem is entirely oral it cannot "become an end in itself"[290] or "be glimpsed as a fixed object."[291] Variability marks orally performed art—absent the possibility of making systematic comparisons of different performances, it could hardly be otherwise.[292] In performance, the oral poem contains the "phonemic string we call *text*" (i.e., the words of the poem), but also

> all the concomitants of spoken language and performance intonations, special pronunciations, melody, musical accompaniment, facial expressions, somatic gestures, special times or seasons for speaking, not to

mention the ambiance created by the entire bodily presence of the living speaker and of a living audience. *In its functions oral poetry has a force that is always dispersed and weakened by purely textual dissemination.*[293]

The preserved Hebrew manuscripts of the Song (MT, DSS fragments: 4QCant[a-c], 6QCant) consist of a wholly consonantal script with words divided by spacing and formatted in columns of running text (figs. 41–42), and although all are belated, it is likely that any earlier written versions in an alphabetic script would have shared this same basic text profile (see chapter 4).[294] What is most striking about this form of textuality is not the implication of unity (of a singular poem) but its utter dependence on active vocalizing in order to transform the alphabetic signs on the manuscript page ("the phonemic string we call text") into language and poetry. This is an inscribed textuality more dependent on the voice and the ear and memory than on the eye. Input from outside what is explicitly written is required. Vowels need supplying to fill out the consonantal frames of the script and to make (sound) actual words. For example, *yšqny* (6QCant = Song 1:2; fig. 40) must be vocalized, either as *yiššāqēnî* "let him kiss me" (as in MT; Qal juss. 3 m. sg. + 1 sg. suffix √*n-š-q* "to kiss") or *yašqēnî* "let him give me to drink" (Hiphil juss. 3 m. sg. + 1 sg. suffix √*š-q-h* "to drink," cf. Song 8:1–2). Or *ddyk* (Song 1:2), performed either as *dōdeykā* "your love" (as in MT) or as **daddeykā* "your breasts" (as in LXX, Vg.; cf. Ezek 23:21; Prov 5:19). In order to make such decisions readers must employ their preperformance knowledge of aural and semantic cues derived from the writing itself (e.g., is the girl likely to be admiring the boy's breasts?), as well as an awareness of what has been written down in the first place (e.g., a love song and not a song of lament). Possible "good" variants—which may reflect oral interference—appear: *šmnym ṭwbym* /šĕmānîm ṭôbîm/ "finest oils" in 6QCant 1.5 (= Vg. *unguentis optimis*; cf. 2 Kgs 20:13 = Isa 39:2; Ps 133:2) for MT's *šĕmāneykā ṭôbîm* "your oils are fine."[295] And the words fill the columns, running continuously from right to left, with only the odd bit of extra spacing (e.g., B19a: after 1:4 [fig. 41]; 4QCant[b]: after 5:1 [frag 3.14])[296] to indicate a possible structural boundary. Such spare writing assumes that the poetry's larger rhetorical structures (e.g., line breaks, couplets, stanzas, poems), as in oral verbal art more generally, will be articulated acoustically, through sound, syntax, and rhythm,[297] with deictic aid possibly provided by accompanying visual or bodily gestures (e.g., a nod or a shout), "to create patterns that unify a movement either by developing a series of parallel and balanced lines or by developing a pattern different from those of the previous and following units."[298] For example, the *waṣf*-like song in Song 4:1–7 stands out from what precedes and follows it in a number of obvious ways: its focus on individual parts of the girl's body, the high density of similes and verbless clauses, and the use of exotic imagery, all set apart by a framing inclusio or ring structure (*hinnāk yāpâ ra'yātî* / *hinnāk yāpâ* [v. 1] // *kullāk yāpâ ra'yātî* / *ûmûm 'ên bāk* [v. 7]), a traditional technique for bringing the strongly additive logic of much oral verbal art to a (momentary) stopping point. Song 3:1–5 offers another good example, standing out as a singularity in its immediate context for the narrative logic it employs and the highly repetitive phrasing by which it shapes its individual lines (e.g., the fourfold repetition of *b-q-š* "to seek," *m-ṣ-'* "to find," and *'et-še'āhăbâ napšî* "him whom my soul loves"). The adjuration to the girlfriends (v. 5) offers a gesture of closure (as also in 2:7 and 8:4), not unlike the famous "shout" that A. B. Lord observed at the end of junctural wholes in so many South Slavic epic songs.[299] Again the outstanding point is the acute sparseness of readerly cues (metascript conventions) within the preserved Hebrew manuscripts themselves. From this perspective the benefit of the LXX tradition, which in a number of uncials (e.g., Vaticanus, Sinaiticus, Alexandrinus) supplies indentation as a visual cue to poetic line structure (see fig. 17), is immense.[300] Here the way of writing (now in translation) begins to be better tuned to the needs of "sight" readers (e.g., the scribe who is doing the translating) and less dependent on assumed readerly knowledge.

The "shout" of Lord's "singer of tales" recalls in a striking way the literal absence from these manuscripts of the singer who would have performed the poetry whose wording they preserve.[301] In fact, much of the love poetry from the ancient Near East shares a similar kind of textuality, with little or no concession made to the singers these poems presume. Still, that there were such singers of love songs seems certain. In the Bible they are sighted only obliquely, for example, in reference to Ezekiel (33:32), imagined as a singer of a literal "song of love" (*šîr 'ăgābîm*)[302] who has a "beautiful voice" (*yĕpê qôl*) and is a skilled instrumentalist (*mēṭîb naggēn* lit. "one who plays pleasantly"); to Isaiah of Jerusalem, whose so-called Song of the Vineyard (Isa 5:1–7) parodies a love song—"Let me sing for my beloved...."; and to the performer-scribe of Psalm 45—editorially labeled a "love song" (*šîr yĕdîdōt*)—who offers a rare bit of compositional self-awareness, "my tongue is the pen of an expert scribe" (v. 2, NJV).[303] In Egypt, there is the one (possible) outstanding reference in P. Chester Beatty I to the "sayings of the great entertainer (*T3 sḥmḥt-ib '3*)."[304] Otherwise, the fact of a singer is an inference that may be drawn on the one hand from the characterization of groups of these poems as "entertainment" (*sḥmḥt-ib* lit. "making the heart forget"; P. Harris 500, groups B and C; P. Chester Beatty I, group A)[305] and what is known about entertainment from such things as the tomb paintings; and on the other hand from what may be inferred by the manner of poetic performance itself, which here and there, as

Fox recognizes, presumes a voicing beyond the various poetic personae (e.g., the girl and the boy) that feature in these poems.[306] Analogously, the opening of CAT 1.24, *ašr. nklwib.* "let me sing of Nikkal-Ib" (l. 1; cf. ll. 37–39, 40) is likely the voice not of any of the main personae (e.g., Nikkal-Ib, Yariḫ; cf. ll. 37–39) but of the singer of the song (cf. Ps 45:2, 18). In Mesopotamia, the fact of a singer is mostly an implication of the mythological projection of these love poems, which presumes a cultic context and thus some kind of performance. In some cases the latter can be posited most confidently, as in the Dumuzi and Inanna songs, which presume the sacred marriage festival,[307] or the "Love Lyrics of Nabû and Tašmetu" (SAA 3 14), which also may be associated confidently with a cultic setting: "The ritual setting of the text is beyond any serious doubt. Without being a detailed ritual description, the Love Lyrics clearly reflect different phases of the love ritual of Nabû and Tašmetu discernible from other sources."[308]

Both Tg. Cant. and LXX explicitly compensate for this lack in different ways. Tg. Cant., taking its clue from Song 1:1, identifies Solomon as the singer: "Songs and praises which Solomon, the prophet, the king of Israel, recited in the holy spirit before the Sovereign of all the World, the Lord."[309] On the other hand LXX, in a number of manuscripts (e.g., Alexandrinus, Codex 161, Sinaiticus, Venetus) adds rubrics identifying the speaker of specific verses (e.g., LXX[S]: "the groom to the bride," 1:15; "the bride to the groom," 1:16; fig. 17). This practice arises, in part, because Greek does not mark gender morphologically with verbs as does Hebrew, and thus literal translation (alone) into Greek is unable to track the change in speaking voices that is otherwise apparent in the Hebrew original (or in actual performance). It also reflects the addition of the kind of explicit explanatory context (*diegesis*) that "literary texts"—texts, that is, that are (mainly) read outside of a performative arena—tend to require. As A. N. Doane explains with reference to manuscripts containing Anglo-Saxon (oral-derived) poetry:

> These same texts appear almost invariably in manuscripts that entirely fail to put them in context, that is, there is no literary or historical message around them. Voiced poems, where poem, poet, and audience are implicated in a specific situation, do not need explanation. In contrast, literary texts…tend to occur in specific "literary" contexts, however imperfectly realized, because texts separated from speakers and performance need explanations.[310]

The lack of such explanatory contexts in the Hebrew manuscripts of the Song (e.g., no superscriptions or introductory glosses—aside, perhaps, from 1:1), do not so obviously implicate a unified singularity—which presumes a kind of high literary textuality designed for nonperformative uses—as an "emergent" or "interfacial" textuality shaped by and still in service to performance: texts that remain "beholden to performance."[311] These have the format, that is, of the kind of aids to memory that J. Herington supposes for written versions of early Greek song texts—a mostly "mechanical means of preserving [the poems'] wording between performances."[312] By their very failure to accommodate to a singer-less environment (namely a readerly or literary textuality) they provide a glimpse—or better, trace—(through absence and noncompensatory gestures) of the still assumed "substance and presence" of the singer. The singer would have "located, contained, and continuously sustained the performance in its shifts among all different types of discourse that any sustained fabula would require."[313] Such a text, made up almost entirely of only the verbal element, "must have appeared brutally paratactic, lacking in all the means that ensure the cohesion and smooth flow of a performance, in which the embedding of one discourse into another is frequently handled by nondiscursive means."[314] What we may have in the Song, then, is perhaps neither a long poem nor a lyric sequence, both high achievements of a distinctly literate art, but a writing still orally and aurally oriented that is on its way to becoming something akin to these other forms—this, too, would be a "new sort" of something (i.e., the writing down of oral performance).[315] C. B. Pasternack coins the phrase "verse sequence" for the inscribed verse of Anglo-Saxon England precisely as a means of deflecting the high literate values otherwise so easily assumed when thinking about poetry and poetry collections. She also writes of "movements" instead of "poems," mindful that such textuality in support of performance has not yet achieved the settled, boxed-in character of written poetry;[316] that such a way of writing, spare with only a minimum of readerly helps, not only requires extratextual input and performance but remains, like oral verbal art, more generally a distinctly open medium, inviting of performance and reperformance, of taking the words and disposing them to one end at one time and to some other end at another time. That is, scholars' failure to agree, for example, on the precise number of "poems"—or "movements"—in the Song (fourteen, thirty-one, forty-two) may be a sign not that there are not multiple singularities but that the form of the textuality in which these songs were transcribed remains open and variable, accommodating multiple ways of composing and recomposing these poems—the very form of the textuality requires readers in performance to make these interpretive moves without setting the expectation that there is one single, verifiable way of composing these songs.[317] It is a way of writing—a first writing—that mimes the way of oral performance.

In the end, it is not crucial for my analysis of the idea of lyric poetry in the Bible to settle on one specific understanding of the Song. If I am partial to the latter perspective, that is, the Song as a verse sequence that is inscribed in an emergent textuality that remains open and malleable,[318] the foregoing discussion at least reveals the fact that textuality is not everywhere just of one kind and that there are at least two modalities for extending the reach and scale of lyric's native conciseness, through writing (whether in collocation or as a longer singularity), which has proved most successful over the long run, and through the embodied presence of a singer in performance, who would guide the listening audience through the various junctures and disjunctures that make up a complex performative piece like the Song.

Beyond Lyric: Toward a Richer Understanding of (Other) Biblical Poems

Even if this chapter's central thesis may be granted (for sake of argument)—namely, that the Bible contains a core of verse that may be accurately (though variably) characterized as lyric and that it is every bit as old as and in some instances older than that far more famous lyric tradition from ancient Greece—this leaves much biblical poetry unaccounted for. What of that poetry? First, it exists. Already at the end of the nineteenth century S. R. Driver had well in view two broad kinds of nonnarrative poetry in the Bible, lyric and what he called *gnomic* verse.[319] By the latter Driver means didactic or wisdom poetry and has Proverbs, Job, and Ben Sira uppermost in mind. He defines this kind of verse broadly as consisting "of observations on human life and society, or generalizations respecting conduct and character."[320] In many respects the basic medium of such verse is similar to the lyric just described. In fact, Driver himself observes that "the line between these two forms cannot always be drawn strictly."[321] Beyond thematic and performative differences (most wisdom literature would not have been sung), different life-settings (e.g., teaching), and a preference for other kinds of genres (e.g., proverbs), the major modal difference is a higher incidence of discursive logic. This leads to a second observation, namely, "that the category *lyric*," as Culler writes, "has the virtue of directing our attention to nonnarrative poetry in general"[322] and providing a (heuristic or pragmatic) model for how to read it, how to apprehend it. That is, given the general overlap in kind (notwithstanding some real differences, e.g., nonmelic quality) between lyric and other varieties of nonnarrative verse, an appreciation of the basic means of lyric discourse has a certain practical usefulness for reading other nonnarrative poems and for making sense of their prosody and poetics.

My own initial interest in lyric was spurred in part by the nineteenth- and twentieth-century commentary tradition on Lamentations, which mostly seemed befuddled by this poetry's general lack of plot or sustained (theological) argument, as if there was some fault in Lamentations for its failure to meet these readers' explicitly narrative and discursive expectations. But these poems are not narratives and are not discursive in orientation. The fault was not theirs but was otherwise. I turned to (predominantly) Romantic and post-Romantic notions of lyric as a ready-to-hand antidote to this history of misreading Lamentations. My intuitive sense was that the vast majority of the biblical poetic corpus, including Lamentations, answered quite nicely to what contemporary critics and theorists call lyric today—almost all poetry that does not obviously tell a story. Hence the opening to my "Psalms and Lyric Verse": "My ambition here is to begin thinking Hebrew poetry through from the lyric point of view out."[323] After some polite prodding by colleagues (esp. Berlin, Linafelt, O'Connor),[324] coaxing me back to my own strongly historicist bent of mind, I have long since given up the urge to stuff all biblical poetry into a single "lyric" sack.[325] In ancient Greece, to take our most scrutinized example, beyond the songs of the archaic period sung to the lyre or *aulos* or even unaccompanied by musical instrumentation, there were also unsung (and undanced) varieties of nonnarrative, nonmimetic verse—poetry recited (*not sung*) in dactylic hexameters, elegiac couplets, and iambic trimeters.[326] Beyond the lyric and gnomic varieties of nonnarrative verse touted by Driver, other subgroups of biblical poetry may also be usefully identified. I have already problematized here the "lyricism" of the lament, in its various guises—individual and communal laments, funeral dirges, laments for destroyed cities (e.g., Lamentations). It was an especially common ancient poetic genre.[327] Prosodically and materially, it shares much with lyric and didactic verse.[328] It may be distinguished, broadly, by its chief thematic concerns (suffering and loss), its typically dark and somber mood, and often (especially in funeral dirges) a fondness for unbalanced couplets—the so-called qinah meter. Some laments—the psalmic laments, for example—were apparently associated with song (e.g., Psalm 13 is labeled a *mizmôr* and includes a reference to singing, v. 6), though others, like gnomic or didactic verse, were not necessarily sung—so, for example, the *qînâ* is never introduced by verbs for singing, but only by q-y-n "to lament, keen" (e.g., 2 Sam 1:17; 2 Chron 35:25) or n-ś-ʾ "to lift up" (e.g., Amos 5:1; Ezek 19:1). However, if I would no longer want to characterize Lamentations, for example, as prototypically lyric, it is a closely related type (and therefore I have referenced it periodically in the foregoing discussion) and reading it through the lens of lyric is hugely beneficial (pragmatically)—my aim here is not to reify classificatory schemes but to get in view more perspicuously precisely what this kind of poetry requires of its audience, to evolve a critical idiom that is maximally useful for reading biblical poems and for making sense of their prosodies.

Another large block of poetry in the Bible is associated with prophets and prophecy (so Lowth)—the "elaborate artifice" of prophetic verse marks "distinctions from the plainness of instrumental speech" and thereby signals its divine authority.[329] One need not insist that such poetry is everywhere in the Bible prototypically lyric in order to recognize that there are some high lyrical moments exhibited among these highly parasitic performers (e.g., Isa 5:1–7),[330] who routinely take up forms and genres from elsewhere and use them to their own ends, or that like gnomic verse prophetic verse, even when it moves most decisively away from any kind of strong lyric sensibility, nonetheless holds much in common with the lyric poetry of the Bible. Therefore, in addition to the "abundance of lyric poetry" in the Bible and the strict absence of "epic poems and drama," as Alonso Schökel observes, there is a range of other kinds of nonnarrative poems in the Bible that differ from the lyric in some important ways (esp. in their nonmelic character) but that also share with it a broad kinship and thus benefit from being considered in light of the habitual practices and tendencies of lyric, because those practices and tendencies are not—descriptively, empirically—exclusive to the lyric genre—so Langer: "there is no device characteristic of lyric composition…that may not also be met in other forms."[331] That is, the various genres and forms of the Bible's nonnarrative poetry hold in common a core of central characteristics and practices, and thus they tend to go about the poetry making business in much the same way. Where distinctions arise among the genres is in how this shared core poetics is enacted (e.g., with song, with discursive or narrative logic, oracularly) and thematized (e.g., love, loss and suffering, generalizations about character and conduct, critique) and where and in what context (e.g., communal, private, cult, education, war camp) and for what reasons (e.g., critique, edification, prayer, love, celebration). There is, in other words, something very much recognizable as *biblical poetry*.[332]

That the nonnarrative verse of the Bible shares a core prosodic profile brings me to a final consideration, which I press in light of the thinking of the comparatist (of East Asian literatures in particular) E. Miner. Miner points out a very "curious" fact: poetics, whether implicit or explicit, everywhere but in the West is "founded not on drama, but on lyric. Western literature with its many familiar suppositions is a minority of one, the odd one out. *It has no claim to be normative*."[333] Miner is on firmest footing with respect to cultures in which "an explicit 'originative' or 'foundational' poetics" (e.g., Aristotle's *Poetics* or Ki no Tsurayuki's Japanese preface to the *Kokinshū*, ca. 910 CE) is found.[334] Not all cultures evolve such an explicit poetics. Certainly nowhere does this happen in the pre-Hellenistic Near East. There, too, there must have been an operative poetics, but it was "implicit in practice," and to date not much attention has been paid by scholars to teasing out what its nature might have been. It is enough, then, for my own project to take Miner's assertion as to the implicitly lyric-based ("affective-expressive") poetics of "near Eastern cultures" (inclusive of the Hebrew Bible)[335] as a hypothesis to be considered and scrutinized. Still, it is a provocative idea and productive in a number of ways even in advance of a full vetting. First, if he is right, then the broad similarities and kinships (family resemblances) that characterize biblical poetry generally—lyric and nonlyric kinds alike—becomes most sensible and the idea of thinking biblical Hebrew poetry through from a lyric point of view ever more attractive. Second, whatever may be made of the poetics implied by ancient Near Eastern and biblical literature, there is no drama extant in these traditional literatures. As is the case generally, "lyric and/or narrative are the genres with which known literary systems originate."[336] Miner elaborates:

> We shall see that it is of no little importance that drama is typically (always!) the last kind of literature to achieve separation. In culture after culture, it is so closely bound to religious and social rituals on the one hand, and so nearly allied with music and dance on the other, that it usually emerges only after narrative and lyric. One can see this in cultures as diverse as the Greek, the European after the fall of Rome, and the great Asian cultures of India, China, and Japan.[337]

We may be confident, then, that the basis of the Bible's implied poetics is non-mimetic,[338] and perhaps as important, that a tacitly assumed mimetic-based criticism, such as has mostly prevailed in the study of literature in the West since Aristotle (including almost all post-Lowthian forms of biblical literary criticism), will only be revealing of nonmimetic genres to a point—"it has no claim to be normative." The archaic Greek situation is tellingly comparable. Although an Aristotelean mode of criticism might be productively applied to archaic Greek lyric (texts may always be read from different angles and to different ends), there is no reason to privilege such a mode uncritically, nor could Aristotle's *Poetics* have emerged from that archaic period, before the advent of drama itself. Western poetics has not been static and did not stop with Aristotle, of course. As Miner emphasizes, Horace's *Ars Poetica* "is of crucial importance, since it introduced a strongly effective...poetics into western currency."[339] That is, even a mimetic-based poetics can be enlarged and made to accommodate nonmimetic forms. Nevertheless, one take-away from Miner

here is the ongoing need to reflect critically on methods and theories of literary study (for me) of the Bible, getting in view as clearly as possible both our
own orienting presuppositions—there are no naive positions from which to
enter into acts of textual interpretation—and the literary history of the Bible
and its implied poetics.

Third, a similar caution arises about the assumed normativity of prose narration. J. Kittay and W. Godzich observe that contemporary scholars and critics "are very much affected by the predominance of prose today—prose
considered as a given or natural state of written language."[340] "Our world,"
Kittay and Godzich state, "is a literally prosaic one, full of prose."[341] This was
not always the case. So Miner: "Drama comes much later as does, usually, *literary* narrative in prose. Not only do drama and prose narrative tend to appear
far later than lyric and poetic narrative, but their normative acceptance lags
even more."[342] Not only has the vast majority of "literary study" of the Bible
since the 1960s (a rebirth of sorts) focused on prose narrative, scholars' tacit
pose toward biblical poetry has been what Kittay and Godzich call a "postprose" view of verse,[343] a view that considers poetry and poetics from the presumed normativity of written prose narrative. The latter is newly emergent
during the biblical period, so the world of the Bible, though not only or purely
"preprose" in orientation, was never fully *après prose*[344] either, as is our world,
and thus a perennial challenge for students of biblical poetry in particular is
the need to continuously negotiate our "postprose" view of verse when reading poetry from a world that prose had yet to fully conquer.

Finally, though lyric and narrative poetry are the originating genres of
all known literary systems, "it is passing strange," writes Miner, "that there
is no originative poetics founded on narrative."[345] Again the thought is provocative, if only for providing yet further warrant for the importance of getting some kind of critical handle on the lyric corpus of the Bible and the nature
of this kind of discourse. One can hardly consider lyric's place in a (implicit)
biblical poetics in the absence of such a critical understanding. A chief outcome sought in the review of the several lyric practices and tendencies I have
discussed in this chapter was to sharpen and extend the critical understanding
of the inner workings of this kind of biblical poetry and to (re)introduce
the notion of "lyric" as a critical idiom. It is not that the presence of lyric
poetry in the Bible has not been well observed in the past. It has, and early
on, too. To cite a famous example, Jerome in his *Preface to Job* compares
Psalms, Lamentations, and "almost all the songs of Scripture" to Greek and
Roman lyric poets, such as Flaccus, Pindar, and Sappho.[346] Rather, what I do
not always perceive on the part of contemporary interpreters of biblical poetry
is a *critical* awareness of the lyric as a distinct mode of discourse, and it is

to this awareness, especially when our default reading strategies are so narratively oriented in this age of novels and Hollywood movies, that I would recall us.

As for the suspicion that the very idea of lyric is somehow foreign to the Bible and the biblical world, Miner's work, like any minimally inclusive survey of oral and written verbal art (literature) from around the world and throughout history, helps to show that such worry is misplaced—indeed, is simply wrong. Lyric, though called by many different names—*šîr, shi, uta, melos, carmen,* song—is widely attested, perhaps even universally so. But Miner also helps in seeing better how and why such a worry might arise in the first place. My hunch is that a (mostly though tacitly) monolithic, explicitly Western notion of poetics is the chief culprit. On the one hand Western scholars are only too aware of both the centrality of the Greek lyric in discussions of lyric poetry in general and its place in the Western (post-Horatian in particular) canon and the Bible's (Near) Eastern and hence non-Greek settings, sensibilities, genres, content. Hence, whatever the psalms, for example, might be, and despite a real "resemblance" to the likes of Pindar, Alcaeus, and Sappho (with deference to Jerome),[347] there are many differences, too, and ultimately no mistaking the one for the other—lyric poetry everywhere is a language-specific act unavoidably enmeshed in historical and cultural particularity. On the other hand the bias of a distinctly Western poetics that in good conscience is being guarded against (so as not to impute it to that which is foreign to it) also occludes the very fact that lyric may have a more surpassing sensibility than what is known from Greece or the larger Western literary tradition, that lyric—not literally using the Greek term, of course, which is already belated and anachronistic when first used by the Alexandrians—might also be attested outside the West, might even be, as Miner maintains, the founding basis for another culture's "originative" and orienting poetics, as, say, in Japan, China, and India, or perhaps even for the incipient impressions of an "implicit" poetics, "as...for near Eastern cultures."[348] In other words, the failure to countenance the idea of lyric in the Bible is in large part a consequence of a certain blindness caused by a lack of critical leverage on the very categories that inform and authorize so much Western literary criticism (of the Bible). Whether or not readers are finally persuaded by my own account of the (biblical) Hebrew lyric, there can be no contestation on principle of the idea of lyric poetry in the Bible. To the contrary, comparative study shows lyric verse almost literally everywhere and at all times. If not all biblical poetry is lyric, which it is not (so Driver's gnomic verse), that some is should be of no surprise. Indeed, that there may even be "an abundance of lyric poetry" in the Bible is perhaps what should have been supposed all along—

whether we consider the Psalter or the Lamentations of Jeremiah, or almost all the songs of Scripture, they bear a resemblance to our Flaccus, and the Greek Pindar, and Alcaeus, and Sappho, let him read Philo, Josephus, Origen, Eusebius of Caesarea, and with the aid of their testimony he will find that I speak the truth.[349]

FIGURE IA–B R. Lowth, *De Sacra Poesi Hebraeorum Praelectiones Academicae Oxonii Habitae* (London: Clarendon, 1753), pp. 185–86, showing his lineation of the Hebrew of Psalm 93:3–4.

FIGURE 2 4QPs^b includes col. XXVI (Ps 112:4–5). Plate 999/1 B-298338. Photo Shai Halevi, COURTESY ISRAEL ANTIQUITIES AUTHORITY. One verse line per column line format.

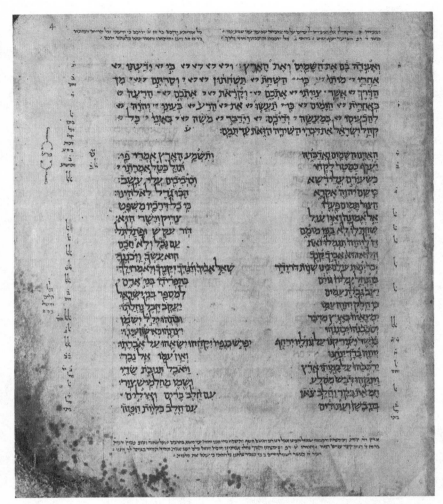

FIGURE 3 Aleppo Codex, folio 4 recto (Deut 32). Courtesy Yad Izhak Ben-Zvi. Illustrates one of the special formatting layouts specifically prescribed by the rabbis during the Middle Ages: two blocks of writing per columnar line with a large intervening span of uninscribed space.

FIGURE 4 B19a (Leningrad Codex), folio 139 recto (Judg 5). D. N. Freedman et al., *The Leningrad Codex: A Facsimile Edition* (Grand Rapids: Eerdmans, 1998). Photograph by Bruce and Kenneth Zuckerman, West Semitic Research, in collaboration with the Ancient Biblical Manuscript Center. Courtesy Russian National Library (Saltykov-Shchedrin). Illustrates the other major special format prescribed by the rabbis during the Middle Ages: a single column of text the width of the folio page with columnar lines composed of either (portions of) three blocks of writing divided by two large spans of white space or (portions of) two blocks of writing separated by one large span of space.

FIGURE 5 B19a (Leningrad Codex), folio 397 recto (Job 1:1–1:21A). D. N. Freedman et al., *The Leningrad Codex: A Facsimile Edition* (Grand Rapids: Eerdmans, 1998). Photograph by Bruce and Kenneth Zuckerman, West Semitic Research, in collaboration with the Ancient Biblical Manuscript Center. Courtesy Russian National Library (Saltykov-Shchedrin). Illustrates the typical manner in which the Masoretes formatted most biblical texts (except for Ps, Prov, Job): three narrow columns per page with columns filled with a running text.

FIGURE 6 B19a (Leningrad Codex), folio 397 verso (Job 1:21B–3:1A). D. N. Freedman et al., *The Leningrad Codex: A Facsimile Edition* (Grand Rapids: Eerdmans, 1998). Photograph by Bruce and Kenneth Zuckerman, West Semitic Research, in collaboration with the Ancient Biblical Manuscript Center. Courtesy Russian National Library (Saltykov-Shchedrin). Typical columnar layout for the three specially formatted poetic books of the Bible (Ps, Prov, Job): two wider columns per page. The last two-thirds of the left-hand column also show the typical spacing that distinguishes the individual verse lines in this formatting convention; the right-hand column, in contrast, is laid out in a running format (with no intervening spacing).

FIGURE 7 P.Oxy. LXV 4443 (LXX, Est E16-9.3). Courtesy of The Egypt Exploration Society and Imaging Papyri Project, Oxford. Typical Greek prose format with narrow, squared-off columns of writing.

FIGURE 8 Timotheos papyrus, U. von Wilamowitz-Möllendorff, *Der Timotheos-Papyrus* (Leipzig: Heinrichs', 1903): col. V (Courtesy Staatsbibliothek zu Berlin— Prussian Cultural Heritage, Shelf mark: 2" Uk 1103-1/4). Early (ca. fourth century BCE) Greek papyrus roll in which verse appears in a running format.

FIGURE 9 P.Mil. Vogl. VIII 309, col. XI. G. Bastianini and C. Gallazzi (eds.), *Posidippo di Pella Epigrammi (P.Mil. Vogl/VIII 309)* (Milan: LED, 2001), 2, Tav. V (digital images included on two CDs). An early example of the one-verse-per-line format, showing wide column with ragged right-hand margin typical of Greek poetic manuscripts.

FIGURE 10 4QH^{c, d, e}. Plates 513, 522, 352 B-284559 (PAM: M-43531). COURTESY ISRAEL ANTIQUITIES AUTHORITY. Running format of a nonbiblical poetic text.

FIGURE 11 MasPs^a col II 3–7 (Ps 82:1–4). (SHR 5255, Courtesy the Israel Museum, Jerusalem). Two verse lines per columnar line separated by medial spacing.

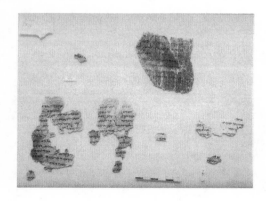

FIGURE 12 4QProv^b (Prov 13:6–15:31). Plate 1153 B-284257 (PAM: M-43016). COURTESY ISRAEL ANTIQUITIES AUTHORITY. Space inserted between individual verse lines but not centered on the column line.

FIGURE 13 Abbott Papyrus, EA 10221, 1 (AN334341001, © Trustees of the British Museum). Late New Kingdom hieratic roll showing typical column layout.

FIGURE 14 A fragment from Gilgamesh, Tablet X, Rm.621 (AN326205001, © Trustees of the British Museum). The fragment displays well the columnar layout typical of cuneiform literary tablets more generally.

FIGURE 15A 11QPsᵃ (recto). Plate 978 B-385953. Photo Shai Halevi, Full Spectrum Color Image, Courtesy of the Israel Antiquities Authority. All psalms in this scroll (except Ps 119) are written in a running format.

FIGURE 15B 11QPsᵃ frag. C II (Ps 102:18–29; 103:1). Plate 977 B-280834 (PAM: M-42180). COURTESY ISRAEL ANTIQUITIES AUTHORITY.

FIGURE 16 B19a, folio 386 reverse (Ps 99:9–102:24A). D. N. Freedman et al., *The Leningrad Codex: A Facsimile Edition* (Grand Rapids: Eerdmans, 1998). Photograph by Bruce and Kenneth Zuckerman, West Semitic Research, in collaboration with the Ancient Biblical Manuscript Center. Courtesy Russian Nattonal Ltbrary (Saltykov-Shchedrin). Shows the customary special formatting for the three poetic books (Ps, Prov, Job) in MT.

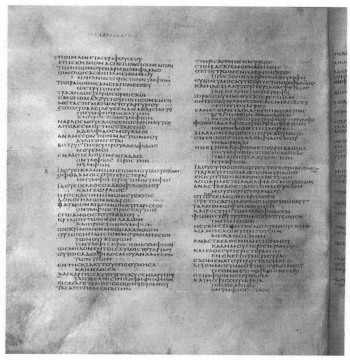

FIGURE 17 Codex Sinaiticus (Song 1:8–2:15). London, British Library folio 148b (scribe A). © The British Library Board. Illustrates *per cola et commata* formatting, with indentation. Rubrics, introducing speakers, are rendered on separate lines in red ink.

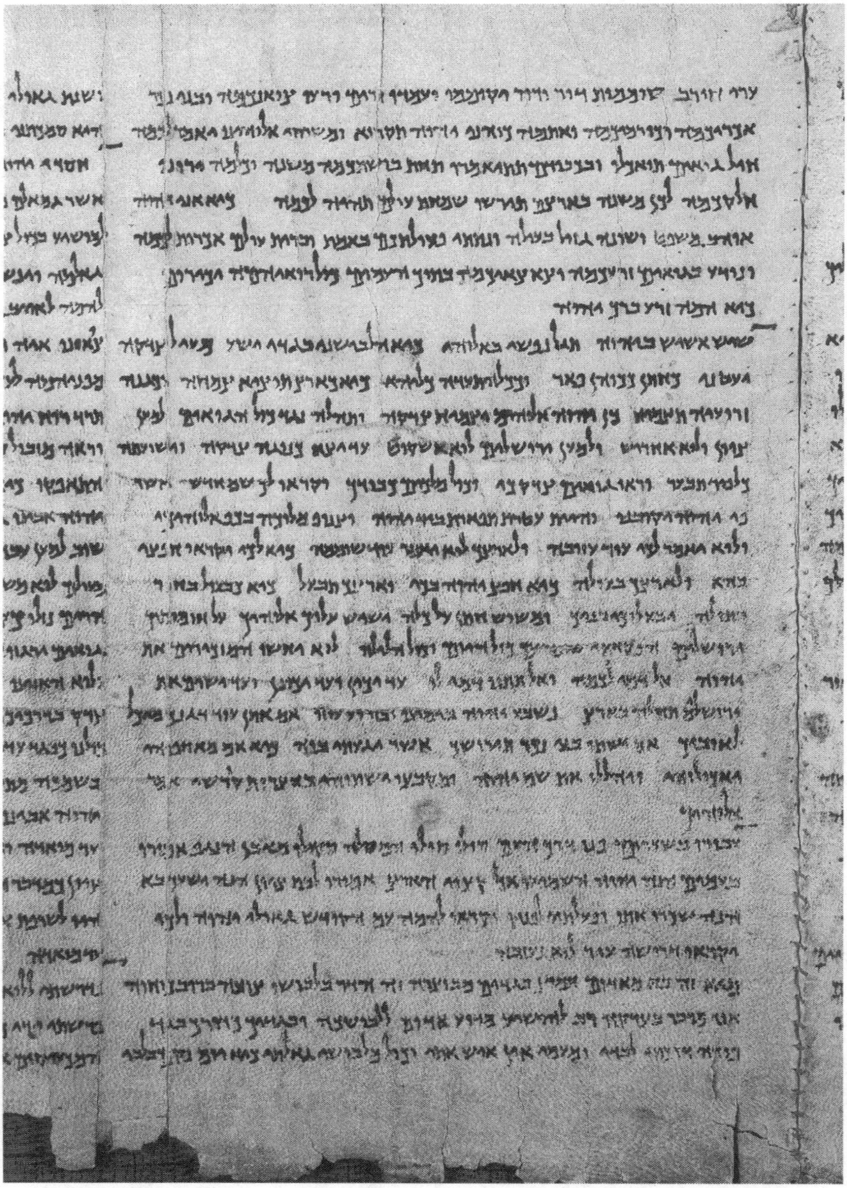

FIGURE 18 1QIsaᵃ (Isa 61:4–63:4) (PAM 43.783). Courtesy Israel Museum, Jerusalem.

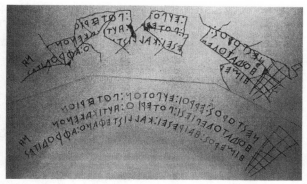

FIGURE 19 Nestor's cup (ca. eighth c. BCE), from www1.unionedu/~wareht/greek3/writing_nestor.jpg, accessed March 5, 2015.

FIGURE 20 Auct. F.I. 15, 57ᵛ (*De consolatione Philosophiae*) (The Bodleian Library, Oxford University). Formatting—one verse line to a line of writing, initial capatals, endpoints—typical for the copying out of Latin verse in Anglo-Saxon England (from the eighth century on).

FIGURE 21 London, British Library, Cotton Vitellius A XV, 1ʳ (Beowulf). © The British Library Board. Exhibits the running format ("long lines across the writing space") typically used in copying Old English verse.

FIGURE 22 First tablet from Kirta (CAT 1.14 obv), showing running format written in horizontal lines and in columns, with word dividers. [InscriptiFact Text ISF_TXT_01254, InscriptiFact Digital Object ISF_DO_17450, 1K14P01]. Photograph by Wayne Pitard, West Semitic Research. Courtesy Department of Antiquities, Syria.

FIGURE 23 From Ahiqar (TAD Cl.1, col. 6) [InscriptiFact Text ISF_TXT_00071, InscriptiFact Digital Object ISF_DO_05705, AT_91_P13446E R_P]. Photograph by Bruce and Kenneth Zuckerman, West Semitic Research. Courtesy Ägyptisches Museum, Berlin.

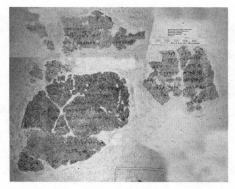

FIGURE 24 Deir ʿAlla (KAI 312). [InscriptiFact Text ISF_TXT_00825, InscriptiFact Digital Object ISF_DO_06542]. Photograph by Bruce Zuckerman and Marilyn Lundberg, West Semitic Research. Courtesy Department of Antiquities, Jordan.

0   5 cm

FIGURE 25 Kuntillet Ajrud 4.2. S. Ahituv, E. Eshel, and Z. Meshel, "The Inscriptions" in *Kuntillet ʿArud (Ḥorvat Teman): An Iron Age II Religious Site on the Judah-Sinai Border* (ed. Z. Meshel; Jerusalem: IES, 2012), 111, fig. 5.53. Reproduced with permission of Zeev Meshel.

FIGURE 26 Carpentras stele (*KAI* 269). S. R. Driver, *Notes on the Hebrew Text and Topography of the Books of Samuel* (Oxford: Clarendon, 1913), pl. 3.

genus populorum rudium et indoctorùm, quibus aut nulla omnino aut minime pervagata erat literarum cognitio, utilitati accommodatum erat, quod aures animofque capturum, et memoriæ firmiter inhæfurum ef- fet; quod non tradendum effet manibus, fed mentibus infundendum.

Eodem modo apud Hebræos etiam fe rem habuiffe, ufumque Poeti- cæ cum valde antiquum, tum mature fuiffe communem et pervaga- tum, ut ex rei natura verifimile eft, ita clare etiam apparet ex reliquiis et veftigiis quibufdam dictionis poeticæ, quæ in fcriptis Mofaicis extant. Primum quod ibi occurrit hujus rei exemplum remotiffimæ atque inti- mæ eft vetuftatis, Lamechi ad Uxores effatum, eo quidem obfcuriffi- mum, quod, qua occafione effet editum, omnino reticetur; cætera au- tem, aptam verborum conftructionem, concinnam totius periodi in tria difticha diftributionem, fententias in fingulis diftichis binas parallelas, alteramque alteri quafi recinentes; ifthæc, inquam, fi fpectetis, agnof- cetis, credo, primævi carminis clariffimum fpecimen : ¹

עדה וצלה שמען קולי
נשי למך האזנה אמרתי:
כי איש הרגתי לפצעי
וילד לחברתי:
כי שבעתים יקם קין
ולמך שבעים ושבעה:

" Hadah et Sillah, audite vocem meam ;
" Uxores Lamechi, aufcultate eloquium meum :
" Quod virum occîdi in vulnus meum,
" Et puerum in livorem meum :
" Quia feptempliciter vindicabitur Cain,
" Et Lamech feptuagefies fepties.

κινηθείσαν. Ουκὶν ἐδὲ μαντικίω κηϊμα και χαϊντας εἰθϊνί ὁ θεος, ἐδὲ ἀεπιλαυσὲν εἰθηεδὲ τιμωεθμενην με- εαν τα τεμπιδός, ἀλλὰ εππμετο, μεἀδοι εερειςων τοις ποιντεημὸς κατεζεῤᾳοϊϊμος φυειος, αυτὸς τε φιερνοτιας ενεδιδε, κρη ενενξωεημ᾽ το ααδιαχον κρη λογιον, ως αεμχϊϊον κρη θωϊμμεζοῤϑμον. P L U T A R C H. Comment. Cur nunc Pythia non reddat oracula carmine. fub fin.

¹ GEN. IV. 23, 24. Cum plane nefciam quæ fit hujus loci fententia, contentus fum fubjun- xiffe Verfionem Interlinearem S A N T I S P A G N I N I.

Alterum

FIGURE 28 Lowth, *De Sacra Poesi Hebraeorum Praelectiones Academicae Oxonii Habitae* (London: Clarendon, 1753), 301. Shows Lowth's lineation of Isaiah 62:5, which corresponds to the extra spacing in the corresponding section of 1QIsaᵃ.

FIGURE 29 Lowth, *De Sacra Poesi Hebraeorum Praelectiones Academicae Oxonii Habitae* (London: Clarendon, 1753), 302. Shows Lowth's lineation of Isaiah 62:5, which corresponds to the extra spacing in the corresponding section of 1QIsaᵃ.

FIGURE 30 Lowth, *De Sacra Poesi Hebraeorum Praelectiones Academicae Oxonii Habitae* (London: Clarendon, 1753), 242. Shows the first portion of Lowth's Hebrew translation of Ben Sira 24.

FIGURE 31 Cambridge University Library T-S 12.871 (B I recto). A Geniza fragment of Ben Sira (Sir 10:19–11:2) showing special formatting for verse. Used with permission of the Syndics of Cambridge University Library.

FIGURE 32 RS 24.281 (CAT 5.20). A double abecedary from Ugarit. © Copyright 2009 Eisenbrauns. Reproduced from Pierre Bordreuil and Dennis Pardee, *A Manual of Ugaritic* (Linguistic Studies in Ancient West Semitic 3; Winona Lake, IN: Eisenbrauns, 2009), 284, pl. 58. Reprinted by permission of Eisenbrauns.

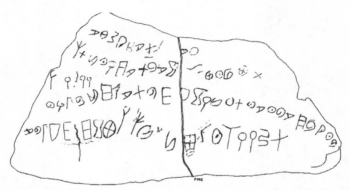

FIGURE 33 Abecedary from Izbet Sartah. F. M. Cross, "Newly Found Inscriptions in Old Canaanite and Early Phoenician," *BASOR* 238 (1980), 8, fig. 9 (complete article can be located on JSTOR). Reproduced with permission of the American Schools of Oriental Research.

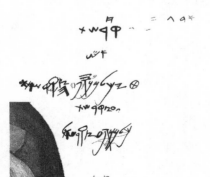

FIGURE 34 Kuntillet Ajrud abecedaries, 3.11–14. S. Ahituv, E. Eshel, and Z. Meshel, "The Inscriptions" in *Kuntillet ʿArud (Ḥorvat Teman): An Iron Age II Religious Site on the Judah-Sinai Border* (ed. Z. Meshel; Jerusalem: IES, 2012), 102, fig. 5.45. Reproduced with permission of Zeev Meshel.

FIGURE 35 11QPs^a, cols. XII–XIII (Ps 119:128–42, 150–64). Plates 979, 975, B-285186 (PAM: M-43784). COURTESY ISRAEL ANTIQUITIES AUTHORITY. A biblical acrostic that is specially formatted.

FIGURE 36 11QPs^a, cols. XVI–XVII (Ps 145:1–7, 13–21). Plates 975, B-285190 (PAM: M-43786). COURTESY ISRAEL ANTIQUITIES AUTHORITY. A biblical acrostic in a running format.

FIGURE 37 Samaria Ostracon 53. [InscriptlFact Text ISF_TXT_00897, Inscripti-Fact Digital Object ISF_DO_06815]. Courtesy Harvard Semitic Museum. Shows typical use of word dividers in the "old Hebrew" script.

FIGURE 38 A tomb-painting from Nebamun (near Thebes, 18th Dynasty). EA37981. Depicts a banquet scene, divided into two registers: upper—men and women sit together and are attended by one standing servant-girl; lower—four musicians (two shown full-face) are shown seated on the ground while two dancers provide entertainment for the guests. © Trustees of the British Museum.

FIGURE 39 Gypsum wall panel relief from the North Palace in Nineveh (Ashurbanipal, 645–35 BCE). 118916. Depicts a harpist and lyre player, one a woman wearing a fillet of great beads, the other a youth (?), wearing feather headdress, with tame lion beneath palms and cypresses. © Trustees of the British Museum.

FIGURE 40 6QCant (Song 1:1–8). Plate 646 B-284841 (PAM: M-42943). COURTESY ISRAEL ANTIQUITIES AUTHORITY.

FIGURE 41 B19a (Leningrad Codex), folio 423 recto (Ruth 4:13B–Song 2:5A). D. N. Freedman et al., *The Leningrad Codex: A Facsimile Edition* (Grand Rapids: Eerdmans, 1998). Photograph by Bruce and Kenneth Zuckerman, West Semitic Research, in collaboration with the Ancient Biblical Manuscript Center. Courtesy Russian National Library (Saltykov-Shchedrin).

FIGURE 42 B19a, folio 394 recto (Ps 133). D. N. Freedman et al., *The Leningrad Codex: A Facsimile Edition* (Grand Rapids: Eerdmans, 1998). Photograph by Bruce and Kenneth Zuckerman, West Semitic Research, in collaboration with the Ancient Biblical Manuscript Center. Courtesy Russian National Library (Saltykov-Shchedrin).

FIGURE 43 Aleppo Codex, folio 267 recto (Ps 133). Courtesy Yad Izhak Ben-Zvi.

FIGURE 44 11QPsᵃ, col. XXIII (Ps 133). DSS Plate 978 B-285198 (PAM: M-43789). COURTESY ISRAEL ANTIQUITIES AUTHORITY.

FIGURE 45 Codex Sinaiticus (Ps 133). London, British Library folio 124b (scribe A). © The British Library Board.

FIGURE 46 Victory stele of Naram-Sin, King of Akkad (Akkadian Period, c. 2250 BCE; ART161684). Musée du Louvre. © RMN-Grand Palais/Art Resource, NY.

FIGURE 47 Gypsum wall panel relief: showing a formal scene. Bearded Ashurnasirpal II appears holding a bow and bowl flanked by a human attendant with a fly-flapper (865–60 BCE). North-West Palace, Room G, Panel 10. London, British Museum ME 124569 © Trustees of the British Museum.

FIGURE 48 Greek coin depicting image of Persian ruler (with beard), presumably Darius 1. London, British Museum ME 1917,1103.6 © Trustees of the British Museum.

FIGURE 49 Upper part of a red granite colossal statue of Ramses II (19th Dynasty, ca. 1280 BCE). London, British Museum ME EA67 © Trustees of the British Museum.

FIGURE 50 Detail (no. 5 of 28) of the bearded King Jehu of Israel paying tribute to Shalmaneser III from the Black Obelisk (825 BCE). London, British Museum ME 118885 © Trustees of the British Museum.

FIGURE 51 Detail (no. 15 of 28) of Israelite porters (all bearded) from the Black Obelisk of Shalmaneser III (825 BCE). London, British Museum ME 118885 © Trustees of the British Museum.

FIGURE 52 Gypsum wall panel from the South West Palace of Sennacherib (700–692 BCE; Room XXXVI (OO) Panel 8). Depicts the siege of Lachish, showing Judaean prisoners moving in families, taking goods and animals into exile. The adult male is bearded. London, British Museum ME 124907 (no. 2 of 16) © Trustees of the British Museum.

4

An Informing Orality

BIBLICAL POETIC STYLE

*we do not question the essential
orality of Canaanite poetry*
—M. O'CONNOR, *Hebrew Verse Structure* (1980)

THE LAST DECADE or so has seen a marked upsurge in interest on the part of biblical scholars in a host of questions having to do with orality, literacy, and textuality in ancient Israel and Judah, though relatively little specific attention has been paid in this discussion to biblical poetry per se (i.e., its nature, style, inscription).[1] This is a little surprising since cross-culturally and transhistorically "poetry" is the preeminent oral art form. M. O'Connor has maintained that much biblical poetry appears "comparably close to the oral poetic situation,"[2] and in what follows I mean to elaborate this idea. Baldly stated, my thesis is that biblical poetic style owes much to an informing orality, an orality that continues to figure significantly and to be "heard" in the written versions of biblical poems preserved in the received tradition.

Some Preliminary Points of Orientation

As a means of orienting the discussion that follows, I begin with a few summary and preliminary observations. First, the outstanding finding that emerges from all recent research (no matter the many differences in emphasis, focus, or theoretical orientation) is that Israel and Judah throughout their histories were always primarily oral (and aural) cultures.[3] That is, the management of knowledge and its verbalization in Israel and Judah was dominantly and prominently oral, communicated in speech, face-to-face, embodied. The world of the Bible and the world in which the Bible took shape was a thoroughgoing oral world. Even in the midst of ever increasing literacy and the emergence of a (more) textual culture, as in Israel and Judah throughout the Iron Age, orality can still be expected to circumscribe, shape, and orient these new written modalities. Cultural change is slow. Oral habits of mind are tenaciously persistent, they do not die out immediately. So just because oral poems, for example, begin to be written down or that poetic composition itself begins to take place in writing does not entail the immediate loss of all (or even most) informing oral sensibilities, for the simple reason that these very sensibilities are the only idioms known for articulating poetry.[4] This is a point I will return to. The chief implication of this (re)new(ed) awareness is that all biblical scholars, no matter the topic of study, will forever need to chasten their tacit and deeply engrained literary biases with knowledge of the Bible's informing orality. No reading of a biblical poem can afford to be unmindful of the myriad ways an informing orality potentially may have impacted said poem, whether in composition, during performance, through transmission, or when it was eventually written down.[5]

Second, and correlatively, at least from the middle of the fourth millennium BCE, when writing emerges in both Mesopotamia and Egypt, orality, however dominant a mode of communication, in the ancient Near East, is always enacted within (and thus is shaped by) a context of literacy (no matter how specialized) and textuality. And thus at no time in the history of the late arriving Israelites and Judahites (ca. 1200 BCE) would writing not have been known and used in some capacity (e.g., among the royal and religious elites, as a kind of craft literacy). These were not what W. J. Ong calls "primary oral cultures"—cultures with no knowledge of writing.[6] In fact, however scant, alphabetic inscriptions from southern inland sites in Canaan do exist from Iron I and IIA (e.g., Gezer Calendar, Tel Zayit abecedary, Qeiyafa ostracon), albeit still in the panregional linear alphabetic script(s) that pervade(s) the southern Levant during this period.[7] Certainly by the early eighth century BCE (and possibly even a little earlier) there are technological means available in Israel and Judah for inscribing poems in vernacular Hebrew (see discussion "Emergent Textuality" below). And then there is that stubborn, unequivocal fact of literary history that whatever founding or enabling orality may be ascribed to biblical poems, those poems have only come down to us textualized, in writing, and thus by their very medium of inscription are indubitably marked by textuality and literacy.[8] Therefore, although for the most part hard information about reading and writing practices for the ancient Levant is lacking and much must be surmised on the bases of the texts that have been preserved and of comparative ethnographic studies, still, as a purely practical matter, some accounting of the literate or textual shaping and reception of biblical poetic material will always be required. Any historical assessment of biblical poetry ultimately will need to be ready, as R. Thomas urges with respect to ancient Greek literature,

"to countenence literacy and orality together."⁹ Indeed, as it turns out, "orality
and literacy" in many cultures (e.g., ancient Greece, medieval England, the
southern Levant during the Iron Age) are not the dichotomous and monolithic descriptors they are sometimes made out to be but are more "parts of a
subtle, complex, lengthy process of change" and thus "do not occupy discrete
and conflicting cognitive spheres."¹⁰ In fact, one of the principal ambitions
of R. Finnegan's *Oral Poetry* was "the denial of a clear-cut differentiation between oral and written literature." To the extent that an oral/written distinction exists, says Finnegan, it "is more like a continuum (or a complex set of
continuums)."¹¹

Third, on occasion in the foregoing chapters I have referenced orality,
often heuristically, as a means of making sense of some aspect of biblical
poetic art (e.g., length of the biblical poetic line, the unmetered nature of biblical poetic rhythm), and in what follows I return to some of these same phenomena as I press my case for an informing orality at the center of the Bible's
poetic style. In the end, of course, I will not be able to prove my thesis in any
strong way, if only because, as just noted, our only access to such orality is
through textuality riven by various dimensions of literacy. The worry that a
literate poem can always mime oral-derived features can never be successfully
deflected. In fact, ethnographically one of the familiar pathways charted in
literate art that emerges out of aboriginal orality involves replication and
emulation (of aspects) of that aboriginal oral style. In the end, then, arguments for an informing orality in biblical poetry can be pressed only so far,
and many questions of interest will not be maximally generative. To presume,
as I do, that biblical poetic art is ultimately rooted in an aboriginal orality will
be very comfortable for most biblical scholars after a century and more of
form criticism inspired above all by H. Gunkel, for whom the conviction that
the poems and stories of ancient Israel and Judah emerged initially as oral
productions was unshakable.¹² While no part of Gunkel's program may be
taken at face value—indeed, the paradigm as a whole is probably no longer
salvageable, and not a few of its aspects were outdated even at their first articulation,¹³ still his strong awareness of an informing orality that has shaped
many aspects of biblical literature, when rethought beyond its highly Romantic conceptualizations, remains a vital and enduring insight. That there
were oral precursors to much biblical literature would seem likely a priori
since, as J. M. Foley reasons, "as far as we know all peoples have composed
and transmitted oral traditions."¹⁴ But again, in trying to tease out more elab-
orately how biblical poetry is "comparably close to the oral poetic situation"
I will only be able to come so close and then no farther. The ultimate quarry
of this investigation—an informing orality—will forever be finally elusive, lost

in ephemerality along with most of the world's oral art produced throughout history.

A final preliminary comment on the natures of oral traditions. They are plural, both the traditions and their natures. They are as diverse and as multi-faceted as the many unique and different cultures that voice them. The Parry-Lord theory of oral formulaic composition was so successfully articulated (especially in A. B. Lord's phenomenally popular *Singer of Tales*)[15] that it had the adverse effect of severely limiting (in the minds of many Western schol-ars) what constituted an oral poem. But as ethnographic study of oral tradi-tions beyond the South Slavic ones reported by Parry and Lord began to be undertaken, other possibilities for conceptualizing oral art also began to emerge. Finnegan's *Oral Poetry* from 1977 was something of a watershed event. In that work she paints an intentionally rich and variegated picture of oral poetry and its natures and social contexts, inclusive of Parry and Lord–styled oral formulaicism but also evidencing other styles of composition, per-formance, and transmission and a range of genres beyond that of narrative poetry. At one point she observes: "The 'oral-formulaic' style of composition (as depicted in *The Singer of Tales* and similar works) is not a sufficient indica-tion for concluding that a given work is 'oral,' nor a necessary condition for the creation of 'oral poetry.'"[16] This broader and richer understanding of what con-stitutes oral poetry, along with a healthy allergy to dichotomizing stagings of oral and written verse, is crucial, I maintain, for a fully empathetic appre-ciation of biblical poetry as verse ("properly so called") and its informing orality—I dare say the latter will remain mostly obscured outside of such a larger view.

Prob(lematiz)ing the Question of Hebrew Narrative Poetry

I begin with the fact of the wholly nonnarrative nature of biblical poetry (see chapter 3). This is quite striking. On the one hand narrative (nonmelic) poetry is the best documented and most studied genre of all oral (and oral-derived)[17] verbal art, and, on the other hand it is a genre that is well attested in the an-cient Near East, not the least from ancient Ugarit (modern Ras Shamra) on the north Syrian coast, where narrative poems are preserved in a West Semitic dialect (e.g., Kirta, Aqhat, Baal Cycle). In fact, the discovery of the Ugaritic tablets beginning in 1929 gave new impetus to questions about the possibility of Hebrew epic verse,[18] and scholars have been debating the issue (off and on) ever since. Short of new articulate information (e.g., recovery of a scrap of nar-rative verse labeled as such), it is unlikely that a fully satisfactory resolution will be found to the question "Was there a Hebrew epic?" Still, the issue remains very much worth probing and problematizing even in the absence of such prospects, both because the questions that are asked and how they are asked matter and because an awareness of the phenomenality of oral narrative verse proves a crucial foil for a fully empathetic and acute appreciation of non-narrative oral (or oral-derived) poetry.

To ask the question alone has an immediate clarifying force. Famously Gunkel depicts the typical setting in which he imagines the "legends" of Genesis first being told before they were ever written down: "In the leisure of a winter's evening the family sits about the hearth; the grown people, but most especially the children, listen intently to the beautiful old stories of the dawn of the world, which they have heard so often yet never tire of hearing repeated."[19] There is probably every reason to suspect that some version of this highly romanticized scenario took place, nor do I doubt that the mostly informal matters likely discussed on such occasions—family lore, tribal politics, folktales, stories of the gods—will have informed in all kinds of ways the written prose narratives that have actually been preserved in Genesis (and elsewhere in the Bible). But this is something very different from the more formally stylized art form studied by Parry and Lord in the former Yugoslavia, or that of Homer or of *Beowulf*, or, indeed, of Kirta, Aqhat, or the Baal Cycle preserved from Late Bronze Age Ugarit. These all would seem to require training and skill and talent. A bard. A storyteller. A singer (of tales, no less). Gunkel, of course, goes on almost immediately to note the "marked artistic style" of these preserved written narratives and then to hypothesize the existence in Israel and Judah of "a class of professional story-tellers."[20] As usual with Gunkel there are keen insights here, but the situation is likely more complex than he realized. The early notice of "artistic style" in biblical prose narrative is not an incidental matter but will have at least two gross sources: the emerging style of written narrative discourse and the inherited style and idioms of oral performative art. The former is part of what Gunkel misses. Prose everywhere is a phenomenon birthed from the technology of writing. And not surprisingly as it evolves it evolves a style. R. Alter, R. Kawashima, and T. Linafelt, among others, have emphasized in particular how deeply stylized biblical prose narrative really is. Kawashima, in his *Death of the Rhapsode*, is especially keen to isolate those stylistic elements that owe their origin to writing (as opposed to oral storytelling), for example *diegesis*, free indirect discourse. Ethnographers and comparatists who study oral traditions often (informally) talk and write about "oral" prose. Usually what they have in mind is the distinction in the way the ethnographer transcribes the text of an oral performance, whether she or he lineates or not. "Oral" prose is that which is unlineated. Most oralists are hypersensitive to the fact that much of the scholarly ("scientific") language they employ is explicitly visually and literately oriented, evolving initially most often in discourse about written literature. Some try to evolve a more neutral vernacular, others accentuate oral-derived terms themselves, and still others are more and less comfortable in extending where prudent the use of literary terms for oral phenomena. There is no hard-and-fast rule here. However, it seems to me that "prose" is one term that should be mostly avoided when speaking about oral verbal art. It carries with it the presumption of too many writing-specific phenomena (e.g., third person narration), risking occluding the very fact of their lack in oral performative art. Biblical prose narrative is not to be equated with either the ordinary language of everyday use or even the perhaps more marked (but not yet poetic) idiom of (some) oral storytelling (folktales and whatnot) as imagined by Gunkel. The latter, as noted, will be among the oral resources readily available to the writing scribe as he (rarely she) practices the writerly art of prose fiction. And so, too, would be an oral poetic narrative tradition, if it existed. But at the least the very posing of the question of oral epic in Israel and Judah requires from biblical scholars a good deal more specificity in their talk about oral tradition and the art forms that make up that tradition.

Now to the merits of the question itself. At the outset the existence of two counterposing realities of oral verbal art, whose implications for consideration of the question of Hebrew epic cannot be totally deflected, requires acknowledgment. One, there are oral traditions that lack formally developed narrative art forms. "Epic has a very wide distribution over the world and throughout a period of several millennia," writes Finnegan. She continues:

> But it does not occur everywhere. Its absence in some cultures disappoints the expectation that "epic" is a universal poetic stage in the development of society. In the usual sense of the term it seems to be uncommon in Africa and in general not to occur in aboriginal America or, to any great extent, in Oceania and Australasia. All in all, epic poetry seems to be a feature of the Old World, where it is, or has been, held in high regard and composed or performed by specific individuals of recognized poetic expertise.[21]

Here it is helpful to recall that there is no such thing as an oral culture in general. Orality and its traditions are riven by difference crossculturally, and thus one reason for the absence of narrative verse in the Bible may be that no such tradition prevailed in ancient Israel or Judah. Two, there is no inherent reason for oral art to ever be written down. Its aboriginal medium is the human body and voice.[22] As Foley emphasizes, the vast majority of oral art produced throughout the world and across the millennia has not been written down. And much oral or oral-derived art from antiquity has often only come down to us in singular copies. This is the case with most of the Anglo-Saxon poetry from medieval England, including *Beowulf,* and also appears true of the narrative poems from Ugarit.[23] So, two, the counter-supposition to a Hebrew oral tradition that did not have narrative epic poetry is that the Hebrew oral tradition did have narrative epic but that part of the tradition simply never got written down (i.e., there was no external excuse or motivation for writing out this narrative poetry)[24]—or if epic poems were written down they have not survived or at least have so far not been recovered. In any event, the absence of narrative verse in the Bible is equally well explained by these counterposing realities from ethnography.

I see no reason why there should not have been an oral narrative and non-melic verse tradition in Israel and Judah, and there are even a number of positive things to say in support of the supposition, beginning with the *insignificance* of the lack of inscription of such poetry. Biblical studies, like other area studies in the humanities, is hypertextual in orientation. So the empirical lack of textuality is often deemed significant, though in this case what is significant is that lack's insignificance. The expectation for oral art is that it would not be written down. So if this were the case in Israel or Judah that would be entirely normal and not significant. This fact complicates scholarly reconstructive endeavors, but that is a different matter. Inscription is what is abnormal, however crucial for historical analysis (not unlike the significance that destruction layers in Middle Eastern tells hold for archeologists). My point: the absence of inscription of any putative oral narrative tradition by itself is not significant, or rather that its significance is other than normally thought.[25]

More positively, though still somewhat suppositionally, Israel and Judah stood at the heart of the "Old World" mentioned by Finnegan, geographically and culturally a part of the ancient Near East, a region within which oral narrative flourished, if one is to judge by the oral-derived bit that did get inscribed. It would be surprising if Israel and Judah, along with their immediate neighbors in the southern Levant during the Iron Age, where alphabetic literacy emerged rather slowly, did not participate in the practice of oral storytelling, folkloristic varieties but also especially more formal, large-scale narrative poems.[26] The general paucity of written remains (even allowing for the loss of what was written on perishable materials) from Israel and Judah during the Iron II period, and their kind (mostly short texts that serve immediate practical purposes, e.g., letters, short-term record keeping, seals), as well as the severely limited extent of literacy (of all kinds) during the period (mostly limited to scribes, royal functionaries, religious elites, and the like), suggests to S. B. Parker that "virtually all 'literature' must have been oral."[27] The Ugaritic narrative poems provide positive, empirical evidence for the existence of oral-derived poetic narrative in the Levant at the end of the Late Bronze Age.[28] All students of the Ugaritic tablets since their discovery have been impressed by the tablets' linguistic, literary, religious, and cultural connections with the slightly later (Iron Age) literature of the Hebrew Bible. U. Cassuto's early expression of the "largely homogeneous"[29] nature of the two traditions in particular— they share "the rhythm of verses, the structure of sentences, parallelism, rhetorical techniques and modes of expression"—remains widely accepted: "Biblical literature was but the continuation of the *antecedent Canaanite literature*."[30] Israel and Judah were Canaanite cultures, and (biblical) Hebrew is a Canaanite dialect. The poetic narrative tradition in evidence at Ugarit is ancestral to the prose and poetry of the Bible (in differing ways) and presumably to any putative narrative poetry that may have existed in the region during the Iron Age as well, no conversion necessary.[31] Or to put it slightly differently, O'Connor writes, on the basis of the Ugaritic poetic narratives and the poetic (mostly nonnarrative) corpus preserved in the Bible, "there was a Canaanite poetic tradition that retained its integrity from the Late Bronze Age through the first part of the first millennium."[32] The question is can anything more empirical be said in support of the supposition of poetic narrative continuing into the first millennium?

Since no such unambiguous narrative verse has yet to be recovered and by all accounts there is no true narrative poetry in the Bible, empirical support for the thesis is limited mainly to exploring vestiges of a putative oral, nonmelic, narrative tradition in extant biblical literature. That biblical Hebrew has the capacity for narrative poetry, though usually presumed (e.g., on the basis of the Ugaritic narrative poems), may actually be shown. Even if there are no true narrative poems in the Bible, there are nonnarrative poems with longer and shorter narrative runs in them. F. M. Cross points to some of the "early Hebrew poetry" in particular: "We possess lyric poems with strong narrative content in the Song of the Sea (Exodus 15) and the Song of Deborah (Judges 5)."[33] In each case the underlying lyric medium must be confronted and negotiated, something that those treating these poems have not always been successful in doing. Still, most would affirm Cross's sense of narrativity in these poems and their closeness to the narrative idiom of the Ugaritic epics.[34] From the other end of the spectrum, certainly later and didactic and not lyric, is the narrative run at the heart of Proverbs 7 (vv. 6–23). Here, too, there is no question of ignorance of writing ("write them [i.e., the speaker's teachings] on the tablet of your heart," v. 3) but no question either of the capacity for poetic narrative in biblical Hebrew—the appeal of story is there to bolster the traditional authority of the wise father figure. These examples may suffice to show that the lack of narrative verse in the Bible is not for the lack of poetic narrative know-how, and perhaps as significant, they themselves, along with other narrative runs that could be cited (e.g., in Ps 78), do exhibit (however minimally) snatches of poetic narrative.

Cassuto pioneered the strategy of looking for signs of epic verse in the Bible. He is mostly theoretically naive, although there is an explicit evolutionary linearity that drives his convictions about the existence of Israelite epic that must ultimately be eschewed. He begins his essay: "Epic poetry…appears among many peoples in the epoch of their youth."[35] But such ideas in fact are not supported by ethnography, as Finnegan stresses.[36] In the main Cassuto's chief insights are ultimately empirical and comparative in nature, inspired by his reading of the Ugaritic narrative poems. He suggests that there are two main categories of evidence in biblical literature that presume the existence of an indigenous poetic narrative ("epic") tradition that continues and is part and parcel of the Canaanite tradition in evidence at Ugaritic: allusions to epic narrative themes/motifs that otherwise are not attested in the Bible and stylistic techniques and diction that may be shown to originate in earlier epic traditions. He exemplifies the first category, initially, with a set of texts (Isa 51:9–10; Ps 74:13–15; Job 7:12) in which each alludes to Yahweh's battle with the (personified/mythologized) sea and/or the sea monsters.[37] What intrigues Cassuto is that nowhere is a full-blown Yahwistic version of this myth attested in the Bible, though other versions are well known from both Ugarit and Mesopotamia. From this he deduces that such a myth must have "existed in an *Israelite* recension."[38] As Y. Zakovitch affirms, such allusions "cannot be explained… except as clear allusions" to a mythic epic of the kind that Cassuto hypothesizes.[39] Myths of any sort do not simply float free on the ether, so to speak, but must be instantiated in some manner—either as a part of an ongoing and live oral tradition or entexted—to have any cultural substantiality. Myth (a story about gods) is an important subgenre in the narrative poetic traditions of the ancient Near East and should not be opposed too sharply by an anachronistic notion of epic proper (a story about heroic human characters). At least "narratologically speaking," writes J. M. Sasson, "ANE myths and epics hardly differ, in form or structure, and even less so in the character-roles of protagonists. Both were regarded as equally historical (or not) and both equally challenge our capacity to disbelieve.… Moreover, they [the scribes] shuttled at will motifs, themes, even globs of material between what we label myths and epics."[40] To wit, a putative narrative poetic tradition in Israel and Judah would have surely included its share of mythological stories.[41] There is a great

amount of such mythological allusions in biblical poetry (as opposed to biblical prose narrative, where there is very little) but never the myths themselves.
In predominantly oral, small-scale, and traditional societies like those of Israel
and Judah, myths like all stories only have reality as long as they are told and
retold, and thus remembered (namely "that which we have heard and known, /
that our ancestors have told us," Ps 78:3). To be sure, written versions can preserve a myth, and even act as an aid to memory, but they would still require
reperformance and reauralization to gain any cultural purchase. Whatever more
may be supposed about such mythic allusions, that the performing poets (and
scribes) anticipated that (at least some part of) their imagined audience would
have the requisite cultural knowledge to place (at least some of the) said allusions seems certain enough.[42] With respect to the "battle against Sea" myth,
there are many more allusions to it in biblical poetry than the three Cassuto
cites initially, many of which he then goes on to tally. In fact from these allusions (and his knowledge of other versions of the myth) he even reconstructs
the Yahwistic "recension" of the myth in great detail.[43] While the latter effort
remains highly speculative, the number of allusions themselves favor Cassuto's premise, namely, that the myth, either in (extrabiblical) texts that have yet
to come to light or as a part of a vital oral tradition, had contemporary currency in a version involving Yahweh. The major insight here is that the allusions must be allusions to a myth (Yahwistic or not) whether textualized or
oralized.

Cassuto's other category of evidence, style and diction, also points concretely to knowledge of a poetic narrative tradition.[44] In particular, he gathers
a number of "set and oft-recurring phrases" that appear frequently in (certain
parts of) biblical prose (but never in the Bible's nonnarrative poetry) and that
are equally stereotyped and common in Ugaritic narrative poetry. For example,
the two corpora share stock phrases for "lifting up the eyes and seeing" and
for "raising the voice and crying out." As E. L. Greenstein notices, "there can
be no doubt of a historical connection between the Canaanite formulas and
their biblical doubles."[45] These are just two of the several that Cassuto brings
forward, and more recently F. Polak (among others) has elaborated and extended this line of inquiry.[46] Polak affirms Cassuto's conclusion: "In short, the
distribution of formulaic phrases confirms Cassuto's thesis"—namely, that
"ancient epic served as the fountain-head for Biblical narrative."[47] Cassuto
notes well that written prose everywhere follows poetry.[48] Greenstein elaborates this point in a most telling way, first, demonstrating explicitly with respect
to the often-remarked-on "early Hebrew poems" (e.g., Exod 15, Judg 5)—which
tend not to have the narrative deictic particles such as the definite article (ha-),
the marker of the direct object ('et-), and the relative particle 'ăšer "which" that

evolve with Hebrew prose writing—that the Bible's prose writers obviously cited from the early corpus of Hebrew lyric or melic verse, and then concludes as follows concerning the stock phrases first identified by Cassuto:

> So how can narrative formulas known from second millennium Canaanite epic get absorbed into biblical prose narrative? Not from the archaic poetry that is found in the Bible, which, as we have seen, is never essentially narrative and contains no such formulas. The only realistic explanation I can imagine is that in the same way that the authors of biblical prose narrative occasionally drew on the corpus of archaic Hebrew poetry, they drew on pre-biblical Hebrew epic, which also belonged to that corpus.[49]

Part of Cassuto's original rationale for identifying these formulas and set phrases was a supposed odd, antiquated feel about them—"like fossilized expressions."[50] Such fossilizations do not so much point backward (e.g., to a putative antecedent tradition)—though they do that—as implicate an ongoing currency of intelligibility in the present (at least at the point of original inscription). So Polak, who concludes, "Apparently, at the time that these [biblical] stories assumed their basic form, the [prose] narrators were still quite conscious of the epic formulaic style."[51] A common characteristic that scholars have noted about both written verse and written prose as they emerge out of oral poetic traditions is their tendency to continue using traditional oral style and idioms. J. Kittay and W. Godzich, in their study of the emergence of written prose in thirteenth-century France (one of the very few historical and critical studies of its kind), emphasize that there is nothing "natural" about prose narrative. Prose everywhere is a product of writing and, as Cassuto well understood, emerges after verse—indeed, emerges *out of* performative verse:

> Historical evidence shows that it is verse that precedes prose. In the linguistic traditions of Hebrew, Greek, Latin, Arabic, Old Icelandic, English, Spanish, German, Wolof, amd Pulaar, and on and on and on, prose comes after verse. There is an epoch in each of these traditions in which there is no prose, and apparently never had been. There is then, subsequently, a time in which prose appears. And the appearance of prose does not at all coincide with the appearance of writing. It is subsequent to the appearance of writing.[52]

This emergence of prose is gradual, not singular but complex, and not necessarily linear in development, self-evident, or easy. And as prose develops and differentiates itself as a new signifying practice, it by necessity and quite naturally will utilize and carry on aspects of the previous signifying practice, that is, oral verbal art. It could hardly do otherwise. What is new everywhere must develop (historically, culturally) out of something, something old, known, given, something ancestral. In this case, prose (written nonverse) has among its ancestors performative verse. For the new writers of prose and their audiences, nurtured in an oral culture, a culture of performance, the only idiom available for telling stories was oral, traditional, poetic. Written prose eventually opens up new possibilities for how to tell a story, but it must begin with what has been known and relied on for generations, the techniques and devices of oral performance.[53] M. C. Amodio makes the same point about the emergence of written verse traditions in Anglo-Saxon England: "Although compositional devices such as formulas and formulaic style serve highly specialized functions within oral performative traditions, poets, both oral and literate, continue to use them because they are the very stuff of poetic articulation and of poetic thought"—these were not conscious attempts to recreate oral poetry but the use of the "only idiom at their disposal for the articulation of poetry."[54] And Foley in a related vein:

> Even when the process becomes one of making oral-derived texts, the traditional phraseology and narrative patterns continue to provide ways for the poet to convey meaning, to tap the traditional reservoir. Poets do not persist in employing traditional structures after the advent of literacy and texts out of a misplaced antiquarianism or by default, but because, even in an increasingly textual environment, the "how" developed over the ages still holds the key to worlds of meaning that are otherwise inaccessible.[55]

So it would seem that Polak's inference about biblical prose emerging (in part)[56] from a living epic tradition is well motivated. The express linearity and tight chronological sequencing of the developmental scheme that he projects out from that imagined originary moment is less compelling to me. It is not obvious that the data at our disposal allow for such fine-grained plotting, though I do not doubt that the basic trajectory articulated (at least in very gross terms) is right. Biblical prose surely evolves such that it develops and exploits those capacities that the new technology of writing makes available to it, which at points includes distinct and tractable movements away from the inherited traditional style of poetic narrative. Cassuto himself identifies one such development. He offers "the love of *repetition*, which is so marked in Biblical narrative," as still further "evidence of the continuation of the epic tradition" in Israel and

Judah.[57] He associates such fondness with the epic's rootedness and origins in oral culture, its aboriginal status as performative art. One kind of typical "epic repetition"—a name Parker gives to this kind of repetition in his own study of Ugaritic narrative poetry—involves "a given command and its execution": "The poet, in such a case, begins by telling us that so-and-so enjoined so-and-so, saying to him: Do thus and thus. After citing the words of the one who issued the order, the narrator continues: And so-and-so did thus and thus. All the details of the action are then repeated in precisely the same words as were used by the poet the first time."[58] Parker provides numerous examples from Aqhat and Kirta of just this sort of epic repetition (e.g., CAT 1.17.V.16–21, 21–25, 28–31),[59] and Cassuto cites as a biblical counterpart the instructions for the construction of the Tabernacle (Exod 25–31, 35–40; cf. Josh 6).[60] Cassuto goes on to notice, then, and this is the main point, that such verbatim repetition is not so prominent in biblical prose precisely because of a difference in technology, as written prose develops capacities that are not open to its oral narrative forebears:

> Prose is intended for reading rather than hearing, and the reader, unlike the listener, does not look forward to passages he already knows by heart. On the contrary, the repetition of the subject in identical words may sometimes be tiresome to him. Hence prose writings tend, for aesthetic reasons, to change the expressions, or to shorten them, or to alter their sequence, when reverting to a given theme.[61]

While there is much more to this development than aesthetics, the observation nevertheless is prescient, anticipating more recent and more sophisticated probings of the development of prose writing as it emerges out of oral performative culture.[62]

The pathway that this development takes, from oral (or oral-derived) narrative verse to written prose narrative, is worth underscoring, as it is not an uncommon one. Cross, in articulating his own understanding of the kinds of oral traditions that underlie and inform the written sources of the Pentateuch, makes this very point. After citing two comparative examples (Russian and Spanish), Cross concludes: "My argument is not that there is a natural evolution from poetic epic to prose epic"—no doubt an observation triggered by the express evolutionary shape given to this idea by Cassuto. "Rather," Cross continues, "I am observing that the recasting of poetic epic in prose narrative and indeed its use as a source for the composition of historical narrative is not an isolated occurrence in Israel; the techniques used here to reconstruct Israel's epic have precise analogies in literary scholarship."[63] Part of what makes Kittay and Godzich's study of the emergence of prose in thirteenth-century France so illuminating is that in several instances (parts of) both the ancestral verse traditions and the emergent prose renditions of the same narratives have survived.[64] In these instances, close comparisons can reveal quite specifically what the new technology of prose writing carried over from its ancestral source and where it diverged and in what manner. It is not to be presumed, of course, that biblical prose will have developed in quite the same way. But these kinds of comparisons provide for an enriched conceptual horizon within which biblical scholars may profitably continue to probe the nature of biblical prose, especially as it emerges from the traditional performative context(s) of oral storytelling. Beyond the presence of epic formulas and epic repetition, other signs that early biblical prose narrative is especially indebted to oral style include the use of type-scenes,[65] traditional tale types,[66] and traditional settings,[67] bursts of rhythmicity and even parallelism,[68] episodic and strongly additive structure,[69] and the prevalence of simpler syntactic structures (e.g., preference for parataxis, shorter noun strings, and few explicit constituents in a clause).[70] Much biblical prose, in fact, is acoustically shaped in no small part because it will still have "listeners" as much in view as "readers"; hence: "and the ears of all the people" were attentive to Ezra as he read the scroll of the Torah to them at the Water Gate (Neh 8:3).[71]

Cross, equally provoked by the study of Ugaritic narrative poetry, articulates an alternative conceptualization of the kinds of oral sources that would have informed the writers of biblical literature. Whereas Cassuto was mostly theoretically naive and paid significant attention to mining the Bible's nonnarrative poetic corpus for signs of mythic narrative antecedents, Cross embraces, wholeheartedly, the Parry and Lord formulaic theory and focuses quite specifically on oral sources that he presumes to underlie the preserved literary sources of the Pentateuch. Cross formulated his ideas at the height of the Parry-Lord influence over the study of oral narrative traditions (from the late 1960s through the mid-1980s). He found in the Parry-Lord theory a compelling antidote to the broadly folkloristic paradigm that otherwise shaped the field's notion of oral traditions. In particular, Cross was convinced that Parry and Lord's ideas had successfully illuminated the originating orality of Ugaritic narrative poetry:

> There can be no doubt that this poetic cycle [the Baal cycle] was orally composed. It is marked by oral formulae, by characteristic repetitions, and by fixed pairs of synonyms (a type of formula) in traditional thought rhyme (*parallelismus membrorum*) which marks Semitic oral literature as well as much of the oral literature throughout the world. Moreover,

their repertoire of traditional formulae overlaps broadly with that of the earliest Hebrew poetry, a circumstance impossible to explain unless a common tradition of oral literature embraced both Israel in the south and Ugarit in the north.[72]

The logic of Cross's thinking here, bolstered by his own status in the field, the unquestioned verity of the Parry-Lord paradigm, and the readily apparent formularity of the texts themselves and the recurrent use of set themes and motifs, has continued to compel assent when it comes to the presumed orality that informs the Ugaritic narratives (which, in light of their having been written down, are best thought of as oral-derived texts). Curiously, however obvious the fact of this informing orality, the thesis itself has not been as robustly interrogated as might be presumed.[73] Much of the work has been comparative in nature, with the chief focus on the Hebrew Bible. Kawashima is a good recent example. While his study focuses primarily on the emergence of biblical prose narrative as a specifically written art form, the narrative poetry of the Homeric epics and of Ugarit are used to exemplify the possibilities/differences of oral (and oral-derived) narrative art.[74] The comparisons are themselves generally insightful, and Kawashima succeeds in revealing important aspects of Ugaritic narrative art (e.g., the foregrounded and forward-moving progression of the action).[75] But the informing orality of the Ugaritic texts itself is mainly asserted, or more accurately, assumed to have been "persuasively argued," though the supporting literature cited is again thin and (in this instance) wholly comparative in nature.[76] Kawashima's best source for the traditional, oral-derived nature of Ugaritic narrative is the single most substantive study of the topic, Parker's work *The Pre-biblical Narrative Tradition*. Parker does not flaunt his theoretical bent. At the outset he simply notes, "I take it as a given that the [Ugaritic] poems as we have them are the products not only of some copying of earlier written version(s) but also of a period of oral transmission; and that as oral poems they used traditional sources."[77] Although Parker labels "literary" the "angle of vision" assumed in his study, its notion of narrative is thoroughly informed by leading oralists of the day (e.g., Lord, Finnegan, J. Vansina). And what he chiefly reveals (with appropriate empirical detail) is just how thoroughly indebted the Ugaritic narrative poems (here mainly Aqhat and Kirta) are to oral, traditional modes of storytelling. Two long summarizing quotes may serve (in lieu of detailed exemplification) to underscore the point. The first quotation comes from Parker's long, initial discussion of the narrative conventions exhibited in Aqhat and Kirta. After making clear his astute awareness of our inability to get behind the texts with any great specificity, he writes the following:

One thin line leading us toward the activity of the poets is the function and adaptation of the conventions discussed in this chapter. For those conventions as we have found them used were all functional for the oral poets who were undoubtedly the main tellers of these tales, even during the period of their written transmission. Such poets would depend on their mastery of a repertoire of formulae, on their skill of echoing cola with parallel cola, on their freedom to repeat with epic prolixity speeches or actions repeated in the plot, and on their knowledge of standard scenes and actions and tale-types—would depend on all of these in order to perform a narrative. For these resources would enable them both to spin it out from memory and to vary it according to their own artistic sense, the demands of the situation and the reactions of the audience. Thus the traditional tale, in which various poets and audiences shared ownership, would be realized in fresh and vital ways from performance to performance. The small deviations from type, which we have noted again and again, may at times betray the poet's inattentiveness or resourcelessness—or that of the scribe who may or may not have been a poet. But often such deviations play a clear aesthetic or rhetorical or narrative or thematic role, giving testimony to the poets' responsiveness, creativity or purposefulness even within the conventional culture of their art. Recognition of the limitations and possibilities of the poets may enable us to appreciate more fully even at our cultural distance the repetitiveness, slower pace, conventionality of much of the poetry.[78]

Then in anticipation of the kind of detailed study undertaken by Kawashima, Parker offers the following counterpointing characterization at the conclusion of his own study:

In Ugaritic literature, the plot progresses through largely stereotyped descriptions of actions which may be extended and slowed down by epic repetition or repetion with a numerical framework, or abbreviated and speeded up by a cluster of selected formulaic cola. Speeches too may be quite conventional and may be repeated to fill out a scene (as in [KTU] 1.17.5). On the other hand, they may be used to portray character and to show changing relationships and so to develop the plot (as in 1.17.6). Fast or slowly, the plot progresses directly forward. There are no asides, no anticipatory confidences to the listener/reader, no summaries or generalizations, no normalizing lessons drawn, no explanations of older customs, no references to the present day.

Biblical narrative, for all its variety, may be characterized generally
by contrast with these features. Though stereotyped language and repetition are used, they are occasional rather than pervasive, and generally used for particular artistic effects rather than as a basic means of
storytelling. Epic repetition is used very selectively and economically
and repetition with a numerical framework never. The more flexible
use of language—a function of prose composition, as against traditional verse composition—allows more sensitive portrayal of character
and more subtle recounting of and commenting on action. The story
line is occasionally punctuated by words directed by the narrator to the
audience.... In every such case, a different point of view is represented.[79]

This mainly by way of affirming the field's general sense of the informing
orality of Ugaritic narrative poetry. Parker has done the most to flesh out this
understanding—and much could still be done, especially now in light of renewed interest in the topic of orality and textuality—though as Parker well
knew, the Ugaritic narratives have only come to us as written hard copies, so
no pure orality here.

In entitling his study of Ugaritic narrative poetry *The Pre-biblical Narrative
Tradition* Parker signals his conviction that the two narrative traditions are
connected. This is not to claim direct connection between the Ugaritic poems
under review (Aqhat and Kirta) and any specific biblical narrative, nor to imply
anything about the dating of the biblical texts (i.e., he is not positing any necessary chronological contiguity). Rather, Parker writes, "*Krt* and *Aqht* simply
happen to be the only two representatives we have of what was doubtless
a rich narrative tradition spread throughout the Northwest Semitic-speaking
settlements of the Eastern Mediterranean countries; and that tradition would
have continued in such communities long after the collapse of the late bronze
age communities of northern Syria."[80] In other words, the Ugaritic poems
represent a narrative tradition ancestral to that found in the Bible. This is a
position, if more carefully stated, consistent not only with that of Cassuto but
also with the alternative (or complementing) hypothesis of Cross. Famously,
Cross pressed a most specific thesis: "We prefer to speak of J and E as variant
forms in prose of an older, largely poetic Epic cycle of the era of the Judges....
No doubt the Epic cycle was originally composed orally and was utilized in the
cult of covenant-renewal festivals of the league, taking on variant forms at different sanctuaries and in different times."[81] This is an idea that Cross held for
an extended period, so it is not without some complexity. In some ways, like
Cassuto's, it is a thesis that is very much a product of its (germinal) time.
Many of its informing suppositions will no longer garner wide assent, for

example the idea of the league, the espousal of high antiquity for many biblical texts and traditions, the narrow construal of orality through the Parry-
Lord model. Some aspects of his exposition seem impossibly naive from our
current standpoint, as when he converts (through the stripping "of a few prose
particles") the prose of Exodus 19:3–6 into "exquisite poetry in epic style."[82]
Cross means this to illustrate his conviction that the JE "epic sources" would
have been "largely poetic." While the exercise is not without imagined heuristic ends to which it might be put,[83] it does not reveal anything about the
putative oral poetic source informing the passage, not the least the poetic
source itself. More detrimental, it exposes that aspect of Cross's thinking that
is most easily caricatured and dismissed, namely the thought that biblical
prose may be easily peeled back to reveal "exquisite" epic verse. And there are
aspects of Cross's hypothesis that are to be rejected. So, still fully enamored
with the Parry-Lord school, even as late as 1998, Cross can remark: "I should
find it surprising indeed if Israel's old epic cycle in its oral presentations did
not rival or even exceed in length the preserved Yahwist source."[84] The problem,
however, as Greenstein observes, is that the assumption is opposed to what is
known empirically about written epic verse from the ancient Near East, namely,
that such poems routinely number less than three thousand lines—and the
preserved Ugaritic narratives are considerably shorter still, no more than
about twelve hundred lines.[85] There are moments where Cross clearly imagines "a long and rich poetic epic" underlying the "truncated and secondary
derivatives" of the prose "variants" preserved in J and E,[86] and at these moments Cross should be resisted—Greenstein is rightly emphatic: "I cannot
accept such a far-reaching theory."[87]

There are also moments of more subtlety and complexity that remain provocative and worthy of probing. For example, almost as a counterpoint to the
singularity of "a long and rich poetic epic" Cross somewhat enigmatically at
the end of "Traditional Narrative" writes: "Israel's ancient epic is not a historical narrative. On the other hand, it is not a collection of fragments."[88] Frus-
tratingly, he does not go on to clarify more precisely what he means. I suggest
that the most charitable gloss of this statement comes in his extended description of the "epic cycle" that is at the heart of the essay.[89] It is far more episodic
and multiformal—even fragmentary—than the unitary gloss(es) of his ideas
would suggest. So he imagines one component of the cycle—a term that itself
presumes plurality—as consisting of a bundle of themes—a recounting of the
exodus, covenant, and conquest based on the mythic pattern exhibited in the
Baal Cycle and in some of the early lyric poems in the Bible (e.g., Exod 15, Judg 5,
Deut 32, Hab 3)—to be performed variously and variably at different locales
(e.g., Gilgal, Shechem, Bethel). This emphasis on multiformity is in Cross

from the beginning—"taking on variant forms at different sanctuaries and in different times"⁹⁰—but has often gotten lost (no doubt in part because of other emphases that are also in Cross). Cross observes, surely indebted to the thought of Lord, "the epic tradition was continuous, new elements expanding and replacing old, a dynamic process with changing times and institutions."⁹¹ Or: "In fact, epic plots and bundles of themes, mythic patterns, and indeed tales sung based on memorable events, throughout the age of epic composition, existed as a background for each new performance of epic tradition."⁹² And again at the close of the essay: "Israel's epic drew on older epic cycles in dynamic change," and "the epic acquired accretions and variants in its recompositions by bards and hierophants, and it developed multiforms in the festivals of the pilgrimage shrines."⁹³ These accents are far more compatible with the kind of episodic cycle of traditions that can be more readily imagined given the examples of the Ugaritic poems and what is known about the evolution of the Gilgamesh Epic, for example.⁹⁴

When it comes to pressing for details about the content of the epic tradition Cross treads on shakier ground. What remains so convincing about Cassuto's theory of an "Israelite epic" is his leveraging of the mythological allusions to point, even if only generally, to content. Cross tries something similar in his espousal of a "mythic pattern" undergirding the narrative traditions in the Tetrateuch ("the P work") as an alternative to the more documentary-based construals of a von Rad or Noth: "An alternative, and I believe superior, approach is open, at least, to the possibility that the battle at the sea and the covenant-making and establishment of divine rule belong to a sequence of events or bundle of themes narrated in the primitive epic cycle."⁹⁵ What is analogous to Cassuto's logic is the leveraging of extratextual knowledge to make sense of an aspect of what may be observed in the text: "That the pattern existed before the elaboration of units in the Israelite epic—and indeed shaped the selection of events to be narrated—can be argued on the basis of the myth of the Divine Warrior from Ugarit, as well as from Hebrew poetry early and late."⁹⁶ The problem for Cross is that patterns can sometimes be even more ephemeral than allusions and thus hard to show. By most accounts Cross's discernment of the pattern in the older biblical poems (e.g., Exod 15) is more convincing than seeing the same in the prose narratives. As for the "patriarchal lore," another significant component of the narrative traditions as they have come down to us, Cross can only assert that such "traditions were an integral element in Israel's early epic," as currently there is no obvious way of similarly leveraging external confirming evidence. R. Hendel, whose study of the Jacob tales is intended to flesh out aspects of Cross's ideas, for example, can show that the birth stories (that he treats) in the Hebrew Bible are rooted

in and show explicit knowledge of one well-documented Eastern Mediterranean oral-based type-scene, which is no small thing.[97] But he has no means
for determining more specifically whether any of the biblical stories themselves reflect actual antecedent oral traditions (e.g., about the births of Jacob
and Isaac) or whether they are free compositions of a prose writer with knowledge both of the type-scene and of the traditional lore.[98] So here one can be
confident of the traditional nature of the storytelling technique—as Kawashima
emphasizes, the sharing of such formal features between written "biblical
narrative" and "oral-traditional epics" likely points "to an actual historical relationship between the two"[99]—without also being able to point more specifically to actual oral poems—so S. Niditch: "We cannot link these [kinds of
oral-derived features]...with strictly poetic texts at all."[100] In general, then,
Cross's theory, like other speculation about Hebrew poetic narrative tradition,
given the lack of textual evidence, is best held loosely and heuristically, while
resisting the desire to press too closely for details.

The foregoing has been a synthetic and selective review of (some) leading
threads in the discussion of an oral-based Hebrew poetic narrative tradition.
It is a topic that still requires a full vetting. But even on the basis of what has
been said here, two large conclusions may be confidently drawn: one, that
an oral poetic narrative tradition existed in Israel and Judah during the first
millennia, and two, that written biblical prose was rooted in this tradition,
emerged out of it, and evolved a style that remains, at points, highly indebted
to it.[101] With regard to the former, which is most germane to my principal concern in this chapter (the informing orality of biblical nonnarrative poetry),
those aspects that most persuasively point to the existence of an ancient
Hebrew narrative poetry may be briefly summarized: that the biblical world
was a thoroughgoingly oral world, even after the advent of writing, and that
the chief outlet even for written compositions was oral performance; the fact
of the empirical preservation of written versions of oral or oral-derived poetic
narrative poems, especially those in a West Semitic dialect from Late Bronze
Age Ugarit; that biblical Hebrew evidences the capacity for narrative poetry;
that mythical allusions (and even "snatches" of verse) and mythic story patterns evident in biblical poems indisputably point to known myths; and with
regard to biblical prose, that the presence of set narrative formulas known
only from other ancient Near Eastern poetic epics, the use of traditional themes,
motifs, settings, type-scenes, and tale types, and the prevalence, especially in
earlier prose materials, of simpler syntactic profiles irrefutably show knowledge of oral narrative traditions—and this even while acknowledging the writerly development of this particular verbal art form. Therefore, Zakovitch's very
emphatic title to his article on the topic may be heartily echoed here: "Yes,

There Was an Israelite Epic in the Biblical Period." The shape, broad extent, and much of the content of this narrative tradition, with some exceptions (e.g., presence of myth, likely episodic nature), remain necessarily elusive. The Ugaritic narrative poems offer the best guide to what slightly later Hebrew narrative poems would look like. Kawashima among recent commentators has emphasized the pastness of this oral tradition—part of the title of his book after all is *The Death of the Rhapsode*—as a precondition for the emergence of a specifically written form of prose narrative.[102] His elucidation of (some of) what biblical prose owes to the new technology of writing is wonderfully illuminating, but nowhere, as far as I can tell, do his insights require the strong version of his historical thesis. Ethnographically, in fact, not only is such a presumption not required, it may well be even more likely to expect a prose narrative tradition (especially with so many telltale signs of traditional storytelling) to emerge in the midst of a living and vibrant oral tradition. The best paradigm for this is the emergence of written prose in archaic and classical Greece (eighth to fourth centuries BCE), which was an extended process (Plato was still reacting to it in the *Republic*) and took place in what was otherwise still very much an overwhelmingly traditional and oral performative culture. As Thomas states specifically for the classical period, "written publication and oral performance jostled side by side."[103] A broadly analogous kind of culture may be presumed for the pre-Hellenistic Levant generally,[104] as suggested, for example, by the myriad of representations within the Bible of even written texts needing to be read out loud, performed for listeners.[105] And if Israel and Judah's storytelling tradition remained alive throughout the biblical period, as some suppose,[106] this might explain how later poets and prophets in particular could allude so knowingly to Yahwistic mythology, given the continuing absence in the material record of written versions of such myths.[107] What may be affirmed with Kawashima is that narrative prose eventually succeeds and survives in writing and narrative verse does not (as far as is currently known)— in no small part, no doubt, because the former is more congenial (in a myriad of ways) to a storyteller-less text.[108] Indeed, the basic trajectory of development—"the gradual undermining of oral culture by the power of writing"—is broadly typical, if not inevitable.[109]

Cassuto quite memorably ends his essay by expressing his fervent desire that some written bits of Israel and Judah's once vibrant oral epic tradition would come to light:

> The epic poetry of Israel was wide in range and variegated in character. Our ancestors possessed a complete epic literature till after the Babylonian Exile and the Return to Zion. One cannot but wish that just as we

were privileged to see the ostraca of Lachish, remants of the correspondence of the last generation of the epoch of the First Temple,
which had remained hidden in the ground for thousands of years and
came to light in our time, so it may be granted to us to behold, through
some fortunate discovery in the near future, relics of the ancient epic
poetry of the people of Israel.[110]

Zakovitch, at the close of his own contribution on the topic (published in the
International Folklore Review) recalls Cassuto's closing wish and writes by way
of counterpoint: "This hope is yet to be fulfilled, but our assuredness of the
existence of an Israelite epic has not lessened: 'O for those who are gone and
forgotten.'"[111] Today, almost seventy years after Cassuto's original publication,
still no extrabiblical written remains of ancient Hebrew narrative poetry have
been recovered. Zakovitch's point is that the lack of written versions of oral
verbal art does not imply that the oral art never existed. As I noted at the
outset, oral art qua oral art does not *ever* require translation into writing. It
may simply be the case, however continually challenging it is for contemporary highly literate and chirographically oriented Western scholars to conceptualize and truly appreciate, that the connection between the one-time
written-out narrative poems from Ugarit and the written prose narratives of
the Bible that are so obviously their cultural heirs was always only traditional
and oral and unaided by writing. If we have learned anything from the now
nearly century-long study of oral narrative traditions since Parry's famous
doctoral dissertation, it is that traditions of oral storytelling can flourish—and
have done so!—in the absence of writing; or perhaps more historically realistic for the ancient Levant, a region not unfamiliar with the technology of
writing, *alongside but unaided by writing*. Given the long familiarity with writing
in the ancient Near East and in the Levant in particular, Cross, who like Cassuto and Zakovitch imagines "a long and continuous tradition of epic singers
and epic cycles" in Israel and Judah,[112] advises nonetheless that "one must
reckon always with the possibility in Israel, as in Ugarit, of written as well as
oral transmission of epic texts."[113] As I turn now to the question of orality and
the nonnarrative poetry of the Bible, here, too, as I will show, it is also a matter
of reckoning orality and literacy together.

Nonnarrative Oral Poetry, Or:
Orality Poeticized Otherwise

In beginning with the question of ancient Hebrew narrative verse I have
meant to underscore that it existed once upon a time, a fact that ultimately

impinges (directly and indirectly) on an appreciation of biblical poetry in a variety of ways, not least, the sharp imprint of orality inscribed in its style and the nature of that orality. One of the more debilitating consequences of the Parry-Lord lockdown on the study of oral poetry for so long was the choice of narrative verse as the chief subject of inquiry. That field in part came of age thinking through the art of oral storytelling, remaining all but deaf to singers of other nonnarrative songs and the possibilities of their singing differently. That is, a chief problem for the study of oral art after *The Singer of Tales*—especially for the comparatist and nonspecialist—was that the then "Yugoslavian guslar" became "the exclusive model of an oral poet." Yet other types of oral songs, songs that do not tell stories even, exist and have always existed. Ancient Greek lyric is a paradigm example; as E. A. Havelock stresses, "a vast body of 'oral' lyric must have circulated which had ephemeral value."[114] He continues with emphasis:

> The scraps that we have represent the work of those poets lucky enough to live late enough to be inscribed and whose manuscripts were deemed worthy of preservation. Their oral ancestory must have been as sophisticated as that of Homer. But because alphabetized, they entered the realm of "literature." It is absurd to suppose in the manner of histories of Greek literature that the forms of "lyric" were suddenly invented in all their perfection at the point where the Alexandrian canon begins in the seventh century B.C.[115]

For comparative purposes it is worth emphasizing what Havelock characterizes as the "multifarious" nature of ancient Greek lyric verse. It was "not the product of any one specialized craft" and included "cult hymns addressed to a deity, festival songs, including processional songs and dancing songs, marriage songs and funeral dirges, birthdays songs, children's songs . . . , lullabies, military and campfire songs, epitaphs, elegies and elegaic homilies—covering all kinds of social communication beyond the casual converse of the vernacular."[116] The litany of types here is not unlike the one Alter offers in describing biblical poetry—seemingly everything but stories.

In a similar vein, J. Opland notices that a large portion of the preserved corpus of Anglo-Saxon poetry "is not narrative at all."[117] If the South Slavic tradition as defined by Parry and especially Lord (i.e., in its explicit narrative mode) provides "useful analogues for much of the narrative poetry that survives in Anglo-Saxon manuscripts"[118]—including, for example, *Beowulf*, which has figured so prominently in discussions of the formulaic, improvisational model of oral poetry—Opland does not think these same analogues are well

suited to the nonnarrative poems in the corpus. This is a crucial point he
makes at the outset of his study of Anglo-Saxon oral poetry. Therefore, in
this work he foregrounds the "eulogistic"—"it deals with the character of [the
poet's] subjects and their deeds"—tradition of the Xhosa- and Zulu-speaking
Bantu peoples of South Africa as a more useful analogue for the nonnarrative
forms in Anglo-Saxon poetry.[119] This eulogistic tradition is highly lyrical in
nature, namely allusive and elliptical and not narratival, mostly short, ritual-
ized, and primarily memorial. It exemplifies well the kind of oral tradition
noticed more generally by Finnegan where narrative (epic) is not at all prominent. At any rate it is hard to counter the force of Opland's argument that
comparisons should be made as much as possible between like and like.[120]

Just as interesting, both historically and critically, is the fact that the Serbo-
Croatian oral tradition, like that of Anglo-Saxon England and ancient Greece,
included both narrative and nonnarrative art forms. So Opland on improvisation, a subject Lord explored fully and illuminatingly:

> It is perhaps unfortunate for the purpose of comparative studies that
> the choice to emphasise only the improvising guslar, excluding from
> his definition of oral poet the memoriser: the memorising guslar cer-
> tainly does exist in Yugoslavia, as do lyric poets . . . , and their exclusion
> from consideration by Lord created the unfortunate impression that
> "the Southslavic poetic tradition" was represented by the guslar alone
> and was accordingly "primarily improvisational."[121]

The critique is sharp. Opland makes clear he thinks the exclusivity of Lord's
focus both was intentional and knowing—"the memorising guslar certainly
does exist in Yugoslavia, *as do lyric poets*" (emphasis added). In support of the
latter, Opland cites the second endnote to Lord's *The Singer of Tales*, which
describes the Milman Parry Collection at Harvard University, which at the
time of Lord's publication (1960) contained over 12,500 texts collected "in various parts of [the then] Yugoslavia in 1934 and 1935"—"both epic and lyric
songs."[122] He also cites a 1977 article by M. P. Coote that demonstrates scholarly knowledge of nonheroic, nonepic Serbo-Croatian verse—ethnographically
designated as "women's songs"—that dates at least to the middle of the nineteenth century.[123] In a later essay, again focusing on the so-called women's
songs though this time based on material from the Parry Collection, Coote reports that the collection, "despite an emphasis on heroic songs in its original
intent, in its publication, and in the seminal studies based upon it," also contains
"approximately eleven thousand dictated and 250 recorded women's songs."[124]
These "women's songs" are not strictly for women but are the unmarked category

for songs in the South Slavic oral tradition and include everything except the marked, heroic narrative songs studied by Parry and Lord (among others). The latter is restricted in the circumstances of performance and in content "to the world of the adult male in a patriarchal and often embattled society."[125] The "women's songs," by contrast, include

> ballads and bawdy songs, laments, lullabies, courting and love songs, songs to hive bees by, songs to spite the next village, ritual songs for rainmaking, seasonal festivals, weddings and circumcisions, and so forth. These are any songs sung outside the special circumstances of performing heroic songs, but often restricted to their own peculiar performance conditions (as, for example, ritual songs).[126]

This is a familiar listing, very much akin to Havelock's for ancient Greek lyric, or Alter's for biblical poetry, or indeed what could be elaborated for either the eulogistic tradition of southeast Africa or the nonnarrative portions of the Anglo-Saxon poetic corpus. Finnegan is adamant: "Lyric is thus an extremely important and wide category of oral poetry."[127]

And it is precisely on the issue of nonnarrativity that Coote places her emphasis in these studies and makes her most incisive observations. For the purpose of text analysis, she argues, "the useful distinction is between narrative (including both heroic songs and non-heroic ballads and romances) and non-narrative (again, everything else)"—which she says, naturally, also may be termed "lyric."[128] Coote goes on to show that in the South Slavic tradition the nature of performance, composition, and transmission varies remarkably depending on whether the songs are stories or lyrics, narratives or not narratives. In many respects, the nonnarrative "women's songs" stand opposed to performative practices reported for heroic narrative. For example, the brevity of the nonnarrative, lyric songs in the Parry Collection (e.g., averaging from seventeen to thirty-two lines) means they can exist as fixed texts, be memorized, and thus there is not the need for recomposition as with the longer heroic epics.[129] The extent and use of formulaic language differs between the two kinds of songs.[130] And so, too, does the nature of composition:

> The technique of composition of a lyric seems to consist in the combination of familiar clusters of lines rather than in the recomposition of an entire song line by line in traditional formulaic language. While the essence of a narrative song is a story outline that the singer fleshes out with a choice of type-scenes and formulas, the lyric has no such backbone of narrative structure. Realizing a single type-scene, it plays upon

an unstated theme that attracts to itself conglomerations of images embodied in clusters of formulas from the common store of traditional
poetry. Each cluster of formulas in the text contributes to the song
both the denotation of the lines themselves and a wealth of connotative
meaning accrued from their contact with other contexts in the poetry
and by association with the society's customs and beliefs.[131]

These few and nondetailed observations reveal the possibility of difference
that may attend different performative art forms, even from the same tradition. The "Yugoslavian guslar," the paradigm of the "oral poet" in Western
scholarship for much of the latter part of the twentieth century, was not the
only kind of oral performer even in his own South Slavic tradition. There were
other performers who performed other kinds of oral songs that, all importantly, voiced their orality differently (in many respects). The differences and
plurality of oral traditions is now well accepted by oralists and folklorists.
Oral culture is not monolithic. And the many different traditions they (have)
produce(d) vary in innumerable ways, from place to place and from time to
time and, crucially, depending on the kind of songs in view. Any comparative ethnography will always need to be awake to the possibility of such differences and intentional about eliciting parallels, analogs, models that are
maximally appropriate and informative. I suspect that a large part of the dis-
inclination on the part of biblical scholars to substantively probe the issue of
orality specifically at the site of biblical poems, and also of the mostly disap-
pointing results of the few studies that have undertaken such efforts, may
be attributed to the dominance of a comparative model—Lord's "singer of
tales"—that is ill suited to the non-tale-like nature of so much poetry in the
Bible. As Coote emphasizes, "the useful distinction is between narrative...and
non-narrative."

Now for the fun part. The first person in the wake of the phenomenal
success of *The Singer of Tales* to make this very observation, and in regard to
biblical poetry specifically, was none other than A. B. Lord himself—his contribution predates Coote's earliest statement by a year (1976). A paper by Lord
entitled "Formula and Non-narrative Theme in South Slavic Oral Epic and the
OT" is included in a collection of essays on *Oral Tradition and Old Testament
Studies* published in an early number of *Semeia* edited by R. C. Culley.[132]
In what must be his only published contribution to the study of the Hebrew
Bible, Lord returns to the broad issue of formularity, in particular as provoked
by R. B. Coote's "The Application of Oral Theory to Biblical Hebrew Literature."[133] In this essay R. B. Coote makes a number of what remain incisive
critiques of the assumed applicability of the Parry-Lord model to biblical

poetry, for example, the problem of meter at the center of Parry's definition of the formula, the inability in the nonmetrical verse of the Bible to adequately measure formulaic density or thrift. R. B. Coote does not doubt the oral heritage of biblical literature, but he also firmly believes that writing eventually has its part to play as well. He concludes: "In a sense the analogy between Homer and the Yugoslav tradition on the one hand and biblical literature on the other fails completely. There is nothing having to do with biblical literature which the oral theory alone completely explains."[134] Not surprisingly, the "fails completely" irks Lord—"[R. B.] Coote is a bit too pessimistic."[135] Quite aside from the merits of the debate—and there are merits on both sides— what is significant for my interest in the question of orality at the site of biblical poems is how R. B. Coote provokes Lord to his (anticipatory) insight about the nonnarrativity of biblical poetry: "The difficulties raised by [R. B.] Coote, it seems to me, are the result of trying to apply the description of the formula in oral traditional *narrative* poetry to what is postulated to be oral traditional non-narrative poetry (lyric, proverbial wisdom, and so on)."[136] Lord reasons, for example, that "metrical usefulness and thrift," however important in long narrative poems, may not be pertinent at all in (short) "non-narrative songs"[137]— particularly when those songs are themselves also not metrical (see chapter 2 here). Lord continues by suggesting recourse to nonnarrative oral traditions and corpora as better models for the kind of orality presumably evident in biblical poems (e.g., Chinese lyric poetry), including referencing the nonnarrative "women's songs" in the Parry Collection: "There is an abundance of lyric song texts from Yugoslavia in the Milman Parry Collection...and an investigation of repeated lines and groups of lines in them might shed some light on this problem."[138] The remainder of his essay gives a number of examples with commentary, to which I will return. He closes, again with R. B. Coote no doubt uppermost in mind:

> The foregoing examples of the structuring of non-narrative themes in Serbo-Croatian oral epic song may, I hope, suggest that the phenomenon of parallel pairs in the OT is closely akin to them. If so, then the analogy to South Slavic oral traditional narrative poetry will not have been in vain.[139]

There are issues to quibble with here, but the central thrust of his insight—that biblical poetry is dominantly nonnarrative and therefore similarly nonnarrative ethnographic parallels are required if this poetry's informing orality is to be adequately and fully fathomed—is well made and early and, as far as I can tell, largely unrecognized and unappreciated.[140]

Signs of (Nonnarrative) Orality in Biblical Poetry

In what immediately follows I canvas a broad range of considerations that point to what I have been calling (somewhat obliquely) the informing orality of biblical poetry—features, contexts, and other signs in biblical poems (or about biblical poems) that may be (more and less) confidently associated with orality (vocality, aurality) in all of its complexity. The fact that orality deeply informs biblical poetics is perhaps easily admitted even on the basis of comparative study using exclusively narrative models of orality. So R. B. Coote: "When, however, the traits of Hebrew poetry which are analogous to the distinguishing traits of Homeric and Yugoslav poetry are summed up, they leave no doubt whatsoever that Hebrew poetry descended from an oral tradition of a particular sort."[141] Still, to detail these traits and say more specifically of what sort they are—to say *how* biblical poetry is "comparably close to the oral poetic situation"—is no bad thing, especially in view of Gunkel's habit of asserting a rather vague and nebulous idea of orality and that primarily as a background to the biblical texts, both habits that the field has long since assimilated and sublimated. The survey recoups (though not necessarily reexplicates) observations made in earlier chapters, elaborating where appropriate and necessary, and gathers a host of other considerations as well. The resulting accumulation, though appropriately "thick" in places, is again finally exemplary and not comprehensive in its ultimate achievement. A distinct representation of the residual orality that informs and shapes biblical poetry is achieved, yet further details and clarifications (and even contestations) are easily imagined. Throughout I am acutely attuned to the possibility of difference in that paradigm of "other modes" of orality—nonnarrative song—and what it may implicate about the character of biblical poetry's orality. In other words, I aim to follow Lord's lead in taking seriously the differences (from a presumed narrative norm) that may inhere in "oral traditional non-narrative poetry."

Performance

In characterizing early Greek poetry, B. Gentili observes, "What distances it most radically from modern poetry is the medium of communication: not a written text for reading but a solo or choral performance, to the accompaniment of a musical instrument, before an audience."[142] Though biblical poetry, like archaic and classical Greek lyric, has only come down to us textualized and thus indelibly marked by writing and literacy, there is little doubt that most of it, too, however composed and even when finally written down, was disseminated and circulated originally orally and performatively—"performance is constitutive of the domain of verbal art as spoken communication"[143] and implicates the temporal coincidence of communication and reception.[144] There was no active book trade or reading public in the ancient Near East until the Hellenistic period at the earliest. Much biblical verse is preserved in decontextualized poetic collections that usually do not allow inference about any putative performative context. Fortunately, however, there are a good many biblical Hebrew poems preserved in written narratives that sometimes more and less explicitly stage the poems they cite or transcribe. Such narrative portrayals do not necessarily reveal anything factual about a putative original performance (though they might). Rather, they offer narrative representations of situations that at least made sense to the scribes at the time the narratives were written down. Such presentations provide us glimpses of the nature of poetic performance in ancient Israel and Judah.

I consider initially the apologetic account in Jeremiah 36 of Baruch's production of a scroll containing prophetic (and poetic)[145] oracles attributed to Jeremiah.[146] Yahweh instructs Jeremiah to write down in a scroll (*mĕgillat-sēper*) "all the words" (*kol-haddĕbārîm*) he had spoken against Israel and Judah and the nations over the previous twenty or so years (vv. 1–2, 4). Communication between deity and prophet is here conceived of as spoken communication, namely "all the words which I spoke to you" (v. 2; visions and dreams are more specifically ocular kinds of divine revelation). And as such the prophet Jeremiah's appointed task was clear: "you shall go to all to whom I send you, / and you shall speak [*tĕdabbēr*] whatever I command you" (Jer 1:7). And several verses later Yahweh says: "Now I have put my words [*dĕbāray*] in your mouth [*bĕpîkā*]" (1:9). The implication is that the oracles whose recording is narrated in Jeremiah 36 had been performed previously and orally by the prophet. The prose narratives collected in MT Jeremiah often depict the prophet delivering such oracles, for example, in the temple (7:2; 26:2), before the king (17:19–27; 21:1–7; 22:1–2), to the people (18:11–12; 22:1–2), before a priest (20:1–6). Original oral performance of prophetic oracles is consistent with the representation of prophecy in the book of Jeremiah and throughout the Hebrew Bible (esp. 1 Kgs 22) and elsewhere from the ancient Near East.[147] The (narrative) purpose for writing down Jeremiah's prophecies is so that Baruch might read them aloud in the temple (from which Jeremiah was banned) "in the hearing of all the people" (*'oznê kol-hā'ām*, v. 10; cf. vv. 5–6, 8). Writing in this instance serves oral performance by another person. Jeremiah himself is represented as reperforming (and thus remembering) his oracles as he "dictates" them to Baruch—literally, "Baruch wrote from the mouth [*mippî*] of Jeremiah" (v. 4).[148] After hearing Baruch's public reading at the temple (vv. 10–11), Micaiah

reports (*n-g-d*) to the king's officials "all the words which he heard" (v. 13)—
another specifically "oral" re-presentation. Baruch is summoned and rereads
aloud (lit. "in their hearing," v. 15) "all the words" from the scroll before the
officials (vv. 15–16). The officials then "report in the hearing of the king"
(*wayyaggîdû bĕ'oznê hammelek*) all the words that they themselves have heard
Baruch recite (v. 20). The scroll was eventually retrieved, and Jehudi "read it
in the hearing of the king" and the officials who were in attendance (v. 21).
And as Jehudi "read three columns or four," the king cut the columns off and
burns them in the fire (v. 23). The account ends with Jeremiah reperforming—dictating—one last time "all the words of the scroll that King Jehoiakim
of Judah had burned in the fire," to which he added many similar "words"
(v. 32).[149] The main point to underscore is that even with the support of writing
in a time of increasing textuality in Judah—as K. van der Toorn most incisively
reveals, the scroll of Jeremiah itself is plainly a scribal production, a product,
that is, of writing—oral performance (public and private) remains the dominant mode of publication and transmission of prophetic oracles (cf. Jer 1:17;
2:2). The "word" of Hebrew prophecy is classically a spoken word, both by the
deity (e.g., *zeh haddābār 'ăšer-dibber yhwh* "this is the word that Yahweh spoke,"
2 Kgs 19:21; *dĕbar-yhwh*, Hos 1:1; *kōh 'āmar yhwh*, Mic 3:5) and by the prophet
(e.g., *dibrê 'āmôs*, Amos 1:1; "Go and speak to this people!" Isa 6:9; "Hear the
word of Yahweh!" 1 Kgs 22:19; cf. *Lach* 3 rev. 3–5;[150] *KAI* 202 A.11–13; 315.1–2;
SAA 9 1.4 ii 16'–40').[151]

Two brief performances of prophetic verse by way of illustration. The first
is embedded in the account of Isaiah's meeting with Ahaz at the fuller's field
(Isa 7:1–9). Yahweh instructs Isaiah to take his son Shear-yashub and go out
to meet (*sē'-nā' liqra't*, v. 3) Ahaz and to "say to him" (*wĕ'āmartā 'ēlāyw*, v. 4),
among other things, a little oracle of salvation (7:7–9), which is introduced
formally by the messenger formula (*kōh 'āmar 'ădōnāy yhwh*, v. 7).[152] The narrative thread structuring the collected oracles of First Isaiah is spare at best,
and often, as here, it is inelegant, or at least its verisimilitude is not fully realized. The narrative never actually tells of Isaiah delivering the oracle to Ahaz,
of doing what Yahweh commands, as was customary in traditionally told stories (e.g., via "epic repetition" as commonly in Ugaritic narrative verse; see the
prose adaptation in Josh 6, Jer 36). Still, the scene implicated is clear: a prophet
confronting a king in person and orally declaiming his oracle. It is a rather
conventional scene (e.g., 1 Kgs 22; Jer 17:19–27; 22:1–2). The Zakkur stela
(*KAI* 202), from the early eighth century BCE, presumes a similar scenario.
Zakkur, his city under siege, prays to Baalshamayn, who "answers" him (*wy'nny*,
A 11)[153] through "seers and messengers" (*ḥzyn... 'ddn*, A 12) and provides him
with a salvation oracle (namely "Do not fear," A 12).[154] That Isaiah did in fact

meet up with Ahaz, though not narrated, is presumed by the exchange between prophet and king related in 7:13–17. This narratological infelicity, interestingly, reveals something of the difference that textuality will begin to usher in during this period. It may be presumed, based especially on the example of the Neo-Assyrian prophetic collections,[155] that at least one impetus for such collections was preservation (e.g., for later consultation)[156]—indeed preservation and communication are the two primary functions of writing in antiquity.[157] Early on, the preservative benefit of writing for royal propaganda was well appreciated. So Zakkur, for example, worries about those who would come after him and efface the written account of his achievements and thus deny him enduring fame or memory (*KAI* 202 B 15–28, C 1–2). The oracle in Isaiah 30:6–7 (cf. vv. 8–17) is commanded to be written down precisely for this purpose, "so that it may be for a time to come as a witness forever" (v. 8, NRSV; cf. Jer 32:10–14; Job 19:23–24). Once textualized, language may be retrieved, time and again, visually by readers and as a consequence preservation no longer depends (solely) on story. The oracle in Isaiah 7:7–9 is there for future consultation by *readers*, irrespective of the narratival ineptitude of its presentation. Writing, in this instance, though not a maximally efficient means for re-presenting a real-life, face-to-face encounter between king and prophet, still gestures in that direction (as noted earlier) and most importantly preserves the crucial aspect of the encounter, what was communicated from Yahweh.[158]

A second example comes from Amos 7:10–17. Here, too, the narrative is inelegant, more "like a fragment of a story"—beginning abruptly and breaking off rather than ending.[159] But again the prose is sufficient to preserve two bits of prophetic verse attributed to Amos and also to allow readers to glean something of this (kind of) poetry's originating performative contexts. The first snatch of verse is but a couplet (v. 11),[160] and it is recollected by Amaziah. J. B. Couey has provided the general background against which the depiction of Amaziah's confrontation with Amos should be read.[161] The kind of report Amaziah sends to Jeroboam with regard to Amos's prophetic activity, as Couey shows, was a commonplace in the ancient Near East, with especially good parallels from Mesopotamia. Kings wanted to be apprised of prophecies, especially when they had direct implications for current concerns. Performance is not explicitly stated, though perhaps implied by the reference to "all of his words" (*kol-dĕbārāyw*, v. 10)—the collection as a whole is editorially entitled "the words of Amos" (*dibrê ʾāmôs*, 1:1)—and by the specific attribution "for thus Amos has said" (*kî-kōh ʾāmar ʾāmôs*, v. 11).[162] Less debatable is the spokenness of the poetry in verses 16–17,[163] which is rendered explicitly as a part of a larger dialogue (namely *wayyaʿan ʾāmôs wayyōʾmer...wĕʿattâ šĕmaʿ dĕbar-yhwh*, vv. 14, 15).

Both narratives with their embedded bits of verse make plain what may otherwise be posited, namely, that oral performance (private or public) was one originating mode of publicizing and communicating oracular poetry in ancient Israel and Judah, although our own belated access to this once oral verse is indebted to and deeply entangled with textuality and writing from the very beginning—the consequences of which, as P. Zumthor underscores, are far-reaching.[164]

Other poetic genres are also (re)presented in the Bible aboriginally as orally performed verbal art. Biblical song (šîr/šîrâ) is placed literally in the mouth of the singer (e.g., Deut 31:21; Ps 40:4), voiced (2 Sam 19:36; Ezek 33:32), and taken in by the listener through the ears (Deut 21:30; Qoh 7:5; see Judg 5:3; 2 Sam 19:36). It is audible (Ezek 26:13; Amos 5:23). Moses and the Israelites "sing" (yāšîr, v. 1) the Song of the Sea in Exodus 15:1–18, which is designated as a "song," haššîrâ (presumably Miriam and the women do the same, accompanied by tambourines and dancing, though only the opening couplet is actually quoted,[165] vv. 20–21). So, too, Deborah and Barak "sing" (wattāšar, Judg 5:1) the Bible's other great old poem, Judges 5. Israel is represented in Numbers 21:16–18 as gathering together and singing the Song of the Well in celebration of the finding of the water source—perhaps only a small "snatch" (here a couplet and a triplet) of the song is quoted (vv. 17–18).[166] David and Saul are serenaded in song by "the women from all the cities of Israel" after David's victory over Goliath (1 Sam 18:6–7; cf. 1 Sam 21:12; 29:5)—only a single couplet is actually quoted ("Saul has killed his thousands / and David his ten thousands"). Exodus 15 and Judges 5 exemplify just this kind of "victory song" (cf. Judg 11:34).[167] The bit of prophetic verse in Isaiah 26:1–6 is introduced as a song to be sung (yûšar haššîr-hazzeh), and Isaiah of Jerusalem famously parodies a love song in Isaiah 5:1–7, namely, "Let me sing ['āšîrâ nā'] for my beloved [lîdîdî] / a song of (my) love [šîrat dôdî] about his vineyard" (v. 1).[168] Psalm 45 is labeled explicitly a "song of love" (šîr yĕdîdōt, v. 1; cf. Ezek 33:32; Ug. mšr. l. dd. aliyn bʿl "a song about the love of Mightiest Baal," CAT 1.3.III.5–6) and the Bible's only collection of love poetry is called šîr haššîrîm "the song of songs" (Song 1:1). Perhaps the most vivid narrative representation in ancient Levantine literature of a love song performance is projected mythologically and tells of Anat singing of Baal's love:

tiḫd. knrh. byd[h.]	She takes her lyre in [her] hand.
[tšt.] rimt. lirth	[She puts] the lyre to her breast.
tšr. dd al[iyn] bʿl	She sings the love of Mightiest Baal.
	(CAT 1.101.16–18; cf. 1.3.III.4–8)

References to singing and musical instruments pervade the Psalms (cf. also CAT 1.3.I.18–22). Many psalms feature first person (e.g., Ps 13:6; 18:50 [= 2 Sam 22:50]; 21:14; 27:6; 89:1; 101:1; 144:9) and imperative (e.g., Ps 33:2, 3; 47:7; 68:5; 96:1; 98:5; 105:2; 137:3) uses of verbs for singing (e.g., *š-y-r*, *z-m-r* 1, *ʿ-n-h* 4). Many psalms are labeled either a *šîr/šîrâ* "song" (e.g., Ps 18:1; 46:1; 67:1; 88:1; 120:1; 134:1) or a *mizmôr* "psalm" (e.g., Ps 3:1; 6:1; 13:1; 19:1; 51:1; 68:1; 83:1; 92:1; 98:1; 101:1; 108:1; 143:1). In the superscription to Psalm 7 David is said to have sung (*šar*, v. 1) the psalm, while Psalm 18:1 maintains that he had "recited the words of this song" (i.e., Ps 18) (*dibber... ʾet-dibrê haššîrâ hazzōʾt*; cf. Judg 5:12). Amos 6:5 contains a difficult couplet that imagines David perhaps "improvising" (*happōrĕṭîm* || *ḥāšĕbû*, cf. Ar. *fāriṭ*) a song on a lyre.[169] David of course was remembered as having been in Saul's service as a lyre player (e.g., 2 Sam 16:23), and the Chronicler credits David with initiating cultic song before Yahweh (e.g., 1 Chron 6:16–18). There is little doubt that song was a part of life at the royal court (2 Sam 19:35; cf. Ps 45; 1 Macc 14:4–15). Within Psalm 35 a couplet is quoted and introduced as song:

> Let them sing [*yārōnnû*][170] and rejoice
> those who delight in my innocence
> and let them say continually:
> "Great is Yahweh
> who delights in the well-being of his servant!" (v. 27)

And the Chronicler, too, twice (2 Chron 5:13; 20:21) explicitly introduces a couplet (a version of Ps 106:1 or 118:1, cf. 1 Chron 16:34, 41; 2 Chron 7:3, 6; Ezra 3:11) as being sung chorally, one as a part of the dedication of Solomon's temple and the other before battle. While there is relatively little of a descriptive nature about the cult in the Bible, it is at least safe to assume that song and music featured as a part of the festivities (e.g., 2 Sam 6:5; Isa 30:29; Ezek 40:44; Amos 5:23; 8:10; Ps 27:6; 81:2–6; 137:1–4; Neh 7:27–43; 12:46; 1 Chron 6:16; 15:16; 2 Chron 23:18; 29:27).[171] Entertainment offered another traditional site for song in the ancient Mediterranean world generally (e.g., at banquets, see CAT 1.3.I.18–22; 16.I.39–43; 17.VI.30–32; 108.1–5),[172] and such singing is also referenced in the Bible (e.g., Isa 5:11–13; 22:13; 23:15–16; Amos 6:4–6; Song 2:4–5; 5:1;[173] cf. Gen 31:27; 1 Sam 16:16, 23; 2 Sam 19:36).

Not all biblical poetry necessarily was literally sung. For example, funeral dirges (*qînâ*, *qînôt* [pl.]) were either "lifted up" (*n-ś-ʾ*: Jer 7:29; 9:9; Ezek 19:1; 26:17; 27:2; 32; 28:12; 32:2; Amos 5:1; cf. Ug. *trm tnqt*, CAT 1.16.II.34) or "keened" (*q-y-n*: 2 Sam 1:17; 3:33; Ezek 19:14; 27:32; 32:16; 2 Chron 35:25).[174]

In the midst of one of Ezekiel's ironized dirges over Tyre the prophet provides a depiction of the kind of scene such lamenting entailed:

> At the sound of the cry of your pilots
> the countryside shakes,
> and down from their ships
> come all that handle the oar.
> The mariners and all the pilots of the sea
> stand on the shore
> and wail aloud over you,
> and cry bitterly.
> They throw dust on their heads
> and wallow in ashes;
> they make themselves bald for you,
> and put on sackcloth,
> and they weep over you in bitterness of soul,
> with bitter mourning.
> In their wailing they raise a lamentation [wĕnāśĕʾû . . . qînâ] for you,
> and lament [wĕqônĕnû] over you: (Ezek 27:28–32, NRSV)

The quotation of the dirge (within a dirge) follows in Ezekiel 27:32–36 (namely "who was ever destroyed like Tyre"). Dirges were distinguished from songs (Amos 8:10; cf. 8:3). Most poems in the Bible are simply introduced by a verb of speaking, usually ʾ-m-r "to say," but sometimes also d-b-r "to speak." These verbs prototypically refer to acts of speaking. They may on occasion, however, simply reference the vocality of a verbal utterance. So Deuteronomy 32, which is plainly called a "song" (i.e., šîrâ, Deut 31:19, 21, 30; 32:44), nonetheless is said to have been "spoken, declaimed, uttered" (waydabbĕr, Deut 31:30; 32:44; lĕdabbēr, Deut 32:45; cf. Judg 5:12; Ps 18:1). And the text of Judges 5, a song that Deborah and Barak sing, is introduced by the familiar lexical marker of quoted speech, lēʾmōr (Judg 5:1; cf. 2 Sam 22:1, 2). The māšāls of Balaam, which the narrative presents as being performed before Balak and "all the princes of Moab" (Num 23:6), are all introduced in the same way, wayyiśśāʾ mĕšālô wayyōʾmar, literally "and he raised his oracle and said" (Num 23:7, 18; 24:3, 15, 20, 21, 23).[175] This introductory idiom with n-ś-ʾ "to lift up" is used elsewhere with other prophetic māšāls (Isa 14:4; Mic 2:4) as well as with two Joban poems, also called māšāls (Job 27:1; 29:1) and appears to predicate above all active vocality—note especially the collocation with "voice" (qôl) (e.g., Gen 21:16; 2 Sam 13:36; Judg 9:7; Isa 24:14; 52:8; Ps 93:3), or on the mouth or lips (Ps 16:4; 50:16). Like the qînâ and māšāl, zimrâ (Ps 81:3), tiplâ (Isa 37:4), *maśśâ* (2 Kgs 9:25), and *'ālâ* (1 Kgs 8:31) may all be so "taken up" and uttered aloud.

Frequently, biblical poems and poetic sayings are simply introduced by verbs of speaking, and thus their spoken-ness may be presumed (e.g., Gen 4:23–25; 16:11–12; 25:23; Num 21:27–30; Josh 10:12–13; Judg 14:14, 18; 15:16; 1 Sam 15:22–23; 2 Sam 20:1; 1 Kgs 8:12–13; 12:16). The little poetic oracle in Numbers 12:6–8 not only announces itself as spoken ("And he said: 'Hear my word'") but hyperliteralizes (precisely because deities outside of myths are not usually caught out speaking) the nature of the spoken interface between Yahweh and Moses: "face-to-face I speak with him" (Num 12:8; cf. Exod 34:6–7). Proverbs 7:13 (*wattō'mar lô* "and she said to him") is an especially enlightening example because it is embedded in a little run of poetic narrative (vv. 6–23) in which the emplotted action is made readily apparent. The *'iššâ zārâ* seizes and kisses the literally "unwitting lad" (*na'ar ḥăsar-lēb*, v. 7) and then erupts into a run of spoken (namely, "and she said to him") verse (vv. 14–20). Indeed, these are the very "smooth words" (*'ămāreyhā heḥĕlîqâ*, v. 5; cf. *bĕḥēleq śĕpāteyhā*, v. 21) that the wise father figure puts at issue in the poem. No matter how the poem in Proverbs 7 was actually performed, if performed, the utterance in verses 14–20 is represented in the poem literally as spoken verse— indeed, the operative conceit in the poem's frame verses (vv. 1:1–5, 24–27) is patently oral and traditional as well (namely store up, say, listen, words of my mouth). The boy's speech in Song 2:10–13 (and also v. 14?), though perhaps part of a performative song, is linguistically staged in the poem by the girl as re-presented speech: *'ānâ dôdî wĕ'āmar lî*, literally "my lover answered and said to me" (v. 10).[176] The girl's restaging of voice—and thus a revoicing—is no accident, as the lexeme *qôl* "voice" is itself repeated fourfold throughout the poem (vv. 8, 12, 14 [two times]). The poetic "speeches" in Job, of course, are mostly posed (if very sparely) dialogically as well (e.g., *wayya'an 'iyyôb wayyō'mar*, 3:2)—regardless of the ultimate writtenness[177] of these poems the operative dialogical conceit is a very traditional one: "Sustained thought in an oral culture is tied to communication" (i.e., interlocution).[178] And in fact there is a great deal of embedded speech generally within the three books that the Masoretes specially formatted as verse (Psalms, Proverbs, Job), for example, "They open wide their mouths against me; / and say, 'Aha, Aha, / our eyes have seen it'" (Ps 35:21, NRSV).[179]

Blessings, curses, and oaths are among the most widely attested poetic genres in traditional societies, and biblical narrative commonly presents them in action, being performed in "face-to-face" contexts or otherwise underscores their vocality: blessings (e.g., Gen 14:19–20; 24:60; 27:27–29; 48:15–16, 20; Num 23:20; 24:9; Deut 33:1, 2, 13, 20, 24; Ps 45:17; cf. CAT 1.15.II.18–28;

17.I.34–37), curses (e.g., Gen 3:14, 17; 27:29; 49:7; Num 23:7; 24:9; Job 3:1–2; Qoh 10:20; cf. CAT 1.19.III.45–48), and oaths (e.g., Josh 6:26; Amos 8:14; Job 31:20; Prov 29:24; cf. CAT 1.14.IV.38–39; 17.I.36–37).[180] The short, often pithily phrased proverb (*māšāl* in biblical Hebrew) is yet another widespread and highly traditional genre, and although often framed verbally with an etymon in the Bible (*m-š-l* "to use, speak, make a proverb," e.g., Ezek 18:2–3), in several places the typical spokenness of the genre is made clear. Solomon literally "speaks" (*waydabbĕr*—perhaps in the sense of oral composition, so NRSV, NJV) "three thousand" such proverbs (*māšāl*). Proverbs may be taken in by the "ear" (Ps 49:5) and articulated with the "mouth" (Ps 78:2; Prov 26:7, 9) and eventually get collected (in writing) under the rubric of "words" (e.g., *dibrê ʾāgûr*, Prov 30:1; cf. *mly ʾḥyqr*, TAD C1.1.1.1); and of course tropes of vocality and aurality generally abound in the biblical book of Proverbs (namely "listen!," "hearing ear," "fool's lips," "mouth of the righteous," "my words"), as they do in Ahiqar (e.g., "more than all guarding, guard your mouth," TAD C1.1.6.82).

The poem in Genesis 49:2–27, which includes blessings (vv. 25, 26; cf. v. 28), is provided with an explicit performative context: "Then Jacob called his sons, and said: 'Gather around, that I may tell (*wĕʾaggîdâ*) you what will happen to you in days to come'" (Gen 49:1; cf. v. 2). The spoken-ness of the poem is emphasized again in the closing narrative frame (namely *wĕzōʾt ʾăšer-dibber lāhem* "and this is what he spoke to them" v. 28) and is registered as well in the doubled call to "hear!" (*šimʿû*) that opens the poem itself (v. 2). Deuteronomy 33 is also called a "blessing" (*habbĕrākâ*) and introduced simply with *wayyōʾmar* "and he said" (v. 2). A number of psalms have been embedded within biblical narratives, sometimes with their narrative performative contexts made explicit. Psalm 18 is instructive, since the psalm is both collected in the psalter (MT 150) and included as a part of the Samuel narrative (2 Sam 22). In this case the narrative embedding is only minimal as the psalm is collected as a part of the miscellany at the end of Samuel. Still, 2 Samuel 22:1 reports that David "spoke" (*wayyĕdabbēr*) the "words of this song" (*ʾet-dibrê haššîrâ hazzōʾt*) to Yahweh (cf. Ps 18:1). We should imagine David's song as being vocalized, even if only mumbled or subvocalized (cf. Ps 1:2), as with Hannah, whose lips moved (*śĕpāteyhā nāʿôt*) even though "she was speaking" her prayer "in her heart" (*hîʾ mĕdabberet ʿal-libbāh*, 1 Sam 1:13). Hannah's song of thanksgiving (1 Sam 2:1–10) is cited in full and spoken ("and she said," 1 Sam 2:1), though whether Eli and Elkanah (1 Sam 1:26–28; 2:11) remain present to hear this prayer is not explicitly remarked on. Prayer, of course, as the narrative in 1 Samuel 1 demonstrates, may be performed individually. And Jonah's prayer (Jon 2:3–10)— oddly a song of thanksgiving—is "said" from the "belly of the fish" (Jon 2:2–3) with only his god as an imagined audience. 1 Chronicles 16:8–36, a psalm made up from parts of three known psalms (Ps 105, 95, 106), is placed within a corporate setting—the Chronicler's retelling of David's installation of the ark in Jerusalem. Asaph and the levitical singers are charged with leading such songs of praise to Yahweh (1 Chron 16:7).

In sum, the Bible (narratively) represents or otherwise stages a great swath of the poetry from ancient Israel and Judah that it preserves as explicitly sung, spoken, or otherwise vocalized—that is, as consisting of (once) orally performed verbal art. This is consistent with the thoroughgoing orality of these Iron Age cultures that scholars have started revealing in detail in recent decades. It is also consistent with many of the leading features of these poems, as I now turn to elaborate.

Parallelism

Since Lowth parallelism has been recognized as a leading characteristic— indeed, even *the* leading characteristic—of biblical Hebrew poetry. It is no small thing, then, that the trope itself is a rather common feature of traditional oral performative art generally. So R. B. Coote writes: "It is in fact a nearly universal characteristic of traditional language and needs no special explanation."[181] No one has seen this more incisively than M. Jousse, who already in 1925 in his book *The Oral Style* writes the following:

> It is precisely such an examination that enables us to establish the psycho-physiological origin of the linguistic phenomenon known, since Lowth, by the name of "parallelism of clauses." But what Lowth could not have realized, when he wrote, was the enormous psychological importance of this phenomenon. One can say without any exaggeration, that it plays as vital a role in the world of thought and human memory as does gravitation in the physical universe. Indeed, the deep-seated laws of the "human compound" of flesh and spirit dictate that each improvised utterance has a curious tendency to trigger, in the phonatory system of the speaking subject, one or more utterances of parallel construction and of similar or opposed meaning.[182]

Jousse stressed throughout his work that "parallelism is but the consequence and transposition of the bilateral structure of the human body onto the oral mechanism,"[183] thus providing perhaps an organic basis for the dominance of couplets in biblical poetry and the dyadic shaping of their parallelistic play.[184]

The human brain is avid for pattern, and parallelism is a massively generative and malleable means of forming patterns out of words, and specifically out of the sounds and senses of words, individually and as they are collected syntactically into ever larger chunks (phrases, clauses, sentences). Repetition is at the heart of pattern and of parallelism and is crucial for the kind of rhythmicity and redundancy required if a person is to remember "carefully ariculated thought" in a purely oral environment. Parallelism is part of the ornamentation of biblical poetic language that calls out for attention and marks it as memorable. Patterns, repetitions, redundancies all allow ideas, images, sentiments, feelings, impressions *as they are heard* to root ever more deeply in embodied human consciousness. So parallelism in all of its varieties functions to facilitate knowledge retention—an aid for memory par excellence, especially in the absence of writing—through its redundancies and antitheses, through the rhythm that it helps to create, and by measuring out thought in bite-size chunks that are easily consumed in short-term memory. The spoken word is like a bird, to borrow an image from Ahiqar (*TAD* C1.1.82), once sent out it needs capturing, and repetition, rhythm, conventionality, and face-to-face interlocutors are the chief tools available for this recapture in the absence of writing, aids to memory for real-time processing and for long-term remembering.

Writing of course is a far more effective and efficient means for this capture and retention, more like an unbroken clay pot with lid in place (another image from Ahiqar, *TAD* C1.1.94). Parallelism in oral verbal art, because it is carried literally (at a basic level) on the backs of words, usually translates successfully into written verbal art. Writing systems generally are designed to efficiently represent (symbolize) words. Certainly, both the "old" Hebrew script known from the extrabiblical inscriptions of the first half of the first millennium BCE and the Aramaic-derived new "Jewish script" used for copying biblical texts at Qumran visually spatialize words—the former through its use of word-dividers (fig. 37), the latter through the use of spacing itself (fig. 44—a practice also exhibited in the much later Masoretic manuscripts from the medieval period, e.g., fig. 42). Not surprisingly, Lowth was able to successfully unlock "line" structure, even in nonspecially formatted manuscripts such as of the Latter Prophets, largely by following the countours of the parallelistic patterns (repetition, elision, chiasm) that the written words would repeatedly resolve themselves into. These poetic lines, after all, are nothing more than the consumable, bite-size chunks of language that the play of parallelism concomitantly creates and reveals, essentially a (common) kind of end-fixing, vocally punctuating the boundaries of those chunks of poetic thought (see chapter 1).

Like Lowth we now mostly "see" parallelism in poetry (biblical and otherwise) and appreciate it chiefly for its linguistic capabilities, capabilities that

are visible in writing but once were adopted and adapted from oral performance. Parallelism's originating vocal character and performative environment
is worth remembering, even if only heuristically, so as to reiterate the fact
of the trope's nonsingularity, its nonidentity with biblical poetry. Even in the
written corpus of biblical poems that has come down to us parallelism is
not omnipresent, and the evidence of other elements of language art (e.g.,
anaphora, soundplay, figuration, stanzaic form, rhythm) is patent. Some of
these language elements overlap with and therefore support the play of parallelism to its various ends, namely, aesthetic, rhythmic, chunking, or end-
fixing. But in addition, oral performance—and even originally written biblical
poems would have been mostly destined for oral performance—would have
involved all manner of nonlanguage elements (e.g., interlocution, musical accompaniment and/or melody, dance, bodily gestures of all sorts, modulation
of tone, silence and pause) that are part and parcel of any oral performance
but get occluded in writing, a notoriously impoverished technology for the
economical recording of nonlinguistic material. These nonlinguistic, textually effaced elements also would have enfleshed and reinforced the poetic play
of parallelism (and of other language elements). To glimpse parallelism as it
is mediated through writing alone—however incredibly crucial that glimpse
has proven to be for our knowledge of biblcal poetics (and our debt to Lowth
here remains immense)—is to see an emaciated parallelism, a parallelism
shorn of an accompanying nod, pointing finger, tapping foot, or pregnant
pause: nontextual means all for ornamenting, calling attention to, making
memorable the poem that they and parallelism help produce.

The topic of parallelism has figured prominently in the discussion of Hebrew
epic, which I reviewed earlier, and some will have noticed the absence there of
any significant treatment of the topic. I have delayed discussion till now because whatever parallelism's presence in biblical poems implicates about the
existence of Hebrew narrative poetry, it de facto typifies biblical nonnarrative
poetry and it is to that corpus that it most directly speaks. In other words,
strictly speaking, the hypothesis of a living oral narrative tradition in ancient
Israel and Judah is not required to account for parallelism (or parallel word
pairs, see next section) in biblical poetry. Parallelism is patently characteristic
of the biblical nonnarrative poetic tradition. Its appearance in Ugaritic narrative verse provides strong warrant for assuming its presence in any putative
Hebrew poetic narrative tradition. Indeed, it would seem that parallelism was
broadly characteristic of the Canaanite poetic tradition, whether narrative or
nonnarrative, since the feature is empirically preserved in both kinds of verse.
Analogous situations prevail in other traditions. For example, alliteration pervades Anglo-Saxon poetry regardless of mode, as does meter in ancient Greek

verse—though in the latter the specific meter (or mixture of meters) used
does often vary depending on the kind of verse. By way of partial confirmation, the one certain (nonnarrative) prayer text preserved from ancient Ugarit
(CAT 1.119.26'–36') stands out as verse from its surrounding context of ritual
prose, in part because of the obvious presence of parallelism:

> "When a strong foe attacks your gate,
> a warrior your walls..." (*COS* I, 284)

A version of this parallelistic couplet is repeated three times over in the short
prayer, especially here at the beginning and again at the close of the prayer,
forming a traditional envelope (ring) structure.[185] Parallelism was surely a part
of an ancient Hebrew tradition of narrative verse (cf. Prov 7:6–23), and the
abundance of parallelism attested in the biblical poetic corpus amply demonstrates knowledge of the trope, and therefore requires consideration in the
larger discussion of Israel and Judah's narrative tradtion. But what needs no
speculation is the facticity of parallelism as a chief characteristic of much *nonnarrative* verse in the Bible, and thus whatever may be surmised about the
originating orality of a putative narrative tradition based on the prominence of
the trope holds all the more for the nonnarrative tradition that is extant. In
other words, parallelism in the Bible's nonnarrative poetry is a strong indicator of the deep rootage of that poetry in a living oral tradition, no matter
what may be concluded about the question of Hebrew epic. Like alliteration in
Anglo-Saxon poetry and formulaicism in Homer, parallelism in biblical poetry
"declares the traditional nature of the verse" and "cues the audience"[186] to its
reception. Its long familiar patterned play of repetition in one instance connects to a multiplicity of other similarly parallelistic expressions and in doing
so enfolds what is expressed in the tradition, "a mode of thought understood
to be long-accepted by the community."[187]

Parallel Word Pairs and the Question of Formularity

Following the decipherment of the Ugaritic tablets scholars began recognizing
that these newly recovered poetic texts shared with the biblical poetic tradition
sets of more or less fixed pairs of words that repeatedly occurred in parallel
lines—hence they were soon dubbed "parallel word pairs." The first pair H. L.
Ginsberg discusses gives a typical example of the phenomenon.[188] More than
two dozen times *ksp* "silver" and *ḥrṣ* "gold" appear in parallel to one another in
Ugaritic (e.g., "he casts silver [*ksp*] by the thousands / gold [*ḥrṣ*] he casts by the
ten thousands," CAT 1.4.I.26–28).[189] In the Bible, whenever *ḥārûṣ* "gold"

occurs, it is always paired in parallel with *kesep* "silver" (Zech 9:3; Ps 68:14; Prov 3:14; 8:10, 19; 16:16).[190] Such shared pairs became one of the stronger pieces of evidence revealing the continuity and identity of the two poetic traditions, and now a great many such shared pairs have been collected. Also from early on the benefit for oral performance of these kinds of associated pairs of terms was generally appreciated. So, for example, consider Psalm 7:6, which features the word pair *'eres* "earth, ground" and *'āpār* "dust":

> "Then let the enemy pursue and overtake me,
> trample my life to the ground [*'āreṣ*],
> and lay my soul in the dust [*'āpār*]." (NRSV)

The pair occurs another eleven times in the Bible (Isa 25:12; 26:5; 29:4; 34:7, 9; 47:1; Ezek 24:7; Mic 7:17; Ps 7:6; 44:26; Prov 8:26; Job 14:8; 39:14) and at least eight more times in Ugaritic (CAT 1.1.II.19–20, IV.7–8; 2.IV.5; 3.III.11–12, IV.52–53, 72–73; 10.II.24–25; 17.I.28–29).[191] The advantage of such stereotyped word pairs is noted already by Cassuto: "A poet who introduced the word *'rṣ* in the first hemistich already knows that in the second hemistich he would have to employ *'pr*. Or, contrariwise, if he used *'pr* first, he would have to conclude with *'rṣ*."[192] The force of Cassuto's point is perhaps better illustrated by the not uncommon practice in both Ugaritic and biblical Hebrew poetry of breaking up conventional phrases and redistributing their elements among the component lines of couplets and triplets. M. Dahood gives the example of the phrase *šemen rôqēaḥ* "perfumer's oil" in Qoheleth 10:1, which also appears in Ugaritic (*šmn rqḥ*, CAT 1.41.21; 1.148.21; 4.91.5; cf. 4.31.2; Aram. *rqḥ zy mšḥ*, ATNS, 45b.5), as motivating the couplet in Isaiah 57:9: "You journeyed to Molech with oil [*šemen*], / and multiplied your perfumes [*riqquḥāyik*]" (NRSV).[193] So analogously the many different collocations of *šāmayim* "heavens" and *'ereṣ* "earth" (e.g., *qōnê šāmayim wā'āreṣ*, Gen 14:22; *bên haššāmayim ûbên hā'āreṣ*, 2 Sam 18:9) motivate the frequency with which the pair figures in poetic parallel expressions (e.g., CAT 1.3.II.39, IV.43; Gen 27:28 [cf. v. 39]; Isa 1:2; Ps 73:9; etc.).[194] Thus R. B. Coote argues that such conventional parallel pairs, like parallelism itself, though characteristic of biblical (and Ugaritic) poetry are always "optional" and not "governed by predetermined restrictions" and function mainly to "facilitate the composition" of the parallel lines themselves— "a conventional resource on which the poet draws as he is disposed."[195]

This analysis leads R. B. Coote to conclude that so-called parallel pairs are not formulas at all. The latter position had been argued by W. Whallon, S. Gevirtz, and P. B. Yoder under the influence of the Parry-Lord model of oral formulaic tradition.[196] But asking about formularity in this narrow, all-or-nothing manner ultimately restricts what may be considered formulaic and indeed how formulas are conceptualized. Other, more productive questions may be asked: How are formulas conceptualized in the first place? What is the nature of the formularity they exhibit? And how formulaic is the larger poetic tradition of which they are a part? In the Parry-Lord theory these are givens. The formula is monolithic, and the tradition is entirely formulaic. Yet if the question of formulas is to be entertained for either Ugaritic or biblical Hebrew verse it will need to be done outside of any consideration of meter, which figured so centrally in Parry's original definition of the formula, since biblical and Ugaritic poetry are nonmetrical verse traditions.[197] Furthermore, O'Connor has severely criticized the tacit understanding of "parallel pairs" in particular (but also formulas more generally) as so many fixed entries in a hypothesized special dictionary learned by poets performing within the tradition. In line with R. B. Coote's thinking already referenced, O'Connor writes:

> The analogy of formulas in other oral poetries to dyads [his preferred term for "parallel pairs"] in Hebrew does not require the notion of a fixed stock of usages. Formulas in all oral poetries are to a large extent involved with the language of use and it is unparsimonious to suppose that a poet in any language learns thousands of poetic collocations which can be "figured out" afresh every time they are needed. If the same solution turns up every time, it is because that best fits the requirements. If there are a number of good fits, they will all turn up.[198]

Several examples may be offered by way of illustrating and fleshing out what O'Connor has in mind here. Consider the epic formulas *wyśʾ qwlw wyqrʾ* (e.g., Judg 9:7) and *wyʿn wyʾmr* (e.g., Gen 18:27; 1 Sam 1:15), which have survived in the written prose of the Bible. Both are used to introduce speech, and it is reasonable to suppose that it is the actuality and naturalness of this "language use"—ready to hand as the situation requires—that primordially drives their conventional usage, although surely habituation and traditioning will also have had a role to play over the long run. Culley's collection of formulaic language in the Psalms features, not surprisingly, various kinds of invocations of the deity, for example, *ʾlhym šmʿ tplty* (Ps 54:4; 84:9; 102:2; 143:1), *ʾlyk yhwh ʾqrʾ* (Ps 28:8; 30:9; Joel 1:19).[199] Again the driver of convention in these cases is language use, speech act. As Culley's study shows, there is indeed quite a wide range of "formulaic" phrases that would serve well in such prayers or hymns to a deity, that would be "good fits."

O'Connor also raises the question of the kind of formularity that a given formula may exhibit, resisting the notion that formulas everywhere are the same. He does not doubt that the parallel pairs (or "dyads") of the Canaanite poetic tradition "are of the same class of phenomena as formulas" in other oral poetries, but they differ in "involving much less syntactic complexity and fixity."[200] This is a crucial insight. He continues: "On a scale of formularity, Hebrew and Ugaritic verse must be set low because the entities which are 'formularized' are smaller."[201] Although O'Connor is focusing specifically on word pairs, his insight has broader applicability, opening up, for example, the possibility that a single oral tradition may use a variety of formula types, with different degrees and kinds of formularity. There is no reason to dismiss out of hand the possibility of even more complex and larger formulas in biblical and Ugaritic verse.[202] In fact, the existence of such has already been well established, for Ugaritic by R. E. Whitaker—recall, too, the tracing of epic formulas into biblical prose narrative by Cassuto, Polak, and others; and for biblical poetry, there is Culley's study of repeated, formulaic phrasing in biblical psalms.[203] Culley himself resisted considering word pairs as formulas in part because the debate had mostly excluded consideration of these larger kinds of repeated phrases he studied in the Psalms. But surely more than one variety of formula can be tolerated, as Lord himself implies in his essay in the *Semeia* volume, where he assumes the formularity of both the parallel word pairs *and* Culley's repeated phrase-level formulas. Moreover, biblical non-narrative verse is noticeably less formulaic in general than Ugaritic narrative verse, and both West Semitic traditions are themselves lower still in formularity than Homeric verse, for example. R. B. Coote's early and strong insistence on a misfit between biblical verse and the Parry-Lord model of oral formulaic poetry offers insight that should not be overlooked. Scholars have now isolated many modes of orality beyond the strictly formulaic Parry-Lord model that suits Homeric verse so well, and even oral formulaic verse varies in the degree and kinds of formularity it entails—here the nature of the language of the tradition is critical.[204] What is signaled by this low(er) degree of formularity in biblical Hebrew poetry, for example, as O'Connor so well understood, is the distinctive character of this poetry's (originary) orality. Taking things very much at face value and (intentionally) naively, biblical verse is simply not highly formulaic. It is, as just noted, far less formulaic than Ugaritic narrative verse. However, many word pairs have turned up that biblical poetry shares with Ugaritic narrative verse, and despite their obvious usefulness in performance and their importance in indexing the shared traditionality of the larger extratextual context, ultimately these are not so many and can in no way anchor biblical poetics. And even the most "formulaic" of the biblical psalms studied by Culley, those (on his estimate) in which 40–60 percent of the psalm consists of formulaic phrasing, are relatively few in number (a dozen or so) and do not approach full formularity, the ideal mark once thought to characterize all authentically oral verse. These observations need not provoke a questioning of "the essential orality" of biblical poetry but reveal instead something of this orality's distinctive character, namely prominence of parallelism, usage of traditional, dyadic pairs (to various, even nonparallelistic ends), some light presence (esp. in the Psalms) of more complex formulaic phrasing. Moreover, attention to the question of formulas indirectly reveals the breadth and importance of all manner of vocal "recurrence" in this poetic tradition—"replays, variation on a stock theme, diversity within sameness, and the laying down of a technique that is everywhere the same and for which only the mechanisms of usage differ, to a greater or lesser extent, depending on the situation"—that typifies so much vocal verbal art.[205]

A Memorial Tradition

While allowing for dyads and more syntactically complex formulas, it remains the case that the poetry that has come down to us in the Bible is mostly not heavily formulaic. In fact, one of the chief characteristics of this poetry's informing orality is precisely its *lack* of formularity. It may be that this lack is best explained along the lines Coote argued in her diagnosis of so many of the Serbo-Croatian "women's songs": these tend not to be formulaic in nature because for fairly short, nonnarrative poems, human memory is more than capacious enough that formulas are not needed.[206] To this point Coote writes: "The brevity of the songs . . . and the frequency and ease with which they may be repeated suggest that the singers would not find it necessary to recompose them in performance as does the singer of heroic songs, who deals in hundreds or even thousands of lines."[207] A certain fixity characterizes memorized poems, for example, variants of a song showing a history of "word-for-word" or "phrase-by-phrase" transmission.[208] When there is variation, it "usually consists in leaving out or inserting lines rather than in the rewording of lines."[209] D. M. Carr has been among those in biblical studies who recently has stressed the importance of memory in the transmission of biblical literature.[210] As Carr notes, "findings by cognitive psychologists" show "that the human mind generally cannot remember more than fifty lines [of poetry/verse] without written aids for accurate recall."[211] Most biblical psalms, the component songs of the Song of Songs, many prophetic oracles, the "snatches" (Ar. *qiṭʿa*) of verse quoted in biblical narratives (e.g., Gen 4:23; Num 17–18; Josh 10:12),[212] and almost all individual proverbs are, as O'Connor observes, short or medium in length,[213] and thus eminently memorizable from a cognitive perspective. That the heart of the preserved biblical poetic tradition is rooted in an oral-based, memorial tradition becomes an attractive possibility. This is not to rule out written composition in any given instance—obviously, short poems have been written—or to ignore Carr's contention that once writing emerges scholars will always need to reckon with the possibility that writing is used as an aid to memory. In fact, in several instances the Bible itself represents just such a situation. In Deuteronomy 31:19 (cf. v. 22) Yahweh is represented as instructing Moses to "write" down the long poem (forty-three verses) in Deuteronomy 32 (*wĕʿattâ kitĕbû lākem ʾet-haššîrâ hazzōʾt*) in order to "teach it to the Israelites" (*wĕlammĕdāh ʾet-bĕnê-yiśrāʾēl*) by literally "placing it in their mouths" (*śîmāh bĕpîhem*) so that the "song may become a witness against" them (*lĕmaʿan tihyeh-lî haššîrâ hazzōʾt lĕʿēd bibnê yiśrāʾēl*). That is, writing is to be used as an aid to memorizing the song, preserving it bodily—the implied medium of the "witnessing" is oral performance,[214] the "placing" of the song in the mouth for resinging, reperforming, re-calling.[215] David's lament over Saul and Jonathan (2 Sam 1:19–27) is significantly shorter and, one may presume, easily memorized. Still, the narrative represents the ultimate writing down of the *qînâ* (*hinnê kĕtûbâ ʿal-sēper hayyāšār*) chiefly as a tool for the "teaching" (*lĕlammēd*) of the song for remembering (v. 17–18).[216] In both cases, the writing down of these songs has also meant their ultimate textual survival for posterity, for us to read and study and even reperform (cf. Ps 102:19–23).

Carr's chief motivation for calling biblical scholars to a readiness to "contend with a mix of oral and written dynamics" when conceptualizing the transmission of biblical literature has to do with the readily apparent fixity of so much of that transmission.[217] That is, there appears to be far, far less variation than one generally associates with purely or predominantly orally performed (and thus transmitted) narratives. That any historically responsible accounting for surviving biblical textuality will need to contend with a messy mixture of "oral and written dynamics" is surely right and has now been in view for some years. But Carr's motivating vision here is one shaped in its expectation strictly in terms of oral narrative. Parry is his premiere stimulus—the opening chapter of *Formation of the Hebrew Bible* begins: "In a seminal article published in 1930, Milman Parry..."[218] Carr nowhere allows for the difference that different genres may make for the kinds of orality realized. So if we posit—even only hypothetically—that some (substantial) portion of the preserved biblical poetic corpus emerges out of a memorial tradition of some sort, then more "fixity" is precisely one characteristic we might anticipate about such poetry. So A. Jabbour already at the end of the 1960s suggests with regard to Old English nonnarrative verse that where "word-for-word" or "phrase-by-phrase" transmission from an archetype can be established, then a "memorial" tradition may well be in evidence.²¹⁹ Consequently, evidence of fixity in the transmission of biblical poems may arise not only from the interference of writing (especially as textuality increases in later periods) but also from the very nature of (at least part of) the poetic tradition itself.

That some part of the biblical poetic tradition is likely memorial in nature I posit on the basis of inferences drawn from the overwhelming orality of the ancient world (with all that this implies about oral performance and transmission), the (comparatively) low degree of formularity evident in the preserved poetic corpus, and the general brevity and nonnarrative nature of that corpus. And yet I raise the possibility of a memorial poetic tradition also heuristically, both to problematize assumptions about poetic production, performance, and transmission in ancient Israel and Judah and to entertain alternative possibilities for these acts. While the kind of "good" variants that Carr, for example, spotlights in *Formation of the Hebrew Bible* bear witness to the facticity of oral performance/transmission, they are not often able to tell us the kind of orality in evidence. So, too, with narrative portrayals such as those in Deuteronomy 31:19, 22 or 2 Samuel 1:18. In both instances writing serves the remembering and re-oralizing of the poem. The written version of Deuteronomy 32, for example, is not sufficient itself as a witness (cf. Exod 17:14; Isa 30:8) because, among other reasons, the largest part of the population could not have read it (i.e., they lacked the necessary skills for reading such texts, mass circulation of written documents was not technologically possible). The written text serves as an aid to a literate reader/writer (Moses as portrayed in 31:22), who then teaches the poem orally—literally "placing it in their mouths" (*śîmāh bĕpîhem*). The written text preserves the words, but the remembering that will serve here as a witness is a bodily, performative, oral remembering on the part of all "Israelites."²²⁰ This is so even for the readers themselves, as the manner of writing—very spare with few metascript conventions besides word division—and scroll technology did not make for easy reference, thus requiring active remembering as an essential component of the act of reading itself.²²¹ Such oral performative remembering surely was the traditional and dominant mode of preserving and transmitting such nonnarrative and mostly short(er) songs in ancient Israel and Judah even without the support of writing. It is not surprising that narrative glimpses of such acts unattached to writing are rare (e.g., 1 Sam 18:7), since writing itself is a major force for stimulating the kind of axial self-reflexivity necessary for staging such self-conscious narrative presentations. What makes traditional modalities for song performance and the ends to which they are put, for example, traditional in the first place is their very givenness, the fact that this is simply how it is done and therefore requires no comment. Invisibility in written remains is not always tantamount to nonexistence.

Still, even without fully revealing metadescriptions of the memorial component of Israel and Judah's song culture that are not also linked explicitly with writing (as in Deut 31:19, 22; 2 Sam 1:18) there are some positive considerations by which aspects of this memorial tradition may be fixed on and (partially) disclosed. Memory, of course, is a critical dimension of human cognition, indispensable for the evolutionary success of the species and for human self-consciousness. H. Eising begins his discussion of *zākar* in *TDOT* (IV, 66) by emphasizing just this dimension of the root's base semantic field, "the active intellectual equipment of a person." Written in the mid-1970s, the entry shows no specific awareness of issues of orality and literacy. But it is at least clear from the texts cited and discussed that the act of cognition implicated by *zkr* is in the first place a human capacity exercisable even in the absence of external aids (such as writing). Job 21:1–6 is striking in its bodily portrayal of remembering. Even if composed in writing itself, the section is narratively staged as dialogue ("And Job answered and said," v. 1), and oral speaking figures prominently in Job's own self-presentation—"listen," "my words," "I will speak," "mouth." Job is complaining about his suffering. The two couplets in verses 5–6 foreground embodiment and the feat of memory that the human brain sponsors—in this case to horrific ends:

> Turn to me and be appalled
> and set hand upon mouth
> and if I remember [*zākartî*] I am terrified (too)
> and shuddering seizes my flesh.

Here we have a brief glimpse of memory at its barest: Job sublimating his suffering, though when he remembers it—brings it to consciousness—it is a bodily act with bodily consequences.[222] Remembering involves allowing something to come (e.g., *ʿlh*) or be placed (e.g., *śym*) in the heart (e.g., 2 Sam 19:19; Isa 46:8; 47:7; 57:11; 65: 17; Jer 51:50; Ps 77:7). Once the technology of writing becomes available, a scribal metaphor may be used to describe the human cognitive capacity for remembering—writing on the heart (Jer 31:31–33) or on a tablet of the heart (Jer 17:1; Prov 3:3; 7:3). The bodily modality of remembering remains the same—the human heart being the chief physiological locale of memory. The use of the scribal image lends a sense of permanence and longevity that became associated with writing almost immediately (Isa 30:8; Jer 32:14; Job 19:23–24; cf. *KAI* 202 B.15–C.2)—writing is a most effective technology for extending the hardwired limitations of human memory.

In death there is no remembering (Ps 6:6) precisely because the biological instrument for remembering has ceased to function, has stopped living. And as for the memory of those who die, that normally fades with death, too (e.g., Isa 26:14; Jer 11:19; Ezek 21:32; Qoh 9:5). Part of what motivated the veneration of ancestors was a desire to counter the natural erosion that memory incurs because of death and time.[223] In these instances, humanity's built-in biological capacity for memory is glimpsed, along with some awareness of human memory's limitations.

Before writing, and after it as well, the chief means for transmitting memories was the human voice. The idiom used in Jeremiah 31:20 reflects (somewhat unwittingly) the primordial association between speaking and remembering: "as often as I speak of him [kî-middê dabbĕrî bô]/ I continue to remember him [zākōr 'ezkĕrennû 'ôd]"—with the embodied consequences of such memories being remarked on immediately in the succeeding lines.[224] And similarly in Joshua 1:13: "Remember [zākôr] the word [haddābār] which Moses the servant of Yahweh commanded [ṣiwwâ] you, saying [lē'mōr]." One of the images employed in Psalm 137—a psalm in which song and memory are directly associated (vv. 1–3)—used to ward off not remembering ('im-lō' 'ezkĕrēkî, literally, "if I do not remember you") gives eloquent expression to the predominantly oral-based nature of active remembering: "let my tongue cling to the roof of my mouth" (v. 6). The upshot of the self-curse is to call down damage on the very organs used primordially for such remembering, the tongue and the mouth. To remember the "fame" (lit. the "name," šēm) of an individual meant to tell of that fame person to person, mouth to mouth (Ps 45:18). In another striking image in Hosea 2:19, the prophet says, "For I will remove the names [šĕmôt] of the Baals from her mouth [mippîhā], / and they will not be remembered [yizzākĕrû] again by their name [bišmām]." Removing names from the mouth implicates an inability to speak those names and therefore being unable to remember them. The earnestness of the image, its matter-of-factness, bespeaks an oral/aural world. Writing significantly counterfeits the limitation of such spoken-ness. By spatializing language and inscribing it in durable materials, for example, a deity's name could be preserved and honored indefinitely (e.g., KAI 6.2; 17.1–2; 201). Kings, too, appreciated the potential durability that writing makes possible. For example, Mati'el of Arpad (ca. eighth century BCE) intends what he has written to serve as a "reminder, memorial" (lzkrn) to his son and grandson after him (KAI 222 A3.1–4). Similarly, Azatiwada of Karatepe (eighth/seventh centuries BCE) concludes his own memorial inscription that details and lauds his royal achievements with the wish that "the name [šm] of Azatiwada may be forever like the name [šm] of the sun and the moon!" (KAI 26 A iv.1–3).[225] But more traditionally a person's fame would have been told or sung. So David, whose success as a warrior meant that "his name became greatly honored" (*wayyîqar šĕmô mĕʾōd*, 1 Sam 18:30), was greeted (along with Saul?) after one successful battle by women "from all the cities of Israel" dancing and singing of his (and Saul's) accomplishments:

> Saul has slain his thousands
> and David his ten thousands! (1 Sam 18:6–7)[226]

The narrative portrayal here remains typically laconic and does not yet explicitly delineate this snatch of verse as memorial in nature, but it is not difficult to imagine it as so. In fact, its traditional nature (e.g., parallel usage of "thousands" // "ten thousands," cf. Deut 32:30; Ps 91:7; 144:13; CAT 1.4.I.27–29), brevity, performative modality (singing and dancing) and the generality of its attribution (i.e., as sung by the women of all the cities of Israel) are consistent with the hypothesis of a memorial tradition.

It is Yahweh himself (e.g., Exod 15:1; Judg 5:2; Jer 20:13; Ps 104:33), Yahweh's deeds (e.g., Ps 96:2; 98:1; Job 36:24), and even Yahweh's name (e.g., Ps 7:18; 9:3; 18:50) that are most frequently sung about in the Hebrew Bible. That such singing at times involved an accounting of Yahweh's acts, and thus a remembering of them, too, is perhaps safely assumed (esp. Job 36:24).[227] In such light, the reading of 2 Samuel 22:50 (MT: *ûlĕšimkā ʾăzammēr* "and of your name I will sing") in LXX[L] as "and your name I will (cause to) remember [ʾzkr]" is perhaps not entirely innocent but another "good" and telling variant.

A final example is Psalm 45, which editorially is labeled a "love song" (*šîr yĕdîdōt*)—it is a song that in lauding an unnamed king presumably in anticipation of his marriage to a Tyrian princess (*bat-ṣōr*, v. 13) means to make that king's "name" (*šimkā*, v. 18—ironically now lost) "remembered in every generation." The body of the poem (vv. 3–17), which admires the allure and attraction of both king (vv. 3–10) and princess (vv. 11–17), is framed by a triplet (v. 2) and a couplet (v. 18) in which the voice of the singer self-consciously stages the poem:

rāḥaš libbî dābār ṭôb	My heart stirs with a good word
ʾōmēr ʾănî maʿăśay lĕmelek	I speak my work for the king
lĕšônî ʾēṭ sôpēr māhîr	my tongue is a pen of a master scribe.... (v. 2)
ʾazkîrâ šimkā bĕkol-dōr wĕdōr	I will cause your name to be remembered in every generation
ʾal-kēn ʿammîm yĕhôdūkā lĕʿōlām wāʿed	therefore peoples will laud you always (v. 18)

The opening triplet leaves no doubt as to the orality informing this work of art, namely "my heart stirs," "good word," "I speak," "my tongue"—though writing is not unknown as the poet/scribe's tongue is metaphorized as the "pen of a master scribe." And the closing couplet expresses the psalmist's ambition that his "work" (of poetic art, lit. *ma ʿăśeh*) will cause the king's "name" to be "remembered,"[228] that others hearing it will admire this king and perhaps themselves take up, memorize, and resing its song, just like the women in 1 Samuel 18:6–7. Yet in the end the poem as given does not fully disclose such reperformative horizons. That at this point remains ultimately an inference that we must draw from the study of a textual corpus largely innocent of metadiscussions of any kind. We gain only partial glimpses here and there. Still, these are informative at points. That memory and teaching were traditionally oral/aural affairs in Israel and Judah is not in dispute. And that textuality—writing—would eventually be used in support of these endeavors is also certain. Even some brief glimpses may be had in the Bible of popular songs being sung from memory or poems whose authorial voice anticipates a reception from an audience. And many of the poems themselves bear the leading characteristics (e.g., brevity, nonnarrativity, spareness of formulas) of other ethnographically known memorial oral traditions. That some portion of Israel and Judah's preserved poetic corpus emerged out of such a tradition seems entirely likely to me, even if I have not been able to catch that tradition fully disclosing itself as such at any one point. The hypothesis by its nature is not entirely falsifiable. It suits the character of much biblical poetry better than the ill-fitting Parry-Lord paradigm, and the various aspects of this poetry's informing orality characterized in this chapter are entirely consistent with it.

However, to suppose that some (even large) portion of the biblical poetic corpus evolved out of a dominantly memorial tradition does not require total dismissal of the possibility of improvisation in the tradition. Opland is critical of those who have failed to entertain the possibility "that there might have been both improvisers and memorisers among the rank of Anglo-Saxon poets, that the tradition might have been complex and not simple."[229] The point is well made, especially from the perspective of what is possible, what constitutes the scholarly horizon of expectation. Opland's severest criticism of Lord, whose work he generally admires, is reserved for Lord's decision to ignore the memorial part of the oral poetic tradition that he knew existed (as is made clear in his *Semeia* contribution)—"the memorising guslar certainly does exist in Yugoslavia."[230] There is no need to insist on monolithic theories. Even Cross, as highly captivated by the Parry-Lord oral formulaic theory as he was, allowed for some old "lyric" songs (e.g., Exod 15, Judg 5, Deut 32), memorializing events important to the evolving "national" tradition, as making up part of Israel and Judah's old, orally performed song corpus, alongside cycles of specifically epic narrative traditions.[231] The oral poetic tradition in Israel and Judah, as Opland supposes for the Anglo-Saxon tradition and for what is known, for example, of the South Slavic tradition, was likely complex, containing a mixture of improvisational and memorial forms. Certainly, the oral narrative tradition, to judge by the remnants of that tradition preserved in biblical prose narrative and by what has been preserved of the Ugaritic narrative poetic tradition, must have been dominantly improvisational and necessarily dominantly formulaic. The work of Cassuto, Cross, and others on the hypothesis of Hebrew epic, provoked anew by the discovery of a highly formulaic kind of narrative poetry at ancient Ugarit but eventually fueled theoretically by the largely compelling force of the Parry-Lord paradigm, on the issue of the tradition's presumed improvisational profile is surely right. Equally obvious is the misfit between the oral formulaic paradigm based on narrative verse tradition and the great bulk of the Bible's nonnarrative poetry. R. B. Coote's critique on this point remains broadly convincing, as does Lord's response pointing up the nonnarrativity of the biblical tradition and the consequences this might have for the kind of orality realized in the tradition. That much of the preserved corpus of poetry in the Bible seems more readily characterized as a broadly memorial tradition is a thesis this chapter as a whole means to champion. But even here purity and monality do not likely prevail. The use of word pairs and some longer formulas in the Psalms, for example, suggests that we might anticipate some degree of improvisation associated with nonnarrative biblical poems as well. Coote also finds those more narrative varieties of Serbo-Croatian "women's songs" employing improvisation techniques (e.g., formulas). Even Lord, belatedly, comes to have a more nuanced understanding of these very same "women's songs," suggesting that the patterning of stability and variation may result from "a remembering of a number of 'more or less fixed' texts and a selection, conscious or unconscious—probably the latter—of elements from them."[232] In other words, a mix of remembering and improvising. That some of Israel and Judah's nonnarrative song tradition would show influence of its narrative song tradition, a priori, would not be surprising. This would explain the general consensus in the field that the so-called archaic (or "old") poems in the Bible (e.g., Exod 15, Judg 5) strongly resemble (mostly in style) Ugaritic verse—indeed, it is this resemblance that is most suggestive of these poems' putative archaism. And that the written prose tradition eventually impacts biblical poems is certain, as shown above all by the increased use of the so-called prose particles in later poems especially and the elongation and complication of poetic syntax. Therefore, even in a dominantly memorial tradition all need not depend on rote memorization. Or to put it differently, conventional, formulaic phrasing would aid the memorizing process itself. And improvisation can be imagined on different scales. I return below to Culley's thesis of formularity in the Psalms to suggest that some of the given forms in the Psalms (e.g., individual lament) may best be construed as largely improvisational forms. In gross terms, I suspect that Israel and Judah's narrative poetic tradition was dominantly improvisational in nature on the one hand, though this tradition is only available to us through some vestiges left in the biblical text and in close analogs like the Ugaritic narrative poems. On the other hand the preserved nonnarrative poetry of the Bible originated in a prominently memorial oral poetic tradition, though one that likely had plenty of space for various forms of improvisation. In both cases, there is every reason to anticipate that one modality would also potentially influence the other and vice versa. So that improvisational characteristics, for example, also appear to varying degrees in the biblical poetic corpus is not surprising and should be anticipated. The eventual advent of written poetic composition still further complicates the picture. My main ambition here, then, is to open up possibilities for future research, to enlarge and complicate the interpretive horizon(s) in which we ask about orality and biblical poetry. We do not possess the kind of rich textual discourse that will enable us to fully reconstruct Israel and Judah's oral poetic past. But there is enough already revealed to make its complexity in these matters safe to assume.

Rhythm

Already by 1925 Jousse had well articulated—if in his own highly idiosyncratic way—the centrality of rhythm to oral poetic style. As Jousse stressed, rhythm is inherent to human physiology and biology—"all [propositional] rhythm is only muscular movement made easier"—and "makes a propositional gesture 'dance' on the laryngo-buccal muscles of an improvisor or reciter" and "'dance' again" in the ears and on the lips and in the dance of auditors and new reciters and memorizers.[233] W. Ong restates Jousse's key insight this way: "To solve effectively the problem of retaining and retrieving carefully articulated thought, you have to do your thinking in mnemonic patterns, shaped for ready oral recurrence. Your thoughts must come into being in heavily rhythmic, balanced patterns, in repetitions or antithesis, in alliterations or assonances, in epithetic and other formulary expressions....Serious thought is intertwined with memory systems."[234] I have emphasized Jousse's work because of its early date but also because he had the Bible in view from the beginning and because his ideas made a strong impression on the young Milman Parry during his stay in Paris.[235] I have already elaborated Jousse's ideas on rhythm as they bear on the poetic rhythm of the Bible (see chapter 2) and will not reprise that discussion here. What I would reiterate is Jousse's characterization of a "rhythmic schema" in oral style generally:

> Each balancing of each rhythmic laryngo-bucall schema is naturally composed of a certain number of syllables which, according to the rate at which they are pronounced, throw into greater or lesser relief the rhythm of energetic expressions necessary for a whole series of muscular movements.... A rhythmic schema, so to speak, elaborates itself by the balanced recitation of two, and sometimes three, approximately parallel gestures.[236]

Jousse does not mean to reify this characterization. Oral style is a "living thing," often complex, and multitudinous and its "rhythm rather free."[237] The "tendency" toward balancing is just that, a tendency, and not a universal given. And the "balancings" can be "fairly loose" and may not even exist—oral verse is not reducible to varieties of parallelism; nonparallelistic, enjambed lines appear not uncommonly in many oral traditions. Nonetheless, the characterization holds broadly for oral style across many traditions. And that this broadly parallelistic profile of oral style fits biblical poetry is readily apparent and was well emphasized by Jousse—"the linguistic phenomenon known, since Lowth, by the name of 'parallelism of clauses.'"[238] Of course, the biblical poetic corpus comes to us ultimately only after having been textualized, so there is no question of the Bible preserving a transcript of pristine orality. Rather, what may be said is that the predominantly balanced thrusts in which the rhythm of so much biblical poetry (however much or little impacted by textuality and literacy) ebbs and flows share a broad kinship with the rhythmic profile of oral style generally and that the prospect that the free rhythms of biblical poetry evolved out of a once living oral tradition is entirely plausible and even likely if finally not provable. Here is yet another specific way we might say with O'Connor that biblical poetry is "comparably close to the oral poetic situation."

Short Lines, Simple Clauses, End-Stopping, Parataxis

In previous chapters (see chapters 1 and 2) I have had occasion to query the animating orality of a cluster of features highly characteristic of biblical poetry, including its variable though ultimately constrained line, mostly simple clause structure, high prominence of end-stopping,[239] and prevalence of parataxis. Without reprising these earlier discussions, what I want to emphasize here is just how redolent of orality these features are and what this implies about biblical poetic style—namely, its deep rootedness in oral poetics. The commonness of such features to traditional verse is amply attested ethnographically (as elaborated earlier), and the overwhelming orality of the ancient world similarly may be stipulated on the basis of ethnography. Therefore, to infer—which is what we must do—the informing orality of an ancient poetic tradition so suffused with such features seems hardly controversial. And yet in the case of biblical poetry it needs saying plainly. Written verse has long since appropriated such features (short lines, etc.) to its own ends, rendering their traditional heritage susceptible to occlusion. The hyperliterate model of textuality supposed by so much Western scholarship has only ramified this susceptibility in its reception and interpretation of biblical poems. That relatively short lines consisting of mostly simple, sentential clauses linked paratactically are characteristic of biblical poetry is not in doubt. That is plain for all to see. That these are also the telltale signs of this verse tradition's informing orality, if equally obvious on reflection, has not been nearly so well appreciated. But this I submit is so. What in part makes biblical poetry "comparably close to the oral poetic situation" is precisely that so much of its stylistic core evinces such strong affinities with oral poetic style. That is, if biblical poetic style is itself not an oral style (preserved in writing, so Jousse),[240] it is "comparably close" to such a style, derived from it, rooted in it, even possibly preserving residues of it.

A Language of Orality, Aurality, and Vocality

The language of biblical poetry is pervasively a language of speaking, singing, and hearing, of embodied performance and of face-to-face interaction. The first sign of this pervasiveness is the comparable lack of language and imagery about reading, writing, and the scribal world. While textuality is increasingly on the rise in Iron II Israel and Judah and does not fail to leave its imprint on the poetic corpus it eventually preserves (see discussion "Emergent Textuality" later), it is relatively sparse in distribution and not so deeply ingrained in the core poetic idioms. So, for instance, exhortations to "write" (k-t-b) in poems are relatively few (e.g., Isa 30:8; Jer 22:30; Hab 2:2; Ps 102:19; Job 19:23–24; 31:35; Prov 3:3; 7:3; Dan 6:26), whereas many, many biblical poems include and often begin with entreaties or acclamations to hear or listen (š-m-ʿ/ʾ-z-n: e.g., Gen 49:2; Num 23:18; Deut 32:1; Judg 5:3; 2 Sam 22:7 = Ps 18:7; Isa 1:2, 10; 18:3; 28:23; 34:1; 42:18; 44:1; 46:3; 48:1; 49:1; 51:1; Jer 5:21; 6:19; 9:19; 10:1; 13:15; 31:10; Hos 4:1; 5:1; Joel 1:2; Amos 3:9, 13; 4:1; 5:1; Mic 1:2; 3:1; 6:1, 9; Ps 5:2; 17:1; 27:7; 39:13; 49:2; 50:7; 54:4; 55:2; 61:2; 77:2; 78:1; 80:2;

84:9; 102:2; 141:1; 143:1; Job 13:6; 15:17; 16:2; 21:2; 33:1; 34:2; 37:14; Prov 1:8; 4:1; 7:24; 8:32; 22:17),²⁴¹ call out (*q-r-*ʾ: e.g., Deut 32:3; 2 Sam 22:4, 7; Isa 1:4; 40:2; Joel 1:19; Jon 2:3; Ps 3:5; 17:6; 22:3; 28:1; 55:17; 57:3; 66:17; 86:3, 7; 88:10; 102:3; 105:1; 130:1; 141:1; Prov 7:4; 8:4), speak (*d-b-r/ʾ-m-r*: e.g., Deut 32:1, 40; Judg 5:12; Isa 40:2; 58:1; 63:1; Jer 13:15; 20:8; Ps 39:4; 42:10; 50:7; Job 7:11; 10:1; 13:3; 16:6; 33:2; Prov 8:6),²⁴² tell (*n-g-d/s-p-r*: e.g., 2 Sam 1:20; Isa 41:22; 48:20; 58:1; Jer 4:5; 5:20; 31:10; 46:14; 50:2; Mic 1:10; Ps 9:2, 12, 15; 26:7; 44:2; 66:16; 71:15; 75:2, 10; 96:3; 119:13; 145:6; 1 Chron 16:24), or sing (*š-y-r/z-m-r*: e.g., Exod 15:1, 21; Judg 5:3; 2 Sam 22:50 = Ps 18:50; Isa 5:1; 12:5; 42:10; Jer 20:13; Ps 9:2; 13:6; 33:2, 3; 59:17; 66:2; 68:5, 33; 89:2; 96:1; 98:1; 101:1; 105:2; 108:2; 138:1; 146:2; 147:1; 149:1; 1 Chron 16:9). Performed poems will all be situated and thus accompanied by all manner of nonverbal cues and guided by the performer. But it is the human voice that ultimately must initiate the poetic utterance and make vocal space for its saying or singing. Such stereotyped acclamations (e.g., "Give ear, O heavens, and I will speak," Deut 32:1; *hôy* "ah!" in Isa 5:8–10 and other so-called *hôy* oracles of the prophets)²⁴³ or other conventional verbal gestures (e.g., *kōh ʾāmar yhwh* "thus says Yahweh," Amos 1:3) at or near the beginnings of biblical poems bespeak an oral/aural register as they very literally call the audience to attention, to pay attention, to join in the shared performance that distinguishes all performative verbal art.²⁴⁴ They kick-start the poem to get it going. This traditional means for starting an oral performance is occasionally thrown into relief when the poem is embedded within a larger prose narrative and supplied with an extra introductory gesture. For example:

> Then Jacob called his sons, and said: "Gather around,
> that I may tell you what will happen to you in days to come.
> Assemble and hear, O sons of Jacob;
> listen to Israel your father...." (Gen 49:1–2, NRSV)

> Then Moses and the Israelites sang this song to the LORD:
> "I will sing to the LORD, for he has triumphed gloriously;
> horse and rider he has thrown into the sea." (Exod 15:1, NRSV)

> Then Deborah and Barak son of Abinoam sang on that day, saying:
> "When locks are long in Israel,
> when the people offer themselves willingly—
> bless the LORD!"
> "Hear, O kings; give ear, O princes;
> to the LORD I will sing,
> I will make melody to the LORD, the God of Israel." (Judg 5:1–3, NRSV)

> Then Moses recited the words of this song, to the very end,
> in the hearing of the whole assembly of Israel:
> Give ear, O heavens, and I will speak;
> let the earth hear the words of my mouth. (Deut 31:30–32:1, NRSV)

Absent a live performative context—where the context itself, the presence of performer and audience, and all manner of nonverbal elements are integral to the poem's staging, including how it begins—such poems need explicit textual orientation (e.g., attribution to a speaker) with respect to their place within a written narrative. The resulting double introductions, though somewhat repetitive and clumsy for readers, disclose the transposition into a new medium.[245]

Much of the imagery for song and poetry in the Bible is performative and embodied in nature. So with respect to the oracles of Balaam, the narrative reports that "Yahweh put a word [*dābār*] in Balaam's mouth [*pî*]" (Num 23:5; cf. vv. 12, 16), a common image for prophetic verse (e.g., Isa 1:20; 49:2; Jer 1:9; Ezek 3:2–3;[246] Mic 4:4). The opening exhortation to hear in Deuteronomy 32 explicitly targets "the words of my mouth" (*'imrê pî*, v. 1; cf. Jer 9:19; Ps 54:4; 78:1; 89:2; Job 33:1). And indeed poetic utterance generally is imagined as originating in the mouth (e.g., 2 Sam 2:1; Ps 19:15; 34:2; 40:4; 49:4; 51:17; 66:14, 17; 71:8, 15; 78:2; 109:30; 119:13; 145:21; Job 3:1; 7:11; 16:5; 33:2; Prov 4:5; 5:7; 7:24), on the tongue (e.g., 2 Sam 23:2; Isa 50:4; Jer 23:31; Ps 35:28; 45:2;[247] 66:17; 119:172; Job 33:2) or lips (e.g., Isa 29:13; Jer 17:16; Ps 17:1; 40:10; 51:17; 63:4, 6; 66:14; 71:23; 119:13, 171; Job 13:6; 16:5; 33:3).[248] It is explicitly "voiced" (*qôl*: e.g., Deut 33:7; Judg 5:11; 2 Sam 22:7; Isa 28:23; 51:3; Jer 9:18; Jon 2:3, 10; Ps 3:5; 5:3; 27:7; 28:2, 6; 64:2; 66:19; 77:2; 98:5; 130:2; 140:7; 141:1; 142:2; Job 33:8; Lam 3:56) and taken in with the ears (e.g., Deut 31:30; 2 Sam 22:7 = Ps 18:7; Jer 6:10; 36:6, 10, 13, 14, 15, 20, 21; Ezek 3:10; Ps 31:3; 44:2; 78:1; 86:1, 2; 102:3; 116:2; 130:2; Job 13:17; 33:8; Prov 2:2; 4:20; 5:1; 22:17).

The aboriginal "spokenness" of biblical verse is suggested as well by the continuity it exhibits in a number of respects with oral-derived Ugaritic verse and more broadly with epistolary discourse and with the dialogic elements (discourse as opposed to narration) of biblical narrative prose. None of these should be (mis)taken as transcripts of everyday speech, but the tacit pose of embodied (face-to-face) discourse implicates a number of shared elements. These include a similar patterning in verbal predication, cooccurrence with certain expressive constructions (e.g., *'ak*), and prominence of first and second person pronouns.[249] That all biblical poetry has come down to us in writing as staged (and thus fictionalized) discourse can obscure the fact that the tradition itself originates in discourse, as the spoken, chanted, or sung verbiage of a live

performer in performance. The "I" of this traditional performer has sometimes been recognized, for example, as in the odd first person voice in some
of the older biblical poems (e.g., Gen 49:3, 6, 9, 18; Exod 15:1–2; Judg 5:3, 9,
13, 15, 21).[250] In these specific instances the singer is no singer of tales, as
sometimes supposed, however, since the songs themselves as we have them,
whatever their narrative content, are finally songs and not tales, and thus the
"poet-reciter's I" in these instances is the "I" of a singer of songs.[251] Still, that
the "poetic I" in these and other biblical poems may be a (now written) reflex
of a once embodied presence (e.g., prophet: Isa 5:1; Hab 3:1; singer of psalms:
1 Sam 2:1; Ps 18:2; 45:2) is a crucial insight and potentially provides another
indicator of the informing orality that animates this poetic tradition. The felt
need to stage so much of this poetic discourse once written down, to provide
a "vicarious voice" for the now absent "poet-reciter" (e.g., Gen 49:1; Exod 15:1;
2 Sam 22:1; Hab 3:1),[252] may itself be viewed as the trace of the once embodied
singer of these songs.[253] More palpable still is the communal "we" that is heard
throughout the poetic corpus, and especially in the Psalms (e.g., 44, 46, 74,
78, 132, 137; cf. Lam 5). Such a "we" emerges most explicitly from performance, either in group singing (e.g., 2 Sam 6:5 [= 1 Chron 8:13]; Isa 26:1–6;[254]
cf. Num 21:17; 1 Sam 18:6–7; 2 Chron 5:13) or from a solo performer in front
of a live audience (e.g., 1 Chron 16:8–36;[255] Num 21:27–30;[256] cf. Deut 31:30; Jer
36:8–10; Ezek 33:32), and epitomizes the shared perspective and knowledge
at the heart of traditional verbal art—"confirmational discourse falling back
on something 'we all know.'"[257] U. Schaefer helpfully explicates the traditionality latent in this mode of expression:

> The deictic value of the first-person plural pronoun is that it includes
> the speaker and those to whom he or she speaks. Hence this pronom-
> inal reference may indeed be interpreted as the manifestation of the
> unity of the knower(s) and the known, comprising the text—or rather,
> utterance—and the whole (potential) context.[258]

There is perhaps no more paradigmatic case of the "poetic I/we" in the Bible
than that found in the hypertraditional opening of Psalm 78:

> Give ear, O my people, to my teaching;
> incline your ears to the words of my mouth.
> I will open my mouth in a parable;
> I will utter dark sayings from of old,
> things that we have heard and known,
> that our ancestors have told us.

> We will not hide them from their children;
> we will tell to the coming generation
> the glorious deeds of the LORD, and his might,
> and the wonders that he has done. (vv. 1–4, NRSV)

The rarity of the communal voice in so much contemporary Western poetries is no doubt in large part due to the nonperformative and highly literate nature of these traditions.[259]

Improvisational Structure: Individual Laments

Here I want to think through the possibility of improvisational forms of biblical poetry, mostly as a heuristic to set beside the expectation of a memorial tradition in Israel and Judah. I do so in light of Culley's early study of "oral formulaic language" in the Psalms, with specific attention given to the individual laments. Culley's study is a revision of his 1963 doctoral dissertation written in the immediate afterglow of Lord's *Singer of Tales*—"it provided an invaluable guide on almost all aspects of oral formulaic composition."[260] I note the influence in order to make clear that it is expressly an improvisational form of oral poetry that Culley has in view throughout. The study succeeds in two large ways. First, and very much in keeping with the spirit of my own thinking here, Culley identifies a number of features in the language of the Psalms (especially its comparatively high degree of formulaic and repetitive phrasing) that are also characteristic of orally performed verbal art and thus suggestive of "a time when there was a living tradition of oral composition" in Israel and Judah. That is, they point to the tradition's informing orality. Second, insofar as the features disclosed are also characteristic ethnographically of improvised composition—(re)composition in the process of performance—it is not "unreasonable" to suppose that a similar mode of composition may have obtained at times in Israel and Judah, though this cannot be finally insisted on outside of explicit contextual commentary, which is completely lacking. Still, there are four leading features of the individual lament that are broadly suggestive of an improvisational tradition: the comparatively high degree of formulaic and repetitive phrasing, the variable but limited set of constituent thematic elements, highly paratactic structure, and the "openness" of the language. Culley has the first three well in view. The chief benefit of formulas is to have a body of phrasing that is widely known and thus ready to hand for on-the-spot composition and for maximally successful auditory reception. Culley's study leaves little doubt that formulaic and repetitive phrasing is prominent in psalmic discourse generally, and in

laments and hymns in particular.[261] Further, the variable shaping of these repetitions is noteworthy—he identifies 176 different combinations of repeated
groups of words—as it exhibits the kind of multiformity characteristic of performed oral art: that capacity to reproduce "with minimum and [yet] countless
variations" (Zumthor).[262] Scholars of textualized, oral-derived traditions are
no longer so quick to assume that formulaic diction presumes (re)composi-
tion in performance without explicit contextual information to this effect. Yet
this mode of composition is well known. There is a rich ethnographic record
of such traditions, not least the South Slavic one studied by Parry and Lord.

Theme, which Lord defines as a group of "ideas regularly used in telling a
tale in the formulaic style of traditional song,"[263] aids the improvisational poet
in a similar way as the formula, though on a larger scale, providing read-
y-made "elements of subject matter or groups of ideas repeated in variable
form."[264] Theme is another recognized feature typical of improvisational
forms of oral verbal art. Lord, of course, developed this notion explicitly in
terms of narrative. The suggestion, however reserved, that "there is no reason...
why similar repeated groups of ideas or elements could not be devices in other
kinds of oral poetry as well"[265]—poetry, that is, that is not narratival and operates on a smaller scale—may be one of Culley's most incisive insights. He
even tentatively points to the thematic components of the individual lament
as possible small-scale, nonnarrative equivalents to the (Parry and) Lord narrative "theme":

> The relative stability in the form of a type such as the individual com-
> plaint might be due to the use of this form as a device for composing
> psalms orally just as the theme is used in narrative poetry. Among the
> elements of the complaint there appears to have been no rigid rule
> about the way the elements may be expressed or the order in which
> they might appear, since there is considerable freedom and variety
> within a general stability among the complaints in the Old Testament.
> Thus, the repeated groups of elements appearing in a variable form in
> individual complaints recalls the definition of the theme.[266]

Though Culley goes on to equivocate and finally resists pressing these impressions too far, his observation has much to commend it. Certainly, the discrete
thematic (and other) movements in smaller scale, nonnarrative oral poems
operate in ways very similar to the ways the themes in larger-scaled epic poems
do.[267] Above all, thematic content is at the heart of most psalmic "forms" like
the individual lament, something oddly often occluded by form criticism (i.e.,
they are not really "formal" at all). And what is so suggestive of improvisational

style is the lack of "rigid rule" about which elements to include and their order and the "repeated groups of elements" within variable form, precisely characteristics that have befuddled form criticism.

The "adding style" evident in most psalms, including laments, is also broadly "characteristic of much oral poetry."[268] J. A. Notopoulos explains:

> The artistic illusion, which he [the oral poet] creates by means of winged words, is ever in flux; neither the poet nor his audience can divert their attention for any period of time to the whole; they cannot pause to analyze, compare, and relate parts to the whole; the whole only exists as an *arrière pensée* which both the poet and his audience share as a context for the immediate tectonic plasticity of the episode. The spoken word, unlike the written word, must be winged, impelled ever onward by the spontaneity and urgency of verbalization in oral poetry. Creation by means of the spoken word leaves the poet little time to pause and appraise the lines he is shaping in terms of the larger pattern.... This technique inevitably results in the λέξις εἰρομένη, the strung-along and adding style, and in the paratactic handling of his material.[269]

The structure of most laments retains the strong impress of speech's boundedness to temporal sequence, the forward-leaning accumulation of uttered language as it falls into chronology. Recognizing that not only most psalms but in fact most biblical poems exhibit this kind of episodic or paratactic structure, Culley suggests that "Hebrew poetry may have achieved this style in an oral period," and then becoming "so well established... it continued to be the normal style well into the literary period."[270] Here Culley gives early expression to the thought that a literate poetic tradition emerging out of an oral tradition would be likely to carry forward, especially initially, elements of that prior, informing oral tradition.

Finally, a fourth feature broadly characteristic of improvisational art may be pointed to in psalmic verse, namely, the openness of the language. This openness manifests itself in two ways in particular. First, with respect to referentiality, meaning is derived in large part from (extratextual) context. P. D. Miller points to this kind of openness, for example, when commenting on the use of lament forms in Jeremiah: "All of this stereotypical language, however, is now placed in a context that serves to give content and reference to the clichés"—"to flesh out the meaning of the lamenters's anguished cries and prayers."[271] The second way psalmic language is open is with respect to the ease of its (re)utter-ability—that capacity of the language that allows for and even invites vocalization by everyone in broadly typical human situations.[272]

Like most biblical poetry, very little is known about how the psalmic laments were actually used. There were likely "professional" poets/scribes/ priests/singers, "well trained in their craft, whose function it was to compose psalms on behalf of people who desired a psalm to be offered."[273] And there would have been accompanying rituals and liturgies, whether at a shrine or temple (e.g., 1 Sam 1:3–4, 9–11) or elsewhere (e.g., Ps 27, 84). But the possibility of nonprofessionally composed laments should not be discounted out of hand. Typically, these are not complex compositions, and most would be easily managed with knowledge of some standard phrasing and the standard set of (very limited) themes used in such prayers—knowledge, one imagines, easily mastered over a lifetime of hearing and reciting such prayers.[274] Opland offers the example of the Xhosa-speaking peoples of southern Africa whose oral poetic tradition is complex.[275] It includes specialists (e.g., the *imbongi*) who are talented and perform more often and at a higher level of sophistication than others, but all Xhosa speakers (men, women, children) perform and compose poems, both memorially and through improvisation. That the broad spectrum of Israelites and Judahites were expected to memorize and (re)vocalize—perform!—poems in a fixed form is an implication that may be drawn from the explicit instructions that Deuteronomy 32 (31:19; cf. v. 22) and 2 Sam 1:19–27 (vv. 18) are to be taught to all the people. Group singing is also explicitly noticed (e.g., 1 Sam 18:6–7)—again presumably a memorial form. The givenness with which the Bible's narrative tradition describes all manner of people using psalmic forms and even sometimes providing the text of the psalm (e.g., 2 Sam 22; Jon 2:3–10; Isa 38:10–20) is consistent with the expectation of an ability to compose and perform such forms—at least, the mediation of a specialists is never explicitly noted. Hannah is the paradigm example of a nonprofessional lamenting. While only the vow is explicitly reported (1 Sam 1:11), there is little doubt that the prayer recounted in 1 Samuel 1:9–18 is a lament.[276] Perhaps Eli (v. 9) provided her with the text of an appropriate psalm, but if so this goes unrecorded and seems contrary to the basic plot line of the story, which presents Eli as seeing Hannah's lips moving and presuming her to be drunk (vv. 13–14) rather than praying. The story continues. A child is born, and Hannah eventually fulfills her vow by giving the boy to Yahweh—the ritual context is explicit (1 Sam 1:24–24). She prays again (1 Sam 2:1), but this time it is a hymn of praise, and the whole text is given (1 Sam 2:1–10). The text of the psalm itself is likely a found piece and placed in Hannah's mouth by the prose writer (cf. v. 10). Nevertheless, as Miller notices, this hymn of praise, along with those of Moses and Miriam (Exod 15) and Deborah (Judg 5:3–5), "however composed," is in its "spirit and character spontaneous, real, and enthusiastic"[277]—which is to say, it is represented in the story in a way that is consistent with an improvisational form.

Jeremiah may get us as close as we can come to fixing narratively on an improvisor of oral laments. Jeremiah, of course, is no ordinary "Joe Judahite" but is himself a specialist of performative art, a prophet. Still, the corpus of oracles and stories associated with this prophet is notable for its rich and deep familiarity with psalmic idioms, imagery, and forms.[278] In particular, there are the so-called confessions of Jeremiah (11:18–12:6; 15:10–12, 15–21; 17:14–18; 18:18–23; 20:7–13, 14–28), which are nothing other than laments.[279] At the narrative level, at least, this shows a certain plausibility (perhaps dating as far back as the time of the late Judahite monarchy, perhaps somewhat later)[280] of imagining an individual who, though a specialist, is not quite the kind of liturgical specialist (singer or scribe) often associated with psalmic verse[281] and yet is familiar enough with psalmic discourse to produce psalmic forms, that is, laments. Moreover, the narrative logic of Jeremiah 36 presumes that the oracles of Jeremiah have not been previously written down, and there is little reason, in any event, to suppose that (an actual) Jeremiah ever wrote anything of substance beyond perhaps affixing his signature to a contract of sale (Jer 32:10, 12) or writing out a brief note of some kind (cf. Jer 29:1–3).[282] Add this to the undoubted fact that oral delivery was normative for (preexilic) prophetic discourse—"for you shall go to all to whom I send you, / and you shall speak [*tĕdabbēr*] whatever I command you" (Jer 1:7)—and it would seem most plausible to assume that (the) Jeremiah (of the Bible) would have likely composed (mostly) without the aid of writing, and perhaps even improvisationally in performance.[283] Form criticism, though aware of the lament's rootedness in orality, nevertheless privileges a distinctly literary manner of perceiving and reading these psalms. And while not entirely out of bounds, as they obviously become textualized and therefore require literary appreciation, to approach these poems the other way around, so to speak, with some initial perception of what in them is owed to an aboriginal oral modality of composition and performance, may open up richer and more empathetic construals of their art and at least will make clear that even in the written forms in which we have them, such laments are not the product of a fully literary sensibility.[284]

Genres of (Oral) Poetic Tradition

Here I can be brief. Any survey of poetic genres found in the Bible[285] will reveal that with only a few notable exceptions (e.g., acrostic poems) most are traditional kinds, broadly typical of oral verbal art generally, for example, work songs (Num 21:17), dirges (2 Sam 3:33–34), the song of the watchman

(Isa 21:12), the song of the harlot (Isa 23:16), drinking songs (Isa 22:13), love songs (Ezek 33:32), victory songs (1 Sam 18:6–7), hymns (Exod 15:21; Isa 6:3), panegyrics (Ps 45), laments (1 Sam 1:9–18; 1 Kgs 8:33–40), prophetic oracles (Num 23:7–10), blessings (Gen 14:19–20), curses (Gen 3:14), oaths (Josh 6:26), riddles (Judg 14:14, 18), proverbs (Ezek 18:2[286]). This is not to say that all such kinds of poetry in the Bible are oral. They are surely not. However, the over-whelming pervasiveness of oral-derived genres points unambiguously to a once thriving oral tradition of poetry and thus furnishes yet more evidence of the tradition's informing orality.

Archaisms, Figures, and Other Special Codes

Oral poems lack the unity, fixity, and spatial sensibility that writing imparts to language. Such verbalizations in performance must distinguish them-selves from the flow of ordinary, everyday discourse. This may be done in a multitude of ways, for example, through the specialness of the performance arena or the time of performance (a particular festival), the presence of special speakers or singers (a prophet), the use of specific verbal cues or signals to begin and to end the poetic utterances ("Give ear, O my people!," "I will sing to Yahweh!," "Thus says Yahweh"), musical accompaniment, facial and other bodily gestures (dancing). The language of the oral poem—"the phonemic string we call 'text'"[287]—also frequently calls attention to itself and thus dif-ferentiates itself (functionally) from the communicative conventions of everyday speech. Ethnographers and oralists often report the presence of archaisms or other special usages that demarcate the special idiom of per-formed verbal art.[288] In the case of linguistic or cultural archaisms, for ex-ample, which exemplify a kind of fossilization, especially in long-lived oral traditions, it is the fact of ongoing performance that allows such "archaisms" to retain their currency. From a functional perspective, as R. Bauman observes, "such usages are no more archaic than the language of everyday speech, in-sofar as they have a vital—if restricted—place in contemporary speaking."[289] Archaisms have often featured as a topic of scholarly interest in commentary on the "old poems" of the Bible (e.g., Exod 15, Num 23–24, Judg 5), though almost always with the end in view of ascertaining the time of original compo-sition.[290] The peculiarity of traditional verbal art is precisely the currency of such "archaisms," which may point to the (general) antiquity of the tradition but nothing necessarily about the time of that tradition's first writing down. So Ajax's shield as depicted in the *Iliad* (*Il.* vii.219–23) is of a kind that had ceased to be used by the Greeks already in the fourteenth century BCE. But this does not imply anything about that epic's first writing in the eighth century BCE.

"It seems clear," writes S. Sherratt, "that an eighth-century Homer knew about such things only because they were an integral part of the inherited bardic (and therefore 'historical') traditions with which he had to work."[291] That many of the Bible's "old poems" are peppered throughout with such archaisms (namely grammatical ambiguities, "Canaanite holdovers," etc., no matter the difficulty in our capacity to assess them as such) may say more concretely about the traditional nature of this poetry than anything specific about a putative date of composition.[292] Indeed, the fact itself of traditionality would seem to militate against the use of archaisms for dating purposes of this kind.

Figurative language figures prominently in standard accounts of leading characteristics of oral verbal art.[293] As Bauman writes, "the semantic density of figurative language, its foregroundedness, make it especially appropriate as a device for performance, where expressive intensity and special communicative skill are essential."[294] And patterning of all kinds and rich imagery (visual, auditory, kinesthetic) help activate cognition and enhance memory processing.[295] Biblical poetry abounds with figures of all manner, while curiously, as T. Linafelt emphasizes, the narrative prose of the Bible "tends to avoid elevated diction or figurative language."[296] This stylistic difference is striking—that the one genre is rooted in oral performance and the other emerges out of the practice(s) of writing is perhaps a not irrelevant datum. Regardless, it is not to be supposed that the mere presence of figurative language, or archaisms for that matter, in a given biblical poem signifies orality in any straightforward way. Not at all. As Zumthor frequently remarks, "oral poetry and written poetry use an identical language."[297] Rather, it is more to be aware that a similar stylistic profile is shared with oral and oral-derived verbal art more generally, and thus is of potential interest to any fully empathetic assessment of the imprint of orality (in all of its variability) on the biblical poetic tradition.

Myth in Biblical Poems

I conclude this (selective) survey by returning to Cassuto's observation about mythological allusions in the Bible. Such allusions become a curious diagnostic of biblical poetry, as they almost always appear in poems and (mostly) not in the narrative prose of the Bible—so L. Alonso Schökel: "The Hebrews do not welcome myths as narratives, but they have no difficulty in incorporating mythical motifs into their lyric texts."[298] For Cassuto the emphasis was placed on the missing myths implicated by the allusions, since they were constitutive of (at least part of) Israel's lost narrative poetic tradition. Yet if

emphasis is placed instead back on the poems in which the mythological allusions appear, the traditionality of these poems is revealed in a new and star-
tling way. "Mythic culture" is aboriginally rooted in orality and may be glossed
after M. Donald as "a unified, collectively held system of explanatory and
regulatory metaphors. The mind has expanded its reach beyond the episodic
perception of events, beyond the mimetic reconstruction of episodes, to a
comprehensive modeling of the entire human universe."[299] The fact of mythological illusions itself is a gross index of orality,[300] and the meanings of these
allusions are context-dependent and intrinsic or immanent. They are not
(maximally) meaning-full on their own or even embedded within their textual
context—the linguistic material does not constitute its own referential system,
not all relevant information is provided in the (linguistic) text itself. Rather,
these allusions, like formulaic expressions in other oral poetic traditions, are
directed externally and "tie the poetic discourse to the extratextual world and
thus depend on this extratextual world for their 'referential system.'"[301] They
presume the myths and the mythic worldview as something given and broadly
shared by the whole community, and thus are strong indicators of the ongoing significance of an oral/aural semiotics, of an informing orality. Biblical
Hebrew nonnarrative poetry is not unique in this matter. Archaic and classical
Greek lyric draws regularly as well on myth, "a constant point of paradigmatic
reference."[302] And there, too, its extratextual reference is apparent, as Gentili
recognizes: "Myth functioned in the same way in maintaining the fabric of
continuity within oral culture and providing a social instrument for interaction between past and present, tradition and modernity, poet and audience."[303]

* * *

THE CHIEF ACCOMPLISHMENT of the preceding survey (by no means exhaus-
tive) has been to begin detailing and specifying the nature of the orality that
informs so much of the Bible's poetry, to say as particularly as possible how
this poetry is "comparably close to the oral poetic situation." Its language, style,
techniques, and primary mode of publication (i.e., vocal performance) all
remain deeply indebted to orality and the traditional poetics orality sponsors
and requires. These characteristics are themselves tangible evidence of a once
vibrant oral tradition in Israel and Judah. And, equally important, their presence presumes that even at the time of textualization the traditional techniques and tropes of orality remained critical to the successful reception of
these poems. That is, they imply an audience habituated to the norms of oral
communication. Writtenness in this case does not exhaust orality or obliterate
it but to the contrary succeeds because of it. It is to the question of writing
biblical poetry that I now turn.

Emergent Textuality

To this point my focus has been fixed chiefly on pointing up what in the biblical poetic tradition may be most positively ascribed to (an informing) orality
and detailing more precisely the nature of that orality (e.g., nonnarrative, etc.),
with only occasional notice taken of presenting issues of textuality. Yet the in-
controvertible fact about biblical poetry is its (ultimate) textuality. The fate of
all biblical poetry was to be written down. And in being written down, to be
preserved. This at least is beyond dispute. The manuscript evidence, whether
in Hebrew (e.g., DSS, MT) or translation (e.g., Targum, Peshitta, LXX, Vulgate) is belated but incontestable. This "belated" textuality provides the beginning point and often the only basis for any act of textual interpretation of
biblical poetry. Still, even in a climate of "minimalism," when scholars are
generally unwilling to accept at face value the Bible's self-assertions as to time
and place of writing, many continue to think that the biblical poems preserved
for the first time in writing in the Dead Sea scrolls mostly predate that particular inscription in the Hellenistic period and can even imagine a sizable portion of these poems originating in the period before the dissolution of the
historic kingdoms of Israel and Judah. Therefore, in what follows I consider
from various angles the possibility of writing poetry in the pre-Hellenistic
southern Levant (especially in Israel and Judah during Iron II), the nature of
its textuality, and the consequences for how we finally construe the informing orality of biblical poetry. The picture revealed—admittedly often only in
broad strokes and with fractured images, since we possess so little historical
documentation—is of an emergent textuality, a textuality at the interface
with orality, and thus a textuality in which the traditional techniques and
tropes of orality remain critical to the production and successful reception
of poetry. Writtenness in this case, as just noted, does not exhaust orality but
succeeds because of it. Indeed, one of the distinguishing characteristics of
biblical poetry is its starkly "interfacial" nature, as a poetry and poetics
deeply rooted in pervasive orality that comes of age in a time of ever increasing textuality.

(Some) Signs of Writtenness in Biblical Poems

One of the tricky parts of apprehending the textuality of biblical poems prior
to their Hellenistic inscription is precisely the absence of manuscripts from
earlier periods. Whatever picture is to be constructed can only be done obliquely,
through inferences and by triangulating from comparative and ethnographic
considerations. I begin by pointing up some of the leading signs of writtenness

embedded already within the biblical text itself. Such signs, to the extent that they are not obviously the products of Hellenism, *may* implicate a preceding textuality, an awareness of a certain writtenness anterior to biblical poetry's otherwise current earliest textualization (at Qumran). The heuristic mode of my inquiry here is to be noted. The *possibility* of an anterior writing is sufficient for my more general argument.

That all biblical poems have survived textually as parts of larger wholes, either embedded in blocks of narrative prose (e.g., Gen 49 from the Torah; Ps 18 in Samuel-Kings, 2 Sam 22; parts of Ps 105, 96, and 106 in Chronicles, 1 Chron 16:8–36) or gathered in poetic collections or sequences of various sorts (e.g., prophetic: Isaiah; love poetry: Song of Songs; proverbs: Proverbs) is an initial indication of writtenness beyond the mere facticity of textuality. Prose narrative is the quintessential writerly genre, a byproduct of the technology of writing, and therefore the preserve of scribes. And the act of collecting is similarly scribal in nature, and an act specifically enabled by writing.[304] That is, the very forms shaped to convey these poems—they are not innocent and could have been otherwise!—themselves evolve only and specifically from acts of writing.

A further index of writtenness at the level of these larger strucutural wholes is the presence of explanatory context provided to situate the poems. Strictly speaking, verbal art destined for oral (or vocal) performance requires no (or little) overt contextualization, given the immediacy of the performative situation and the presence of a "live" performer (author, singer, poet, reader, scribe) responsible for sustaining and situating such discourse. So Kittay and Godzich, "Now, when an utterer stands in a given place at a given time, with us, we the receivers of the verbal message also receive everything necessary to know about the empowerment of the situation," and therefore there is no need for the overt specification of context or situation, it is known implicitly by all participants.[305] By contrast, poems "separated from speakers and performance need explanations" and thus habitually "occur in specified 'literary' contexts, no matter how imperfectly realized.[306] The evolution of prose and its accompanying *diegesis* ("description" or "recounting of action") in particular is a direct consequence of needing to accommodate performer-less discourse outside of a performative context.[307] As written versions of poems become increasingly separated from their originating contexts of performance, the pressure builds to compensate *in writing* for the absence of the nonverbal behavior and myriad of reportorial acts by which the performer anchored and guided verse performances. Hence, an increased need for deixis (e.g., "and he said," Deut 33:2) and situational specification (e.g., "This is the blessing with which Moses, the man of God, blessed the Israelites before his death," Deut 33:1), for example. The foregoing survey of the various performative modalities for the delivery of biblical poems draws heavily from this kind of explanatory comment. The detail and dexterity of the comment is variable, though on the whole it remains on the sparse side, since the written poems are often situated in functionally equivalent circumstances to that in which they (are imagined to have) originated and vocal performance of some kind is in view even once poems are embedded within narratives or gathered into collections— and thus active extratextual and nonverbal contributions are always anticipated, albeit perhaps nonoriginary in nature and now involving textual mediation. As a rule biblical poems embedded in narratives are usually explicitly situated in their larger literary contexts, even if only by way of a brief introduction (e.g., 2 Sam 22:1). Collections (and sequences) vary greatly in the amount of narrative *diegesis* provided to orient the poems they gather. For example, the collection of Jeremiah's oracles stands out precisely because of the overall amount of narrative context provided. Many details remain undisclosed, of course (e.g., ambiguity about oracle boundaries, dates of composition or performance), but other prophetic collections (e.g., Amos, the oracles of Isaiah of Jerusalem—Isaiah 1–39) are much more sparing in the amount explanatory comment provided.[308] The poetic dialogues of Job (Job 3–42:6) are oriented by a frame story (Job 1–2, 42:7–17) and then the barest narrative thread to introduce new speakers (e.g., "And Eliphaz the Temanite answered and said," Job 4:1).[309] A still different model is offered by many of the superscriptions to the Psalms (in MT), which situate a psalm in terms of the biography of David (e.g., Ps 3:1: "A psalm of David, when he fled from his son Absalom"). MT-Song of Songs may be cited by way of counterpoint, as MT-Song—aside perhaps from the opening line (*šîr haššîrîm 'ăšer lišlōmōh*, Song 1:1), which most commentators understand as an editorial gloss—is completely devoid of narrative presentation: "there is no literary or historical message around" the verbal text of component songs.[310] Changes in speaker or scene are not indicated or situated. Individual songs run together without editorial signs (e.g., superscriptions, extra spacing) of beginnings or endings, creating a parataxis of the wording as it appears on the page that is extreme and difficult to negotiate because of its failure to provide cues to guide the discourse. Such a bare text—just the verbal material alone—suggests a kind of minimal transcription in service of active performance, which is always more than the words themselves and where a singer can be counted on to guide and situate the songs that are sung.[311] But in any case it points up the "excess" of such explanatory comment when it does occur and thus the need for some kind of critical accounting (once the preserve of redaction criticism).

The ability of scholars to situate satisfactorily such explanatory comment (redaction) is not uncomplicated, and I will refrain from attempting in-depth analyses here. It will be enough to indicate that the capacity for such scribal contributions predates Hellenism in the southern Levant. The possibility for writing extended narratives in vernacular alphabetic scripts (Phoenician, Hebrew, Aramaic) dates at least as far back as the mid- to late ninth century BCE, when first person conquest narratives in royal memorial inscriptions begin to appear (e.g., *KAI* 24, 181, 202).[312] And the Deir ʿAlla plaster texts (*KAI* 312, ca. 800–750 BCE; fig. 24) provide stunning evidence of an early extrabiblical collection of prophetic oracles dating from the same general period.[313] Other extant extrabiblical literary collections from the southern Levant in the first millennium (outside of Qumran) include the miscellany of poems, hymns, laments, rituals, and narrative prose found in Papyrus Amherst 63 (ca. third century BCE) and the proverbs collection associated with Ahiqar from Elephantine (ca. fifth century BCE; fig. 23).[314] The Bible itself mentions at least one well-known (extrabiblical) poetic collection, the so-called book-scroll of Jashar (Josh 10:13; 2 Sam 1:18; cf. 1 Kgs 8:53 [LXX]), which presumably gathered together a number of poems beyond those explicitly cited in the biblical text.[315]

In some instances the pattern of preservation itself at Qumran implicates prior inscription of manuscripts containing biblical poems. Such is the case, for example, with the thirty-nine psalms scrolls recovered from Qumran and its environs (roughly dating between 175 BCE and 70 CE).[316] These reflect multiple collections, not just (proto)versions of the MT-150 Psalter, though that, too, is in evidence (e.g., MasPs^b). Some are clearly smaller in size and differ in content. 11QPs^a is the parade example (fig. 15). It is the longest surviving Psalms scroll from Qumran (measuring almost five meters in length). It appears to be nearly complete and contains most of the psalms known from books IV and V of the MT-150 Psalter (i.e., parts of psalms from Ps 93–150), albeit often in different sequences and with differences in content, including an additional ten or eleven psalms not contained in MT. Perhaps most interesting, as P. W. Flint details, the collection of Psalms as known from MT was still very much in flux throughout the Qumran period. Or more specifically, at least the final half of the collection, Psalms 90–150, seems not yet to have been fully stabilized, there being a good many manuscripts like 11QPs^a at Qumran that exhibit divergences both in content and order from that known in the MT-150 Psalter. Fluidity prevails in this part of the Psalter throughout the period. Not so, however, in the first half of the received Psalter. Psalms 1–89 are relatively stable in Psalms manuscripts from Qumran, with minor and few divergences. Together these two facts (the stability of Pss 1–89, the lack of stability of Pss 90–150) imply that the practice of collecting psalms attested at Qumran did not start at Qumran. The existence of a shorter, earlier collection containing Psalms 1–89 (or thereabouts) is to be assumed (cf. 4QPs^a).

Moreover, given the plurality of Psalms collections in evidence at Qumran, it seems very likely that a shorter Psalms 1–89 collection would not have been the only Psalms collection in existence. Certainly the scribe responsible for piecing together the psalm in 1 Chronicles 16:8–36 from parts of Psalms 105, 96, and 106 was drawing on a collection other than the short Psalms 1–89 collection. So at the time of the composition of Chronicles (ca. fourth/third century BCE), for example, a second earlier Psalms collection must be posited.[317]

Some singular poems, of course, also likely got written down on their own, either for display purposes (as with the Greek "Nestor's cup" or Aramaic Capentras stele, figs. 19, 26) or in a small papyrus or leather roll, for example. The plaster wall inscription from Kuntillet Ajrud (*KA* 4.2 ca. 800 BCE, fig. 25), if poetic, offers a good example of singular preservation for display purposes. It is very fragmentary and written in a Phoenician script, though the language is Hebrew, and appears to exhibit several instances of parallelism and a strong resemblance in theme and imagery to several of the theophanic hymns from the Bible (esp. Deut 33, Judg 5, Ps 24 and 68).[318] Prophetic collections likely presume written recordings of singular oracles (as in the Neo-Assyrian prophetic corpus)[319]—Lachish 3 (rev. 3–5) references a "letter" (*spr*) from a prophet containing the report of an oracle, though whether that report also contained some of the poetic oracle itself (e.g., as sometimes in letters from Mari) is not stated. There may be as many as three manuscripts containing only the one long Psalm 119 at Qumran (4QPs^g, 4QPs^h, and 5QPs), though admittedly the unusual length of this particular psalm probably accounts for its singular inscription. The Elephantine corpus, however, does attest an abundance of (relatively) short, single document scrolls, albeit all of a documentary (nonliterary) nature (e.g., the collection of Aramaic legal papyri from the Brooklyn Museum; *TAD* B),[320] and thus warrant exists for supposing that perhaps some of the (relatively) numerous Iron II provenanced seals and bullae from the region may have once sealed singular poetic documents.[321]

In sum, then, the "editorial" packaging of biblical poetry manifests a certain writtenness in two large ways: in the structuring genres that enfold this poetry, narrative prose and poetic collections, and in the impulse to narrate and situate these poems, to surround them with a "literary or historical message," however meager or mangled. And even without sustained scrutiny the likelihood that these writerly manifestations inhered, at least to some degree, already in writings that antedate Hellenism and Qumran has warrant.

Moving to the poems themselves, there are instances in which the language or tropes used in a poem implicate knowledge of writing. Several striking examples of this may be briefly considered. Occasionally, there are references within poems to acts of writing (e.g., Isa 10:1, 19; 30:8; 44:5;[322] 65:6; Jer 17:13;

22:30; Hos 8:12; Hab 2:2; Ps 40:8; 69:29; 87:6; 102:19; 139:16; 149:9; Job 13:26; 19:23; 31:35; Prov 3:3; 7:3; 22:20³²³). In Psalm 45:2, in a rare moment of poetic self-reflexivity, the speaker of the psalm metaphorizes his "tongue" as "the stylus of an expert scribe" (*lĕšônî ʿēṭ sôpēr māhîr*). That the "tongue" is the tenor of the metaphor is confirming of an anticipated vocal performance, which follows as well from the presence of idioms for speaking and hearing (e.g., *ʾōmēr ʾănî*, v. 2; *šimʿî-bat*, v. 11),³²⁴ use of direct discourse throughout, and a closing boast to personally cause the king's name to be remembered (*ʾazkîrâ šimkā*; i.e., through the vocal performance of the "I"). Characterizing the speaker's tongue in terms of the materiality of writing—a reed stylus—makes apparent that this poem emerges in a world knowledgeable of writing. Indeed, it is a stylus belonging to a master or accomplished (*māhîr*) scribe (so also Ezra, Ezra 7:6; Ahiqar: *spr ḥkym wmhyr*, *TAD* C1.1.1.1), someone whose skill is appreciated and praiseworthy. There can be a tendency in our modern imaginations to conceptualize scribes as subsidiary figures and their work as mainly facilitatory, mechanical, reproductive. But in antiquity, and especially in cultures where textuality is emerging, it is probably more accurate to think of them as traditional performers of verbal art (on par with singers, storytellers, priests, prophets, and the like), whose productions, though manifestly the product of a rare and valuable skill, writing, also exercise a certain "'communicative competence' within the tradition that normally resides in speaking and traditional memory" and thus are content-full and eventful in all the ways that typify oral performance more generally in traditional cultures.³²⁵ The psalmist's image in Psalm 45:2, then, is perhaps more apt than generally thought, as it likely means to attribute to the tongue not only the dexterity of a fine hand but also the "dynamic and determinative" achievement of what is wrought by that hand—Jeremiah's reference to *ʿēṭ šeqer sōpĕrîm* (8:8), no matter how the syntax is resolved, focalizes content.

Equally striking and evocative of writing is the pair of images used at the beginning of Proverbs 7 (v. 3) to graphically underscore the wise teacher's enjoinder to "keep my words" and to "store up my commandments with you" (v. 1), that is, to remember them. The first imagines these spoken "words" bound on the fingers—*qošrēm ʿal-ʾeṣbĕʿôteykā* (cf. Job 31:35–36). The objectification of words as things (i.e., that can be tied to a finger, carried on the shoulder) is only conceivable after language becomes fixed and spatialized in writing—spoken utterances are ephemeral and precisely lacking any thing-like objectivity.³²⁶ The second image, that of the heart metaphorized as a writing tablet (*kotbēm ʿal-lûaḥ libbekā*; cf. Prov 3:3; Jer 17:1), trades on the greatly enhanced capacity for preservation that writing as a technology enables, a capacity the ancients had well in view (esp. Isa 30:8; Jer 32:14; Job 19:23–24; also evident

in the habitual worry over erasure in West Semitic royal monumental inscriptions, e.g., *KAI* 24.13–16; 202 B.16–28).[327] The so-called prose particles
(e.g., ʾet-, the *nota accusativi*; ha-, definite article; ʾăšer, relative particle), insofar
as they originate or increase in usage with the advent of prose composition,
offer yet additional signs of the impress of writing when they occur in poems,
at least at the point of inscription.[328] That is, once these particles enter the
written language they become available for poets to use, regardless of the
mode of composition. For example, for Lamentations, which ranks fairly low
in the usage of these particles,[329] it may be confidently posited that the use of
ʾōtî (*nota accusativi* + 1 sg. suffix) "me" in 3:2 and of hāʾōkĕlîm (definite article
+ participle) "the ones who eat" in 4:5 is intentional, since in both instances
the particles conform to the constraints of the alphabetic acrostic (appearing
in the *aleph* and *he* stanzas of their respective poems). The lack of these particles in biblical poetry more generally may reflect the tradition's rootedness in
an oral tradition antecedent to the emergence of written prose, and therefore
one long accustomed to discourse in the absence of such particles. The poetic
usage of these "prose particles" that does occur indexes the steady rise in the
prominence of written prose narrative over the course of the biblical period.

The last example of this kind that I will mention is the alphabetic trope that
structures the acrostic poems in the Bible (e.g., Pss 9–10, 25, 34, 37, 111, 112,
119, 145; Lam 1–4). The trope itself is a product of writing, modeled after the
scribal school texts known as abecedaries (e.g., Izbet Sartah, *KA* 3.11–14, figs.
33–34) and features the traditional sequence(s) of (twenty-two) letter forms in
the Hebrew alphabet. It plays graphically for the eye,[330] featuring the letter
forms themselves, and not sonically for the ear, as the biblical Hebrew phonemic inventory is larger than the twenty-two-letter linear alphabet which was
adapted to write out Hebrew (see esp. the *śin/šin* stanzas),[331] and thus presumes literal "readers."[332] Here there can be no question as to writing's impress on poetic production and reception. These are poems, like none other
in the Bible, whose shaping trope visually inscribes the presence of writing, or
at least the individual letter forms out of which writing is constructed. In fact,
the acrostic poems may well be, as van der Toorn supposes, the most obvious
examples of "scribal inventions" in the Bible—that is, written compositions of
some scribe's "own contrivance."[333] If so—like most biblical poems the acrostics lack any explicit comment as to specific mode of composition or production—it is to be observed that the poetic style of these poems, with whatever
innovations are owed to writing (e.g., an architectural structure in which the
parts are expressly related through the alphabetic conceit to the whole), remains continuous with that of the biblical tradition more generally—"shaped to
the requirements of oral comprehension and oral memory" (e.g., relatively

short lines, parallelism, some kind of mostly parsing enjambment, episodic structure).[334] That is, then, in these instances—*if* the acrostics were *in fact* composed in writing—writing does not consume or exhaust or overwrite the tradition's informing orality but rather starts from that orality, is at first a writing of the biblical poetic oral tradition, albeit without suppressing the innovative impress of its writtenness, that is, as manifested in the letter signs of the written alphabet. In other words, continuity of (a primarily oral) style is an outstanding characteristic of the whole corpus of (eventually written) biblical poetry.

Such indications (metaphors, tropes, prosaic inflections), by dint of their associations with writing, at the very least call attention to poems created in a world of writing, though the poems need not be written themselves—*although they could be that, too.* There are a handful of instances where the facticity of a written poem—a poem that has been written down, placed into writing—is noted, as with some of the component poems in the thrice mentioned "scroll of Jashar," for example "Is this not written in the scroll of Jashar" (*hălō᾿-hî᾿ kĕtûbâ ʿal-sēper hayyāšār*, Josh 10:13; cf. 2 Sam 1:18; 1 Kgs 8:53 [LXX]), or the thanksgiving psalm attributed to Hezekiah in Isaish 38:10–20, which uniquely is called a *miktāb*, literally a "writing" (v. 9). In such instances the ultimate writtenness of the poem in question is plainly named—in the latter case probably signifying the medium in which the votive was likely offered (cf. Ps 40:8; *Qom* 3; *KAI* 201, 202)[335]—but without any implications as to mode of production (e.g., the term *miktāb* itself signifies only the medium of writing, esp. Ezra 1:1; 2 Chron 36:22).[336] The specific acts of writing that produced biblical poems mostly go unrecorded in the Bible—most biblical poems, if presented narratively, are presented as extempore performances. Moses is said to have written down the song in Deuteronomy 32: "And Moses wrote [*wayyiktōb*] this song on that day" (Deut 31:22; cf. v. 19). The larger context (esp. v. 24), a confusing patchwork of disparate written accounts, seems to imply that Moses himself is the writer, actually writing out the song and not having someone write in his stead—the root *k-t-b* may signify both nuances (e.g., as in Jer 36:2, 4). The source of the writing, however, goes unnoted—almost as if the poem was preexistent, as it surely was for the prose writer of Deuteronomy. Similarly, the Aramaic poem recorded in Daniel 6:27–28, however composed, was eventually written out (*kĕtab*) and circulated throughout the "whole land" (Dan 6:26). Proverbs 22:20 contains a unique reference to the writing down of the sayings of Proverbs 22:17–24:22, "Have I not written (*kātabtî*) for you thirty sayings...?" (NRSV);[337] and Job expresses the desire that his "words" (*millāy* lit. "my words") be written down (*yikkātĕbûn*) in a *seper* (Job 19:23)—a "self-reference" to the book of Job itself?[338]

Written poetic texts would have been produced through a number of different modalities in antiquity. Perhaps the commonest, a speaker dictating directly to a scribe,[339] is the only of these that is explicitly narrativized in the Bible. The depiction of Baruch "writing from the mouth of Jeremiah" (*wayyiktōb bārûk mippî yirmĕyāhû*, v. 4) in Jeremiah 36 is the paradigmatic example of dictation in the Bible (cf. Isa 8:1; Hab 2:2).[340] When interrogated (v. 17) Baruch describes precisely what such dictation entailed: "From his mouth [*mippîw*] he was uttering [*yiqrā'*] to me all these words and I was writing (them) [*wa'ănî kōtēb*] on the scroll in ink" (v. 18). The source is explicitly oral—Jeremiah recollecting and reperforming ora(cu)l(ar) performances from the past (cf. v. 2) —and it is above all the authorizing source to which the Hebrew idiom *k-t-b* + *mippî* PN chiefly gives expression.[341] The process is likely to have been interactive and collaborative, and we are not to imagine some kind of verbatim recording of Jeremiah's precise words, namely minus Baruch's scribal interventions. In part this is so because technologically such recordings are impossible before the invention of mechanical sound recording instruments. But also it likely misunderstands the nature of scribal performances in antiquity. Baruch would have been acting from within what Doane calls the culture's "social penumbra,"[342] and therefore would have been familiar with Jeremiah's prophetic discourse and a competent native speaker of Hebrew, both of which would have impinged on his act of writing in a myriad of ways (e.g., spelling, grammar, formatting, suggestions about phrasing and content). And at any rate there can be no question of recovering Jeremiah's unmediated original "words" or intent, as Doane makes clear in a discussion of a analogous situation from medieval England:

> When an "auctor" dictates his words to a secretarial scribe and then reads them over, he cannot say that the scribe has not written them exactly, for the dictated words have vanished and only the written ones remain. All he can say is that he doesn't like this or that expression or this or that meaning and must negotiate further writing with the writer. In a chirographic culture there can be no fixed authorial intention, because the author's is always mediated by a scribal intention.[343]

The same point is argued by van der Toorn using examples drawn from the Mari archive.[344] Indeed, one of van der Toorn's outstanding achievements in *Scribal Culture* is to show just how thoroughgoing the Bible's debt is to scribes and scribalism.[345] There is no question of ever fully circumventing the scribal mediation that has produced and preserved biblical poetry.

Dictation presumes an oral source—somebody speaking and somebody transcribing what is spoken into writing. The originating source also could be (already) in writing.[346] As mentioned earlier, sometimes preexisting written versions of poems are explicitly remarked on (e.g., Josh 10:13; 2 Sam 1:18). Several modes of text production involve specifically written sources. Three may be considered by way of example. Translation involves generating a new text in a language different from that of the source text. By most accounts Proverbs 22:17–23:11 represents a translation of a portion of the Egyptian composition, the *Teachings of Amenemope*,[347] and it may be that (parts of) Psalm 20 also originated in translation of a Phoenician *Vorlage*. "New" poems also may be created by combining parts of preexisting written poems, as is likely with the psalm in 1 Chronicles 16:8–36, which is made up from parts of Psalms 105, 96, and 106 (inclusive of the editorial doxology tagged to the end of Ps 106, v. 48 = 1 Chron 16:36),[348] or as van der Toorn supposes for much of the material in Jeremiah 50–51.[349] M. V. Fox believes those who collected and edited Proverbs knew and used a written version of the proverbs collected in the name of Ahiqar (e.g., Prov 23:13–14 ≈ *TAD* C1.1.176–77; see fig. 23).[350] Compiling or recombining in this manner is a practical extension in writing of what otherwise often happens as improvised oral texts are (re)performed. Copying is another common modality of producing written texts from already existing texts and, especially in the context of scribal education, is responsible for much of the textual production in the large-scale polities of the ancient Near East (e.g., Babylon, Egypt).[351]

Significantly, prior to Qumran, there is a remarkable absence of multiple copies of biblical or any other nondocumentary text in West Semitic from the southern Levant. And only rarely does the Bible ever assume multiple copies of a single text—Deuteronomy 17:18 perhaps recognizes a second copy of the Torah—*mišnê hattôrâ*—written for the king; Joshua 8:32 recognizes a working draft for the "copy" (*mišnê*) of the "Torah of Moses" he had inscribed on stone (a similar kind of fair copy is implied for the display inscriptions from Deir 'Alla); and there are the "sealed" and "open" copies of the *sēper hammiqnâ* in Jeremiah 32. But these are clearly exceptional. More typical is Jeremiah 36. The narrative logic of having Jehoiakim burn the scroll of Jeremiah's oracles (Jer 36:23) would make no sense if five or six other copies existed, as have survived, for example, at Qumran (2QJer, 4QJer[a,b,c,d,e]), let alone twenty- or thirty-odd copies as with Psalms, Deuteronomy, and Isaiah at Qumran. In fact, the narrative is entirely innocent of such an idea. The only technological response that could be made to the king's actions was to dictate again and to make another, different compilation (Jer 36:32). Similarly, the story of the discovery of the "scroll of the Torah" in 2 Kings 22–23 also "presumes a single copy," as van der Toorn well emphasizes.[352] Wider "publication" was mediated through public readings (2 Kgs 23:2). References to *sēper* "(book-)scroll" in biblical Hebrew are normally singular and definite, for example, "the scroll of Jashar," 1 Samuel 2:18; "the book of the law," 2 Kings 22:11; "this book" (*hassēper hazzeh*), 2 Kings 23:3; "scroll of the covenant," Exodus 24:7. Distinct, singular scrolls are almost always in view. Of the 191 occurrences of the noun in the Bible, only twenty-one are pluralized (*sĕpārîm*), and almost all of these are references to "letters" (e.g., 1 Kgs 21:8; Isa 39:1; Esth 1:22; 2 Chron 32:17). There is also a reference to documents of sale in Jeremiah 32 (v. 14). Otherwise only Qoheleth 12:12 and Daniel 9:2 provide possible references to multiple, non-pragmatic (e.g., letters, contracts) documents. The overwhelming oralit of daily life, the relative expense of writing materials and general onerousness of their manipulation, the comparatively small numbers of readers and writers, and the relative dearth of extrabiblical written remains from the region are all consistent with this picture of unique text editions prior to Qumran (or perhaps a little earlier).[353] Some copying, of course, will have gone on, but not likely on the (large) scale presumed in much biblical scholarship.

The aforementioned modalities all involve preexisting sources, either written or oral. Yet a written poem could be generated in the absence of explicit sources, a scenario van der Toorn treats under the rubric "invention"—"the scribe who invents composes a text of his own contrivance."[354] This might entail an initial writing down of unmediated oral tradition, as D. Pardee supposes is the case with Ilimilku's version of the Baal Cycle at Ugarit.[355] There is no doubt that scribes in ancient Israel and Judah, like other performers of traditional verbal art (e.g., prophets), possessed individual talent and thus the capacity to create original works of art based on traditional materials brought together in new ways,[356] though such acts are not narrated as such in the Bible. And by virtue of their abilities to read and write, scribes also could draw on the incipient textual tradition as source material for new poetic creations. 1 Chronicles 16:8–36 has already been cited as an example of a "new" psalm created from part of the written tradition available to the Chronicler—namely, a psalms scroll inclusive of Psalms 105, 96, and 106. The much later 11QPsᵃ 151 A (col. xxviii 3–12, ca. first century CE; cf. LXX Ps 151:1–5), as a "poetic midrash on 1 Sam 16:1–13" (*DJD* IV, pp. 53–60), provides a different but equally obvious example of a psalm "invented" from a specifically written tradition. There is also the use of Amenemope and Ahiqar in Proverbs. The ability to write also means that writing may potentially factor in the composition of poetry.[357] Oral modes of composition (without the aid of writing)[358] would have been aboriginal and would have persisted, potentially, as long as a predominantly performative culture remained in place, and likely long after the advent of writing. J. Herington, for example, presumes the use of writing in the composition of lyric poetry from archaic and classical Greece to be minimal at best, "with the act of writing down occurring toward the end" of the composi- tion process or even after the composing itself was finished.[359] It is perhaps not accidental that the portrayal of written poetry in the Bible often has a be- lated sense about it, that is, a sense of its having been *written down* as opposed to *written out* in any sort of initiating effort (e.g., 2 Sam 1:18; cf. Job 19:23). I presume that much of the initial writing of biblical poetry was specifically a writing down of the oral tradition, for example, Baruch's writing down of Jeremiah's prophecies. So D. R. Olson from a more general perspective:

> With the introduction of writing, important parts of the oral tradition were written down and preserved in the available literate forms. The important cultural information, the information worth writing down, consisted in large part of statements shaped to fit the requirements of oral memory such as the epics, verse, song, orations, and since readers already knew, through the oral tradition, much of the content, writing served primarily for the storage and retrieval of information that had already been committed to memory, not for the expression of original ideas.[360]

And much of the "inventiveness," therefore, was of a kind consistent with the protean nature of oral verbal art more generally. The act of writing, in "sepa- rating the knower from the known" (to use Ong's oft-repeated phrase),[361] even- tually opens up space for new content and new ideas—traditional formulations could be leveraged to traditional ends, as always, but those formulations and ends now, outside the lifeworld of the performative arena and through introspec- tion and revision afforded by the fixity of writing, also could be scrutinized, countered, critiqued, supplemented, and vitiated.[362] Such an "inventiveness," expressly born of textuality, must be entertained (if even only incipiently) for the written prose of the Bible—"the biblical [prose] writers demonstrate the telling freedom to break" the generative "rules" of traditional oral verbal art[363]— and thus is a possibility, too, for the written poetry of the Bible. Deciding which poems (if any—Deutero-Isaiah? Job—though see Job 19:23) were com- posed *in* writing (e.g., as opposed to being written *down* after composition) is a difficult task, especially absent explicit comment (which is wholly missing— "no text from the Hebrew Bible is explicitly the invention of a scribe")[364] and given the general continuity of style that pervades the biblical poetic corpus, a style broadly "shaped or biased to fit the requirements of oral communication and auditory memory,"[365] as all biblical poems (regardless of medium or com- positional mode) emerged out of "an orally constituted sensibility and tradi- tion"[366] and in service to a culture always primarily oral and aural.[367] Indeed,

the prominence of "pseudonymity and anonymity," as R. F. Person emphasizes, signals that these texts remain (largely) "related to the ongoing traditional culture rather than to individual creative literary geniuses."[368]

* * *

THESE SIGNS, DISPARATE and not equally consequential, to be sure, nonetheless
in the aggregate may serve as an initial brief in support of the supposition of
a writing of (some) biblical poetry anterior to our current earliest manuscript
evidence (from Qumran and environs). They locate or implicate acts of writing
of various kinds and to varying degrees embedded already within the received
text of these poems. Such writtenness, of course, has been widely supposed by
generations of biblical scholars and will not be seen as a controversial hypothesis. And yet from the perspective of the oral (and aural) world out of which
this poetry comes, that it should get written down is not at all self-evident and
is an event of note,[369] in need of as thick and elaborate diachronic description
as possible, especially given the absence of early manuscripts. Even in advance of such a description, some of the differences (from the perspective of a
fully literary textuality) of the kind of textuality that will have characterized
written biblical poems initially may already be perceived, for example, written
out in unique copies, gathered in larger wholes, still abounding with an abundance of oralism. Other aspects will be disclosed as I continue to probe the
emerging textuality of Hebrew poetry in ancient Israel and Judah.

On the Possibility of Writing Biblical Poetry

Here I scrutinize the possibility of writing biblical poetry in light of what is
known about the emergence of writing more generally and the use of written
texts in the southern Levant over the course of the first millennium in particular. The angle of inquiry, as it were, is from the outside looking in. The terminus post quem for the writing down of poetry in a vernacular Hebrew script
(the "old Hebrew" script) is established by the development of that script,
which only begins to evolve paleographically (e.g., in comparison to and in
part away from the Phoenician script) during the mid- to late ninth century
BCE at the earliest (e.g., Mesha Stela, ca. 850 BCE, *KAI* 181).[370] Prior to this time
written poems would have been inscribed either in some version of the tran-
sregional linear alphabetic script used throughout the greater Levant during
Iron I and IIA (customarily simply referred to as "linear Phoenician"),[371] or
if earlier still, during the Late Bronze Age, then in a language ancestral to
Hebrew (a West Semitic dialect known only from the first millennium BCE)
and either in a form of the early alphabetic script used throughout the latter

half of the second millennium,[372] or in syllabic cuneiform, the international cosmopolitan writing system of the period.[373] However, to date no such early written poems in any of the latter scripts have survived. This is a point that deserves underscoring and elaborating. Of the various Late Bronze corpora, Sanders writes: "There is extensive evidence that speakers of languages ancestral to Hebrew encountered writing in Palestine over and over again. Yet among the hundreds of texts they produced there is not a scrap of native literature preserved, nor is there any sign of the kind of systematizing such a literature would entail."[374] With regard more specifically to the use of syllabic cuneiform in the Levant during the Late Bronze Age, Sanders observes: "The evidence shows three main uses for the writing system: education, administration, and communication. Self-expression and literature were not among them."[375] The linear alphabetic corpus from the Late Bronze Age through Iron IIA is similarly devoid of local literature. R. Byrne concludes his survey of the Iron I core of this material in this way: "The Iron I corpus of applied alphabetic writng consists of two basic categories: prestige objects (possessive, martial, votive, funerary) commissioned by elites, and curricular instruments used to preserve the very profession of scribalism during an era in which it existed on the margins of dominant exchange patterns."[376] The Late Bronze/ Iron I corpus of linear alphabetic inscriptions, it should be emphasized, is very small (numbering only in the tens of inscriptions) and consists of mostly short and often enigmatic epigraphs.[377] In Iron IIA longer, articulate alphabetic writings (e.g., the tenth-century Byblian sequence) begin to emerge, though still not in large numbers and strictly circumscribed in genre and function. And again, no written verse is extant. Indeed, there is no social-historical evidence that either syllabic cuneiform or early linear alphabetic was used to transmit native traditional verbal art in the southern Levant during this broad period.

Only at Late Bronze Ugarit, in alphabetic cuneiform, do local poetic materials get written down. These are all traditional materials (e.g., myths, heroic tales, prayers, songs) with an obvious oralism about them, and they appear only in single copies. As Pardee emphasizes with respect to the mythological texts inscribed by Ilimilku, "there is at present no clear evidence for a written tradition that would have preceded *Ilimilku*'s work."[378] Indeed, Ilimilku inserts a scribal (extranarratival) notation between horizontal lines at CAT 1.4.V.42–43 that appears to require the reader to supply the missing messenger type-scene from memory (*wtb lmspr.. ktlakn* / *ǵlmm* "And return to the recitation, 'when the lads / are sent'"; cf. CAT 1.19.IV. 63 [left-hand edge at l. 23]; 1.40.35).[379] This suggests that a chief function, at least of the Baal Cycle (and likely the other mythological texts inscribed by Ilimilku as well), was as an aid to memory, as Herington supposes for written versions of early Greek song texts—a mostly "mechanical means of preserving [the poems'] wording between performances."[380] While a smattering of alphabetic cuneiform tablets with a reduced graphemic inventory and nearly all written from right to left (like Phoenician and Hebrew) have been recovered from locations mostly outside of Ugarit proper (e.g., CAT 1.77; 4.31, 710; 7.60),[381] no texts in the standard Ugaritic alphabet have been found outside the immediate vicinity of Ugarit itself. As Sanders stresses, alphabetic cuneiform at Ugarit served a distinctly "particularizing" function: "It would have been difficult, even impossible to use this alphabet anywhere but home. Rather than being universal it would most likely have been unintelligible outside of the immediate region. The writers of Ugarit did not send their alphabetic texts abroad."[382] And in any event, it does not survive the Late Bronze cultural collapse. The writing down of local West Semitic traditional lore before Iron IIB, as far as we currently know, was a one-time, isolated occurrence at Ugarit.

The implication to be drawn from the foregoing is the strong likelihood that traditional, local verbal art of the kind (partially) in evidence (in mostly one-time written versions) at Ugarit circulated in the southern Levant during the Late Bronze and early Iron Ages predominantly (if not exclusively) in oral form, just as it surely had for centuries at Ugarit (including during the brief period in which alphabetic cuneiform was in use)[383] and elsewhere in the southern Levant. The existence of the Ugaritic tablets themselves, as well as the fact that alphabetic writing was often transcribed on perishable materials (e.g., papyrus, animal skins), means that the possibility of written poems of native genres in Hebrew (or a language ancestral to Hebrew) prior to Iron IIB cannot be ruled out. If such a poem did somehow manage to get written down it almost certainly would be a unique artifact, the odd product of elite patronage. Perhaps one might even dare to imagine some Israelite (cultural) heir of Ilimilku writing down in a one-off version a number of old oral poems in a scroll, maybe not unlike the (in)famous "scroll of Jashar" mentioned in the Bible (Josh 10:13; 2 Sam 1:18; cf. 1 Kgs 8:53 [LXX]). However, to date no such written poems have survived from the period (outside of Ugarit), and there is no empirical evidence that writing (whether in the linear alphabetic or syllabic cuneiform) was used to record local poetic genres. Rather, given the overwhelming orality of the pre-Hellenistic Levant, the residue of oral semiotics still patently manifest in biblical poems (see previous discussion "Signs of (Nonnarrative) Orality in Biblical Poetry" in this chapter), and the general dearth of extrabiblical written remains from the regions of ancient Israel and Judah prior to Qumran (and especially from the thirteenth through ninth centuries BCE),[384] it is far more plausible to assume that local tales, myths, love songs, hymns, prayers, dirges, oracles, proverbs, and the like—all of which surely existed!—circulated (mainly) orally during the period. They all are traditional art forms and quintessentially performative in nature, and thus not needing to be written down at all as long as contexts of performance persisted.[385] Indeed, oral performance and transmission of such genres was the norm well after poems also started being transcribed (or composed) in writing (cf. Deut 31:28, 31; 32:44–46; 2 Sam 1:17–18; Jer 36). Oralists studying ancient cultures often emphasize the need for empathy and imagination because of the ephemeral nature of oral culture and oral verbal art in particular—most of it eventually simply vanishes. The challenge for a hyperliterate scholarship culturally attuned to the empirical appeal of textuality is to give appropriate counterweight to the dominant oral components of ancient culture(s) that are now mostly missing from the historical record.[386] The linkage between the verbal art of Late Bronze Age Ugarit and that of Iron Age Israel and Judah has long been established. It was certainly cultural, traditional, and oral.[387] It need not have been scribal; in fact, presently there is no empirical evidence that it was scribal.[388]

The earliest written copies of biblical poems from Qumran (e.g., 4QDeut[b], ca. 150–100 BCE; 4QpaleoJob[c], ca. 225–150 BCE) provide the terminus ante quem for the writing down of biblical poetry, though linguistic and cultural considerations alone make clear that most of this poetry did not originate at Qumran. And that so much of it does survive in writing (and in multiple copies) into the Hellenistic period suggests that at least some of it must have been written down at an earlier time, perhaps in some cases even as early as the poems' original composers/performers/transcribers.[389] How much earlier, of course, depends on a complex of factors, including, most important, which poems are in view, their kind, and their *Sitz im Leben*.[390] The oldest poems in the Bible are usually thought to include some or all of the following: Genesis 49, Exodus 15, the oracles of Balaam in Numbers 23–24, Deuteronomy 32 and 33, Judges 5, 1 Samuel 2:1–10, 2 Samuel 1:19–27, 2 Samuel 22 (= Ps 18) and 23, Habakkuk 3, Psalm 29, and Psalm 68. For many it has become axiomatic to attribute extremely early dates of composition (Iron I, ca. 1200–1000 BCE) to the oldest of these "old poems," especially since the discovery of the Ugaritic texts when many stylistic and linguistic resemblances to Ugaritic poetry have been noted.[391] In several essays and a newly published monograph dedicated to the study of two of these poems (Judg 5 and 2 Sam 1:19–27), M. S. Smith severely critiques the claims for high antiquity:

> Overall, the data in these matter are all too few, resulting in the unavoidable problem of lacking sufficient material for making historical

judgments. In older discussions, the judgment of antiquity perhaps relied on implicit standards involving the density of the features considered to be old. It was this perceived density that tilted the balance in judgment from a simple matter of a vestige or two (or archaizing) and toward claims of for a genuinely old poem. The standard for such density was rarely discussed, much less defined. There are arguably neither enough specimens of this so-called "old poetry" nor understanding of their historical circumstances to develop a sufficient basis for dating them to specific centuries prior to the eighth century when prophetic books begin to play a significant role in the understanding of Hebrew poetry.[392]

Smith's larger reading of the two poems and the "warrior" culture he believes provoked them is comprehensive, appropriately complex, and wonderfully multifaceted and models well a sensitivity to issues of orality, literacy, and textuality and the complex nature of their interaction in ancient Israel and Judah. He argues that both poems originated as oral compositions and supposes that they would have been performed and reperformed for an extended period of time before being inscribed for the first time in Iron II. Smith summarizes his position on Judges 5, which he treats extensively, in this way:

> Given that apart from vv. 4–5, the old material, whether linguistic or cultural, is largely concentrated in the composition in vv. 14–30 and in select, older bits embedded in vv. 2–13, these may be Iron I; but the material of the [scribal] composer contains little or no such older material and thus may well be Iron II, perhaps even the ninth century (arguably older-looking than eighth-century poetry).[393]

This position is modified slightly in Smith's *Poetic Heroes*, where he presses more specifically for an Iron IIA (tenth century BCE) inscription of both poems, presumably under the pressure of his sense that "the tenth century would seem to be a fitting setting" for 2 Samuel 1:19–27 in particular.[394]

The allure of the tenth century remains hard for biblical scholars to resist. Even someone like Carr, for example, who is not insensitive to the deep impress of orality on biblical traditions, nevertheless maintains a fairly maximal view of what he imagines being written down in the the tenth century:

> This also would be the obvious time for the textualization of probable prestate poems like the song of Deborah, the emergence of an early Israelite corpus of royal and Zion Psalms, the development of early

collections of poems like the often-cited book of Yashar..., the creation
of preforms of parts of Proverbs as part of Israelite early education,
and the possible development of an early prose curriculum as well,
including early forms of the creation-flood narratives and narratives
centering on figures like Jacob, Moses, and David.[395]

This is starkly incongruous with what is currently known (materially, culturally, historically) about the tenth century in the southern Levant and especially
about alphabetic writing during the period, which is only sparsely attested at
best and strictly circumscribed in terms of both use and genres.[396] Comparative ethnography also cautions against assuming that the mere evidence of
writing necessarily implies its maximal usage—some sense of the differences
that may attend writing as it first emerges is already apparent from the foregoing discussion.[397] Still, written remains there are (no matter how meager),
and thus the *possibility* that *some* biblical materials were first inscribed at this
point cannot be fully deflected.[398] And *if* we are to imagine some odd bits of
the Bible getting written down initially as early as Iron IIA, then perhaps there
are no better candidates than one (or more) of the "old poems."

   Like Smith, I do not doubt the comparative antiquity of these "old poems"
(most definitely "older-looking" than the "eighth-century poetry" of biblical
prophecy). However, nothing in them, as far as I can tell, requires a specific
time of initial inscription—so Smith on Judges 5: "Both grammatical and cultural features in the poem *could* reflect a northern, early monarchic representation of oral memories of a pre-monarchic conflict, *though they need not.*"[399]
To the contrary, even in the written forms that have survived, they are engineered for oral recitation and for aural reception (see earlier discussion "Signs
of (Nonnarrative) Orality in Biblical Poetry"), and thus for preservation through
time in the traditional technology of rhythmic speech.[400] That is, as long as
there were performance contexts for such poems oral techniques (whether
memorial or improvisational) were adequate for long-term preservation. And
in the main most of these old poems evince the kind of political and/or religious (ritual) linkage that typically facilitates long-term, nonwritten preservation of verbal art in traditional societies. So Cross, for example, imagines
Judges 5 circulating "in the context of the rites of Holy War, or their equivalent, the re-enactment of the epic victory of Yahweh which I have labeled the
'ritual conquest,' celebrated in the pilgrimage festivals."[401] And even the somewhat more mundane setting for the "site of collective memory" imagined by
Smith (e.g., Judg 5:11) is rife with political/historical significance.[402] The
narrative presentations of both Deuteronomy 32 (Deut 31:19) and 2 Samuel
1:19–27 (vv. 17–18), though belated in insisting on the need to teach these

poems to the larger community, index the poems' communal significance. At the same time, these narratives also explicitly record the eventual writing down of these two old and once oral poems, which is at least contemporaneous with the written narrative blocks in which they are embedded and likely antedates these inscriptions—2 Samuel 1:18 even names a preexisting written source, the "scroll of Jashar."[403]

Generally speaking, then, Iron IIB—and specifically the late ninth or early eighth through the seventh and into the sixth centuries BCE—to my mind remains the likeliest period during which to imagine that poetic materials from the Bible, including the "old poems," start being gathered and written down.[404] The ink on plaster display inscriptions in poetic register (which contrasts noticeably with the workaday register of West Semitic epigraphs)[405] from Kuntillet Ajrud (*KA* 4.2; fig. 25) and Deir ʿAlla (*KAI* 312; fig. 24) date from this general period (ca. 800–750 BCE), though the question of the nature of the underlying medium—prose or poetry—remains open and debated for both— of the two, the Kuntillet Ajrud plaster text is the more suggestive of poetry, given its use of parallelism and the presence of hymnic themes and imagery.[406] Regardless, both evidence (in writing) knowledge of two prominent poetic genres well known from the Bible, psalmic and prophetic verse. From the same period also comes the royal commemorative stela of Zakkur, king of Hamath (in Aramaic; *KAI* 202). Although not a verse composition, the first seventeen lines or so (Side A) are composed of leading elements of what Gunkel called the thanksgiving song: the self-characterization of Zakkur as the petitioner (cf. esp. Ps 34:6), an account of troubles, and the declaration that the deity heard Zakkur and delivered him from his troubles (e.g., Ps 18, 30, 31, 34, 116, 118; cf. Isa 38:10–20).[407] Knowledge of this one psalm type is plainly indicated. And there are late ninth-century bullae (with papyrus imprints), recovered from Jerusalem,[408] that indicate the existence of papyrus rolls, a medium used for writing nondocumentary (as well as documentary) works[409]—in fact, the Deir ʿAlla display inscription mirrors the layout of a papyrus roll (fig. 24).[410] It is only during this general period, as Sanders (among others) has shown, that writing in Israel and Judah "attests a constellation of tools for *reproducing* a standard written Hebrew" and thus the wherewithal for the inscribing and collecting of traditional poems and local lore. So, for example, at Kuntillet Ajrud (ca. 800 BCE) there are practice texts (abecedaries, letters; *KA* 3.6, 11–14, see fig. 34), a letter (*KA* 3.1), a prayer (*KA* 3.9), and the apparent hymn previously mentioned (*KA* 4.2, see fig. 25), and at Samaria (ca. 770 BCE) we have for the first time evidence for bureaucratic record keeping (fig. 37). Textualized versions (of various sorts) of small-scale traditional genres, such as blessings (*KA* 3.1.2), curses (e.g., *Silw* 1.2–3), and proverbial sayings (e.g., *Lach* 6.3), also begin to appear at this time. In fact, it is throughout this period (Iron IIB) that a substantial upsurge in writing more generally may be detected in the extrabiblical epigraphic corpus[411] and that most still date the written prophecies of the likes of Hosea, Amos, Isaiah of Jerusalem, and Micah—arguably the earliest writings from the Bible that can be dated with any confidence and much of which is in verse (following Lowth).[412] And the process of consolidating the great swath of narrative prose that now constitutes the Torah and Deuteronomistic History (roughly Genesis through Kings) is most often imagined to have begun during this same period of time (usually associated with either Hezekiah or Josiah)—though the corpus as a whole would not have reached its final shape until sometime in the sixth or fifth centuries BCE (at the earliest) in response to the events surrounding the 586 capture of Jerusalem.[413] The latter conglomerations, though largely prosaic and narrative in orientation, contain, here and there, individual poems, including many of the "old poems" referenced earlier (e.g., Exod 15; Judg 5; 2 Sam 1:19–27), and many smaller snippets of poems (e.g., Gen 4:23–24; Exod 15:21; Num 21:27–30; Josh 10:12–13; Judg 14:14, 18).

With the Babylonian capture of Jerusalem and the destruction of the Judahite political infrastructure, including the forced exile of many of the ruling elite and artisans of various sorts (e.g., Jer 29:2), Hebrew totally disappears from the the epigraphic record until the Hellenistic period. Sanders astutely recognizes the "very bond" between "written Hebrew" and the "spoken language" during the Iron II period more generally—"it [i.e., the written language] had always been represented as isomorphic with and iconic of speech"—and the "limit" this causes once Aramaic becomes a "main spoken language" in the region: "the switch to Aramaic as the script-language for daily activity seems almost a foregone conclusion."[414] And in fact epigraphic Aramaic from the Persian period in particular is abundant with just the expected sorts of everyday documents, namely letters, legal contracts, economic documents, ownership markers (e.g., as abound in the Elephantine corpus). Yet internal evidence from the Hebrew Bible witnesses (the result of) intense scribal activity (e.g., editing, collecting) involving extended texts in the Hebrew language pervaded by allusions to themes of exile and return—and a few poetic compositions even explicitly situate their discourse in terms of exile (e.g., Ps 137). A substantial portion of the biblical poetic corpus is preserved in collections or sequences of poems that mostly postdate 586, including the three books formatted as verse by the Masoretes, Psalms, Proverbs, and Job,[415] and Lamentations and the Song of Songs.[416] And there are late prophetic collections, too (e.g., Jeremiah, Second Isaiah), as well as the late (fourth/third centuries BCE) prose retelling of Israel's history, Chronicles, which includes some

poetry (e.g., 1 Chron 16:8–36).[417] Poetic production in Hebrew clearly persists
after the destruction of Jerusalem, though the precise nature of its supporting
textuality, especially initially, if any ("songs don't require scribes" or "pen and
parchment"),[418] remains at issue. Presumably that textuality would have had a
dominant Aramaic inflection, both scribally and linguistically,[419] and would
have continued to interface with speech and to be engineered for aural reception (though now that speech is multilingual). The nature of textual production in the Hebrew language, then, shifts subtly but importantly during
the runup to Qumran. And by Qumran yet another shift is noticeable. The
new "Jewish script" there in use evolves out of the fifth- and fourth-century
Aramaic "script-language for daily activity," and the poetic productivity of the
exile and the postexile is for the first time now plainly exhibited in multiple
copies (e.g., Psalms, thirty-nine scrolls; Deuteronomy, thirty-one scrolls; Isaiah,
twenty-two scrolls)—written transmission of biblical poetry at this time is
beyond doubt, albeit still in a dominantly oral culture and with a mostly "oral
mind-set."[420]

Inscribed in Vocality

To describe the textual productivity just sketched as "emergent" is to emphasize its nascent and fluid nature and to resist the idea that mere textuality
immediately gives way to full-fledged literate or monolithic conceptions. To
be sure, the modern literary study of the Bible almost from its very inception
with Lowth has proceeded (mostly tacitly) as if the texts it studies were in fact
just like modern, post-Gutenberg texts, and though the achievements gained
from such an angle of vision have been considerable,[421] so, too, have been the
costs, not least in the misapprehension of the historical phenomenon in view.
However sublime we judge biblical poems to be they are the products of what
Doane calls a distinctly "interfacial moment":

> At certain discrete historical moments a culture that has adopted
> writing as a privileged or as a secondary mode for the production and
> preservation of texts may form an "interface"…with a primar(ily) oral
> culture or with an oral strain of culture within itself. An interface is the
> moment when the oral text and the technology of literacy are capable of
> penetrating and interpreting each other. The result of these encounters
> is the gradual undermining of the oral culture by the power of writing
> and literacy. Once it comes into contact with writing, the orality of oral
> cultures tends to bifurcate into written traces, the production of high
> formalism being replaced by the power of writing, and into ordinary

language which is not considered worth preserving in writing. At the same time, during these interfacial moments (moments which may last for months, years, centuries—even millennia, as in the case of India), many performative situations may migrate into written residue. These "oral-residual texts" are always particular reflexes of specific, individual historical encounters at the oral/written interface and constitute the body of the various "oral literatures" available for study in contemporary lettered culture.[422]

In the case of the Bible, the interfacial moment was prolonged—"biblical literature seems for the most part to belong to a transitional stage during which there developed an interplay among oral tradition, MS tradition, and memory"[423]—and the written poetic texts that were produced, though neither fully oral nor fully written, nevertheless do remain (to use again O'Connor's phrase) "comparatively close to the oral poetic situation." That is, in a number of important aspects these poems, even once written down, are decidedly more oral than not. The chiefest evidence here is the prevailing vocality of written biblical poems. However ultimately composed, biblical poems, like their archaic and classical Greek and medieval European vernacular (e.g., English, German, French)—and ancient Near Eastern, too[424]—counterparts, were written to be read aloud, vocalized, and thus heard. That is, reading in ancient Israel and Judah and in the greater southern Levant, certainly through the Persian period, was normally a vocal practice and publication (reception) inevitably still performative and aural in nature—biblical poems were distinctly more dependent on the ear than the eye for their reception.

This state of affairs is now widely observed, as I have noted already in this chapter and follows from various considerations.[425] In particular, as many have noticed, the etymology of the biblical Hebrew verbal root that becomes used with the meaning "to read," *q-r-ʾ*, aboriginally means simply "to call, cry out, make a noise"—a meaning it retains throughout, for example, "all the people...called [*qārěʾû*] a fast.... And then Baruch read [*wayyiqrāʾ*] in the scroll the words of Jeremiah...in the hearing of all the people" (Jer 36:9–10). Further, the representations of reading preserved in the Bible routinely make the vocality of the reading experience explicit, as in Jeremish 36:9–10. Most spectacular is the couplet from Isaiah 29:18: "On that day the deaf shall hear / the words of the scroll" (NRSV). Vocal performance is also in view in these lines from Habakkuk: "Write down [*kětôb*] the vision and make it plain on tablets / so that a herald [lit. 'a crier,' *qôrēʾ*] might run with it (and proclaim it)" (2:2). One read "in the hearing" (*běʾoznê*) of an audience (e.g., Exod 24:7; Deut 31:11; Jer 36:6, 10, 13–15, 21; 2 Kgs 19:14–16) or "before" (*neged, lipnê*) one (e.g.,

Josh 8:35; 2 Kgs 22:10; Esth 6:1). Words are proclaimed from the "mouth" (*peh*, Josh 1:8) and "muttered, mumbled" vocally (*y-g-h*) even if alone (Ps 1:2; cf. Josh 1:8).

What has not been emphasized as much is the very vocality required by the manner of the inscription itself, how the poetry was physically encoded on the page (as it were). The "old Hebrew" script (like all other forms of vernacular alphabetic writing in the Levant, e.g., Phoenician, Aramaic) was always consonantal (see fig. 37)[426] and thus requires active vocalization in order to render the spoken language, that is, to provide the vowel sounds, articulate syllable structure, intonation, stress contours, and the like that make any (spoken) language linguistically comprehensible. For example, every written lexeme requires on the part of a reader literal vocalization—providing the appropriate vowels—in order for the graphic symbols on a potsherd or a piece of papyrus to be translated into a Hebrew word—to turn *mlk* into a linguistically meaningful word, *melek* (<*malk-) "king" (*Lach* 3.19) or to distinguish *zrˤ*/zĕrôaˤ/"arm" (*Arad* 88.2) from *zrˤ*/zeraˤ/"seed" (*Lach* 5.10).[427] The advent of *matres lectionis* begins to provide some minimal readerly cues for vocalization (e.g., *ʾrr*, *BLei* 3.1 v. *ʾrwr*, *Silw* 1.2 for /ʾārūr/ "cursed!"), but these never become widespread prior to Qumran.[428] The running format that would have likely prevailed for writing Hebrew poetry in pre-Hellenistic manuscripts (see figs. 22–25)[429] is virtually devoid of any kind of punctuation or metascript conventions to aid readers in navigating sentence contours, let alone mapping larger discourse structures (e.g., poetic lines, paragraphs, stanza or poem boundaries). In such a manner of writing readers need to hear (as they vocalize) the rhythm, syntax, and meaning of words in order to perceive the poetry's structure. Some aid is provided lexically. For example, the transition to a new topic is sometimes headed by (*w*)ʿt "(and) now" (e.g., *Arad* 2.1; 40.4; *Lach* 4.2) and direct discourse is often introduced explicitly (e.g., *lʾmr* "saying," *Lach* 3.14, 20–21; 6.4–5, 9). These, too, are the telltale signs of active readerly oralization and contrast distinctly with visually oriented cues such as lineal indentation (e.g., for marking new paragraphs) or quotation marks (for distinguishing quoted speech or direct discourse) that evolve to maximize fluidity for ocular processing. The word divider itself, which is characteristic of writing in the "old Hebrew" script (see fig. 37—though by no means unfailingly systematic),[430] is one kind of visually oriented metascript convention—an early precursor to the period, comma, and colon that eventually develop to guide predominantly optically oriented—sight—reading. In this case, then, the consonantal components of a word (or closely bound phrase) are graphically distinguished for readers.[431] Such writing is practical and decodable even without maximal vocalizing for many everyday uses in relatively short texts, for example ownership markers, basic record keeping (e.g., Samaria ostraca), short letters or memoranda (e.g., Arad, Lachish). This kind of readerly ability may well lie behind Hoshayahu's boast in Lachish 3 (namely "By the life of Yahweh, no one has tried to read for me a letter—ever!" ll. 9–10). However, for more extended and complex texts, whether poems or prose narratives, the "old" Hebrew-script language is mostly useless absent a reader with prior extratextual knowledge of the text in question.[432] A. Ford offers a similar assessment of written manuscripts of early Greek song texts: "Altogether, a lyric song text of the archaic period was fairly useless to anyone who had not already heard the song."[433] The same point has been made about written versions of Anglo-Saxon poetry from the Middle Ages.[434] In fact, one idiom preserved in biblical Hebrew for the ability to read is literally "to know the document" (*y-d-ʿ* "to know" + *sēper* "document, scroll"): "The vision of all this has become for you like the words of a sealed document [*dibrê hassēper heḥātûm*]. When it is given to one who knows the document [*yôdēaʿ hassēper*], with the command, 'Read this [*qěrāʾ nāʾ-zeh*],' he says, 'I am unable for it is sealed.' And when the document [*hassēper*] is given to one who does not know the document [*ʾăšer lōʾ-yādaʿ sēper*], saying, 'Read this [*qěrāʾ nāʾ-zeh*],' he says, 'I do not know the document [*lōʾ yādaʿtî sēper*]'" (Isa 29:11–12).[435]

One tangible, albeit belated, measure of the difficulty caused by this spare manner of writing—just the spatialized words (set off by word dividers) with little else—is the consternation often expressed by contemporary biblical scholars over the amount of biblical poetry found in the received tradition (MT) in a running format (esp. in the Latter Prophets), which can make it difficult to know (and always contestable) where line or couplet boundaries are, or to distinguish poems from other poems (or sections of poems) or even from passages of narrative prose. Some have even gone so far as to suggest that the general lack of special formatting for biblical poems may mean that the West's familiar distinction between prose and poetry (verse) is not appropriate to this material.[436] However, in my view, it is more likely a bout of (mostly unintended) ethnocentrism that ignites this consternation in the first place, both in its hyperliterate orientation, which assumes all writing is optimized for sight-reading, and therefore poems somehow are naturally distinguishable in writing from prose, and in the specificity of how this distinction is realized—verse is to be written out stichically (i.e., in lines). But writing everywhere is a local and highly culture-specific technology, as previously discussed (see chapter 1). There are no universal rules for its development. Scripts and metascript conventions optimally fashioned for fluid sight-reading with a minimum of presumed extratextual knowledge are relatively late phenomena and everywhere historically tractable. And the stichic lineation of verse that is now ubiquitous in the West is the cultural heir to one very specific tradition, that of ancient Greece. Other conventions for writing out verse are amply attested historically, and even in ancient Greece verse was not always specially distinguished in writing (e.g., Timotheos papyrus, ca. fourth century BCE). There are surely genres in the Bible that defy being neatly characterized as poetry or prose, but they are not so many. And poetry is among the world's oldest and most widely attested forms of verbal art, oral and written. To suppose its presence in the Bible, while requiring substantiation (so Lowth), is hardly a cultural imposition.[437]

In any case, the troubles for even highly educated scholars (i.e., readers with a high degree of extratextual knowledge) provoked by the Masoretes' consonantal script and running formats are at least emblematic of those faced by ancient readers of Hebrew poems set out in a similarly "bare" script-language—"fairly useless" to anyone who did not already know the poem. The advent at Qumran of the use of extra spacing for the delineation of lineal units in some written biblical poems is a huge boon for readers. Lines of biblical verse, engineered (initially) to accommodate human memory constraints and vocal capacities, routinely uncoil in clausal or sentential wholes, and therefore to signify these junctures textually, graphically is to provide information about verse units and syntactic rhythms and structures that in a running format could only be supplied by active oralization from a reader already familiar with the aural patterns of the poem and prepared to interpret them for a listening audience. Yet even such special formatting remains relatively spare (and inconsistent) in the information conveyed ocularly, far from that required for the autoreferentiality characteristic of fully written and literate poetic discourse.

Doane in his work on Anglo-Saxon poetry uses the term "chirograph" to distinguish this kind of bare writing that evolves from a primar(il)y oral context, writing as he notices that remains comparatively close to oral utterances, as it emerges similarly from embodied activity and shows the traces of this (e.g., in the handwriting, individual layout, (in)consistency of word and line division). Chirographs are always unique materially, both in the language material they contain (e.g., full of variation, mechanical errors) and how that language material is laid out and in the actual material used for the writing surface itself, whether potsherd, papyrus, leather, stone, or wood—no two surfaces are ever exactly alike.[438] Moreover, he emphasizes that chirographs "are 'performative productions' by which a relatively valuable or rare skill (that of the scribe) is brought to bear in a direct communicative link with a reading or hearing audience that cannot or does not write for itself, in many cases a specific individual or corporate audience (though we in many or most cases do not know who these audiences were)."[439]

The requirement of active vocalization demanded by the very writtenness of biblical poems—a writing that stubbornly requires extratextual investment, input to make sense of what is written—resolves a crucial dimension of the orality that informs so much biblical poetry diagnosed in earlier sections of this chapter. My pose initially was intent on establishing the deep rootedness of biblical poetic style in oral tradition, all the while remaining mindful of the belatedness of this poetry's textualization—minus actual contemporary poetic manuscripts from the region embedded in maximally informative metadiscussions it is imprudent to assume that any of the Hebrew poetry preserved in the Bible represents the transcripts of actual oral performances.[440] Indeed, by dint of their very writtenness they all evidence scribal mediation and intervention of a sort that could only alter the oral text, if only by adding writing to it. However, the very vocality of these poems' writtenness helps us to see that the "informing orality" of biblical poetry is not only the trace of something in the past, bits of performative contexts that have migrated into a written residue (as Doane emphasizes), though it is this, too; but such signs of orality also point ineluctably to the ongoing relevance of oral semiotics even for the written versions of the poetic texts that have survived in the Bible. That is, the informing orality of biblical poetry is there both because it is a poetry, and thus a style, that emerges out of a primar(il)y oral environment and because oral tradition (with all that this phrase connotes) remains vital to the production and successful vocal reception of this poetry, even once entexted. Said differently, an expressly oral semiotics is still required on the one hand because it could hardly have been otherwise for writing poets/scribes for whom the very sensibility of poetry—namely *šîr, māšāl, qînâ*—was only traditional and oral. Scribes (at least initially) wrote (down) the oral poetry they knew and in which they were immersed. Writing changes the semiotic equation, but the pace of that change is gradual, and nowhere in the biblical poetic corpus does textuality (and the literacy it unleashes) fully overwrite and thus mute the tradition's informing orality. On the other hand, as van der Toorn stresses, "the oral delivery of the texts" was also determinative for "their style"[441]—the reception of this poetry was always ultimately aural and thus requiring a semiotics that would facilitate such uptake, a language shaped "to fit the requirements of oral communication and auditory memory."[442] The signs of (an informing) orality in these poetic texts (e.g., short lines, rhythmic speech, parallelism, repetitive phrasing, archaisms, episodic structure), then, are themselves the very evidence of the ongoing importance of orality (cum vocality) for biblical poetry and its successful reception and form the core of what may be described as biblical poetic style.

* * *

IN BRINGING THIS chapter to a close I am keenly aware that the discussion about orality, literacy, and textuality that I have joined and focalized specifically in terms of biblical poetry is in many ways a discussion still in its infancy, even after a century and more of research. That there is much more to say on these topics is an understatement. What I would claim by way of an interim statement in light of the preceding exposition may be summarized as follows. First, orality is not a singular phenomenon, and where it is sighted (culturally, historically, generically) makes all the difference. Biblical poetry is almost wholly nonnarrative in nature, and therefore if the orality that informs it is to be fully fathomed it will require comparisons with similarly nonnarrative forms of oral poetry. Though Lord made this very point about biblical poetry in the mid-1970s, as far as I am aware no one has seriously followed up on his insight, undoubtedly blinded by the irresistible allure of his *Singer of Tales*. The possibility of Hebrew oral narrative verse is an old topic in the field, though continuing to probe it, from new angles and with different assumptions, remains productive and illuminating, not least in bringing starkly into view the non-narrative-ness of the orality informing so much biblical verse. Second, the leading features of biblical poetic style (e.g., short lines, simple clause structure, parataxis, parallelism, rhythmicity) are also characteristics of oral verbal art more generally and nonnarrative oral poetry in particular. In other words, biblical poetic style is at heart an "oral style" (as Jousse stressed already before Parry launched his influential program), both because it emerges out an overwhelmingly oral world as a specimen of oral verbal art and because even once written down it was transmitted in vocality and thus remained subject to the semiotics of orality. Third, a chief advantage of writing as a technology is its greatly enhanced preservation capacities. That the Bible's nonnarrative poetic tradition was eventually written down means that aspects (residues) of an otherwise ephemeral art form have been conserved and are available for scrutiny. Gathering and identifying these features, even if only in a preliminary fashion, is crucial as a means of concretizing in what this orality consisted, saying more specifically how biblical poetry is "comparably close to the oral poetic situation." To move beyond Gunkel's mostly nebulous conception of Israel and Judah's oral past is important for the field and for the comparative study of oral (and oral-derived) verbal art more broadly. Finally, the facticity of this eventual textualization must always be faced. We only know biblical poetry as a textualized artifact, and that only belatedly so (e.g., DSS, MT). There is no question of completely confounding this textuality, yet an anterior textuality also may be presumed and sometimes even isolated. The initial writing of the biblical poetic tradition likely occupied a prolonged moment in which orality, literacy, and textuality intersected one another in diverse and complex ways, the details of which we are likely never to know fully. We mostly get the odd glimpse here and there that can then be refracted or triangulated by way of comparative ethnography. What is viewable in these snapshots, at times more clearly than others, is an emergent textuality that both anticipates and differs from (often strikingly so) that which is more familiar to our own post-Gutenberg textual sensibilities.

The Way of Poetry in Psalm 133

a poet's words are of things that do not exist without the words
—WALLACE STEVENS, "The Nobel Rider and the Sound of Words" (1942)

THE ART OF reading remains the paradigmatic practice of literary criticism, even (and perhaps especially) on this, the thither side of theory. The principal thrust, for example, of T. Eagleton's recent poetry primer is to call students of literature back to the practices and habits of close reading.[1] In biblical studies, too, kindred voices have been raised urging scholars and students of biblical poetry to move from a preoccupation with matters of underlying structure and prosody (never irrelevant issues) to a pursuit of "the poetry per se," a pursuit, that is, of reading.[2] Readings (always in the plural) are at once the stuff out of which all construals of prosody and poetics are necessarily made and what complete said construals. They are the ultimate justification of poetry, the gift of poetry. Readings of biblical poems, and especially close, deep, lusciously savored, highly imaginative readings, are still too few in the field. Such a reading of Psalm 133 is what I put forward in this closing chapter. It is elaborated, in the first place, as a cashing out of my efforts to think through the several facets of biblical poetics on offer throughout this book (i.e., the line, rhythm, lyricism, oral-derived style), an exemplification of how poetics can open onto reading; and thus the chapter brings the whole collection to a certain culmination. And yet the reading is not wholly naive—no reading ever really is—but has an argument of its own to make, which is thematized under the rubric "the way of poetry." The chief way of poetry for me is a way of words; it is, as has often been said (e.g., Stevens), a making out of words—*poesy* (cf. *ma'ǎśay*, Ps 45:2). I parse the phrase "the way of poetry" in two principal ways. The first is the more mundane (though not less interesting for that) and is revealed through the close (and slow) reading of the psalm that constitutes the first several sections of the chapter in particular. Here "the way of poetry" is the literal path through this particular piece of poetic discourse, how the psalm gets from beginning to end, word by word, and what happens along the way. The "word itself" is very much the "motor" of this "poetic discourse."[3] The second "way" of this poem is tackled in the chapter's shorter third section. This way of poetry, if also by necessity a way of words, does not lie in the words alone but emerges, as well, because of them and in between them, literally in the spans of uninscribed space that isolate and surround these ancient words as we meet them in actual manuscripts (see figs. 42–45).[4] Here I aim to capture something of how the poem amounts to more than the sum total of its words, to celebrate what happens, not just in the words but because of them, as they are specially assembled and performed in this particular psalm within an ancient context.[5]

I am alert throughout to the peculiarities of this psalm's traditional "word-power." That is, that the words of this psalm, having likely been shaped at the interface of orality, literacy, and textuality, are not the product of high literary achievement. Rather, they are stubbornly tradition-bound. Therefore, another part of the "way" of this poem that I chart throughout is precisely the "how" and "what" of this traditionality, its situated-ness (in part) "within a set of associations and expectations formally extrinsic but metonymically intrinsic" to the experience of this work of "verbal art."[6] In other words, much of what gets done in my "close" reading[7] of this psalm is a laying bare of the metonymic, extratextual sensibilities of this accumulation of poetic "words"—the "unusual Near Eastern coloring" that H. Gunkel found so delightful though not so easily understood.[8]

Still more "ways" of poetry, other ways by which this particular poem stages discourse—through sound, retrospection, and shape-shifting—are briefly explicated, especially in the treatment of the poem's closing lines in the final section of the chapter.[9] And thus, if my reading of this psalm *as a reading* provides this book with one kind of conclusion, its claims about the (heterogenous) way of poetry in Psalm 133 reveal it as yet another in this series of essayistic probings of biblical poetics, and therefore whatever closural force is registered at chapter's end is only of a temporary kind, a momentary pause until the next chapter, essay, or book is written. The work of literary criticism,[10] whether in reading or in critical assessment, happily, is never truly finished.

I

The only claim made in the short Psalm 133[11] comes in the opening couplet,[12] where the beauty of brothers dwelling together is extolled:

hinnê[13] *mah-ṭṭôb ûmah-nnāʿîm*	Wow, how good and how pleasant is
šebet ʾaḥîm gam-yāḥad	the dwelling of brothers all together—[14]

What is most striking about this claim is its unmistakable hyperbole and its thoroughgoing aesthetic character. As J. Culler observes, lyric discourse generally exhibits a strong attraction to extravagance, exaggeration, sublimity: "the tiger is not just orange but 'burning,'" and "the wind is the very 'breath of Autumn's being.'"[15] In the first line of our poem the hyperbolic register is signaled by the twofold use of the exclamatory *mah* ("How!"), headed by the presentative *hinnê* ("Wow!").[16] If the semantics of such an additive strategy appears "strangely redundant,"[17] a more satisfying sum is achieved when the arithmetic is factored in terms of rhetorical force. One plus one plus one, in this poetic math, yields a threefold underscoring of the attraction of brothers dwelling together. Indeed, this piling up of exclamatory particles coupled with the withholding of the object of admiration means that the resulting surfeit of exultation seems to explode from the line as auditors move on to the second line in search of the unnamed topic so extravagantly hymned.

Among the closest parallels to the line are Numbers 24:5, *mah-ṭṭōbû ʾōhāleykā yaʿăqōb* "How good are your tents, O Jacob," and especially Song 7:7 (cf. 4:10), *mah-yyāpît mah-nnāʿamtā* "How beautiful are you, how pleasant!" In both instances, the phrasing itself nicely throws into relief the added rhetorical force of *hinnê* in Psalm 133:1,[18] but it is the obviousness of the line's aesthetic interest in the Song (though also true of Num 24:5) that proves so crucial for our appreciation of Psalm 133 more generally. As the line in the Song is said of the beloved girl, we easily acquiesce to its defining aesthetic bent—after all she is repeatedly admired and found beautiful by her lover throughout the Song (e.g., 1:15; 4:1–7; 7:2). It is the aesthetic appeal of the less tangible "brothers dwelling together" that is front and center in the psalm. This is plainly indicated by the only two content words in the line, *ṭôb* and *nāʿîm*, both of which have pronounced aesthetic valences. The root *n-ʿ-m* in biblical Hebrew chiefly signifies high aesthetic value, as is well evidenced by Song 7:7 (cf. Gen 49:15; 2 Sam 1:26; Ps 16:6, 11; 135:3; 147:1; Job 36:11; Prov 9:17; 24:4; Song 1:16). By contrast, the semantic range of *ṭôb* is considerably broader. The term often conveys a positive ethical evaluation (e.g., Gen 2:17; 3:5, 22; 1 Kgs 8:36; Isa 7:15)—and indeed it is hard not to hear at least the faintest echo of Micah's more obviously ethically oriented *mah-ṭṭôb* (6:8). But *ṭôb*, of course, implicates high aesthetic esteem as well (e.g., Gen 1:4; 2:9; 31:24; Num 24:5; 2 Sam 19:28; Song 1:2; Qoh 11:7), and this is the range of meaning on which *nāʿîm* (see esp. Gen 49:15; Ps 135:3) and the similes in Psalm 133:2–3 so clearly focus attention.[19]

The second line of the couplet, *šebet ʾaḥîm gam-yāḥad*, provides the subject of this opening exultation (cf. Num 24:5). The line is especially close to a clause in Deut 25:5: *kî-yēšĕbû ʾaḥîm yaḥdāw* "when brothers dwell together."

The formal differences between the two are telling. In the Deuteronomic version, a circumstantial clause, normal prose syntax prevails: temporal particle (*kî*) + finite verb (*yēšĕbû*; Qal impf. 3 m. sg.) + subject (*'aḥîm*) + adverbial (*yaḥdāw*). In Psalm 133:1, the syntactic norms are slightly bent, as is customary in poetry, and the line as a whole is noticeably figured and shaped.[20] The verb is now nonfinite (*šebet*; Qal inf. const.), and the phrase has a more concise feel to it—especially noticeable when the added *gam* is bracketed and the late Tiberian segholation in *šebet* (< **šibt*) is dispensed with.[21] As a nonfinite form, the infinitive construct here focuses the "bare verbal action" of dwelling, without regard being paid (linguistically) to aspect, the agent, or circumstances (*IBHS* sec. 35.2.2a). The dynamicity of dwelling, then, is emphasized, all the while allowing it to be packaged nominally. The clause functions as the subject of the exclamations in the first line, providing the first instance of the poem's defining rhythm of enjambment.[22] The words *nā'îm* and *'aḥîm* rhyme, the patterned cadences of their half-line phrasing (*ûmah-nnā'îm* / *šebet 'aḥîm*) enhance this sonic effect. Even the additive particle *gam* is figured to good effect: the note of emphasis that *gam* contributes (frequently when "giving an exaggerated, aggravated or extreme case")[23] both heightens still further the couplet's already highly exclamatory rhetoric and focuses the accent most particularly on the "unity, togetherness" of the brothers' dwelling (cf. Deut 25:5; Gen 13:6; 36:7),[24] while its climatic position[25] at line-end pleasantly balances the opening *hinnê*.

Deuteronomy 25:5 provides the phrase *šebet 'aḥîm . . . yāḥad* with its most concrete sense, that of the patrimonial house—in biblical Hebrew, the *bêt 'āb*. In ancient Israel and Judah, as throughout the ancient Levant, the patrimonial house was society's chief socioeconomic unit. Ideally, it spanned three generations, consisting of a senior conjugal couple with their unmarried children, together with their married sons and the latter's wives and children, as well as other dependents (e.g., paternal kinsfolk, servants). Such a family would have lived in a large, single, multiroomed house or in a compound of smaller houses built closely together with shared courtyards, external walls, and so on.[26] It is just such a joint family that is assumed in Deuteronomy 25:5. That passage is concerned specifically with the practice of Levirate marriage and the division of family property after the death of the paterfamilias. The phrase *kî-yēšĕbû 'aḥîm yaḥdāw* itself refers to the period of time after the father's death but before the division of property when the brothers would have continued to live together on the undivided family estate.[27] It is precisely the ideal of the multigeneration, joint family that most commentators privilege in their reading of the phrase as it appears in Psalm 133.[28] Family is extolled as well in the larger sequence of the Songs of Ascents (esp. Ps 127:3–5; 128:3), and is one of the key elements in Qoheleth's *carpe diem* speech (9:7–10, esp. v. 9; cf. Gilg M iii 6–14).[29] And yet in the absence of the delimiting issue of Levirate marriage, which is nowhere in view in Psalm 133, and in awareness of the tendency for kinship language in Israel and Judah to get extended into other spheres (e.g., politics, cf. Amos 1:9) and used figuratively in various ways (e.g., Song 4:10), the phrasing in Psalm 133:1 is considerably more capacious than normally thought. It may focus on the prototypical joint family, but it can as easily take into its purview other patterns of coresidence (e.g., whole villages, neighborhoods in walled towns),[30] larger (potentially non-kinship-based) political alliances, and the like.[31] In the end, much will depend on the specific context in which the poem is heard.[32] The Hebrew phrasing (esp. *yāḥad*) does appear to have in view a specifically spatial sense of dwelling together (see Gen 13:6; 36:7; Jer 31:24)—of which unity (Tg. *kḥd*ʾ, Syr. ʾ*yk ḥd*ʾ, Vg. in uno) is only one dimension.

In sum, the opening couplet exclaims the aesthetic appeal of brothers (literal and metaphorical) dwelling spatially together. This is the voice of tradition, appropriately ornamented in high hyperbole, asserting what all know, the "good"-ness of the flourishing family household (e.g., Ps 127:3–5; 128:3; Prov 17:5)—despite (and in real knowledge of) the fractious realities that can nevertheless obtain in a lived-world.

II

The body of the poem (vv. 2–3) features two similes:

kaššemen haṭṭôb[33] ʿ*al-hārōʾš*	like fine oil on the head
yōrēd[34] ʿ*al-hazzāqān*	running down over the beard
zēqan-ʾahărōn šeyyōrēd[35]	the beard of Aaron which is running down
ʿ*al-pî middôtāyw*[36]	over the collar of his robes
kĕṭal-ḥermôn šeyyōrēd[37]	like the dew of Hermon running down
ʿ*al-har(ĕ)rê*[38] *ṣiyyôn*[39]	over the mountains of Zion!

There are three couplets[40] in all and enjambment pervades the whole. In each couplet, the participle *yōrēd* stands on either side of a (couplet internal) line juncture,[41] effectively escorting readers via its projection of the pure durative force of descending through the juncture (and eventually across and down the page, see figs. 42–44). The participle's nonfinite framing of bare action answers to the related focus of the infinitive construct in the opening couplet. Both, then, contrast with the single finite verb, *ṣiwwâ*, that comes in the poem's concluding lines. And beyond accentuating and reinforcing the effect of enjambment, the threefold repetition of *yōrēd* eases the transition from the image of fine oil to that of dew, as the one liquid melds into the other, and further gives the little poem its basic trajectory: moving most emphatically from the opening exclamation (down) through (and via) the overflowing oil and dew and spilling (as it were) onto Yahweh's "blessing"[42] at the end of verse 3. In addition to this patterned play of line type, cohesion is built into this section of the poem through word (*kĕ-*, *yōrēd*, *zāqān*) and phrase ('*al* + prepositional object) repetition—the word chaining identified by A. Berlin.[43]

At the heart of this song—and ultimately one of the chief ways that it means—are two similes, one picturing "the finest oil" and the other "dew." The initial image of oil cascading viscously but bountifully over head and beard (ultimately spilling, we are led to imagine, down onto the unnamed figure's clothes) continues the beginning couplet's hyperbolic accent. It does so in two principal ways. First, by designating the oil—which in the ancient Levant meant olive oil[44]—as the finest and most expensive variety of olive oil (virgin oil), here *šemen ṭôb* (esp. 2 Kgs 20:13 = Isa 39:2; cf. Song 1:3; 4:10; Qoh 7:1) but also called *rē'šît šĕmānîm* (Amos 6:6) and *šemen kātît*, literally "crushed oil" (Exod 27:20; 29:40; Lev 24:2; Num 28:5; 1 Kgs 5:25), in the Bible and *šmn rḥṣ*, literally "washed oil," in the Samaria ostraca (16a.3; 16b.3; 17a.2; 18.2; 21.2; etc.). The first two phrases represent quality designations known from elsewhere in the ancient Near East,[45] while the latter two are derived from the production process itself. P. J. King and L. E. Stager describe this process this way:

> The picked olives are first crushed and then pressed. In the case of virgin oil they are crushed, not pulverized, to avoid getting pulp-paste into the oil. Crushing is achieved by rolling a large stone…over the olives spread on a flat rock or on the floor of a rectangular crushing basin.…The oil was extracted by pouring hot water over the crushed olives, stirring the mixture, and then skimming the floating oil off by hand. *šemen rāḥūṣ* equals "crushed and washed"; whereas *šemen zayit zāk kātît* (Ex. 27:20; Lev. 24:2) equals "crush only"; both equal virgin oil. The first oil from the batch of olives is superior; the quality declines with successive pressings.[46]

Each of these designations, then, signifies superiority, and thus the poem's auditors are cued that the high arc of the rhetoric continues. Indeed, the connection with the opening couplet is not left to chance but is made plain to see and to hear through the verbatim repetition of the word *ṭôb* "good"—the first of Berlin's "word chains" that help formally bind this poem together.[47] The

"good" (*ṭôb*) of the extended family is literally—at the surface of the poem—
"like the good oil" (*kaššemen haṭṭôb*) that is poured over the head;[48] the two *ṭôbs*
materially, physically linking the two sentiments, underscoring their shared
fineness. Such "recurrence" is the "constant and perhaps universally definitive of oral poetry,"[49] and thus an unabashed sign of the tradionality of the
psalm's art.

Olive oil ultimately becomes a source of economic prosperity in the region
of Syria-Palestine.[50] Since the climate in other parts of the Mediterranean
world (e.g., Egypt, Mesopotamia) was not suitable for growing olives (too consistently warm), olives and olive oil were among the Levant's chief luxury
items coveted by the social and political elites and thus exported, either for
profit or trade, or through gift exchange (Hos 12:2; Ezek 27:12; cf. EA 161.56;
TAD B3.8.20),[51] and commonly counted among other valuables (gold, silver,
and the like, see 2 Kgs 20:13; cf. CAT 4.438.4; EA 1.70; *TAD* B3.8.20). Thus, it
is not surprising that olive oil carries mostly positive symbolic associations in
the Hebrew Bible, signifying prosperity (Ezek 16: 13, 20; Prov 21:17;), high
value and plenty (Deut 32:13; 33:24; 1 Kgs 17:12, 14, 16; 2 Kgs 2:4, 6, 7; Job
29:6), joy and well-being (Isa 61:3; Ps 92:11; 104:15). The gesture of anointing
the head with oil (sacral and nonsacral alike), the image of which is specifically evoked in this verse, is a case in point. It is a high sign of richness, sufficiency, superabundance, and, above all, high pleasure (Ps 23:5; Qoh 9:8; cf. Ps
141:5). This pleasurable quality is especially at the fore in the banqueting
scenes in Psalm 23 and in Qoheleth's *carpe deim* speech (in chapter 9) and is
echoed impressively in a description of Esarhaddon's banquet celebrating the
dedication of his new palace: "I drenched their heads with finest oil and perfumes" (ì.sag *igulâ muḫḫašunu ušašqi*, Borger Esarh. 63 vi 53, as cited in *CAD*
R, 431b).[52] Here in Psalm 133:2, then, not only does the oil's specific designation as the finest (*šemen ṭôb*) match and thus redouble the preceding couplet's
rhetoric of extravagance, but so does the gesture of drenching the head with a
superfluity of this fine oil, a literal image of over-the-topness, extravagance,
superabundance par excellence.

There is still a subtler connection between the evocation here of olive oil
and that of the extended family household in verse 1. The olive itself (Heb.
zayit) was a mainstay of the Israelite and Judahite diet, and the oil extracted
from it was similarly omnipresent in everyday life (Deut 8:8; 1 Kgs 17:12;
2 Kgs 4:2; *Arad* 4.1; 6.5; 7.8; 10.3; 12.1; EA 55:12), being put to any number of
uses, including as a foodstuff (1 Kgs 17:12; Ezek 16:13, 19), a fuel for lamps
(Exod 25:6; 35:8), a salve for the softening of skin (Isa 1:6; Ezek 16:9) or the
leather on a shield (2 Sam 1:21), and a base (cf. Exod 30:23–25) for perfumes,
cosmetics, and oils (Song 1:3; 4:10; Qoh 10:1; Est 2:12)—men and women

anointed the body with scented oil[53] both to condition the skin against the effects of the hot, dry climate and to perfume the body (after washing).[54] On ritual occasions, oil was also used for the anointing of kings (1 Sam 10:7; 16:1, 3; 1 Kgs 1:39; 2 Kgs 9:1, 3; Ps 89:21) and priests (Exod 30:24, 25; Lev 8:2, 10, 12) and to accompany offerings of various sorts (Gen 35:14; Num 7:31, etc.).[55] Indeed, so basic a commodity is oil in the ancient world that a husband's duty to provide it for his wife, alongside food and clothing, is enshrined in ancient Near Eastern legal practice (e.g., *ANET*, 160), a convention that surely lies behind the more figurative elaboration in Hosea 2:7 ("those who provide my bread and my water, / my wool and my flax, / my oil and my drink"; cf. Ezek 16:18–19).[56]

It is in this givenness, the very commonality of olive oil in the lifeworld of the ancient inhabitants of the southern Levant, that its mention in Psalm 133:2 resonates almost covertly with the reference to the extended family household in the psalm's opening lines. In fact, olive presses have been found interspersed among private houses at any number of Iron II sites in Palestine (e.g., Tell Beit Mirsim, Tell en-Naṣbeh, Shechem, Timnah).[57] D. Schloen estimates that the proportion of Iron II households with presses was 20 percent or more and infers from this that oil pressing at this time was chiefly a local affair, a part of the area's subsistence economy:

> The seasonal workforce needed to harvest the olives and man the presses must have been greater than any individual household could supply, suggesting that neighbors, probably in their role as kinsmen or clients, assisted the press owners and were allowed to press oil for their own use in return.[58]

The commonness of family, house, and oil, then, did not detract from the ancients' valorization of these necessities. Rather, it is in part this very quality, especially given the principally subsistence-based economy of the region, that endears them so. In fact, the valorization of everyday pleasures is a well-attested, traditional wisdom theme (e.g., Qoh 9:7–10; Gilg M iii 6–14).

The image of oil running down over the head and onto the beard foregrounds movement, energy—especially given the threefold repetition of *yōrēd* in the song and the eventual melding with another liquid figure, that of a plentiful, abounding dewfall, the combination of which Z. Zevit vividly— and apropos of the poem's deployment of these images—describes as chasing "a chain of similes into a verbal whirlpool."[59] This is not so very far from the hyperbole of Job's "streams of oil" (*palgê šāmen*, Job 29:6) or Ezekiel's likening of rivers to flowing oil (*wěnahărôtām kaššemen ʾôlîk* lit. "like oil I cause their rivers to flow," Ezek 32:14).[60] Energy and force—the raw stuff of movement—are at the heart of "life" (ḥayyîm), which is the ultimate blessing of the poem (v. 3) and, interestingly, a figure of choice in the Hebrew Bible for rendering "running, fresh water," that is, "living water" (mayim ḥayyîm, e.g., Gen 26:19; Lev 14:5; Jer 2:13).

Poetic imagery is not monolithic—especially that which is rooted in oral tradition where it is characteristically "protean." If the oil's treacly movement is figuratively and literally critical to how this poem gets from beginning to end, other sensorial dimensions of the image are important to the poem as well and also would likely have been elicited in the minds of ancient auditors—especially given traditional meaning's typical metonymic bent. Two stand out. Touch is one of the actual consequences of oil poured on the head. The experiencer feels the oil as it comes in contact with the hair follicles and oozes down over ears, forehead, and face (or as here, over the beard). Oil has a palpable tactility about it. Though it is vain to try to contain oil in the human hand (Prov 27:16), it is soft and soothing to the hand's touch (Isa 1:6; Ps 55:22; Prov 5:3), a well-known healer's balm (Isa 1:6; cf. Ezek 16:8);[61] it moistens, soaks (bw') into the body (Ps 104:15). Oil can be collected in jars (nbl šmn, throughout the Samaria ostraca) and then handled and handed over (Arad 17.rev.1–2). And not only is there feel but there is smell, too. The finest oils are fine in part because of their sweet fragrance (Song 1:3; 4:10; cf. Qoh 10:1; cf. LXX's myron). The highly figured representation of the male lover's beard in Song 5:13 precisely accents the beard's pleasing erotic scent—presumably reflecting the fact that the beard would have been routinely oiled as with other parts of the body. These tactile and olfactory dimensions of the image flood in mostly through cognitive (and extratextual) associations, the poem's auditors calling to mind (or projecting from) their own practical experiences with olive oil as the latter is evoked in the words of the poem.[62] And thus, the image of cascading oil not only lends an energetic substantiality to the psalm (however viscous) but also sensualizes the poem's meaning, literally making it sensible, available to and through the senses—here to and through touch and smell as conjured in human mental activity and practical experience.

The addition of a second couplet in verse 2 forms what may be described as a kind of run-on simile, a simile in which the original meaning or imagery is expanded in some way, or even moves off in an entirely new direction. In either case, the expansion takes its cue from some aspect or element of the simile proper.[63] In this case the tag element is the term zāqān "beard," which takes on a specific identity, as belonging to Aaron. The major interpretive issue raised in the secondary literature concerns the nature of this new, run-on part of the image. Does the image of overflowing oil continue, the oil now running down Aaron's beard (as the dew in v. 3 will flow from Hermon to Zion)?[64] Or is an overflowing, and thus full, beard now in view, with the beard itself running down over Aaron's robes?[65] That is, is the antecedent of *šeyyōrēd* the phrase *šemen haṭṭôb*, or is it *zĕqan-ʾahărōn*? Linguistically, both are possible.[66] The latter is more proximate, and it is often the case that dependent relative clauses follow closely on their antecedents in biblical Hebrew. On this reading a full beard that runs down over the collar is imagined.[67] It was customary for mature Israelite and Judahite males, as elsewhere in the Levant and Mesopotamia, to wear a beard. The biblical text simply presumes the presence of a beard on adult males (e.g., Lev 13:29), but aside from a few prohibitions (addressed to both priests and laity) against shaving specfically in relation to rites for the dead (Lev 19:27–28; 21:5; Deut 14:1; Ezek 44:20), there is little of a descriptive nature that might help us visualize how the beard was actually worn.

Nonetheless, hair, in general, because it continues to grow throughout life, was considered by the ancients as one seat of human vitality and life force (so Samson), and, as J. Milgrom reminds us, in some ancient societies, including Israel, more particularly "the beard was the prized symbol of manhood."[68] To have it forcibly shaved off was a great disgrace and humiliation (esp. 2 Sam 10:4; cf. Isa 7:20). In fact, in one of Sennacherib's inscriptions, the king boasts of cutting off his enemies' "beards" (here *sapsapāte* lit. "lower lip") and thereby destroying their "vitality, life force" (Akk. *baštu/baltu*; see *CAD* B, 143a; S, 167a). Accordingly, I. Winter, commenting specifically on the ideological significance of the representation of the king in the Stela of Naram-Sin (fig. 46), suggests that "what is manifest in men's beards...is precisely their fully developed manhood."[69] And it is very much the case that representations of the king in Mesopotamia standardly depict him with a full beard (fig. 47). Indeed, as O. Keel remarks,[70] gods, kings, and dignitaries are commonly shown with a full beard in the art of the ancient Near East (down through the end of the Persian period, see fig. 48). Even in Egypt, where it was more customary to shave, the pharaohs are frequently depicted with fake, ceremonial beards (fig. 49).[71] Western Asiatics (e.g., Canaanites, Arameans, Ammonites) in Egyptian representations are often shown with beards that "as a rule" fall down over the neckline. And similar beards are donned by the prostrate Jehu and the Israelite porters on the Black Obelisk (figs. 50–51), as well as by the adult male Judahite prisoners in the Lachish reliefs (fig. 52).

In sum, as Keel contends,[72] there may well be an intentional evocation of a long, flowing beard here. That is, the evocation of Aaron in particular is meant to summon the (ideal) image of a hoary old Israelite cultural icon, with the beard itself symbolizing vigor and vitality, just as with the flowing oil earlier. Note, to this end, that the appositional structure (i.e., "beard, / beard of"; especially as accented in MT)[73] extends by a whole again the physical length of the beard's linguistic representation in the poem. That is, length of the beard is effectively mimed in its very linguistic representation, as the Hebrew word for beard, *zāqān*, is repeated, resounded.

Still, as Berlin observes with regard to the phrase *kaššemen haṭṭôb*, "it is, of course, not necessary or even desirable to limit the sense of a poetic image."[74] Multivalence, after all, is one of the hallmarks of the poetic the world over. That the image of overflowing oil is here evoked alongside that of a beard running down a man's cheeks and chin remains an attractive possibility. There is no syntactic obstacle inhibiting *šeyyōrēd* from picking up on the less proximate antecedent *šemen haṭṭôb*.[75] And several of the poem's nonsemantic features positively coerce such a reading. In particular, the repetition of *zāqān* and the phrase *yōrēd ʿal* strongly compels auditors to assume the continuation (repetition) of the same subject matter, flowing oil. That the oil now spills down the beard and over the robe's collar seems only natural—indeed, the two images, flowing beard and flowing oil, fit well together and to some extent have already been given in the first couplet of verse 2, namely *oil* flowing over a *beard*. The continuation of the oil image is consistent, as well, with the prominence of liquified imagery in this poem more generally and follows, straightforwardly, as a consequence of the poem's informing enjambment—that is, the oil and dew follow in the wake, as it were, of the syntax's pronounced pull forward. Finally, besides the fact that nowhere in the Bible are there explicit references focusing on length as a notable characteristic of beards, the one other time that *y-r-d* is used in connection with a beard, it describes the spittle that runs down David's beard in 1 Samuel 21:14 (as he pretends to be mad): *wayyôred rîrô ʾel-zěqānô* "and let his spittle run down his beard" (NRSV). Such usage makes it extremely difficult to ignore the strong attraction of the oil image in this context. Thus, imagery, line play, word repetition, and diction all conspire to keep the image of flowing oil before the auditor's consciousness.[76]

If the question of *šeyyōrēd* and its antecedent(s) has preoccupied scholars' philological interests, it is surely the identification of the beard as belonging to Aaron that is the most striking aspect of the couplet. To this point the imagery has been nonspecific—unnamed brothers living together somewhere, oil, even the finest olive oil, poured over the head and beard of an unidentified man. Against such a background the sudden mention of a specific and even legendary figure commands attention.[77] But to what effect? Aside from his ability to speak (*kî dabbēr yědabbēr hûʾ*, Exod 4:14), which could resonate, though most obliquely, with the "pleasing words" of the song itself (as in Ps 45:2, *dābār ṭôb*; cf. 1 Kgs 12:7; 18:24; 2 Kgs 20:19; Zech 1:13; Ps 141:6; Prov 12:25; 15:23), Aaron is not known for any outstanding physical attribute, such as the beauty of David's ruddy skin (1 Sam 17:42) or the disfigurement of Mephibosheth's crippled feet (2 Sam 4:4). In fact, the biblical tradition pays no attention whatsoever to Aaron's physicality, suggesting that the reference here to Aaron's beard in one respect is conventional (traditional) and iconic, following the representational trajectory better witnessed to in the two- and three-dimensioned representational art from the wider ancient Near East. This is not to downplay the beard's symbolic significance—a specific emblem of (manly) vitality and weal, as suggested by Milgrom, Winter, and others. To the contrary, the identification of the beard as belonging to Aaron, a cultural hero remembered as one of Israel's founding patriarchs (alongside Moses; Num 33:1; Josh 24:5; 1 Sam 12:6, 8; Mic 6:4; Ps 77:21; 105:26) and first chief priest (Num 18:1; Josh 21:13; Ps 99:6; Ezra 7:5; Neh 10:39; 1 Chron 6:34; 24:19; 2 Chron 31:19), only heightens this symbolism. This is not just any beard but the beard of Aaron. And thus the poem's high arc of hyperbole continues still, the mention of Aaron upping the rhetorical ante just as in the opening couplet's surfeit of exultation, the specification of an overabundance of fine virgin olive oil, and the mimetic figuration (through repetition) of a doubly long beard. Even the momentary fixation on the anointing of Aaron as high priest (Exod 29:7; Lev 8:12),[78] which his naming here elicits allusively, retrospectively, traditionally, follows this same trajectory, the already buoyant and beatific image of anointing becoming itself bathed in the extra specialness of a treasured sacral moment.

Such specificity appears to flood the second half of this little poem—Aaron, Hermon, Zion (note the /-ōn/ ending that sonically links the three), though always from the background; that is, the poetic focus stays trained specifically on the *beard* of Aaron, the *dew* of Hermon, and the *mountains* of Zion. Still, this turn away from the hitherto abiding anonymity is unmistakable, and the poem's second (explicit) simile, that of dew, as a consequence, takes shape against a more immediately recognizable backdrop. Its chief effect is to draw the audience in, quicken their attention, through the force of familiar names and places. The image itself—dew—maintains the poem's liquid texture, with the repetition of the comparative *kĕ*- unleashing, as it were, a new surge of watery energy. The less viscous nature of dew itself, along with the final repetition of *y-r-d*, gives the strong impression of increased velocity and force— necessary, perhaps, to propel the dew (and auditor, too) down its imaginary course from Hermon to Zion. Dew, "the deposit of water droplets on objects the surface of which is sufficiently cool, generally by nocturnal radiation, to bring about the direct condensation of water vapour from the surrounding air,"[79] provides a critical water source in the subtropical and semiarid climate regimes that typify most of the Levant (especially important during the dry season).[80] And though specific dewfall amounts and incidences vary across the region (due to any number of local factors, such as season, cloud cover, wind influence, ground canopy, relative humidity), the steady, moist prevailing west winds from the Mediterranean ensure a relatively stable number of dew events in general, and in some places (e.g., Jerusaelm) the disposition amounts are relatively high.[81] The ancients were well aware of this critical importance. Job uses the image of nightly dew on branches to figure his prior vigor and vitality (29:19; cf. Hos 14:6; Zech 8:12; Prov 19:12). The regularity and plenitude of dewfall was one of the characteristics of the land that made it so attractive for human habitation and therefore worthy of celebration:

> So Israel lives in safety,
> untroubled is Jacob's abode
> in a land of grain and wine,
> where the heavens drop down dew. (Deut 33:28; cf. Zech 8:12)

Indeed, dew, as a gift from the heavens (*tal haššāmayim* "dew of heaven," Gen 27:28, 39; Deut 33:13; Hag 1:10; cf. Dan 4:12; Ug. *ṭl šmm*, CAT 1.3.II.39) with no dependence on human agency (Mic 5:6; cf. Exod 16:13–14; Num 11:9), was thought of as a blessing of the gods and often factored itself as a blessing (Gen 27:28; Deut 33:13), a wishing well (cf. Isa 26:19; Hos 14:5) and its lack as a curse (2 Sam 1:21; 1 Kgs 17:1). The mention of Yahweh's commanded blessing in the immediately following lines will focus more precisely (if retrospectively) on this aspect of dew's symbolism. Other characteristics traded on in biblical images are dew's nightly regularity (Exod 16:13; Num 11:9; Judg 6:37–38, 40; 2 Sam 17:12; Ps 110:3; Job 29:19; Song 5:2), refreshing quality (Deut 32:2; Prov 19:12; Sir 43:2), typical heaviness (Judg 6:38; 2 Sam 17:12), relatively quick evaporation (Hos 6:4; 13:3), and formation into droplets (Job 38:28; Song 5:2).

In Psalm 133 it is as an emblem of weal and well-being that the image of cascading dew registers initially, especially coming so close on the beatific evocation of a superfluity of the finest virgin olive oil in verse 2. In fact, M. Dahood may be correct that the joining here of bountiful images of oil and dew is not all happenstance.[82] As he notices, the phrasing echoes closely the parallelism between *šmn arṣ* "the oil of earth" and *ṭl šmm* "the dew of heaven" that is found at least twice in the mythological texts from ancient Ugarit (CAT 1.3.II.39; IV.43):

[t]ḥspn.mh.wtrḥṣ	[She] draws water and washes
[ṭ]l.šmm.šmn.arṣ.	[With D]ew of Heaven, Oil of Earth
rbb [r]kb.ʿrpt.	Showers of the Cloud[r]ider (CAT 1.3.II.38–40)[83]

The dew and oil (and also rain showers) are (hyperbolic) figures for Anat's bath water (*mh*) mentioned in the first line of the triplet (cf. CAT 1.6.III.6–7). A probable biblical reflex of this same phrasing comes in Genesis 27:28:

wĕyitten-lĕkā hāʾĕlōhîm	May God give to you
miṭṭal haššāmayim	from the dew of heaven
ûmišmānê[84] *hāʾāreṣ*	and from the oil(s) of the land
wĕrob dāgān wĕtîrōš	and much grain and wine, too.

Only here the "dew of heaven" and "oil of earth" would appear to be far more literal in nature,[85] uttered as a part of a "fertility blessing," a wishing of weal that makes good sense in a traditional agricultural setting (see esp. the matching characterization of the land in Deut 33:28). So the knowing auditor of Psalm 133 will not only appreciate the distinct symbolism of each of the poem's focal similes but will also hear something of the tradition's long habit of twinning the two images as a merism of plenitude—bounty from above and from below (esp. Hag 1:10; Deut 33:13). The melding of the two liquids prompted by the poem's repetitive phrasing, then, also has deeper informing roots.

The poem's rhetoric continues its hyperbolic reach. The dew, like the oil and beard before it, though of ordinary stuff (here another inflection of the quotidian that circulates through the images in the psalm) cannot be truly ordinary but in the end also must be exceptional in some way. The exceptionality in this case is achieved through association with Mount Hermon, the high (ca. 2,814 meters), southernmost part of the Anti-Lebanon range, whose snowcapped peaks are visible to many parts of Palestine. Literally, dewfall in the Hermon is renowned for its copiousness, especially below the snowline.[86] So the "dew of Hermon" is a literal cipher for heavy dew disposition. But beyond actual dewfall amounts, this dew gains a certain exceptionality from Hermon's stunning iconicity. It is surely the iconic image of this mountain, with its imposing height and the hoary beauty of its high peaks covered almost year round with snow (so it is called in Arabic *Jabal al-Thalj*, "snowy mountain"; cf. Aram. *ṭwr tlgh*, Tg. *Onq.* Deut 3:9; Tg. *Cant.* 4:8), always present, whether up close or off on the horizon, perpetually a part of the area's landscape, perpetually providing sensory input (conscious and otherwise) to the viewer's visual system, that impresses itself most tenaciously and pervasively on the imaginations of any who have visited or lived in the region. And the views from Hermon are equally magnificent and stunning. In the Bible Hermon most frequently serves to demarcate the furthest reaches of Israel's northern extremity (Deut 3:8; 4:48; Josh 11:3, 17; 12:1,5; 13:5, 11; 1 Chron 5:23).[87] But some glimpse of its iconicity may be seen in Psalm 89:13, where, along with Tabor, the mountain is imagined as hymning Yahweh as creator. The sense of this passage must be something like the idea that even the most extraordinary landmasses in the region celebrate Yahweh and Yahweh's marvelous deeds—of which, of course, they would be a part. It may also be that the two mountains were themselves thought of as the homes of deities (e.g., the mountain of Baal Hermon, Judg 3:3),[88] as was customary in the ancient Levant, adding to their specialness. In other words, it would not suffice, given the psalm's hymnic ambitions here, to have just any place personified. What is called for are locales whose specialness befits the specialness of the one hymned. And therefore, however ultimately resistant to precise calculation, the dew in Psalm 133 sparkles (cf. Isa 26:19) ever more brilliantly because it is linked with Hermon.

The last repetition of *yōrēd*, finely balanced at the line's end, can be heard in two ways. Since the ancients understood dew to be a meteorological phenomenon related to rain (esp. 1 Kgs 17:1; Mic 5:6; Prov 3:20; CAT 1.19.I.44; *Sanh.* 96b(52); *FPT* Deut 23:28[04]), they conceptualized it, like rain, as water that falls down (specifically with *y-r-d* in Num 11:9; cf. Deut 32:2; 33:28; 2 Sam 17:12; Job 38:28; Prov 3:20; Dan 4:12) from the heavens (esp. Zech 8:12). This lexical association between the verb *y-r-d* and the noun *ṭal* is troubled initially by phrasing and syntax. The phrase "dew of Hermon" is itself a little surprising and even puzzling when heard instead of the commonplace "dew of heaven" (Gen 27:28, 39; Deut 33:13; Hag 1:10; cf. Dan 4:12; Ug. *ṭl šmm*, CAT 1.3.II.39) and the role that the phrase plays—goal, as would be more natural, or source—is not clarified until the prepositional object is given in the second line of the couplet. When the prepositional phrase does come ("upon the mountains of Zion"), it becomes apparent that Hermon is the source of the dew that descends on Zion. Here the more natural *y-r-d*-ing of dew (i.e., falling out of the sky like rain) gives way to an image of the dew collected (cf. Judg 6:37–40) in the Hermon streaming (somehow) down onto Zion. Auditors now feel the force of the earlier image of oil running down over head and beard, as well as the general association of the Lebanon and Anti-Lebanon mountains as a source of flowing water (e.g., Song 4:15)—the runoff from the Hermon, of course, actually feeds the headwaters of the Jordan, hence the "waters of the Jordan" (*mê hayyardēn*) literally "run down" (*yôrĕdîm*) from their source "above" (*milmāʿlâ*; Josh 3:13; cf. Ps 42:7).

Having the dew spill down onto Zion some hundreds of kilometers to the south is a fabulous image.[89] It accentuates the already high hyperbole and at the same time concretizes the image of superfluity, measures it, makes it is graspable, imaginable to the mind's eye. And as a felicitous consequence, the several ridges on which the ancient city of Jerusalem is situated (cf. Ps 125:2), rising no higher than eight hundred meters, are made more noble, more majestic as they are bathed in the superabundance of Hermon's copious dewfall. The magnificence imparted through this association is not unlike that when Zion elsewhere (Ps 48:3) is imagined to rival in height the loftiest peaks of the towering Mount Zaphon—present-day Mount Cassius (Ab. *Jabal al-'Aqra'*) on the north Syrian coast, which rises some 1,950 meters above sea level.[90] And all three mountains are divine mountains, homes to local deities,[91] and thus it is no surprise that this spilling over of dew onto Zion ultimately leads to Yahweh's blessing in the psalm's closing triplet—according to the old Zion tradition, one of the more felicitous consequences of Yahweh's residence on Zion is the beneficence and weal—the blessing (cf. Ps 128:5; 134:3; 135:21; Jer 31:23)—that devolves to Zion's inhabitants.[92]

III

Beyond a shared interest in aspects of everyday life, there is little of substance in the content of the two similes in Psalm 133:2–3—one involving fine oil, the other dew—that necessarily connects them with the exaltation in 133:1.[93] Rather, the connection lies in syntax and the force of juxtaposition, word repetition (*ṭôb*) and plays (the echoing of *šebet* in *kaššemen*), and perhaps even a common rhetoric of extravagance. To what end? Surely, A. Weiser is correct in thinking that auditors are won over to the poem's opening exclamation (in part) precisely "by means of" the "colourful images" of fine oil and dew.[94] But the latter do not only illustrate the "harmonious beauty and charm" exclaimed in verse 1, though they do that, they concretize it, making it sensual (through figures of taste, feel, smell, and sight) and thus sensible, imaginable. What is key, then, is the combination of exclamation *and* similes. A great deal of what this poem achieves comes about expressly through the joining of elements, emerges in the uninscribed space between the poem's entexted words[95] and in the time that elapses during the song's performance.[96] R. P. Blackmur observes in a comment on a similar figure in Wallace Stevens's poem "The Death of a Soldier" that what is achieved is "not exactly in the words" themselves but "because of them."[97] The force of the similes in our little poem is not so much "for example" but "just like" or "as" (in Hebrew, literally *kě-*), and because of them the exclamation in verse 1 ("how good...!") is fitted out with qualities and feelings that ornament and bolster the traditional sentiment. That is, the goodness of brothers dwelling together is beyond the sense of the actual words used to express it. What is good and praiseworthy is made known and knowable, finds its purchase in the variable sensibilities (as traced here)

conjured by a superfluity of fine virgin olive oil and the fecundity of overflowing dew. This extraordinary goodness—trebly hyped—is the goodness of
"good oil," its feel and smell, its rich associations of richness, daily sufficiency,
a life well and long lived with family and among the gods, against the majestic
backdrop of snowcapped Hermon and amid the surety of life promised in the
dewy runoff so abundant that it finds a catch-point even amid the hills of
Zion. This begins to approach—*but only approach!*—the goodness and pleasantness of "brothers dwelling together" hymned in this psalm. What is here
put in words, then, as Blackmur observes, is at the same time put "beyond
words and beyond the sense of words,"[98] and herein lies the second "way" of
this poem and the words out of which it is made—and thus of poetry (written
and oral) more broadly, too. That is, I want to claim for poetry—and here specifically biblical Hebrew poetry—the critical importance of its way of saying
and what emerges as a product of that saying, a saying that necessarily says
things one way—with specifc words—and not another, chooses in this case to
think goodness and pleasantness of family, an image that itself is already
given very particularly, namely "brothers living together," through selected
images of fine virgin olive oil, a long flowing beard, and heavy Mediterranean
dewfall, and as a result gives rise to an idea, a sensibility, a knowing above and
beyond (but always in light of, too) what is literally said (namely the goodness,
etc.) that is new—that does not exist apart from this (particular) way of saying
it, in these words—and not new—that is traditional and protean, that leverages knowledge and ideas that are well known. To ventriloquize Blackmur one
last time, "we cannot say abstractly, in words, any better what we know" about
this goodness and pleasantness, "yet the knowledge has become positive and
the conviction behind it indestructible, because it has been put into words,"
into these specific words in this most particular way.[99]

IV

But this is not yet the end of the poem (or my reading of it), though the change
in feel and form of the final three lines[100] signals an impending ending:

kî šām[101] *ṣiwwâ*	There[102] Yahweh
yhwh ʾet-habbĕrākâ	commands the blessing—
ḥayyîm[103] *ʿad-hāʿôlām*[104]	life always!

Compact to this point, orchestrated around the patterned play of couplets, the
psalm now uncoils just a bit, as the closing declaration ("there Yahweh commands the blessing, life always") spreads out over three lines instead of two,

the extended reach enabled by the added bulk of the so-called prose particles (e.g., *ha-*, *'et-*).[105] And the syntax here, still enjambed but now unfettered by the earlier lines' rhetoric of repetition, straightens out noticeably, becoming more obviously sententious, plainer even—standard prose word order (VSO) prevails. With these subtle changes as signal guides—terminal modification is a quintessential mechanism of closure[106]—the poem glides to its seemingly inevitable (*'ad-hā'ōlām* "always") close.[107]

Beyond implications of closure (cf. Isa 5:7; Ps 1:6; 2:11; 4:9; 5:13; 82:8; 127:5; Job 3:25; Lam 5:22), the force of *kî* here may be taken asseveratively (esp. Gen 22:17; Deut 2:7; 1 Sam 26:16; Isa 1:27, 29–30; 7:15–16; Jer 22:5, 24; 31:18–19; Amos 4:2; Ps 49:16; 77:12; Lam 3:22)[108]—in which case we have yet one further (obvious) inflection of the poem's rhetoric of extravagance—or logically and causally (esp. Gen 11:9; 21:31; Num 11:34; 2 Sam 1:21; Joel 4:12),[109] wherein the simile-laden goodness so far hymned is provided with a kind of explanation, one loaded (the citation of divine blessing) such that it will brook no argument.[110] And I see no reason why both senses are not to be heard here. But in either case (or even in both cases) the extended *kî* clause itself motivates what precedes it. Its target may be construed locally, as modifying the immediately preceding image (esp. 2 Sam 1:21; Joel 4:12).[111] The poet/singer has already used a run-on simile with regard to the elaboration of the beard as belonging to Aaron, so to see another here is unproblematic. The "there" (*šām*), then, on this reading would point back explicitly to the "mountains of Zion."[112] Most often the antecedent of this deictic particle (*šām*) in biblical Hebrew is local and proximate. And, of course, it is precisely from Zion (most especially in the so-called Zion tradition),[113] the mountain home of Yahweh, that the deity's commands and teachings are issued (Isa 2:1–4) and a bounteous life promised for Zion's inhabitants (Ps 48:12–14; 132:13–18; 147:12–20; Isa 33:17–24). In fact, *šām* echoes through several of the psalms in the small collection of Songs of Ascents (Ps 122:4, 5; 132:17), each time referencing Zion/Jerusalem, and thus *šām* is given a most specific semantic gloss as it is read across the surface of this particular sequence of poems.[114] Further, the blessing of Yahweh is a motif that bunches noticeably toward the latter part of the Songs of Ascents (Ps 128:4, 5; 129:8; 132:15; 134:3). And twice again is the source of this divine blessing specifically located in Zion (Ps 128:5; 134:3), with the last notice in Psalm 134:3, which itself actually closes the sequence as a whole.[115] The blessing that is in focus in these poems is often exemplified more specifically. So, for example, in Psalm 128 it results in goodness and prosperity (vv. 2, 5) for Jerusalem, epitomized by a flourishing family, that is, projecting the ideal three-generation household ("May you see your children's children," Ps 128:6). In Psalm 132 on the other hand Yahweh's blessing is parsed more politically and includes the promise of food for the hungry (v. 15). In Psalm 133 the content of the blessing Yahweh commands is spelled out most proximately in the immediately following line that concludes the poem: "life always" (*ḥayyîm ʿad-hāʿôlām*). The phrase is stacked paratactically in apposition next to *ʾet-habbĕrākâ*, literally as if it were a gloss.[116] This is the psalm's second significant use of apposition, the first coming back in verse 2 and there also straddling a line boundary, namely *hazzāqān / zĕqan ʾaḥărōn*. This is not the "eternal life" of later tradition (only in Dan 12:2)[117] but the finite existence (i.e., life and not death, cf. Deut 30:15–20) that Yahweh, "maker of heaven and earth" (Ps 134:3), established and blessed for human beings. Psalm 21:5 more explicitly glosses this notion of "life" with the standard royal leitmotif of "length of days" (e.g., *KAI* 4.5–6; 5.2; 6.2–3; cf. Deut 30:20; *TAD* A4.7.3), days, it is often implied, which are also full, abundant, satisfying.[118] The expression "forever and ever" in that psalm is well explained by P. Craigie as implying "that such life would extend into the future as far as conceivable."[119] This is the basic sense of *ʿôlām* more generally—especially apparent in the legal literature from around the ancient Near East[120]—and it holds for the expression in Psalm 133: life, good and whole and abundant, for as long into the future as possible, unto such a time that is not presently conceivable.

Šām has a less proximate antecedent as well. This one cued by the ears, through the voiced quality of the word itself. The /-ām/ sound of *šām*'s single syllable, redoubled and thus sonically underscored in the /-ām/ of the triplet's (and poem's) final syllable, *ʿôlām*, echos the /-am/ of *gam* in the poem's opening couplet. An alertness to the possibility of sound play is provoked, however briefly, in the rhyming /-ōn/ endings that connect the three named figures in the body of the poem—*ʾaḥărōn, ḥermôn, ṣiyyôn*. But for the most part, at least to this point, the poem's play with sound happens covertly, piggybacking, as it were, on the poem's more overt play of word (and phrase) iteration, namely *ṭôb // ṭôb, yōrēd // yōrēd // yōrēd, še- // še-, zāqān // zĕqan, kĕ- // ka-, ʿal // ʿal // ʿal // ʿal*. And yet once the ear hearkens back to that initial couplet it will hear the rhyme and chime of other sounds, too, chains of sound (to match the word chains already noticed) that appear to reach back over the body of similes to link the opening couplet to the closing triplet: the final /-â/ in *ṣiwwâ* and *habbĕrākâ* echoing the doubled *mah* in verse 1 and the /-îm/ of the plural morpheme in *ḥayyîm* resounding in the /-îm/ of *nāʿîm* and *ʾaḥîm*.[121] Repetition here, too, is the means by which these sounds re-sound across the surface of the poem, the hearing of them helped by the absence of word-final /-am/, /-â/, and /-îm/ in the body of the poem. Thus, in addition to the sheer pleasantness of this burble of sound, auditors are seduced by its thrum into hearing the closing *kî* clause as if in answer to the psalm's initial exclamation:

Wow, how exquisite and how pleasant is
the dwelling of brothers all together—
…
—there Yahweh
commands the blessing—
life always!

The "there" of the divine blessing so heard resides, it now seems clear, also
in the brothers' residing (together).[122] That is, family, literally and in its many
possible metaphorical and metonymic extensions, is one place where Yahweh's blessing of life is made manifest (e.g., Gen 12:2; 2 Sam 7:29; Zech 8:13;
Ps 37:26). The household and family life are valorized elsewhere in the Songs
of Ascents (esp. Ps 127 and 128). In fact, the image of the happy household
conjured in Psalm 128:3 is explicitly linked to divine blessing in the very next
line: *hinnê kî-kēn yĕbōrak* "Wow! Surely thus will he be blessed" (Ps 128:4).
And then an even more resonant triplet follows in verse 5: "May Yahweh bless
you from Zion / and may you see in goodness (*bĕṭûb*) Jerusalem / all the days
of your life." Hence, it is hard not to hear in Psalm 133's vocalic valorization of
family the tradition's long pattern of linking family and blessing, a pattern
that itself reaches back as far as Israel's earliest ancestral memories, to the
household of Abraham, whom Yahweh promises to make into a great nation
(*gôy gādôl*) and to bless and through whom, through this political household,[123]
Yahweh promises as well to bless "all the families [*mišpĕḥōt*] of the earth" (Gen
12:1–3)—"I will bless you [*'ăbārekkă*]...that you will be a blessing [*bĕrākâ*]."[124]
And so H. W. Wolff may famously conclude: "'Blessing' becomes the catch-
word of the whole of Israel's history."[125] And if we listen hard enough, we may
even hear in this commanded blessing the murmured *kî-ṭôb ... kî-ṭôb ... kî-
ṭôb ... kî-ṭôb ... kî-ṭôb ... kî-ṭôb ... wĕhinnê ṭôb mĕ'ōd* that Elohim pronounces
over all creation, all life (Gen 1). This is the very stuff of tradition and a paradigm of the echoic poetics of traditional verbal art.

Here, then, several other ways by which poetry—and this poem in particular—means come into view. The way of sound, as it infects and affects thought
and sense, Culler observes, is precisely one of the scandals of lyric verse.[126] In
this case, the "chaos of paronomasia, sound-links, ambiguous sense-links,
and memory-links" (to borrow N. Frye's words) refocuses the site of blessing
in the psalm (euphonically relocating its *šām* in the opening couplet's *gam*)
and at the same time discloses an alternative formal structure operative in the
poem. With *šām*'s most proximate antecedent uppermost in mind (i.e., the
"mountains of Zion"), the poem may be read (and heard) as consisting of an
opening exclamation followed by two run-on similes.[127] Yet when the links of

sound are noticed, the initial couplet and closing triplet resolve into a frame, enveloping the images of oil, beard, and dew.¹²⁸ Such framing is common-place in biblical poems (and sections of poems), a traditional technique rooted in oral art, occurring in numerous guises, such as the refrain of Psalm 8 (*yhwh 'dnynw / mh-'dyr šmk / bkl-h'rṣ*, vv. 2, 10), the intentionally not-quite-perfect inclusio of Song 4:1–7 (*hinnāk yāpâ ra'yātî / hinnāk yāpâ // kullăk yāpâ ra'yātî / ûmûm 'ên bāk*), and the set of couplets (vv. 3, 10) that enclose (and extin-guish) the chaos of triplets in the first section of Job 3 (vv. 3–10). Exclamations, vocatives, and hortatory gestures of various sorts not infrequently find their warrant in a *kî* clause, a pattern that may be exploited for structural purposes, as in the (imperative) hymn of praise (e.g., Ps 100, 117) or Job's "curse of the day" (3:3–10). And if *šām* routinely takes a local and proximate antecedent in standard biblical Hebrew usage, it may also point more remotely and even generically. The triply repeated *šām* in Job 3:17 and 19 is a parade example. For the "there" in question is surely the underworld figured throughout this sec-tion of the poem (vv. 11–19) though nowhere precisely named.¹²⁹ That is, *šām* in that poem has no single linguistic item to which it literally points, and so the antecedent does not lie in any of the actual words of the poem but in what those words imagine, create, conjure. Similarly remote is the antecedent of the sequence of *šām... šammâ... šām* in Isaiah 34:14–15 (cf. v. 12), which ultimately refers back to Edom, named explicitly only at the beginning of the oracle (Isa 34:5–6) but referenced throughout by a web of third person feminine forms, especially pronominal suffixes. *Kî šām // kî šāmâ* in the shorter-compassed Psalms 137 (v. 3) and 122 (v. 5), which are more generally reminiscent of Psalm 133, also ultimately find their antecedents less proximately, though in these instances the identity of each antecedent is hardly in doubt.¹³⁰

Once cued to the more expansive purview of Yahweh's blessing in the poem, it may also occur to some auditors—especially those steeped in the stories and poems of ancient Israel and Judah, in their songs, psalmody, pro-verbial lore, and even royal annals—that fine olive oil (Deut 8:6–10; 33:24; cf. 28:1–15) and copious dew (Gen 27:28, 39; Deut 33:13; Zech 8:12–13; cf. Deut 28:1–15; Judg 6:37–38; Hos 14:6; Prov 19:12) are themselves often thought of as a blessing or the marks thereof. Indeed, Hermon and Zion as divine moun-tains are inherently blessed (cf. Gen 49:26; Jer 31:23), or more properly, become sites of blessing as a felicitous consequence of their divine resident(s), and sites from which blessings are effected (Ps 128:5; 134:3; 135:2; cf. Deut 27:2; Josh 8:33).¹³¹ Aaron, too, is a (verbal) source of blessing (Lev 9:22), and his posterity, the "house of Aaron," even attracts blessing (Ps 115:12; 135:19), and blessings may themselves be characterized as "good" (Ps 21:4; Prov 24:25).¹³² And thus here again a glimpse may be had of how biblical Hebrew poems through their words (and the worlds they open onto) can achieve something more than what those words literally say. It is as if once commanded by Yahweh the blessing is released and ricochets,[133] echoically or retrospectively,[134] back through the psalm, pinball fashion, hitting and catching hold on words (momentarily) wherever it might, first through the attraction of sound and then through a rich if spasmodic and nonlinear array of association and implication.[135] There is a substance and density that lyric verse takes on "by virtue of the quickenings or subtle gradations of sense established by the choice of words and the patterns they enter into—as overt syntax and as elements thickening the texture of the attitudes projected by such gradations."[136] As a consequence, any fully empathetic, close reading of single items in a poem, words in particular, but also images, sounds, rhythms, and the like, will always require attending to their potential resonances, both prospective and retrospective; a detailed following out, that is, of the multiple, often discontinuous, and complex meanderings of sense and sensibility that are enacted in the event of the poem.[137] This, too, is a prototypical way of poetry, and of (oral and oral-derived) lyric poetry most especially.

It is worth stressing here one last time that even this more capacious purview of *šām* as staged in MT is itself a matter of words and their specific deployment, performance. This may be appreciated most spectacularly from a comparison with the song as inscribed in 11QPs[a]. I have noted (mostly in the notes) a number of variations from MT present in the latter version of the psalm. The most significant comes at the end. 11QPs[a] reads *hr ṣywn* instead of the more enigmatic *har(ĕ)rê ṣiyyôn* of MT—clearly identifying the mountain of Israel and Judah's God—and then subtly (so subtle that scholars have not seemed to notice) but substantially rewriting (and thus reperforming) the closing triplet:

ky šmh ṣwh yhwh	For there YHWH commanded
't hbrkh 'd 'wlm	the blessing forever:
šlwm 'l yśr'l	"Peace (be) upon Israel!"

Here the local construal of *šām*'s (or **šammâ*'s, as the case may be) antecedent is ramified. The sound play that cues auditors to hear other, earlier possibilities for the location of *šām* in MT are all but obliterated in 11QPs[a]. The chain of /-īm/'s is no more; the echoing of /-ām/, though still to be heard in **šammâ* and *'ôlam*, is a bit more muffled, lacking its pounding, word-final accent; and the extra emphasis given to /-ā/ (*šmh, ṣwh, hbrkh*) seems as much to keep attention focused on this ending as pointing back to the beginning. As a consequence readers and auditors do not quite have the aural impetus for rethinking

the location of *šammâ. Neither is the notion of "blessing" ignited and allowed to bounce around the poem as in MT. And not only is the "blessing" not
glossed with the notion of "life" (as in MT), or even conjoined with it (as in
LXX, Syr., and Tg.), but it now becomes a placeholder, a name for what then is
exemplified, given as the blessing, which is now literally pronounced: "Peace
(be) upon Israel!" Thus, the closing of the song in 11QPs^a is completely different. The whole can only have the shape of an exclamation followed by two
run-on similes. The triplet, as in the version reflected in MT, swerves away
from the patterned repetition of couplets, but in a more complicated fashion.
The lines ky šmh ṣwh yhwh / 't hbrkh 'd 'wlm themselves could have formed a
couplet (cf. Ps 72:19; 145:1), with 'd 'wlm (as 'ad-hā'ôlām in MT) providing the
underscored force of closure through allusion to the very epitome of termination and extremity, the future that cannot yet be foreseen (namely "until such
a time …"). The addition of šlwm 'l yśr'l, then, creates the triplet and effects the
swerve away from the poem's prevailing pattern of couplets. The citation itself
redoubles the closing gesture, as similarly in Psalms 125:5 and 128:6.[38] The
poem ends most emphatically with Yahweh's blessing ringing forth: "Peace
(be) upon Israel!"

     And so, too, I hope my own point rings forth equally eloquently: the chance
for Yahweh's blessing to reverberate back through the poem as given in MT,
for the "thereness" of šām to acquire its more capacious purview, is a chance
afforded by word choice. The words are themselves the heart of the matter.
Change (enough of) them and the poem changes, becomes a different poem.
The variations in the version of Psalm 133 found in 11QPs^a are more than a
text-critical curiosity. They reconfigure—reperform—how the poem sounds,
looks, and ultimately means. Chance *there* changes. Reperformance of traditional art, in this case by a scribe copying 11QPs^a, often results in just such
variability, fluidity, multiformity—"'indifferent' variations," as A. N. Doane
calls them, as they are "the product not only of the power of writing, but also
of the power of speaking," and therefore subject to "ongoing reformulation"
(with attendant variation) of a traditional kind, that is, "that normally resides
in speaking and traditional memory."[39]

     In sum, and on the reading of the poem as witnessed to in MT, Psalm 133's
bold exclamation of the goodness and pleasantness of family (in its multiple
manifestations), successively shaped, instantiated, and elaborated through
images of fine virgin olive oil, a long flowing beard, and heavy Mediterranean
dewfall, is finally suffused with the radiating (if retrospective) intoxication of
divine blessing. Quite literally, brothers dwelling together is so stunningly
good and wonderful because there (in that dwelling together of brothers)
Yahweh commands the blessing of "life" unto a time not yet imagined. And

yet to say this, which this psalm most affirmatively does say,[140] is but to scratch the surface of the way of saying in this poem, the way of poetry in Psalm 133.

* * *

I HAVE LINGERED long over this psalm, in part, as I indicated at the outset, to savor the gift of reading that it sponsors. Along the way I hope to have illustrated as well some of the possibilities that accompany a reading attentive both to the words that make the poem, words in their manifold dimensions of meaning, form, and sound, and to what happens in the spaces between those words, what happens, for example, because of them, as a result of their being fitted together in one way and not another and as they are bathed in a traditonal vernacular. And like all readings, my reading, however intentionally patient and mindful of larger horizons of interpretation, in the end is but a reading, singular, limited in how it sees, what it celebrates and luxuriates in. Other readers, bringing different eyes and ears, different sensibilities to bear on this small poem, have read and will read it differently.

Psalm 133, in its varied versions (e.g., MT, 11QPs^a) and however late, remains a not untypical specimen of traditional verbal art. Its achievement is not that of an autonomous or fully literary textuality but more what U. Schaefer calls a "confirmational discourse falling back on something 'we all know'"[141]—namely "how good it is…" Meaning in such discourse is marked by a dominantly extratextual orientation (and is not to be found in the text alone as a contemporary audience might suppose). Much of my "close" attending to the words of this short song text has been in an effort to retrieve (as maximally as possible) the extratextual sensibilities that these words would have held for ancient auditors. Such a retrieval, a close reading that takes advantage of whatever historical knowledge is currently available, is made necessary by the chronological distance between the "now" of my reading and the "then" of the psalm's first uttering. "We" now no longer "all know" what the psalm's context-dependent discourse presumes of us, and thus some kind of historicizing intervention is required.[142] Curiously, however, though such an intervention will always be anachronistic, fallibilistic, and may need to take advantage of modalities of knowledge unimaginable to the ancients (e.g., philology, text criticism, literary criticism), the basic trajectory of reading that it charts (i.e., from the text outward) is isomorphic to the trajectory of (metonymic) meaning that the psalm itself plots.

Notes

INTRODUCTION

1. The lectures were collected and initially published in 1753 (London: Clarendon; the third edition [1775] is now conveniently reprinted in *Robert Lowth (1710–1787): The Major Works* [ed. D. A. Reibel; London: Routledge, 1995]). An English translation was eventually brought out in the year of Lowth's death (1787) by G. Gregory, entitled *Lectures on the Sacred Poetry of the Hebrews* (2 vols.; London: J. Johnson, 1787; reprinted in *Robert Lowth (1710–1787): The Major Works*. The quotation comes from *Lectures*, II, 34.

2. *Isaiah. A New Translation; with a Preliminary Dissertation*, and Notes (London: J. Nichols, 1778; reprinted in *Robert Lowth (1710–1787)*, iv–v—the "subject" is Lowth's diagnosis (of much) of the prophetic corpus as verse, which importantly involves his initial analysis of parallelism; he cites Lectures XVIII and XIX specifically (p. v, n. 1). The *Preliminary Dissertation* serves as an introduction of sorts to Lowth's translation and commentary on Isaiah. Roman numerals in citations reference the dissertation; Arabic numerals reference the translation and notes.

3. *Isaiah*, xiv.

4. M. Roston, *Prophet and Poet: The Bible and the Growth of Romanticism* (Evanston, Ill.: Northwestern University Press, 1965), esp. 21, 133–38; see B. Hepworth, *Robert Lowth* (Boston: Twayne, 1978).

5. *Lectures*, I, 113.

6. See T. R. Preston, "Biblical Criticism, Literature, and the Eighteenth-Century Reader," in I. Rivers (ed.), *Books and Their Readers in Eighteenth-Century England* (Leicester: Leicester University Press, 1982), 100. The roots of historical criticism reach back into the seventeenth century (e.g., Spinoza, Simon).

7. Cf. Roston, *Prophet and Poet*, 71–72, 87; D. B. Morris, *The Religious Sublime: Christian Poetry and Critical Tradition in 18th-Century England* (Lexington: University of Kentucky, 1972), 162; D. Norton, *A History of the English Bible as Literature* (Cambridge: Cambridge University Press, 2004), 119, 124.

8. So Lowth figures in J. Turner's story of *Philology: The Forgotten Origins of the Modern Humanities* (Princeton: Princeton University Press, 2014), esp. 79–80.

9. Cf. F. W. Dobbs-Allsopp, "Rethinking Historical Criticism," *BibInt* 7 (1999), 235–71.

10. Roston, *Prophet and Poet*, 21.

11. "The Name and Nature of Comparative Literature," in *Discriminations: Further Concepts of Criticism* (New Haven: Yale University Press, 1970), 2.

12. S. S. Friedman, "Why Not Compare?," in R. Felski and S. S. Friedman (eds.), *Comparison: Theories, Approaches, Uses* (Baltimore: Johns Hopkins University Press, 2014), 52.

13. See M. C. Legaspi, *The Death of Scripture and the Rise of Biblical Studies* (Oxford: Oxford University Press, 2010), 121–27.

14. See J. J. M. Roberts, "The Ancient Near Eastern Environment" and "The Bible and the Literature of the Ancient Near East," in *The Bible and the Ancient Near East: Collected Essays* (Winona Lake, Ind.: Eisenbrauns, 2002), 3–43, 44–58.

15. E.g., B. Hrushovski, "On Free Rhythms in Modern Poetry," in T. Sebeok (ed.), *Style in Language* (New York: Wiley, 1960), 173–90; M. O'Connor, *Hebrew Verse Structure* (Winona Lake, Ind.: Eisenbrauns, 1997 [1980]) (Google Books ed.); R. Alter, *The Art of Biblical Poetry* (New York: Basic Books, 1985); D. Peterson and K. Richards, *Interpreting Hebrew Poetry* (Minneapolis: Fortress, 1992).

16. *The Challenge of Orpheus* (Baltimore: Johns Hopkins University Press, 2008), 1–14, esp. 7.

17. See esp. T. V. F. Brogan's formulation in "Verse and Prose," in A. Preminger and T. V. F. Brogan (eds.), *The New Princeton Encyclopedia of Poetry and Poetics* Princeton: Princeton University Press, 1992) (*NPEPP*), 1348—he tries to remain descriptively neutral, not privileging one kind of presentation mode, e.g., isolating the verse line graphically in writing. Interestingly, S. R. Driver's (*Introduction to the Literature of the Old Testament* [Cleveland: Meridian, 1956 (1892)], 361) own explication of the biblical Hebrew verse line, discussed explicitly with reference to biblical poetry's informing rhythm, closely presages Brogan's description: "The onward movement of emotion is not entirely irregular or unrestrained; it is *checked*, or interrupted, at particular intervals; and the flow of thought has to accommodate itself to a certain degree to these recurring interruptions; in other words, it is divided into *lines*."

18. So widespread is the phenomenon that T. S. Eliot can offer his seemingly tautological observation that "the only absolute to be drawn is that poetry is written in verse and prose is written in prose" ("The Borderline of Prose," *New Statesman* 9 [1917], 158). The distinction is now a commonplace, cf. T. V. F. Brogan, "Line," in *NPEPP*, 694; "Poetry," in *NPEPP*, 938; "Verse and Prose," 1348; C. O. Hartman, *Free Verse: An Essay on Prosody* (Princeton: Princeton University Press, 1980), 11; M. Kinzie, *A Poet's Guide to Poetry* (Chicago: University of Chicago, 1999), 51, 433.

19. Brogan, "Line," 694; "Verse and Prose," 1348.

20. The great bulk of oral verbal art never gets written down. P. Zumthor (*Oral Poetry: An Introduction* [trans. K. Murphy-Judy; Minneapolis: University of Minnesota Press, 1990], 147), wishing to avoid privileging chirographically derived terminology, describes the equivalent of the written verse line in oral poetry as "an autonomous unit between what comes before and what after."

21. Esp. O'Connor, *Hebrew Verse Structure*.

22. Contra J. Kugel, *The Idea of Biblical Poetry* (New Haven: Yale University Press, 1981).

23. Esp. Hartman, *Free Verse*; J. Longenbach, *The Art of the Poetic Line* (St. Paul: Graywolf, 2008); B. H. Smith, *Poetic Closure: A Study of How Poems End* (Chicago: University of Chicago Press, 1968).

24. *Lectures*, I, 65.

25. D. Attridge, *Poetic Rhythm: An Introduction* (Cambridge: Cambridge University Press, 1995,) 7.

26. Hartman, *Free Verse*, 24–25.

27. Hrushovski, "Free Rhythms."

28. J. F. Hobbins's "Regularities in Ancient Hebrew Verse: A New Descriptive Model," *ZAW* 119/4 (2007), 564–85, is a recent exception that begins to reappreciate and redeploy Hrushovski's germinal ideas.

29. *Revue Anglo-Americaine* 6 (1933), 490–507.

30. See D. Wesling and E. Bollobaś, "Free Verse," in *NPEPP*, 425.

31. E.g., Attridge, *Poetic Rhythm*; C. Beyers, *A History of Free Verse* (Fayetteville: University of Arkansas Press); R. D. Cureton, *Rhythmic Phrasing in English Verse* (London: Longman, 1992); Hartman, *Free Verse*; D. Wesling, *The Scissors of Meter: Grammetrics and Reading* (Ann Arbor: University of Michigan Press, 1996).

32. *Art of Biblical Poetry*, 27.

33. *Art of Biblical Poetry*, 29–38.

34. *Introduction to the Literature of the Old Testament*, 360.

35. *Introduction to the Literature of the Old Testament*, 360–61: "the line between these two forms [i.e., lyric and gnomic] cannot always be drawn strictly."

36. E.g., C. Altieri, "Taking Lyrics Literally: Teaching Poetry in a Prose Culture," *New Literary History* 32 (2001), 259–81; "Tractus Logico-Poeticus," *Critical Inquiry* 33 (2007), 527–43; J. Culler, *Structural Poetics* (Ithaca: Cornell University Press, 1975), 161–88; "Lyric, History, and Genre," *New Literary History* 40/4 (2009), 879–99; Dubrow, *Challenge of Orpheus*; B. Gentili, *Poetry and Its Public in Ancient Greece* (Baltimore: Johns Hopkins University Press, 1988); W. R. Johnson, *The Idea of Lyric* (Berkeley: University of California Press, 1982); S. Langer, *Feeling and Form; A Theory of Art* (New York: Scribner, 1953), 259–79; E. Miner, *Comparative Poetics: An Intercultural Essay on Theories of Literature* (Princeton: Princeton University Press, 1990); R. von Hallberg, *Lyric Powers* (Chicago: University of Chicago, 2008).

37. Gunkel's most elaborate statement on the topic comes in his *The Legends of Genesis* (trans. W. H. Carruth; Chicago: Open Court, 1901).

38. See esp. S. Niditch, *Oral World and Written Word: Ancient Israelite Literature* (Louisville: Westminster John Knox, 1996); W. Schiedewind, *How the Bible Became a Book* (Cambridge: Cambridge University Press, 2004); D. M. Carr, *Writing on the Tablet of the Heart: Origins of Scripture and Literature* (Oxford: Oxford University Press, 2005); *The Formation of the Hebrew Bible: A New Reconstruction* (Oxford: Oxford University Press, 2011); K. van der Toorn, *Scribal Culture and the Making of the Hebrew Bible* (Cambridge, Mass.: Harvard University Press, 2007); S. Sanders, *The Invention of Hebrew* (Urbana: University of Illinois Press, 2009); R. D. Miller, II, *Oral Tradition in Ancient Israel* (Eugene, Ore.: Cascade Books, 2011).

39. "Parallelism," in *NPEPP*, 878.

40. Cf. R. Thomas, *Literacy and Orality in Ancient Greece* (Cambridge: Cambridge University Press, 1992), 28; M. C. Amodio, *Writing the Oral Tradition: Oral Poetics and Literate Culture in Medieval England* (Notre Dame: University of Notre Dame Press, 2004), 22.

41. Amodio, *Writing the Oral Tradition*, 22.

42. Amodio, *Writing the Oral Tradition*, 30.

43. See J. Kittay and W. Godzich, *The Emergence of Prose: An Essay in Prosaics* (Minneapolis: University of Minnesota Press, 1987). There is no mistaking some of these telltale signs in early biblical prose narrative, e.g., its pronounced rhythmicity, prominence of simple and constricted clause structure, traditional phrasing, commonality of little runs of parallelism.

44. So E. Said, "The Return to Philology," in *Humanism and Democratic Criticism* (New York: Columbia University Press, 2004), 57–84; cf. S. Pollock, "Future Philology? The Fate of a Soft Science in a Hard World," *Critical Inquiry* 35/4 (2009), 931–61.

45. *Daybreak: Thoughts on the Prejudices of Morality* (trans. R. J. Hollingdale; Cambridge: Cambridge University Press, 1982), 5.

CHAPTER I

1. (2 vols.; trans. G. Gregory; London: J. Johnson, 1787; reprinted in *Robert Lowth (1710–1787): The Major Works*, vols. 1–2 [London: Routledge, 1995]).

2. *Lectures*, I, 56.

3. *Lectures*, I, 65.

4. *Lectures*, I, 65.

5. *Lectures*, I, 57.

6. *Isaiah. A New Translation; with a Preliminary Dissertation, and Notes* (London: J. Nichols, 1778; reprinted in *Robert Lowth (1710–1787): The Major Works* (London: Routledge, 1995).

7. *Isaiah*, v.

8. *Isaiah*, vii.

9. *Isaiah*, vii.

10. *Lectures*, I, 65; *Isaiah*, esp. ix–x.

11. *Lectures*, I, 55.

12. *The Singularity of Literature* (London: Routledge, 2004), 71; so, too, B. Hrush-ovski, "On Free Rhythms in Modern Poetry," in T. Sebeok (ed.), *Style in Language* (New York: Wiley, 1960), 185: "Purity of principle is not a feature of poetry…it is impossible to name a differentia which will appear in all poetry and which cannot appear even in greater numbers in certain texts of prose."

13. See T. V. F. Brogan, "Poetry," in *NPEPP*, 938.

14. *Isaiah*, v.

15. *Isaiah*, v–vi.

16. *Isaiah*, x.

17. *Isaiah*, vii (emphasis added).

18. *De Sacra Poesi Hebraeorum Praelectiones Academicae Oxonii Habitae* (London: Clarendon, 1753; the third edition [1775] is now conveniently reprinted in *Robert Lowth (1710–1787): The Major Works*.

19. For details see the discussion of manuscript evidence for the poetic line below, and with greater elaboration, F. W. Dobbs-Allsopp, "Space, Line, and the Written Biblical Poem in Texts from the Judean Desert," in M. Lundberg et al. (eds.), *Puzzling Out the Past: Studies in Northwest Semitic Languages and Literatures in Honor of Bruce Zuckerman* (Leiden: Brill, 2012), 19–61.

20. See his own English translations of Psalm 112:1 and 10 (*Isaiah*, xiii, xv) and his discussion of Psalm 111:4 (*Isaiah*, xxxvi–xxxvii).

21. P. Skehan, E. Ulrich, and P. W. Flint, "Psalms," in *DJD* XVI (Oxford: Clarendon, 2001), 23–48, pls. III–VI.

22. Lowth, *Isaiah*, x.

23. T. V. F. Brogan, "Line," in *NPEPP*, 694; "Verse and Prose," in *NPEPP*, 1348. The distinction is a commonplace, see C. O. Hartman, *Free Verse: An Essay on Prosody* (Princeton: Princeton University Press, 1980), 11; M. Kinzie, *A Poet's Guide to Poetry* (Chicago: University of Chicago Press, 1999), 51, 433. Famously, T. S. Eliot gave voice to this understanding: "the only absolute to be drawn is that poetry is written in verse and prose is written in prose" ("The Borderline of Prose," *New Statesman* 9 [1917], 158). And Brogan emphatically states, "It is impossible that there could be verse not set in l[ines]" ("Line," 694). Interestingly, Lowth himself (*Isaiah*, vii) instinctively points up the contrast with "Prose" in his effort to characterize the Hebrew "Verses properly so called."

24. "Verse and Prose," 1348.

25. "Verse and Prose," 1348.

26. T. V. F. Brogan, "Poetry," 938; see M. O'Connor, "The Contours of Biblical Verse: An Afterword to *Hebrew Verse Structure*," in *Hebrew Verse Structure* (Winona Lake, Ind.: Eisenbrauns, 1997 [1980]) (Google Books ed.), 629. B. Boyd: "The only common feature of verse across languages is that in verse, poets determine

where lines end—in accordance with their sense of what audiences can take in at a given moment" (*Why Lyrics Last: Evolution, Cognition, and Shakespeare's Sonnets* [Cambridge, MA: Harvard University Press, 2012], 16). Not all verse gets specially formatted (i.e., written out in lines) in writing, however.

27. For my own (brief) accounting of a broader understanding of biblical Hebrew poetry and of what it consists, see F. W. Dobbs-Allsopp, "Poetry, Hebrew," in K. D. Sakenfeld (ed.), *The New Interpreter's Dictionary of the Bible*, vol. 4, *Me–R* (Nashville: Abingdon, 2009), 550–58; see O'Connor, "Afterword."

28. J. Longenbach, *The Art of the Poetic Line* (St. Paul, Minn: Graywolf, 2008), xi.

29. For example, see the discussion in A. Baker, "Parallelism: England's Contribution to Biblical Studies," *CBQ* 35 (1973), esp. 433–38.

30. *Hebrew Verse Structure* (Winona Lake, Ind.: Eisenbrauns, 1980), 31.

31. *Poetic Closure: A Study of How Poems End* (Chicago: University of Chicago Press, 1968), 38.

32. Hrushovski, "Free Rhythms," 186 ("the differentia of poetry is the verse line"); Hartman, *Free Verse*, 11; R. Holscher and R. Schultz, "A Symposium on the Theory and Practice of the Line in Contemporary Poetry," *Epoch* (Winter 1980), 161–224; "The Poetic Line: A Symposium," in S. Friebert and D. Young (eds.), *A Field Guide to Contemporary Poetry and Poetics* (New York: Longman, 1980); A. Holder, *Rethinking Meter: A New Approach to the Verse Line* (Lewisburg, Pa.: Bucknell University Press, 1995), esp. 135–36 ("It seems fair to say that the overwhelming majority of prosodists and poets, if only implicitly, regard the use of the line as a *sine qua non* of poetry"); Kinzie, *Poet's Guide*, 51; R. von Hallberg, *Lyric Powers* (Chicago: University of Chicago, 2008), 100; M. K. Blasing, *Lyric Poetry: The Pain and the Pleasure of Words* (Princeton: Princeton University Press, 2007), 121; Boyd, *Why Lyrics Last*, 15–16.

33. Esp. O'Connor, *Hebrew Verse Structure*. Several reviews of *Hebrew Verse Structure* have pointed out how that study assumes the *line* to be the basic unit of Hebrew poetry (J. L. Kugel, *The Idea of Biblical Poetry* [Baltimore: Johns Hopkins University Press, 1981], 315–23; S. Geller, "Theory and Method in the Study of Biblical Poetry," *JQR* 73 [1982], 71; E. L. Greenstein, "Aspects of Biblical Poetry," *Jewish Book Annual* 44 [1986–1987], 38). And O'Connor himself, in the afterword to his reprinted edition of *Hebrew Verse Structure* (639), specifically states that "the line" is "the basic unit of the verse."

34. Esp. D. L. Petersen and K. H. Richards, *Interpreting Hebrew Poetry* (Minneapolis: Fortress, 1992), 4–5; see now J. B. Couey, "The Line in First Isaiah," in "'The Most Perfect Model of Prophetic Poetry': Studies in the Poetry of First Isaiah" (Ph.D. diss., Princeton Theological Seminary, 2009), 22–73; E. Grosser, "The Poetic Line as Part and Whole: A Perception-Oriented Approach to Lineation of Poems in the Hebrew Bible" (Ph.D. diss., University of Wisconsin, Madison, 2013).

35. The first half of the essay aims to flesh out the summary statement in F. W. Dobbs-Allsopp, "The Enjambing Line in Lamentations: A Taxonomy (Part I)," *ZAW* 113/2 (2001), 222, n. 15.

36. Eventually, both terms get used to designate the segmented block of writing, see Kugel, *Idea*, 122, n. 62.
37. Kugel, *Idea*, 122.
38. Kugel, *Idea*, 121.
39. *Idea*, 123.
40. In reality, of course, the realization is highly variable, depending on such factors as the length of individual poetic lines and the presence of triplets. Sometimes, then, space limitations prohibit larger spans of space, or limits them to one per manuscript line even when two are required. Of course, spacing is only one kind of visual cue provided for readers of these manuscripts. Accentuation marks (esp. the presence of the *sillûq* and *'atnāḥ*) also aid in the visual demarcation of poetic lines. In fact, the combination of the columnar set, the presence (or absence) of spacing, and accentuation markings is highly effective (though by no means infallible) in visually signaling the presence of poetry and demarcating the individual poetic lines.
41. This difference in spatial arrangement is apparent on even the most cursory of glances. For example, compare the two columns on folio 397 verso of B19a (fig. 6). In the first (right-hand) column (and the first third of the second column), which contains portions of the prose material from Job 1 and 2, the text is written continuously *without white spaces* appearing in the manuscript lines. By contrast, in the last two-thirds of the second column, containing the first half of the opening poem in Job 3, the columnar lines are routinely punctured with spacing, which usually helps distinguish the individual poetic lines.
42. *Oral Poetry: An Introduction* (trans. K. Murphy-Judy; Minneapolis: University of Minnesota Press, 1990), 147.
43. LSJM 1646b; T. V. F. Brogan and R. J. Getty, "Stichos," in *NPEPP*, 1214.
44. For standard descriptions of these writing conventions, see F. W. Hall, *A Companion to Classical Texts* (Oxford: Clarendon, 1913), 11–12; F. G. Kenyon, *Books and Readers in Ancient Greece and Rome* (2d ed.; Oxford: Clarendon, 1951), 56; E. G. Turner, *Greek Papyri: An Introduction* (Princeton: Princeton University Press, 1968), 63; *Greek Manuscripts of the Ancient World* (Princeton: Princeton University Press, 1971), 8; see W. A. Johnson, *Bookrolls and Scribes in Oxyrhynchus* (Toronto: University of Toronto Press, 2004), 100–130. Interestingly, Masoretic practice enshrines a variation on the latter practice, arranging all biblical compositions in three columns per codex page, except the several festival songs (e.g., Exodus 15, Judges 5) and the "אמ״ת books"—the latter are written in two (wider) columns per codex page; for details about the origins and evolution of the codex, see E. G. Turner, *The Typology of the Early Codex* (Philadelphia: University of Pennsylvania Press, 1977), esp. 10, 35–37; Gamble, *Books and Readers*, 42–81; C. Serat, *Hebrew Manuscripts of the Middle Ages* (Cambridge: Cambridge University Press, 2002).
45. A. T. Cole, "Colon," in *NPEPP*, 223. On Aristophanes of Byzantium, see R. Pfeiffer, *History of Classical Scholarship* (Oxford: Clarendon, 1968), 171–209, esp. 181–89.

Prior to Aristophanes, lyric verse, unlike hexameter (and other stichic) verse, apparently was written out in continuous lines like prose. For an example of a papyrus roll containing poems by Bacchylides written out according to cola, see F. G. Kenyon, *The Poems of Bacchylides, from a Papyrus in the British Museum* (London, 1887); see G. Nagy, "Reading Greek Poetry Aloud: Evidence from the Bacchylides Papyri," *Quaderni Urbinati di Cultura Classica* NS 64 (2000), 7–28.

46. See the discussion in G. B. Gray, *The Forms of Hebrew Poetry* (Ktav, 1972 [1915]), 12 and n. 1.

47. See the comment by S. Mowinckel regarding his assessment of the rise of the term "colon" in English-language scholarship in *The Psalms in Israel's Worship* (trans. D. R. Ap-Thomas; Nashville: Abingdon, 1962), I, 159.

48. The use of the term to comment on biblical poetry likely dates back to the earliest period of classical scholarship. M. B. Parkes (*Pause and Effect: An Introduction to the History of Punctuation in the West* [Aldershot, England: Scolar Press, 1992], 97) notices that "the presentation of verse" in manuscripts from late antiquity "seems to reflect accounts of verse found in the works of grammarians, who discussed structure in terms of *colon* and period." Even Lowth on the rare occasion speaks in the *Praelectiones* of a *Mononcolon, Tricola, Tetracola*, and the like.

49. LSJM 773b; T. V. F. Brogan, R. A. Hornsby, and T. Cable, "Hemistich," in *NPEPP*, 514–15. *OED* dates the earliest use of the term to reference biblical verse ("the first hemistich, or former part of the verse") in English to 1609 CE. Presumably, such usage takes its cue from a layout scheme analogous to that used by the Masoretes in their usual manner of formatting the columnar line (construed as the stich) in the three poetic books, which prototypically consists of a variable span of space separating (parts of) two blocks of writing (the hemistichs). Other formats (e.g., as a running text or one verse line per columnar line) do not lend themselves so readily to such terminology.

50. *Psalms in Israel's Worship*, I, 159. Of course, Mowinckel's way of stating the "ambiguity" already privileges his own sense of how the terms "stichos" and "hemistichos" should be used when applied to biblical Hebrew verse structure. It should be underscored that the use of "stichos," of which Mowinckel would appear to disapprove, dates back at least to Origen, and therefore Mowinckel's judgment as to what constitutes correct usage need not be taken at face value. Further, the ambiguity is compounded by the fact that "stich," for those for whom "hemistich" is the base term, must take on yet an added sense, that of the combination of two (usually) or even three hemistichs.

51. Esp. Cole, "Colon," 223.

52. LSJM 1016b–17a.

53. M. L. West, *Greek Metre* (Oxford: Clarendon, 1982), 5–6; R. S. Garner, "Studies in Early Greek Colometry: Traditional Techniques of Composition and Word Placement in Archaic Epic and Other Verse Forms" (Ph.D. diss., Princeton Uni-

versity Press, 2003), 22–25, now published as *Traditional Elegy: The Interplay of Meter, Tradition, and Context in Early Greek Poetry* (Oxford: Oxford University Press, 2011); Parkes, *Pause and Effect*, 302—as West's and Garner's discussions exemplify, the term *with this sense* retains a currency in scholarship about Greek meter and prosody more generally.

54. West, *Greek Metre*, 5. That is, as with the verse period in antiquity, the character of the colon was variable, its extent depending on the nature of the verse form in question (whether hexameter, elegiac, lyric, etc.), see Parkes, *Pause and Effect*, 97.

55. Parkes assumes that these must have been teaching copies (as Cicero, for example, was apparently scornful of the use of punctuation), though none survive from the period. However, there is a ninth century CE copy of Cicero's *De senectute* written out *per cola et commata* (*Pause and Effect*, 15–16, pl. 14).

56. J. C. Treat, "Lost Keys: Text and Interpretation in Old Greek Song of Songs and Its Earliest Manuscript Witnesses" (diss., University of Pennsylvania, 1996), 394. Latin text available in R. Weber, ed., *Biblia Sacra* (Stuttgart, 1983), 1096.

57. Parkes, *Pause and Effect*, 16.

58. H. B. Swete, *An Introduction to the Old Testament in Greek* (rev. ed.; New York: KTAV, 1968), 346; Treat, "Lost Keys," 394.

59. *Pause and Effect*, 16, pl. 10.

60. Swete, *Old Testament in Greek*, 346; Treat, "Lost Keys," 394.

61. Swete, *Old Testament in Greek*, 346. Even parts of the New Testament could be formatted *per cola et commata*, especially Greek-Latin bilingual manuscripts (B. M. Metzger, *The Text of the New Testament* [4th ed.; Oxford: Oxford University Press, 2005 (1954)], 45–46).

62. Swete, *Old Testament in Greek*, 344.

63. Lowth, *Lectures*, I, 57; compare *Praelectiones*, 32.

64. Baker, "Parallelism," 430; see Parkes, *Pause and Effect*, 305.

65. *Lectures*, I, 98.

66. *Lectures*, I, 101.

67. *Lectures*, I, 99. Note that the last clause in the quotations offers what is perhaps Lowth's most explicit statement as to how important the line is to his conception of biblical Hebrew verse. D. R. Hillers makes much the same point in writing about the problem of knowing where to divide the poetic lines in Lamentations in the absence of parallelism as a guide. In such cases, which are dominant in this poetic collection, Hillers says, "it seems impossible to define syntactically where the division between cola . . . is to be made" (*Lamentations* [AB 7A; 2d rev. ed.; New York: Doubleday, 1992], 20).

68. The Latin is *Compositio*, meaning literally, "putting together" (*Chambers Murray Latin-English Dictionary*). So the sense of "conformation" in Gregory's translation must be "the manner in which a thing is formed with respect to the disposition of its parts" (*OED*), which only underscores the chief focus of Lowth's analysis.

69. Lowth, *Lectures*, II, 34.

70. *Lectures*, II, 65.

71. *Lectures*, II, 68.

72. *Lectures*, II, 51; see *Praelectiones*, 260; also compare Gregory's rendering of Lowth's initial description of parallelism in Lecture XIX quoted earlier (*Lectures*, II, 34) in which the phrase "so that in two lines (or members of the same period)" is a reworked and glossed version of the original Latin *ita ut in duobus plerumque membris* (lit. "such that in the two members") (see *Praelectiones*, 242).

73. *Lectures*, II, 32, n. 10.

74. *Isaiah*, x.

75. In Baker's estimate, the phrase "parallelism of members," entirely intelligible to an educated eighteenth-century English gentleman, is mostly a "pedantic curiosity" for contemporary speakers of English ("Parallelism," 439).

76. Quite literally so, for example, according to G. Fohrer, who gives the following equation: "member = half line = stich = colon" (*Introduction to the Old Testament* [trans. D. Green; Nashville: Abingdon, 1968], 45). A. Weiser even goes so far as to speak about how "the division into separate members is emphasized by the way they are written" (*The Old Testament: Its Formation and Development* [New York: Association, 1961], 24). While Lat. *membrum* is the equivalent of Gk. *kōlon* in rhetoric (Baker offers the following from Cicero [*Orat.* 62.211]: "quae Graeci kommata et kōla nominant nos recte incisa et membra dicimus" ["Parallelism," 436, n. 41]; that Lowth, too, well understood this is made clear in his *A Short Introduction to English Grammar* [(London: J. Hughs, 1762), 115]: "The colon or member, is a chief constructive part, or greater division of a sentence"), unlike *kōlon* (after Aristophanes of Byzantium) it never develops a comparable paleographic connotation, i.e., it does not designate a specific means for writing out a clause. Hence, Jerome's use of the Greek *cola* and *commata* in his *Preface to Isaiah*.

77. *The Art of Biblical Poetry* (New York: Basic Books, 1985), 9. Unfortunately, Alter's own preferred term, "verset," while (unwittingly?) mirroring Lowth's use of Lat. *versiculus*, is nonetheless equally obsolete in current English usage (according to *OED*).

78. "Stichos," 1214.

79. *Art of Biblical Poetry*, 9.

80. Swete, *Old Testament in Greek*, 345; Parkes, *Pause and Effect*, 302.

81. The treatment of the Psalms as "prose" in the Codex Amiatinus discussed by Parkes (*Pause and Effect*, 16, pl. 10) exemplifies well the kind of ambiguity that may result.

82. As applied to the nonmetrical verse of the Bible, "colon" can only signify (1) a division of sense that (2) is then available for graphic representation in writing, whether in singular lines, as paradigmatic in the Greek (and Latin) based traditions, or through other means of formatting, as with the spacing of the Masoretes.

Of course, the outdated nature of the term in English occludes and deflects the very literary sensibilities that pervade its classical use.

83. Lowth's later usage is followed, most notably, by S. R. Driver (*Introduction to the Literature of the Old Testament* [Cleveland: Meridian, 1956 (1892)], esp. 359–67), Gray (*Forms of Hebrew Poetry*), T. H. Robinson (*The Poetry of the Old Testament* [London: Duckworth, 1947]), O'Connor (*Hebrew Verse Structure*), S. A. Geller ("Hebrew Prosody and Poetics," in *NPEPP*, 509–11), and Petersen and Richards (*Interpreting Hebrew Poetry*, esp. 23).

84. *Isaiah*, vii.

85. *Poetic Line*, xi (emphasis added).

86. *Hebrew Verse Structure*, 31.

87. Lowth himself mentions viewing and collating (or having others collate for him) actual manuscripts (see esp. Lowth's notes to Lecture XVIII [*Praelectionis*, 227–28; *Lectures*, II, 7–8] in which he remarks on his consultation of actual manuscripts, e.g., a Vatican MS dating to 1479 CE. He also used Michaelis's 1720 CE printed edition of the Hebrew Bible (Io. Heinr. Michaelis [ed.], *Biblia hebraica: ex aliqvot manvscriptis et complvribvs impressis codicibus; item masora tam edita, qvam manu-scripta...recensita...; accedvnt loca Scriptvrae parallela...brevesqve adnotatio-nes...* [Halae Magdebvrgicae, Typis & sumtibus Orphanotrophei, 1720]), which reflects the columnar and stichographic conventions of the manuscripts on which it is modeled. See comments in the notes to the *Praelectionis* (e.g., p. 228) and at the end of the *Preliminary Dissertation* (*Isaiah*, lxix).

88. *Idea*, 123.

89. "Special Layout of Poetical Units in the Texts from the Judean Desert," in J. Dyk (ed.), *Give Ear to My Words: Psalms and Other Poetry in and around the Hebrew Bible* (Amsterdam: Societas Hebraica Amstelodamensis, 1996), 115–28; *Scribal Practices and Approaches Reflected in the Texts Found in the Judean Desert* (Leiden: Brill, 2004), 166–78; "The Background of the Stichometric Arrangements of Poetry in the Judean Desert Scrolls," in J. Penner, K. Penner, and C. Wassen (eds.), *Prayer and Poetry in the Dead Sea Scrolls and Related Literature: Essays in Honor of Eileen Schuller on the Occasion of Her 65th Birthday* (Leiden: Brill, 2012), 409–20.

90. Esp. *Scribal Practices*, 168 and table 8; "Stichometric Arrangements," 411–12, table 1.

91. In his discussion, Tov assumes that 4QPs[b] contains remains of Psalm 119, which is lined differently from the other psalms in this scroll. According to the editors of the editio princeps, however, this scroll contains no remains from this psalm (Skehan, Ulrich, and Flint, "Psalms," 23–48, pls. 3–6; see P. Flint, *The Dead Sea Psalms Scrolls and the Book of Psalms* (Leiden: Brill, 1997), 33–34.

92. Flint (*The Dead Sea Psalms Scrolls*, 32, n. 23) adds the tiny and fragmentary 3QPs to this list—"on the basis of the relative positions of the remaining letters in verses 6 and 7, which begin on successive lines."

93. So there are a good many nonbiblical poetic compositions that are *not* format-ted specially (e.g., 1QH[a, b]; 4Q380; 4Q381; 4QShirShabb[a–f]; see fig. 10).

94. Tov, *Scribal Practices,* 169 and table 9; "Stichometric Arrangements," 413–14, table 2; see Flint, *Dead Sea Psalms Scrolls,* 49, n. 153.

95. I have only tallied manuscripts from biblical books in running format for which there are also extant manuscripts in a special format. This leaves out, then, the great bulk of the Latter Prophets, for example, which simply appears in a running format.

96. Kugel (*Idea,* 121) makes the same point with respect to the Masoretic manu-scripts: "while stichography may well have been the rule in certain books, it was not *required*" (emphasis in the original). The flexibility at Qumran is much more pronounced.

97. Interestingly, this line format presages the formatting scheme that is used by Lowth in his *Praelectiones* (e.g., figs. 1a-b) and modern poets writing in Hebrew (see T. Carmi, *The Penguin Book of Hebrew Verse* [New York: Penguin Books, 1982]).

98. Notice, however, that in Psalm 119 in 11QPs[a] a number of the component lines of a couplet are sometimes separated by space (e.g., VII, 4; VII, 6; XI, 7; XII, 12), see Tov, "Special Layout," 120.

99. Mistakenly listed by Tov with the first group; but internal spacing is clearly present in the line formatting of this scroll (see Skehan, Ulrich, and Flint, "Psalms," 50–51).

100. Tov, "Special Layout,"121.

101. Tov, *Scribal Practices,* 82.

102. See esp. R. Parkinson and S. Quirke, *Papyrus* (Austin: University of Texas Press, 1995), 44. Of the two, it is Egyptian practice that ultimately serves as the model informing the columnar layout of the leather manuscripts from the Judean Desert. Consider J. Cerny's description of the layout of hieratic rolls written in horizontal lines (a practice that begins in the Middle Kingdom): "For horizontal lines therefore a suitable length was chosen which varies from book to book and even within the same book. A number of horizontal lines were written each time, one below the other, and when the bottom of the papyrus had been reached, a blank space was left at the left of this sequence of lines [direction of writing was from right to left] and then a new series of lines was written, this procedure being repeated till the text was completed. The book [i.e., the papyrus roll or scroll] is in this way divided into a number of columns or pages with blank spaces of 1.5 to 3 cm. between them.... In Egyptian manu-scripts, even in the best ones, the blanks are sometimes so narrow that the ends of the lines of one column nearly touch the beginnings of those of the next, and the scribe thought it advisable to separate them in places by irregular vertical lines." (*Paper and Books in Ancient Egypt* [London: K. Lewias, 1952], 20; see Parkinson and Quirke, *Papyrus,* 38). The chief difference between writing

on papyrus and writing on leather is that in the latter the individual sheets were (normally) stitched together only after inscription (Tov, *Scribal Practices*, 35–37). It is likely that Egyptian influence on columnar layout in Levantine writing dates back at least into the earliest part of the first millennium (see in chapter 4 on the format of the Deir 'Alla plaster texts and its significance; see M. Haran, "Book-Scrolls in Israel in Pre-Exilic Times," *JJS* 33 [1982], 161–73).

103. See Hall, *Companion to Classical Texts*, 11–12; Kenyon, *Books and Readers*, 56; Turner, *Greek Papyri*, 63; *Greek Manuscripts*, 8; see Johnson, *Bookrolls*, 100–130.

104. Tov, *Scribal Practices*, 83.

105. "The stichographic representation of specific texts probably mainly reflects a recognition of the poetical nature of these units" (Tov, *Scribal Practices*, 167).

106. *Scribal Practices*, 166.

107. For details, see Alan D. Crown, "Studies in Samaritan Scribal Practices and Manuscript History: III. Columnar Writing and the Samaritan Massora," *Bulletin of John Rylands Library* 1 (1984), 349–81; Tov, "Special Layout," 127–28.

108. In an appendix to his *Scribal Practices* (app. 5, pp. 303–15), Tov examines all of the Greek papyri containing biblical texts known to him dating from the fourth century CE or earlier and comments on, among other things, whether or not poetic texts receive special formatting of any kind. In total, he lists eighteen papyri in which the poetry is written out stichographically: P.Fouad 266b (Deut 32); P.Bodl. MS. bibl. Gr. 5 of Psalms 48–49; P.Antinoopolis 7 of Psalms; P Leipzig 170 of Psalm 118 LXX; P.Vindo. Gr. 26035B of Psalms 68–69 LXX; P.Alex. 240 (PSI 921) of Psalm 77 LXX; P.Berlin Inv. 21265 of Ps 144 LXX; P.Antinoopolis 8 of Proverbs 5–20; P.Mil. 13 of Qoh + P.Mich. 135 of Qoh 6; P.Laur. Inv. 140 (34) of Psalm 1; P.Oxy. 10.1226 of Psalms 7–8; P.Lit. London 207 of Psalms 11–16; P.Bonn Coll. P147v of Psalm 30 LXX; P.Flor. BL. 1371 of Psalm 36 LXX; P.Vindob. Gr. 35781 of Psalm 77 LXX; P.Berlin 18196 Cant 5–6; P.Oxy. 6.845 of Psalms 68–70 LXX; P.Oxy. 24.2386 of Psalms 83–84 LXX; P.Damsc. VII of Canticles 2, 5. R. Kraft adds the third-or fourth-century CE PHarris 31 (Ps 23), see "Some Observations on Early Papyri and MSS for LXX/ OG Study," http://ccat.sas.upenn.edu/rak/earlypaplist.html, accessed February 1, 2015.

109. For details, see Treat, "Lost Keys," esp. 393–98. He lists the following manuscripts as exhibiting the Song in *commata* in his critical edition of OG: 924, PBer(lin), PDam(sc.), B, S, A, C, and 147 ("Lost Keys," 394).

110. Treat, "Lost Keys," 394.

111. Treat, "Lost Keys," 394. This generally agrees with other early lineated Greek papyrus fragments, e.g., he cites the second-century CE PBodl. 5 (Ps 48–49).

112. For details, see Treat, "Lost Keys," esp. 393–98.

113. Treat, "Lost Keys," 397.

114. Tov, *Scribal Practices*, 136.

115. O'Connor, *Hebrew Verse Structure*, 30.

116. O'Connor, *Hebrew Verse Structure*, 29.

117. For this notion and supporting literature, see M. W. Green, "The Construction and Implementation of the Cuneiform Writing System," *Visual Language* 15 (1981), 345–72, esp. 348–49.

118. Green, "Construction."

119. See W. J. Ong, *Orality and Literacy: The Technologizing of the Word* (London: Routledge, 1982), esp. 83–85.

120. Hall, *Companion*, 9–14; Kenyon, *Books and Readers*, 78; K. O'Brien O'Keeffe, *Visible Song: Transitional Literacy in Old English Verse* (Cambridge: Cambridge University Press, 1990); Parkes, *Pause and Effect*, 97–98; R. Huisman, *The Written Poem: Semiotic Conventions from Old to Modern English* (London: Cassell, 1998), 99–126.

121. C. Watkins, "Observations on the 'Nestor's Cup' Inscription," *Harvard Studies in Classical Philology* 80 (1976), 25–40; see M. L. West, *The East Face of Helicon: West Asiatic Elements in Greek Poetry and Myth* (Oxford: Clarendon, 1997), 26.

122. *Before the Muses: An Anthology of Akkadian Literature* (Bethesda: CDL, 1993), vol. 1, 14; for details, see K. Hecker, *Untersuchungen zur akkadischen Epik* (AOAT 8; Neukirchen-Vluyn: Neukirchener Verlag, 1974), 101–41.

123. See A. R. Millard, "In Praise of Ancient Scribes," *BA* 45 (1982), 146.

124. In point of fact, as E. G. Turner observes (*Greek Papyri*, 63), even Greek verse conventions are not entirely uniform. Though the line unit "usually" is "the length of the complete [metrical] verse" (with the hexameter being the longest such unit), exceptions arise in the case of "very early texts" and "in lyric verse, where the colometry may be a matter of opinion."

125. *Pause and Effect*, 97.

126. Parkes, *Pause and Effect*, 98.

127. Parkinson and Quirke, *Papyrus*, 44; R. B. Parkinson, *Poetry and Culture in Middle Kingdom Egypt.* (London: Continuum, 2002), 112–17, esp. 113–14.

128. Parkinson and Quirke, *Papyrus*, 44.

129. See A. E. Robertson, "Word Dividers, Spot Markers and Clause Markers in Old Assyrian, Ugaritic, and Egyptian Texts: Sources for Understanding the Use of Red Ink Points in Two Akkadian Literary Texts, Adapa and Ereshkigal, Found in Egypt" (Ph.D. diss., New York University, 1993).

130. Parkinson and Quirke, *Papyrus*, 44.

131. Parkinson, *Poetry and Culture*, 113.

132. Parkinson and Quirke, *Papyrus*, 44 (emphasis added).

133. The use of nonlinguistic spatial and graphic conventions as aids for decoding and reading in Old English manuscripts develops only gradually over time, from the eighth through the eleventh centuries CE. For details, see esp. O'Brien O'Keeffe, *Visible Song*, and Huisman, *The Written Poem*, 99–126; see Parkes, *Pause and Effect*, 97–98.

134. Esp. S. L. Sanders, *The Invention of Hebrew* (Urbana: University of Illinois Press, 2009), 142; also see the opening thoughts of E. L. Greenstein on the Kuntillet Ajrud text in his "Signs of Poetry Past: Literariness in Pre-biblical Hebrew Literature" (unpublished manuscript); see M. Dijkstra, "Response to H.-P. Muller and M. Weippert," in *The Balaam Text from Deir ʿAllā Re-evaluated* (ed. J. Hoftijzer and G. van der Kooij; Leiden: Brill, 1991), 211–17 (on Deir ʿAlla); P. K. McCarter, "Kuntillet ʿAjrud Plaster Wall Inscription (2.47D)," in *The Context of Scripture: Monumental Inscriptions* (vol. 2; ed. W. W. Hallo; Leiden: Brill, 2000), 173 (on *KA* 4.2). Whether either is in verse remains a debated issue. Of the two, the Kuntillet Ajrud plaster text (apparently written in a Phoenician script but in the Hebrew language) is the more suggestive of poetry, with several possible instances of parallelism and the general likeness in theme and imagery to a number of poems in the Bible (esp. Deut 33; Judg 5; Ps 24 and 68). For preliminary transcriptions, translations, and general discussions, see Z. Meshel, *Kuntillet ʿAjrud: A Religious Center from the Time of the Judaean Monarchy on the Border of Sinai* (Jerusalem: Israel Museum, 1978) (unpaginated); McCarter, "Kuntillet ʿAjrud," 173; F. W. Dobbs-Allsopp et al., *Hebrew Inscriptions: Texts from the Biblical Period of the Monarchy with Concordance* (New Haven: Yale University Press, 2005), 286–89; S. Ahituv, *Echoes from the Past: Hebrew and Cognate Inscriptions from the Biblical Period* (Jerusalem: CARTA, 2008), 324–29. The editio princeps has now appeared: S. Ahituv, E. Eshel, and Z. Meshel, "The Inscriptions," in *Kuntillet ʿArud (Ḥorvat Teman): An Iron Age II Religious Site on the Judah-Sinai Border* (ed. Z. Meshel; Jerusalem: IES, 2012), 73–142—references to inscriptions from this site follow this volume's enumeration, e.g., *KA* 4.2. As for the Deir ʿAlla texts, while there is no mistaking their high(er) literary register, syntactically they have more of a narrative feel about them, suggestive of the kinds of prophetic reports well known from the Bible and its environs.

135. See G. del Olmo Lete, *Mitos y leyendas de Canaán según la tradición de Ugarit* (Madrid: Cristiandad, 1981), 463 and n. 3; W. G. E. Watson, "Lineation (Stichometry) in Ugaritic Verse," *UF* 14 (1982), 311–12; "Ugaritic Poetry," in *Handbook of Ugaritic Studies* (ed. W. G. E. Watson and N. Wyatt; Leiden: Brill, 1999), 166. This happens periodically anyway, as the typical width of a column is roughly equivalent to the average length of a verse line (on average 9–12 consonants, see O. Loretz, "Die Analyse der ugaritischen und hebräischen Poesie mittels Stichometrie und Konsonaenzählung," *UF* 7 [1976], 267), and sometimes there are even runs of lines where the verse line and columnar line match up (e.g., CAT 1.15.III.1–23). For the abnormal use of word dividers in CAT 1.24 and its possible implications for verse formatting, see A. Robertson, "Non-word Divider Use of the Small Vertical Wedge in *Yariḥ and Nikkal* and in an Akkadian Text Written in Alphabetic Cuneiform," in *Ki Baruch Hu* (ed. R. Chazan, W. W. Hall, and L. Schiffman; Winona Lake, Ind.: Eisenbrauns, 1999), 89–109.

136. U. von Wilamowitz-Möllendorff, *Der Timotheos-Papyrus* (Leipzig: J. C. Heinrichs', 1903).

137. L. D. Reynolds and N. G. Wilson (*Scribes and Scholars: A Guide to the Transmission of Greek and Latin Literature* [3d ed.; Oxford: Clarendon, 1991], 4–5) note that even without finds like the Timotheos papyrus the prevailing running format of early Greek lyric (i.e., mostly stanzaic) verse would be inferable from the tradition that Aristophanes of Byzantium (ca. 257–ca. 180 BCE) devised the colometry that distinguishes Greek verse structure; see Hall, *Companion*, 11–12; Turner, *Greek Papyri*, 63; West, *East Face of Helicon*, 26. For an early example of the one-verse-per-line format, see P.Mil. Vogl. VIII 309 (fig. 9), a beautifully preserved, late third-century BCE papyrus poetry book containing epigrams of Posidippus (G. Bastianini and C. Gallazzi [eds.], *Posidippo di Pella Epigrammi (P.Mil. Vogl/VIII 309)* [2 vols.; Milan: LED, 2001]). Both J. Herington (*Poetry into Drama: Early Tragedy and the Greek Poetic Tradition* [Berkeley: University of California Press, 1985], 46), and A. Ford ("From Letters to Literature: Reading the 'Song Culture' of Classical Greece," in H. Yunis [ed.], *Written Texts and the Rise of Literate Culture in Ancient Greece* [Cambridge: Cambridge University Press, 2003], 21), for example, note that only stichic verse (e.g., hexameter, iambic trimeter) from the classical and archaic periods would have likely been lineated in writing, and even this, as Herington stresses (*Poetry into Drama*, 236, n. 14), cannot be proved on present evidence.

138. From the shapes of the letters to the materials used for writing (e.g., papyrus, ink) to the very manner in which the writing was formatted (e.g., in columns of horizontal lines written right to left—as in hieratic), all betray an obvious debt to Egyptian models (see the general overview in W. M. Schniedewind, *A Social History of Hebrew: Its Origins through the Rabbinic Period* [New Haven: Yale University Press, 2013], 55–60).

139. See O'Brien O'Keeffe, *Visible Song*, x.

140. "Verse and Prose," 1348.

141. See Kenyon, *Books and Readers*, 68–69; Green, "Construction," 359–60; O'Brien O'Keeffe, *Visible Song*, x–xi, 21; Parkes, *Pause and Effect*, 10–11; Parkinson and Quirke, *Papyrus*, 46; P. Saenger, *Space between Words: The Origins of Silent Reading* (Stanford: Stanford University Press, 1997), 1–51. Parkes's examples of how readers of Latin negotiated the bare *scriptio continua* of written texts are most illuminating for imagining analogous ways in which readers of ancient Hebrew verse might have gone about analyzing and interpreting unformatted manuscripts. Ford ("From Letters to Literature," 21), noting the impoverished nature of how early Greek songs were written down, observes, "Altogether, a lyric song text of the archaic period was fairly useless to anyone who had not already heard the song"—that is, readers needed to bring an abundance of nontextual knowledge to bear on the reading of these texts (so also Herington, *Poetry into Drama*, esp. 44, regarding the lack of musical notation in archaic and classical song texts).

142. Esp. Serat, *Hebrew Manuscripts*, 147–48. D. Boyarin ("Placing Reading in Ancient Israel and Medieval Europe," in *Sparks of the Logos* [Leiden: Brill, 2003], 59–88), well captures the overriding orality of ancient Israelite and Judahite reading practices.

143. See O'Brien O'Keeffe, *Visible Song*, 40; Huisman, *The Written Poem*, 110. So, for example, 4QLam[a], which is formatted as a running text and makes no visual accommodation whatsoever to the acrostic that constrains the initial word in the first line of each six-line (three-couplet) stanza, presumes a priori knowledge of the acrostic on the part of any who would read this manuscript and perform (in whatever manner) the poem it contains most felicitously.

144. Parkes, *Pause and Effect*, 99. Ford ("From Letters to Literature," 21), as noted, makes the same basic point with regard to the running formats of early lyric texts from Greece. Also R. Bauman on the distinguishing features of performative oral verbal art of the Chamula: "it is stylistically marked by a degree of verbatim repetition of words, phrases, and metaphors, and in certain subcategories, or genres, by parallelism in syntax and metaphorical couplets" (*Verbal Art as Performance* [Long Grove, Ill.: Waveland, 1977], 23)—here, of course, there is no question of inscription, and yet the "marked" nature of poetic performance is recognizable, nonetheless, even in the absence of graphic distinctiveness.

145. For details, see Dobbs-Allsopp, "Space, Line," 19–61; W. M. Schniedewind, "Aramaic, the Death of Written Hebrew, and Language Shift in the Persian Period," in S. L. Sanders (ed.), *Margins of Writing, Origins of Cultures* (Chicago: Oriental Institute of the University of Chicago, 2006), 137–47, esp. 139–40; D. Vanderhooft, "'el mĕdînâ ûmĕdînâ kiktābāh: Scribes and Scripts in Yehud and Achaemendi Transeuphratene," in *Judah and the Judeans in the Achaemenid Period: Negotiating Identity in an International Context* (ed. O. Lipschitz, G. N. Knopers, and M. Oeming; Winona Lake, Ind.: Eisenbrauns, 2011), 529–44.

146. Tov's suggestion that it is the mixed nature of these compositions, containing both prose and verse materials, that might account for why a tradition of verse formatting never developed with respect to this material (*Scribal Practices*, 166) is worth considering seriously (see fig. 6). Similarly, in Greek papyrus rolls with mixed compositions standard formatting conventions often were discarded (see Hall, *Companion*, 8–13)—in the early Derveni papyrus (ca. fourth century BCE), for example, very wide columns are used in order to accommodate typical hexameter lines that are mixed in with the prose commentary.

147. Kugel, *Idea*, 121; see Lowth, *Isaiah*, lv.

148. See Brogan, "Line," 696.

149. *Pause and Effect*, 9.

150. See K. van der Toorn, *Scribal Culture and the Making of the Hebrew Bible* (Cambridge, Mass.: Harvard University Press, 2007), esp. 109–41. The role of writing in the composition of nondocumentary texts is difficult to gauge (for

lack of evidence)—though we should probably not think of it as overly prominent. Herington, for example, presumes the use of writing in the composition
of lyric poetry from archaic and classical Greece to be minimal at best, "with
the act of writing down occurring toward the end" of the composition process
or even after the composing itself was finished (*Poetry into Drama*, 47).

151. To put it perhaps too kindly, Lowth had a fairly low opinion of the Masoretic
      tradition, especially with regard to vocalization and accentuation (e.g., *Lectures*,
      II, 7–9; *Isaiah*, liv–lxiii; and similar comments may be found throughout the
      commentary section of the *New Translation*; see B. Hepworth, *Robert Lowth*
      (Boston: Twayne, 1978), 145–46; Reibel, introduction to Lowth, *Isaiah*, ix–x, xv–
      xvii). From our own contemporary perspective, Lowth was plainly mistaken in
      this judgment. MT (especially as embodied in the Ben-Asher group of manu-
      scripts) is unexceptionally our best witness to the text(s) of the Hebrew Bible
      (see Reibel, introduction to *Isaiah*, xvi–xvii). And yet it seems fairly obvious
      that without this particular cultural blindness ("Lowth was…following the
      most recent and reliable scholarship," Reibel, introduction to Lowth, *Isaiah*,
      esp. xv) Lowth would never have had the necessary audacity to think and repre-
      sent biblical Hebrew verse beyond the constructions of the Masoretes.

152. *Hebrew Verse Structure*, 30.

153. *Hebrew Verse Structure*, 30.

154. *Hebrew Verse Structure*, 31.

155. *Isaiah*, iv.

156. *Isaiah*, xi, see ii.

157. *Isaiah*, iii, iv–x, x–xxxiv; *Lectures*, I, 57–66; II, 33–35. The term "analogy" itself
      appears already in Lecture IV of the *Lectures* (I, 88) and is used later in the *Pre-
      liminary Dissertation* to explain the significance of the acrostics: "we may draw
      some conclusions, which plainly follow from the premises, and must be admit-
      ted in regard to the Alphabetical Poems themselves; which also may by Analogy
      be applied with great probability to other Poems, where the Lines and Stanzas
      are not so determined by Initial Letters; yet which appear in other respects to
      be of the same kind" (*Isaiah*, vi–vii).

158. Crucially, the Hebrew, perhaps on Lowth's own example in the *New Transla-
      tion*, is left out of Gregory's (and all successive editions are predicated on him)
      English translation of the *Lectures*, and thus this aspect of Lowth's work has
      been underappreciated.

159. Lowth, *Praelectiones*, 250.

160. Lowth, *Praelectiones*, 275.

161. Lowth, *Praelectiones*, 322.

162. Lowth, *Praelectiones*, 154.

163. Hepworth, *Robert Lowth*, 20–25, 63–76. J. D. Michaelis, one of the foremost
      philologists of the day, saw Lowth chiefly "as a poet speaking about poetry"
      (Hepworth, *Robert Lowth*, 39). Though unknown to Lowth, of course, it bears

mentioning that, as described above, there now exists ancient evidence for the one-verse-per-line format for biblical verse as well. Interestingly, West in his *East Face of Helicon* (26), speculates that now lost (as they were presumably written on perishable materials) early first millennium West Semitic poetic manuscripts from the Levant "may well have mediated the one-verse-per-line format to the eighth-century Greeks." It should be noted that currently we have neither Semitic nor Greek lineated manuscripts from such an early period. My own suspicion, at least for the West Semitic side of things, is that, assuming some verse did in fact get written down in an early period, it would have most likely been arranged in a running format—this is suggested by, among other things, known scribal conventions of the period, the likely expense of writing materials, and the kinds of literacy imaginable for these cultures. Still, West's notion of a connection between East and West in terms of poetic line layout remains intriguing, especially now in light of the manuscript evidence from the Judean Desert—though perhaps a downward adjustment to his chronology is required.

164. Compare, respectively, Aleppo Codex, folio 258 verso and B19a, folio 385 verso (Ps 93:4); Aleppo Codex, folio 270 verso and B19a, folio 397 verso (Job 3:3); Aleppo Codex, folio 290 verso and B19a, folio 419 recto (Prov 27:19); Aleppo Codex, folio 4 recto (Deut 32:2). The spacing for the latter passage in B19a (folio 118 verso) is mechanical or decorative and does not appear to display an (overtly acute) awareness the poem's line structure.

165. *Praelectiones*, 52–53.

166. (Lipsiae: J. C. Hinrichs, 1905–).

167. See N. K. Gottwald, "Hebrew Poetry," *IDB* 3:830; O'Connor, *Hebrew Verse Structure*, 32.

168. *Praelectiones*, 407–8.

169. *Isaiah*, iv, xi; see ii. Lowth's understanding of the underlying verse structure of the larger passage, which like MT agrees broadly with the spacing in 1QIsaᵃ, may be inferred from his own English translation in the *Isaiah* (161–63), as it, too, is lineated.

170. Lowth, *Lectures*, II, 177.

171. *Praelectiones*, 329–32.

172. Esp. A. E. Cowley and A. Neubauer, *The Original Hebrew of a Portion of Ecclesiasticus* (Oxford: Oxford University Press, 1897); S. Schechter and C. Taylor, *The Wisdom of Ben Sira* (Cambridge: Cambridge University Press, 1899); for further bibliographic details, see conveniently P. C. Beentjes, *The Book of Ben Sira in Hebrew* (Leiden: Brill, 1997), 13–19.

173. See conveniently the images at www.bensira.org, accessed February 1, 2015.

174. Y. Yadin, *The Ben Sira Scroll from Masada* (Jerusalem: IES, 1965).

175. *Hebrew Verse Structure*, 32.

176. Lowth well appreciated this point: "The Masoretic Punctuation...is in effect an Interpretation of the Hebrew Text made by the Jews of a late age...and may

be considered as their Translation of the Old Testament....and the sense
which they give is Their sense of the passage; just as the rendering of a Translator into another language is His sense; that is, the sense in which in His
opinion the original words are to be taken; and it has no other authority, than
what arises from its being agreeable to the rules of just interpretation" (*Isaiah*,
liv). Lowth goes on to underscore his respect for MT: "We do not deny the usefulness of this interpretation, nor would we be thought to detract from its
merit by setting it in this light: it is perhaps upon the whole preferable to any
one of the ancient Versions" (lv)—a most substantial estimate for Lowth.

177. See esp. his comment in *Isaiah*, lvii.
178. *Literacy and Orality in Ancient Greece* (Cambridge: Cambridge University Press, 1992), 5.
179. Brogan, "Line," 696.
180. "Verse and Prose," 1348.
181. *Poetic Rhythm: Structure and Performance; An Empirical Study in Cognitive Po- etics* (Berne: Peter Lang, 1998), 221 (emphasis added).
182. But as Smith stresses, "it is just as evident that not all free verse depends on typography for its form or determination of its lines" (*Poetic Closure*, 88). The quote from Tsur above is taken from a passage in which he, too, is contesting the general "misconception" that free verse, for example, is "only verse for the eyes" (*Poetic Rhythm*, 221).
183. J. Hollander, *Vision and Resonance: Two Senses of Poetic Form* (New Haven: Yale University Press, 1985).
184. See F. W. Dobbs-Allsopp, "Acrostic," in *The Encyclopedia of the Bible and Its Re- ception* (ed. H.-J. Klauck et al.; Berlin: de Gruyter, 2009).
185. M. Perloff, "The Linear Fallacy," *Georgia Review* 35/4 (1981), 855–69.
186. For example, see D. Levertov, *Light Up the Cave* (New York: New Directions, 1981), 78; Hollander, *Vision and Resonance*; Brogan, "Line," 696; "Verse and Prose," 1348; R. Pinsky, *The Sounds of Poetry: A Brief Guide* (New York: Farrar Straus and Giroux, 1998), 43, 46, 52—J. B. Couey has usefully adapted the lat- ter's ideas to his construal of line structure in First Isaiah ("Poetry of First Isaiah," ch. 1); Hallberg, *Lyric Powers*, 177 ("lines cohere and take sound shapes" even "without strict adherence to a metrical norm").
187. "Word-Power, Performance, and Tradition," *Journal of American Folklore* (1992), 279.
188. Students of oral poetry are less inclined today to make broad, sweeping gener- alizations about this art form. Indeed, the accent is now on the diversity of oral literature—much vaster than that of written literature (esp. R. Finnegan, *Oral Poetry: Its Nature, Significance, and Social Context* [Cambridge: Cambridge Uni- versity Press, 1977])—and the importance of local inflection (i.e., in terms of history, language, culture, conventions, etc.). The question of line structure is clearly important to many traditions of oral poetry. As with written verse, the

line is (often) the differentia of oral verse, a point that may be illustrated in a comment by J. M. Foley on Zuni and Northwest Coast poetry: "In each case queries about the nature of the poetic line become more than theoretical inquiries, more even than credible attempts to 'get it right.' If we don't know what a line is in the Zuni and Northwest Coast oral performance, we can't really 'read' them. We can't even identify them as *poetry*" (emphasis added; *How to Read an Oral Poem* [Urbana: University of Illinois, 2002], 54; see D. Tedlock, *Finding the Center: Narrative Poetry of the Zuni Indians* [New York: Dial, 1972]; D. Hymes, *"In Vain I Tried to Tell You": Essays in Native American Ethnopoetics* [Philadelphia: University of Pennsylvania Press, 1981]; J. Sherzer, "Poetic Structuring of Kuna Discourse: The Line," in *Native American Discourse* [Cambridge: Cambridge University Press, 1987], 103, 136–37; W. Bright, "'With One Lip, with Two Lips': Parallelism in Nahuatl," *Language* 66 [1990], 437–38; B. Hayes and M. MacEachern, "Are There Lines in Folk Poetry," *UCLA Working Papers in Phonology* 1 [1996], 125–42). Naturally, not all scholars of oral discourse concur. P. Zumthor (*Oral Poetry: An Introduction* [Minneapolis: University of Minnesota Press, 1990], 135), for example, is much less interested in distinguishing hard and fast between verse and prose. While helpfully stressing the conventional and thus historico-cultural nature of all versification systems (including that which would distinguish between verse and prose)—they are not determined "on some natural fact" (135)—Zumthor nonetheless talks about "versification systems," "strophic forms," "couplets," "tercets," and the like (136–40), all of which presumes the notion of the line, or at least its equivalent, "an autonomous unit between what comes before and what after" (147). There, too, is something of the mismatch in terminology probed earlier with regard to the notion of a biblical Hebrew line of verse that in the Masoretic verse formats, for example, does not receive its own line of writing. Not surprisingly, the study of oral art forms has inherited much of its methods and terminology from literary criticism, a discipline of study whose roots, however far back one goes, are mostly literate in orientation. Hence, the terminology is often ill-fitting. Namely "oral literature." So when speaking about "lines" in oral verse it is well to recall that the phenomenon itself is only manifested in writing after the fact and may be described without any reference to writing: the fundamental rhythmic and auditory unit whose segmentation interrupts the otherwise continuous flow of sense (as in prose) "so as to increase information density and perceived structure" (Brogan, "Line," 694). In fact, Driver's (*Introduction*, 361) own explication of the biblical Hebrew verse line, discussed explicitly with reference to biblical poetry's informing rhythm, closely presages Brogan's description: "The onward movement of emotion is not entirely irregular or unrestrained; it is *checked*, or interrupted, at particular intervals; and the flow of thought has to accommodate itself to a certain degree to these recurring interruptions; in other words, it is divided into *lines*."

189. For example, see Tedlock, *Finding the Center*, xv–xxxii.

190. Foley, *Oral Poem*, 101; see Sherzer, "Poetic Structuring," 105, 106, 107, 110, etc.; D. Tedlock, "On the Translation of Style in Oral Narrative," *Journal of American Folklore* 84 (1971), 127–29; A. C. Woodbury, "Rhetorical Structure in a Central Alaskan Yupik Eskimo Traditional Narrative," in Sherzer and Woodbury, *Native American Discourse*, 182; F. Turner and E. Pöppel, "The Neural Lyre: Poetic Meter, The Brain, and Time," in F. Turner (ed.), *Natural Classicism: Essays on Literature and Science* (New York: Paragon, 1985), 74; Brogan, "Line," 695. For the significance of silence ("real or potential") in Hebrew prosody, see S. Geller, "Hebrew Prosody," 509–10.

191. J. Scully, *Line Break: Poetry as Social Practice* (Willimantic, Conn.: Curbstone, 2005 [1988]), 143.

192. J. Dewey, *Art as Experience* (New York: Perigee, 1934), 155, 172. Dewey also emphasizes the recuperative and connective nature of pauses, a dynamism that propels forward as much as it arrests. Pauses as they punctuate and cut across and cut up streams of language are crucial to the effectuation of poetic rhythm.

193. See Brogan, "Line," 695.

194. GKC sec. 29i–v; I. Yeivin, *Introduction to the Tiberian Masorah* (trans. E. J. Revel; Chico: Scholars Press, 1980), 170. W. G. E. Watson (*Classical Hebrew Poetry: A Guide to Its Techniques* [London: T. and T. Clark, 2001 (1984)], 14) explicitly notes the importance of "pausal forms" as guides "to marking off lines in Hebrew" verse.

195. See Yeivin, *Tiberian Masorah*, 267.

196. GKC sec.15h; Yeivin, *Tiberian Masorah*, 264, 265–66.

197. See Geller, "Hebrew Prosody," 509. E. J. Revell details the specifics of how pausal forms articulate line structure in biblical verse ("Pausal Forms and the Structure of Hebrew Poetry," *VT* 31 [1981], 186–99). His most striking finding concerns couplets (his "distichs") in Psalms, Job, and Proverbs, the most common form of line grouping in these collections. "In such cases," writes Revell, "the last word in either stich [i.e., line] regularly ends in a pausal form where this is possible" (188–89). By his calculations, "a pausal form could occur in some 1700 cases" and "contextual forms occur in less than 2% of these," a most "negligible proportion of exceptions" (189).

198. Kinzie, *Poet's Guide*, 51; Brogan, "Line," 694.

199. Though as R. D. Cureton remarks, meter "is usually restricted to lower levels of [linguistic] structure" (*Rhythmic Phrasing in English Verse* [London: Longman, 1992], 124; see M. H. Thaut, *Rhythm, Music, and the Brain* [New York: Routledge, 2005], 9).

200. A point stressed particularly in Foley, *Oral Poem*, esp. 153, 155.

201. Kinzie, *Poet's Guide*, 51—biblical Hebrew verse is her choice to illustrate poetic traditions in which syntactic units generally coincide with line units; see Smith, *Poetic Closure*, 85; Hartman, *Free Verse*, esp. 72–73; Turner and Pöppel, "Neural Lyre," 77; Brogan, "Line," 695–96; Pinsky, *Sounds of Poetry*, 25–49.

202. R. Jourdain, *Music, the Brain, and Ecstasy* (New York: Harper Perennial, 1997), 138–39.

203. *Poet's Guide*, 68.

204. Esp. O'Connor, *Hebrew Verse Structure*, 85–86, 120–21, 129; see Dobbs-Allsopp, "Enjambing Line," 223; Geller, "Hebrew Prosody," 510.

205. There is also a way in which a sentential style may evolve its own rhythmic signature such that recognition of that signature may become yet one more sign of line boundary in predominantly end-stopped verse. Cicero provides exquisite testimony as to the capability that such recognition affords: the end of the sentence "ought to be determined not by the speaker's pausing for breath, or by a stroke interposed by a copyist, but by the constraint of the rhythm" (as cited in Parkes, *Pause and Effect*, 12).

206. Garner, "Early Greek Colometry," 102; W. L. Chafe, "Linguistic Differences Produced by Differences between Speaking and Writing," in D. R. Olson et al. (eds.), *Literacy, Language, and Learning* (London: Cambridge University Press, 1985), 106–8, 111–12. Chafe calls these sententious wholes "idea units" ("Linguistic Differences," 106–8), and M. Jousse (*The Oral Style* [trans. E. Sieneart and R. Whitaker; New York: Garland, 1990], 53–61) "propositional gestures" or "semiological wholes." In action propositions these are composed prototypically of "three phases," which Jousse generalizes in the formula "the agent acting the acted" (e.g., "the dog-hunts-the hare"). Syntactically, such chunks generally correspond to "the basic grammatical proposition: subject-verb-object" (E. Sienaert, "Marcel Jousse: The Oral Style and the Anthropology of Gesture," *Oral Tradition* 5 [1990], 95)—to what E. B. Voigt terms the "fundament," the essential, deep-structure of a chunk of syntax (e.g., in English consisting of a subject and predicate, *The Art of Syntax: Rhythm of Thought, Rhythm of Song* [Minneapolis: Graywolf, 2009], 10). As Chafe underscores, these base "idea units" contain "all the information a speaker can handle in a single focus of consciousness" ("Linguistic Differences," 106). The largest percentage of verse lines in O'Connor's corpus contain just such "fundaments," composed of a single clause (75 percent), two (48 percent) or three phrases (40 percent), and/or two, three, or four words (98 percent) (*Hebrew Verse Structure*, 316). In other words, the most common line types in biblical Hebrew verse have a decidedly oral shape to them.

207. Jousse, *Oral Style*, 60–61; see Voigt, *Art of Syntax*, 25. W. S. Merwin's practice of foregoing all forms of punctuation in his poetry except line structure offers an illuminating contemporary (and very literate) example of the line's (whether graphically or aurally signaled) capacity to punctuate and parse poetic discourse. This is perhaps the closest lineal parallel to the use of spacing in Qumran and Masoretic manuscripts of biblical poems.

208. Kinzie, *Poet's Guide*, 407.

209. Hartman, *Free Verse*, 24–25.

210. See Hartman (*Free Verse*, 14–15) on the notion of "boundary" and its prosodic importance.

211. Esp. Ong, *Orality and Literacy*, 38–41.

212. As reported by C. Higbie (*Meaning and Music: Enjambment and Sentence Structure in the Iliad* [Oxford: Clarendon, 1990]), taken from the table in Garner, "Early Greek Colometry," 103; see M. Parry, "The Distinctive Character of Enjambement in Homeric Verse," in *The Making of Homeric Verse: The Collected Papers of Milman Parry* (Oxford: Clarendon, 1971), 266–324; A. Lord, "Homer and Huso III: Enjambement in Greek and Southslavic Heroic Song," *Transactions of the American Philological Association* 79 (1948), 113–24; G. S. Kirk, "Verse-Structure and Sentence-Structure in Homer," *Yale Classical Studies* 20 (1966), 105–52; H. R. Barnes, "Enjambement and Oral Composition," *Transactions of the American Philological Association*, 109 (1979), 1–10.

213. Longenbach, *Poetic Line*, 55.

214. "Rhetorical Structure," 189.

215. "Rhetorical Structure," 190.

216. O'Connor (*Hebrew Verse Structure*, 421–22) refers to this as the "supralinear-level trope of mixing"; see Genesis 49:10a–d; Numbers 23:24a–d; Deuteronomy 32:30a–d; 33, 4b–5c; Judges 5:7a–d; 2 Samuel 1:20a–d.

217. Esp. O'Connor, *Hebrew Verse Structure*, 409; see S. A. Geller, *Parallelism in Early Biblical Poetry* (HSM, 1979), 6, 30, 295, 379; Watson, *Classical Hebrew Poetry*, 332–36; J. F. Hobbins, "Regularities in Ancient Hebrew Verse: A New Descriptive Model," *ZAW* 119/4 (2007), 573–76; Couey, "Poetry of Isaiah," 108–13. For an extended treatment of the topic of "enjambment" and biblical Hebrew verse, see my "Enjambing Line," 219–39, and "The Effects of Enjambment in Lamentations (Part 2)," *ZAW* 113/5 (2001), 370–85—though the focus there is explicitly on Lamentations, which, given its use of the alphabetic acrostic (esp. in Lamentations 1–2) and the density and complexity of the poetry, was likely composed as much for the eye, i.e., to be read, as for the ear, i.e., since if ever performed it would have been read *aloud*.

218. See Dobbs-Allsopp, "Enjambing Line," 229–33, esp. 231.

219. See D. R. Hillers, "Observations on Syntax and Meter in Lamentations," in H. N. Bream et al. (eds.), *A Light unto My Path* (Philadelphia: Temple University Press, 1974), 270 (reprinted in D. R. Hillers, *Poets before Homer: Collected Essays on Ancient Literature* [ed. F. W. Dobbs- Allsopp; Winona Lake, Ind.: Eisenbrauns, 2015], 277–82); see Dobbs-Allsopp, "Enjambing Line," 229–33.

220. Esp. Garner, "Early Greek Colometry," 101–8, which focuses on nonepic Greek verse.

221. "Possibilities of Isochrony" (Ph.D. diss., Washington University, 1974), 108 (as cited in Hartman, *Free Verse*, 74).

222. Two additional observations may be made. First, fixing the end of lines in biblical verse, whether end-stopped or enjambed, is always a matter of more than just syntactic considerations. Second, though the biblical verse line is unquestionably

constrained syntactically, as shown by O'Connor (*Hebrew Verse Structure*), and these constraints can be described, analyzed, and known, this does not entail that individual lines, as they occur in a poem, can be predicted syntactically. The constraints tell us what is possible and proscribe broad parameters but cannot be wielded into an algorithm for predicting or generating the occurrence of any one specific line.

223. *Hebrew Verse Structure*, 104, 160. O'Connor references P. Kiparsky, "Oral Poetry: Some Linguistic and Typological Considerations," in *Oral Literature and the Formula* (ed. B. Stolz and R. Shannon; Ann Arbor: University of Michigan Press, 1976), 73–106.

224. *Oral Formulaic Language in the Biblical Psalms* (Toronto: University of Toronto Press, 1967).

225. Culley himself is already critical of the model in his dissertation (e.g., resisting stipulation of meter at the heart of Parry's much quoted definition of the formula) and remained throughout his career one of the best informed and most thoughtful commentators on issues of orality and the Bible.

226. *The Psychology Review* 63 (1956), 81–97 (www.musanim.com/miller1956/, accessed February 1, 2015); see B. Boyd, *Why Lyrics Last: Evolution, Cognition, and Shakespeare's Sonnets* (Cambridge, Mass.: Harvard University Press, 2012), esp. 15–16; Turner and Pöppel, "Neural Lyre," 61–105; "Metered Poetry, the Brain, and Time," in *Beauty and the Brain: Biological Aspects of Aesthetics* (ed. I. Renchler et al.; Basel: Birkhäuser, 1988), 71–90; O'Connor, "Afterword," 629. P. C. Hogan, *The Mind and Its Stories: Narrative Universals and Human Emotion* (Cambridge: Cambridge University Press, 2003). D. E. Brown: "The UP [Universal People]… have poetry in which lines, demarcated by pauses, are about 3 seconds in duration. The poetic lines are characterized by the repetition of some structural, semantic, or auditory elements but by free variation too" ("The Universal People," in *Evolution, Literature, and Film: A Reader* [ed. B. Boyd, J. Carroll, and J. Gottschall; New York: Columbia University Press, 2010], 85).

227. S. J. Willett, "Working Memory and Its Constraints on Colometry," *Quaderni Urbinati di Classica* NS 71 (2002), 9—relevant literature on the research since Miller is cited throughout, and also in S. J. Willett, "Reconsidering Reuven Tsur's *Poetic Rhythm: Structure and Performance—An Empirical Study in Cognitive Poetics*," *Journal of Pragmatics* 37 (2005), 497–503. E. Grosser is developing Tsur's insights and applying them in a wonderfully stimulating study of lineation in biblical poetry (preliminarily, see her "Perceptions and Expectations of the Biblical Hebrew Poetic Line: A Cognitive Poetics Approach to Lineation of David's Lament in 2 Samuel 1:19–27," paper presented at the annual meeting of the SBL, Nov 18, 2012; "Poetic Line as Part and Whole").

228. This is Tsur's example (*Poetic Rhythm*, 15), which is apparently a little shorter than the two-second duration now supported by recent experimental data (see Willett, "Working Memory," 10–11, n. 12).

229. Willett, "Working Memory," 9; "Reconsidering Reuven Tsur," 501; Tsur, *Poetic Rhythm*, 15, 72–73—noting the amount of time the brain takes to transmit sense impressions to higher-order ganglia, roughly two to four seconds, see Turner and Pöppel, "Neural Lyre," 74.

230. *Poetic Rhythm*, 15.

231. Esp. Willett, "Working Memory," 11; Tsur, *Poetic Rhythm*, 15, 72–73. Also see the observations of Turner and Pöppel in "Neural Lyre" (74), who find that the line "nearly always takes from two to four seconds to recite, with a strong peak in distribution between two-and-a-half and three-and-a-half seconds." They correlate this observation with the amount of time the brain takes to transmit sense impressions to higher-order ganglia—their chief interest lies in the auditory system. The upshot, as Turner and Pöppel explain, is that "a human speaker will pause for a few milliseconds every three seconds or so, and in that period will decide on the precise syntax and lexicon of the next three seconds. A listener will absorb about three seconds of heard speech without pause or reflection, then stop listening briefly in order to integrate and make sense of what he has heard" (88). Hrushovski ("Free Rhythms," 188) adds grouping effects to the consideration of line length: "a line of more than four stresses cannot be kept as a single unit," and "eight or nine syllable (or so) are the normal syntactical unit ('Kolon,' or 'syntagma')."

232. Esp. Jourdain, *Music, the Brain, and Ecstasy*, 139.

233. Turner and Pöppel understand themselves to be contesting this analysis: "It is, we believe, highly significant that this analysis of the fundamental line in human verse gives little or no significance to breath, or 'breath-units,' as a determinant of the divisions of human meter" ("Neural Lyre," 77).

234. *Oral Poem*, 153; see 15; on the basic verse unit in Egyptian verse, see G. Fecht, "The Structural Principle of Ancient Egyptian Elevated Language," in *Verse in Ancient Near Eastern Prose* (ed. J. C. de Moor and W. G. E. Watson; AOAT 42; Neukirchen-Vluyn: Neukirchen Verlag, 1993), 69–94, esp. 76: "that component of the stream of speech divided by possible pauses for breath." Willett ("Working Memory," 10) stresses that the perception of poetic rhythm even in ancient Greek verse, the very bedrock of Western poetics, is "essentially an auditory phenomenon" and exists not in the visual scansion of symbols on a page (i.e., in writing) but "when we hear a poem recited or we read it aloud."

235. "The Acoustical Prehistory of Poetry," *NLH* 35 (2004), 367.

236. It may well be that the two (i.e., breath-groups and the constraints of short-term memory) are not unrelated. Jourdain observes that there is a tendency in the natural rhythms of speech to slow down the tempo at the beginnings and endings of phrases, this partly to facilitate breathing (*Music, the Brain, and Ecstasy*, 145). So when phrase-endings correspond with line-ends, as they do so routinely in biblical poetry (and in other oral or orally derived poetry), the pause necessitated by cognitive constraints overlaps and is reinforced by the equally

necessary taking of a breath. Breath-groups and the needs for cognitive uptake, not surprisingly, are often in coordination in orally performed language art.

237. Correlatively, the evolution of the long, potentially endless free verse line is itself a technological innovation of written culture and the changes in human cognition that writing permits and stimulates, i.e., the capacity to read and reread supplements and compensates for the hard constraints of short-term memory.

238. "Working Memory," 11; also see Willett, "Reconsidering Reuven Tsur."

239. "Hebrew Prosody," 509.

240. Lowth already notes well the defining concision of biblical verse in his discussion of "sententious style": "The Hebrew poets frequently express a sentiment with the utmost brevity and simplicity" (*Lectures*, I, 100; see 98). Of course, such concision likely owes something to the demands of oral style and the needs of cognitive perception without the aid of writing. See the interesting observations toward this end in F. H. Polak, "The Oral and the Written: Syntax, Stylistics and the Development of Biblical Prose Narrative," *JANES* 26 (1998), 59–105. The capacity for enhanced (here syntactic) complexity accompanies written discourse.

241. Prose is a genre of writing and the later arriving art form in ancient Israel and Judah. That is, there is no "natural" reason to think of prose as the norm or standard from which biblical poetry varies. So, for example, the lack of the so-called prose particles in a specific biblical poem may always potentially reflect the fact that poetry is an art form that predates the advent of prose narrative.

242. Syllable, word, and stress counts are given here in a purely descriptive manner as rough indicators of line length. Each varies in the sensitivity of the measure effected, and the manner of counting itself can deviate from scholar to scholar in defensible ways. The aim here is chiefly heuristic: to give a rough indication of the range of typical line lengths encountered in biblical poems. Furthermore, there is a short-line kind of verse in the Bible that regularly falls at the lower end of the length continuum, see G. Fohrer, "Über den Kurzvers," *ZAW* 66 (1954), 205–7; *Introduction to the Old Testament*, 46–47. It is mainly used in combination with and as an auxiliary (for purposes of emphasis and the like) to lines of more standard lengths.

243. This is the range of tallies registered by D. Pardee in his analysis of CAT 1.3.I and Proverbs 2 (*Ugaritic and Hebrew Poetic Parallelism: A Trial Cut ('nt I and Proverbs 2*) (Leiden: Brill, 1988), 4, 71.

244. "In books like Job or Psalms, most clauses [which regularly delimit lineal units] consist of two to six words, the majority having from three to five" (Geller, "Hebrew Prosody," 509).

245. "The basic units [i.e., lines] almost never consist of one or of more than four stresses, that is, they are simple groups of two, three, or four stresses.... The stresses are strong, being major stresses of words (in a synthetic language) and

being reinforced by the syntactic repetition. Thus the groups can be felt as similar, simple, correlated units. As the number of stresses in such a unit is small, they become conspicuous, giving special weight to the words" (Hrushovski, "Free Rhythms," 189. Hobbins ("Regularities in Ancient Hebrew Verse," 567) resists the idea of a four-stress line in his adaptation of Hrushovski's ideas, since such a line is always potentially decomposable into two two-stress lines, especially given the prominence of couplets in the tradition. Heuristically, at least, I am still inclined to hold open the possibility of four-stress lines (as per Hrushovski's original statement), though Hobbins's accent on the prosodic significance of "twos and threes" generally in biblical poetry is well made.

246. So Willett ("Working Memory," 13) on the "12-syllable colon with some 3–6 words" that typifies the Alexandrian colometry for Greek choral lyric as represented in the medieval manuscript tradition.

247. As but a single example, R. C. Culley ("Metrical Analysis of Classical Hebrew Poetry," in *Essays on the Ancient Semitic World* [ed. J. Wevers and D. Redford; Toronto: University of Toronto Press, 1970], 12–28) reports an average couplet (or bicolon) length of seventeen syllables in Psalm 119, which falls outside the generally estimated perceptual capacity of working memory. This is significant since at Qumran this psalm, given that the acrostic frames each couplet in eight-couplet stanzas, is almost always written out with a couplet placed on its own columnar line. Hence, the columnar line, in this instance, does not correspond to a unit that is perceivable as a rhythmic whole. In other words, literal lineation cannot be taken, a priori, as if it has some extratraditional, metaphysical value. Certain traditions may well choose to graphically represent lineal units in writing with literal lines (e.g., ancient Greek verse), but there is no need for poetic verses to be so lined out. And sometimes lines of writing may have no relationship to lines of verse (e.g., as in the continuous writing of Ugaritic narrative poetry), let alone a one-to-one correspondence.

248. See Hrushovski, "Free Rhythms," 188, 189.

249. *Music, the Brain, and Ecstasy*, 139.

250. Geller, "Hebrew Prosody," 509–10.

251. Brogan, "Line," 694–95.

252. Kinzie explains well the line-fixing force of anaphora (though she is not especially concerned with oral poetry): "anaphora secures the sense of each line by encouraging comparison between it and other lines beginning with the same words, while also drawing attention to the larger enumerative sequence" (*Poet's Guide*, 393).

253. The alphabetic acrostic (Nah 1:2–9; Ps 9–10, 25, 34, 37, 111, 112, 119, 145; Prov 31:10–31; Lam 1–4; Sir 51:13–30), especially as in Psalms 111 and 112 where a new letter of the alphabet begins each new line, is surely the most effective (and obvious) means for demarcating the beginning of a line, though this is an irredeemably graphic conceit (see Dobbs-Allsopp, "Acrostic").

254. O'Connor, "Parallelism," in *NPEPP*, 878: "P[arallelism] plays a role in structuring the line." See Sherzer, "Poetic Structuring," 105; D. Tedlock, "Toward an Oral Poetics," *NLH* 8 (1977), 507–8; "Hearing a Voice in an Ancient Text: Quiche Maya Poetics in Performance," in Sherzer and Woodbury, *Native American Discourse*, 146 and n. 4; Bright, "Parallelism in Nahuatl," esp. 437–38; Foley, "Word-Power," 286, 296, n. 16; Brogan, "Line," 694–95; *OED*, s.v. "parallelism," esp. definition no. 3. Parallelism may also (help) fix lines in written verse traditions as well, as it does, for example, in the verse of Walt Whitman. G. W. Allen says that parallelism's "first" function in Whitman is to provide "the basic structure for the lines" (*The New Walt Whitman Handbook* [New York: New York University Press, 1986], 221).

255. For an explication of how echo, repetition, formulas, parallelism, and the like enable oral poetic communication, see the discussion in E. A. Havelock, *Preface to Plato* (Cambridge, Mass.: Harvard University Press, 1963), esp. chs. 8–9.

256. C. B. Pasternack also well appreciates how parallelism "prompts a [vocalizing] reader or listener to recognize starting or stopping points within the linguistic sequence" (*The Textuality of Old English Poetry* [Cambridge: Cambridge University Press, 1995], 131).

257. See O'Connor, "Parallelism," 877.

258. Formal patterns (through repetition) more generally have this power to elicit the participation of an audience by the arousal of an "attitude of collaborative expectancy.... Once you grasp the trend of the form, it invites participation" (and knowledge), as K. Burke recognizes (*A Rhetoric of Motives* [Berkeley: University of California Press, 1969], 58).

259. As cited in Foley, *Oral Poem*, 89.

260. Foley, *Oral Poem*, 89.

261. See *CTA*, 64, n. 6.

262. See Brogan, "Line," esp. 695.

263. Sherzer, "Poetic Structuring," 105.

264. "Warm Springs Sahaptin Narrative Analysis," in Sherzer and Woodbury, *Native American Discourse*, 68.

265. The likelihood that the Bible's prose tradition evolves a style that in part is indebted to the region's oral epic tradition(s) (see conveniently F. Polak, "Orality: Biblical Hebrew," in *The Encyclopedia of Hebrew Language and Linguistics*, vol. 2, *G–O* [ed. G. Khan; Leiden: Brill, 2013], 930–37; see chapter 4 here) may explain some of this usage.

266. This was seen already by Lowth, even if his idea of "synthetic parallelism" greatly obscured matters: "sometimes the parallelism is more, sometimes less exact, sometimes hardly at all apparent" (*Isaiah*, xx). D. Norton, a nonbiblicist, acutely draws out the logical implication of Lowth's more complicated and nuanced appreciation of biblical parallelism that has all too often been missed even by specialists: "if there are unparalleled lines, and parts of the poetry

where parallelism is not apparent, it would seem that parallelism is not to be found everywhere in the poetry: consequently parallelism cannot be taken as the general system it is often thought of as being" (*A History of the English Bible as Literature* [Cambridge: Cambridge University Press, 2004], 227). There is more to biblical poetry than parallelism; indeed, much more. Driver (*Introduction*, 362) sees things very similarly: "so that the *parallelismus membrorum*, though an important canon of Hebrew poetry, is not the *sole* principle by which its form is determined" (see also Culley, *Oral Formulaic Language*, 119).

267. Ong, *Orality and Literacy*, esp. 104–5; see E. A. Havelock, *The Greek Concept of Justice: From Its Shadow in Homer to Its Substance in Plato* (Cambridge, Mass.: Harvard University Press, 1978).

268. Most notably, J. Marböck, "קו—Eine Bezeichnung für das hebräische Metrum?," *VT* 20 (1970), 236–39; see *HALOT* s.v.

269. For most of the history of Western biblical scholarship, the "rule" or "measure" in question would have been assumed to be a reference to meter (as explicitly even in Marböck, "Bezeichnung"). If Heb. *qaw* can have this meaning (presumably as an extension from the use of the term in the sense of a "measuring line," e.g., 1 Kgs 7:23; Isa 28:17; Jer 31:39; Lam 2:8), the reference in Ben Sira would be similar in kind (i.e., accommodating Hebrew verse to the Greek metrical tradition) to other Hellenistic sources (Philo, etc.).

270. For details, elaboration, and relevant bibliography, see F. W. Dobbs-Allsopp, "Psalms and Lyric Verse," in *The Evolution of Rationality: Interdisciplinary Essays in Honor of J. Wentzel van Huyssteen* (ed. F. L. Shults Grand Rapids: Eerdmans, 2006), 346–79 (and chapter 3 here). Of course, the idea of lyric verse is not solely a Western idea. E. Miner elaborates a broadly comparative notion of lyric (inclusive in particular of Far Eastern literary traditions and practices) in *Comparative Poetics: An Intercultural Essay on Theories of Literature* (Princeton: Princeton University Press, 1990), esp. 82–134.

271. S. Langer, *Feeling and Form: a Theory of Art* (New York: Scribner, 1953), 259.

272. See P. King and L. Stager, *Life in Biblical Israel* (Louisville: Westminster John Knox, 2001), 290–98; J. Braun, *Music in Ancient Israel/Palestine* (trans. D. W. Stott; Grand Rapids: Eerdmans, 2002), 8–32.

273. Alan Cooper, "Biblical Poetics: A Linguistic Approach" (Ph.D. diss., Yale University Press, 1976), 10; see *Lectures*, II, 189–90.

274. As Cooper notes ("Biblical Poetics," 43, n. 13), the use of *māšāl* to designate nonpoetic (i.e., prosaic) parables is a postbiblical development.

275. So, too, M. Haran, "Mashal" (in Hebrew), *Encyclopedia Biblica* (Jerusalem, 1968) vol. 5, 551 (as cited in Cooper, "Biblical Poetics," 5)—though as Psalm 49:5 suggests the *māšāl* may not have been entirely incompatible with music (see Cooper, "Biblical Poetics," 5).

276. See Alter, *Art of Biblical Poetry*, 12.

277. Compare *mʿbd* "work(s)" in the Tell Siran Bottle inscription (*CAI* 78.1 = Ber xxii 120.1), likely referring to royal work projects (vineyards, gardens, etc., mentioned

in ll. 4–5), which in royal inscription are construed as bringing joy and renown to the sponsoring king. Some have even considered the inscription to be poetic, and thus construe *m'bd* as "poem." Regardless, the sensibility of *ma'ăśay* in Psalm 45 and *m'bd* in Tell Siran are the same: both are practical artifacts, products of human labor, that may bring joy (see Ps 45:16) or cause renown.

278. Alter, *Art of Biblical Poetry*, 12.

279. See for overviews, J. Döller, *Rhythmus, Metrik und Strophik in der bibl.-hebr. Poesie* (Paderborn, 1899), 18–35; Gray, *Forms of Hebrew Poetry*, 9–17; Ernst R. Curtius, *European Literature and the Latin Middle Ages* (London: Routledge and Kegan Paul, 1953), 72–73, 446–57; Kugel, *Idea*, 135–70; D. R. Vance, *The Question of Meter in Biblical Hebrew Poetry* (SBEC 46; Lewiston, N.Y.: Edward Mellen, 2001), 41–62.

280. In his *Preface to Job* (J.-P. Migne, *Patrologiae Latina*, vol. 28, 1140), Jerome explicitly distinguishes between the prose portions of the book ("from the beginning to the words of Job" [at Job 3:3] and the small section from Job 42:7 "to the end of the book") and those written as verse (*versus*), Job 3:3–42:6—he even uses layout (according to Migne's facsimile edition) to distinguish verse (lineated) from prose (set as a running text).

281. Otto Eissfeldt, *The Old Testament: An Introduction* (trans. P. Ackroyd; New York: Harper and Row, 1965]), 59; see Gray, *Forms of Hebrew Poetry*, 9–17, esp. 16–17.

282. Again Jerome is perhaps the most explicit on this point, as he observes in the *Preface to Job* (Migne, *Patrologiae Latina*, vol. 28, 1141), for example, that "almost all the songs of Scripture...bear a resemblance to our Flaccus, and the Greek Pindar, and Alcaeus, and Sappho" (translation in Gray, *Forms of Hebrew Poetry*, 15, n. 1)—one can hardly get more comparative.

283. Origen in his scholion on Psalm 119:1 is quite explicit about his own awareness of a difference. After observing that Deuteronomy 32 was written in lines of hexameter and the Psalms in trimeters and tetrameters, he says: "The Hebrew verses [lit. *stichoi*], nevertheless, are different than ours" (translation in Vance, *Question of Meter*, 52, n. 143); see Gray, *Forms of Hebrew Poetry*, 13, and esp. 14, where Gray writes with regard to Jerome's comparisons to classical meters: "these statements occur in such connexions, or are accompanied by such qualifying phrases, as to indicate that Jerome did not intend them to be taken too strictly, or as exactly assimilating Hebrew poetry in respect of its measurements to classical poetry."

284. *Forms of Hebrew Poetry*, 10.

285. Jerome is explicit, as in his *Preface to Job*, that he is basing his translation on Hebrew manuscripts—*voluminis*.

286. Esp. A. Berlin, *Biblical Poetry through Medieval Jewish Eyes* (Bloomington: Indiana University Press, 1991); see Cooper, "Biblical Poetics," app.; Kugel, *Idea*, 95–286.

287. Berlin, *Through Medieval Jewish Eyes*, 8–9.

288. Berlin, *Through Medieval Jewish Eyes*, 37.

289. A convenient sampling of postbiblical Hebrew poetry may be found in Carmi, *Hebrew Verse.*

290. Berlin, *Through Medieval Jewish Eyes,* 11.

291. Berlin, *Through Medieval Jewish Eyes,* 43–44.

292. Berlin, *Through Medieval Jewish Eyes,* 43; see 89–93.

293. Sir Philip Sidney, "An Apologie for Poetrie," in G. G. Smith (ed.), *Elizabethan Critical Essays* (Oxford: Oxford University Press, 1904), 158. I. Baroway in commenting on this passage notes that the reference to the Tremellius-Junius Bible, which followed the English Protestant custom of separating out the poetical "third" part of the Bible (see B. Lewalski, *Protestant Poetics and the Seventeenth-Century Religious Lyric* [Princeton: Princeton University Press, 1979], 32), shows that Sidney had verse specifically in mind here ("The Bible as Poetry in the English Renaissance: An Introduction," *Journal of English and German Philology* 32/4 [1933], 463, n. 29).

294. Esp. Lewalski, *Protestant Poetics,* and the series of early articles by Baroway: "Bible as Poetry"; "The Hebrew Hexameter: A Study in Renaissance Sources and Interpretation," *ELH* 2/1 (1935), 66–91; "The Lyre of David: A Further Study of Renaissance Interpretation of Biblical Form," *ELH* 8/2 (1941), 119–42; "The Accentual Theory of Hebrew Prosody: A Further Study in Renaissance Interpretation of Biblical Form," *ELH* 17/2 (1950), 115–35; see D. B. Morris, *The Religious Sublime: Christian Poetry and Critical Tradition in 18th-Century England* (Lexington: University Press of Kentucky, 1972), 17–18.

295. Lewalski, *Protestant Poetics,* 4. How widespread this knowledge was is truly impressive, even if much was "vague, repetitive and devoid of analytical method," as M. Roston (*Prophet and Poet: The Bible and the Growth of Romanticism* [Evanston, Ill.: Northwestern University Press, 1965], 56) contends.

296. A point Lewalski, in particular, makes throughout her *Protestant Poetics*—Job, however, was thought of as an epic poem, see Lewalski, *Protestant Poetics,* 32; and esp. B. Lewalski, *Milton's Brief Epic: The Genre, Meaning, and Art of Paradise Regained* (Providence: Brown University Press, 1966), 10–28.

297. In the Christian tradition during the sixteenth and seventeenth centuries, Job, Psalms, Proverbs, Qoheleth, and Song of Songs were often identified as the poetic "third part" of the Bible, as in the Tremellius-Junius Bible (see I. Baroway, "Tremellius, Sidney, and Biblical Verse," *MLN* 49/3 [1934], 145–49), and even published separately. Indeed, such a conception, according to Lewalski (*Protestant Poetics,* 32), underlies the divisions of the KJB of 1611 in which Psalms is set apart from Job (considered epic and assimilated to the historical parts of the Bible), with a similar division occurring after the Song.

298. Esp. Baroway ("Accentual Theory," 116), who notes that knowledge of Jewish scholarship "would have been channeled to Christendom through converts like Tremellius, as well as by Christian Hebraists."

299. See Baroway, "Hebrew Hexameter."

300. Sidney, "Apologie for Poetrie," 155.

301. *A Preparation to the Psalter* (London: Nicholas Okes, 1619), 59; see 61 (online access through EEBO: http://eebo.chadwyck.com/home; also on: archive.org). Wither can be even more blunt: "the language of the *Hebrew* and the phrases thereof are so different from the two learned Tongues of *Europe. Greeke* and *Latine*, that in my opinion, there should not be any likelinesse in the Scansion or manner of their *Verse*" (61).

302. "Accentual Theory."

303. H. Smith, "English Metrical Psalms in the Sixteenth Century and Their Literary Significance," *Huntington Library Quarterly* 9 (1946), 249–71; L. B. Campbell, *Divine Poetry and Drama in Sixteenth-Century England* (Berkeley: University of California Press, 1959); Roston, *Prophet and Poet*, esp. 15–41, 126–42; Morris, *Religious Sublime*, 14–22, 104–14; Lewalski, *Protestant Poetics*, esp. 31–71; R. Zim, *English Metrical Psalms: Poetry as Praise and Prayer, 1535–1601* (Cambridge: Cambridge University Press, 1987).

304. Lewalski, *Protestant Poetics*.

305. Smith, "English Metrical Psalms," 251–53; Roston, *Prophet and Poet*, 126.

306. As it is with the more original poems of the period that borrowed from the Bible (e.g., style, themes, imagery) but were themselves not versions (however loose) of specific biblical poems. On the place of imitation in the literary thought world of the eighteenth century in particular, see Morris, *Religious Sublime*, 18–21.

307. Morris, *Religious Sublime*, 19.

308. *Prophet and Poet*, 134—Roston's larger treatment of this topic, which I have echoed here, may be found on 133–42.

309. Interestingly, Roston (*Prophet and Poet*, 134–35) well emphasizes the significance for English poetry of Lowth's decision to set his English translation of Isaiah "line by line."

310. *Preparation to the Psalter*, 59–60.

311. Baroway, writing in ignorance of the Qumran evidence (e.g., P. W. Skehan's initial publication of 4QPs[b] only appeared in 1964: "A Psalm Manuscript from Qumran [4QPs[b]]," *CBQ* 26, 313–22 + plate; the material on Deuteronomy appeared even later), called attention to the presumed lineation disparity in Wither's transcription of Deuteronomy 32:2, the other example cited in full in chapter IX of *Preparation to the Psalter* (60): "Each two lines of the translation [actually referencing Wither's transliteration] represent one line of the Hebrew; the whole passage [rendered by Wither in four lines] represents two Hebrew lines" ("Accentual Theory," 134, n. 59). But here, as well, Qumran provides manuscripts of Deuteronomy where the individual verse line is set on a single manuscript line in conformity with Wither's practice (e.g., 4QDeut[c]; see Deut 32 in the Greek p.Fouad inv. 266; 4QDeut[q] [contains a combination of one and two lines per columnar line]).

312. Wither, *Preparation to the Psalter*, 60.

313. Wither, *Preparation to the Psalter*, 61.

314. My summation of Wither's larger point, see *Preparation to the Psalter*, 61.

315. *Idea*, esp. 59–95.

316. *Idea*, 86; see 69.

317. *Lectures*, I, 57.

318. *Isaiah*, v.

319. There are good reasons to think that the acrostic is itself a trope of writing as it appears based on a quintessential scribal genre, the abecedary (see Dobbs-Allsopp, "Acrostic"; see figs. 32–34). But in counter-distinction to the use of *littera notabilior* to mark the heads of verse lines in copies of medieval Latin poems, for example, which is purely a graphic phenomenon, the succeeding graphemes of the alphabet in biblical acrostics also have phonemic value (e.g., see the acrostic of Lamentations 1 in 4QLam^a, which is written out in a running format, that is, without special graphic distinction; also the several Babylonian acrostics that spell out a name or sentence).

320. As cited in Parkes, *Pause and Effect*, 98; see pl. 42.

321. For example, see Parkes's comments on rhyme in medieval Latin and vernacular poetry: "In medieval Latin and vernacular poetry rhyme became a structural feature, since it coincided with, and so marked, the ends of verse *cola* or periods. In stichic verse the periods were linked by end-rhymes, and in poems produced from the eleventh century [CE] onwards leonine rhymes at the regular caesura indicated the *cola* as well" (*Pause and Effect*, 98). It is perhaps worth underscoring that this whole bit with respect to the acrostics and line structure remains a matter of interpretation. That it is the verse line that provides the structural basis for the deployment of the alphabetic acrostic is an inference made from a weighing of multiple factors (e.g., other cues about line structure in the tradition, the nature of acrostics in other literary traditions). It is not simply a given, no matter the apparent obviousness of the posited connection.

322. O'Connor, "Parallelism," 878.

323. My analysis is concentrated at the surface level of the line. For a deep structure analysis of the workings of parallelism, see E.L. Greenstein, "How Does Parallelism Mean?," in *A Sense of Text* (*JQR* supp., 1982), 41–70; and now in "Parallelism," in *PEPP*.

324. As applied to prosody, the *OED* glosses "parallelism" as "correspondence, in sense or construction, of successive clauses or passages" and cites Lowth as its earliest exemplar with this sense: "The correspondence of one Verse, or Line, with another, I call Parallelism. When a Proposition is delivered, and a second is subjoined to it, or drawn under it, equivalent, or contrasted with it, in Sense; or similar to it in the form of Grammatical Construction" (*Isaiah*, x).

325. Esp. Zumthor, *Oral Poetry*, 111.

326. "Parallelism," 877.

327. *Biblical Poetry*, esp. 3–61; see Kugel, *Idea*, 1–58.
328. *Biblical Poetry*, 23.
329. Ong, *Orality and Literacy*, 40; see Jousse, *Oral Style*, 95–107; Finnegan, *Oral Poetry*, 130–33; Zumthor, *Oral Poetry*, 110–13.
330. *Lectures*, II, 34.
331. Lowth, *Isaiah*, x.
332. The possibility of repeating is constitutive of identity, according to J. Derrida ("Signature Event Context," in *The Margins of Philosophy* [trans. A. Bass; Chicago: University of Chicago Press, 1982], 315, 318). Though such "identity" is also riven by difference, the capability of occurring again, there being another, a second iteration by its very nature introduces an "essential dehiscence" (326), and thus the identity so constituted is never quite identical with itself, not a "unity of self identity" or a "pure singularity" (318, 326). And so the difference that Alter so creatively and wonderfully exploits in his analysis of the Bible's poetic parallelism is itself constitutive of the very iterability that lies at the heart of how parallelism means.
333. Lowth, *Isaiah*, x.
334. *Lectures*, II, 42–43; see O'Connor, "Parallelism," 878.
335. Jousse connects this to human bilateralism, see *Oral Style*, 95–100, 238, 239–40; see Antomarini, "Acoustical Prehistory," 363–65.
336. Not accidentally, G. W. Allen (*New Walt Whitman Handbook*, 218) in comparing Whitman's use of parallelism—where parallel lines may be reiterated many times over, such as in one part of the "Song of the Broad-Axe," which contains sixty-two consecutive lines in parallel (G. W. Allen, *American Prosody* [New York: American Book, 1935], 223)—to that of the Bible recognizes well the logic of parallelism: "the fact that in parallelism, or in the 'rhythm of thought,' *the single line must by necessity be the stylistic unit.*" That the line is a unit of sense in Whitman is told mostly by its end-stopped nature, which in turn, for Allen, provides one piece of "evidence that parallelism is Whitman's first rhythmical principle" (*American Prosody*, 222).
337. R. Gordis, "Studies in the Relationship of Biblical and Rabbinic Hebrew," in *Louis Ginzberg Jubilee Volume* (New York: American Academy of Jewish Research, 1945), vol. 1, 184–86; M. Gruber, "The Meaning of Biblical Parallelism: A Biblical Perspective," *Prooftexts* 13 (1993), 289–93.
338. Gordis, "Studies," 186.
339. See Gruber, "Biblical Parallelism," 291.
340. Gordis, "Studies," 185. V. 20 reads: "Only grant two [*šĕtayim*] things to me, / then I will not hide myself from your face" (NRSV). Others think the "two" refers to vv. 21–22 taken together, see C. L. Seow, *Job 1–21* (Illuminations; Grand Rapids: Eerdmans, 2013), 661.
341. Gruber, "Biblical Parallelism," esp. 291.
342. Kugel, *Idea*, 42.

343. Brogan, "Line," 696; "Verse and Prose," 1348.
344. *Poetic Line*, 18; see xi–xii, 16, 26–27.
345. So, for example, Brogan, "Verse and Prose," 1348; Longenbach, *Poetic Line*, 18–19; Antomarini, "Acoustical Prehistory," esp. 367—"the hemistich is the fossil of that short breath specific to poetry."
346. Esp. Smith, *Poetic Closure*, 9; P. Valery, *The Art of Poetry* (trans. D. Folliot; New York: Pantheon, 1961), 162; see D. Attridge, *Poetic Rhythm: An Introduction* (Cambridge: Cambridge University Press, 1995), 1–3; S. Stewart, *Poetry and the Fate of the Senses* (Chicago: University of Chicago Press, 2002), 68–69—"we will bring to a text [of a poem] our memories of speech experience."
347. Esp. Hollander, *Vision and Resonance*.
348. *Light Up the Cave*, 78.
349. Hartman, *Free Verse*, 65; see Watson, *Classical Hebrew Poetry*, 227; Couey, "Poetry of First Isaiah," 41–42.
350. O. Borowski, *Every Living Thing: Daily Use of Animals in Ancient Israel* (Walnut Creek, Calif.: Altamira, 1998), fig. 5.4.
351. This is as in MT, which is suspect, see Seow, *Job 1–21*, 722–23.
352. For a brief analysis of this poem's structure, see F. W. Dobbs-Allsopp, "The Delight of Beauty and Song 4:1–7," *Interpretation* 59 (2005), 261–63; "Song of Songs," in *New Interpreter's Bible One Volume Commentary* (ed. B. Gaventa and D. Peterson; Nashville: Abingdon, 2010).
353. See Smith, *Poetic Closure*, 44.
354. Longenbach, *Poetic Line*, 28.
355. *Poet's Guide*, 75.
356. For details, consult O'Connor's own in-depth statement in *Hebrew Verse Structure* (pp. 86–87 contain the briefest account of the defining syntactic constraints); see W. L. Holladay, "*Hebrew Verse Structure* Revisited (I): Which 'Words' Count?," *JBL* 118 (1999), 19–32; "*Hebrew Verse Structure* Revisited (II): Conjoint Cola, and Further Suggestions," *JBL* 118 (1999), 401–16. But for my argument the details themselves are not paramount. One can change up the variables in view or define them differently, quibble with readings of specific verses, champion other theories of syntax, even evolve a more elegant syntactic description of the biblical poetic line, but a syntactic description it would be all the same, and therein lies the chief significance for the argument mounted above (e.g., Hobbins, "Regularities in Ancient Hebrew Verse," esp. 582–83).
357. Though sometimes the Masoretic spacing can be decorative or ornamental, as, for example, in the special layout of Deuteronomy 32 in B19a (folio 118 verso), which does not appear to display an (overtly acute) awareness of the poem's line structure.
358. O'Connor, "Parallelism," 878.
359. For some general discussion, see A. M. Dale, "Stichos and Stanza," *Classical Quarterly* NS 13 (1963), 46–50; T. V. F. Brogan and R. J. Getty, "Stichos," in

NPEPP, 1214; T. V. F. Brogan, "Stanza," in *NPEPP*, 1211–13; E. Haublein and T. V. F. Brogan, "Strophe," in *NPEPP*, 1215; Kinzie, *Poet's Guide*, 403; E. Hirsch, *How to Read a Poem* (New York: Harcourt Brace, 1999), 313–14.

360. Whether couplets are counted as stanzas depends on the critic, e.g., West, *Greek Metre*, 44; Kinzie, *Poet's Guide*, 463.

361. Esp. M. Oliver (*A Poetry Handbook* [New York: HBC, 1994], 60–61), for whom "there are no absolutely right or wrong ways to divide a poem into stanzas"— outside, of course, of the purely given forms (e.g., sonnet, Spenserian stanza). She stresses that beyond designating the grouping of lines that form the "divisions" of a poem, "there is no further *exact* definition" of the term "stanza." In ancient Egyptian stanzas were called *ḥwt* "mansions" and sometimes even made visible in the manuscripts, see Parkinson, *Poetry and Culture*, 114.

362. So already Lowth (*Lectures*, I, 100): they dispose the corresponding sentences in regular distichs adapted to each other, and of an equal length, in which, for the most part, things answer to things, and words to words." Interestingly, Lowth cites as confirmation Ben Sira's characterization of the works of God in Sirach 33:15 as δύο δύο, ἓν κατέναντι τοῦ ἑνόσ (in Gregory's English rendition: "two and two, one against the other")—interesting because Ben Sira's verse is shaped so regularly in couplets or di stichs, a point Lowth makes well in his own Hebrew rendition of Ben Sira 24 (see fig. 30). Also Driver (*Introduction*, 362; see 364): "The fundamental (and predominant) form of the Hebrew verse is the couplet of two lines....The Hebrew verse does not, however, consist uniformly of two lines; the addition of a third line is apt especially to introduce an element of irregularity." More recently, Hobbins ("Regularities in Ancient Hebrew Verse," 568), too, emphasizes the importance of "twos and threes" to the overall biblical verse system, including line structure, though (following Alter) he prefers to think of a line as consisting of two and three versets.

363. "Signs of Poetry Past."

364. "Free Rhythms," 188; see Voigt, *Art of Syntax*, 25.

365. The term is taken from S. A. Geller, "The Dynamics of Parallel Verse: A Poetic Analysis of Deut 32:6–12," *HTR* 75 (1982), 35, n. 1, but in fact, as Berlin stresses (*Through Medieval Jewish Eyes*, 44; see 43–44, 53, n. 6), an awareness of the informing binariness of biblical verse is long-standing in Jewish scholarship; Kugel also emphasizes aspects of binarism throughout his *Idea*.

366. "Couplet," in *NPEPP*, 244.

367. See Couey, "Poetry of First Isaiah," 76–78.

368. Brogan and Piper, "Couplet," 244; see Hirsch, *Read a Poem*, 275–76; Kinzie, *Poet's Guide*, 401–2; Smith, *Poetic Closure*, esp. 70–78; T. V. F. Brogan, "Distich," in *NPEPP*, 299.

369. Esp. Smith, *Poetic Closure*, 41, 47–48, 70–78. Smith draws explicitly on the still seminal work of gestalt theorist M. Wertheimer, especially "Laws of Organization

in Perceptual Forms," in W. Ellis, *A Source Book of Gestalt Psychology* (London: Routledge and Kegan Paul, 1938), 71–88 (http://psychclassics.asu.edu/Wertheimer/Forms/forms.htm; I cite throughout from the online version, accessed February 1, 2015).

370. Smith, *Poetic Closure*, 48, n. 14.

371. *Greek Metre*, 44.

372. "Another Factor is that of past experience or habit. Its principle is that if—*AB* and—*C* but not—*BC* have become habitual (or 'associated') there is then a tendency for—*ABC* to appear as—*AB/C*" (Wertheimer, "Laws of Organization").

373. Grouping patterns tend to resolve themselves more clearly when there are sufficiently long strings. As Wertheimer notices, in shorter strings containing fewer stimuli "we find that the arrangement is not so imperatively dictated" ("Laws of Organization").

374. Text taken from M. L. West, *Iambi et Elegi Graeci* (2d ed.; Oxford: Oxford University Press, 1989). Also see www.gottwein.de/Grie/lyr/lyr_tyrt_gr.php, accessed February 1, 2015.

375. M. L. West, *Greek Lyric Poetry* (Oxford: Oxford University Press, 1993), 24.

376. Ben Jonson, *Poems of Ben Jonson* (ed. G. B. Johnston; Cambridge, Mass.: Harvard University Press, 1955), 7.

377. See Smith, *Poetic Closure*, 47–48.

378. E.g., Watson, *Classical Hebrew Poetry*, 174, 177; Geller, *Parallelism*, 5–6; Kugel, *Idea*, 1; O'Connor, *Hebrew Verse Structure*, 134–35, 392; Petersen and Richards, *Interpreting Hebrew Poetry*, 23–24.

379. Smith, *Poetic Closure*, 48.

380. Lines and groups of lines in nonmetrical verse normally do not fall into constant patterns, see Smith, *Poetic Closure*, 86.

381. See Dobbs-Allsopp, "Enjambing Line," 219–39; "Effects of Enjambment," 370–85.

382. Note how the rhyming at the beginning and ending of Song 1:9 reinforces this sense of couplet wholeness (*lĕsūsātî . . . raʿyātî*).

383. The poems in Lamentations 1 and 2 are dominated by the unbalanced qinah couplet (see esp. Dobbs-Allsopp, "Enjambing Line") and thereby illustrate well how repetition, if sufficiently prolonged, can be most effective in conveying knowledge of this couplet type, even to the uninitiated auditor.

384. See H. L. Ginsberg, "The Rebellion and Death of Baʿlu," *Orientalia* NS 5 (1936), 180–81; "Baʾl and Anat," *Orientalia* NS 7 (1938), 7; "Ugaritic Studies and the Bible," *BA* 8 (1945), 54; S. E. Loewenstamm, "The Expanded Colon in Ugaritic and Biblical Verse," *JSS* 14/2 (1969), 176–96; Y. Avishur, "Addenda to the Expanded Colon in Ugaritic and Biblical Verse," *UF* 4 (1972), 1–10; E. L. Greenstein, "Two Variations of Grammatical Parallelism in Canaanite Poetry and Their Psycholinguistic Background," *JANES* 6 (1974), esp. 96–105; "One More Step on the Staircase," *UF* 9 (1977), 77–86; Watson, *Classical Hebrew Poetry*, 152–56. Of the two, Exodus 15:11 is the more prototypical example of this variety of parallelism.

385. Note the line lengths throughout these three examples, which are all slightly longer than the more concise lines, say, of Judges 5:10 or Psalms 133:3. To be sure, these still fit the performance constraints discussed earlier. But it is clear from examples like these (also prominently in Second Isaiah) that biblical poetry features two prominent line types, one shorter and one longer (though both remain relatively concise).

386. One of the gains in these larger groupings is expanded discursive space. The examples from Proverbs are most telling on this point since the pithy couplet is otherwise by far the preferred form of line grouping in this poetic collection. Not all pertinent knowledge is optimally communicated within the relatively brief span of two lines. The added space of these larger forms allows for elaboration of all kinds, e.g., expanded complexity, added nuance, further exemplification.

387. See O'Connor, "Parallelism," 878.

388. So already Fohrer: "The single long verse [Fohrer's designation for the typical line in biblical poetry, which he then goes on to contrast with a "short verse" or short line] constitutes the basic poetic and stylistic unit that can exist independently. In point of fact, we always find at least two long verses joined together" (*Introduction to the Old Testament*, 46). Though his "always" is perhaps too confident, he is clearly aware that a singularity (here Fohrer's "long verse") may have substance without also being independent (i.e., a line that predominantly comes joined together with one or more other lines). Fohrer does allow for singular short lines (47), and a little earlier, using slightly different terminology (derived ultimately from Lowth), he says: "A verse need not have more than one member, even though most extant verses do in fact have two or three" (45).

389. *Classical Hebrew Poetry*, 168; see Driver, *Introduction*, 364.

390. So O'Connor, *Hebrew Verse Structure*, 185.

391. Watson (*Classical Hebrew Poetry*, 171) notices that one of the places where single lines may be found is at the end of structural units, though the three examples that he specifically cites (Isa 63:9; Jer 12:11; 14:9), not surprisingly, are all debatable. The last line in Jeremiah 6:16 cited below is one of the more conspicuous examples of a single line closing a distinct structural unit, since it so obviously deviates from the assortment of elements that join the preceding quatrain.

392. B19a is ambiguous since there is no internal spacing involved. The column margin separates *šātûl* and *'al-*. Either way *BHS* goes its own way.

393. Preliminary observations to this end are offered in F. W. Dobbs-Allsopp, "The Art of Poetry in Jer 17:5–8" (paper presented at the annual meeting of the SBL, November 20, 2012). One of the earliest explicit construals of the Jeremiah line as a line is that of Lowth in his *Notes on Isaiah* (18):

He shall be like a tree planted by the water-side,
And which sendeth forth her roots to the aqueduct:

She shall not fear, when the heat cometh;
But her leaf shall be green;
And in the year of drought she shall not be anxious,
Neither shall she cease from bearing fruit.

This anticipates B. Blayney's more general delineation of verse in Jeremiah in his 1784 commentary (*Jeremiah and Lamentations* [3d ed.; London, 1836]).

394. J. F. Creach, "Like a Tree Planted by the Temple Streams: The Portrait of the Righteous in Psalm 1:3," *CBQ* 61 (1999), 37; see R. P. Carroll, *Jeremiah* (OTL; Philadelphia: Westminster John Knox, 1986), 351.

395. That the line is remembered variably, as a multiform, is no surprise in a primarily oral culture—this even amid a rise in textuality (see chapter 4).

396. That the same line is attached as an additional lineal unit to the version of Psalm 133 preserved in 11QPsᵃ is further suggestive of this line's singular identity.

397. M. V. Fox, *Proverbs 10–31* (AB18B; New Haven: Yale University Press, 2009), 867–68.

398. The extra spacing in B19a is not as dramatic but is there.

399. Undoubtedly, the quotative frame is used because the boy's entreaties are represented as the girl's recollection, i.e., what her lover said to her from outside the wall. The whole poem (2:8–17) is voiced by the girl.

400. There is no doubt that quotative frames are at times scripted as lineal units in couplets (e.g., Isa 43:14a; 44:6a), triplets (e.g., Isa 43:16), and quatrains (e.g., Isa 3:7; 18:4; 29:13a; see Couey, "Poetry of First Isaiah," 121).

401. All of these involve the prophetic "messenger formula" (*kōh 'āmar yhwh*), mainly as a convenient sampling, but also because the formula's genealogy in epistolary discourse makes clear that the formula is separate from the quoted material that follows. In all of these cases the strongly coherent nature of the line groupings that follow reinforce the impression of separation. It is possible, of course, to expand the messenger formula and thereby group it with additional lines, e.g., by elaborating the introduction of speech (Isa 43:1; 43:14; 44:6), by adding words that tie in thematically with the quoted material (Isa 45:1; Jer 14:10).

402. Esp. Watson, *Classical Hebrew Poetry*, 170–71. In fact, a strong reason to expect isolated, single lines in the biblical poetic tradition is because they so obviously occur in Ugaritic narrative poetry—the genre difference (narrative vs. nonnarrative) is likely to account in part for the distribution difference. Not surprisingly, the formula itself has strong oral, epic roots, see F. H. Polak, "Epic Formulas in Biblical Narrative: Frequency and Distribution," in *Actes du Second Colloque International "Bible et Informatique: Méthodes, Outils, Résultats" (Jérusalem 9–13 Juin 1988)* (ed. R. F. Poswick et al.; Geneva: Slatkine, 1989), 437, 447–48, 482, n. 1, 484, n. 7.

403. E.g., M. V. Fox, *The Song of Songs and the Ancient Egyptian Love Songs* (Madison: University of Wisconsin Press, 1985), 162.

404. E.g., J. C. Exum, *Song of Songs* (OTL; Louisville: Westminster John Knox, 2005), 240.

405. So Fox, *Song of Songs*, 162.

406. Or couplet, as in Exum's understanding of the lines (*Song of Songs*, 240).

407. See Fox, *Song of Songs*, 162.

408. Exum, *Song of Songs*, 213; Fox, *Song of Songs*, 159–60.

409. Such repetitive or formulaic phrasings are typical in much oral/oral-derived verbal art. The opening line of the Song (*šîr haššîrîm ʾăšer lišlōmōh*) is also obviously a single entity, though most take it to be a later editorial addition.

410. Not all large groupings of lines are always decomposable into groupings of couplets and triplets.

411. Esp. Gruber, "Biblical Parallelism," 289–93.

412. The implications of Hrushovski's observation that "two or three are not divisible into smaller groups" (i.e., they are only divisible by themselves; "Free Rhythms," 187) are very much of the same vein.

413. For details and a full discussion of what follows, see F. W. Dobbs-Allsopp, "So-Called 'Number Parallelism' in Biblical Poetry" (unpublished manuscript). The central thrust of that essay is to counter the standard understanding of graded or ascending numerical sequences of the kind exemplified by Proverbs 30:18–19 as quasi-synonymous word-pairs. The numbers are always different and therefore not synonymous. Rather, I propose that what is being troped through this parallelistic play is not (chiefly) synonymity but number knowledge of various kinds (e.g., the numeral system, basic arithmetic), including especially counting—M. Pope points up the correct framework in his entry "Number, Numbering, Numbers," in *IDB* (vol. K–Q, 561–67, esp. 562–64), though his own explanation of the numerical sequences under review finally follows the standard interpretation.

414. G. Ifrah, *From One to Zero: A Universal History of Numbers* (trans. L. Bair; New York: Viking Penguin, 1985), 21.

415. T. Dantzig, *Number: The Language of Science* (New York: Plume Penguin, 2007 [1930]), 8.

416. Lowth, *Lectures*, II, 51–52; see esp. W. M. W. Roth, "The Numerical Sequence x/x+1 in the Old Testament," *VT* 12 (1962), 300–311.

417. O'Connor, *Hebrew Verse Structure*, 378; see Kugel, *Idea*, 42.

418. *The Universal History of Numbers: From Prehistory to the Invention of the Computer* (trans. D. Bellos, E. F. Harding, S. Wood, and I. Monk; New York: Wiley, 2000 [1998]), I, 20. The fact of abbreviation here should cause no problems. It is essentially the same process that lies behind such common contemporary English idioms as "One, two, three, go!," but also well attested in antiquity. For example, in Ugaritic narrative poetry, the passage of time is usually relayed in increments of seven (days, years) and the seven units literally counted out (e.g., CAT 1.14.III.2–4; 1.17.I.1–6). However, abbreviations of various sorts

occur, including various renditions of seven year/day periods with only the literal mention of the seventh increment (CAT 1.17.V.3–4; see 1.19.IV.13–18), renditions in which the period of elapsed time is telescoped to three- and four-day increments (e.g., CAT 1.14.IV.32–33, 44–46), and even once where Baal's absence is rendered in a parallel couplet as lasting for "seven years…, / (and) eight…" (CAT 1.19.I.42–44; see D. N. Freedman, "Counting Formulae in the Akkadian Epics," *JANES* 3 [1970–71], 75–80, esp. 81; S. B. Parker, *The Pre-biblical Narrative Tradition* [Atlanta: Scholars Press, 1989], 46–52).

419. See esp. Freedman, "Counting Formulae."

420. Here I intentionally overemphasize to make clear that the following pair of verse lines is the divine speech being referenced (see F.-L. Hossfeld and E. Zenger, *Psalms 2* [Hermeneia; Minneapolis: Fortress, 2005], 111, n. g). Most add "thing" in English (e.g., NJV) for the implicit noun, which is fine. Clearly, what are literally spoken and heard are words, *dābār / dĕbārîm* in biblical Hebrew, which can have either a general or more specific (e.g., promise, 1 Kgs 2:4; command, Gen 24:33; precept, Ps 50:17; see *TDOT*, III, 104) meaning depending on context. Here the "words" are the uttered chunks of poetry belatedly called a "line."

421. On the expansive and flexible notion of what counts as a "word" in primarily oral cultures, see R. F. Person, "The Ancient Israelite Scribe as Performer," *JBL* 117/4 (1998), 601–9. In reference to the short bit of South Slavic epic poetry quoted earlier and the "discrete" nature of the poem's component lines, Foley writes the following: "the *guslari* as much as told us the same thing [i.e., the discrete nature of the lineal units] when they insisted on the integrity of whole lines as 'words,' explaining that our [i.e., Western, literate] concept of the word just didn't square with theirs" (*Oral Poem*, 89).

422. Roston, *Prophet and Poet*, esp. 72; Morris, *Religious Sublime*, 160–61; Norton, *History of the English Bible*, 220.

423. *Hebrew Verse Structure*, 149.

424. *Poetic Line*, 33.

425. Esp. Gruber, "Biblical Parallelism," 291.

426. See Brogan and Piper, "Couplet," 244–45; Brogan, "Distich," 299.

427. *Poetic Line*, 27–28.

428. Bits of poems are also obviously quoted at various points in the Bible as well. These normally go unattributed and therefore it is frequently difficult to know for certain whether they are in fact quotations from larger poems or themselves very short poems (and to some extent the dominant orality of the informing tradition blunts even this distinction). But there are a handful of times where we can be a good deal more certain about the quotative process. The reprise of the Song of the Sea's (Exod 15:1–18) opening couplet in Exod 15:21 is perhaps the parade example: *šîrû l-yhwh kî-gā'ōh gā'â / sûs wĕrōkĕbô rāmâ bayyām* "Sing to Yahweh for he has triumphed gloriously, / horse and rider he cast into the sea." That this is a quotation is made clear because we also happen

to have the whole poem from which it is taken. And that such quotes usually come in groupings of two lines or more follows from and reveals in a most pointed manner the distichic base of biblical poetry. Even the variation in initial verb form (*šîrû*, v. 21 // *ʾāšîrâ*, v. 1) is consistent with biblical poetry's originary performative environment, where reperformances of poems (written and oral) would inevitably involve variation of just this sort.

429. Couey ("Poetry of First Isaiah," 24–26) also emphasizes the instability of our notion of the line and the need to always construe it, though in a different way, using ideas inspired by Pinsky's thinking (especially in *Sounds of Poetry*, 35, 46).

CHAPTER 2

1. So most recently, M. Miller, *Collage of Myself* (Lincoln: University of Nebraska Press, 2010), 25.

2. August 4, 1860 (p. no. unknown), reprinted in R. M. Bucke, *Walt Whitman* (Philadelphia: David McKay, 1883), 200–201; and now also in M. Hindus, *Walt Whitman* (New York: Routledge, 1997), 103–4; cf. K. M. Price, *Walt Whitman: The Contemporary Reviews* (Cambridge: Cambridge University Press, 1996), 108. There is also a slightly earlier passing notice of Whitman as "too Hebraic to be polite" by his friend G. S. Phillips ("Literature. Leaves of Grass—by Walt Whitman," *New York Illustrated News* 2 [May 26 1860], 43; reprinted in Walt Whitman, *A Child's Reminiscence* [ed. T. O. Mabbott and R. G. Silver; Seattle: University of Washington Press, 1930], 33).

3. "Biblical Analogies for Walt Whitman's Prosody," *Revue Anglo-Americaine* 6 (1933), 490–507; "Biblical Echoes in Whitman's Works," *American Literature* 6 (1934), 302–15.

4. "Biblical Analogies," 491.

5. "Biblical Analogies."

6. "Biblical Analogies," 490, n. 3.

7. "Biblical Analogies," 505.

8. G. W. Allen, *American Prosody* (New York: American Book, 1935), 221.

9. For details, see F. W. Dobbs-Allsopp, *Walt Whitman and the King James Bible: A Biblicist's Perspective* (in preparation).

10. "The prosody of a poem," according to C. O. Hartman (*Free Verse: An Essay on Prosody* [Evanston, Ill.: Northwestern University Press, 1980], 13), "is the poet's method of controlling the reader's temporal experience of the poem, especially his attention to that experience." Cf. T. V. F. Brogan, "Prosody," in *NPEPP*, 980–94.

11. *American Prosody*, 220; see Allen, "Biblical Analogies," 491; Hartman, *Free Verse*, 90. The truth, of course, is that such "free" rhythms—such nonmetrical verse—are attested even earlier than the Bible, as they are characteristic of ancient Mesopotamian, Ugaritic, and Egyptian poetry as well (e.g., D. Wesling and

E. Bollobás, "Free Verse," in *NPEPP*, 425; G. B. Cooper, "Free Verse," in *PEPP*).
Allen also stresses in his comments here that Whitman's verse (and by extension free verse more generally) is not entirely "free" either. This is a point
I return to later at a number of places. Here it will suffice to direct readers to
B. H. Smith's discussion of free verse in which she, too, emphasizes the common
misapprehension of freedom when directed at nonmetrical verse (*Poetic Closure: A Study of How Poems End* [Chicago: University of Chicago Press, 1968],
84–95). As she observes, "the distinction between metrical verse and free verse
is a relative, not an absolute, one" (87).

12. For example, C. Beyers rightly emphasizes that Whitman was not the originator of
free verse (*A History of Free Verse* [Fayetteville: University of Arkansas Press, 2001],
39–40)—though certainly one of its better known practitioners (in English).

13. Of course, Whitman himself notices the rhythmic and specifically nonmetrical
nature of biblical verse—"rhyming" and "metre" were not "characteristic[s] of
Hebrew poetry at all"—via a reference culled from a New York rabbi, Frederick
de Sola Mendes, in the late essay "The Bible as Poetry," first published in the
Critic (3 3, 1883), 57, and then later included as part of *November Boughs* (Philadelphia: David McKay, 1888), 45–46. And this was consistent with scholarly
knowledge of the day, see M. Stuart, *A Hebrew Chrestomathy* (Andover, Mass.:
Codman Press, 1829), 193–94 (Stuart's *Chrestomathy* was eventually included
[minus the Hebrew text] at the end of his translation *Hebrew Grammar of Gesenius* (ed. E. Roediger; trans. M. Stuart; Andover, Mass.: Allen, Morrill, and
Wardwell, 1846], 352). George Wither (1588–1667 CE) is an outstanding example of a premodern who recognized the nonmetrical nature of biblical verse:
"The *Hebrews* are full of variety in their *Numbers*, and take great liberty in their
Verses. For as *Marianus Victorius* reports, they are not alwaies measured out by
the same Number or quality of Syllables, as the *Greeke* or *Latine Verses* are"
(*A Preparation to the Psalter* [London: Nicholas Okes, 1619], 59).

14. E. E. Grier (ed.), *Notebooks and Unpublished Prose Manuscripts* (6 vols.; New York:
New York University Press, 1984), 1:353. For discussion, see E. Folsom, *Whitman
Making Books/Books Making Whitman: A Catalog and Commentary* (Iowa City:
Obermann Center for Advanced Studies, University of Iowa, 2005), www.whit-
manarchive.org/criticism/current/anc.00150.html, accessed February 19, 2015.

15. See the convenient review in D. R. Vance, *The Question of Meter in Biblical
Hebrew Poetry* (Lewiston, NY: Edwin Mellen, 2001).

16. (2 vols.; trans. G. Gregory; London: J. Johnson, 1787; reprinted in *Robert Lowth
(1710–1787): The Major Works*, vols. 1–2 [London: Routledge, 1995]), I, 55–73.

17. *Lectures*, I, 56.

18. *Lectures*, I, 65.

19. Hartman, *Free Verse*, 24–25.

20. Unfortunately, Allen's strong dependence for his understanding of Lowth on
the likes of J. H. Gardiner (*The Bible as Literature* [New York, 1906]) and R. G.

Moulton (*Modern Reader's Bible for Schools* [New York: Macmillan, 1922]), both of whom exhibit a tendency to simplify and thereby distort Lowth's actual thinking on matters (cf. D. Norton, *A History of the English Bible as Literature* [Cambridge: Cambridge University Press, 2004], 227), often vitiates his insights into Whitman.

21. Esp. in the *Preliminary Dissertation* to the *New Translation* of Isaiah (*Isaiah. A New Translation: with a Preliminary Dissertation, and Notes* [London: J. Nichols, 1778; reprinted in *Robert Lowth (1710–1787): The Major Works* (London: Routledge, 1995)], x–xxviii).

22. See H. Smith, "English Metrical Psalms in the Sixteenth Century and Their Literary Significance," *Huntington Library Quarterly* 9 (1946), 249–71; L. B. Campbell, *Divine Poetry and Drama in Sixteenth-Century England* (Berkeley: University of California Press, 1959); M. Roston, *Prophet and Poet: The Bible and the Growth of Romanticism* (Evanston, Ill.: Northwestern University Press, 1965), esp. 15–41, 126–42; D. B. Morris, *The Religious Sublime: Christian Poetry and Critical Tradition in 18th-Century England* (Lexington: University of Kentucky, 1972), 14–22, 104–14; B. K. Lewalski, *Protestant Poetics and the Seventeenth-Century Religious Lyric* (Princeton: Princeton University Press, 1979), esp. 31–71; R. Zim, *English Metrical Psalms: Poetry as Praise and Prayer, 1535–1601* (Cambridge: Cambridge University Press, 1987).

23. *Prophet and Poet*, 134—for details, see 133–42.

24. *Fragments of Ancient Poetry, Collected in the Highlands of Scotland, and Translated from the Garlic or Erse Language* (Edinburgh: G. Hamilton and J. Balfour, 1760); *Fingal, an Ancient Epic Poem, in Six Books: Together with Several Other Poems* (London: Becket and P. A. De Hondt, 1762); *The Works of Ossian, the Song of Fingal, in Two Volumes* (London: Becket and P. A. De Hondt, 1765).

25. For example, see the essays in H. Gaskill (ed.), *Ossian Revisited* (Edinburgh: Edinburgh University Press, 1991), and in J. Porter (ed.), "Special Issue: James Macpherson and the Ossian Epic Debate," *Journal of American Folklore* 114/454 (2001).

26. Esp. D. S. Thomson, *The Gaelic Sources of Macpherson's Ossian* (Edinburgh: Edinburgh University Press, 1952); D. E. Meek, "The Gaelic Ballads of Scotland: Creativity and Adaptation," in *Ossian Revisited*, 19–48.

27. J. Porter, "'Bring Me the Head of James Macpherson': The Execution of Ossian and the Wellsprings of Folkloristic Discourse," *Journal of American Folklore* 114/454 (2001), 399; cf. Meek, "Gaelic Ballads in Scotland."

28. Roston, *Prophet and Poet*, esp. 145–46; R. Bauman and C. Briggs, *Voices of Modernity: Language Ideologies and the Politics of Inequality* (Cambridge: Cambridge University Press, 2003), 155, n. 20; S. L. Sanders, *The Invention of Hebrew* (Urbana: University of Illinois Press, 2009), 26. Not only is the content often very reminiscent of the Bible (e.g., see the passage cited by Roston, *Prophet and Poet*, 144, which is strikingly like the Song of Songs) but apparently Macpherson even supplies references to biblical parallels in the notes to his "translation"

(Morris, *Religious Sublime*, 165). It is quite certain that Hugh Blair, who actively encouraged Macpherson's work and defended the authenticity of the presumed originals (*Critical Dissertation on the Poems of Ossian* [Garland, 1765]), was very knowledgeable of Lowth—indeed, almost his entire assessment is carried out in Lowthian terms (Roston, *Prophet and Poet*, 144–46).

29. Originally published in *November Boughs*, 12–13 (the essay was also included at the end of the so-called deathbed edition of *Leaves of Grass* [Philadelphia: David McKay, 1891–2], 425–38). An 1839 edition of *The Poems of Ossian* (Philadelphia) was found in Whitman's book collection at his death (see D. S. Reynolds, *Walt Whitman's America* [New York: Vintage, 1995], 314; see P. Zweig, *Walt Whitman: The Making of the Poet* [New York: Basic Books, 1984], 150).

30. For the connection of Smart and Blake to Lowth, see Roston, *Prophet and Poet*, 135, 148, 165; it is not clear whether Whitman actually knew Smart's work at all, and it is likely that he came to know Blake only later in his career, see Zweig, *Walt Whitman*, 150; C. K. Williams, *On Whitman* (Princeton: Princeton University Press, 2010), 6–7; cf. Beyers, *History of Free Verse*, 39. F. Stovall (*The Foreground of Leaves of Grass* [Charlottesville: University Press of Virginia, 1974] 185–88) entertains the possibility that Whitman's knowledge of the Bible was learned from "books and articles on Hebrew poetry." He comes to no firm conclusion, but surveys possible secondary sources to which Whitman could have had access. Of the two premier eighteenth-century discussions, Lowth's *Lectures on the Sacred Poetry of the Hebrews* (original Latin 1753; translated into English in 1787 by G. Gregory) and J. G. Herder's *The Spirit of Hebrew Poetry* (1782; translated into English in 1833 by J. Marsh), Whitman's own aesthetic sensibilities align more naturally with Herder's. But neither work is an easy read, and I think it doubtful that Whitman, apparently not always the most studious of readers, would have had the patience to wade through either book, let alone distill their essential insights—Lowth has been as misappreciated as appreciated by biblical specialists. Stovall is unable to tie Whitman to any of the secondary sources he considers.

31. See Zweig, *Walt Whitman*, 149–50; Reynolds, *Walt Whitman's America*, 315–17; M. Cohem, "Martin Tupper, Walt Whitman, and the Early Reviews of *Leaves of Grass*," *WWRQ* 16 (1998), 22–31; Miller, *Collage of Myself*, 25–26.

32. B. Hrushovski, "On Free Rhythms in Modern Poetry," in T. Sebeok (ed.), *Style in Language* (New York: Wiley, 1960), 173–90. M. Kinzie even calls it "biblical free verse," saying that this is how "it is more commonly known"—though I do not know what common knowledge she is referencing (*A Poet's Guide to Poetry* [Chicago: University of Chicago Press, 1999], 337).

33. Esp. Hrushovski, "On Free Rhythms," 189–90; A. Cooper, "Biblical Poetics: A Linguistic Approach" (Ph.D. diss., Yale University, 1976), 30–31; T. Collins, *Line-Forms in Hebrew Poetry: A Grammatical Approach to the Stylistic Study of the Hebrew Prophets* (Rome: Biblical Institute, 1978), 251; M. O'Connor, *Hebrew Verse Structure* (Winona Lake, Ind.: Eisenbrauns, 1980), 138; J. Kugel, *The Idea*

of Biblical Poetry (New Haven: Yale University Press, 1981), 141; D. Pardee, "Ugaritic and Hebrew Metrics," in G. D. Young (ed.), *Ugarit in Retrospect: Fifty Years
of Ugarit and Ugaritic* (Winona Lake, Ind.: Eisenbrauns, 1981), 115; R. Alter, *The
Art of Biblical Poetry* (New York: Basic Books, 1985), 9; D. Peterson and K. Richards, *Interpreting Hebrew Poetry* (Minneapolis: Fortress, 1992), 37–47; Vance,
Question of Meter; J. F. Hobbins, "Meter in Ancient Hebrew Poetry: A History
of Modern Research," 2005, http://ancienthebrewpoetry.typepad.com/ancient_
hebrew_poetry/files/meter_in_ancient_hebrew_poetry_a_history_of_modern_
research.pdf, accessed February 19, 2015.

34. J. F. Hobbins's "Regularities in Ancient Hebrew Verse: A New Descriptive Model,"
    ZAW 119/4 [2007], 564–85) is a recent exception. He, too, builds consciously on
    Hrushovski's (esp. as viewed through Alter, i.e., the "Harshav-Alter Description")
    basic understanding of Hebrew verse structure ("the most fitting description of
    ancient Hebrew verse known to the present writer," 565), often in ways most con-
    genial to my own thinking, though with a far more emphatic linguistic focus.

35. As R. D. Cureton stresses, critical comment on free verse prosody generally is
    disturbingly thin (*Rhythmic Phrasing in English Verse* [London: Longman, 1992],
    70–71, n. 6). In what follows, in addition to Hrushovski's seminal ideas, and
    also Cureton's pioneering work, I am most heavily influenced in my thinking
    about rhythm and free verse prosody by S. K. Langer, *Feeling and Form: A Theory
    of Art* (New York: Scribner, 1953), esp. chs. 7 and 8; Smith, *Poetic Closure*, esp.
    84–92; Hartman, *Free Verse*; D. Attridge, *The Rhythms of English Poetry* (London:
    Longman, 1982); *Poetic Rhythm: An Introduction* (Cambridge: Cambridge Uni-
    versity Press, 1995); A. Holder, *Rethinking Meter: A New Approach to the Verse
    Line* (Lewisburg: Bucknell University Press, 1995); D. Wesling, *The Scissors of
    Meter: Grammetrics and Reading* (Ann Arbor: University of Michigan Press,
    1996); R. Tsur, *Poetic Rhythm: Structure and Performance* (Berne: Peter Lang,
    1998); G. B. Cooper, *Mysterious Music: Rhythm and Free Verse* (Stanford: Stanford
    University Press, 1998); Beyers, *History of Free Verse*. My account is ultimately
    aimed at facilitating richer, more perspicuous, more rewarding readings of bib-
    lical poems and thus remains practical and decidedly not technical (in the
    manner of either Cureton's *Rhythmic Phrasing* or Tsur's *Poetic Rhythm*, for ex-
    ample), though substantial enough to answer Hrushovski's call to elaborate his
    (brief) "remarks" on this topic ("On Free Rhythms," 188).

36. *Poetic Rhythm*, 3. Related conceptions of rhythm are articulated in O. Barfield,
    "Poetry, Verse and Prose," *New Statesman* 31 (1928), 793; Langer, *Feeling and
    Form*, 126; Hrushovski, "On Free Rhythms," 179 ("the whole impact of the
    movement of the language material in the reading of a poem"); Smith, *Poetic
    Closure*, 84–92; Cooper, "Biblical Poetics," 30–31; Hartman, *Free Verse*, 14 ("Rhythm,
    in poetry, is the temporal distribution of the elements of language"), 22, 24–25;
    P. Zumthor, "The Text and the Voice," *New Literary History* 16 (1984), 83–84;
    R. Cureton, "Rhythm: A Multilevel Analysis," *Style* 19 (1985), 242–57; "A Definition

of Rhythm," *Eidos* 3 (1987), 7–17; *Rhythmic Phrasing*, 121; J. Hollander, *Rhyme's Reason* (enlg. ed.; New Haven: Yale University Press, 1989), 26; T. V. F. Brogan, "Rhythm," in *NPEPP*, 1066–67; Cooper, *Mysterious Music*, esp. 16–42.

37. Attridge, *Poetic Rhythm*, 7; cf. Barfield, "Poetry, Verse and Prose," 793; Smith, *Poetic Closure*, 87; Cooper, "Biblical Poetics," 30–31; Hartman, *Free Verse*, 22 30; T. V. F. Brogan, "Meter," in *NPEPP*, esp. 768–69; Cureton, *Rhythmic Phrasing*, 123–24; Cooper, *Mysterious Music*, 28–29. The basic orientation of most of these thinkers is to treat metrical and nonmetrical verse holistically: "No absolute distinction may be made between the sources of rhythm in free verse and metrical poetry" (Smith, *Poetic Closure*, 85; see also the somewhat idiosyncratic but often insightful Wesling, *Scissors of Meter*, esp. 52–53). It is also worth noting that the Greek metrical tradition—which is an utterly diverse and not monolithic tradition—likely evolved itself out of nonmetrical traditions, see esp. G. Nagy, "Formula and Meter," in *Oral Literature and the Formula* (ed. B. A. Stolz and R. S. Shannon; Ann Arbor: University of Michigan Press, 1976), 239–60.

38. "On Free Rhythms," 179.

39. Esp. Brogan, "Rhythm," 1068.

40. Attridge, *Poetic Rhythm*, 6.

41. This obviously means to reverse the emphasis that Lowth makes in the title of his third lecture, "The Hebrew Poetry Is Metrical." As I illustrate later, some Hebrew poetry is metrical, but not the biblical variety.

42. For convenient surveys of this literature, see Cooper, "Biblical Poetics," 19–34; Vance, *Question of Meter*; Hobbins, "Meter in Ancient Hebrew Poetry."

43. See—perhaps most (in)famously—K. Budde, "Das hebräische Klagelied," *ZAW* 2 (1882), 1–52.

44. "Prosody, Hebrew," in *EcyJud* (1971–72), 13: 1201–2.

45. Lowth, *Lectures*, I, 57–58.

46. *Psalm 119: The Exaltation of Torah* (Winona Lake, Ind.: Eisenbrauns, 1999), 63. J. P. Fokkelman provides syllable tallies for the psalm, and again the numbers never align (*Major Poems of the Hebrew Bible at the Interface of Prosody and Structural Analysis. Volume III: the Remaining 65 Psalms* [SSN; Assen: Van Gorcum, 2003], 373–79). His counts by verse for the first stanza (Ps 119:1–8) are as follows (p. 373):

   1. $6 + 9 = 15$
   2. $8 + 7 = 15$
   3. $7 + 6 = 13$
   4. $9 + 4 = 13$
   5. $8 + 5 = 13$
   6. $8 + 6 = 14$
   7. $7 + 9 = 16$
   8. $6 + 8 = 14$

Tallying words or stresses fares no better in bringing these lines and couplets into regular alignment.

47. *Psalms 1–59* (trans. H. Oswald; Minneapolis: Fortress, 1993), 269.
48. "The Contours of Biblical Verse: An Afterword to *Hebrew Verse Structure*," in *Hebrew Verse Structure* (Winona Lake, Ind.: Eisenbrauns, 1997 [1980]) (Google Books ed.), 632, n. 2.
49. *Hebrew Verse Structure*, 201.
50. *Hebrew Verse Structure*, 209. For this analysis, see B. Hrushovski, "Note on the Systems of Hebrew Versification," in T. Carmi, *The Penguin Book of Hebrew Verse* (New York: Penguin Books, 1982), 60.
51. "Note on the Systems of Hebrew Versification," 57–68.
52. Precisely to this point, C. L. Seow reports (email, February 5, 2014) that Moses ibn Ezra, a renowned paytan from Andalusia, already in the eleventh century questioned the notion of biblical poetry as metrical: "We have found nothing [in Scripture] departing from prose save . . . Psalms, Job, and Proverbs. And these . . . employ neither meter nor rhyme in the manner of the Arabs," *Kitāb al-Muḥāḍara wal-Mudhākara: Sefer ha-ʿIyyunim we-ha-Diyyunim* [*The Book of Discussion and Conversation*] (ed. and trans. A. S. Halkin; Jerusalem, 1975).
53. There is also quite an abundance of fully unfettered free verse in postbiblical Hebrew poetry, especially in more recent times, which provides a still further means of meaningfully triangulating on the biblical verse tradition. In this latter instance, there are broad continuities in overall prosody, though the later, non-biblical free verse typically lacks the constraint on overall line length that is evidenced in its biblical counterpart. Other resources on postbiblical Hebrew poetry include R. F. Mintz, *Modern Hebrew Poetry: A Bilingual Edition* (3d ed.; Berkeley: University of California Press, 1982); S. Burnshaw et al. (eds.), *The Modern Hebrew Poem Itself* (new and updated ed.; Detroit: Wayne State University Press, 2003); P. Cole, *The Dream of the Poem* (Princeton: Princeton University Press, 2007); T. Keller, *Poetry on the Edge: An Anthology of Contemporary Hebrew Poetry* (Albany: State University of New York Press, 2008).
54. "On Free Rhythms," 189; elaborated some in his entry "Hebrew Prosody," in the *Encyclopedia Judaica*, and again in his "Note on the Systems of Hebrew Versification." Interestingly, Hrushovski was anticipated in his insights by the musicologist C. Sachs (*Rhythm and Tempo: A Study in Music History* [New York: Norton, 1953], 69–70), who said of biblical poetry that it "is the classic example of a free accentual rhythm." He even elaborates: "It never squeezes emotion or meaning into formal, regular patterns of meter or stress. No frigid, monotonous sequence of uniform iambs or dactyls, no constant number of feet in a verse, no even distribution of accents" (70). Cf. Cooper, "Biblical Poetics," 34–35.
55. "On Free Rhythms," 173.
56. "On Free Rhythms," 178, 179, n. 13, 180. In fact, it is not too much to say that ametrical rhythm *requires* appreciation on its own terms. Both J. Frigyesi and M. R. L. Clayton, for example, have stressed the naivete of approaching free rhythm forms of non-Western music solely from the perspective of metricity, the dominant perspective of Western music theory (Frigyesi, "Preliminary

Thoughts toward the Study of Music without Clear Beat: The Example of 'Flowing Rhythm' in Jewish 'Nusah,'" *Asian Music* 24 [1993], esp. 64–66; Clayton, "Free Rhythm: Ethnomusicology and the Study of Music without Metre," *BSOAS* 59 [1996], 325–27). Wesling mounts a similar critique from the perspective of contemporary avant-garde poetries (*Scissors of Meter*, 32–38).

57. See Smith, *Poetic Closure*, 85; Cureton, *Rhythmic Phrasing*, 71, n. 6, 120; Wesling, *Scissors of Meter*. 51–54; Attridge, *Poetic Rhythm*, 6–7, 176; cf. Hartman, *Free Verse*, 10–28. The sources of rhythm in language arts are everywhere the same, the elements of language themselves. Musicologists similarly have begun thinking through rhythm in these more holistic terms as well, e.g., R. Jourdain, *Music, the Brain, and Ecstasy* (New York: Harper, 2002 [1997]), 122–23; E. F. Clarke, "Rhythm and Timing in Music," in D. Deutsch (ed.), *The Psychology of Music* (2d ed.; San Diego: Academic, 1999), 473–500; M. A. Thaut, *Rhythm, Music, and the Brain* (New York: Routledge, 2005), 4–5. In fact, Cureton models his own thinking about rhythm in poetry most explicitly on the work of music theorists (123), and it is clear that a richer understanding of rhythm generally will result from an exploration of the phenomenon mindful of its nature in these (and other) art forms. Smith's work in *Poetic Closure* is also informed by an awareness that poetry and music both produce "experiences that are temporally organized" (9). Jourdain even offers a statement about the existence of nonmetered song that mirrors Hrushovski's about nonmetered verse: "Music can exist in the absence of strict temporal patterning" (*Music, the Brain, and Ecstasy*, 125).

58. As Brogan underscores ("Rhythm," 1068), this is very much now the "established view." So already M. Jousse, *The Oral Style* (trans. E. Sienaert and R. Whitaker; New York: Garland, 1990 [French original, 1925]), 240: "All metre is rhythm, but not all rhythm is metre."

59. Hrushovski, "On Free Rhythms," 180.

60. *Scissors of Meter*, 102.

61. Attridge, *Poetic Rhythm*, 1–3. For a related image with similar consequences, see Zumthor, "Text and the Voice," 74–75 ("Each syllable acquires a rhythm from the pulsing of blood in our veins, and the energy arising from this converts the question into a declaration, memory into a prophecy, and covers up the tracks the loss of which irreparably affects our language and our time"); R. Pinsky, *The Sounds of Poetry: A Brief Guide* (New York: Farrar, Straus and Giroux, 1998), 8; Thaut, *Rhythm, Music, and the Brain*, 3 (emphasizing the physicality of the sound "vibrations transduced in our hearing apparatus into electrochemical information"); M. K. Blasing, *Lyric Poetry: The Pain and the Pleasure of Words* (Princeton: Princeton University Press, 2007), 58 ("we cannot physically experience verbal rhythm in a way that is distinguishable from a mental experience"). Jousse (*Oral Style*, 17) anticipates all such descriptions: "Vocal sound is the result of a struggle that takes place at certain determinate points between the organs of speech and pressurised air expelled by the lungs. It is therefore natural that we should observe . . . the column of air employed in each sound and

for the same sound in different places that it may occupy in the various vocal groups [in the laryngo-bucal gestures]." (Jousse's work consists of a series of quotations—culled from some five hundred separate sources—with his own contributions folded in brackets.) Here it is quite apparent that the explosion of sound that constitutes human speech is inherently and necessarily rhythmic.

62. *Orality and Literacy: The Technologizing of the Word* (London: Routledge, 1982), 32.

63. *Orality and Literacy*, 34; cf. E. A. Havelock on the importance of "rhythmic speech" to memory and oral tradition throughout his *Preface to Plato* (Cambridge, Mass.: Harvard University Press, 1963).

64. *Oral Style*, 125, 127; cf. 20–21. "Memories are nothing but [gestural reviviscences, more or less incomplete repetitions of past receptions] which we re-enact in ourselves.... Thus, when we bring to mind a dramatic scene which we witnessed..., we act it out [or, more precisely, we *re*-enact it].... We not only resuscitate...emotions felt in the past, with all of their physiological and physical accompaniment [set off in the order in which they previously occurred], but also [by combing prior gesticulations in new ways] we evoke new emotions...without precedent in our past life." Memory in this way is not only "reproductive," but "in fact essentially creative, [or, better, it selectively abbreviates and combines] and manifests itself as creative always, from the very beginning" (Jousse, *Oral Style*, 29–30).

65. Esp. Ong, *Orality and Literacy*, 85. Scripts of course mainly record linguistic data. Much rhythmicity in oral performance would not have been restricted to language elements alone but would have been signaled by any number of other means as well, e.g., musical instrumentation, melody, dance, foot-tapping, head-bobbing. My focus in this chapter by necessity will be on the language material of biblical poetry, as that is what has been preserved. Nonetheless, keeping in mind the richer performative environment that would have customarily enfleshed and enlivened these elements is of heuristic value, if only as a reminder of the relative impoverishment of our evidence.

66. *Poetic Closure*, 9; cf. P. Valery, *The Art of Poetry* (trans. D. Folliot; New York: Pantheon, 1961), 162.

67. Smith, *Poetic Closure*, 9, 16–17 ("the poem, *as an utterance*,...is, was, and always will be the script for its own performance").

68. *Poetry and the Fate of the Senses* (Chicago: University of Chicago Press, 2002), 68–69. Stewart here is strictly opposing the notion of the poem as "a representation of an utterance" or the need to imagine it as "a score or script," both ideas that are prominent in Smith's thinking. But Smith, I think, better grasps the consequences of writing as a graphic means of spatializing language. Moreover, Stewart's leading insights (e.g., her emphasis on the humanly authored nature of all discourse) stand regardless. For other illuminating insights on how writing complicates and supplements poetic discourse, see B. Antomarini, "The Acoustical Prehistory of Poetry," *NLH* 35 (2004), 355–72 (Stewart is Antomarini's translator), especially in her exposition of Amelia Rosselli's "Spazi metrici" (366–67).

69. *Oral Style*, 19; cf. 7–25, esp. 14–15. In this instance, Jousse's source in part is W. James (*Principles of Psychology* [2 vols.; New York: Holt, 1890], II, 372), whose ideas on these matters remain vital, see C. Petitmengin, "Towards the Source of Thoughts: The Gestural and Tramsmodal Dimension of Lived Experience," *Journal of Consciousness Studies* 14 (2007), 54–82, esp. 59 (and Jousse is another of her sources, 67, 69).

70. Esp. Jousse, *Oral Style*, 10–11; Thaut, *Rhythm, Music, and the Brain*, 5.

71. *Rhythmic Phrasing*, 121; 98–106.

72. E.g., J. Dewey, *Art as Experience* (New York: Perigee, 1934), esp. 163, 177; Langer, *Feeling and Form*, 126–29; Hrushovski, "On Free Rhythms," 187; Smith, *Poetic Closure*, esp. 8–14; Tsur, *Poetic Rhythm*, 13–16, 23–54; Attridge, *Poetic Rhythm*, esp. 1–4; Brogan, "Rhythm," 1067; Stewart, *Poetry and the Fate of the Senses*, 67–69; Antomarini, "Acoustical Prehistory."

73. *Art as Experience*, 162.

74. *Poetry and the Fate of the Senses*, 68–69.

75. *Art as Experience*, 176–77.

76. *Music, the Brain, and Ecstasy*, 137.

77. *Art as Experience*, 147; cf. 154; Langer, *Feeling and Form*, 126.

78. "Definition of Rhythm," 7.

79. Langer, *Feeling and Form*, 128.

80. Langer, *Feeling and Form*.

81. Smith, *Poetic Closure*, 10; cf. Cureton, *Rhythmic Phrasing*, 98–106.

82. See the essays collected in P. Desain and L. Windsor, *Rhythm Perception and Production* (Lisse, Netherlands: Swets and Zeitlinger, 2000)—the title underscores the bifold perspective of rhythm as a phenomenon. Jousse would have surely resisted such strict bifurcation, since for him, as Antomarini nicely phrases it, "oral language is a corporeal gesture that reproduces the actions of perception. Thanks to the natural rhythm of imitation, the listener in turn hears and imitates and remembers the gesture and continues the chain," "Acoustical Prehistory," 357; cf. H. You, "Defining Rhythm: Aspects of an Anthropology of Rhythm," *Culture, Medicine and Psychiatry* 18 (1994), 371. Language in humans, like all other gestures, begins in mimicry, miming the external world that confronts sentient life: "At each reception: 'in the presence of the object our whole body [reacts with a more or less visible gesticulation] and assumes an attitude that imitates it'" (Jousse, *Oral Style*, 23). In this way, E. Sienaert ("Marcel Jousse: The Oral Style and the Anthropology of Gesture," *Oral Tradition* 5 [1990], 95) elaborates: "man plays out what was played in him, plays out his receptions.... Play, then, is the osmosis of man and the reality that imposes itself upon him, it is the way by which reality is progressively instilled into him from childhood. It is this act of playing out, this play, that is at the origin of all art, for man needs to reproduce what he sees. He cannot but play out, he cannot do without art." Such artful playing and replaying, such mimicry, always gestural, even in its most latent stage, courses through human consciousness with

energy, movement, and thus rhythm. There is in Jousse, then, a stronger emphasis on the holism of rhythm's sourcing in human motor activity and a reluctance to pry its various components too far apart. Recent researchers, like Jourdain, concur. Though the sound of spoken language is a product of the vocal apparatus, language itself "clearly originates in the brain" (*Music, the Brain, and Ecstasy,* 149).

83. Thaut, *Rhythm, Music, and the Brain,* 4; cf. Dewey, *Art as Experience,* 162–69; Sachs, *Rhythm and Tempo,* 14.

84. *Music, the Brain, and Ecstasy,* 123.

85. The "natural" rhythm of human bodily movement figures frequently in discussions of rhythm (e.g., Wesling, *Scissors of Meter,* 39–47). Interestingly, S. Mithen, in *The Singing Neanderthals: The Origins of Music, Language, Mind, and Body* ([Cambridge, Mass.: Harvard University Press, 2006], 139–59), argues that one of the chief consequences of the evolution of bipedalism in *Homo ergaster* (1.8 million years ago) was to "take the role of rhythm," which is indispensable to efficient walking, running or any complex coordination of the human body, "to a new order of magnitude" (158). "Efficient bipedalism requires a brain that is able to supply temporal control to the complex coordination of muscle groups," and as "our ancestors evolved into bipedal humans so, too, would their inherent musical abilities [and eventually linguistic abilities, too] evolve—they got rhythm" (152). This all by way of underscoring that rhythm (and not meter) is a capacity crucial to human (bipedal) bodily existence and deeply embedded in our evolution as a species. That the temporal arts (e.g., music, poetry) should tap into and exploit our evolved sense of rhythm is not at all surprising. Indeed, it is most "natural," at least in an evolutionary sense.

86. Jourdain, *Music, the Brain, and Ecstasy,* 122–23.

87. For him rhythm includes two dominant phenomena, what he calls phrasing, the organic kind of rhythm just described, and meter, the more strictly patterned rhythm of accentuated beats. Cureton will also adopt a componential analysis of rhythm and develops the notion of phrasing in a very productive way, but not from Jourdain.

88. Jourdain, *Music, the Brain, and Ecstasy,* 123.

89. This is Attridge's formulation, *Poetic Rhythm,* 183.

90. For brief overview of typical "functions of rhythm in poetry," see Attridge, *Poetic Rhythm,* 11–19; cf. Smith, *Poetic Closure,* 87.

91. E.g., Cureton, "Definition of Rhythm," 8–10; Brogan, "Rhythm," 1067–68; Cooper, *Mysterious Music,* 16–42.

92. "Multilevel Analysis," 244.

93. *Feeling and Form,* 126; cf. Cureton, *Rhythmic Phrasing,* 124, 146–53.

94. *Feeling and Form,* 127.

95. *Feeling and Form,* 126–27; cf. Jourdain, *Music, the Brain, and Ecstasy,* 122–23.

96. *Primitive Music: An Inquiry into the Origins and Development of Music, Songs, Instruments, Dances, Pantomimes of Savage Races* (London: Longmans, 1893), 233.

97. Dewey, *Art as Experience*, 155; cf. Wallaschek, *Primitive Music*, 234.

98. *Primitive Music*, 233–34—Wallaschek is quoting G. Allen, *Physical Aesthetics* (New York: Appleton, 1877), 114.

99. Esp. Cureton, "Definition of Rhythm," 8; *Rhythmic Phrasing*, 124; Cooper, *Mysterious Music*, 30–35.

100. "Rhythm," 1067.

101. Smith, *Poetic Closure*, 13; for the operation of the mind reading and processing in short-term memory, see very similarly Brogan, "Rhythm," 1067: "in reading a text, the mind makes a rapid series of predictions each second about what it ought to see next based on what it has just previously seen (and still holds in short-term memory), and if the expected signal is delayed or missing, the mind often supplies it anyway."

102. So Cureton ("Definition of Rhythm," 8): "Recurrence multiplies opportunities for both structural anticipation and the rise and fall of … saliences."

103. *Mysterious Music*, 30.

104. *Feeling and Form*, 129.

105. Smith, *Poetic Closure*, 38; cf. M. Shapiro, "Repetition," in *NPEPP*, 1035–37.

106. Dewey, *Art as Experience*, 166; Langer, *Feeling and Form*, 129; Cooper, *Mysterious Music*, 19; Cureton, "Definition of Rhythm," 8 (though Cureton also emphasizes that rhythmic structure is not necessarily recurrent, 7); *Rhythmic Phrasing*, 106–10; Brogan, "Rhythm," 1067.

107. L. Windsor and P. Desain, "Introduction: Multiple Perspectives on Rhythm Perception and Production," in Desain and Windsor, *Rhythm Perception and Production*, xii.

108. Smith, *Poetic Closure*, 39.

109. Langer, *Feeling and Form*, 129, and Cureton, *Rhythmic Phrasing*, 107.

110. "Definition of Rhythm," 8.

111. *Art as Experience*, 154; cf. Langer, *Feeling and Form*, 66, 127; Brogan, "Rhythm," 1067; Attridge, *Poetic Rhythm*, 3; Hrushovski, "Prosody," 1201.

112. *Art as Experience*, 154–55; cf. Brogan, "Rhythm," 1067.

113. Cf. Jourdain, *Music, the Brain, and Ecstasy*, 130; Thaut, *Rhythm, Music, and the Brain*, 11—"changes of contour" is what distinguishes the various groupings of rhythmic events of which so much non-Western, free rhythmic music consists.

114. "Definition of Rhythm," 8.

115. *Music, the Brain, and Ecstasy*, 126; cf. Frigyesi, "Flowing Rhythm," 63.

116. Jourdain, *Music, the Brain, and Ecstasy*, 126.

117. Jousse, *Oral Style*, 14; Attridge, *Poetic Rhythm*, 3; Brogan, "Rhythm," 1067.

118. Clayton, "Free Rhythm," 330; cf. Frigyesi, "Flowing Rhythm," 63, 66.

119. Cureton, "Definition of Rhythm," 8; cf. *Rhythmic Phrasing*, 121–23; Cooper, *Mysterious Music*, 27–28.

120. *Art as Experience*, 166.

121. "On Free Rhythms," 187.

122. Cureton, "Definition of Rhythm," 8, and in detail in *Rhythmic Phrasing*, 124, 135–46; cf. Hrushovski, "On Free Rhythms," 187–88; Smith, *Poetic Closure*, 41, 47–48, 70–78, 84, 90; Brogan, "Rhythm," 1067–68.

123. G. A. Miller, "The Magical Number Seven, Plus or Minus Two," *Psychology Review* 63 (1956), 81–97 (available at www.musanim.com/miller1956/, accessed February 19, 2015)—Miller stands at the head of the line of "psychologists" implicated in Cureton's comment ("Definition of Rhythm," 8). Jourdain discusses the topic under the rubric of the "perceptual present," a psychological experience of time that "arises from the nervous system's perception of its own interaction with the world"; "the minimum time it takes to sense and perceive and categorize, and it is dictated by the speed at which neurons fire" (*Music, the Brain, and Ecstasy*, 136; cf. 135–41).

124. Jourdain emphasizes that "memory is music's canvas" (*Music, the Brain, and Ecstasy*, 132). The same of course might be said of orally performed poetry.

125. *Music, the Brain, and Ecstasy*, esp. 124–25; cf. E. B. Voigt, *The Art of Syntax: Rhythm of Thought, Rhythm of Song* (Minneapolis: Graywolf, 2009), 8–11. Jourdain illustrates chunking in the perception of language in this way: "Our brains grasp individual words as they appear, but not yet the meaning of a whole sentence. Yet we achieve some degree of understanding before the sentence is completed by formulating partial understandings of phrases and subphrases.... Rhythmic markers amplify our perception of such hierarchies, and therefore make them possible" (*Music, the Brain, and Ecstasy*, 125).

126. *Rhythmic Phrasing*, 124.

127. Thaut, *Rhythm, Music, and the Brain*, 6; cf. Attridge, *Poetic Rhythm*, 2–3; Cureton, "Definition of Rhythm," 7.

128. Smith, *Poetic Closure*, 4, 122–28; Hartman, *Free Verse*, 13.

129. Smith, *Poetic Closure*, 4. By the "representation of an utterance" Smith means to emphasize that however narrative or dramatic lyric poems may be in certain respects, they ultimately are not structured like events or actions (e.g., lyrics cannot end in death) but like "personal discourse"—so they are typically brief, resemble direct discourse, and take place in the present (esp. 122–23).

130. See Windsor and Desain, "Introduction," xii; J. A. Michon, "Introduction [to Part II: Tapping and Synchronization]," in Desain and Windsor, *Rhythm Perception and Production*, 84; Smith, *Poetic Closure*, 10–14, 119.

131. Cureton, *Rhythmic Phrasing*, 123–24; cf. P. Fraisse, *The Psychology of Time* (trans. J. Leith; Harper and Row, 1963).

132. "Rhythm," 1068; cf. Cureton, "Definition of Rhythm," 10; *Rhythmic Phrasing*, 121–23; Cooper, *Mysterious Music*, 35–42; Wedling, *Scissors of Meter*, 58–60.

133. Esp. Cureton, *Rhythmic Phrasing*, 121–23.

134. Jourdain, *Music, the Brain, and Ecstasy*, 143.

135. Esp. Jourdain, *Music, the Brain, and Ecstasy*, 120–22; cf. Dewey, *Art as Experience*, 166.

136. *Feeling and Form*, 126.
137. *Art as Experience*, 147.
138. S. T. Coleridge, "Shakespeare's Judgment Equal to His Genius," in D. A. Stauffer (ed.), *Selected Poetry and Prose of Samuel Taylor Coleridge* (New York: Random House, 1951), 432–33.
139. Dewey, *Art as Experience*, 155.
140. Hartman, *Free Verse*, 86.
141. Cureton, *Rhythmic Phrasing*, esp. 79–98.
142. E.g., Hrushovski, "On Free Rhythms"; Smith, *Poetic Closure*, esp. 84–95; Hartman, *Free Verse*, esp. 81–105; Wesling, *Scissors of Meter*; Attridge, *Poetic Rhythm*; Cureton, *Rhythmic Phrasing*.
143. *Mysterious Music*, 72; cf. Langer, *Feeling and Form*, 129: "it is just the sort of play on a basic pattern...that is characteristic of organic forms."
144. Attridge, *Rhythms of English Poetry*, 309.
145. Jousse (*Oral Style*, 113–22), too, connects the freer rhythms of modern free verse (explicitly mentioning Whitman!) with those of the Bible, but also with Assyrian and Babylonian poetry from ancient Mesopotamia and with the various oral poetries he knew from traditional, nonchirographic cultures. And all almost a decade before Allen.
146. Indeed, as Hobbins emphasizes, the kinds of rhythmic variability typical of biblical poetry also characterize "earlier periods" (in particular) of other poetic traditions even outside of the ancient Near East ("Regularities in Ancient Hebrew Verse," 579 and n. 30.
147. E. A. Havelock (*The Literate Revolution in Greece and Its Cultural Consequences* [Princeton: Princeton University Press, 1982], 115–19) has a Joussean sensibility with regard to this same topic, though he nowhere cites Jousse. Havelock notes that writing's great boon is its ability to preserve language—an inscribed document can be changed only "by an act of physical destruction." In oral culture, on the other hand, there is only one way to fix language, "by the arrangement of words in a rhythmic sequence which is independent of the words, but in which they have to respond acoustically."
148. *Oral Style*, 113. The quote is from A. Condamin, *Le livre de Jérémie* (Paris, 1920), 238.
149. *Literate Revolution in Greece*, 116.
150. As cited in Havelock, *Literate Revolution in Greece*, 117—presumably based on some form of the KJB.
151. Havelock, *Literate Revolution in Greece*, 117.
152. Thaut, *Rhythm, Music, and the Brain*, 11.
153. Clayton, "Free Rhythm," 330.
154. Thaut, *Rhythm, Music, and the Brain*, 11.
155. Frigyesi, "Flowing Rhythm," esp. 60–65; Clayton, "Free Rhythm," 328–30. Jourdain (*Music, the Brain, and Ecstasy*, 120–24) opens his discussion by pointing up just this difference between meter and rhythm proper. He contrasts the regularity

of beat in an imagined performance of the *Nutcracker* with the clear but nonperiodic beat of an imagined drum performance in a Central African village.

156. Esp. Thaut, *Rhythm, Music, and the Brain,* 11–14.

157. *Rhythm and Tempo,* 20.

158. "Flowing Rhythm," 67.

159. *Rhythm and Tempo,* 21.

160. Thaut, *Rhythm, Music, and the Brain,* 11.

161. Frigyesi, "Flowing Rhythm," 65.

162. Frigyesi, "Flowing Rhythm," 68.

163. "On Free Rhythms," 189; cf. Cooper, "Biblical Poetics," 34–35.

164. Hrushovski, "On Free Rhythms," 183. "Free rhythms" is an English gloss of the German *freie Rhythmen,* which Hrushovski prefers to either the French *vers libre* or its English counterpart, *free verse*—mainly because "free rhythms" offers a more positive take on the prosody of nometrical poems ("On Free Rhythms," 183–84). My own use of "free rhythms" is very much intended in the spirit of Hrushovski's (and to recognize his contribution), as a broad cover term for nonmetrical verse, and not meaning to implicate more specifically its German etymon (see D. H. Chisholm, "Freie Rhythmen," in *NPEPP,* 427; D. H. Chisholm and K. Bowers, "Freie Rhythmen," in *PEPP*)—though interestingly Friederich Gottlieb Klopstock, whose poetry from the 1750s the term came to describe, was very much influenced in his prosodic orientation by the Bible, and especially the Psalms (see K. M. Kohl, *Rhetoric, the Bible, and the Origins of Free Verse: The Early "Hymns" of Friedrich Gottlieb Klopstock* [Berlin: de Gruyter, 1990]).

165. See M. Schneider, "Primitive Music," in *The New Oxford History of Music,* vol. I, *Ancient and Oriental Music I* (Oxford: Oxford University Press, 1957), 31; B. Nettl, *Music in Primitive Culture* (Cambridge, Mass.: Harvard University Press, 1956), 57; G. Nagy, *Pindar's Homer: The Lyric Possession of an Epic Past* (Baltimore: Johns Hopkins University Press, 1990), esp. 34–35; M. L. West, *Ancient Greek Music* (Oxford: Clarendon Press, 1992), 39.

166. "On Free Rhythms," 183–84; cf. 176.

167. Chisholm, "Freie Rhythmen," 427.

168. *Origins of Free Verse,* 1; for the coinage of the term, see 1, n. 1.

169. Kohl, *Origins of Free Verse,* 1.

170. See now Cooper, "Free Verse," who does tip his hat to the Bible: "Scholars have pointed to possible predecessors such as ancient Heb[rew] lit[erature] and its mod[ern] trans[lations], esp. the King James Bible; the *Epic of Gilgamesh;* very early Gr[eek] poetry."

171. Hrushovski, "Prosody," 1201.

172. This is one of the chief consequences of Cureton's critique of traditional prosody, see *Rhythmic Phrasing,* 76–117; cf. Wesling, *Scissors of Meter,* 9–38.

173. Hrushovski, "On Free Rhythms," 180–81. Others writing on rhythm have also stressed these features, so Smith (*Poetic Closure,* 87) on holism and the need to always (re)embed prosodic theory in the reading of whole poems (cf. Wesling,

Scissors of Meter, 33, 53, 103), and Cureton ("Multilevel Analysis") on the multi-dimensional nature of rhythm. Smith's exemplary list of other "linguistic features" that factor more importantly than meter in the creation of "rhythmic effects of free verse" include "pitch levels, the relative value of junctures, assonance, internal rhyme, and simple word-repetition" (*Poetic Closure*, 87; cf. Cooper, *Mysterious Music*, 188–89).

174. *Rhythmic Phrasing*, 123.
175. Cureton borrows the musical idea of "reduction" in an effort to lay bare the different rhythmic layers that can be decomposed in poems, *Rhythmic Phrasing*, 200–11.
176. Hrushovski, "On Free Rhythms," 180. I am also indebted to Cureton's early "Rhythm: A Multilevel Analysis," in which he undertakes (in much briefer compass) a similar kind of phenomenally oriented exposition—although there, and also in the graphic analyses in his *Rhythmic Phrasing* (277–422), his treatment follows the hierarchical organization of rhythmic phenomena (lower to higher, higher to lower). While mindful of rhythmic hierarchies throughout, my own exposition begins with those elements that feature as the base for much biblical poetry or are otherwise most salient and then moves on to treat elements that get used to fine-tune and complicate a biblical poem's chief rhythmic layers. My aim in doing this is to give a more perceptive presentation of how rhythm gets layered and activated in most biblical poems than a strictly hierarchical treatment would allow.
177. No transcripts of the spoken language obviously exist. The written prose of the Bible is already stylized (e.g., carrying forward features from oral epic, see F. Polak, "Epic Formulae in Biblical Narrative and the Origins of Ancient Hebrew Prose" (in Hebrew), in M. A. Friedman (ed.), *Studies in Judaica* [Te'uda 7; Tel Aviv: Tel Aviv University Press, 1991], 9–54 [English summary, vii–viii], and therefore would not necessarily have been isomorphic with the spoken language of the day. Knowledge of the latter can perhaps be fine-tuned a bit by considering the workaday documents (such as letters) in epigraphic Hebrew (and even from later dialects). But in the main biblical prose, especially the dialogic portions, offers us a better approximation of the spoken dialect than most of the Bible's poetic corpora.
178. Attridge, *Poetic Rhythm*, 24. As illustrated earlier, consonance and alliteration are not uncommon in biblical poetry. In part, this is a consequence of the very shape of the syllables in biblical Hebrew, which must always begin with a consonant. Runs of assonating vowels can and do occur (e.g., /-ī/i/ in *pithî-lî ʼăḥōtî raʽyātî yônātî tammātî*: "Open to me my sister, my friend, / my dove, my perfect one," Song 5:2) but not quite with the commonality or punch that is achievable in languages that permit syllables to open with a vowel (e.g., ancient Greek, modern English) and never in the absence of the complicating clutter of consonants.
179. Cooper, "Biblical Poetics," 31; cf. Sachs, *Rhythm and Tempo*, 69–70; Hrushovski, "Prosody," 1201; J. Blau, *Phonology and Morphology of Biblical Hebrew* (Winona

Lake, Ind.: Eisenbrauns, 2010), 70–71—and for a convenient overview of the historical development of stress in biblical Hebrew, see 143–55. Hobbins in "Regularities in Ancient Hebrew Verse" leverages a far more formalized linguistic accounting of Tiberian Hebrew phonology (esp. references at 570, n. 16).

180. Attridge, *Poetic Rhythm*, 1, 4.
181. Blau, *Phonology and Morphology*, 70.
182. Attridge, *Poetic Rhythm*, 2.
183. *Hebrew Verse Structure*, 102—this is not to deny that the language of orally performed verbal art is marked or "italicized," as R. Finnegan says (*Oral Poetry: Its Nature, Significance, and Social Context* [Cambridge: Cambridge University Press, 1977], 25), "set apart from everyday life and language," but rather to stress with A. N. Doane ("Oral Texts, Intertexts, and Intratexts: Editing Old English," in *Influence and Intertextuality in Literary History* [Madison: University of Wisconsin Press, 1991], 77–78) that such language, however "marked," nevertheless, involves "more or less everyday language elements" and evolves out of "the ordinary language."
184. So similarly Smith (*Poetic Closure*, 90) in her exposition of a section from Whitman's *Leaves* ("Twenty-eight young men...") where she notes that the stress patterns and syllable counts, "though not repeated exactly, are more highly controlled...than in discursive prose."
185. Little work has been done specifically on the rhythm of narrative prose in the Bible, but it exists, as in all other written narrative prose traditions the world over (see G. Josipovici, "The Rhythm Established: *Bereshit Bara*," in *The Book of God: A Response to the Bible* [New Haven: Yale University Press, 1988], 53–74). The complicating factor is the closeness of the rhythmic profiles projected by biblical poetry and biblical prose. This in part reflects a common origin in native oral performative art. While biblical Hebrew prose is a specifically written genre, it quite clearly evolves (certainly initially and in part) by borrowing and elaborating oral epic features of various sorts, including syntax (Polak, "Epic Formulae," esp. vii–viii; "The Oral and the Written: Syntax, Stylistics and the Development of Biblical Prose Narrative," *JANES* 26 [1998], 59–105). Such a trajectory is far from unique in the emergence of prose narrative cross-culturally (esp. J. Kittay and W. Godzich, *The Emergence of Prose: An Essay in Prosaics* [Minneapolis: University of Minnesota Press, 1987]). Sometimes the closeness of the rhythmic profiles has given rise to assertions about the lack of clear-cut boundaries between biblical prose and poetry. But such are naive, failing, in this instance, to account fully for the genealogy of these art forms. If there is a place where biblical prose approaches the spoken register of vernacular speech in ancient Israel and Judah, it is as R. Kawashima notices (*Biblical Narrative and the Death of the Rhapsode* [Bloomington: Indiana University Press, 2004], 64) in quoted speech (dialogue, discourse)—though even here much remains stylized and elevated.

186. Hrushovski, "On Free Rhythms," 189; cf. "Prosody," 1201; "Note on the Systems of Hebrew Versification," 58. As Hobbins notices, Hrushovski's characterization is not absolute, since there are occasions where two stressed syllables are immediately juxtaposed in the received tradition (e.g., *hôy gôy ḥōtē'*, Isa 1:4), though "the rule works remarkably well" ("Regularities in Ancient Hebrew Verse," 567; for an explication of some of the facilitatory processes, see B. E. Dresher, "The Word in Tiberian Hebrew," in K. C. Hanson and S. Inkelas (eds.), *The Nature of the Word: Essays in Honor of Paul Kiparsky* [Cambridge, Mass.: MIT Press, 2009], 95–111). In Egyptian verse, according to G. Fecht, the number of unaccented syllables in a verse line are also variable, though the number of accented syllables are fixed ("The Structural Principle of Ancient Egyptian Elevated Language," in *Verse in Ancient Near Eastern Prose* [ed. J. C. de Moor and W. G. E. Watson; AOAT 42; Neukirchen-Vluyn: Neukirchener Verlag, 1993], 70–75).

187. *Rhythm and Tempo*, 71. This variability alone tells against the metrical hypothesis. As Cureton emphasizes, meter involves "patterns of regularity" and "is strictly limited to duple and triple patterns, and is usually restricted to the lower levels of structure" (*Rhythmic Phrasing*, 124; cf. Attridge, *Poetic Rhythm*, 97–146). The restriction to duple and triple patterns is likely perception based. Jourdain states that the "perception of meter hinges on prime numbers" (*Music, the Brain, and Ecstasy*, 127). Two and three are obviously prime numbers. Four-beat meters are usually heard as two duples. And five-beat meter, though a prime number, is significantly longer than either duple or triple, but when the brain tries to break it down into smaller groups, the uneven patterns simply confuse the brain. No such patterns of regularity, especially at these lower levels of linguistic structure, exist in biblical Hebrew poetry, and the patterns' alternations are obviously not limited to duple and triple patterns. Hobbins's understanding of the "regularities" in biblical verse foregrounds an appreciation for the strong prominence of such duple and triple patterns ("Regularities in Ancient Hebrew Verse").

188. Hrushovski, "On Free Rhythms," 189; cf. "Prosody," 1201; "Note on the Systems of Hebrew Versification," 58.

189. Cooper, *Mysterious Music*, 57.

190. The organization of the accents never advances in regularity to the point of becoming metrical. "For the accents to constitute a meter, they have to be measured. At least on a clear average the number must remain constant" (Hartman, *Free Verse*, 30). What is constant in moving from line to line in biblical verse is precisely the variation in the number of accents. Biblical verse is not metrical.

191. See esp. M. M. Barry, *An Analysis of the Prosodic Structure of Selected Poems of T. S. Eliot* (rev. ed.; Washington, D.C.: Catholic University Press, 1969), 1–2.

192. Thaut defines periodicity as "repetition rates that establish the sensation of a regular, cyclic pulse sequence" (*Rhythm, Music, and the Brain*, 7).

193. Clayton, "Free Rhythm," 327–31; cf. Frigyesi, "Flowing Rhythm," 64, 66.
194. *Rhythm and Tempo*, 69–70.
195. Hartman, *Free Verse*, 92. Smith places the emphasis somewhat differently (like Hrushovski), thinking the sources of rhythm to be much the same in metered and unmetered verse, but with a similar appreciation of the role of the verse line as a leading "unit" of rhythmic patterning (*Poetic Closure*, 85–86; cf. Cureton, "Rhythm," 250–52, 255, n. 4; Wesling, *Scissors of Meter*, 60; Cooper, *Mysterious Music*, 92–101).
196. Hartman, *Free Verse*, 92; cf. Cooper, "Free Verse."
197. S. A. Geller, "Hebrew Prosody and Poetics," in *NPEPP*, 509. See the supporting thoughts of P. P. Byers, "A Formula for Poetic Intonation," *Poetics* 8 (1976), 367–80; I. Lehiste, "Rhythm of Poetry, Rhythm of Prose," in V. Fromkin (ed.), *Phonetic Linguistics* (Orlando: Academic, 1985), 145–55; "Speech Research: An Overview," in J. Sundberg et al. (ed.), *Music, Language, Speech, and Brain* (Basingstoke: Macmillan, 1991), 98–107; Cooper, *Mysterious Music*, 63–66.
198. So the elongated syntax (e.g., embedded clause, v. 1; stacking of adjuncts, v. 3; listing, v. 5) of the later prose dialect of biblical Hebrew here helps to accentuate the difference (cf. Polak, "Oral and the Written," 59–105). Earlier biblical prose narrative will often stand much closer to the Bible's poetic style since it initially emerges (in part) out of this style.
199. There can be a tendency to reify the formal idea of the line, whether because of the appearance of plasticity that writing lends it, or the mathematical assurance that its generation through metrical figuring can suggest, or the concreteness that our necessarily belated and hypostasized critical expositions and characterizations impute to it. In reality lines of verse, even metrical verse, are never arbitrary or self-identical but always emerge dynamically, in process, as a part of whole poems, conjoint with other poetic elements and in relation to preceding and succeeding lines. Poetic lines, like sentences, are ultimately made up of language, of words and phrases that have particular sounds and meanings. Consequently, the line does not exist outside of its enabling interface with morphology, syntax, semantics, and the like. Here my abstracting away from the line's constitutive linguistic content is a convenience intended to spotlight the potential shaping force of form alone, i.e., length and grouping patterns (cf. Smith, *Poetic Closure*, 85; Cooper, "Free Verse").
200. D. Pardee, *Ugaritic and Hebrew Poetic Parallelism: A Trial Cut ('nt I and Proverbs 2)* (Leiden: Brill, 1988), 4, 71.
201. Geller, "Hebrew Prosody," 509.
202. Hrushovski, "On Free Rhythms," 189.
203. Smith, *Poetic Closure*, 86.
204. "Upon an *average*, the lines of Hebrew poetry consist of 7 or 8 syllables; but (so far as apparent) there is no *rule* on the subject; lines may be longer or shorter, as the poet may desire; nor is there any necessity that the lines composing a

verse should all be of the same length" (S. R. Driver, *Introduction to the Litera-ture of the Old Testament* [Cleveland: Meridian, 1956 (1892)], 365). This squares with Hobbins's more recent estimate of typical poetic line lengths in the Bible, on average "between four to nine syllables," though the latter emphasizes the importance of aggregation for the "parameterization of varieties" of biblical verse ("Regularities in Ancient Hebrew Verse," 577–78).

205. H. Wildberger (*Isaiah 1–12* [trans. T. H. Trapp; Minneapolis: Fortress, 1991], 179) makes essentially the same point, though his structural analysis and divi-sion of lines differ from my own and he uses the vocabulary of "meter" and measures by the number of stresses.

206. The length anomaly is partially set off by the line only having two major stresses.

207. On the latter point, see F. M. Cross's discussion of the terms *longum* and *breve* as his preferred manner of distinguishing longer and shorter lines of biblical verse ("The Prosody of Lamentations 1 and the Psalm of Jonah," in *From Epic to Canon: History and Literature in Ancient Israel* [Baltimore: Johns Hopkins University Press, 1998], 99–102). So in Lamentations, for example, a seven-syllable line will be long (1:2a) or short (1:2c) depending especially on the nature of the line it is paired with (see Cross, "Prosody," 107).

208. See J. Longenbach, *The Art of the Poetic Line* (St. Paul: Graywolf, 2008), 32, 70.

209. Esp. Beyers, *History of Free Verse*, 38–42; cf. Voigt, *Syntax*, 23–42. Beyers's insist-ence on the need to be sensitive to differences of kind—genre!—when analyz-ing even nonmetrical poetry is a point well made. Not all free verse is the same.

210. Esp. G. Fohrer, "Über den Kurzvers," *ZAW* 66 (1954), 199–236; and for the short line as a standard component of the *qinah* couplet, see Budde, "Klage-lied," 1–52. Consequently, sometimes this short line will be compared to the otherwise normal "long" line of biblical poetry (so G. Fohrer, *An Introduction to the Old Testament* [trans. D. E. Green; Nashville: Abingdon, 1968], 45–47). Such a "long" line is only long by comparison with the short line of biblical verse and should not be confused with the long-line version of modern free verse high-lighted by Beyers and others, which, of course, tends to be much, much longer.

211. For this convenient overview, see Fohrer, *Introduction to the Old Testament*, 46–47. Fohrer isolates the oracles of Jeremiah and Ezekiel as poems that are often composed either "in short verses or combined long and short verses" and the Song of Songs (via a notice of W. Rudolph) as a body of "late lyric poetry" that features short-line verse—lines often averaging only six or seven syllables in length. Interestingly, Fohrer remarks that "short verse came to be employed for 'narrative poetry' (for which long verse is not suited)." Since the Bible is not rich in narrative poetry, presumably he has in mind short narrative runs, such as in Ezekiel 17:3–6 (containing lines with syllable counts ranging from four to nine syllables and a total of nine *wayyiqtol* forms), or perhaps the example of Ugaritic narrative poetry. Regardless, it is not readily apparent why narrative

verse should prefer short lines, except in that in the ancient Near East epic narrative was birthed explicitly as an oral genre. Therefore, the short line, to the extent that it dominates (short) poetic narrative runs in the Bible, is likely ultimately indebted to the medium's oral roots, even in the case of explicitly written verse such as in Ezekiel.

212. Cooper, *Mysterious Music*, 46.
213. Beyers, *History of Free Verse*, 42; Voigt, *Syntax*, 24.
214. For a convenient collection of examples and discussion of the phenomenon, see W. G. E. Watson, *Traditional Techniques in Classical Hebrew Verse* (JSOTSS 170; Sheffield: Sheffield Academic, 1994), 144–91. Since parallelism involving only two elements is difficult to recognize as such on such a small scale, the trope usually requires four elements at a minimum (gapping, too, is hard to pull off in the course of only a single, relatively brief line), and thus a longer line. Allen early on observed how "*Leaves of Grass* contains more internal parallelism than the poetry of the Bible" ("Biblical Analogies," 497). This is precisely the kind of thing that Whitman's long line readily accommodates.
215. Psychophysiological constraints, according to Hrushovski, mean that wherever possible language material is organized rhythmically into "hierarchies of simple groups." Such groups usually consist of two or three smaller units (two and three being prime numbers and therefore not divisible into smaller groups), and occasionally four, which allows for an "innerbalanced composite unit" (e.g., 2 + 2). Larger groupings of lines are also sometimes encountered, but tracking such larger groups, which are made up already of quite complex patterns, becomes difficult for the human brain in an oral performative context, aside perhaps from lines of highly repetitive material—the sameness of the language material at lower levels facilitating the ability to group in larger numbers.
216. Cf. C. L. Seow, *Job 1–21* (Illuminations; Grand Rapids: Eerdmans, 2013), 315.
217. The resulting rhythmic complexity is enabled (at least in part) by language's capacity for simultaneous signifying. Language as a complex symbol system has the capacity to signify in multiple ways at the same time. A poetic stanza with an *abab* rhyme scheme offers a very basic example of such linguistic simultaneity: the semantic elements are marshaled to one end (i.e., what the stanza actually says or means), while sound is marshaled to another end (i.e., the rhyming). This is done at the same time and using the very same elements. These ends, in turn, can be choreographed (i.e., synchronized, counterpointed) or not as desired. This capacity of language can and often is exploited in poetry to explicitly rhythmic ends. The line itself, though strictly speaking not a linguistic element per se but rather a nonlinguistic mechanism of textual (written or oral) organization, nevertheless participates in the simultaneous play of poetic language. That is, it shapes rhythm in two ways simultaneously, (1) as a perceptual unit amenable to patterning (e.g., in biblical poetry through variation

in line length and line grouping), and (2) as a frame for the staging of the language material that is constitutive of the line. Thaut (*Rhythm, Music, and the Brain*, esp. 3–4) stresses the role of simultaneity in musical rhythm. Linguistic simultaneity is of a different kind, though it is no less relevant rhythmically.

218. The key insight of J. Kurylowicz's theory of biblical Hebrew poetic meter is precisely the significance of syntax, the prosodic consideration of stress within "word-complexes" (*Studies in Semitic Grammar and Metrics* [London: Curzon Press, 1973], 167–77); see Cooper, "Biblical Poetics," 32–34; O'Connor, *Hebrew Verse Structure*.

219. *Poetic Closure*, 84, 90.

220. So, for example, Kinzie (*Poet's Guide*, 51–74, 75–110), Longenbach (*Poetic Line*, 3–44, 45–82) and Voigt (*Syntax*, 23–42) all feature chapters dedicated to the interface of line and syntax in studies of poetry generally. Also Wesling's "grammetrics" focuses explicitly on "sentencing" as it features rhythmically in metrical and nonmetrical poems alike (*Scissors of Meter*, esp. vii–viii, 66–67, 74–79, 90, 166). Cooper (*Mysterious Music*, 92–115) dedicates an entire chapter to the topic in his own study of rhythm in free verse, and Cureton's *Rhythmic Phrasing* engages syntax throughout. Cf. Cooper, "Biblical Poetics," 32–34 (here commenting on the work of Kurylowicz).

221. Attridge, *Poetic Rhythm*, 21.

222. Voigt, *Syntax*, 8–9. I build on Voigt's general discussion throughout, along with S. Pinker's *The Language Instinct: The New Science of Language and Mind* (Penguin Books, 1995), esp. 83–125, and Jourdain, *Music, the Brain, and Ecstasy*, 120–54—these are Voigt's principal sources. See also N. Chomsky, *The Minimalist Program* (Cambridge, Mass.: MIT Press, 1995).

223. Here I conveniently draw on the descriptions found in *IBHS*, secs. 4.1–8.

224. See R. D. Holmstedt, "The Typological Classification of the Hebrew of Genesis: Subject-Verb or Verb-Subject?," *JHS* 11 (2011), 14, and, in more detail, the author's "Pro-Drop," in G. Khan (ed.), *Encyclopedia of Hebrew Language and Linguistics* (Leiden: Brill), 265–67.

225. For a convenient overview, see Holmstedt, "Typological Classification," with references to other literature, including T. Givón's early and still insightful "The Drift from VSO to SVO in Biblical Hebrew: the Pragmatics of Tense-Aspect," in C. N. Li (ed.), *Mechanisms of Syntactic Change* (Austin: University of Texas Press, 1977), 184–254.

226. *Syntax*, 10.

227. *Syntax*, 12. This is language and ideas ultimately derived from Chomsky and generative grammar. For a readable overview, see Pinker, *Language Instinct*, esp. 83–125.

228. For this basic trajectory, see Polak, "Oral and the Written," 59–105.

229. See *CTA*, 64, n. 6.

230. *Syntax*, 24.

231. *Poet's Guide*, 51.

232. Esp. O'Connor, *Hebrew Verse Structure*, 129–32, 409–22; cf. S. A. Geller, *Parallelism in Early Biblical Poetry* (Missoula: Scholars Press, 1979), 6, 30, 295ff., 379; W. G. E. Watson, *Classical Hebrew Poetry: A Guide to Its Techniques* (London: T. and T. Clark, 2001 [1984]), 332–36; F. W. Dobbs-Allsopp, "The Enjambing Line in Lamentations: A Taxonomy (Part 1)," *ZAW* 113 (2001), 219–39; "The Effects of Enjambment in Lamentations (Part 2)," *ZAW* 113 (201), 370–85; Hobbins, "Regularities in Ancient Hebrew Verse," 573–76.

233. *Poetic Line*, 55; cf. Voigt, *Syntax*, 24.

234. Though even in much (most) contemporary free verse, as Cooper observes (*Mysterious Music*, 94–95; cf. "Free Verse"), the coincidence of line and syntactic phrase is broadly normative (unmarked), and certainly in the poets he focuses on, T. S. Eliot, James Wright, Robert Lowell.

235. Cf. J. Scully, *Line Break: Poetry as Social Practice* (Willimantic: Curbstone, 2005 [1988]), 143.

236. See chapter 1 here; cf. F. W. Dobbs-Allsopp, "Space, Line, and the Written Biblical Poem in Texts from the Judean Desert," in M. Lundberg et al. (ed.), *Puzzling Out the Past: Studies in Northwest Semitic Languages and Literatures in Honor of Bruce Zuckerman* (Leiden: Brill, 2012), 19–61.

237. W. S. Merwin, *Migration: New and Selected Poems* (Port Townsend, Wash.: Copper Canyon, 2005), 223.

238. *The Moving Target: Poems* (New York: Atheneum, 1963). Merwin himself emphasizes how the lack of punctuation allows the words to do the punctuating "for themselves, as they do in ordinary speech" (see the interview with Merwin in *Paris Review*, www.theparisreview.org/interviews/2692/the-art-of-poetry-no-38-w-s-merwin, accessed February 20, 2015). The connection Merwin here makes with orality is insightful, though I think he misses the crucial shaping force that the line has for his own work, precisely as it punctuates his poems.

239. Wesling, who is also mindful of how lineation may punctuate poems, remarks that unpunctuated poems, or even less fully (or archaically—he's thinking of Shakespeare here) punctuated poems, "put unusual pressure on naked grammar as the maker of sentence sense" (*Scissors of Meter*, 102). This emphasizes in its own way that both lineation (or spacing in the case of most extant ancient Hebrew manuscripts) and punctuation are metascript conventions designed to aid the reading (decoding) of written material. Less fully punctuated versions of a poem are still performable as a poem, but their (written) cues for performance depend on the language material itself ("naked grammar"), or extratextual special knowledge.

240. Hartman (*Free Verse*, 93–94; cf. 73, 76) uses a Williams poem ("Exercise") to illustrate how "line division" may "substitute for punctuation"—though the syntactic cuts Williams makes in this poem are not so radical.

241. "Biblical Analogies," 505.

242. See the discussion in *IBHS*, sec. 4.8a.

243. As Lowth well understood, see *Lectures*, I, 98.

244. Cf. Dobbs-Allsopp, "Enjambing Line," 233–38.

245. Such a pattern prevails more generally in other distichic structures such as, for example, the Anglo-American tradition of verse rendered in rhymed couplets (see Smith, *Poetic Closure*, 70–78; T. V. F. Brogan and W. B. Piper, "Couplet," in *NPEPP*, 244–45), or the ancient Greek elegiac distich (see M. L. West, *Greek Metre* (Oxford: Clarendon, 1982), 44–46, 157–59; T. V. F. Brogan and A. T. Cole, "Elegiac Distich," in *NPEPP*, 321).

246. Cf. *IBHS*, sec. 19.1c–d; 37.5.

247. For details, see Dobbs-Allsopp, "Effects of Enjambment," 371; cf. Dobbs-Allsopp, "Enjambing Line," 219, n. 3.

248. Dobbs-Allsopp, "Effects of Enjambment," 370–71.

249. T. V. F. Brogan, "Catalexis," in *NPEPP*, 174.

250. Enjambed but closed couplets are not unique to ancient Hebrew poetry, see D. W. Harding, *Words into Rhythm: English Speech Rhythm in Verse and Prose* (Cambridge: Cambridge University Press, 1976), 21 (e.g., "Golden lads and girls all must / As chimney-sweepers, come to dust.").

251. For a similar use of enjambment in English poetry, see J. Hollander, " 'Sense Variously Drawn Out': On English Enjambment," in *Vision and Resonance: Two Senses of Poetic Form* (New York: Oxford University Press, 1975), 112.

252. As O'Connor has recognized, this psalm contains a fair amount of enjambed lines (*Hebrew Verse Structure*, 129–31).

253. T. V. F. Brogan and C. Scott note well enjambment's general suitability to effecting extended runs of narrative verse ("Enjambment," in *NPEPP*, 359).

254. Cf. Alter, *Art of Biblical Poetry*, 27–61.

255. See Dobbs-Allsopp, "Enjambing Line," 224–26.

256. Dobbs-Allsopp, "Enjambing Line," 228–30.

257. For convenience, my reading broadly follows that of D. R. Hillers, *Micah* (Hermeneia; Philadelphia: Fortress, 1984), 16–21.

258. *IBHS*, sec. 20.1a.

259. See P. J. King and L. E. Stager, *Life in Biblical Israel* (Louisville: Westminster John Knox, 2001), 31, Ill. 16.

260. Additional syntactic scrutiny (e.g., distinguishing between finite and nonfinite verbal forms) may reveal yet further rhythmic nuance.

261. Voigt, *Syntax*, 11–12. Voigt herself understands parallelism specifically as a patterning "in … syntax" (11; cf. Cooper, "Free Verse"), but O'Connor's notion that syntax is "the core of a p[arallelism]" is the more precise diagnosis of the phenomenon ("Parallelism," in *NPEPP*, 877).

262. *Oral Style*, 95; cf. 95–96, 238, 239–40; and in detail in M. Jousse, "Les Lois psycho-physiologiques du Style oral vivvant et leur utilisation philologique," *L' Ethnographie* 23 (1931), 1–18.

263. And he coined the term, see A. Baker, "Parallelism: England's Contribution to Biblical Studies," *CBQ* 35 (1973), 429–40.

264. In the corpus of biblical poems studied by O'Connor, parallelism, as a line-level trope, "holds together somewhat over a third of the lines" (*Hebrew Verse Structure*, 391).

265. *Oral Style*, 238–39. And of course since Allen's "Biblical Analogies" parallelism has featured prominently in many accounts of free verse rhythm, e.g., Smith, *Poetic Closure*, 84–92; Hartman, *Free Verse*, 121–22; Attridge, *Poetic Rhythm*, 169–70; Cooper, *Mysterious Music*, 99–101.

266. *Oral Style*, 95. More recent expositors of the centrality of the human body to human thinking are easy to come by. See, for example, A. Damasio, *Descartes' Error: Emotion, Reason, and the Human Brain* (New York: Quill, 1994), M. Johnson, *The Body in the Mind: The Bodily Basis of Meaning, Imagination, and Reason* (Chicago: University of Chicago Press, 1987), and G. Lakoff, *Women, Fire, and Dangerous Things: What Categories Reveal about the Mind* (Chicago: University of Chicago Press, 1987).

267. *Oral Style*, 109.

268. Translated into O'Connor's syntactic vocabulary, for example: "One line of given constituent or unit structure is followed by one or more of identical structure" (*Hebrew Verse Structure*, 391).

269. Compare J. M. Foley's related characterization of the rhythmic pulse of parallelism in so much orally performed South Slavic epic verse, *How to Read an Oral Poem* (Urbana: University of Illinois Press, 2002), 89.

270. *Rhyme's Reason*, 26. I have relineated Hollander's version to accommodate my own understanding of the shape of the underlying biblical verse line (which is pertinent to my interest here though not necessarily to Hollander's) and to conform to my manner of citing actual biblical examples more generally in this chapter. Hollander, as made evident in the final triplet quoted (i.e., "One half-line..."), follows a still common nomenclature tradition that assumes the biblical verse line is broken up into two and three parts (see chapter 1 here).

271. P. Fussell, *Poetic Meter and Poetic Form* (New York: Random House, 1979), 15.

272. So Smith (*Poetic Closure*, 90), for example, highlights the role of "syntactic parallelism" as it contributes to the rhythm of a Whitman poem: "We should also note that syntactic parallelism creates patterns of intonational cadence which again are not repeated exactly in succeeding lines but recur frequently enough to have rhythmic effects."

273. Cooper, *Mysterious Music*, 72–76.

274. S. Heaney, *Beowulf: A New Verse Translation* (New York: Farrar, Straus, and Giroux, 2000).

275. Carmi, *Hebrew Verse*, 424. It is worth noting that systematic or stanzaic rhyme schemes of this kind, despite the paradigmatic association of rhyme with poetry (especially in modern Russian, English, and French verse traditions),

are relative latecomers to poetry, arising perhaps earliest in Arabic and Chinese traditions. Rhyme, in fact, is lacking in most of the world's poetries. It is not employed significantly originally in any of the Indo-European languages, and it occurs only rarely in ancient Greek poetry (see. T. V. F. Brogan, "Rhyme," in *NPEPP*, esp. 1061–62).

276. For example, this easily predates Thomas Wyatt's first sonnets in English from the first half of the sixteenth century, and even Chaucer's translation of Sonnet 132 from Petrarch's *Canzoniere*, "Cantica Troili" (composed in the rhyme royal used throughout *Troilus and Criseyde*, which likely dates to the last quarter of the fourteenth century).

277. Cf. T. P. McCreesh, *Biblical Sound and Sense: Poetic Sound Patterns in Proverbs 10–29* (JSOT 128; Sheffield: Sheffield Academic, 1991).

278. Seow, *Job 1–21*, 653.

279. See F. W. Dobbs-Allsopp, *Lamentations* (IBC; Louisville: Westminster John Knox, 2002), 79–91.

280. For a treatment of the "irregular rhythm of the words," see A. Welsh, *Roots of Lyric: Primitive Poetry and Modern Poetics* (Princeton: Princeton University Press, 1978), 133–61.

281. Cureton gives an example of such rhythmic manipulation, Wallace Stevens's "The Lord of the Sugar Cane," in which all the disyllabic words share the same trochaic stress contour, and thus dramatizing rhythmically the theme of "ebbing" in the poem ("Rhythm," 248). Such scripting becomes more prevalent in postbiblical Hebrew poetry.

282. Cf. Smith, *Poetic Closure*, 87; Cooper, *Mysterious Music*, 90–91.

283. "*Leitwort* Style in Pentateuch Narrative," in M. Buber and F. Rosenzweig, *Scripture and Translation* (trans. L. Rosenwald and E. Fox; Bloomington: Indiana University Press, 1994), 114 (the selection is excerpted from a larger lecture entitled "The Bible as Storyteller" that Buber delivered in 1927).

284. For an explication of the multiple purpose of *Leitwort* in Buber's thought, see Y. Amit, "Multi-purpose 'Leading Word' and the Problems of Its Usage," *Prooftexts* 9 (1989), 99–114.

285. Buber, "*Leitwort* Style," 114.

286. Buber, "*Leitwort* Style," 114.

287. Singular, isolated lines in biblical Hebrew poetry are very rare, as the tradition is dominantly distichic. So on those occasions when they seem to occur such unaffiliated lines are always closely scrutinized. In this case, though the manuscript evidence is of a piece, the number of proposed conjectural emendations are legion. Surely, in light of the sevenfold repetition of *qôl yhwh* at the heads of lines in this psalm, the possibility that a second line (of an original couplet) could have dropped out as a result of haplography is very real—though if this happened the manuscript tradition has not left any telltale signs of it, nor aside from new manuscript evidence can there be any hope of knowing the

content of the now lost line. An original couplet here would regularize this threefold run of *qôl*, spacing them out more evenly at the heads of the two resulting couplets and one triplet. Alternatively, v. 7 could be joined to v. 8 forming another triplet (cf. vv. 3, 9). Rhythmically, this would result in a more irregular pace—two immediately successive claps of thunder, followed at a distance by a third—not unlike the interruptive force I associated with the use of a singular line. In any case, taking v. 7 as an isolated line is only one possible construal. That the different grouping possibilities result in slightly different rhythmic effects underscores the componential nature of rhythm.

288. "*Leitwort* and Discourse Type: An Example," in Buber and Rosenzweig, *Scripture and Translation*, 143 (originally dates from 1935).

289. The latter offers a slightly different rendering of Buber's original German phrasing (M. Buber, "The 'Leading Word' Device in the Narratives of the Torah," in *Darko shel miqra': 'iyunim bidfusey-signon batanakh* [Jerusalem: Bialik Institute, 1964], 284).

290. See esp. the comments of Amit, "Multi-Purpose," 100. For Buber "the possibility of presenting unity by means of repetition" could be focused at many levels, including that of the original compositions (though his own emphasis is mostly placed elsewhere).

291. For this description of the Semitic root, see J. Fox, *Semitic Noun Patterns* (HSS 52; Winona Lake, Ind.: Eisenbrauns, 2003), 37, 44.

292. The analysis is essentially that of L. C. Allen, *Psalms 101–150* (Word; Waco: Word Books, 1983), 88–93.

293. It may not be accidental that Psalm 111 is a written psalm (see comments hereafter on the acrostic as an explicitly scribal genre). Root play of this kind is more acutely observable in writing. This is not to say that it is unimaginable in oral art, since root sequences will have an aural reality as well. But informally it appears that a great deal of root play in biblical poetry remains mostly restricted to the local level (e.g., line, phrase). And of course Buber's early statement on *Leitwort* style focuses explicitly on written narrative prose.

294. "Biblical Analogies," 492; cf. 505. Here it is likely in part that Allen is parroting a common idea from biblical scholarship—so H. Ewald already in the middle of the nineteenth century glosses biblical poetic parallelism as *gedankenrhythmus* "thought-rhythm" (*Die Dichter des Alten Bundes* [Göttingen: Vändenhoeck und Ruprecht, 1866], I, 111). But it also gets picked up in Whitman scholarship and in discussions about free verse more broadly.

295. Cf. E. Isaacs, "The Origin and Nature of Parallelism," *AJSL* 35 (1919), 116.

296. *The Literary Study of the Bible* (London: Isbister, 1896), 73.

297. *Oral Style*, 127.

298. "On Free Rhythms," 181. Recall that one of Hrushovski's shorthand glosses for the free rhythms of biblical verse was a "semantic-syntactic-accentual" system—semantics being one of the more important contributing elements.

299. *Poetic Closure*, 4–5. See also Cureton, *Rhythmic Phrasing*, esp. 195–200; Wesling, *Scissors of Meter*, 79–82; Attridge, *Poetic Rhythm*, 21, 182–209; Zumthor, "Text and the Voice," 83–84.

300. There are textual problems at the end of the narrative in vv. 22–23, where a triplet or two can be construed. Though if so, they function mainly to signal the impending close to the narrative, and thus support the narrative's thematic development—the boy "thoughtlessly . . . follows her" (v. 22). For the sake of the foregoing reading, I follow the couplet logic underlying the translations in NRSV and NJV, for example.

301. Cf. Smith, *Poetic Closure*, 132.

302. For discussion of logical sequence in a poem's thematic structure, see Smith, *Poetic Closure*, 131–39.

303. Smith, *Poetic Closure*, 131–32. Joban poetry is not classically lyrical, however indebted is its scribal art to the lyric core of the biblical poetic tradition. But the fit between Job and Smith's broad-brush description of logical sequence in lyric is not surprising. For Smith lyric above all is conceptualized as "the representation, not of an action or the chronicle of an action," and therefore its structure is not related to the structure of events (as in plays or novels) but to "that of personal discourse" (*Poetic Closure*, 122). And, of course, Job is precisely a representation of discourse—argument, debate, dialogue—among persons.

304. *Poetic Closure*, 132.

305. *Poetic Closure*, 28, 43–44, 107; and on paratactic structure more generally, 98–109.

306. *Rhythmic Phrasing*, 197. Cureton goes on to claim that "all prominence relations in or rhythmic grouping of language are primarily informational relations" (198)—this, of course, is broadly consistent with the idea that language always comes enfleshed in meaning.

307. They may be habitually associated with some grammatical feature (e.g., petitions are often rendered with imperative or jussive forms) and other formal features may figure in realizing an individual psalm's larger structure—though these will vary from lament to lament; but in no way is there a givenness, a constancy to the structure *as form* that these psalms habitually take, i.e., they are nothing like the sonnet or sestina of the metrical (European) tradition, for instance. Thematic structure, in fact, is at the heart of all the psalmic given forms (e.g., laments, hymns, thanksgiving songs, royal psalms) isolated in the form critical program initiated by H. Gunkel at the turn of the twentieth century. Of the three elements central to Gunkel's classification scheme—content or theme, linguistic form, and life situation—Gunkel emphasized thematic content, although his expository habit of explicating the life context prior to the discussion of content (and form) often obscured the importance of theme to his genre analysis. And even the very name given to Gunkel's program, "form criticism," which apparently Gunkel himself was not entirely happy about,

badly obscures the centrality of theme to these so-called psalmic "forms"—
Gunkel's own restriction of form to strictly linguistic matters ignores the fact
that matters of form in language art are considerably more capacious than
grammar alone. To be sure, Gunkel's insights into psalmic verse (in particular)
are manifold (e.g., their originating orality). Perhaps one of his most important
contributions to psalm study is his classification scheme. He saw that not all
psalms were the same and devised a vocabulary and schema for grouping and
classifying these different types—or forms. In the end, the whole form critical
enterprise now needs to be rethought in light of contemporary genre theory,
see T. Longman, "Form Criticism, Recent Developments in Genre Theory, and
the Evangelical," *WTJ* 47 (1985), 46–67. For a thorough and critical overview of
Gunkel and his scholarship, see M. Buss, "Gunkel in His Context," in *Biblical
Form Criticism in Its Context* (JSOTSS 274; Sheffield: Sheffield Academic,
1998), 209–62. My summary assessment of Gunkel's brand of "form criticism" draws generously on Buss's study.

308. Smith, *Poetic Structure*, 99. *Listenwissenschaft* is one of the original "sciences"
of the ancient Near East, see W. von Soden, "Leistung und Grenze sumerischer
und babylonischer Wissenschaft," *Die Welt als Geschichte* 2 (1936), 411–64,
509–57.

309. Smith, *Poetic Structure*, 109.

310. Smith, *Poetic Structure*, 99.

311. Of course, in a performative context there would likely have been (many) extratextual clues that would leave little doubt about the identity of the ensuing
psalm, e.g., occasions that call for lamentation usually are very different from
occasions of praise and rejoicing.

312. E. Berry notices how asymmetrically shaped stanzas visually "may suggest
movement in a direction" ("Visual Poetics," in *NPEPP*, 1364).

313. *Poetic Closure*, 88; cf. Hartman, *Free Verse*, 15, 60, 74; Attridge, *Poetic Rhythm*,
52; and esp. Hollander, *Vision and Resonance*.

314. For much of what follows and with more details, see F. W. Dobbs-Allsopp,
"Acrostic," in H.-J. Klauck et al. (ed.), *The Encyclopedia of the Bible and Its Reception* (Berlin: de Gruyter, 2009).

315. Cf. J. A. Sanders, *The Psalms Scroll of Qumran Cave 11* (Oxford: Clarendon,
1965).

316. P. W. Skehan, *Studies in Israelite Poetry and Wisdom* (CBQMS 1; Washington,
D.C.: Catholic Biblical Association of America, 1971), 74.

317. B. R. Foster, *Before the Muses: An Anthology of Akkadian Literature* (2 vols.;
Bethesda: CDL, 1993), 806. More generally on the *Babylonian Theodicy*, see
W. G. Lambert, *Babylonian Wisdom Literature* (Oxford: Clarendon Press, 1960).
Sibylline Oracles 8.217–50 provides a good example of such a name/sentence
acrostic from later Greek literature; and for acrostics in postbiblical Hebrew
verse traditions, see Carmi, *Hebrew Verse*, esp. 61.

318. Writing itself is no guarantee, either, that such an alphabetic frame will be made visible. 4QLamᵃ, which preserves a version of most of Lamentations 1, is written in a running format such that the acrostic pattern is all but obscured. Any would-be reader of this manuscript, in order to fully appreciate/perform this version of Lamentations 1, would need to bring a prior understanding of the acrostic's presence to the reading process.

319. The oldest datable acrostics come from ancient Mesopotamia and can be dated to the reigns of Ashurbanipal and Nebuchadnezzar II during the middle of the first millennium BCE (e.g., K 7592 + K 8717 + DT 363 and BM 55469). For the possibility that the acrostic in the *Babylonian Theodicy* may be even older, see Lambert, *Babylonian Wisdom*, 67. For a broad-ranging treatment of visual tropes in the Western poetic tradition, see J. Hollander, *Vision and Resonance*; Berry, "Visual Poetics," 1365.

320. See D. Pardee, "Ugaritic Alphabetic Cuneiform in the Context of Other Alphabetic Systems," in C. L. Miller (ed.), *Studies in Semitic and Afroasiatic Linguistics Presented to Gene B. Gragg* (Chicago: University of Chicago Press, 2007), 181–200.

321. M. Kochavi, "An Ostracon of the Period of the Judges from ʿIzbet Ṣarṭah," *Tel Aviv* 4 (1977), 1–13.

322. Z. Meshel, "Kuntillet Ajrud," in *ABD* 4, 107; P. K. McCarter, *Ancient Inscriptions: Voices from the Ancient World* (Washington, D.C.: BAS, 1996), 109; Dobbs-Allsopp et al., *Hebrew Inscriptions*, 293–95. Now: S. Ahituv, E. Eshel, and Z. Meshel, "The Inscriptions," in Z. Meshel (ed.), *Kuntillet ʿArud (Ḥorvat Teman): An Iron Age II Religious Site on the Judah-Sinai Border* (Jerusalem: IES, 2012), 102–3.

323. R. E. Tappy, P. K. McCarter, M. L. Lundberg, and B. Zuckerman, "An Abecedary of the Mid-tenth Century B.C.E. from the Judaean Shephelah," *BASOR* 344 (2006), 5–46. The site is in the Beth Guvrin Valley (in the Shephelah, approximately seven kilometers north of Lachish). The script is antecedent to the Hebrew script that does not begin to evolve in earnest until the late ninth century BCE (see discussion in chapter 4) and the variant orders for letter pairs attested provides further evidence of the unsettled nature of early linear alphabetic writing through Iron IIA.

324. The comparative evidence also supports a scribal origin for the form. The Akkadian acrostics are obviously scribal in origin, as it was mainly only the scribes who could read syllabic cuneiform—not to mention the inherent difficulty (e.g., use of rare words) of these poems, which further presumes a literate base of knowledge only imaginable for scribes.

325. *Poetic Closure*, 88; cf. Hartman throughout *Free Verse* for comments on Williams and especially at 65–66 with regard to typography and spatial matters.

326. *Poetic Closure*, 88.

327. For details, see P. Saenger, *Space between Words: The Origins of Silent Reading* (Stanford: Stanford University Press, 1997), esp. 1–13. Saenger's chief focus is

on word separation, but the neurophysiological benefit that he lays out for word spacing is germane to other spatial dimensions of textual organization and page layout, as his own comments suggest (6).

328. Saenger, *Space between Words*, 11–12.

329. Some minimal, additional information is conveyed even when the extra spacing does not quite align, e.g., cuing a poetic performance (albeit one still in need of extratextual knowledge).

330. Cureton, "Rhythm," 245.

331. Cureton, *Rhythmic Phrasing*, 123.

332. *New York Daily Tribune*, supp. (March 22, 1850), 1.

333. *New York Daily Tribune* (June 14, 1850), 3.

334. *New York Daily Tribune* (June 21, 1850), 3. Of the three poems, "Resurgemus" is the most mature, exhibiting in particular the rhythmic instinct that characterizes Whitman's later poetry, and not surprisingly, then, it is the only one of the three to be included (albeit in revised form) in the 1855 *Leaves of Grass* (Brooklyn, 1855), 87–88.

335. From a manuscript fragment entitled "Rules of Composition," likely dating to the early 1850s, see Grier, *Notebooks and Unpublished Prose Manuscripts*, 1:103.

336. *Leaves*, v.

337. From sec. 13 of "As I Sat Alone By Blue Ontario's Shore," in *Leaves of Grass* (New York, 1867), and also in the poem's final version, "By Blue Ontario's Shore," in *Leaves of Grass* (Boston: Osgood and Company, 1881–82).

338. (Camden, N.J., 1876), 29.

339. "Bible as Poetry," 57.

340. *Daybooks and Notebooks* (ed. W. H. White; 3 vols.; New York: New York University Press, 1978), 3:776.

CHAPTER 3

1. L. Alonso Schökel, *A Manual of Hebrew Poetics* (Subsidia biblica 11; Rome: Editrice Pontificio Istituto Biblico, 1988), 11; see R. Lowth, *Lectures on the Sacred Poetry of the Hebrews* (2 vols.; trans. G. Gregory; London: J. Johnson, 1787; reprinted in *Robert Lowth (1710–1787): The Major Works*, vols. 1–2 [London: Routledge, 1995]), II, 189–210; S. R. Driver, *An Introduction to the Literature of the Old Testament* (Cleveland: Meridian Books, 1956 [1897]), 359–91. J. W. Johnson treats it in his survey of ancient Near Eastern lyric traditions ("Lyric," in *NPEPP*, 716).

2. For my own earlier attempt at a more comprehensive statement on the poetics of lyric verse in the Bible, specifically at the site of psalms, see F. W. Dobbs-Allsopp, "Psalms and Lyric Verse," in F. L. Shults (ed.), *The Evolution of Rationality: Interdisciplinary Essays in Honor of J. Wentzel van Huyssteen* (Grand Rapids: Eerdmans, 2006), 346–79. This chapter is a revised and adapted version of the earlier essay.

3. Tracing and demystifying the history of this three-way distinction in Western literary criticism is the project of G. Genette's *The Architext: An Introduction* (trans. J. E. Lewin; Berkeley: University of California Press, 1979). For a now seminal reworking of these classic categories, see N. Frye, *Anatomy of Criticism* (Princeton: Princeton University Press, 1957). For a defense of the three-genre typology beyond its inherited Western lineage, see E. Miner, *Comparative Poetics: An Intercultural Essay on Theories of Literature* (Princeton: Princeton University Press, 1990).

4. See G. Nagy, *Pindar's Homer: The Lyric Possession of an Epic Past* (Baltimore: Johns Hopkins University Press, 1990), 3; Johnson, "Lyric," 714. But even in the Alexandrian period it is more a matter of inferring the theories of lyric implied in the gathering, sorting, and ordering of the lyric poets of old (by then) than anything explicitly articulated, see W. R. Johnson, *The Idea of Lyric: Lyric Modes in Ancient and Modern Poetry* (EIDOS; Berkeley: University of California Press, 1982), 76–95, esp. 83–84.

5. Genette, *Architext*, 11; his initial discussions of Plato and Aristotle are on 8–9 and 10–14, respectively.

6. "Lyric and Greek Myth," in R. D. Woodard (ed.), *The Cambridge Companion to Greek Mythology* (Cambridge: Cambridge University Press, 2007), 19.

7. R. Finnegan, *Oral Poetry: Its Nature, Significance and Social Context* (Bloomington: Indiana University Press, 1992 [1977]), 13; cf. A. B. Lord, "Oral Traditional Lyric Poetry," in M. L. Lord (ed.), *The Singer Resumes the Tale* (Ithaca: Cornell University Press, 1995), 22–68; P. Zumthor, *Oral Poetry: An Introduction* (trans. K. Murphy-Judy; Minneapolis: University of Minnesota Press, 1990), 76, 103–6.

8. Johnson, "Lyric," 715; see B. Boyd, *Why Lyrics Last: Evolution, Cognition, and Shakespeare's Sonnets* (Cambridge, Mass.: Harvard University Press, 2012), esp. 9–23. Though Johnson does not proceed to thematize "oral" lyric as such, his awareness of the genre's millennia-old roots in human culture presupposes it. And while lyric's oral pedigree has not received nearly the amount of scholarly attention paid to the genre's nonmelic oral cousin, epic verse, there is no question that lyric is just as old and widespread in the oral traditions of the world as epic, if not more so. At any rate, the Bible's lyric tradition is most definitely rooted in orality (see chapter 4 here) and its central practices and characteristics, as I elaborate over the course of this chapter, betray this heritage in any number of telling ways.

9. Johnson, "Lyric," 713–27.

10. This is epitomized by the narrow focus of V. Jackson's entry "Lyric," in *PEPP*, especially as it replaces Johnson's more expansive entry from the earlier edition of the encyclopedia.

11. See M. K. Blasing, *Lyric Poetry: The Pain and the Pleasure of Words* (Princeton: Princeton University Press, 2007), 4, 20–21, n. 12.

12. See esp. H. Dubrow, *The Challenges of Orpheus: Lyric Poetry and Early Modern England* (Baltimore: Johns Hopkins University Press, 2008), 1–14. For my own

thoughts on genre, see F. W. Dobbs-Allsopp, *Weep, O Daughter of Zion: A Study of the City-Lament Genre in the Hebrew Bible* (BibOr 44; Rome: Editrice Pontificio Istituto Biblico, 1993); "Darwinism, Genre Theory, and City Laments," *JAOS* 120/4 (2000), 625–30. My approach throughout is distinctly pragmatic and heuristic, much in the vein of R. von Hallberg in *Lyric Powers* (Chicago: University of Chicago Press, 2008), esp. 1–7—"opportunistically use whatever distinctions serve understanding and appreciation of particular poems" (2).

13. D. Lindley, *Lyric* (London: Methuen, 1985), 5.

14. Cf. Lindley, *Lyric*, 22. So, for example, J. Culler glosses "poetic" with "lyric" in his own discussion of the three overarching modes or genres (*Literary Theory: A Very Short Introduction* [Oxford: Oxford University Press, 1997], 69). But more to the point, lyric is simply assumed to be the prototype of poetry in most critical discussions today (a holdover from the Romantic era and from New Criticism?).

15. Cf. Blasing, *Lyric Poetry*, 8—Blasing emphasizes the historical rootedness of all lyric speech (esp. 1–24; cf. 45–77).

16. "Genre: Lyric," in R. Warhol (ed.), *The Work of Genre: Selected Essays from the English Institute* (English Institute, 2011), http://quod.lib.umich.edu/cgi/t/text/text-idx?c=acls;idno=heb90055.0001.001 (accessed February 28, 2015), par. 35; see par. 58. Culler here provides the most thoughtful reflection on the importance of thinking lyric and genre through together. From par. 60 he writes the following:

> Foregrounding the lyric helps promote the possibility of comparisons with other traditions. In the afterword to the 2007 *PMLA* [122: 1648] issue, "Remapping Genre," Bruce Robbins compares notions of genre to the norms in the socioeconomic realm that allow, for instance, transnational comparison of living standards and argues that the case of genre in a nutshell is that of historical comparison. Genre, he argues, is a crucial instrument combating the professional inclination to focus on a literary period—which he calls "a sort of pseudo-anthropocentric norm that has been adopted for a long time out of laziness. It is one level of magnification among others, no less valid than any other but also no less arbitrary." Genre, he insists, offers us "versions of history that take us beyond the period-by-period agenda of our ordinary studies." "Why," he concludes, "would criticism voluntarily deprive itself of the additional scale of transperiodic vision and the aggregations it brings into view?" Why indeed? Genre remains an essential notion for trans-linguistically broadening critical horizons, connecting various narrower modes of reading and interpretation and enlarging discursive possibilities.

17. Lindley, *Lyric*, 22.

18. Heuristically, I operate with an (ideal) discourse continuum in mind. It is composed of narrative at one extreme and lyric at the other, with much mixing in

between. This is obviously but one way to look at literature, focusing on one set of variables; it is not intended to be a comprehensive interpretive strategy. I find warrant for such an approach both in contemporary literary theory and criticism (e.g., J. Culler, *The Pursuit of Signs* [Ithaca: Cornell University Press, 1981], 149–52) and especially in the prose/poetry dichotomy that pervades biblical Hebrew literature and breaks down mostly along a narrative/nonnarrative divide. More broadly (and from a specifically linguistic perspective), K. Hanson and P. Kiparsky argue that verse is the "unmarked form of literary language" and prose the "marked form"; and correlatively, that the "unmarked function of verse is lyric" ("The Nature of Verse and Its Consequences for the Mixed Form," in J. Harris and K. Reichl (eds.), *Prosimetrum: Cross-cultural Perspectives on Narrative in Prose and Verse* (Cambridge: D. S. Brewer, 1997), 17–18. H. Dubrow, who also works with such a continuum, nonetheless does so precisely to emphasize the mixture of narrative and lyric moments in early modern English lyric (*Challenges of Orpheus*, 191–227). P. Zumthor also emphasizes that "the oral text seems to fight against its model" (namely lyric, narrative, gnomic) and "there always subsist an uncertain fringe, heterogeneous bands, reflections: 'lyric' in narration, or the reverse" (*Oral Poetry*, 105).

19. *The Challenge of Comparative Literature* (trans. C. Franzen; Cambridge, Mass.: Harvard University Press, 1993), 142.

20. S. Langer, *Feeling and Form; A Theory of Art* (New York: Scribner, 1953), 259. And similarly, D. Levertov remarks that lyric verse is constructed out of the everyday language of normal discourse—idle chat, news briefs, dinner table conversation (*The Poet in the World* [New York: New Directions, 1973], 87).

21. *Lyric Poetry*, 116. Hence, G. Genette prefers to speak of the the broad (macro) genres (namely epic, drama, lyric) as modes of "enunciation" (*Architext*, 61).

22. Von Hallberg, *Lyric Powers*, 143, 144.

23. Finnegan, *Oral Poetry*, 13; cf. A. Welsh, *Roots of Lyric: Primitive Poetry and Modern Poetics* (Princeton: Princeton University Press, 1978), 135.

24. *Idea of Lyric*, 28. Others also emphasize the orality of ancient Greek lyric, e.g., C. M. Bowra, *Greek Lyric Poetry: From Alcman to Simonides* (2d ed.; Oxford: Oxford University Press, 1961); J. Herington, *Poetry into Drama: Early Tragedy and the Greek Poetic Tradition* (Berkeley: University of California Press, 1985); E. A. Havelock, *The Literate Revolution in Greece and Its Cultural Consequences* (Princeton: Princeton University Press, 1982), 17; B. Gentili, *Poetry and Its Public in Ancient Greece: From Homer to the Fifth Century* (trans. A. T. Cole; Baltimore: Johns Hopkins University Press, 1988), esp. 3–49; Nagy, *Pindar's Homer*; "Lyric and Greek Myth," 19; R. S. Garner, *Traditional Elegy: The Interplay of Meter, Tradition, and Context in Early Greek Poetry* (Oxford: Oxford University Press, 2010). For an elaboration on the oral roots of lyric discourse, see chapter 4 here.

25. *The Legends of Genesis* (trans. W. H. Carruth; Chicago: Open Court, 1901), 38; cf. 41.

26. Cf. D. Pardee, "Preliminary Presentation of a New Ugaritic Song to 'Aṯtart (RIH 98/02)," in K. L. Younger (ed.), *Ugarit at Seventy-Five* (Winona Lake, Ind.: Eisenbrauns, 2007), 30.

27. The musicality of Sumerian love poetry is suggested by its occasional designation as "composition for a TIGI (harp)" or "for a KUN.GAR instrument" and by the likelihood that the Inanna-Dumuzi poems were chanted as a part of the cult (see J. Goodnick Westenholz, "Love Lyrics from the Ancient Near East," in J. M. Sasson (ed.), *CANE*, IV [New York: Scribner, 1995], 2474, 2476). A second-millennium catalog from Asshur attests to the musical quality of Akkadian love songs. Many of the compositions listed in the catalog are labeled *zamāru* "song" and were sung to musical accompaniment (cf. E. Ebeling, *Ein Hymnen-Katalog aus Assur* (Berlin, 1929). For the song quality of Egyptian love poetry, see M. V. Fox, *The Song of Songs and the Ancient Egyptian Love Songs* (Madison: University of Wisconsin, 1985), 244–47. Ugaritic (e.g., *mšr. l. dd. aliyn b'l*, "a song about the love of Mightiest Baal," CAT 1.3.III.5–6; cf. 1.101.16–18) and biblical love poetry (e.g., Song 1:1; Isa 5:1; Ps 45:1) is also explictly labeled as "song."

28. A. Cooper, "Biblical Poetics: A Linguistic Approach" (Ph.D. diss.; Yale University, 1976), 3. It is tempting to replace the belated and specifically Greek derivation "lyric" with the more indigenously rooted term "song" (e.g., *šîr*) when referencing the lyric forms of biblical verse. However, it is quite likely as Gunkel supposes that oral Hebrew narrative poetry (see chapter 4 here) was also "sung" and thus equally referenced as "song." U. Cassuto, in fact, suggests that the reference in Job 36:24 ("Remember to extol his work, / of which mortals have sung [*šōrĕrû*]," NRSV) is specifically to such a sung mythic narrative song about Yahweh ("The Israelite Epic," in *Biblical and Oriental Studies* [Jerusalem: Magnes, 1975 (1943)], II, 73–74). Certainly, at ancient Ugarit *š-y-r* was used explicitly for both narrative (e.g., CAT 1.23.1; 24.1) and nonnarrative (*RIH* 98/02.1) songs. Furthermore, "lyric" has evolved as the preferred literary critical term for designating such songs regardless of tradition or indigenous terminology. In fact, as noted earlier, the Greek term itself was not yet in use when the archaic and classical forms it came to designate were initially composed. The broader term used in these earlier periods would have been *melos* "song," which is a good deal closer to the biblical (and Ugaritic) designations (e.g., Nagy, "Lyric and Greek Myth," 19–20). In other words, the term "lyric" is no less appropriately used of Hebrew than of Greek poems. "Lyric" here, like "line," "verse," and "poetry," is used chiefly as an idiom of current critical discourse, mindful of its particular (Greek) etymology but not captivated by it. To talk about biblical Hebrew *lyric* poetry is not to ascribe Greek parochial characteristics to it but to identify a kind or genre of poetry via a conventional idiom of literary criticism.

29. *Lectures*, II, 189.

30. Cf. P. King and L. Stager, *Life in Biblical Israel* (Louisville: Westminster John Knox, 2001), 290–98; J. Braun, *Music in Ancient Israel/Palestine* (trans. D. W. Stott; Grand Rapids: Eerdmans, 2002), 8–32.

31. Cooper, "Biblical Poetics," 3–4; Braun, *Music*, 37–42.
32. See King and Stager, *Life in Biblical Israel*, 286.
33. See A. D. Kilmer, "Music and Dance in ancient Western Asia," *CANE* IV, 2601–13; King and Stager, *Life in Biblical Israel*, 285–300; Braun, *Music*, 47–320. On the hymn recovered from ancient Ugarit, see A. D. Kilmer, R. L. Crocker, and R. R. Brown, *Sounds from Silence: Recent Discoveries in Ancient Near Eastern Music* (Berkeley: Bit Enki, 1976). Levantine lyre-players may be seen in Sennacherib's reliefs (ME #124947).
34. M. Schneider, "Primitive Music," in *The New Oxford History of Music I, Ancient and Oriental Music* (Oxford: Oxford University Press, 1957), 31; B. Nettl, *Music in Primitive Culture* (Cambridge, Mass.: Harvard University Press, 1956), 57; Nagy, *Pindar's Homer*, esp. 34–35; M. L. West, *Ancient Greek Music* (Cambridge: Clarendon, 1992), 39. Nagy points out that accompaniment by instrumental music is another way in which song is marked (and thus distinguished) from speech (*Pindar's Homer*, 33–34).
35. Nettl, *Music in Primitive Culture*, 57.
36. One may suppose that as in Greece knowledge of the melodies and such were likely handed down orally (lacking an established written notation system for music), see A. Ford, "From Letters to Literature: Reading the 'Song Culture' of Classical Greece," in H. Yunis (ed.), *Written Texts and the Rise of Literate Culture in Ancient Greece* (Cambridge: Cambridge University Press, 2003), 20–21; Herington, *Poetry into Drama*, 45.
37. As Nettl notes (*Music in Primitive Culture*, 6–7), the most important role of music in "primitive" culture is "assisting in religious rituals," which, of course, is precisely the generative context for much of the lyric verse preserved from the ancient Near East, and especially in the biblical psalms.
38. Johnson, "Lyric," 714.
39. About rhythm Nettl writes, it "is in some ways the most basic musical principle" (*Music in Primitive Culture*, 62). For my account of the basic rhythm(s) of Hebrew verse, see chapter 2, which elaborates on the seminal insights of B. Hrushovski, especially his notion of "free rhythms" (see "Prosody, Hebrew," in *EcyJud* [1971–72], 13: 1200–1203; "On Free Rhythms in Modern Poetry," in T. Sebeok (ed.), *Style in Language* [New York: Wiley, 1960], 173–90). At the core of Hrushovski's thesis is the idea that the rhythmic organization of biblical verse is analogous to that of free verse poetries more generally. That is, it is variable and organized by other than numerical (i.e., metrical) modes and involving any number of features (e.g., lineation, stress or accent, syntax). The resulting asymmetry is precisely the "most conspicuous characteristic" of primitive musical rhythm (Nettl, *Music in Primitive Culture*, 63; Bruce Zuckerman put me onto the connection between the free-verse-like rhythms that typify Hebrew verse and the dominant rhythmical shape of preclassical music).
40. Langer, *Feeling and Form*, 260; cf. Lindley, *Lyric*, 43; Johnson, "Lyric," 714–15.
41. Johnson, *Idea of Lyric*, 26–29.

42. Johnson, *Idea of Lyric*, 27.

43. On rhythm and musicality, see von Hallberg, *Lyric Powers*, 167–68.

44. S. Brewster, *Lyric* (New York: Routledge, 2009), 19; E. Hirsch, *How to Read a Poem* (New York: Harcourt Brace, 1999), 17. For the musicality of Sumerian verse, see P. Michalowski, "Ancient Poetics," in M. Vogelzang and M. Vanstiphout (ed.), *Mesopotamian Poetic Language: Sumerian and Akkadian* (Groningen: STYX, 1996), 145–46.

45. E.g., Welsh, *Roots of Lyric*, 134–35.

46. See H. Jahnow, *Das hebräische Leichenlied im Rahmen der Völkerdichtung* (BZAW 36; Giessen: A. Toppelmann, 1923).

47. See D. Boyarin, "Placing Reading in Ancient Israel and Medieval Europe," in *Sparks of the Logos* (Leiden: Brill, 2003), 59–88. For more extended discussion, see chapter 4 here.

48. Cf. Culler, "Genre: Lyric," par. 37.

49. "Approaching the Lyric," in C. Hošek and P. Parker (ed.), *Lyric Poetry: Beyond New Criticism*, (Ithaca: Cornell University Press, 1985), 31.

50. E.g., Langer, *Feeling and Form*, 259; B. H. Smith, *Poetic Closure: A Study of How Poems End* (Chicago: University of Chicago Press, 1968), 122; M. P. Coote, "On the Composition of Women's Songs," *Oral Tradition* 7 (1992), 333, 334; Johnson, *Idea of Lyric*, 35; M. L. Rosenthal and S. M. Gall, *The Modern Poetic Sequence: The Genius of Modern Poetry* (New York: Oxford University Press, 1983), 11; Johnson, "Lyric," 713, 714; Race, "Melic," in *NPEPP*, 755; Culler, *Literary Theory*, 70; "Why Lyric?," 203; "Genre: Lyric," par. 46.

51. *Literary Theory*, 73; cf. Smith, *Poetic Closure*, 122. Or, as Langer puts it, the lyric creates a "virtual history"—"the occurrence of a living thought, the sweep of an emotion, the intense experience of a mood" (*Form and Feeling*, 259).

52. *The Art of Biblical Poetry* (New York: Basic Books, 1985), 27; cf. Driver, *Introduction*, 360–61.

53. This is a point well stressed by Genette in his discussion of modes (*Architext*) and is the cornerstone of most contemporary genre theorists (e.g., A. Fowler, *Kinds of Literature* [Cambridge, Mass.: Harvard University Press, 1982]).

54. E. S. Gerstenberger, *Psalms, Part 2, and Lamentations* (FOTL 15; Grand Rapids: Eerdmans, 2001), 281. Cf. 1 Samuel 10:2; Ezekiel 1:19, 21; 5:16; Jonah 2:8; Esther 1:5; 2:12, 15, 19; Daniel 10:15. It is very common with *wayhî* (e.g., Gen 35:17, 18, 22; 38:28; Exod 13:17; Judg 13:20; 1 Sam 16:6; 23:6; 1 Kgs 11:15; Ezek 10:6; Est 2:8; Dan 8:15). The construction without *wayhî* is fairly common in poetic texts (e.g., Judg 5:2; Ps 4:2; 9:4; 27:2; 68:15; 76:10; 105:12; 109:7; 142:4; Job 29:7; cf. CAT 1.17.V.9), evidencing something of the typical compactness of Hebrew poetry. Given the obvious creation imagery that pervades the psalm, e.g., sanctuary (v. 2), imagery drawn from the mythology of the *Chaoskampf* (vv. 3, 5; see S. A. Geller, "The Language of Imagery in Psalm 114," in T. Abusch et al. (eds.), *Lingering over Words* [HSS 37: Atlanta: Scholars Press, 1990], 179–94, esp. 182–84),

it is tempting to hear the faintest echoes of a very specific kind of story, the epic of creation, e.g., *bĕrē'šît bārā' 'ĕlōhîm* "When God first created" (Gen 1:1), *e-nu-ma e-liš la na-bu-u ša-ma-mu* "When on high the heavens had not been created" (*Enuma elish* I 1).

55. *Psalms 60–150: A Commentary* (Minneapolis: Augsburg, 1989), 316.

56. "Disturbing is the plethora of terms referring to the nation" (Geller, "Language of Imagery," 182).

57. Such fundamental dependence on extratextual knowledge—the need to infer a "referential tie between text and context" (U. Schaefer, "Hearing from Books: The Rise of Fictionality in Old English Poetry," in A. N. Doane and C. B. Pasternack (eds.), *Vox Intexta: Orality and Textuality in the Middle Ages* [Madison: University of Wisconsin Press, 1991], 121)—also epitomizes traditional, performative verbal art more generally.

58. *Psalms 60–150*, 370; cf. Gerstenberger, *Psalms, Part 2*, 283.

59. Both Langer (*Feeling and Form*, esp. 260–79) and R. Greene (*Post-Petrarchism: Origins and Innovations of the Western Lyric Sequence* [Princeton: Princeton University Press, 1991], 23–62) include interesting discussions of temporality and its linguistic manifestations (e.g., tense, deixis) in lyric verse. In this sense, the presence or absence of the *wayyiqtol* form in biblical psalms (especially in standard biblical Hebrew) can be a good barometer of "narrativity." There are clearly psalms (e.g., Ps 105–6) whose narrative ambitions are announced by their liberal use of the *wayyiqtol*.

60. *Psalms 60–150*, 371.

61. At least since Gunkel (*Die Psalmen* [5th ed.; Göttingen: Vändenhoeck, 1968], 493).

62. E.g., Culler, "Genre: Lyric," par. 38; von Hallberg, *Lyric Powers*, ch. 2 ("Praise," esp. 51–55 on the Psalms).

63. *Lectures*, II, 189.

64. *Lectures*, II, 190.

65. The *kî* clause, which prototypically initiates the second movement in Israel's hymns of praise and thanksgiving (cf. P. D. Miller, *They Cried to the LORD* [Minneapolis: Fortress, 1999], 206), grammatically and semantically gives the reason for the praise. The underlying grammar and syntax is made clear by passages such as Judges 16:24, where the Philistines "praised their god" (*wayhalĕlû 'et-'ĕlōhêhem*) Dagan, "because they said, '…'" (*kî 'āmĕrû*…), or even Ezra 3:11, where the priests and Levites sing "with praise and with thanksgiving [*bĕhallēl ûbĕhôdōt*] to Yahweh because [*kî*] he is good, because [*kî*] his steadfast love endures forever over Israel" (cf. 2 Chron 5:13). Especially since F. Crüsemann's *Studien zur Formgescichte von Hymnes und Danklied in Israel* ([WMANT 32; Neukirchen-Vluyn: Neukirchener Verlag, 1969], esp. 32–35), it has been customary to construe the *kî* clauses here as a direct quote (e.g., NRSV; cf. Miller, *They Cried to the LORD*, 358–62). However, this is unlikely for several reasons. First, nowhere else does *hll* "to praise" introduce direct discourse. Second,

though *kî* may introduce either direct or indirect discourse in biblical Hebrew (see C. L. Miller, *The Representation of Speech in biblical Hebrew Narrative: A Linguistic Analysis* [HMS 55; Atlanta: Scholars Press, 1996], 97–116), the presence of "transparent deixis" (Miller, *Representation of Speech*, 65) here favors the indirect construal. And in fact one of the tendencies of late biblical Hebrew is to favor indirect discourse (see M. Eskhult, "Verbal Syntax in Late Biblical Hebrew," in T. Muraoka and J. F. Elwolde (eds.), *Diggers at the Well* [Leiden: Brill, 2000], 86, 90 and n. 31). Moreover, as P. D. Miller observes, "in the several [other] examples where there is a call to praise and those so called are explicitly told what to say, there is never … any use of the *kî* particle" (*They Cried to the LORD*, 359). But the discursive logic here is subordinated (pragmatically) to the poem's larger lyric ambition, which is to offer praise to Yahweh. And as such, the literal reasons given for praise (the steadfast love and faithfulness of Yahweh) are at the same time—by dint of their lyric framing, as it were—themselves expressions of praise. In other words, the poet's chief aim is not to argue a theological point (namely the nations *should* praise Yahweh *because* his steadfast love is mighty and his faithfulness enduring) but to offer that argument as part and parcel of the poem's expression of praise.

66. Many would emend to *millipnê ʾ̌ădôn kol-hāʾāreṣ* based on the phrase's resemblances to *ʾ̌ădôn kol-hāʾāreṣ* in Joshua 3:11 and Psalm 97:5 (e.g., F. M. Cross, *Canaanite Myth and Hebrew Epic* [Cambridge, Mass.: Harvard University Press, 1972], 138, n. 91; Kraus, *Psalms 60–150*, 371; Geller, "Language of Imagery," 180). However, there is no textual support for such a reading and MT makes good sense, especially when the poem is read as a hymn (if the imperative is emended away, a significant basis for identifying the poem as a hymn is lost—the so-called hymnic participle in v. 8 is "hymnic" only by virtue of being in a hymn!). Besides, I suspect that the emendation is motivated by narrative assumptions about discourse continuity and logic, e.g., Cross ("The hills like lambs [danced], / Before the lord") and Kraus ("Why do you [skip] … / O hillocks, like the lambs of the flock?— / in the presence of the Lord") make v. 7 a prepositional phrase dependent on v. 6, while Geller construes v. 7 as the explicit answer given to the question in vv. 5–6 ("Why … ? / It's from the Lord"). However, Geller, at least, concedes that MT is construable as is—a "bold apostrophe" ("Language of Imagery," 188, n. 25). As Michael Carasik has emphasized to me (in person and via email, October 6, 2013), though MT is readable and "makes sense" as is, the "emendation" is nonetheless obvious and "was meant to be so by the poet."

67. LXX construes the concluding *halĕlû yāh* of Psalm 113 as belonging to Psalm 114.

68. In Jeremiah 51:29 "the land of Babylon" (*ʾereṣ bābel*) is said to "writhe" (*wattāḥōl*) at the news of the Yahweh's impending onslaught, and it is this deity's terrible theophany that causes "the earth to writhe" (*wattāḥēl hāʾāreṣ*) in Psalm 97:4; cf. D. R. Hillers, "A Convention in Hebrew Literature: The Reaction to Bad News," *ZAW* 77 (1965), 86–90 (reprinted in D. R. Hillers, *Poets before Homer: Collected*

Essays on Ancient Literature [ed. F. W. Dobbs-Allsopp; Winona Lake, Ind.: Eisenbrauns, 2015], 29–33).

69. Geller ("Language of Imagery," 187–90) also recognizes the psalm's darker moments.

70. Esp. Cross, *Canaanite Myth and Hebrew Epic*, 138–39.

71. Gerstenberger's (and others) assertion that the "mountains and hills jumping like lambs…should be taken as an expression of joy" (*Psalms, Part 2*, 283) seems to me to ignore the significance of the biblical (and extrabiblical) literary parallels and to misread the psalm's basic tenor. Indeed, the nature of the image in Psalm 29:6 (the only other place where the image explicitly appears in the Hebrew Bible) is unmistakable: it registers "the convulsions and travail" (Cross, *Canaanite Myth and Hebrew Epic*, 152; note also the threefold use of the root *ḥ-y-l* in Ps 29:8–9) that accompany the theophany of the Storm God—similar upheavals attend the march of the Divine Warrior from the southland, too (Judg 5:4–5; Hab 3:3–6). In sum, the reactions of Sea and Mountains in Psalm 114 seem to me to be very much of a piece.

72. *Feeling and Form*, 259.

73. Or perhaps even better, a combination of apostrophe and personification not unlike that in "With how sad steps, O Moon, thou climb'st the skies," cited from Sidney's *Astrophil and Stella* (31) by T. V. F. Brogan and A. W. Halsall in "Poropopoeia," in *NPEPP*, 994.

74. Geller, "Language of Imagery," 188, n. 25.

75. See Culler's discussion of what *"distinguishes* the lyric from other speech acts" (*Literary Theory*, 74).

76. Cf. Geller, "Language of Imagery," 181.

77. *Light Up the Cave* (New York: New Directions, 1981), 60; cf. Blasing, *Lyric Poetry*, 28.

78. *Psalms 60–150*, 375.

79. L. C. Allen, *Psalms 101–150* (Waco: Word, 1983), 105.

80. So Gerstenberger, *Psalms, Part 2*, 282.

81. The same thing would appear to be at issue in Numbers 20:2–13, though there the point is made through the failure of Moses and Aaron to follow Yahweh's instruction literally (see the comments by E. Greenstein in *The HarperCollins Study Bible* [San Francisco: HarperCollins, 1993], 111).

82. *Idea of Lyric*, 35; cf. Langer, *Feeling and Form*, 261.

83. Many psalms, of course, are far less interested in narrative, while some others move a long way toward narrative. Psalms 105 and 106 are good examples of the latter. Both contain multiple narrative runs, in which a variety of devices (the *wayyiqtol* form and the like) are used to emplot action, resulting in what R. Alter aptly calls "incipient narrativity" (*Art of Biblical Poetry*, 27–61).

84. Culler, "Why Lyric?," 205; cf. Blasing, *Lyric Poetry*, 2–3. This is to focus the language material of the lyric outside of a consideration of putative extralinguistic contributions made in performance (e.g., gestures).

85. *Feeling and Form*, 259; cf. Johnson, *Idea of Lyric*, 23; R. P. Draper, *Lyric Tragedy* (New York: St. Martin's, 1985), 4–5; Blasing, *Lyric Poetry*, 34. Langer, of course, has modern lyric principally in mind, whose resurces are almost wholly verbal—linguistic. Lyric in it aboriginal state as oral art could draw on nonverbal resources as well—a wink or nod, a tapping foot, musical accompaniment—but so, too, could oral epic, and thus the differences in the deployment of verbal resources remains.

86. *A Poet's Guide to Poetry* (Chicago: University of Chicago Press, 1999), 142.

87. Boyd, *Why Lyrics Last*, ch. 1; J. Culler, "Lyric, History, and Genre," *New Literary History* 40/4 (2009), 896.

88. *Anatomy of Criticism*, 275; von Hallberg (*Lyric Powers*, 19) speaks of "charm."

89. *Anatomy of Criticism*, 271; cf. Culler, *Literary Theory*, 74.

90. I. M. Casanowicz, *Paronomasia in the Old Testament* (Boston, 1894); E. König, *Stilistik, Rhetorik, Poetik* (Leipzig, 1900); A. Berlin, "Motif and Creativity in Biblical Poetry," *Prooftexts* 3 (1983) 231–41; E. Greenstein, "Wordplay, Hebrew," in *ABD* VI, 968–77; D. Grossberg, *Centripetal and Centrifugal Structures in Hebrew Poetry* (SBLMS; Atlanta: Scholars Press, 1989).

91. See F. W. Dobbs-Allsopp, *Lamentations* (IBC; Louisville: Westminster John Knox, 2002).

92. The major difference between *ṭippuḥîm* "to be reared" and *tappûaḥ* "apple" is the initial phoneme, the former beginning with the emphatic interdental stop and the latter with the voiceless interdental stop.

93. *Lamentations* (AB 7A; 2d. rev. ed.; New York: Doubleday, 1992), 87.

94. "The Rhetoric of Lamentations and the Representation of Catastrophe," *Prooftexts* 2/1 (1982), 4; *Hurban: Responses to Catastrophe in Hebrew Literature* (New York: Columbia University Press, 1984), 25.

95. In more detail, see F. W. Dobbs-Allsopp and T. Linafelt, "The Rape of Zion in Lam 1:10," *ZAW* 113/1 (2001), 77–81.

96. Cf. Culler, *Literary Theory*, 79–81.

97. *Reading for the Plot* (Cambridge, Mass.: Harvard University Press, 1984), 5; cf. Greene, *Post-Petrarchism*, 49.

98. Psalm 45:2 is one of the rare instances in which a biblical poet shows some conscious awareness of craft. Here the poet prefaces the poem with a statement about how his mind is teeming with a "good word" (*dābār tôb*) and that he proclaims to/for the king "my work" (*maʿăśay*). The latter offers a rough equivalent to the Greek notion of poesy.

99. There are occasions, as well, when the tropological density on display is more than doubled, as in Psalm 9:2–3, where the opening *aleph* stanza also intentionally alliterates the guttural sound of the *aleph* in the sequence of five verbs: *ʾôdâ, ʾăsapperâ, ʾeśmĕḥâ, wĕʾeʿelṣâ, ʾăzammĕrâ* (cf. *ṣôd ṣādûnî kaṣṣippôr* in the *ṣade* stanza in Lam 3:52).

100. As elsewhere in the Psalms, it is not easy to discern whether this inclusio is compositional or editorial.

Notes to Pages 192–193

434

101. For this notion of conventional form, see esp. K. Burke, *Counter-Statement* (2d ed.; Chicago: Phoenix Books, 1953), 126.

102. E.g., Miller, *They Cried to the LORD*, 205–6.

103. A sign of this form's conventionality (though not precisely "as form") is the frequency with which it is quoted (in part or whole) in later biblical compositions (e.g., Jer 33:11; Ezra 3:11; Neh 9:5; 2 Chron 7:3, 6; 20:21). Moreover, a compelling case can be made that the Joban poet uses the model hymn of praise (though semantically inverted) to shape the opening stanza of the curse of Job's day of birth (3:3–10; an initial jussive, "let it perish," followed after much elaboration by a closing *kî* clause), which if correct shows the hymn's significance "as form" (for some details, C. L. Seow, *Job 1–21* [Illuminations; Grand Rapids, Mich.: Eerdmans, 2013], 315, 321–22).

104. The quote is taken from "Shakespeare's Judgment Equal to His Genius," in *Selected Poetry and Prose of Samuel Taylor Coleridge* (ed. D. A. Stauffer; New York: Random House, 1951), 432–33, as cited in C. O. Hartman, *Free Verse: An Essay on Prosody* (Evanston, Ill.: Northwestern University Press, 1980), 92 and esp. 183, n. 4.

105. See Smith (*Poetic Closure*, 38) for the idea that "repetition is the fundamental phenomenon of poetic form."

106. Nettl notes that "one of the best known and most widely recognized characteristics of primitive music" is "its frequently asymmetrical and irregular structure" (*Music in Primitive Culture*, 62).

107. *Poetic Closure*, 10, 12, 13.

108. Though stanzaic form in metrical verse traditions are routinely associated with rhyme schemes, metrical constraints, line counts, and the like, as M. Oliver reminds us, the term itself designates "a group of lines in a poem" and "is used to indicate the divisions of a poem," but beyond this "there is no further *exact* definition" and "there are no absolutely right or wrong ways to divide a poem into stanzas" (*A Poetry Handbook* [New York: Harcourt Brace, 1994], 60–61). She continues by suggesting—and this seems especially apt for free verse poetries—that "it may be useful, when considering the stanza, to recall the paragraph in prose, which indicates the conclusion of one thought and the beginning of another, a *sensible* division" and that the "sensible paragraph" be thought of "as a kind of norm...from which to feel out the particular divisions that are best for a particular poem" (61).

109. See King and Stager, *Life in Biblical Israel*, Ill. 16.

110. Whatever one makes of the compositional techniques on display in this poem—a notoriously difficult matter to discern without the evidence of explicit comment—the poem itself hangs together as a whole. Thematically, vv. 12 and 15 play key roles in unifying the two parts. Verse 12 makes explicit and implicit connections with the main foci of the poem—nature and Torah. *Nizhār*: NRSV, for example, glosses as "is...warned," construing as a Niphal Part ms √ *zhr* II

"to be warned," which given the context of the second part of the poem makes sense, as it is precisely Torah that guides the psalmist in his or her life. And yet, deriving from *zhr* I "to shine" also makes good sense, as this root is used explicitly in the Bible (e.g., Dan 12:3) and elsewhere of the sun shining! The latter sense is especially relevant as *bāhem* comes at the end of the line, formally—though not semantically, as different antecedents are involved—pointing back to *bāhem* in v. 5c. The tone of "illumination, seeing, shining" also fits well the adoring tone of the poem as a whole. But it is not likely a matter of choosing between the two, except perhaps for translation purposes (it is hard to get both senses into English) and for determining which is primary (i.e., at the surface of the poem), since the poet would appear to have intended both senses to resonate. I would emphasize the derivation from *zhr* I "to shine" only because this has not been routinely appreciated and because there are those who still continue to insist that we have two poems here instead of one. Note, too, how the notion of guarding, etc. is precisely one of the activities that is predicated of Shamash in the Mesopotamian hymn.

The closing triplet in v. 15 is well known. What may be missed is that the invocation of Yahweh as "rock and redeemer" points rather clearly—if metaphorically—to the two dominant movements in the poem—nature and Torah. Redemption, of course, is itself a legal concept. Here, what is intended (at least in part) is that it is precisely through Torah that the psalmist finds well-being, salvation.

111. Free verse compositions come most generally in long-line and short-line varieties (e.g., C. Beyers, *A History of Free Verse* [Fayetteville: University of Arkansas Press, 2001], esp. 39–42).

112. Note further how the repetition of 3ms suffixes syntactically tracks the main actor of the stanza—the sun—but in doing so also builds (formal) coherence into the stanza. A more elaborate use of this kind of anaphora is evidenced in Lamentations (cf. Dobbs-Allsopp, *Lamentations*, 49).

113. As a way of valorizing the image as a vehicle for thought, it may be helpful to recall that according to neurobiologists like A. Damasio, "having a mind means that an organism forms neural representations which can become images" of various kinds (e.g., visual, sound, olfactory) but which only latterly become translated into language (see *Descartes' Error* [New York: Quill, 1995], 83–113, esp. 89–90). That is, image—and presumably even linguistically stimulated images—is itself a most natural and congenial mode of thought for the human organism and one that should not be disparaged on account of our current love affair with all things linguistic.

114. On the "densely patterned" ways in which biblical verse typically means, see Alter's comment in *Art of Biblical Poetry*, 113.

115. *Psalms, Part 2*, 372.

116. *Psalms 60–150*, 485.

117. In H.-J. Kraus, *Psalms 1–59* (trans. H. Oswald; Minneapolis: Fortress, 1993), 115 (citing Buber).

118. It is perhaps crucial to underscore two things here: one, that such tropological density arises in the lyric chiefly in *compensation* for the absence of other discourse features, and two, that such "babbledness," if typical of lyric discourse, also appears in other discourse mediums—in other words, we need not essentialize this characteristic in order to appreciate its typicality and significance for the lyric. Furthermore, such ornamentation, as it turns out, also characterizes oral and oral-derived verbal art, because it aids both aural intake and in distinguishing such art from everyday speech.

119. *Literary Theory*, 71.

120. "The Text and the Voice," *New Literary History* 16/1 (1984), 69.

121. *The Sounds of Poetry: A Brief Guide* (New York: Farrar, Straus and Giroux, 1998), 8. And Blasing throughout her *Lyric Poetry* stresses the embodied nature of lyric art generally, and importantly for her, this includes the cognitive dimensions of human biology.

122. Pinsky, *Sounds of Poetry*, 8.

123. For example, Zumthor writes with regard to medieval oral poetry of "that fullness of the voice, its concreteness, the sensual tactile quality of a puff of air and the vibration of breathing" and that "each syllable acquires a rhythm from pulsing of blood in our veins" ("Text and the Voice," 74).

124. *Literary Theory*, 75. Similarly, Frye notes that what is distinctively "lyrical" is the "union of sound and sense" (*Anatomy of Criticism*, 272; cf. Blasing, *Lyric Poetry*, 28; Frye's additional notion of poetic creation as specifically "oracular," though but one way of conceptualizing the creative process, does flesh out quite vividly the lyrical fusion of "sound and sense": "an associative rhetorical process, most of it below the threshold of consciousness, a chaos of paronomasia, sound-links, ambiguous sense-links, and memory-links very like that of a dream," 271–72; cf. Levertov, *Light Up the Cave*, 29–45). Levertov also stresses the importance of sound to the lyric poet: "All words are to some extent onomatopoeic" (*Light Up the Cave*, 60). And: "The primary impulse for me was always to make a structure out of words, words that *sounded* right. And I think that's a rather basic foundation of a poet's word" (78). Further, the idea of the "oracular" offers pragmatic benefit when focusing on ancient poetic phenomena, such as from the Bible, since so much of this poetry literally would have been rooted in oracular contexts where "sound and sense" could have never been un-/re-fused.

125. Greene, *Post-Petrarchism*, 5.

126. *Sounds of Poetry*, 8.

127. *Sounds of Poetry*, 5–6.

128. *Sounds of Poetry*, 6.

129. *Sounds of Poetry*, 9; cf. Johnson, *Idea of Lyric*, 59, 74.

130. Schaefer, "Hearing from Books," 124.

131. "Direct Discourse and Parallelism," in A. Brenner-Idan (ed.), *Discourse, Dialogue, and Debate in the Bible: Essays in Honor of Frank H. Polak* (Sheffield: Sheffield Phoenix Press, 2014), 79.

132. *Interpreting the Psalms* (Philadelphia: Fortress, 1986), 50–51; cf. R. Greene, "Sir Philip Sidney's *Psalms*, the Sixteenth-Century Psalter, and the Nature of Lyric," *Studies in English Literature, 1500–1900* 30/1 (1990), 23.

133. *The Dramatic Monologue* (New York: Twayne, 1966), 6.

134. R. Pinsky, *Democracy, Culture and the Voice of Poetry* (Princeton: Princeton University Press, 2002), 23.

135. "Lyric, History, and Genre," 886, 887; cf. Culler, "Apostrophe," in *Pursuit of Signs*, 135–54.

136. A. Grossman, "Summa Lyrica: A Primer in the Commonplaces in Speculative Poetics," *Western Humanities Review* 44 (1990), 7.

137. In fact, toward the end of the chapter I raise the possibility, following the thinking of comparatist (of Asian literatures) E. Miner, that biblical (and other ancient Near Eastern) poetics is predicated primarily on ideas founded on lyric assumptions. For the moment it is enough to deconstruct the givenness of the postprose orientation of much modern scholarship, see esp. J. Kittay and W. Godzich, *The Emergence of Prose: An Essay in Prosaics* (Minneapolis: University of Minnesota Press, 1987), xii–xiii.

138. Pinsky, *Voice of Poetry*, 23.

139. Johnson himself stresses the pragmatic ("somewhat dubious even to me") nature of his categories here; they are but one grid through which to view lyric discourse and therefore should not be pressed too far or reified (*Idea of Lyric*, 2–3).

140. For this assessment of the pronominal orientation of much lyric poetry, see Johnson, *Idea of Lyric*, 1–23.

141. H. Vendler, *Soul Says* (Cambridge, Mass.: Harvard University Press, 1995), 2; H. Fisch, *Poetry with a Purpose* (Bloomington: Indiana University Press, 1988), 104–35.

142. Brewster, *Lyric*, 17.

143. *The English Ode from Milton to Keats* (New York: Columbia University Press, 1940), 11–12 (as cited in Brewster, *Lyric*, 17).

144. Some of the most detailed narrative representations of performed poetry in the Bible appear in prophetic literature (e.g., Jeremiah 36), though how prototypically "lyric" prophetic poetry is depends on which poem (or oracle) is in view (see my thoughts in Beyond Lyric and in chapter 4).

145. Cf. Schaefer, "Hearing from Books," 123; Culler, "Why Lyric?," 204. As elsewhere in antiquity but especially in ancient Greece, the voice heard in biblical lyric comes in two predominant varieties: solo and choral (e.g., individual laments vs. communal laments). Both varieties, as Johnson claims, "were equally valid and equally important, each of them necessary to the total shaping of the human personality" (*Idea of Lyric*, 177).

146. S. Mowinckel, *The Psalms in Israel's Worship* (trans. D. R. Ap-Thomas; Nashville: Abingdon, 1962), II, 91; cf. R. C. Culley, *Oral Formulaic Language in the Biblical Psalms* (Toronto: University of Toronto Press, 1967), 113; S. Niditch, *Oral World and Written Word: Ancient Israelite Literature* (Louisville: Westminster John Knox, 1996), 122–23.

147. Note Culler's metonymic description of typical concerns met in lyric poems: "They provide a panoply of poetic speech acts of praise, invocation, celebration, and complaint" ("Genre: Lyric," par. 38).

148. Kathy Rowe of Bryn Mawr College named this for me most explicitly a number of years ago while I was working on Lamentations; cf. Fisch, *Poetry with a Purpose*, 108.

149. Von Hallberg claims that this "you" of the beloved stands (emblematically perhaps) "at the core of lyric poetry"—"an ideal of desire fulfilled in an allegory present in all lyric" (*Lyric Powers*, 160).

150. Culler, "Genre: Lyric," par. 45; see Greenstein, "Direct Discourse," 88–89.

151. W. J. Ong, *Orality and Literacy: The Technologizing of the Word* (London: Routledge, 1982), 34.

152. For details on this poem itself, cf. Seow, *Job 1–21*, 312–79.

153. In his chapter on the Psalms ("Psalms: The Limits of Subjectivity") in *Poetry with a Purpose*, Fisch says much that is consonant with my own approach to the Psalms as lyric, including that "the one book of the Bible that...seems to offer itself as a model of lyrical subjectivity...is the book of Psalms" (106), though his own understanding of lyric discourse is profoundly shaped by Romantic ideology. And since the lyric subjectivity of the Psalms is not that of the Romantic poets and thinkers, he eventually prefers to characterize the Psalms as "covenantal discourse" (120), which hardly clarifies the nature of psalmic discourse.

154. *Lyric*, 3.

155. See the various rough statistics reported by Johnson himself throughout his *Idea of Lyric* (e.g., Catullus: 70 percent I-You; 14 percent meditative; 16 percent dialogic, etc.).

156. Cf. Lindley, *Lyric*, 12–13.

157. E. Bowie, "Lyric and Elegiac Poetry," in J. Boardman et al. (eds.), *The Oxford History of the Classical World* (Oxford: Oxford University Press, 1986), 99. Besides, the idea that a poet could speak through different personae was already well articulated by Plato (Lindley, *Lyric*, 2).

158. Esp. M. Jeffreys, "Songs and Inscriptions: Brevity and the Idea of Lyric," *Texas Studies in Literature and Language* 36/2 (1994), 117–34—though his chief focus is on written lyrics from the fourteenth century on; von Hallberg, *Lyric Powers*, 17, 83. Zumthor (*Oral Poetry*, 103–6) also focuses explicitly on the "short poem" in oral verbal art.

159. "Approaching the Lyric," 31; cf. Langer, *Feeling and Form*, 260; Rosenthal and Gall, *Modern Poetic Sequence*, 3; Johnson, "Lyric," 714; Culler, *Literary Theory*, 70;

B. Hardy, *The Advantage of Lyric: Essays on Feeling in Poetry* (London: Athlone, 1977), 2–4; Dubrow, *Challenges of Orpheus*, ch. 4.

160. Critical research into the nature, dynamics, and extent of the lyric sequence is still very much in its infancy. Scholars have for the most part focused on the Western poetic tradition (e.g., Rosenthal and Gall, *Modern Poetic Sequence*; Greene, *Post-Petrarchism*; T. L. Roche, Jr., *Petrarch and the English Sonnet Sequences* [New York: AMS, 1989]; D. Fenoaltea and D. L. Rubin, *The Ladder of High Designs: Structure and Interpretation of the French Lyric Sequence* [Charlottesville: University Press of Virginia, 1991]). Nevertheless, the potential for identifying other non-Western lyric sequences is good, see the comments to this effect by M. L. Rosenthal and S. M. Gall ("Lyric Sequence," in *NPEPP*, 729) and J. Rothenberg, "Ethnopoetics and Politics/The Politics of Ethnopoetics," in C. Bernstein (ed.), *The Politics of Poetic Form* [New York: Roof, 1990], 13).

161. See esp. C. B. Pasternack, *The Textuality of Old English Poetry* (Cambridge: Cambridge University Press, 1995). See my discussion later in the chapter, "Lyric *in extenso*: Probing (Some) Possibilities in the Song."

162. *Poetic Closure*, 96–150. Aristotle identified the same two organization structures in prose, which he termed *lexis eiromenaā* "strung-on or continuous" style and *lexis katestrammenā* "periodic or rounded" style (see R. L. Fowler, *The Nature of Early Greek Lyric: Three Preliminary Studies* [Toronto: University of Toronto Press, 1987], 53—Fowler helpfully goes on to make clear that parataxis need not imply a lack of logic or rationality).

163. *Poetic Closure*, 110.

164. *Poetic Closure*, 57–59, 98–99; cf. Zumthor, *Oral Poetry*, 107 ("the lyric register does so [i.e., juxtapose elements through parataxis] by cutting the discourse into short affirmations, exclamations, imperatives, and series of discontinuous accumulations; in the extreme, verbs disappear; there are no more phrases but rather a parade of liberated nominal elements").

165. Smith, *Poetic Closure*, 98–99.

166. *Anatomy of Criticism*, 270ff.

167. J. A. Notopoulos, "Parataxis in Homer: A New Approach to Homeric Literary Criticism," *Transactions and Proceedings of the American Philological Association* 80 (1949), 15; cf. Ong, *Orality and Literacy*, 37–38; Culley, *Oral Formulaic Language*, 97; W. G. E. Watson, *Classical Hebrew Poetry: A Guide to Its Techniques* (London: T. and T. Clark, 2001 [1984]), 75, 81.

168. Pasternack, *Textuality of Old English Poetry*, 120.

169. "Lyric Sequence"; cf. Rosenthal and Gall, *Modern Poetic Sequence*, 15. Alter's discussion of "structures of intensification" in biblical poetry offers another way of articulating the generative dynamic that most distinguishes lyrical structure (*Art of Biblical Poetry*, 62–84).

170. Greene, *Post-Petrarchism*, 18.

171. In performance, this "adding style" is under the control and guidance of a singer who helps negotiate these (dis)junctions, thus meliorating and defusing

some of the extreme fragmentation that can arise when written lyric poems become solely works of words alone.

172. My discussion of the fragmenting effects is dependent on Greene, *Post-Petrarchism*, esp. 20. His own discussion at this point has lyric sequences principally in view. But insofar as lyric sequences are essentially lyric poems writ large, his observations, as he himself would maintain, are very much applicable to the structure of individual lyric poems.

173. Greene's focus is on written lyric poems. It is likely that the disjunction made manifest on a written page full of only the lyric's linguistic material would have been blunted aboriginally in performance where the "full existential contexts" (Ong, *Orality and Literacy*, 38), including, most important, the embodied presence of the singer, would suffuse the lyric poem with meaning (and cues) beyond the words alone. That is, in performance there is more to guide an audience through the tumbled and fragmented parataxis of lyric's dominant "adding style."

174. *Poetic Closure*, 99.

175. E.g., H. Gunkel, and J. Begrich, *Introduction to Psalms: The Genres of the Religious Lyric of Israel* (trans. J. D. Nogalski; Macon: Mercer University Press, 1998), 30–31, 34–35.

176. Miller, *They Cried to the LORD*, 57.

177. Alter uses the analogy of film montage in his discussion of the "composite artistry" of Hebrew prose (*The Art of Biblical Narrative* [New York: Basic Books, 1981, 140–41). But the analogy is equally (if not more) applicable to paratactic verse of the kind found in much biblical poetry (e.g., Lamentations).

178. Alter, *Art of Biblical Narrative*, 140 (quoting S. Eisenstein, *The Film Scene* [ed. and trans. J. Leyda; London, 1943], 17; emphasis in Eisenstein's original).

179. For an insightful discussion of this phenomenon in oral-derived Old English poetry, see Pasternack, *Textuality of Old English Poetry*, 11–12, 120–46.

180. The reading is that of J. Levenson, *Creation and the Persistence of Evil: The Jewish Drama of Divine Omnipotence* (Princeton: Princeton University Press, 1988), 17–20.

181. The quote is Levenson's taken from Y. Kaufmann, *The Religion of Israel* (New York: Schocken, 1972), 60.

182. *Persistence of Evil*, 18.

183. *Persistence of Evil*, 19.

184. *Persistence of Evil*, 18.

185. "Lyric," *NPEPP*, 715.

186. I borrow the language Hillers uses to describe Lamentations (*Lamentations*, 6).

187. *Post-Petrarchism*, 5, 11, 12.

188. *Post-Petrarchism*, 15; cf. Culler, "Genre: Lyric," par. 46.

189. *Post-Petrarchism*, 13.

190. *Post-Petrarchism*, 10. My use of Greene's notion of the fictional is pragmatic, a means to spotlight the rituality of so much biblcal lyric. The concept of "fiction"

is more generative than Greene's usage and has yet to be fully exploited by interpreters of the Bible.

191. M. C. Nussbaum, *The Fragility of Goodness* (Cambridge: Cambridge University Press, 1986), 69.

192. *Post-Petrarchism*, 5; Greene, "Sir Philip Sidney's *Psalms*," 20.

193. *Lyric Poetry*, 12.

194. Greene, *Post-Petrarchism*, 5, 8.

195. So broadly on this topic, see the classic study of Mowinckel, *Psalms in Israel's Worship*.

196. Greene, "Sir Philip Sidney's *Psalms*," 23.

197. See esp. Dobbs-Allsopp, *Lamentations*, 12–23.

198. *Lamentations*, 6. Of course, Lamentations has long served ritual ends in Judaism as a part of the Ninth of Ab services.

199. There are two four-couplet stanzas: 1:7 and 2:19.

200. D. Attridge, *Poetic Rhythm: An Introduction* (Cambridge: Cambridge University Press, 1995), 1, 9.

201. F. W. Dobbs-Allsopp, "The Effects of Enjambment in Lamentations (Part 2)," *Zeitschrift für die alttestamentliche Wissenschaft* 113/5 (2001), 2–4.

202. Greene, *Post-Petrarchism*, 5–6.

203. Greene, *Post-Petrarchism*, 7–8.

204. Greene, *Post-Petrarchism*, 5–6.

205. Greene, *Post-Petrarchism*, 6.

206. Greene, *Post-Petrarchism*, 9; cf. Johnson, *Idea of Lyric*, 59, 74.

207. Greene, *Post-Petrarchism*, 6. Greene's express "readerly" pose is not totally inappropriate to Lamentations, which is composed of written acrostic poems intended at one level for actual readers (of some variety)—the alphabetic acrostic is a visual trope.

208. Greene, *Post-Petrarchism*, 10, 11.

209. *Lamentations*, 122.

210. H.-J. Kraus, *Klagelieder* (BK; 3d ed.; Neukirchen-Vluyn: Neukirchener Verlag, 1968), 50–54; Hillers, *Lamentations*, 123.

211. In more detail, see Dobbs-Allsopp, *Lamentations*.

212. Blasing, *Lyric Poetry*, 70.

213. For the beginnings of such a reading, see Dobbs-Allsopp, *Lamentations*.

214. Blasing argues more generally, "The lyric poet is both an individuated/socialized speaker in the mother tongue *and* a discursive 'I,' individuated and socialized over again in a tradition to ensure the linguistic community's historical truth and its reproduction" (*Lyric Poetry*, 52).

215. Johnson, *Idea of Lyric*, 53–71.

216. Johnson, *Idea of Lyric*, 177, 182.

217. See further, Dobbs-Allsopp, *Lamentations*.

218. Greene, *Post-Petrarchism*, 6.

219. Johnson, *Idea of Lyric*, 16.; Culler, "Genre: Lyric," par. 45; von Hallberg, *Lyric Powers*, 21; cf. Dubrow, *Challenges of Orpheus*, ch. 3.
220. Greene, *Post-Petrarchism*, 31 (emphasis in the original).
221. Greene, *Post-Petrarchism*, 26 (emphasis in the original).
222. Greene, "Sir Philip Sidney's *Psalms*," 24. Contrast Greene's discussion of Petrarch's deictic program, which builds toward a more prominently fictional type of lyric sequence, see *Post-Petrarchism*, 22–62.
223. Esp. Greenstein, "Direct Discourse," 79–91.
224. L. Ryken, *The Literature of the Bible* (Grand Rapids: Zondervan, 1974), 123–24. So also Driver (*Introduction*, 360): "In lyric poetry, the poet gives vent to his personal emotions or experiences—his joys or sorrows, his cares or complaints, his aspirations or his despair."
225. *Form and Feeling*, 259; cf. Culler, *Literary Theory*, 72.
226. Ryken, *Literature of the Bible*, 123–24; see Blasing, *Lyric Poetry*, 50. Greenstein underscores the correlation between heightened emotiveness and direct discourse in the biblical lyric, "Direct Discourse," esp. 89–90.
227. M. L. Rosenthal, *The Poet's Art* (New York: Norton, 1987), 96; cf. Johnson, *Idea of Lyric*, 37.
228. *Idea of Lyric*, 197, n. 5.
229. "On Biblical Style," *St. John's Review* 54/1 (2012), 39; cf. T. Linafelt, "The Bible's Literary Merits," *Chronicle of Higher Education* 55/31 (April 10, 2009), B6, http://chronicle.com; "Private Poetry and Public Eloquence in 2 Samuel 1:17–27: Hearing and Overhearing David's Lament for Jonathan and Saul," *Journal of Religion* 88/4 (2008), 506–8.
230. Linafelt, "On Biblical Style," 39; cf. Driver, *Introduction*, 368 (specifically with respect to Psalms).
231. Linafelt, "On Biblical Style," 39; "Private Poetry," 508.
232. E.g., M. C. Nussbaum, *Upheavals of Thought: The Intelligence of Emotions* (Cambridge: Cambridge University Press, 2001); Damasio, *Descartes' Error*.
233. *Literary Theory*, 72–74; cf. von Hallberg, *Lyric Powers*, 12.
234. *Literary Theory*, 72–74.
235. *Art of Biblical Poetry*, 62–84.
236. *Art of Biblical Poetry*, 66 (emphasis added).
237. *Literary Theory*, 73.
238. Cf. F. W. Dobbs-Allsopp, "Daughter Zion," in J. J. Ahn and S. L. Cook (eds.), *Thus Says the LORD: Essays on the Former and Latter Prophets in Honor of Robert R. Wilson* (LHBOTS 502; London: T. and T. Clark, 2009), esp. 125.
239. R. Wilbur, "On My Own Work," in *Responses: Prose Pieces 1953–1976* (New York: Harcourt Brace Jovanovich, 1976), 122 as cited in Kinzie, *Poet's Guide*, 200.
240. As S. Heaney writes, "it is obvious that poetry's answer to the world is not given only in terms of the content of its statement. It is given perhaps even more emphatically in terms of metre and syntax, of tone and musical trueness; and it is given

also by its need to go emotionally and artistically 'above the brim', beyond the established norm" (*The Redress of Poetry* [New York: Farrar, Straus and Giroux, 1995], 25).

241. For my own sense of the Song's lyricism, see my entry "Song of Songs," in K. Doob Sakenfeld (ed.), *The New Interpreter's Dictionary of the Bible*, vol. 5, *S–Z* (Nashville: Abingdon, 2009).

242. J. C. Exum, *Song of Songs* (OTL; Louisville: Westminster John Knox, 2005), 33.

243. *Song of Songs*, 35.

244. Esp. Grossberg, *Centripetal and Centrifugal Structures*.

245. T. Gardner, "Long Poem," in *PEPP* (Kindle ed.). Dubrow (*Challenges of Orpheus*, ch. 4) problematizes the strong distinction between sequence or collection and long poem already in the early modern period in England.

246. C. Altieri, "Motives in Metaphor: John Ashbery and the Modernist Long Poem," *Genre* 11/4 (1978), 653.

247. Or "backward scanning" as J. Goody termed it, see *The Domestication of the Savage Mind* (Cambridge: Cambridge University Press, 1977), 49–50.

248. Consider the so-called great hymns from the Akkadian tradition (e.g., "Great Hymn to Shamash," cf. B. R. Foster, *Before the Muses* [Bethesda: CDL, 1993], II, 536–44), which as B. R. Foster notes," are so called because of their exceptional length, about two hundred lines each, whereas most other hymns are seldom more than fifty lines long" ("Akkadian Literature" in C. Erhlich (ed.), *From an Antique Land: An Introduction to Ancient Near Eastern Literature* [Lanham, Md.: Rowman and Littlefield, 2009], 137–214 [Kindle ed.]). These are explicitly "literary" and thus written hymns—in some cases the written sources drawn on have even been identified (Foster, *Before the Muses*, I, 39). That is, the length of these hymnic "long" poems is precisely enabled by writing.

249. Fox, *Song of Songs*, esp. 195–226.

250. *Love Songs in Sumerian Literature: Critical Edition of the Dumuzi-Inanna Songs* (Ramat Gan: Bar-Ilan University Press, 1998), 28.

251. Sefati, *Love Songs*, 24.

252. "Love Lyrics of Nabû and Tašmetu: An Assyrian Song of Songs?," in M. Dietrich and I. Kottsieper (eds.), *"Und Mose schrieb dieses Lied auf." Studien zum Alten Testament und zum Alten Orient* (AOAT, 250; Münster: Ugarit- Verlag, 1998), 585–634; "Akkadian Rituals and Poetry of Divine Love," in R. M. Whiting (ed.), *Mythology and Mythologies: Methodological Approaches to Intercultural Influences* (Helsinki: Neo-Assyrian Text Corpus Project, 2001), 93–136; "Song of Songs and Sacred Marriage," in M. Nissinen and R. Uro (eds.), *Sacred Marriages: The Divine-Human Sexual Metaphor from Sumer to Early Christianity* (Winona Lake, Ind.: Eisenbrauns, 2008), 173–218; "Akkadian Love Poetry and the Song of Songs: New Sources, New Perspectives" (unpublished manuscript; presented at the annual meeting of the SBL, San Diego, November 23, 2014).

253. See A. Livingstone, *Court Poetry and Literary Miscellanea* (SAA 3; Helsinki: Helsinki University Press, 1989), 35–37; Nissinen, "Love Lyrics," 587–92,

http://oracc.museum.upenn.edu/saao/saao3/P223388/, accessed December 3, 2014; hand-drawing: http://oracc.museum.upenn.edu/cdli/P223388/image, accessed December 3, 2014. For the ritual background of these "love lyrics," see Nissinen, "Love Lyrics," 592–96; "Akkadian Rituals and Poetry," 95–97. CAT 1.24, the Ugaritic poem about the marriage of Yariḫ and Nikkal-Ib, similarly is of small compass, less than fifty lines (not counting the "hymn" that is added after the horizontal line on the reverse of the single-column tablet, ll. 40–50).

254. Fox, *Song of Songs*, 226.

255. See K. van der Toorn, *Scribal Culture and the Making of the Hebrew Bible* (Cambridge, Mass.: Harvard University Press, 2007), 118–25—note in particular his comments on Proverbs and Psalms (118–19, 124–25). The Mesopotamian penchant for collection and organization is well known and exemplified by the existence of numerous literary catalogues of various kinds, including hymnic literature (for bibliography, see A. L. Oppenheim, *Ancient Mesopotamia: Portrait of a Dead Civilization* [rev. ed.; Chicago: University of Chicago Press, 1977], 377, n. 16; G. H. Wilson, *Editing of the Hebrew Psalter* [Chico: Scholars Press, 1985], 25–61), and of a multitude of scholarly collections of all kinds—laws, omens, incantations, and so on (see Oppenheim, *Ancient Mesopotamia*, 206–331; cf. van der Toorn, *Scribal Culture*, 119–22, nn. 38–43).

256. For example, see the relevant entries in *NPEPP* and *PEPP*.

257. See van der Toorn, *Scribal Practice*, esp. 177–78; M. Nissinen et al., *Prophets and Prophecy in the Ancient Near East* (WAW; Atlanta: SBL, 2005), esp. 97–124.

258. Fox, *Song of Songs*, 204—the consensus opinion as Fox reports (195) is that Egyptian love poetry consists primarily of "independent songs, some of which are assembled in loose collections." Love poetry in Akkadian is mostly attested only in individual compsoitons (see the catalogue of love poems, KAR 158; cf. B. Groneberg, "Searching for Akkadian Lyrics: From Old Babylonian to the 'Liederkatalog,' KAR 158," *Journal of Cuneiform Studies* 55 [2003], 55–74).

259. Nissinen ("Akkadian Love Poetry") well emphasizes the scribal context of the preserved Akkadian love poems: "Whatever the social or religious context, function, and purpose of each ancient text may have been, the first material context of every text is the workshop of the scribe. This is often the only context of a cuneiform tablet we can be sure about. The song lists and the colophons indicate that tablets containing love poetry were part of organized libraries, and as several colophons indicate, love songs were sometimes compiled in thematic collections such as the *irtum* songs and the *pārum* songs."

260. N. Fraistat, "Introduction: The Place of the Book and the Book as Place," in N. Fraistat (ed.), *Poems in Their Place: The Intertextuality and Order of Poetic Collections* (Chapel Hill: University of North Carolina Press, 1986), 44–65.

261. See J. Van Sickle, "The Book-Role and Some Conventions of the Poetic Book," *Arethusa* 13 (1980), 5–42.

262. Fraistat, "Introduction," 14, n. 5.

263. Å. Sjöberg and E. Bergman, *The Collection of Sumerian Temple Hymns* (Locust Valley, N.Y.: J. J. Augustin, 1969).

264. Sjöberg and Bergmann, *Temple Hymns*, 5.

265. H. Zimmern, "Ein Zyklus altsumerischer Lieder auf die Haupttempel Babyloniens," *ZA* 5 (1930), 247; C. Wilke, "Der aktuelle Bezug der Sammlung der sumerischer Tempelhymnen und ein Fragment eines Klagelieds," *ZA* 62 (1972), 39, 48–49.

266. Sjöberg and Bergman, *Temple Hymns*, 12, 149.

267. The classic Mesopotamian city laments offer additional examples of collective poetic works which evidence larger integrities, structures, and teleologies, see M. Green, "Eridu in Sumerian Literature" (Ph.D. diss., University of Chicago, 1975); cf. Dobbs-Allsopp, *Weep, O Daughter of Zion*.

268. E.g., Wilson, *Editing of the Hebrew Psalter*; D. M. Howard, Jr., "Recent Trends in Psalm Study," in D. Baker and B. Arnold (ed.), *The Face of Old Testament Studies: A Survey of Contemporary Approaches* (Grand Rapids: Baker Books, 1999), esp. 332–44. Some of this "shaping" appears in the presumed additions of Psalm 1, as a kind of introduction to the collection as a whole, and of the several closely related doxologies that stand at the seams of the various subcollections of psalms (Pss 41:14; 72:18:20; 89:53; 106:48), and the editorial interventions in the latter part of the collection that are revealed when comparing MT 150 Psalms with the various psalms scrolls preserved from Qumran. The additions, in particular, suggest the possibility of editorial activity for other than archival purposes.

269. Such narrative staging stands out precisely because it is contrary in practice to the roughly contemporary Neo-Assyrian oracle collections (esp. van der Toorn, *Scribal Culture*, 184). However, the individual prophetic reports from Assyria (and Mari) do share with the biblical tradition the basic impetus to situate prophetic utterance with a specific prophet, albeit restricted in scale and scope to a singular occasion.

270. For thoughts on the function of "written" frame stories for "readers," see Ong, *Orality and Literacy*, 103.

271. Sefati, *Love Songs*, 218–35.

272. Sefati, *Love Songs*, 28–29 and n. 69.

273. R. C. Steiner, "The Aramaic Text in Demotic Script: The Liturgy of a New Year's Festival Imported from Bethel to Syene by Exiles from Rash," *JAOS* 111/2 (1991), 362–63; *COS* I, 309–27. For the relevance of the sacred marriage poem in col. 17 (= col. 16 in Steiner) to Akkadian love poetry more generally, see Nissinen, "Akkadian Rituals and Poetry," 101–2. Curiously, the last six columns of the papyrus consist of a narrative about the two brothers Assurbanipal and Shamash-shum-ukin.

274. R. Greene, "Lyric Sequence," in *PEPP* (Kindle ed.).

275. See C. T. Neely, "The Structure of English Renaissance Sonnet Sequences," *ELH* 45 (1978), 360–61; Greene, *Post-Petrarchism*, 22–62; Roche, *Petrarch*.

276. Greene, "Lyric Sequence."
277. See the articles in *Arethusa* 13 (1980); W. S. Anderson, "The Theory and Practice of Poetic Arrangement from Vergil to Ovid," in Fraistat, *Poems in Their Place*, 44–65.
278. "Shakespeare's Sonnets' Perjured Eye," in C. Hoĵek and P. Parker (eds.), *Lyric Poetry* (Ithaca: Cornell University Press, 1985), 120.
279. Rosenthal and Gall, *Modern Poetic Sequence*, 25–44; cf. Greene, *Post-Petrarchism*, 133–52.
280. "Some Issues for Study of Integrated Collections," in Fraistat, *Poems in Their Place*, 18; "Poetic Collections," in *NPEPP*, 222.
281. For example, I have expressed my sense of the Song's wholeness in these precise terms, see my "Song of Songs" both in *NIDB* and in B. Gaventa and D. Peterson (eds.), *New Interpreter's Bible One Volume Commentary* (Nashville: Abingdon, 2010), 375–86.
282. "Lyric Sequence."
283. *Lyric Powers*, 83. Von Hallberg elaborates: "Lyric poems are traditionally comprised of smaller units: striking phrases, lines, shapely stanzas; lyrics tend to break down into their parts, and their parts even to move away from each other toward enigmas"—fragmentation and disunity is as much a part of the lyric's fiction as of the lyric sequence.
284. Dubrow problematizes the question of size altogether for the lyric in early modern England, arguing that the connections between the "parts" is more important: "the potentialities for fluidity and malleability that in effect shape and reshape the dimensions of a single lyric by breaking it into parts or inserting it into larger entities" (*Challenges of Orpheus*, ch. 4). She, of course, is working with highly literate poems, as is Greene.
285. Greene, "Lyric Sequence."
286. Fox, *Song of Songs*, 202; cf. Exum, *Song of Songs*, 33. Of course, the issue of unity ceases to be a determining factor once it is admitted that unities are imaginable for collective as well as singular entities. That is, the Song can be a unified whole and also be a collocation of independent poetic integers.
287. Schaefer, "Hearing from Books," 124—presumably quoting Ong, though I have not been able to track the quotation.
288. Zumthor, "Text and the Voice," 86, 76; cf. Finnegan, *Oral Poetry*, 28.
289. Finnegan, *Oral Poetry*, 28.
290. Zumthor, "Text and the Voice," 75.
291. A. N. Doane, "Oral Texts, Intertexts, and Intratexts: Editing Old English," in J. Clayton and E. Rothstein (eds.), *Influence and Intertextuality in Literary History* (Madison: University of Wisconsin Press, 1991), 78; cf. Zumthor, "Text and the Voice," 76–77, 87; A. N. Doane, "The Ethnography of Scribal Writing and Anglo-Saxon Poetry: Scribe as Performer," *Oral Tradition* 9 (1994), 435.
292. Kittay and Godzich, *Emergence of Prose*, xviii.

293. Doane, "Oral Texts," 77 (emphasis added).

294. Dobbs-Allsopp, "Space, Line," 49–61. In the "old Hebrew" script word division was marked by points instead of spacing, though whether written versions of the Song date back to such an early period is an open question. Linguistically, the language of MT seems late (see F. W. Dobbs-Allsopp, "Late Linguistic Features in the Song of Songs," in A. C. Hagedorn (ed.), *Perspectives on the Song of Songs—Perspektiven der Hoheliedauslegung* [BZAW; Berlin: de Gruyter, 2005], 27–77; for a contrasting point of view, see S. B. Noegel and G. Rendsburg, *Solomon's Vineyard: Literary and Linguistic Studies in the Song of Songs* [Atlanta: SBL, 2009]; D. M. Carr, *The Formation of the Hebrew Bible: A New Reconstruction* [Oxford: Oxford University Press, 2011], 442–48), and the lack of editorial interventions in the preserved manuscripts and a better understanding of scribal practice in the ancient southern Levant make the presumption of transmission through generations of copying the Song hard to sustain. That traditional love poetry was known in ancient Israel and Judah seems safe to assume (e.g., Isa 5:1–7; Ezek 33:32; Ps 45:1; for the possible influence of love poetry on Hosea and Deuteronomy, see Carr, *Formation*, 434–38). Transmission may have been predomnantly oral, through performance—"songs don't require scribes" (W. Schniedewind, *How the Bible Became a Book* [Cambridge: Cambridge University Press, 2004], 149). The Song, however late, may simply be one instantation of this "stream of tradition" that also happended to get written down. The fact of word division is no small matter. Orally, words come in continuous streams, phrases. It is writing that begins to resolve words into distinct entities.

295. On "good variants," see Carr, *Formation*, esp. 13–35.

296. The final letters visible in 4QCant[b] frag 3.14 are ום\ד[], in which the *mem* is "much larger" than the letters in the preceding lines. This sequence is then followed by a space that has been left intentionally blank. Further, Tov ("Canticles," in E. C. Ulrich et al. [eds.], *Qumran Cave 4/XI: Psalms to Chronicles* [DJD XVI; Oxford: Oxford University Press, 2000], 217) calculates that this also constitutes the final line of the column. Assuming the word is related to the preceding literary context (and thus not taken to be related to the root דום "to be silent"), one can reconstruct ד[וד]ים "love," the final word in the previous poem (4:8–5:1). The larger size of the final *mem* followed by the *vacat* would then signal the end of the poem. After the blank space at the extreme left edge of the fragment, Tov also notices "the traces of what looks like a Greek *gamma* (Γ) or a sign similar in shape to a *diple obelismene* (a paragraph sign used in the Greek scribal tradition for separating different sections in tragedies and comedies)" (218). (Other such signs appear in the margins to this fragment.) MT also has extra spacing after 5:1, and again after 6:3, thus nicely isolating 5:2–6:3 as a literary unit—MT's extra spacings (mostly *sětumôt* in MT[A] and MT[L]) often coincide with what may be considered structural wholes on internal literary criteria, e.g., 1:2–4, 1:5–8, 2:1–7, 3:1–5, 4:1–7, 5:2–6:3, 6:4–10 (I. Yeivin [*Introduction to the*

Tiberian Masorah (E. J. Revell; Scholars Press, 1980] also notices that the *sĕtumôt* and *pĕtuḥôt* commonly function to frame sense units; see P. W. Flint, "The Book of Canticles (Song of Songs) in the Dead Sea Scrolls," in Hagedorn, *Perspectives*, 102). OG lacks a major enumerated divison at this point, though several smaller divisions cluster at 5:1–3.

297. "Rhythm has an indexical function and enables hearing—ensures the audibility of—what is meant by what is said" (Blasing, *Lyric Poetry*, 54).

298. Pasternack, *Textuality of Old English Poetry*, 11; cf. A. B. Lord, *Singer of Tales* (Cambridge, Mass.: Harvard University Press, 1960), 55–58.

299. Lord, *Singer of Tales*, 55.

300. See J. C. Treat, "Lost Keys: Text and Interpretation in Old Greek Song of Songs and Its Earliest Manuscript Witnesses" (Ph. D. diss., University of Pennsylvania, 1996).

301. Schaefer stresses that even without any compensatory gesture "the simple act of writing down had already transformed the 'singer's' existence onto parchment," though this is not a maximally efficient means of negotiating a singerless text as it still depends on reoralization, i.e., it "had to be brought to life again by somebody who usually was not this singer" ("Hearing from Books," 124; cf. Kittay and Godzich, *Emergence of Prose*, 17).

302. The reading of MT is supported by all the versions, though none of them understand *ʿăgābîm*—Syr. does not even try but simply renders *zmyrtʾ* "song." Many suggest emending MT to read *kĕšar ʿăgābîm* "like a singer of love (songs)" (e.g., *BHS, HALOT*, 1482) or something analogous (cf. W. Zimmerli, *Ezekiel 2* [Hermeneia; trans. J. D. Martin; Philadelphia: Fortress, 1983], 197). However the textual difficulties are resolved, the informing image of the prophet as a singer of love songs is at least clear.

303. On related imagery from Mesopotamia, see D. M. Carr, *Writing on the Tablet of the Heart: Origins of Scripture and Literature* (Oxford: Oxford University Press, 2005), 28–29. There is also the two triplets from the "song of the harlot" (*šîrat hazzônâ*, v. 15) recorded/adapted in Isa 23:16 that imagine Tyre as a "forgotten harlot" singing and playing "many songs." Though the songs are not explicitly called love songs—and may in fact be entirely different—the explicit image of the performer is illuminating nonetheless. And from a much later time there is Rabbi Akiba's famous complaint about the Song ("the Holy of the Holiest") being sung at banquets, which, beyond everything else, foregrounds a sung performance and thus presumes a singer.

304. For details, see Fox, *Song of Songs*, 52, 55–56, n. a.

305. Fox, *Song of Songs*, 244 and n. 18.

306. Fox, *Song of Songs*, 253–55.

307. Sefati, *Love Songs*, 30–49.

308. Nissinen, "Akkadian Rituals and Poetry," 115; cf. 97–99.

309. P. S. Alexander, *The Targum of Canticles. Translated, with a Critical Introduction Apparatus, and Notes* (Aramaic Bible 17A; Collegeville: Liturgical Press, 2003), 75.

310. "Oral Texts," 86.
311. Kittay and Godzich, *Emergence of Prose*, 17.
312. *Poetry into Drama*, 45. The characteristic use of word dividers in alphabetic cuneiform, as also in the later "old Hebrew" script, is to be noted, since they are among the few metascript conventions that appear in these texts and they specifically, graphically distinguish "words." That is, they do quite literally what Herington supposes of early Greek song texts, they preserve the "words" of the poems—recall any oral performance of poetry would have involved much, much more than just the words of the poem (e.g., music, dance, gestures of all kinds, poetic ad-libs, audience participation). It is noteworthy that sometimes in the Bible it is precisely the "words" of a song or oracle that are said to be recited or written down (e.g., Deut 31:30; 2 Sam 22:1; Jer 36:2, 4; Ezek 33:32; Ps 137:3).
313. The language is from Kittay and Godzich, *Emergence of Prose*, 13, who have the medieval French jongleur in view—Kittay and Godzich emphasize throughout their work the real difficulty for written verse and prose to make such accommodations (esp. 14–106). M. Leuchter ("Persian Imperial Mythology and the Levites: Implications for the Origins of Jewish Midrash," unpublished manuscript, paper presented to Old Testament Research Colloquium, Princeton, December 5, 2014), understands the Levites (in the Second Temple period) in an analogous fashion in their singing/reading of psalm texts (Pss 24, 48, 82, 94, 81, 93, and 92, according to Mishnah Tamid 7:4) as a part of the Tamid rite (Lev 6:8–13; cf. Mishnah Tamid 7:3). That is, the ritual performance of these texts required and included more than just what was provided by the (alphabetic) marks on the page, e.g., vocalization of words. Or as Leuchter emphasizes, following the insight of M. Gertner ("The Masorah and the Levites," *VT* 10 [1960], 252–72), "the role occupied by the Levites as readers/chanters of liturgical texts immediately provided them with an opportunity to make choices about how those texts should be read and subsequently understood." And: "if the Levites were entrusted with the vocalization of these written works upon their performance or pronouncement, then even the *peshat* of a given text could be refracted through an interpretive or exegetical lens" ("Persian Imperial Mythology"; cf. Neh 8:7–8). On such a view, midrash could be understood as evolving (in part at least) as a consequence of the kind of textuality at its disposal and the ongoing performative environment of reading *out loud* (Leuchter: "these texts were probably primarily performed or read in ritual contexts").
314. Kittay and Godzich, *Emergence of Prose*, 17.
315. I wonder whether the textuality of the "Love Lyrics of Nabû and Tašmetu" (SAA 3 14), the Akkadian composition that can claim the "closest kinship" with the Song of Songs, should be considered in a similar vein. Nissinen has emphasized the impression of a "literary composition" that "the arrangement of the episodes" in a "rather loose and not always quite coherent" fashion suggests

("Love Lyrics," 595). But given the obvious ritual background of the text (its "cultic affiliation," Nissinen, "Love Lyrics," 592–95; "Akkadian Rituals and Poetry," 97–99; Sefati, *Love Songs*, 46–47) and Nissinen's comparison to the usage of "hymns in Christian churches," I am more struck by the nonliterariness of this poem's textuality. Its writtenness, of course, is beyond doubt (Nissinen rightly stresses the scribal setting of Akkadian love poetry, esp. "Akkadian Love Poetry"), but the question is what kind of textuality is exhibited by this writing? It seems to me to be one that, like that of the Song, presumes a great deal of extratextual input from the ritual singer(s) of this poem. This is most evident in the use of KI.MIN and KI.MIN-*ma* (lit. "ditto, repetition") as a kind of refrain throughout the composition—the content of what is to be repeated is not given and therefore must be supplied by the performer(s)—and in a number of second and first person plural references (e.g., "As for us [*anīnu*]... What is ours [*ša attūni attūni*]...," ll. 2–5; "to Tašmetu say [*qibânišši*]," l. 6; cf. ll. 22–24), which epitomize a performative environment. Such a supposition is also consistent with the "dramatic" and dialogic character of the composition, as well as its "loose" and not "quite coherent" design (Nissinen, "Love Lyrics," 592, 595)—all of which demand/suppose extratextual staging.

316. Pasternack, *Textuality of Old English Poetry*, 10–11.

317. Interestingly, a number of the Song manuscripts from Qumran (4QCant[a] and 4QCant[b]) exhibit scribal "performances" of the Song that differ from that reflected in MT, shortenings of the text (the omission of 4:8–6:10 in 4QCant[a] and 4:4–7 in 4QCant[b]) that do not seem to result from typical kinds of scribal errors (e.g., homoioteleuton), i.e., they are "good variants" (see Tov, "Canticles," 202, 216; Flint, "Book of Canticles," 99–103). Carr also emphasizes the fluidity of the Song's textual transmission (*Formation*, 432–33), though to slightly different ends.

318. This is not to oppose the scribal artifactuality that has preserved the Song (and as emphasized, for example, by Nissinen) but to conceptualize it as it interfaces with and supports orality and operates in realms beyond education (for the possibility of the latter in particular, see Carr, *Formation*, 432–48). Scribes were themselves traditional performers (e.g., R. Person, "The Ancient Israelite Scribe as Performer," *JBL* 117 [1998], 601–9) for whom writing, speaking, and memory were equally consequential (cf. Ps 45:2).

319. Driver, *Introduction*, 360–61.

320. Driver, *Introduction*, 361.

321. Driver, *Introduction*, 360–61. So today such "wisdom" poetry would be folded into a broader understanding of lyric (esp. von Hallberg, *Lyric Powers*, 105–42). Von Hallberg well emphasizes the long tradition of wisdom and poetry and the idea that "poetry yields knowledge" (105), an idea easily forgotten after philosophy. It is worth stressing that poetry, and lyric poetry in particular, offers resources for thinking that are not so readily available to essayists, such as "figures, dramatic dialogue, juxtaposition, paradox, and all the devices of resonance."

322. "Why Lyric?," 202.
323. "Psalms and Lyric Verse," 346.
324. In a discussion of an early version of the essay that was eventually published as "Psalms and Lyric Verse": "Psalms as Lyric," in the Psalms group at the annual meeting of the SBL, November 2004. I also benefited immensely from a discussion of the same paper with colleagues from the Biblical Research Colloquium at their annual summer meeting, Harvard University, August 2005.
325. See esp. F. W. Dobbs-Allsopp, "Poetry, Hebrew," in Sakenfeld, *New Interpreter's Dictionary of the Bible*, vol. 4, *Me–R* (Nashville: Abingdon, 2009), 550–58.
326. Cf. M. L. West, *Greek Lyric Poetry* (World Classics; Oxford: Oxford University Press, 1994), vii; cf. Bowie, "Lyric and Elegiac Poetry," 99–100; H. Fränkel, *Early Greek Poetry and Philosophy* (trans. M. Hadas and J. Willis; New York: Harcourt Brace Jovanovich, 1973), 133, n. 4; Nagy, "Lyric and Greek Myth," 19–20; Garner, *Traditional Elegy*.
327. See Dobbs-Allsopp, *Weep, O Daughter of Zion*, esp. 1–29; "Darwinism," 625–30.
328. Dobbs-Allsopp, *Lamentations*, 12–20.
329. Cf. von Hallberg, *Lyric Powers*, 23.
330. Cf. K. M. Heffelfinger, *"I Am Large, I Contain Multitudes": Lyric Cohesion and Conflict in Second Isaiah* (Leiden: Brill, 2011).
331. Langer, *Feeling and Form*, 259.
332. This insight I owe in particular to A. Berlin's penetrating critique of one of my early presentations on lyric verse in the Bible in which she basically made allowances (in the same vein as I do above) for the obvious differences in some of the genres (e.g., song or not song) and ended by urging me (and the audience) to simply recognize this for what it was, biblical Hebrew poetry. This, of course, does not mean that there is no such thing as lyric verse in the Bible. There is. It is just that the Hebrew lyric shares much with other kinds of specifically unsung or nonmelic biblical verse.
333. Miner, *Comparative Poetics*, 8 (emphasis added); cf. "Why Lyric?," in *The Renewal of Song: Renovation in Lyric Conception and Practice* (ed. E. Miner and A. Dev; Calcutta: Seagull Books, 2000); "On the Genesis and Development of Literary Systems: Part I," *Critical Inquiry* 5/2 (1978), esp. 349, 353. For an informative discussion of the triadic genre conception that is mostly assumed in Western scholarship, see esp. Genette, *Architext*. Culler, too, points to the mostly unfathomed significance of Miner's work, "Lyric, History, and Genre," 899, n. 37.
334. Miner, *Comparative Poetics*, 7.
335. Miner, *Comparative Poetics*, 8–9.
336. Miner, "Literary Systems: Part I," 349.
337. Miner, "Literary Systems: Part I," 344. For the emergence of Greek tragedy in particular, see esp. Herington, *Poetry into Drama*.

338. Miner: "mimesis is one of the least frequent systematic ideas about literature" ("Literary Systems: Part I," 349).

339. *Comparative Poetics*, 9.

340. *Emergence of Prose*, xii–xiii.

341. *Emergence of Prose*, xiii.

342. Miner, "Literary Systems: Part I," 349; Kittay and Godzich, *Emergence of Prose*, xi–xii.

343. *Emergence of Prose*, xiii.

344. *Emergence of Prose*, xiii.

345. Miner, *Comparative Poetics*, 9; "Literary Systems: Part I," 353. Such strangeness, nevertheless, is predicted by Hanson and Kiparsky's argument that verse is used "for narrative functions only if it is also used for lyric functions" ("Nature of Verse," 18). In other words, what Miner finds from a comparative literature perspective also follows linguistically, and both emphasize in their way the urgency for biblical scholarship to have lyric and what is required to read it intelligently better in view.

346. P. Schaff (ed.), *Nicene and Post-Nicene Fathers, Series II* (vol. VI; New York: Christian Literature Company, 1893), 491.

347. See Jerome's *Preface to Job*, in Schaff, *Nicene and Post-Nicene Fathers, Series II*, 491.

348. Miner, *Comparative Poetics*, 8.

349. From Jerome's *Preface to Job*, see Schaff, *Nicene and Post-Nicene Fathers, Series II*, 491.

CHAPTER 4

1. The emphasis here is to be placed on the per se. Almost all of the post-1990s studies that have so enriched the field's understanding of orality in Israel and Judah obviously engage biblical poems to one degree or another. What they do not do is problematize or theorize this engagement. As a result there is a certain naivete that haunts these studies when it comes to the topic of poetry. They are framed tacitly in light of the givenness of today's postprose world and informed by oral theory nourished (almost) exclusively on narrative art. Biblical poems are rooted in a distinctly preprose verse tradition and are nonnarrative. Both facts require a more intentional staging of the question of orality at the site of biblical poems.

2. "Parallelism," in *NPEPP*, 878.

3. Recent major works include: S. Niditch, *Oral World and Written Word: Ancient Israelite Literature* (Louisville: Westminster John Knox, 1996); W. Schiedewind, *How the Bible Became a Book* (Cambridge: Cambridge University Press, 2004); D. M. Carr, *Writing on the Tablet of the Heart: Origins of Scripture and Literature* (Oxford: Oxford University Press, 2005); *The Formation of the Hebrew Bible: A New Reconstruction* (Oxford: Oxford University Press, 2011); K. van der Toorn, *Scribal Culture and the Making of the Hebrew Bible* (Cambridge, Mass.: Harvard

University Press, 2007); S. Sanders, *The Invention of Hebrew* (Urbana: University of Illinois Press, 2009); R. D. Miller, II, *Oral Tradition in Ancient Israel* (Eugene, Ore.: Cascade Books, 2011).

4. Cf. M. C. Amodio, *Writing the Oral Tradition: Oral Poetics and Literate Culture in Medieval England* (Notre Dame: University of Notre Dame, 2004), 30.

5. So already W. J. Ong, *Orality and Literacy: The Technologizing of the Word* (London: Routledge, 1982), 169–70—namely "orality-literacy theorems challenge biblical study perhaps more than any other field of learning."

6. *Orality and Literacy*, 1, 6, 11.

7. This script is sometimes simply called Phoenician (so recently esp. C. A. Rollston, "The Phoenician Script of the Tel Zayit Abecedary and Putative Evidence for Israelite Literacy," in R. E. Tappy and P. K. McCarter (eds.), *Literate Culture and Tenth-Century Canaan: The Tel Zayit Abecedary in Context* [Winona Lake, Ind.: Eisenbrauns, 2008], 61–96). However, two of the diagnostic features of this script tradition, unidirectional writing (from right to left) in horizontal lines and the reduction to twenty-two alphabetic signs (graphemes), predate the classic Byblian sequence of the tenth century (see Izbet Sarta; the inscribed bronze arrowheads). And now P. K. McCarter ("Paleographic Notes on the Tel Zayit Abecedary," in Tappy and McCarter (eds.), *Literate Culture and Tenth-Century Canaan* [Winona Lake: Eisenbrauns, 2008], 45–59) and G. Hamiton ("Reconceptualizing the Periods of Early Alphabetic Scripts," in J. A. Hackett and W. Aufrecht (eds.), *"An Eye for Form": Epigraphic Essays in Honor of Frank Moore Cross* [Winona Lake, Ind.: Eisenbrauns, 2014], 39–50) have argued forcefully that a (significant) number of the twenty-two-letter forms in tenth-century hinterland inscriptions like the Tel Zayit stone and the Gezer calendar cannot be derived morphologically from linear Phoenician as known in the Byblian sequence and instead have their best prototypes in earlier inland alphabetic epigraphs in what Hamilton describes most neutrally as "Early Alphabetic B." The latter may well show the wisdom in F. M. Cross's admonition about the derivation of the vernacular Hebrew script, namely, that "it may be best not to draw a single line of derivation in a single period" ("The Origin and Early Evolution of the Alphabet," in *Leaves from an Epigrapher's Notebook: Collected Paeprs in Hebrew and West Semitic Paleogaphy and Epigraphy* [Winona Lake: Eisenbrauns, 2003], 321). The vernacular Hebrew script does not start to evolve until the end of the ninth century (see Sanders, *Invention of Hebrew*, esp. 103–56)—it is only at this point, when there are meaningful paleographic departures from the so-called Phoenician *Mutterschrift* in the developing old Hebrew and Aramaic scripts, that the Phoenician script resolves itself as such, that is, as distinct from these other newly evolving "national scripts" (see R. Byrne, "The Refuge of Scribalism in Iron I Palestine," *BASOR* 345 [2007], 20; W. Schniedewind, *A Social History of Hebrew: Its Origins through the Rabbinic Period* [New Haven: Yale University Press, 2013], 55—Schniedewind favors the term "Canaanite" for the prenational script(s) of the Iron I–IIA Levant; J. Naveh's

habit of calling the script used to write Aramaic during this same period [i.e., prior to the divergence of a distinctly Aramaic script in the mid-eighth century] "Phoenician-Aramaic" [e.g., *Early History of the Alphabet* (Jerusalem: Magnes, 1987), 80] also helpfully gestures toward the wider regional purview of this manner of alphabetic writing).

8. Cf. R. Thomas, *Literacy and Orality in Ancient Greece* (Cambridge: Cambridge University Press, 1992), 28; Amodio, *Writing the Oral Tradition*, 22.

9. Thomas, *Literacy and Orality*, 5; cf. Niditch, *Oral World*, 98. S. Mowinckel gives early expression to this very sentiment with respect to biblical prophecy (in particular), see "Tradition and Writing," in K. C. Hanson (ed.), *The Spirit and the Word: Prophecy and Tradition in Ancient Israel* (Minneapolis: Fortress, 2002) (Kindle ed.).

10. Amodio, *Writing the Oral Tradition*, 22.

11. R. Finnegan, *Oral Poetry: Its Nature, Significance and Social Context* (Bloomington: Indiana University Press, 1977), 272; cf. P. Zumthor, "The Text and the Voice," *NLH* 16/1 (1984), 85–86.

12. Gunkel's most elaborate statement on the topic comes in his *The Legends of Genesis* (trans. W. H. Carruth; Chicago: Open Court, 1901). But the assumption pervades most of his writings from the turn of the century on, including those on the Psalms. For a thorough and critical overview of Gunkel and his scholarship, see M. Buss, "Gunkel in His Context," in *Biblical Form Criticism in Its Context* (JSOTSS 274; Sheffield: Sheffield Academic, 1998), 209–62. Both Ong (*Orality and Literacy*, 173) and R. C. Culley ("An Approach to the Problem of Oral Tradition," *VT* 13 [1963], 113) credit Gunkel's influence with the widespread assumption in the field about the informing orality of so much biblical literature, and Zumthor ("Text and the Voice," 71) credits "biblical exegetes" of the 1920s with early awareness of the need to reckon with a textual tradition deeply saturated with orality—which is to emphasize that biblical studies has a place in this conversation that antedates Parry. S. Mowinckel and the "Scandinavian" school represents another prominent stream of biblical scholarship awake early on to issues of orality, literacy, and textuality as they impinge on the formation and transmission of biblical literature, see D. A. Knight, *Rediscovering the Traditions of Israel* (Atlanta: SBL, 2006), esp. 165–286.

13. Esp. Buss, "Gunkel in His Context," 252–53.

14. *How to Read an Oral Poem* (Urbana: University of Illinois Press, 2002), 25.

15. (Cambridge, Mass.: Harvard University Press, 1960).

16. *Oral Poetry*, 86; cf. P. Zumthor, *Oral Poetry: An Introduction* (Minneapolis: University of Minnesota Press, 1990), 97; "Text and the Voice," 81–82.

17. All surviving traditional poetry from antiquity, no matter how confident we may be of emergence out of a vital oral tradition, by dint of being preserved in writing exhibits an oral-derived form of art—an art form that has been impacted by writing (e.g., Foley, *Oral Poem*, 8, 10).

18. "Epic" is a term frequently encountered in the secondary literature. I use it in a very minimalist way, as a bare synonym for "narrative" or "nonmelic" poetry, i.e., not necessarily inclusive of more elaborate characterizations (e.g., heroic) typically found in discussions of the genre (e.g., J. K. Newman, "Epic," in *NPEPP*, 361–75). The attested narrative or epic poetry of the ancient Near East tends to focus either primarily on human characters (though with the gods as general participants in the stories) or on the gods themselves—that is, the myths of the ancient Near East were (mostly) accommodated in poems (see J. M. Sasson, "Comparative Observations on the Near Eastern Epic Traditions," in J. M. Foley (ed.), *A Companion to Ancient Epic* [Malden: Blackwell, 2005], 215–32).

19. *Legends of Genesis*, 41.

20. *Legends of Genesis*, 41.

21. *Oral Poetry*, 10.

22. A. N. Doane ("The Ethnography of Scribal Writing and Anglo-Saxon Poetry: Scribe as Performer," *Oral Tradition* 9 [1994], 425) makes the same point about Anglo-Saxon narrative poems.

23. Sanders, *Invention of Hebrew*, 216, n. 38; F. W. Dobbs-Allsopp, "Space, Line, and the Written Biblical Poem in Texts from the Judean Desert," in M. Lundberg et al. (eds.), *Puzzling Out the Past: Studies in Northwest Semitic Languages and Literatures in Honor of Bruce Zuckerman* (Leiden: Brill, 2012), 52, n. 82; D. Pardee, *The Ugaritic Texts and the Origins of West Semitic Literary Composition* (Oxford: Oxford University Press, 2012), 48.

24. Whatever else may have stimulated Ugaritic scribes to begin writing down their local cultural heritage (see S. L. Sanders, "What Was the Alphabet For? The Rise of Written Vernaculars and the Making of Israelite National Literature," *Maarav* 11 [2004], 42–47), the script itself—alphabetic cuneiform—strongly suggests that the impress of syllabic cuneiform textuality was an important interruptive factor.

25. It is perhaps germane to recall here that although copies of oral or oral-derived narrative poems survive in Ugaritic, these are unique (singular) manuscripts, and almost nothing of what we must presume to have been a vibrant oral non-narrative poetic tradition got written down at Ugarit (e.g., *RIH* 98/02). So in certain respects this is a contrasting image with the Bible that preserves no narrative verse but has collections of proverbs, psalms, prophetic oracles, and even a sequence of love poems.

26. So already F. M. Cross, *Canaanite Myth and Hebrew Epic* (Cambridge, Mass.: Harvard University Press, 1972), 124, n. 38.

27. *Stories in Scripture and Inscriptions: Comparative Studies on Narratives in Northwest Semitic Inscriptions and the Hebrew Bible* (Oxford: Oxford University Press, 1997), 8–9; cf. Niditch, *Oral World*, 45–59.

28. The content of these poems, their style (esp. R. E. Whitaker, "A Formulaic Analysis of Ugaritic Poetry" [Ph.D. diss., Harvard University Press, 1969]), and that they are all singular copies (cf. Sanders, *Invention of Hebrew*, 216, n. 38; Dobbs-Allsopp,

"Space, Line," 54–55, n. 100) is consistent with their ascription as oral or oral-derived poetry. D. Pardee understands the partially damaged colophon of RS 92.2016 (ll. 40'–43') as identifying Ilimilku as "an oral poet" who "learned the stories ... by listening to other oral poets until he was able to recite the poems on his own" and then write them down (*Ugaritic Texts*, 47–48). Regardless of what is ultimately made of Pardee's construal of this particular colophon, the underlying supposition about the nature of these poetic narratives requires consideration. And Pardee's expertise answers one of the sharp criticisms of Parry-Lord supporters, who were mostly ignorant of the ancient Near East (see D. R. Hillers and W. H. Marsh, "Homeric Dictated Texts: A Reexamination of Some Near Eastern Evidence," *Harvard Studies in Classical Philology* 80 (1976), 19–23 (reprinted in D. R. Hillers, *Poets before Homer: Collected Essays on Ancient Literature* [ed. F. W. Dobbs- Allsopp; Winona Lake, Ind.: Eisenbrauns, 2015], 45–49).

29. The language is M. O'Connor's (*Hebrew Verse Structure* (Winona Lake, Ind.: Eisenbrauns, 1980), 25).

30. "Biblical and Canaanite Literature," in *Biblical and Oriental Studies* (Jerusalem: Magnes, 1975 [1942–43]), II, 17; also in "The Israelite Epic," in *Biblical and Oriental Studies* [1943], II, 70. And almost fifty years later S. B. Parker, not naively, entitles his study of Ugaritic narrative poetry *The Pre-biblical Narrative Tradition: Essays on the Ugaritic Poems Keret and Aqhat* (Atlanta: Scholars Press, 1989). And still more recently, this obvious close connection gives R. Kawashima warrant in *Biblical Narrative and the Death of the Rhapsode* (Bloomington: Indiana University Press, 2004), 15, to use the Ugaritic epics "as a synecdoche for the pre-biblical Canaanite narrative tradition."

31. The latter clarification is Y. Zakovitch's in his effort to deflect any latent ethnocentrism that might remain in Cassuto's expression of the thesis of an Israelite epic, with which Zakovitch is in general agreement: "In contrast to Cassuto, then, I do not think that the Hebrew epic was first 'converted' in order to fit into a monotheistic framework" ("Yes, There Was an Israelite Epic in the Biblical Period," *International Folklore Review* 8 [1991], 20).

32. *Hebrew Verse Structure*, 25.

33. "Traditional Narrative and the Reconstruction of Early Israelite Institutions," in *From Epic to Canon: History and Literature in Ancient Israel* (Baltimore: Johns Hopkins University Press, 1998), 32.

34. Cross in fact does better than most in emphasizing the lyricism of these poems: "I am not claiming that these two songs are 'epics in miniature.' They are lyric pieces" ("Traditional Narrative," 32, n. 26). In contrast, Kawashima's discussion of Judges 4 and 5 as a means of showing one trajectory of how prose narrative might develop in Israel ("from song to story") would have been all the more incisive had he kept the informing lyricism of Judges 5 more to the fore (*Death of the Rhapsode*, 17–34). That is, the differences in medium (lyric vs. narrative) have as much to do with the distinctiveness of the two treatments as do either

the orality and narrativity in Judges 5 or the emerging writerly prose of Judges 4. That is, the lyricism of the former is an interfering feature that requires accommodation. Compare the analogous discussions in J. Kittay and W. Godzich, *The Emergence of Prose: An Essay in Prosaics* (Minneapolis: University of Minnesota Press, 1987) with respect to the emergence of prose writing in Old French (ca. thirteenth century CE). Only Kittay and Godzich have both the oral poetic narrative and the emerging prose versions of the same stories to work with. One should also note that part of Cross's (and others') appeal to the "early Hebrew poems" was their presumed high antiquity—dates in the twelfth or eleventh centuries were not uncommon in mid-twentieth-century scholarship in particular. Such high antiquity would put these poems very close chronologically to the late thirteenth-century Ugaritic texts. But even those scholars most sympathetic to the early dating hypothesis (see most recently M. S. Smith, "Why was 'Old Poetry' Used in Hebrew Narrative? Historical and Cultural Considerations about Judges 5," in *Puzzling Out the Past*, 197–212) can no longer support the supposition of such early dates for any of the so-called old Hebrew poems.

35. "Israelite Epic," 69. Also: "Poesy issues from the youthful strength of young peoples, whereas prose is the product of the experience reflection of adult notions" (74). This is nonsense, of course. But even where motivation or explanatory horizons are flawed insights may yet prevail. What Cassuto gets right in this instance—that is, what is borne out by historical, comparative, and ethnographic research—is "that prose-writings should begin to appear after poetry is a commonplace phenomenon in the history of world literature" (74).

36. *Oral Poetry*, 9–10, 246–50.

37. "Israelite Epic," 71–73.

38. "Israelite Epic," 73. Cross's own detection of the same "mythic pattern" in both the Baal Cycle and Exodus 15 provides additional support for Cassuto's thesis (*Canaanite Myth and Hebrew Epic*, 112–44).

39. "Israelite Epic," 20.

40. "Comparative Observations," 220. Other epic traditions also routinely include the participation of the gods (e.g., Greece). E. A. Havelock offers a narratological accounting for the gods in Homer in a chapter of *A Preface to Plato* (Cambridge, Mass.: Harvard University Press, 1963 [Kindle ed.]), which emphasizes metaphor—the "most common metaphor" in Greek epic "is a god"—and the importance of action and agency in aural reception and cognition.

41. J. Herington in his wonderfully empirical sketch of the song culture of archaic and classical Greece dedicates an entire chapter to the treatment of myth because mythology suffuses the Greek world and was everywhere assumed (*Poetry into Drama: Early Tragedy and the Greek Poetic Tradition* [Berkeley: University of California Press, 1985], 58–78). There can be little doubt that the same was true of the southern Levant during the Iron Age and also later into the Persian period, all the mid-twentieth-century chatter about "demythologizing" notwithstanding.

42. Since Western scholars have only come to ancient myths through versions that eventually became textualized, it is worth emphasizing with Malinowski (*Myth in Primitive Psychology* [London, 1926], 23, 43) and others (cf. J. Goody and I. Watt, "The Consequences of Literacy," *Comparative Studies in Society and History* 5 [1963], 310) that myth is a prototypically oral genre (even "the seminal folk genre," E. Yassif, *The Hebrew Folktale* [trans. J. Teitelbaum; Bloomington: Indiana University Press, 2009], 10) and succeeds in its present-oriented chartering function so well precisely because of its oral-ness. Further, the fact of these mythological allusions themselves point to the ongoing relevance of traditionality (even when entexted). These are themselves markers of an original orality. Written myth is always belated. Pindar's (mid-fifth-century CE) victory odes contain similar kinds of abrupt, partial, and elusive allusions to myth (see R. Thomas, "Performance and Written Literature in Classical Greece: Envisaging Performance from Written Literature and Comparative Contexts," *BSOAS* 66/3 [2003], esp. 352–57), and thus offer quite analogous parallels to the kind of performative, nonnarrative, myth-infused poetry of the Bible.

43. "Israelite Epic," 80–102. The reconstruction has heuristic benefits, suggesting what such a myth might look like. More compelling is E. L. Greenstein, who points up possible "snatches" from the old epic tradition quoted in the emerging prose tradition (e.g., Gen 7:11b; see "The Formation of the Biblical Narrative Corpus," *AJS Review* 15/2 [1990], 157–58).

44. "Israelite Epic." 74–80.

45. "Signs of Poetry Past: Literariness in Pre-biblical Hebrew Literature" (unpublished manuscript); cf. E. L. Greenstein, review of D. Pardee, *The Ugaritic Texts and the Origins of West Semitic Literary Composition*, *BASOR* 371 (2014), 217.

46. "Epic Formulae in Biblical Narrative and the Origins of Ancient Hebrew Prose," in M. A. Friedman (ed.), *TE'UDA VII: Studies in Judaica* (Tel-Aviv: Tel-Aviv University Press, 1991), 9–53 [in Hebrew with English summary, vii–viii]; see F. H. Polak, "Epic Formulas in Biblical Narrative: Frequency and Distribution," in R. F. Poswick et al. (eds.), *Actes du Second Colloque International "Bible et Informatique: Méthodes, Outils, Résultats" (Jérusalem 9–13 Juin 1988)* (Geneva: Slatkine, 1989), 435–88; "On Prose and Poetry in the Book of Job," *JANES* 24 (1996), 61–97; "Formulaic Style," in J. Khan (ed.), *Encyclopedia of Hebrew Language and Linguistics* (vol. 1; Leiden: Brill, 2013), 906–11.

47. "Epic Formulae," viii. Others concur, esp. Zakovitch, "Israelite Epic," 20; Greenstein, "Signs of Poetry Past."

48. The basic trajectory (from oral to written) is well expressed in the Mesopotamian Enmerkar myth from the eighteenth century BCE, which provides an indigenous etiology for writing. Writing on cuneiform tablets was invented for sending letters. After numerous exchanges of oral messages with the lord of Aratta, Enmerkar invents written cuneiform to ensure the verbatim transmission of his complicated and important message through time and at a distance—

"the spoken words were mere wedges." Historically, of course, written letters do not show up artifactually until almost a millennium (twenty-fourth century BCE) after the earliest cuneiform tablets in Mesopotamia. But the trajectory mapped from oral to written is correct. And indeed letters turn out to be one of those places where we can track some of this development with assurance. Some of the formulaic substructure that necessarily facilitated oral and memorized communication in the verbal exchange of messages becomes conventionalized stylistic features of written letters. Something (however stylized, e.g., parallelism) of what such an exchange would entail may be glimpsed from Ugaritic narrative poetry, where the exchange of messages is a frequently encountered type-scene (e.g., CAT 1.5.II.8–20). The instruction to "say (*rgm*) to PN/GN" and the so-called "messenger formula" (*thm* PN/DN) introducing the message itself both become standard conventions in written letters in alphabetic cuneiform (e.g., CAT 2.10.1–3—as here these conventions are often separated from the body of the letter by an inscribed line running horizontally across the tablet). That is, the narrative representation plus the knowledge that messages were originally (and no doubt also contemporarily) exchanged verbally via messengers (namely Enmerkar) makes clear the oral lineage of the attested epistolary phrasing (cf. Pardee, *Ugaritic Texts*, 50–61; and to a similar end with the prophetic messenger formula in view, see Schniedewind, *How the Bible Became a Book*, 13). Further, note that a certain economy of expression is also facilitated by the technological innovation of a written (nonnarrative) prose (esp. Pardee, *Ugaritic Texts*, 59). Here it is worth underscoring as well that what Havelock calls "ordinary speech" (*Preface to Plato*) is to be distinguished from written prose and from narrative prose (both are stylized and not simply "transcripts" of the spoken vernacular) in particular and our own stridently postprose perspective on the givenness of prose needs chastening and bracketing when it comes to dealing with ancient literature (oral or written) where poetry was foundational and aboriginal. Pardee's high estimate of the achievement of written narrative prose in biblical Hebrew is well made (*Ugaritic Texts*, 35–40).

49. "Signs of Poetry Past."
50. Cassuto, "Israelite Epic," 74.
51. Polak, "Epic Formulae," viii.
52. Kittay and Godzich, *Emergence of Prose*, xi–xii. Interestingly, Cassuto also references continuities in idiom exhibited between early French historical and literary prose and "French epos," "Israelite Epic," 74.
53. Kittay and Godzich, *Emergence of Prose*, 5–7, 28, 63, 83–84.
54. *Writing the Oral Tradition*, 30.
55. *Immanent Art: From Structure to Meaning in Traditional Oral Epic* (Bloomington: Indiana University Press, 1991), 7.
56. This is to recognize that there were also likely written, textual influences that helped to shape biblical prose style. Sanders recognizes the influence of

Neo-Assyrian royal inscriptions on the inauguration of historical narrative in West Semitic more generally (*Invention of Hebrew*, 113–22; cf. N. Na'aman, "Three Notes on the Aramaic Inscription from Tel Dan," in *Ancient Israel's History and Historiography: The First Temple Period* [Winona Lake, Ind.: Eisenbrauns, 2006], 173–86, esp. 173–76). It is likely that another Mesopotamia genre, the chronicle, may have also impacted the historical prose of the Bible (see M. S. Smith, "Recent Study of Israelite Religion in Light of the Ugaritic Texts," in K. L. Younger, Jr. (ed.), *Ugarit at Seventy-Five* [Winona Lake, Ind.: Eisenbrauns, 2007], 5–11; and more broadly, D. Damrosch, *The Narrative Covenant: Transformations of Genre in the Growth of Biblical Literature* [Harper and Row, 1987]). And for nonannalistic prose narratives, see E. L. Greenstein, "On the Genesis of Biblical Prose Narrative," *Prooftexts* 8/3 (1988), 347–54. The likely impress of less formal, folkloristic modes of oral storytelling on the Bible's emergent written prose narrative tradition is not to be discounted either.

57. "Israelite Epic," 77.

58. "Israelite Epic," 77–78.

59. *Pre-biblical Narrative*, 28–21.

60. The latter is not an entirely convincing example but illustrates Cassuto's point nonetheless. A better example is Joshua 6, discussed by Greenstein ("Formation," 159–60), which evidences the "epic repetition" and the trend toward abbreviation (v. 14ff.) that tends to emerge with writing—written narrative prose in the Bible generally develops toward a leaner, more economic means of storytelling.

61. Cassuto, "Israelite Epic," 78; cf. Parker, *Pre-biblical Narrative*, 54.

62. Esp. Kittay and Godzich, *Prosaics*, 27–45. Kawashima begins charting some of these prose departures in biblical prose in *Death of the Rhapsode*.

63. "Epic Traditions," 34; cf. Cassuto, "Israelite Epic," 74.

64. See especially *Emergence of Prose*, 27–106.

65. Parker, *Pre-biblical Narrative*, 63–70, 100–104; R. S. Hendel, *The Epic of the Patriarch: The Jacob Cycle and the Narrative Traditions of Canaan and Israel* (Atlanta: Scholars Press, 1987), 35–67; Kawashima, *Death of the Rhapsode*, 161–89; cf. M. Parry, "On Typical Scenes in Homer," in *Making of Homeric Verse*, 404–7.

66. Cross, "Traditional Narrative," 32, and esp. Parker, *Pre-biblical Narrative*, chs. 3 and 4.

67. Cassuto, "Israelite Epic," 79.

68. Cassuto remarks explicitly on the issue of rhythmicity ("Israelite Epic," 79), which admittedly would be a difficult topic on which to carry out a sustained investigation. And many have observed the prevalence of bouts of parallelism in biblical prose (e.g., Greenstein, "Formation," 158–59). What I find provocative about these notations is that their presence becomes less remarkable if one assumes that biblical prose emerges (in part) out of a highly rhythmic and parallelistic poetic narrative tradition.

69. J. A. Notopoulos, "Parataxis in Homer: A New Approach to Homeric Literary Criticism," *Transactions and Proceedings of the American Philological Society* 80 (1949), 1–23; Havelock, *Preface to Plato*, esp. chs. 9–10; Ong, *Orality and Literacy*, 37–38; M. H. Lichtenstein, "Episodic Structure in the Ugaritic Keret Legend: Comparative Studies in Compositional Technique" (Ph.D. diss., Columbia University, 1979).

70. With regard to the latter, F. H. Polak's study "The Oral and the Written: Syntax, Stylistics and the Development of Biblical Prose Narrative" (*JANES* 26 [1998], 59–105) is especially revealing and in contrast to some others (e.g., Miller, *Oral Tradition*, 10, 69) I find it most compelling (particularly in light of the cognitive constraints placed on oral communication by human anatomy) and surely to be critical for any serious investigation of the topic moving forward. I return to the issue of syntax later, where I probe in particular Polak's worry over our ability to track syntactic style in poetry (61). For some literature in support of Polak's project, see J. Goody, *The Interface between the Written and the Oral* (Cambridge: Cambridge University Press, 1987), 262–72; W. L. Chafe, "Linguistic Differences Produced by Differences between Speaking and Writing," in D. R. Olson et al. (eds.), *Literacy, Language and Learning: The Nature and Consequences of Writing and Reading* (London: Cambridge University Press, 1985), 105–23; "Integration and Involvement in Speaking, Writing and Oral Literature," in D. Tannen (ed.,), *Spoken and Written Language: Exploring Orality and Literacy* (Norwood, N.J.: Ablex, 1982), 35–53. My sense is that more remains to be said both about the debt biblical prose owes to an informing oral narrative tradition (continuing the line of inquiry initiated by Cassuto and extended by Polak, among others) and the ways it develops beyond this ancestral inheritance (following on Kawashima's project, but also building on insights from scholars who have studied biblical prose from explicitly literary perspectives, e.g., Alter, Greenstein, Linafelt).

71. See esp. D. Boyarin, "Placing Reading: Ancient Israel and Medieval Europe," in Boyarin (ed.), *The Ethnography of Reading* (Berkeley: University of California Press, 1993), 10–12.

72. *Canaanite Myth and Hebrew Epic*, 112–13.

73. So Cross has one publication dedicated specifically to the topic, "Prose and Poetry in the Mythic and Epic Texts from Ugarit," *HTR* 67 (1974), 1–15. Most of his own research into the orality of Ugaritic narrative, as well exemplified by *Canaanite Myth and Hebrew Epic*, like that of many of his students (e.g., Hendel, *Epic of the Patriarch*), is pursued in a comparative mode with the biblical corpus receiving primary attention (for a critique of this habit of the field, see D. R. Hillers, "Analyzing the Abominable: Our Understanding of Canaanite Religion," *JQR* 75/3 (1985), 253–69 [reprinted in Hillers, *Poets Before Homer*, 230–44]). R. E. Whitaker's "Formulaic Analysis" is the odd exception—a study that deserves renewed attention in light of the more diversified and sophisticated discussions

of orality today. See also Lichtenstein, "Episodic Structure in the Ugaritic Keret Legend"; K. Aitken, "Oral Formulaic Composition and Theme in the Aqhat Narrative," *UF* 21 (1989), 1–16; "Word Pairs and Tradition in an Ugaritic Tale," *UF* 21 (1989), 17–38; Pardee, *Ugaritic Texts*, 47–48 (he explicitly construes Ilimilku as an "oral poet" who is writing down local Ugaritic mythology for the first time).

74. *Death of the Rhapsode*, esp. 15.

75. *Death of the Rhapsode*, 154–56; cf. Havelock, *Preface to Plato*, ch. 10 and n. 27.

76. *Death of the Rhapsode*, 15, n. 54; cf. 73, n. 96. See Hillers's general worry about this dominant pose in the field, "Analyzing the Abominable," 253–69.

77. *Pre-biblical Narrative*, 1.

78. *Pre-biblical Narrative*, 58–59.

79. *Pre-biblical Narrative*, 228.

80. *Pre-biblical Narrative*, 4. The scribalism of Ugarit did not survive this collapse, suggesting that oral transmission (of some sort) would have been the likeliest and most viable means for these storytelling traditions to continue to survive.

81. Cross, *Canaanite Myth and Hebrew Epic*, 293; cf. 124, n. 38; "Traditional Narrative," 31–32.

82. Cross, "Traditional Narrative," 32–33.

83. For example, as a means of beginning to think about what Israel's emerging prose narrative tradition owes more specifically to oral poetic (as opposed to folkloristic) techniques and content.

84. "Traditional Narrative," 36. In context, Cross is trying to deflect the prevailing view in the field that original sources must be short, which is not a bad thing. But that he has in mind the "length"—a concept that is only really sensible when speaking of *written* epic verse—of some epic traditions (above all Homer) is implied and made explicit in his early note on the idea from *Canaanite Myth and Hebrew Epic*: "In any case, we possess long poetic epics from old Canaan, from ancient Mesopotamia, and Homeric Greece, and to find the same phenomenon in Israel would not be surprising" (124, n. 38).

85. Greenstein, "Signs of Poetry Past."

86. Cross, *Canaanite Myth and Hebrew Epic*, 124, n. 38. So a version of this gloss of Cross's hypothesis would seem to be what chiefly informs Hendel's study of the Jacob cycle: "The bulk of the following chapters will tend to support the view of a full and complex oral tradition underlying the final Pentateuchal compositions" (*Epic of the Patriarch*, 32).

87. Greenstein, "Signs of Poetry Past."

88. "Traditional Narrative," 50.

89. "Traditional Narrative," 39–50.

90. Cross, *Canaanite Myth and Hebrew Epic*, 293.

91. "Traditional Narrative," 47.

92. "Traditional Narrative," 36.

93. "Traditional Narrative," 52.

94. See Greenstein, "Signs of Poetry Past."

95. "Traditional Narrative," 39.

96. "Traditional Narrative," 39.

97. Hendel, *Epic of the Patriarch*, 37–59. R. Alter has perceptively analyzed the literary developments of this particular type-scene ("How Convention Helps Us Read: The Case of the Bible's Annunciation Type-Scene," *Prooftexts* 3 [1983], 115–30; cf. Alter, *The Art of Biblical Narrative* (New York: Basic Books, 1981], 55–78; Kawashima, *Death of the Rhapsode*, 161–89), but Hendel is correct to note and emphasize its rootedness in oral verbal art (esp. 42, n. 21; cf. Parker, *Pre-biblical Narrative*, 63–70, 100–107). The "vow" is another traditional motif that gets taken up and utilized by the prose writer in the Bible, see Hendel, *Epic of the Patriarch*, 61–67; Parker, *Pre-biblical Narrative*, 70–87.

98. See R. Kawashima, "Verbal Medium and Narrative Art in Homer and the Bible," *Philosophy and Literature* 28 (2004), 103–17, esp. 110–15.

99. *Death of the Rhapsode*, 163.

100. "Oral Register in the Biblical Libretto: Towards a Biblical Poetic," *Oral Tradition* 10 (1995), 388–89.

101. Again, this is not to discount the impress of other oral (e.g., folkloristic) and/or specifically written (e.g., epistolary and administrative genres) influences on the emerging biblical prose narrative style.

102. *Death of the Rhapsode*, 10, 14, 15.

103. "Prose Performance Texts: *Epideixis* and Written Publication in the Late Fifth and Early Fourth Centuries," in H. Yunis (ed.), *Written Texts and the Rise of Literate Culture in Ancient Greece* (Cambridge: Cambridge University Press, 2003), 162; cf. Thomas, *Literacy and Orality*, 34; "Performance and Written Literature," 348–57; Havelock, *Preface to Plato*, chs. 1–3; Yunis, *Written Texts*. The medieval period provides another paradigm example of a context in which writing and textuality (of prose and poetry) emerge not at the death of an oral tradition but very much within its midst, e.g., Kittay and Godzich, *Emergence of Prose*; Amodio, *Writing the Oral Tradition*, 22; A. N. Doane, "Oral Texts, Intertexts, and Intratexts: Editing Old English," in *Influence and Intertextuality in Literary History* (Madison: University of Wisconsin Press, 1991), 139; Ong, *Orality and Literacy*, 112–13.

104. Note R. C. Culley's early statement: "It should be added that the coming of writing to a society need not cause an immediate revolution, for the change from a completely oral society to a fully literate one may be slow" (*Oral Formulaic Language in the Biblical Psalms* [Toronto: University of Toronto Press, 1967], 5). See also Schniedewind, *How the Bible Became a Book*, esp. 1–23; F. H. Polak, "Book, Scribe, and Bard: Oral Discourse and Written Text in Recent Biblical Scholarship," *Prooftexts* 31/1 (2011), 126–27.

105. Esp. Boyarin, "Placing Reading"; Havelock, *Preface to Plato*, ch. 3, esp. n. 8; Thomas, "Prose Performance Texts," 162–88; "Performance and Written Literature,"

348–50; H. Yunis, "Writing for Reading: Thucydides, Plato, and the Emergence of the Critical Reader," in Yunis, *Written Texts*, 189–212.

106. E.g., Cassuto, "Israelite Epic," 109; Cross, "Traditional Narrative," 36; Zakovitch, "Israelite Epic," 20.

107. Zakovitch suggests that the oral traditon may even persist into much later times, see "Israelite Epic," 20. On the other hand, there are no extant extended descriptions of epic singers or their epic songs in the Bible. Cassuto suggests that there may be several more oblique references to epic song. Job 36:24 is his lead example: "Remember to extol his work [*poʿŏlô*] / of which mortals have sung [*šôrĕrû*]" (NRSV) ("Israelite Epic," 73). It is impossible from our current vantage point to infer precisely what kind of song the Joban poet has in mind. That Heb. *šyr* was historically more capacious than its current biblical attestation allows for, almost always referencing nonnarrative or lyric song, is suggested by the cognate languages where the same verbs for singing (e.g., Ug *šyr*, Akk. *zamāru*) may be used of both lyric and epic song. Still, the reference in Job could as easily be to a lyric song like Exodus 15 as to an epic telling of Yahweh's mighty deeds (cf. Ps 105:2; 143:5).

108. See Kittay and Godzich, *Emergence of Prose*, 3–23, esp. 17. Sanders has emphasized the importance of social and political history for a maximally informed appraisal of the vernacular revolution that is given view in the Hebrew Bible (*Invention of Hebrew*). Surely one of the important factors in the ultimate success of biblical prose locally was the disruption and dismantling of traditional culture in Iron II Israel and Judah caused by Neo-Assyrian and Babylonian incursions into the region and especially their heinous policies of population displacement. Traditional verbal art becomes impossible once the spaces for those traditional performances have been obliterated. The complaint of Psalm 137 is quite telling on this point: "How can we sing the songs of Yahweh / on foreign soil?" (v. 4). That a form of written verbal art engineered for flourishing outside the arena of performance (especially in the economy of expression and the advent of *diegesis* that it facilitates) should survive the Babylonian exile should be of no real surprise.

109. Doane, "Oral Texts," 79; cf. Ong, *Orality and Literacy*, 139.

110. "Israelite Epic," 109.

111. Zakovitch, "Israelite Epic," 24.

112. "Traditional Narrative," 36.

113. "Traditional Narrative," 38; cf. Greenstein, "Signs of Poetry Past." To reiterate, the example of Ugarit is enough to alert us to the possibility. However, the cultural context of the souther Levant in Iron I and IIA is quite distinct from that of LB Ugarit. And to date there is no extant written narrative verse from the region during this time (or even later in Iron IIB–C). The point that needs constantly underscoring is that continuity in a formal, poetic storytelling tradition between Ugarit and Israel, as I and many others presume, *does not require*

writing, even though writing is known and put to some very particular uses during the period. The traditional, embodied technology of ongoing oral performance is sufficient to the task of preservation.

114. E. A. Havelock, *The Literate Revolution in Greece and Its Cultural Consequences* (Princeton: Princeton University Press, 1982), 17. Others also emphasize the orality of ancient Greek lyric, e.g., C. M. Bowra, *Greek Lyric Poetry: From Alcman to Simonides* (2d ed.; Oxford: Oxford University Press, 1961); Herington, *Poetry into Drama*; B. Gentili, *Poetry and Its Public in Ancient Greece: From Homer to the Fifth Century* (trans. A. T. Cole; Baltimore: Johns Hopkins University Press, 1988), esp. 3–49; G. Nagy, *Pindar's Homer: The Lyric Possession of an Epic Past* (Baltimore: Johns Hopkins University Press, 1990); "Lyric and Greek Myth," in R. D. Woodard (ed.), *The Cambridge Companion to Greek Mythology* [Cambridge: Cambridge University Press, 2007]), 19; R. S. Garner, *Traditional Elegy: The Interplay of Meter, Tradition, and Context in Early Greek Poetry* (Oxford: Oxford University Press, 2010.

115. Havelock, *Literate Revolution*, 17. The "scraps" he refers to is the line of "lyric" poets extending from Archilochus to Simonides known to the Alexandrians. If anything the facticity of early oral Greek lyric should be emphasized (Nagy, "Lyric and Greek Myth," 19), and, indeed, as discussed in chapter 3 here, it is entirely likely that if any of the broad genres deserves privileging it is the lyric, which has strong claims to priority.

116. Havelock, *Literate Revolution*, 17.

117. J. Opland, *Anglo-Saxon Oral Poetry: A Study of the Traditions* (New Haven: Yale University Press, 1980), 12. This nonnarrative part of the tradition comes in for special treatment in particular in C. B. Pasternack's *The Textuality of Old English Poetry* (Cambridge: Cambridge University Press, 1995).

118. Opland, *Anglo-Saxon Oral Poetry*, 12.

119. Opland, *Anglo-Saxon Oral Poetry*, 9–27; cf. J. Opland, *Xhosa Poets and Poetry* (New Africa Books, 1998).

120. Cf. F. H. Bäuml, "Medieval Texts and the Two Theories of Oral-Formulaic Composition: A Proposal for a Third Theory," *New Literary History* 16/1 (1984), 32, 36. This is not to discount what can be revealed even when the comparisons are not optimally close. There is no denying, for example, that A. Lord's *The Singer of Tales* (Cambridge, Mass.: Harvard University Press, 1960) is informative about oral performance broadly and that aspects of oral lyric may well be illuminated, even though that is not at all his focus.

121. *Anglo-Saxon Oral Poetry*, 10.

122. Lord, *Singer of Tales*, 279, n. 2. Also mentioned in the same note is B. Bartok and A. B. Lord, *Serbo-Croatian Folk Songs* (New York, 1951), which contains the transcriptions of seventy-five nonnarrative, non-male-only guslar-accompanied heroic songs (i.e., lyric songs) from the collection.

123. M. P. Coote, "Women's Songs in Serbo-Croatian," *Journal of American Folklore* 90 (1977), 331–38.

124. "On the Composition of Women's Songs," *Oral Tradition* 7 (1992), 334.

125. "Composition of Women's Songs," 333.

126. "Composition of Women's Songs," 333.

127. *Oral Poetry*, 13.

128. "Composition of Women's Songs," 333, 334; cf. Finnegan, *Oral Poetry*, 13—"Lyric poetry, in the general sense of a (relatively) short non-narrative poem that is sung, is of extremely wide occurrence; it can probably be regarded as universal in human culture."

129. "Composition of Women's Songs," 337.

130. "Composition of Women's Songs," 338.

131. "Composition of Women's Songs," 339.

132. A. B. Lord, "Formula and Non-narrative Theme in South Slavic Oral Epic and the OT," *Semeia* 5 (1976), 93–106.

133. *Semeia* 5 (1976), 51–64.

134. Coote, "Application of Oral Theory," 62.

135. Lord, "Non-narrative Theme," 99.

136. Lord, "Non-narrative Theme," 98.

137. Lord, "Non-narrative Theme," 99.

138. Lord, "Non-narrative Theme," 99.

139. Lord, "Non-narrative Theme," 105.

140. Miller's recent *Oral Tradition* (9 and n. 68) is an exception. Lord offers the same sensible advice about comparing like with like in his comments in B. Stolz and R. Shannon (eds.), *Oral Literature and the Formula* (Ann Arbor: University of Michigan Press, 1976), 66–68 (the book is a compilation of papers and discussion from a conference held in 1974). More recently, J. M. Foley has underscored how crucial genre considerations are to a fully empathetic and revealing exploration of oral performative art (*Immanent Art*, 15). W. G. E. Watson (*Classical Hebrew Poetry: A Guide to Its Techniques* [London: T. and T. Clark, 2001 (1984)], 78, n. 44) does note that "most Hebrew poetry is non-narrative" in his own discussion of "ancient Hebrew oral poetry." A late essay by Lord, "Oral Traditional Lyric Poetry" (included in his *The Singer Resumes the Tale* [Ithaca: Cornell Univeristy, 1995], 22–68), offers his most extensive comment on nonnarrative oral poetry; see also his comments in his entry "Oral Poetry," in *NPEPP*, 863–66.

141. "Application of Oral Theory," 57; cf. Watson, *Classical Hebrew Poetry*, 78.

142. *Poetry and Its Public*, 3.

143. R. Bauman, *Verbal Art as Performance* (Long Grove, Ill.: Waveland, 1977), 11.

144. Esp. Bauman, *Verbal Art as Performance*, esp. 7–14, 25–36; D. R. Olson, "From Utterance to Text: The Bias of Language in Speech and Writing," *Harvard Educational Review* 47/3 (1977), 257–81; Zumthor, "Text and the Voice," 67–92; Doane, "Ethnography of Scribal Writing," 420–39; U. Schaefer, "Hearing from Books: The Rise of Fictionality in Old English Poetry," in A. N. Doane and

C. B. Pasternack (eds.), *Vox Intexta: Orality and Textuality in the Middle Ages* (Madison: University of Wisconsin Press, 1991), 117–18.

145. At least many of the oracles preserved in the received text are poetic, as is true for much of the prophetic corpus preserved in the Hebrew Bible (which contrasts with the written remains of prophetic texts from Mari and Assyria, which are all prose summaries or reports of prophetic activity, see esp. M. Nissinen et al., *Prophets and Prophecy in the Ancient Near East* [WAW; Atlanta: SBL, 2005]).

146. See esp. van der Toorn, *Scribal Culture*, 110–11, 173–204; cf. Y. Hoffman, "Aetiology, Redaction and Historicity in Jeremiah XXXVI," *VT* 46 (1996), 179–89.

147. This is not to discount the possibility that prophetic texts could emerge originally as written compositions (e.g., Ezekiel), and certainly the form of prophetic books that have survived in MT (and the versions) and at Qumran are scribal productions, the products of writing, as Jeremiah 36 represents.

148. Such dictation should not necessarily be conceived of as a wholly mechanical or one-way affair. In all likelihood it would have been highly collaborative, as suggested, for example, by the legal contracts recorded at Elephantine, which commonly are said to have been written by a scribe "according to the mouth of" (*kpm*) someone else, though presuming that scribe's knowledge of legal formulary and points of law. Many of the Neo-Assyrian prophecy texts conclude by referencing the source of the utterance recorded, *ša / issu pî* PN "by/from the mouth of PN" (e.g., SAA 9 1.3 ii 13'–15'; 1.7 v 10–11).

149. The latter notice is not unimportant as it suggests what otherwise might be expected, namely, that we should not imagine these various readings and rereadings, tellings and retellings, and writings and rewritings to necessarily be verbatim renderings, one of the other. Oral communication and performances are typically messier affairs.

150. This ostracon appears to reference a "letter" (*spr*) from one Tobiah to Shallum ben Yaddua containing the report of a prophetic utterance (*mʾt. hnbʾ*, see F. W. Dobbs-Allsopp et al., *Hebrew Inscriptions: Texts from the Biblical Period of the Monarchy with Concordance* (New Haven: Yale University Press, 2005), 313).

151. So already Gunkel and especially Mowinckel (see Knight, *Rediscovering the Traditions*, esp. 64–65, 169–70, n. 2, 192–93—Mowinckel: "prophets did not write; they talked"); and more recently, Niditch, *Oral World*, 120; M. Nissinen, "Spoken, Written, Quoted, and Invented: Orality and Writtenness in Ancient Near Eastern Prophecy," in E. Ben Zvi and M. Floyd (eds.), *Writings and Speech in Israelite and Ancient Near Eastern Prophecy* (Atlanta: SBL, 2000), 268; W. Doan and T. Giles, *Prophets, Performance, and Power: Performance Criticism of the Hebrew Bible* (London: T. and T. Clark, 2005), esp. 5. Kittay and Godzich's generic analysis of oracular speech in performance is illuminating of the very mechanics of such speech in its originating orality, namely a prophet as medium through which divine speech takes place (*Emergence of Prose*, 8–9).

152. For an early rendering of these verses as poetry, see R. Lowth, *Isaiah. A New Translation; with a Preliminary Dissertation, and Notes* (London: J. Nichols, 1778; reprinted in *Robert Lowth (1710–1787): The Major Works* (London: Routledge, 1995), 17–18.

153. The presumption is to take *ʿ-n-y* "to answer" literally, and thus two verbs of speaking are usually reconstructed in the lacunae in ll. A 11–12 (*wymll, wyʾmr*).

154. The oracle, though revealed through intermediaries, is attributed directly to Baalshamayn and related as his speech. The Isaianic passage continues in a not dissimilar way in 7:10 (*wayyôsep yhwh dabbēr ʾel-ʾāḥāz lēʾmōr* "and Yahweh continued speaking to Ahaz, saying"). The conceit would seem to be appropriate to the ancient context, even though it becomes clear, as the passage continues, that Isaiah is the prophetic intermediary (esp. 7:13–17—though NRSV feels the need to make this explicit and adds "Isaiah" in its rendering of v. 13). The unease with this transition (e.g., Tg) would seem to be misplaced stylistically.

155. See conveniently, Nissinen, "Spoken, Written, Quoted, and Invented," 249–50; van der Toorn, *Scribal Culture*, 173–204.

156. So also J. B. Couey, "Amos vii 10–17 and Royal Attitudes toward Prophecy in the Ancient Near East," *VT* 58 (2008), 308.

157. Zumthor, "Text and the Voice," 69.

158. It remains an open question as to when the oracles of Isaiah of Jerusalem started being collected and written down. That this could have happened during the prophet's lifetime should not be dismissed out of hand. Certainly by the latter half of the eighth century (when most still place this prophet) the capacity for such scribal activity is well in evidence in Judah, and especially around the capital (Sanders, *Invention of Hebrew*, 122–26; Parker, *Stories*, 8–9, 145, n. 15). Prophetic collections are extant from the general era, both from Deir ʿAlla (*KAI* 312) and from Mesopotamia (see Nissinen et al., *Prophets and Prophecy*, esp. 97–199). Jeremiah 36 shows that at a slightly later period (taking the general chronology within the text at face value) the idea of such a prophetic collection is plainly conceivable. Isaiah 30:8 may show awareness of the writing down of a single prophetic oracle, something, again, imaginable given the written reports of individual oracles extant from contemporary Assyria (SAA 9 5–11). And indeed it is difficult to imagine a scenario in which the oracles themselves could be preserved after the prophet ceased being active outside of them having been written down. Though the prophetic oracles associated with Isaiah of Jerusalem suppose an overwhelmingly oral world, they are not totally ignorant of textuality. Besides the reference already noted in Isaiah 30:8 and the inclusion in the collection of a "writing of Hezekiah" (*miktāb lĕḥizqiyyāhû*, Isa 38:9; cf. vv. 10–20), the material in Isaiah 8:1–4 (closely related to the concerns of Isa 7:1–9) turns on a bit of textuality. Isaiah is instructed to write (*kĕtōb*) on a *gillāyôn gādôl*, the identity of which remains obscure—often glossed as a large tablet or sheet of papyrus (cf. Syr. *gellāyônāʾ* "writing tablet"). What the prophet is told to write looks at first to be miming a

simple ownership notice or tag, "belonging to Maher-shalal-hosh-baz" (*lĕmaḥēr šālāl ḥoš baz*), common to seals and frequently inscribed on all manner of things, e.g., storage jars, bowls, and the like. If so the prophet would appear to be playing on the simpleness of such writing (i.e., exaggerating the size, using a symbolic name—see J. J. M. Roberts, "Isaiah and His Children," in *Biblical and Related Studies Presented to Samuel Iwry* [ed. A. Kort and S. Morschauser; Winona Lake, Ind.: Eisenbrauns, 1985], esp. 195–96). Other interpretations are also imaginable. The mention of witnesses in v. 2 may suggest that *lĕmaḥēr šālāl ḥoš baz* could be, alternatively, a summary (scribal) reference to a longer document, i.e., "to/ for Maher-shalal-hosh-baz." So legal contracts from Elephantine, for example, by convention list the names of those who witnessed the (oral) transaction re-counted in the document and often contain external endorsements summariz-ing the document's content (e.g., *TAD* B3.5.25). Or perhaps the reference is to a prophetic scroll that was sealed (so now J. J. M. Roberts, email, April 23, 2013; cf. Isa 8:16–18). Note that editorial superscriptions of a related kind sometimes are found introducing prophetic oracles, e.g., *lannĕbī'îm* "for/to/concerning the prophets" (Jer 23:9; cf. 21:11; 46:1; 49:1, 7). The Isaianic tradition prefers the label *maśśā'* plus a noun (e.g., Isa 13:1; 15:1; 17:1). Interestingly, the oracle in Isa 30:6–7 that Isaiah is instructed to write down (Isa 30:8) is provided with just such a summary introductory notice: *maśśā' bahămôt negeb* "an oracle of the animals of the Negeb." In any event, it seems assured that even Isaiah's dominantly oral world will have been intersected in a myriad of ways and to differing degrees by an increasing significance of textuality, some signs of which are inscribed in the preserved corpus of this prophet's words.

159. So F. I. Andersen and D. N. Freedman, *Amos* (AB 24A; New York: Doubleday, 1989), 763.

160. What is and is not verse in prophetic literature will always be a contested ques-tion, especially since specially formatted manuscripts are mostly lacking for this material. This couplet has the unbalanced shape (short/long) of a qinah-shaped couplet, appropriate for an oracle of judgment (cf. Amos 5:1–2), and is structured chiastically: PP + V + N // N + V + PP. The second line is quoted again quite intentionally in v. 17, where it is a part of a balanced couplet (both lines containing twelve syllables). Commentators habitually search the pre-served corpus of the "words of Amos" for Amaziah's quotation. And the basic themes are there (e.g., 4:2–3; 5:5, 26–27; 6:7; 7:9; 9:4). But the lack of a precise match should not be disconcerting in such a dominantly oral world, where Amos, like Jeremiah a little later, can be presumed to have prophesied "many more similar words" (cf. Jer 36:32), most of which would have been lost at the moment of their uttering.

161. Couey, "Amos vii 10–17," 300–314.

162. Commentators frequently suggest that the latter means to parody or otherwise play off the standard prophetic messenger formula (e.g., Andersen and Freedman,

Amos, 768; S. Paul, *Amos* [Hermeneia; Minneapolis: Fortress, 1991], 240). This may be true. But the attribution should be taken at face value as well. Mesopotamian prophetic reports may be analogously introduced: "PN the prophetess (says) thus" (PN *raggintu [m]ā*, SAA 9 7.1–2), and more frequently such reports will conclude by affirming that the report came "from/by the mouth" (*ša pî / issu pî*) of a person (e.g., SAA 9 1.10 iv 31; 2.3 ii 28). Both most naturally implicate initial spoken communication, even though these reports are eventually written down. Further, the Mari letters, in particular, reveal the commonness with which prophets are associated with temples and often are reported to have uttered oracles or seen visions in a temple (Nissinen in *Prophets and Prophecy*, 16).

163. Of v. 16, Andersen and Freedman (*Amos*, 776) say, "a single bicolon with simple parallelism." For the shapeliness of the curses in v. 17, see P. D. Miller, *Sin and Judgement in the Prophets: A Stylistic and Theological Analysis* (SBLMS 27; Chico: Scholars Press, 1982), 25.

164. "Text and the Voice," 69.

165. The variation in verb forms in the two versions of the couplet may well be an oral tick, the kind of good variant not untypical of remembered and orally transmitted art (cf. Carr, *Formation*, esp. 13–36).

166. O. Eissfeldt (*The Old Testament: An Introduction* [trans. P. Ackroyd; New York: Harper and Row, 1965], 88) believes this originally may have been a work song sung while digging wells. No doubt such work songs were a common part of daily life in the ancient Levant, though only an occasional odd reference has survived in the Bible (e.g., Judg 21:21; Isa 16:10; Song 2:12—a possible allusion to singing during the harvest). Eissfeldt's discussion of the "pre-literary stage" of biblical literature (9–127) remains a rich resource (with older bibliography) very much worth consulting in light of the more recent work done in the field on orality and textuality. His ideas about orality and oral tradition mainly represent ideas developed in the field up until the time of his writing, with no awareness of the Parry and Lord oral formulaic theory. Exodus 15:21 is just such a "snatch" of Exodus 15:1–18.

167. Eissfeldt, *Old Testament*, 99–101.

168. Zumthor, after reviewing the genres typical of traditional verbal art, emphasizes how all the types may give way as well (with or without modificationn) "to irony and parody" (*Oral Poetry*, 75).

169. For details, see Paul, *Amos*, 206–7.

170. The vocalic character of the root *r-n-n* is not in doubt, and it is used verbally in parallel with *š-y-r* (Ps 59:17).

171. See Eissfeldt, *Old Testament*, 102–24.

172. Egyptian tomb paintings show music and singing as customary parts of banqueting scenes (fig. 38), see M. V. Fox, *The Song of Songs and the Ancient Egyptian Love Songs* (Madison: University of Wisconsin Press, 1985), figs. 3, 9, 10; R.B. Parkinson, *Poetry and Culture in Middle Kingdom Egypt: A Dark Side to Perfection* (London: Continuum, 2002), 56.

173. "Entertainment" (*sḫmḫ ib*) is mentioned explicitly in the headings to three groups of Egyptian love songs, see Fox, *Song of Songs*, 244.

174. Amos 8:10 even contrasts "song" and "dirge"—though by the Chronicler's time "singers" could be associated with dirges as well (2 Chron 35:25).

175. The Deir 'Alla plaster texts (*KAI* 312; ca. eighth century BCE) do not self-evidently preserve "verse." But the communication between Balaam and the gods is presented as spoken (*wyʾmrw*, l. I, 3), and Balaam is consulted by "his people" (*ʿmh*, l. I, 4) in person, and he reveals to them what he knows from the gods by speaking to them (*wyʾmr lhm*, l. I, 4–5).

176. Though the Song is made up of poetic dialogue throughout, this is the only time the dialogue is formally (explicitly) introduced as such—probably precisely because it is the girl's re-presented (remember, recollected, quoted) speech of the boy (i.e., he is not imagined here as actually speaking, but it is the girl recollecting, reperforming him speaking). The introductory formula itself has strong oral, epic roots, see Polak, "Epic Formulas," 437, 447–48, 482, n. 1, 484, n. 7 (in other poetic texts: Isa 14:10; 21:9; Jer 11:5; Hab 2:2; Joel 2:19).

177. The imprint of textuality on Job is no more starkly displayed than in these (third person!) formally narrated introductions of the speakers, hardly necessary in oral performance. Contrast the Song of Songs, similarly thoroughgoingly dialogic, though there is no narrative voice here that breaks into the interior of these poems to stage the dialogues. The one formal introduction of speech (Song 2:10) is not narratorial but embedded within the girl's speech and is necessitated deicticly because it is her recollection of her lover's words. The grip of tradition and convention remains tightly felt in these poems.

178. Ong, *Orality and Literacy*, 34. The conceit of the sufferer being consoled by friends and family (Job 2:11) is also traditional, see *KAI* 312 1.4.

179. See more generally on this topic in the Psalms, R. Jacobson, *"Many Are Saying": The Function of Direct Discourse in the Hebrew Psalter* (London: T. and T. Clark, 2004). For a wonderfully imaginative and illuminating reconstruction of a poetry recitation in Middle Kingdom Egypt, see R. B. Parkinson, *Reading Ancient Egyptian Poetry: Among Other Histories* (Oxford: Wiley, 2009), 20–68.

180. See Eissfeldt, *Old Testament*, 75–76.

181. Eissfeldt, *Old Testament*, 59–60; cf. Finnegan, *Oral Poetry*, 98–109; Bauman, *Verbal Art as Performance*, 18–19; Zumthor, *Oral Poetry*, 111, 137; Foley, *Oral Poem*, 89–90; Miller, *Oral Tradition*, 72.

182. M. Jousse, *The Oral Style* (trans. E. Sienaert and R. Whitaker; New York: Garland, 1990 [1925]), 95; cf. Ong, *Orality and Literacy*, 40; Buss, *Biblical Form Criticism*, 112, n. 47. Jousse apparently exerted a great deal of influence on the young M. Parry during the latter's stay in Paris working on his doctoral dissertation that would eventually usher in a whole new paradigm for understanding the oral origins of Homeric verse, cf. T. de Vet, "Parry in Paris: Structuralism, Historical Linguistics, and the Oral Theory," *Classical Antiquity* 24 (2005), 257–84.

183. *Oral Style*, 95.
184. Finnegan also reports the commonness with which individual verse lines are grouped as couplets and triplets in oral poems cross-culturally (*Oral Poetry*, 108–9). In her only comment on Jousse specifically, Finnegan worries over the possible biological reductionism that she sees in Jousse's thought (91). While there is much in Jousse that needs redacting, editing, rephrasing, nevertheless the central thrust of his animating ideas would seem to be broadly consistent with current research in the cognitive sciences and neurobiology. This is not to reduce all to biology but to be aware of the very real constraints that human physiology places on oral performance.
185. The parallelism that often courses through the short narrative runs preserved in some biblical poems possibly provides a similar kind of cross-grain confirmation of the trope's broader parlance beyond any single mode. However, in the absence of attested ancient Hebrew narrative poetry, it remains mostly an open question as to how different modes or genres (e.g., narrative and nonnarrative) interacted. For example, there are traditions of long narrative poetry that embed nonnarrative genres while retaining some/many of the embedded genre's identifying markers, while other traditions fully assimilate the embedded genres to the norms of the narrative tradition (for a convenient discussion with bibliography, see Garner, *Traditional Elegy*, 79–81). For example, biblical prose narrative certainly embeds Hebrew nonnarrative song in ways that retains the distinctive poetic markers of the latter. But whether the use of parallelism in narrative runs in biblical nonnarrative poetry says anything about parallelism in narrative verse depends on the nature of the embedding practice, which is hard to determine given the lack of attested Hebrew narrative poetry. And it may simply be that with respect to parallelism the question of mode or genre is irrelevant. It is noteworthy, in light of the complete lack of narrative poetry in the Bible, that almost the reverse situation exists with the preserved poetic corpus at Ugarit, with but a handful of nonnarrative poems preserved (e.g., *RIH* 98/02). For example, there is every reason to expect prayers (i.e., laments, hymns) to have been performed at Ugarit. There are plenty of extant ritual texts that imply this and story elements that assume it (esp. CAT 1.14.III.52–IV.8), yet there is but the single clear example of a cultic prayer in CAT 1.119. 26'–36'.
186. Pasternack, *Textuality of Old English Poetry*, 62 (with the Anglo-Saxon tradition specifically in view); Foley, *Oral Poem*, 89 (commenting on parallelism in South Slavic epic verse).
187. Pasternack, *Textuality of Old English Poetry*, 62; cf. Bäuml, "Medieval Texts," 31–49, esp. 43; Doane, "Ethnography of Scribal Writing," 420–39; Olson, "From Utterance to Text," 277; Schaefer, "Hearing from Books," 120–23, 125–26.
188. Ginsberg was among the first to recognize this phenomenon. See H. L. Ginsberg and B. Maisler, "Semitized Hurrians in Syria and Palestine," *JPOS* 14

(1934), 248–40, n. 11; H. L. Ginsberg, "The Victory of the Land-God over the Sea God," *JPOS* 15 (1935), 327; "The Rebellion and Death of Ba'lu," *Orientalia* NS 5 (1936), 172.

189. For a convenient listing of occurrences, see M. Dahood, "Hebrew-Ugaritic Parallel Pairs," in L. Fisher (ed.), *Ras Shamra Parallels* (vol. 1; Rome: PBI, 1972), 234–35.

190. Ginsberg and Maisler, "Semitized Hurrians," 248, n. 15; Cassuto, "Biblical and Canaanite Literature," 51.

191. Cassuto, "Biblical and Canaanite Literature," 43–45; cf. S. Gevirtz, *Patterns in the Early Poetry of Israel* (Chicago: University of Chicago Press, 1963), 38. Cassuto's compilations of word pairs in "Biblical and Canaanite Literature" and in "Parallel Words in Hebrew and Ugaritic," [1947] in *Biblical and Oriental Studies* (vol. 2, 60–68), remain the seminal collections of such pairs. For other treatments, with references to later literature, see esp. P. B. Yoder, "A-B Pairs and Oral Composition in Hebrew Poetry," *VT* 21 (1971), 470–89; O'Connor, *Hebrew Verse Structure*, 96–109; Y. Avishur, *Stylistic Studies of Word Pairs in Biblical and Ancient Semitic Literatures* (Neukirchen-Vluyn: Neukirchener Verlag, 1984); W. G. E. Watson, "The Unnoticed Word Pair 'Eye(s)' // 'Heart,'" *ZAW* 101 (1989), 398–408; Zakovitch, "Israelite Epic," 20, 25, n. 16; Polak, "Formulaic Style," 907–8.

192. "Biblical and Canaanite Literature," 45.

193. "Parallel Pairs," 81.

194. "Parallel Pairs," 356.

195. "Application of Oral Theory," 59–60. The formulation here shares with much of the early studies of orality a chief fixation on oral composition. More recent work is more attendant to the larger performative context, in which reception, for example, is just as interesting as composition. The formulism of much oral verbal art, from this perspective, whatever it may reveal about the putative oral composer, also says something important about "language use which was meaningful for the receivers" (Schaefer, "Hearing from Books," 121). Hence, the significance of formulaic language may be measured beyond the question of composition, about which we are generally ignorant with regard to most biblical poems.

196. W. Whallon, "Formulaic Poetry in the Old Testament," *Comparative Literature* 15 (1963), 1–14; Gevirtz, *Patterns*; Yoder, "A-B Pairs," 470–89.

197. So already Culley, *Oral Formulaic Language*, 10–12; see also P. Kiparsky, "Oral Poetry: Some Linguistic and Typological Considerations," in Stolz and Shannon, *Oral Literature and the Formula*, 87–88; Coote, "Application of Oral Theory," 54–56; O'Connor, *Hebrew Verse Structure*, 104–6.

198. *Hebrew Verse Structure*, 103. O'Connor's thoughts here are generally consistent with the tendency of oralists since Parry and Lord to broaden and generalize the concept of the oral formula. Zumthor is emblematic: "In that [medieval]

society formulaicness refers to everything within the discourses and the modes of utterance which has the tendency of being resaid continuously in a manner hardly diversified, of reproducing itself with minimal and [yet] countless variations" (*La lettre et la voix: De la "littérature" médiévale* [vol. 44; Paris: Éditions du Seuil, 1987], 216, as given in Schaefer, "Hearing from Books," 121).

199. Culley, *Oral Formulaic Language*, 36, 39.

200. *Hebrew Verse Structure*, 105.

201. *Hebrew Verse Structure*, 105. cf. Gevirtz, *Patterns*, 3, 8; Whallon, "Formulaic Poetry," 2.

202. A good example is the stereotyped phrasing of the birth announcement, which is found both in Ugaritic (e.g., *kyld. bn. ly. km aḫy. / wšrš. km. aryy* "for a son is to be born to me like my brothers, / an offspring like my fellows," (CAT 1.17. II.14–15; cf. 17.I.18–19; 23.52–53) and in the Bible (e.g., in Isaiah's announcement of a new king, *kî-yeled yullad-lānû / bēn nittan-lānû* "for a child is born to us, / a son is given to us," Isa 9:5; in Jeremiah's curse of his birthday, *yullad-lĕkā bēn zākār* "a boy is born to you," Jer 20:15; cf. Job 3:3; and in the announcement of Obed's birth in Ruth, *yullad-bēn lĕno ŏmî* "a son is born to Naomi," Ruth 4:17). Here it is likely the commonality of the circumstances (i.e., birth) and a ready way of expressing them that informs the stereotyped phrasing (cf. Parker, *Pre-biblical Narrative*, 62; O'Connor, *Hebrew Verse Structure*, 103).

203. Culley, *Oral Formulaic Language*, esp. 32–101; Whitaker, "Formulaic Analysis." Cf. Polak, "Formulaic Style."

204. One consequence of this larger exposure has been that the definition of the oral formula "has progressively become more flexible and more concise" (Zumthor, "Text and the Voice," 79).

205. Zumthor, "Text and the Voice," 83.

206. There are narrative as well as nonnarrative "women's songs," see Coote, "Women's Songs," 333. The emphasis on the role of memory and lack of formulas pertains chiefly in her analysis to the nonnarrative portion of the tradition, esp. Coote, "Composition of Women's Songs," 333.

207. "Composition of Women's Songs," 337. The songs she is specfically commenting on here are by three singers, and each song has multiple attestations in the collection. These songs average in length from seventeen to thirty-two lines.

208. A. Jabbour, "Memorial Transmission in Old English Poetry," *Chaucer Review* 3 (1969), 168; cf. Coote, "Composition of Women's Songs," 337; Opland, *Anglo-Saxon Oral Poetry*, 10.

209. Coote, "Composition of Women's Songs," 337.

210. Esp. *Tablet of the Heart*. Carr also stresses how memorial transmission would have been aided and intersected by writing throughout the biblical and post-biblical periods.

211. *Tablet of the Heart*, 7; see esp. n. 18, where Carr cites the following studies: I. M. L. Hunter, "Lengthy Verbatim Recall (LVR) and the Myth and Gift of

Tape-Recorder Memory," in P. Niemi (ed.), *Psychology in the 1990's* (Amsterdam: North Holland, 1984), 425–40; "Lengthy Verbatim Recall: The Role of Text," in A. Ellis (ed.), *Psychology of Language* (Hillside, N.J.: Erlbaum, 1985), vol. 1, 207–35; D. Rubin, *Memory in Oral Traditions: The Cognitive Psychology of Epic, Ballads, and Counting-Out Rhymes* (New York: Oxford, 1995), 6–7.

212. The terminology is Greenstein's, from "Signs of Poetry Past."

213. O'Connor, *Hebrew Verse Structure*, 27–28.

214. See esp. Deuteronomy 32:46, where Moses explicitly references his oral "witnessing" in his saying the song (Deut 31:30; 32:44). And all legal witnessing was originally oral (cf. Josh 24:22; Niditch, *Oral World*, 90; Byrne, "Refuge of Scribalism," 15 and n. 63). Even once legal contracts and the like begin to be written down, they usually are simply evidentiary reports that themselves do not effect legal matters, e.g., the witnesses are listed in case their testimony needs retelling.

215. Moses's performance is staged in the narrative as the first, original performance (Deut 31:30; 32:44–45). The metaphorical imagery with regard to Deuteronomy 32 is all oral—speaking, placing in mouth/heart, in the hearing of, song, etc. Indeed, teaching/learning in traditional societies is chiefly an oral, face-to-face event, see esp. Deuteronomy 4:10; 5:1, 31; Isaiah 29:13; Jeremiah 9:19; 31:34; Psalms 34:12; 71:17–18; Proverbs 5:13; 2 Chronicles 17:9. Cf. Carr, *Tablet of the Heart*.

216. For the difficulties in 2 Samuel 1:18, see P. K. McCarter, *2 Samuel* (AB 9; New York: Doubleday, 1984), 67–68, 74.

217. *Formation*, 17.

218. *Formation*, 13.

219. "Memorial Transmission," 178.

220. A similar kind of interfacial relationship between orality and writing is attested in the many legal contracts preserved from different periods throughout the ancient Near East, where human witnesses for most of antiquity remained the traditional force of the law. By contrast, the written summaries of the legal proceedings, which typically include a list of witnesses, served as an aid to memory and by themselves did not effect law. At Elephantine one can begin to see glimpses of a change in this traditional manner of verification, as deictic references to the legal matters contained within the document become more frequent (e.g., *znh spr' 'nh 'nny ktbt lky hw yṣb* "this document which I Anani wrote for you is valid," *TAD* B3.11.16–17) and witnesses begin to sign their own names (e.g., *TAD* B3.10.23–26—as opposed to having the scribe write them out on their behalf).

221. So, too, for inscribed Old English poetry, see Pasternack, *Textuality of Old English Poetry*, 73.

222. For philological commentary on the passage, see C. L. Seow, *Job 1–21: Interpretation and Commentary* (Illuminations; Grand Rapids: Eerdmans, 2013), 877–80.

223. For example, on the cult of the dead, see K. van der Toorn, *Family Religion in Babylonia, Ugarit and Israel: Continuity and Changes in the Forms of Religious Life* (Leiden: Brill, 1996), 206–35.

224. For a general discussion of these lines, see W. L. Holladay, *Jeremiah 2* (Minneapolis: Fortress, 1986), 191–92.

225. Writing entails its own worries about preservation, namely that someone may "erase the name of Azatiwada" (*ymḥ šm 'ztwd*, KAI 26 A iii.13–14) and set their own name in its place (*wšt šm*, KAI 26 A iii.14) or that someone would "pull down the gate" itself (*wys' tš'r*, KAI 26 A iii.15) on which Azatiwada's fame is inscribed. And Jehoiakim thought to get rid of Jeremiah's words by burning the scroll on which they were written (Jer 36:22–23).

226. The text is not without its problems, see P. K. McCarter, *1 Samuel* (Anchor Bible 8; New York: Doubleday, 1980), 310–13. Exodus 15:20 casts Miriam's version of the Song of the Sea (only quoting the initial line in v. 21) in a related fashion—the difference between the imperfect of *šyr* in v. 1 (*'āšîrâ*) and the imperative in v. 21 (*šîrû*) may be one of those "good" oral variants.

227. 1 Chronicles 25:7 mentions "those who were taught songs to/for/of Yahweh" (*mĕlummĕdê-šîr l-yhwh*; cf. *miššîr ṣiuuôn*, Ps 137:3), though the nature of the learning and the songs is left unspecified.

228. The superscriptions in Psalms 38 and 79 label these songs (lit. *mizmôr* in 38:1) as *lĕhazkîr*, the significance of which is not entirely clear. However, since both are addressed to the deity, they are likely intended to invoke the deity, to make the deity remembered (*wyzkr. šm. [hdd. z]n*, KAI 214.16), or to cause the deity to remember the petition and/or petitioner (so frequently in the mortuary inscriptions from Palmyra and Hatra, albeit not often with the causative, see DNWSI 1, 323–28). In either case, the psalms so designated are thus editorially associated with causing a remembrance of some kind.

229. *Anglo-Saxon Oral Poetry*, 10.

230. *Anglo-Saxon Oral Poetry*, 10.

231. Esp. "Traditional Narrative," 32, 44.

232. "Oral Traditional Lyric Poetry," 39.

233. *Oral Style*, 125, 109. And: "in living matter, rhythm is the recurrence of the same physiological phenomena at biological equivalent intervals.... In man, it is necessarily biological: profound pulsations of life from which we cannot escape. Cessation means death" (232, n. 5).

234. *Orality and Literacy*, 34. The central importance of rhythmicity to oral tradition and oral performance is widely attested to by folklorists, oralists, and ethnographers generally, e.g., Havelock, *Preface to Plato*, 88–89, 91–93, 148–54, 160–67; F. H. Bäuml, "Varieties and Consequences of Medieval Literacy and Illiteracy," *Speculum: A Journal of Medieval Studies* 55 (1980), 248; Pasternack, *Textuality of Old English Poetry*, 60–89.

235. So Jousse remarks early on in *Oral Style*, "throughout this work I prefer to cite Jewish examples"—in this case the parenthetical comment comes by way of

introducing "the oral preaching" of Jeremiah (80). As for Jousse's influence on Parry, T. de Vet writes: "But the author who most convinced Parry, and who was later also revered by Albert Lord, his student and successor, is Marcel Jousse, a Jesuit priest who until 1950 held a chair in linguistic anthropology at the École d'anthropologie" ("Parry in Paris," 272). And A. B. Lord: "A work on oral style that was an early influence on Milman Parry and that he assigned me to read as a student was Marcel Jousse" (*Epic Singers and Oral Tradition* [Ithaca: Cornell University Press, 1991], 15, n. 1). See also E. R. Sienert, "Marcel Jousse: The Oral Style and the Anthropology of Gesture," *Oral Tradition* 5/1 (1990), 91: "Milman Parry…was [Jousse's] student in Paris."

236. *Oral Style*, 114.

237. *Oral Style*, 113.

238. *Oral Style*, 95.

239. And even when the syntax carries past line boundaries, the resulting enjambment is mild and always follows the larger contours of biblical Hebrew phrasal and sentential structure. This, too, is typical oral, oral-derived, and oralized or vocalized poetry.

240. *Oral Style*, 231.

241. So Gunkel on the prophets: "They were originally orators, as can be seen from the expression 'Hear!' with which their speeches begin. We must try and imagine their sayings being uttered orally" ("The Israelite Prophecy from the Time of Amos," in *Twentieth Century Theology in the Making* [ed. J. Pelikan; trans. R. Wilson; New York: Harper and Row, 1969], vol. 1, 69).

242. On biblical Hebrew *dābār* "word" as (aboriginally) signifying a distinctly oral utterance, see R. F. Person, "The Ancient Israelite Scribe as Performer," *JBL* 117/4 (1998), 604.

243. For some details and orientation to literature, see D. R. Hillers, "*Hôy* and *Hôy*-Oracles: A Neglected Syntactic Aspect," in C. Meyers and M. O'Connor (eds.), *The Word of the Lord Shall Go Forth: Essays in Honor of David Noel Freedman in Celebration of His Sixtieth Birthday* (Winona Lake, Ind.: Eisenbrauns, 1983), 185–88 (reprinted in Hillers, *Poets Before Homer*, 288–92).

244. For poetry's need to ever secure cognitive attention, see B. Boyd, *Why Lyrics Last: Evolution, Cognition, and Shakespeare's Sonnets* (Cambridge, Mass.: Harvard University Press, 2012), 36. Compare what Foley calls the "*Hwæt* paradigm" of the Anglo-Saxon poetic corpus, which consists of the interjection *hwæt* "lo!," a verb of aurality/orality, and a first person pronoun (singular or plural) and starts no fewer than nine poems (*Immanent Art*, 214–23). Cf. Bauman, *Verbal Art as Performance*, 21; Zumthor, *Oral Poetry*, 102–3; Doane, "Oral Texts," 77–78; Miller, *Oral Tradition*, 73.

245. I do not presume that these poems were necessarily encountered orally by the prose writers responsible for their inclusion (cf. 2 Sam 1:17–18), only that these traditional beginnings are ultimately rooted in oral tradition. Such tropes may always be maintained and continue in use in written verse. It is also worth

stressing that the ability to conceptualize the spatial and physical fixity or unity of a text as such, especially when the text is reduced to a phonemic string of language alone, is largely a product of writing itself (cf. Doane, "Oral Texts," 78; Zumthor, "Text and the Voice," 87). Therefore, perceived ambiguities about where so many prophetic oracles from the Bible begin and end, for example, may arise from our ignorance of the poetic oracle's larger informing performative context, the inherent fuzziness and fragmentary nature of orally performed verbal art, and/or the impoverished nature of the transcription, preserving mainly only the words of a poem, which may or may not have been crucial to defining a poetic utterance's larger shape.

246. Here even the written word of Yahweh must be first placed in the mouth—literally eaten—before the prophet can speak it.

247. The metaphor here is scribal in nature ("the pen of a ready scribe"), but the psalm itself is understood in terms of oral performance—heart, word, speaking, tongue.

248. Contrast the presumption of written law in Ezra 7:14 "which is in your hand" (*dî bîdāk*), i.e., presumably in a scroll of papyrus or leather.

249. Esp. Kawashima, *Death of the Rhapsode*, 49, 232–33, n. 41; T. Linafelt, "On Biblical Style," *St. John Review* 54/1 (2012), 38–39.

250. P. Machinist, "The Voice of the Historian in the Ancient Near East and Mediterranean World," *Interpretation* 57/2 (2003), 121, 126; S. Niditch, *Judges* (OTL; Louisville: Westminster John Knox, 2008), 9–10, 77–78; M. S. Smith, "What Is Prologue Is Past: Composing Israelite Identity in Judges 5," in J. J. Ahn and S. L. Cook (ed.), *Thus Says the Lord: Essays on the Former and Latter Prophets in Honor of Robert R. Wilson* (LHBOTS 502; London: T. and T. Clark, 2009), 43–58; *Poetic Heroes: The Literary Commemoration of Warriors and Warrior Culture in the Early Biblical World* (Grand Rapids: Eerdmans, 2014), 234–66.

251. So Linafelt appropriately figures this "I" as "a precursor of the modern 'lyric I'" ("On Biblical Style," 38). For the "I" of a singer specifically of tales at Ugarit, see especially CAT 1.23.1; 24.1; cf. 1.3.I.18–22—and for the "I" of the singer of songs at Ugarit, see *RIH* 98/02.2: *iḏmr šm* "let me sing the name..." (see D. Pardee, "Preliminary Presentation of a New Ugaritic Song to ʿAṯtartu (RIH 98/02)," in Younger, *Ugarit at Seventy-Five*, 27–39, esp, 30). In the Bible, perhaps the most widespread sign of such tellers of tales is the rise of free indirect discourse (and anonymous third person narration) in prose narratives, which is a consequence of and compensation for the absence of an actual storyteller who staged and guided the performance (the telling), both physically and vocally (for a striking analysis of the mechanics of the emergence of narrative *diegesis*, see Kittay and Godzich, *Emergence of Prose*, esp. 13–23, 49, 56, 116–17; Bäuml, "Varieties and Consequences," 250–53). The coincidence of writtenness and the emergence of anonymous third person narration as a means of successfully and efficiently negotiating a speaker-less signifying practice ungrounded in the nonverbal

figures prominently in Kawashima's explication of biblical narrative prose (*Death of the Rhapsode*, 9, 12–13, 72–73, 74; cf. Greenstein, "Biblical Prose Narrative," 349; Sanders, *Invention of Hebrew*, 161–62; T. Linafelt, "The Bible's Literary Merits," *Chronicle of Higher Education* 31 [April 10, 2009], B6).

252. Such stagings may be minimal, the scribe retaining the "I" that delivers what was told (see Schaefer, "Hearing from Books," 125; Bäuml, "Varieties and Consequences," 253, n. 43—"The development of the 'poetic I' [and its fictionality] ... is an automatic and inevitable consequence of the independent existence of the written text").

253. For the reasoning, see in particular, Schaefer, "Hearing from Books,"esp. 119, 124–25; cf. Bäuml, "Varieties and Consequences," 250–53; Pasternack, *Textuality of Old English Poetry*, 4, 13–14.

254. The fact of the song's singing is all that is made explicit (v. 1), but it has the character of some of the psalms that appear to assume a processual setting and group singing (e.g., Ps 24, 46, 48, 122), and of course the narrative presentation in 2 Samuel 6:5 imagines just such a situation, though the songs that would have been sung are not recorded.

255. Presumably the psalm is voiced by Asaph (and perhaps his relations, cf. v. 7). The explicit report of the the people's response in v. 36 would seem to implicate that the psalm itself was not communally recited.

256. The context in which the *mōšĕlîm* habitually perform is not stated, but I presume it would be in front of some group or another—the context in the other passages cited are explicitly stated, though in these cases the communal "we" is not used.

257. Schaefer, "Hearing from Books," 123.

258. Schaefer, "Hearing from Books," 123.

259. Cf. W. R. Johnson, *The Idea of Lyric: Lyric Modes in Ancient and Modern Poetry* (Berkeley: University of California Press, 1982), 177. The trick for contemporary readers is learning to appreciate the strong communal ethos that is now missing from many of our present-day Western societies but that infused ancient lyric verse without at the same time losing track of the also mostly assumed singularity of the human organism that lies behind first person phenomena (see A. Damasio, *The Feeling of What Happens* [San Diego: Harcourt, 1999], 3–31, esp. 12, 19)—the lyric-I in both of its ancient modalities gives compelling expression to these two lived-realities.

260. *Oral Formulaic Language*, vii.

261. *Oral Formulaic Language*, 31–101, 103.

262. Cf. J. M. Foley, "Word-Power, Performance, and Tradition," *Journal of American Folklore* 105 (1992), 279–80.

263. Lord, *Singer of Tales*, 68; cf. Watson, *Classic Hebrew Poetry*, 75, 81.

264. Culley, *Oral Formulaic Language*, 17–19, 100.

265. Culley, *Oral Formulaic Language*, 18.

266. Culley, *Oral Formulaic Language*, 100.
267. Lord's late "Oral Traditional Lyric Poetry" in fact makes the very same kind of move that Culley makes, i.e., applying the Parry-Lord paradigm (with all necessary adjustments, which Lord already anticipates in his *Semeia* contribution) to nonnarrative verse. In fact, Culley's original thesis becomes far more convincing when read in light of more recent ethnography with nonnarrative verse specifically in view, e.g., Pasternack, *Textuality of Old English Poetry*, 10–12, 113–19.
268. Culley, *Oral Formulaic Language*, 97.
269. Notopoulos, "Parataxis in Homer," 15; cf. Zumthor, *Oral Poetry*, 107; Watson, *Classical Hebrew Poetry*, 75, 81.
270. Culley, *Oral Formulaic Language*, 97.
271. *Interpreting the Psalms* (Philadelphia: Fortress, 1986), 60. The referential openness of oral verbal art is widely assumed, e.g., Schaefer, "Hearing from Books," 120, 135, n. 10.
272. Cf. Miller, *Interpreting the Psalms*, 22–23, 51.
273. Culley, *Oral Formulaic Language*, 113.
274. Not unlike what S. Mowinckel, for example, supposes for what he designates as "free prayer" (*The Psalms in Israel's Worship* [trans. D. R. Ap-Thomas; Nashville: Abingdon, 1962], II, 108), though he strictly distinguishes such prayers from the "learned psalmography" of the temple singers—the professionals.
275. *Anglo-Saxon Oral Poetry*, 19–21; cf. J. Opland, "Xhosa Poetry," in *PEPP* (Kindle ed.). The troubadour lyric tradition of medieval France is another broad-based (a possession of both high and low culture) lyric tradition, see S. Brewster, *Lyric* (New York: Routledge, 2009), 23. The *banjanje* or "healing charms" of Yugoslavia (in the 1970s) discussed by Foley ("Word-Power," 287–89) offer yet another (if more complicated) example. Such charms are performed only by postmenopausal women but were learned by the women in their home villages before the onset of puberty.
276. Esp. Miller, *Interpreting the Psalms*, 56–57, who uses Psalm 6 by way of illustrations, as a stand-in of sorts for the unrecorded lament.
277. Miller, *Interpreting the Psalms*, 70.
278. So esp. W. L. Holladay, "Indications of Jeremiah's Psalter," *JBL* 121 (2002), 245–61.
279. Esp. H. Gunkel and J. Begrich, *Introduction to Psalms: The Genres of the Religious Lyric of Israel* (trans. J. D. Nogalski; Macon: Mercer Universiy, 1998), 121.
280. On the question of historicity and the narrative portrayal of Jeremiah, see most recently, E. Silver, "The Prophet and the Lying Pen: Jeremiah's Poetic Challenge to the Deuteronomic School" (Ph.D. diss, University of Chicago, 2009), esp. 63–99 (focusing on Jer 36).
281. E.g., Mowinckel, *Psalms in Israel's Worship*, II, 91; cf. Niditch, *Oral World*, 122–23.

282. I do not doubt that (some) preexilic prophets could have the functional ability to write short, pragmatic documents (cf. van der Toorn, *Scribal Culture*, 179–82; Mowinckel is on point already by 1916: "If the prophets wrote at all, it was the short, mysterious oracle…such an inscription consisted of one or two words (Isa 8:1f.; 30:7f.)," in Knight, *Rediscovering the Traditions*, 169, n. 2; see Mowinckel, "Form, Tradition, and Literary Criticism," in Hanson, *Spirit and the Word*). But this is quite different from undertaking larger-scaled written assignments, which would have usually been left to trained scribes (if only for practical reasons, e.g., ready access to writing materials). Jeremiah 32:10 reads lit. "I wrote in the document" (*wāʾektōb bassēper*), which could mean that Jeremiah either (1) wrote out the sale document himself, (2) had someone else write out the document, or (3) signed his name along with the other witnesses (v. 12). The first scenario is unlikely. We have lots of legal material preserved from the ancient Near East and the southern Levant, and these documents are almost all the products of trained scribes. The verb *k-t-b* "to write" itself in biblical Hebrew (and in West Semitic more generally) has the broader sense "to have somebody write," given the restricted and function-oriented nature of literacy at the time. The story in Jeremiah 36 provides a good example. Yahweh instructs Jeremiah to write out his oracles (v. 2), and Jeremiah responds by dictating them to his scribe, Baruch (v. 4). No contradiction here. Jeremiah still bears responsibility for the oracles. From fifth-century Elephantine all the contracts are written by scribes, who usually explicitly take credit for the writing: "Haggai son of Shemiah wrote [*ktb*] this document in Elephantine at the fortress at the instruction [*bpm* lit. 'in/from the mouth of'] Anani son of Azariah, the servitor of YHW the God" (*TAD* B3.10.22–23). There is no question that Haggai b. Shemiah was the scribe and he wrote out the bequest on behalf of Anani b. Azariah. And yet the endorsement reads as follows: lit. "Document of a house which Anani son of Azariah the servitor wrote [*ktb*] for Jehoishma his daughter" (*TAD* B3.10.27). Clearly *ktb* in the endorsement means "to have written." So Jeremiah's comment in 32:10 might simply mean he had the contract drawn up on his behalf, just as at Elephantine. Or it could mean he wrote his name as one of the witnesses in the contract (so NRSV)—which the idiom certainly means in v. 12. The actual signatures of witnesses (as opposed to the scribe writing out the names) feature for the first time in West Semitic legal contracts at Elephantine (e.g., *TAD* B3.2.11–14). The practice may antedate the fifth century—signatures in Demotic are attested in the sixth century. As for Jeremiah 29:1–3, it only reports that Jeremiah "sent" a letter. This need not imply that he personally wrote the letter out. Further, reading is a practice that need not imply the practical ability to write as well, though in modern, literate societies the two practices are often combined. Which is to say, Jeremiah may have been able to read without also evidencing advanced writing skills (or having a reason to practice them if capable).

283. I am mindful that the collection itself as it has come down to us in writing was certainly the product of scribes—a "scribal artifact," as van der Toorn well observes (*Scribal Culture*, esp. 184–85, 188–204). So none of this need necessarily imply anything about an actual, historical Jeremiah. I have wanted to keep my focus on the narrative representation of Jeremiah, though assuming that that representation could date back as early as the late Judahite monarchy. Nonetheless, what few threads can be teased out of the text are entirely consistent with what might be reconstructed otherwise for the time period, namely: that preexilic prophets were predominantly speakers and not writers and thus the likelihood is that they would not have depended heavily on writing during composition.

284. S. Niditch's reading of Isaiah 1:2–31 ("The Composition of Isaiah 1," *Biblica* 61/4 [1980], 509–29) exemplifies just the kind of altered perception I have in mind. She cannot prove in any hard and fast way that the two utterances she identifies (Isa 1:2–3, 2–31; 4–20) originated as oral art. But her familiarity with oral verbal art allows her to deploy field-knowledge (e.g., form criticism) to other than (tacitly assumed) high modernist literary ends. For example, her intuition that the distinct blocks of material visible in Isaiah 1 are explainable other than by assuming multiple (written) authorship is on point. Traditional nonnarrative poems often operate in such blocks or chunks of wording that share patterns of sound, rhythm, syntax, and content with borders between these constituent "smaller pieces of content" often emphasized in some way (e.g., change in rhythm, syntax). The role of the prophet as performer would have been to guide the audience through the performance with verbal as well as nonverbal cues. Of course, texts containing only words can offer only a relatively impoverished version of an oral performance. What often looks jumbled and chaotic on the page would have been smoothed and made to cohere in person by the presence of the poet/prophet. Where Niditch succeeds in her reading of Isaiah 1 is in calling on the field to chasten its explicit literary reading practices with more awareness of traditional and oral modes of poetic production. For a rich study that analyzes such modes, see Pasternack, *Textuality of Old English Poetry*, esp. chs. 3–5.

285. E.g., Eissfeldt, *Old Testament*, 64–127; L. Alonso Schökel, *A Manual of Hebrew Poetics* (Subsidia biblica 11; Rome: Editrice Pontificio Istituto Biblico, 1988), 8–19.

286. I cite Ezekiel 18:2 because it specifically uses the term *māšāl* "proverb" (i.e., "a traditional saying, pithily or wittily expressed," *PEPP* [Kindle ed.) and is shaped as a poetic couplet: "The fathers eat sour grapes, / and the children's teeth are set on edge" (NIV; cf. Jer 31:29, NRSV). The latter is to be underscored, since it is sometimes assumed that the so obviously poetically shaped proverbs collected in the biblical book of Proverbs owe their shaping to writing and literacy. To be sure, the impulse to collect is an impulse born of writing and textuality

(van der Toorn, *Scribal Culture*, 118–19). But the poetic tradition in Israel and Judah was always distichic, and thus if that tradition is aboriginally an oral tradition (which is the central thesis of this chapter), then such shaping cannot *by itself* be taken to implicate writing and/or literacy (though written proverbs no doubt are also a part of the biblical collections). That is, proverbs are among the widest attested forms of oral verbal art in the world, and there is no reason not to assume that biblical proverbs are not also similarly rooted in orality. (R. Lowth, *De Sacra Poesi Hebraeorum Praelectiones Academicae Oxonii Habitae* [London: Clarendon, 1753, 3rd ed. (1775) now conveniently reprinted in *Robert Lowth (1710–1787): The Major Works* (ed. D. A. Reibel; London: Routledge, 1995)], 238, cites 1 Sam 24:14 [*mērĕšāʾîm yēṣē rešaʿ* "Out of the wicked comes wickedness"] as a one-line poetic proverb.)

287. Doane, "Oral Texts," 77.

288. E.g., Bauman, *Verbal Art as Performance*, 17; Zumthor, *Oral Poetry*, 108–9; Foley, *Oral Poem*, 85–86.

289. *Verbal Art as Performance*, 17.

290. D. A. Robertson, *Linguistic Evidence in Dating Early Poetry* (SBLDS 3; Missoula: Society of Biblical Literature, 1972). For a critique of the expansive claims in such studies, see now Smith, "Old Poetry," 197–205.

291. "Archaeological Contexts," in *Companion to Ancient Epic*, 136.

292. Smith (*Poetic Heroes*, 211–33, 267–83) and Miller (*Oral Tradition*, 83–93) adduce such "archaisms" in their identification of several of these "old poems" (e.g., Gen 49, Num 21 and 24, Judg 5, and 2 Sam 1:19–27) as traditional and orally derived. On the problem of dating oral traditional poetry, see Lord, "Oral Poetry," in *NPEPP*, 865.

293. E.g., Bauman, *Verbal Art as Performance*, 17–18; Finnegan, *Oral Poetry*, 112–16; Zumthor, *Oral Poetry*, 107; Foley, *Oral Poem*, 87–88.

294. *Verbal Art as Performance*, 17–18.

295. Boyd, *Why Lyrics Last*, 21–22; R. Jourdain, *Music, the Brain, and Ecstasy* (New York: Harper Perennial, 1997), 161–63, 171, 226–31.

296. "On Biblical Style," 36.

297. *Oral Poetry*, 106.

298. *Hebrew Poetics*, 17; T. Linafelt has been stressing this very fact more recently.

299. *Origins of the Modern Mind and Three Stages in the Evolution of Culture and Cognition* (Cambridge, Mass.: Harvard University Press, 1991), 214.

300. By "gross" I mean to signify my awareness that myth continues to flourish after the advent of writing, not least in the pre-Hellenistic Near East because literacy of all kinds was severely limited. In Donald's schema "theoretic culture" can arise only after writing and the invention of a technology for "external memory" (*Modern Mind*, 269–72).

301. Schaefer, "Hearing from Books," 124 (writing about formulaic expressions in Anglo-Saxon poetry); cf. Olson, "From Utterance to Text," 277.

302. Gentili, *Poetry and Its Public*, 3; cf. Herington, *Poetry into Drama*, 58–78; Nagy, "Lyric and Greek Myth," 19–51.

303. Gentili, *Poetry and Its Public*, 46.

304. As van der Toorn notices, "the primal form" of collection (or "compilation") "is that of the list" (*Scribal Culture*, 119), a genre J. Goody long ago connected with writing (*The Domestication of the Savage Mind* [Cambridge: Cambridge University Press, 1977], 74–111). The pattern of preservation of Neo-Assyrian prophecy texts, either on small, single oracle tablets or large multicolumn tablets containing multiple oracles, suggests "the recording of separate oracles preceded the composition of the collections" (van der Toorn, *Scribal Culture*, 178), which in turn spotlights the writtenness of collections from yet a different angle.

305. Kittay and Godzich, *Emergence of Prose*, 21—they use the the term "deixis" in its broadest sense of a pointing to what is outside the utterance. Cf. Doane, "Oral Texts," 86.

306. Doane, "Oral Texts," 86; and in detail, Kittay and Godzich, *Emergence of Prose*, 14–23, esp. 21–22.

307. Zumthor: "oral poetries, no matter where they come from, display a common ineptness at verbalizing descriptions" (*Oral Poetry*, 102).

308. Van der Toorn (*Scribal Culture*, 177) offers this general description of the typical "composite nature" of prophetic collections, which underscores the lack of *diegesis* and thus the presumption of a high degree of readerly preknowledge "manifesting itself in the juxtaposition, often without any apparent transition, of oracles about different subjects and from different periods. Interspersed between and among the oracles, moreover, are laments, prayers, eulogies, and more of the like, as a result of which most books give an impression of incoherence and disorder."

309. The wording of these bare speech introductions likely reflect the conventional formula used in the oral poetic narrative tradition in Israel and Judah, see Polak, "Epic Formulas," 448.

310. Doane, "Oral Texts," 86.

311. The thought that MT-Song as a written text is principally intended as a script in support of oral performance (i.e., a writing that "is just to be recited by the original or equivalent speaker, under functionally equivalent circumstances," Kittay and Godzich, *Emergence of Prose*, 22) is consonant with a number of other features of the Song with strong oral resonances (e.g., generic or impersonal nature of the speakers, echoic and repetitive phrasing, episodic structure) and might explain some of the Song's peculiarities as well (e.g., the reference in Song 6:4 to the old northern capital, Tirzah—the very kind of fossilized "archaism" that typifies traditional, oral verbal art, cf. Miller, *Oral Tradition*, 73–74; D. Pioske, *David's Jerusalem: Between Memory and History* [London: Routledge, 2015], esp. 43–46). That is, the Song of Songs, though as preserved (in MT) is a comparatively late textualization (Persian period at the

earliest in my opinion, cf. Dobbs-Allsopp, "Late Linguistic Features in the Song of Songs," in A. C. Hagedorn (ed.), *Perspectives on the Song of Songs—Perspektiven der Hoheliedauslegung* [BZAW; Berlin: de Gruyter, 2005], 27–77; for a contrasting point of view, see S. B. Noegel and G. Rendsburg, *Solomon's Vineyard: Literary and Linguistic Studies in the Song of Songs* [Atlanta: SBL, 2009]), may represent a tradition of oral love poetry in Israel and Judah that could date back to a much earlier period—certainly love songs were popular enough during the eighth century that Isaiah of Jerusalem could parody one (Isa 5:1–7). The narrativizing rubrics added in several LXX manuscripts of the Song (e.g., Alexandrinus, Sinaiticus, Venetus) would appear to be another instantiation of the need for explicit situatedness as writing moves away from its supporting role in live performance—LXX like all the other versions represents explicitly written acts of translation (see further in chapter 3 here).

312. Esp. Sanders, *Invention of Hebrew*, 113–22.

313. M. Weippert, "The Balaam Text from Deir ʿAllā and the Study of the Old Testament," in J. Hoftijzer and G. van der Kooij (eds.), *The Balaam Text from Deir ʿAllā Re-evaluated* (Leiden: Brill, 1991), esp. 177–78; Nissinen, "Spoken, Written, Quoted, and Invented," 249–50; van der Toorn, *Scribal Culture*, 175–76. For Assyrian prophetic collections from the time of Esarhaddon, see Nissinen, "Spoken, Written, Quoted, and Invented," 250–54.

314. Note the mixture of prose and poetry evident in both of the latter collections, which is reminiscent of many of the extended compositions found in the Bible (e.g., DtrH, with poetry embedded in larger blocks of narrative prose; Job, with narrative prose framing the poetic dialogues; Jeremiah, with prose and poetry interspersed throughout).

315. See Eissfeldt, *Old Testament*, 132–33; M. Haran, "The Book of the Chronicles 'of the Kings of Judah' and 'of the Kings of Israel': What Sort of Books Were They?," *VT* 49 (1999), 159–60; Schniedewind, *How the Bible Became a Book*, 52–54. As Schniedewind suggests (53), Hebrew *sēper hayyāšār* could well reference the contents of the scroll, namely, songs (cf. 1 Kgs 8:53 [LXX]; Haran, "The Book of Chronicles," 159, n. 5). Van der Toorn (*Scribal Culture*, 173–75) raises the possibility that the apparent citations from Micah in 1 Kings 22:28 (= Mic 1:1) and Jer 26:18 (= Mic 3:12) presume the prior existence of a scroll of Micah oracles.

J. J. M. Roberts sees in Isa 8:1–4 a reference to another collection of biblical poems: "I think the reference is to a small scroll that was sealed (vss. 16–18) with the identifying tag on the outside "with reference to Maher-shalal-hosh-baz." The internal contents of the scroll were witnessed by Uriah the priest and Zechariah the son of Berechiah, and I think those contents included Isaiah's oracles about Shear-yashub, Immanuel, and the last child, Maher-shalal-hosh-baz. The purpose of the witnessed and sealed scroll was to prove to later doubters what Isaiah had said to Ahaz and his court during the early stages of the

Syro-Ephraimitic crisis, just as the later writing (Isa 30:8), done at the beginning of Hezekiah's revolt against Sennacherib, was to prove the same to the
court of Hezekiah." (Email, April 23, 2013; see in detail in Roberts's forth-
coming commentary on Isaiah 1–39 in the Hermeneia series). By "a small
scroll" Roberts means "in contrast to a scroll the size of the big Isaiah scroll."
He continues, "If it contained all the oracles concerning Isaiah's three children,
it would certainly be larger than a normal business contract or loan contract,
which is what I think the text is comparing it to. In that sense, it would be a
large scroll, i.e., large for a business contract scroll" (email, April 23, 2013).

316. For details, see P. W. Flint, *The Dead Sea Psalms Scrolls and the Book of Psalms*
(Leiden: Brill, 1997).

317. Chronicles itself would appear to reference psalms and laments or dirges
(2 Chron 29:30; 35:25).

318. See in particular the opening thoughts of Greenstein on this text in his "Signs
of Poetry Past"; cf. P. K. McCarter, "Kuntlllet 'Ajrud," in *COS*, II, 173. For tran-
scrlptions, translations, and general discussions, see now esp. the editio princeps: S. Ahituv, E. Eshel, and Z. Meshel, "The Inscriptions," in Z. Meshel (ed.),
Kuntillet 'Ajrud (Ḥorvat Teman) (Jerusalem: IES, 2012), 73–142; cf. Z. Meshel,
*Kuntlllet Ajrud: A Religious Center from the Time of the Judaean Monarchy on the
Border of Sinai* (Jerusalem: Israel Museum, 1978); McCarter, "Kuntlllet 'Ajrud,"
173; Dobbs-Allsopp et al., *Hebrew Inscriptions*, 286–89; S. Ahltuv, *Echoes fiom
the Past: Hebrew and Cognate Inscriptions from the Blbhcal Period* (Jerusalem:
Carta, 2008], 324–29. Sanders (*Invention of Hebrew*, 142) captures well the potential historical significance of this kind of display inscription: "The genres of
cosmic battle hymns and apocalyptic revelations known from the archaic religious poetry of the Hebrew Bible find their first physical setting in public display on the walls of shrines, located on Iron Age pilgrimage routes."

319. Van der Toorn, *Scribal Culture*, 178.

320. E. Kraeling (ed.), *The Brooklyn Museum Aramaic Papyri* (New Haven: Yale University Press, 1953).

321. For a convenient collection of these materials, see N. Avigad and B. Sass,
Corpus of West Semitic Stamp Seals (Jerusalem: Israel Academy of Sciences and
Humanities, 1997). Obviously the seals and bullae alone say nothing about the
content of the scrolls they once sealed.

322. *l-yhwh* mimes the most common kind of written artifact found in the southern
Levant, an ownership marker or tag—*l* "belonging to" + PN (the tattooing of
slaves with such ownership markers is attested at Elephantine).

323. The list is a quintessential written genre, see Goody, *Domestication*, 74–111; cf.
Niditch, *Oral World*, 94.

324. The psalmist uses *maʿăśay* lit. "my works" (v. 2) to describe the content of this
vocal performance, which connotes embodied activity, potentially inclusive of
writing, although the vocabulary of writing is strikingly absent here, even with

an obvious awareness of its practice (cf. Nagy's comments on Gk. *poiein* "to make" in relation to poetic composition in archaic Greece in "Lyric and Greek Myth," 23).

325. The concept of the "performing scribe" is developed in Doane, "Ethnography of Scribal Writing," 420–39; "Oral Texts," 83–87. The language quoted comes from "Ethnography of Scribal Writing," 423, 430. Cf. Person, "Israelite Scribe," 601–9; van der Toorn, *Scribal Culture*, 14, 272, n. 24; Doan and Giles, *Prophets, Performance, and Power*, 30–33. See Bar-Rakib's scribe on *KAI* 218 (ca. 730 BCE).

326. Ong, *Orality and Literacy*, 91: "It represents sound itself as a thing, transforming the evanescent world of sound to the quiescent, quasi-permanent world of space." (Ong is commenting here specifically on alphabetic writing, but the insight holds for all writing systems.)

327. W. J. Ong, "Writing Is a Technology That Restructures Thought," in G. Bauman (ed.), *The Written Word: Literacy in Transition* (Oxford: Clarendon, 1986), 31.

328. Scholars have long appreciated that these particles are characteristic of prose and generally lacking in biblical poetry. For statistical data, see F. I. Andersen and A. D. Forbes, " 'Prose Particle' Counts of the Hebrew Bible," in Meyers and O'Connor, *The Word of the Lord Shall Go Forth*, 165–83.

329. Andersen and Forbes, "'Prose Particle' Counts," 166.

330. Cf. Gunkel and Begrich, *Introduction to Psalms*, 128.

331. The "old" Hebrew script is traditionally presumed to have derived from Phoenician. Recent finds, such as the Tel Zayit abecedary and the Qeiyafa ostracon, however, have stimulated renewed interest in the question, and may eventually require a more complex understanding of script evolution in the Levant during the Iron Age. For details on the acrostic, see F. W. Dobbs-Allsopp, "Acrostic," in H.-J. Klauck et al. (eds.), *The Encyclopedia of the Bible and Its Reception* (Berlin: de Gruyter, 2009).

332. Acrostics in other literary traditions, including in the postbiblical Hebrew tradition (cf. T. Carmi, *The Penguin Book of Hebrew Verse* [New York: Penguin, 1981], 61), frequently spell out names or entire sentences (e.g., from the *Babylonian Theodicy*: "I, Saggilkinamubbib, am adorant of god and king," B. R. Foster, *Before the Muses: An Anthology of Akkadian Literature* [2 vols.; Bethesda: CDL Press, 1993], 806), making the trope's presumption of readerly reception even more patent. But even here the range of imagined readers had to be severely circumscribed—limited to the scribal elite. It would have been extremely difficult for the uninitiated reader to discern the presence of the acrostic in the running format of 4QLam^a. And this is not to discount the possibility of vocally performing an acrostic poem. Indeed, if these poems had any kind of circulation beyond the scribal elite they would have had to be vocalized, read aloud. Such peformances would have required the reader/performer to indicate the presence of the acrostic in some extratextual manner (e.g., "this is the *aleph* stanza," "*bet*," "each stanza of the song begins with a new letter of the alphabet").

333. *Scribal Culture*, 115–16.

334. Olson, "From Utterance to Text," 264.

335. See P. D. Miller, *They Cried to the LORD: The Form and Theology of Biblical Prayer* (Minneapolis: Fortress, 1994), 199–201.

336. Cf. Niditch, *Oral World*, 94.

337. For the emendation *šĕlōšîm* "thirty," see M. V. Fox, *Proverbs 10–31* (AB 18B; New Haven: Yale University Press, 2009), 710–12.

338. Cf. Seow, *Job 1–21*, 822.

339. Lord, *Singer of Tales*, 124–28; Doane, "Oral Texts," 80; Amodio, *Writing the Oral Tradition*, 23–27; J. D. Niles, *Homo Narrans: The Poetics and Anthropology of Oral Literature* (Philadelphia: University of Pennsylvania, 2010), 89–119; Hillers and McCall, "Homeric Dictated Texts," 19–23; Watson, *Classical Hebrew Poetry*, 70; Niditch, *Oral World*, 94–95, 117–20. As Ong remarks, "longstanding oral mental habits of thinking through one's thoughts aloud encourages dictation" (*Orality and Literacy*, 95).

340. Hillers and Marsh ("Homeric Dictated Texts," 23) early on call attention to the value of this text when thinking through the Parry-Lord model of oral poetry.

341. The use of a different preposition (*k-* "like, according to") in the Aramaic version of the idiom (*ktb* + *kpm* lit. "to write according to the mouth") well attested only a century or so later from Elephantine perhaps more clearly emphasizes this intent, namely "to write according to the instruction of PN" (*DNWSI*, I, 543–45; II, 917). And in any case, the scribal contributions to these legal summaries (e.g., technical phrasing, special formulae) are more readily acknowledged.

342. Doane, "Ethnography of Scribal Writing," 431.

343. "Oral Texts," 83–84.

344. *Scribal Culture*, 112–13.

345. For his treatment of Jeremiah, see *Scribal Culture*, 171–203, and see also 109–41 on modes of textual production in ancient Israel and Judah more generally, on which I draw in the following discussion. Mowinckel is an early predecessor on this theme: "Here it is of the greatest importance to note that the prophetic books are not written by the prophet in question himself. They therefore have nothing whatsoever to do with autobiography or memoirs or pages from a diary. The prophets did not write; they talked" (as given in Knight, *Rediscovering the Traditions*, 169, n. 2).

346. Cf. Niditch, *Oral World*, 127–29.

347. So originally, A. Erman, "Eine ägyptische Quelle der 'Spruch Salomos,'" *SPAW* 15 (1924), 86–93; see Fox, *Proverbs 10–31*, 753–56. The process of creating, translating, collecting, and editing was likely complex (Fox, *Proverbs 10–31*, 756–62, 764–65) and may have involved mediation through Aramaic (there are a hgih frequency of Aramaic loanwords in this section of Proverbs), whether in the seventh century (Fox, *Proverbs 10–31*, 764) or the Persian period (Erman, "Eine ägyptische Quelle," 92).

348. The case is complicated, as oral interferences are likely, and mostly circumstantial—Chronicles is a prose composition, itself a genre of writing; as a composition it clearly draws on and uses (identifiable) written sources (e.g., Samuel-Kings); the piecing together of a composition so precisely from three separate and known psalms is itself suggestive of scribal (and not oral performative) activity; and it seems likely that there would have been multiple Psalms scrolls available to the Chronicler, and perhaps even one in which the psalms being drawn on (Ps 105, 96, 106) were contiguous (being mindful both of the constraints of scroll technology, e.g., difficulty of search and find, and the empirical fluidity of this part of the Psalter at Qumran).

349. *Scribal Culture*, 193–94—importantly van der Toorn allows for a complicated situation in which memory and orality mix with and effect the manipulation of the written tradition.

350. *Proverbs 10–31*, 767–69. Certainly, Aramaic becomes the lingua franca of the Near East during the first millennium, and likely would have been known by scribal elites in Judah even before the sacking of Jerusalem (e.g., 2 Kgs 18:26–27—see Vanderhooft ("Scribes and Scripts," 534–38; see Schniedewind, *Social History of Hebrew*, 130–31) on the use of the lapidary Aramaic script on official seals already in the sixth century and the Elephantine corpus (which preserves the oldest extant version of Ahiqar) explicitly shows Jews using Aramaic by the fifth century.

351. Cf. D. Charpin, *Reading and Writing in Babylon* (trans. J. M. Todd; Cambridge, Mass.: Harvard University Press, 2010), 37.

352. *Scribal Culture*, 147.

353. Esp. M. Haran, "Book-Scrolls in Israel in Pre-exilic Times," *JJS* 33 (1982), 161–73, and "More Concerning Book-Scrolls in Pre-exilic Times," *JJS* 35 (1984), 84–85. Both van der Toorn (*Scribal Culture*, esp. 145–48) and Carr (*Formation*, 145), among recent scholars, have emphasized the strong likelihood that the number of text editions extant at any one time would have been limited. This understanding of a distinctly limited notion of text productivity in the regions of Israel and Judah prior to the Hellenistic period contrasts starkly with basic working assumptions of most biblical scholars, who tacitly assume norms of modern (print-based) text production, or even that generated by scribal schools of ancient, large-scale polities like Babylon, Assyria, or Egypt, and has many potential consequences. For example, text criticism as traditionally conceived in biblical studies only becomes practicable with the kind of text production witnessed at Qumran. When conceiving of putative texts that originate prior to this time, operative notions of text editing will require some substantive reformulation, see esp. Doane, "Oral Texts," 75–113.

354. *Scribal Culture*, 115.

355. *Ugaritic Texts*, 47–48. Cf. Watson, *Classical Hebrew Poetry*, 70; Doane, "Oral Texts," 79–80; Amodio, *Writing the Oral Tradition*, 23–30.

356. Esp. Amodio, *Writing the Oral Tradition*, 46–53. G. S. Kirk emphasizes the idea of "creativity" with respect to the singers of Homeric epic verse in light of the depictions of Phemius and Demodocus in the *Odyssey* (*Homer and the Oral Tradition* [Cambridge: Cambridge University Press, 1976], 125).

357. The written composition of documentary texts (e.g., lists) is certainly attested (Niditch, *Oral World*, 94), and narrative prose by definition is composed in writing.

358. See Finnegan, *Oral Poetry*, 52–88—the variability of these modes is to be stressed.

359. *Poetry into Drama*, 47; cf. van der Toorn, *Scribal Culture*, 22; D. Redford, "Scribe and Speaker," in E. B. Zvi and M. H. Floyd (eds.), *Writing and Speech in Israelite and Ancient Near Eastern Prophecy* (Atlanta: SBL, 2000), 205.

360. "From Utterance to Text," 264. Olson writes the following specifically about the Bible: "In turn, it was recognized that large sections of the Bible possessed a similar oral structure. The books of Moses and the Prophets, for example, are recorded versions of statements that were shaped through oral methods as part of an oral culture" (263; cf. Ong, *Orality and Literacy*, 99).

361. Ong, *Orality and Literacy*, 105; "Writing Is a Technology," 36–45.

362. Esp. Bäuml, "Varieties and Consequences," 249–53. Kawashima (*Death of the Rhapsode*, 11) appreciates well the difference that separation and distance create in the act of writing (biblical) prose, namely, "the simple fact that writing allows an author to edit, to rewrite, whereas speech exists instantaneously and irrevocably in the act of utterance. The ability to manipulate language and... narrative forms gives rise in written narrative to techniques foreign to the traditional, improvisational art of [oral] epic, techniques premised on the impulse to innovate." Kawashima, like Alter and others, rightly places biblical narrative prose on a trajectory of art that leads ultimately to modern novelistic fiction. But differences remain not least because the materiality of writing at the time—ink on papyrus or leather for this kind of verbal art (Deir ʿAlla [fig. 24] offers a gorgeous snapshot of just the kind of papyrus scroll that would have been used; see Haran, "Book-Scrolls," 111–22; R. L. Hicks, "*Delet* and *Megillah*: A Fresh Approach to Jeremiah XXXVI," *VT* 33 [1983], 46–66)—was likely not inexpensive (e.g., the Ahiqar manuscript from Elephantine is written on a palimpsest) nor very easy to manipulate (esp. M. T. Clanchy, "The Technology of Writing," in *From Memory to Written Record: England 1066–1307* [2d ed.; Oxford: Blackwell, 1993], 114–44; cf. van der Toorn, *Scribal Culture*, 9–49). Drafting and revision could certainly take place. Two drafts of the Jerusalem letter have survived at Elephantine (*TAD* A 4.7, 8 = Cowley 30, 31), and presumably yet a third must have been actually sent. But this was likely not normative. The legal summaries from Elephantine reveal the lengths to which scribes would go in order *not* to rewrite—erasures, marginal and interlinear additions, pasted on addenda, etc.

363. Kawashima, *Death of the Rhapsode*, 11.

364. Van der Toorn, *Scribal Culture*, 115. The grandson, of course, presents Ben Sira in the prologue to his Greek translation explicitly as a "writer" (*autos suggrapsai*) of proverbs, instructions, and other didactic poetry.

365. Olson, "From Utterance to Text," 263.

366. Ong, *Orality and Literacy*, 99.

367. Cf. Watson, *Classical Hebrew Poetry*, esp. 69, n. 13; Niditch, *Oral World*, 120. Indeed, a continuity in style is to be anticipated if the scribe responsible for such a written poem was the "special kind of speaking performer" that Doane supposes for Anglo-Saxon England, since such written productions need not add anything new to the piece of verbal art (a "fresh event" made out of "traditional material") beyond the writing itself (see Doane, "Ethnography of Scribal Writing," 421; "Oral Texts," 83–84).

368. *The Deuteronomic History and the Books of Chronicles: Scribal Works in an Oral World* (Atlanta: SBL, 2010), 50—though as noted traditional performers (scribes or otherwise) surely could be creative and inventive but still not in ways we commonly associate with high literacy, namely "literary geniuses."

369. The vast majority of oral literature produced throughout history, of course, has simply vanished, see Foley, *Oral Poem*.

370. Naveh, *Early History*, 65–66; C. A. Rollston, *Writing and Literacy in the World of Ancient Israel* (Atlanta: SBL, 2010), 42–44.

371. The transition from early (and highly variable) alphabetic writing to the (more stable) linear alphabetic script(s) used eventually to write Phoenician, Hebrew, and Aramaic, for example, occurs over the course of Iron I (see esp. Hamilton, "Reconceptualizing," 39–50)—the stabilization of the inscribed arrowhead sequence in the mid-eleventh century BCE has traditionally been focalized and emphasized (esp. F. M. Cross, "The Origin and Early Evolution of the Alphabet," *Eretz Israel* 8 [1967], 8*–24*; *Leaves from an Epigrapher's Notebook: Collected Papers in Hebrew and West Semitic Paleography and Epigraphy* [Winona Lake, Ind.: Eisenbrauns, 2003], esp. 200–203; Naveh, *Early History*, 42). Cross devised the term "Early Linear Phoenician" to reference the stabilized script of the arrowheads that was also "used broadly in Syria-Palestine" (*Leaves*, 226) chiefly in deference to the later Byblian sequence (so Hamilton, "Reconceptualizing," 42). There is an oddity (even an "anachronism") to privileging "Phoenician" as an identifier before the Phoenician script resolves itself as such, especially given the general dearth of early alphabetic epigraphs from Late Bronze/Iron I contexts on the coast (e.g., McCarter emphasizes that many of the arrowheads themselves likely come from the Beqaʿ, "Paleographic Notes," 47 and n. 3) and given that a number of important diagnostic indicators (e.g., single-direction writing, reduction in number of alphabetic signs) need not be tied directly to Phoenician scribalism (alone). For convenience I use the traditional chronology of Albright (and others) for periodizing the Iron Age, i.e.,

Iron IIA = 1000–925 BCE (the lower date is the traditional date for Sheshonq I's raid into the Levant; now 918 or 917 BCE). I recognize that the debates over chronology that have ensued over the last several decades (for an overview, see A. Mazar, "The Debate over the Chronology of the Iron Age in the Southern Levant," in *The Bible and Radiocarbon Dating: Archaeology, Text and Science* [London: Equinox, 2005], 15–42) have consequences. But consideration of writing and writing practices in Israel and Judah during the first half of the first millennium BCE does not change appreciably (if at all) according to the different chronological schemes.

372. For details and general descriptions of early alphabetic writing (with references to earlier literature), see esp. G. J. Hamilton, "W. F. Albright and Early Alphabetic Epigraphy," *NEA* 65 (2002) 35–42; *The Origins of the West Semitic Alphabet in Egyptian Scripts* (CBQM 40;Washington, D.C.: CBA, 2006); "Reconceptualizing"; J. C. Darnell, F. W. Dobbs-Allsopp, M. Lundberg, P. K. McCarter, and B. Zuckerman, *Two Early Alphabetic Inscriptions from the Wadi el-Ḥôl* (AASOR 59.2; Boston: ASOR, 2005); F. W. Dobbs-Allsopp, "Asia, Ancient Southwest: Scripts, Earliest," in K. Brown (ed.), *Encyclopedia of Language and Linguistics* (2d ed.; Oxford: Elsevier, 2006), I, 495–500.

373. For a broad overview of this corpus, see esp. W. Horowitz, T. Oshima, and S. L. Sanders, *Cuneiform in Canaan: Cuneiform Sources from the Land of Israel in Ancient Times* (Jerusalem: IES, 2006).

374. *Invention of Hebrew*, 76.

375. *Invention of Hebrew*, 83; see K. van der Toorn, "Cuneiform Documents from Syria-Palestine: Texts, Scribes, and Schools," *ZDPV* 116 (2000), 108; Byrne, "Refuge of Scribalism," 15, n. 16. As Sanders remarks, the sole bit of literature found in Canaan/Palestine from the period, a fragment from Tablet VII of Gilgamesh found at Megiddo, "is telling in its isolation" (85)—and in its nonnativeness!

376. "Refuge of Scribalism," 22; cf. 17–22; S. L. Sanders, "Writing and Early Iron Age Israel: Before National Scripts, Beyond Nations and States," in Tappy and McCarter, *Literate Culture and Tenth-Century Canaan*, 97–112. Indeed, Byrne's principal thesis is that the linear alphabet survives into the Iron Age precisely because of its "irrelevance," as a craft industry—"i.e., its relevance to those who could afford the *luxury*" (23). Or as Sanders summarizes: "The [linear] alphabet during the Late Bronze Age was a local craft technique that acquired increasing prestige during the retrenchment of the Egyptian empire and the collapse of the major city-states. Indeed, for the writers of the alphabet, a low-budget and multimedia technology, there may have been no collapse, since it was tied to a local, less differentiated social structure that was far less vulnerable. It was only for Babylonian users that the transition between the Late Bronze and early Iron Ages was a 'dark age'" (*Invention of Hebrew*, 101). Byrne's focus is on the "dark age" of Iron I, but the scope of his essay is broader still, inclusive of considerations germane to the Late Bronze and Iron IIA peri-

ods as well. In particular, it is important to note that on Byrne's analysis the use
of alphabetic writing in the southern Levant during Iron IIA continues the
patterns of use noted for Iron I. So, too, N. Na'aman, "Sources and Composition in the History of David," in *Ancient Israelite History and Historiography*,
23–37, esp. 23–25: "Writing in the tenth-ninth centuries BCE must have been
confined to a small group of scribes in the court of Jerusalem and was mainly
used for administration and for diplomatic exchange" (25).

377. For inventories of these inscriptions, see G. Hamilton, "The Development of
the Early Alphabet" (Ph. D. diss., Harvard University, 1985), 213–89, 311–38;
"Reconceptualizing," 34–50; E. Puech, "Origine de l'alphabet," *RB* 93 (1986),
161–213; B. Sass, *The Genesis of the Alphabet and Its Development in the Second
Millennium B.C.* (AAT 13; Wiesbaden: Harrassowitz, 1988), 53–105; Cross,
Leaves, 213–30; Byrne, "Refuge of Scribalism," 17–22.

378. *Ugaritic Texts*, 48; cf. W. H. van Soldt, "Babylonian Lexical, Religious and Literary Texts and Scribal Education at Ugarit and Its Implications for the Alphabetic Literary Texts," in M. Dierich and O. Loretz (eds.), *Ugarit: Ein ostmediterranes
Kulturzentrum in Alten Orient* (Muenster: Ugarit-Verlag, 1995), 186–87. Pardee
construes the fragmentary colophon of RS 92.2016 (ll. 40'–43') as identifying
Ilimilku as an oral poet writing down the mythological stories for the first time.
Here is Pardee's transliteration and translation (47):

[*spr. ilmlk. š*]*bny. lmd. atn. prln*	[The scribe: Ilimilk the Shu] banite, disciple of Attenu the diviner.
[ ]*r. b b* [ ]. *w. mspr. hnd. hwm*	[ ] and this recitation, it
[ ] *rbh. wind ylmdnn*	[ ] and no one ever taught him (it)/ taught it (to him).
[ ]*b spr*	[ ] document.

The more common assumption in the field is that some amount of copying
will have likely preceded the written versions of the narrative poems preserved
from ancient Ugarit (e.g., Parker, *Pre-biblical Narrative*, 1; cf. S. Segert, "Die
Schreibfehler in den ugaritischen literarischen Keilschrifttexten in Anschluss
an das textkritische Hilfsbuch von Friedrich Delitzsch klassifiziert," in *Von
Ugarit nach Qumran: Beiträge zur alttestamentlichen und altorientalischen Forschung* [BZAW 77; ed. J. Hempel and L. Rost; Berlin: Töpelmann, 1958], 193–212).
Such analyses generally tacitly assume models of text production predicated on
large-scale bureaucratic societies (e.g., Babylon, Egypt), as well as a text-
centered orientation to text criticism and editing more generally. Whether or
not Pardee's position proves compelling in the long run (cf. E. L. Greenstein,
review of D. Pardee, *The Ugaritic Texts and the Origins of West Semitic Literary*

Composition, BASOR 371 [2014], 216–17), at a minimum, conventional assumptions about alphabetic text production at Ugarit will require rethinking in light of much more sophisticated understandings of the complex interplay that may obtain between textuality, literacy, and orality in highly traditional and primarily oral cultures (e.g., J. M. Hutton, review of D. Pardee, *The Ugaritic Texts and the Origins of West Semitic Literary Composition: The Schweich Lectures of the British Academy 2007*, *RBL* (August 2014); R. F. Person, *The Deuteronomic School: History, Social Setting, and Literature* [Leiden: Brill, 2002]). The situation at Ugarit will also be complicated by interference from syllabic cuneiform textuality, literacy, and scribalism, which of course will have inspired the very invention of alphabetic cuneiform and the writing down of the indigenous tradition.

379. M. S. Smith and W. T. Pitard, *The Ugaritic Baal Cycle*, vol. 2 (Leiden: Brill, 2009), 572–74.

380. *Poetry into Drama*, 45. The characteristic use of word dividers in alphabetic cuneiform, as also in the later "old Hebrew" script, is to be noted, since they are among the few metascript conventions that appear in these texts and they specifically, graphically distinguish "words." That is, they do quite literally what Herington supposes of early Greek song texts, they preserve the "words" of the poems—recall any oral performance of poetry would have involved much, much more than just the words of the poem (e.g., music, dance, gestures of all kinds, poetic ad-libs, audience participation). It is noteworthy that sometimes in the Bible it is precisely the "words" of a song or oracle that are said to be recited or written down (e.g., Deut 31:30; 2 Sam 22:1; Jer 36:2, 4; Ezek 33:32; Ps 137:3; Job 19:23).

381. The reduction to twenty-two graphemes may suggest derivation from the main alphabetic cuneiform script used at Ugarit "for the purpose of writing Phoenician" (D. Pardee, "Ugaritic Alphabetic Cuneiform in the Context of Other Alphabetic Systems," in C. L. Miller (ed.), *Studies in Semitic and Afroasiatic Linguistics Presented to Gene B. Gragg* [Chicago: University of Chicago Press, 2007], 185)—the jar-handle inscription from Sarepta (written left to right with the shorter alphabet) appears to be in Phoenician (note especially the use of the verb *p'l* "to make," see E. L. Greenstein, "A Phoenician Inscription in Ugaritic Script?," *JANES* 8 [1976], 49–57). As Pardee further notices, this could mean "that the consonantal phonetic inventory of Phoenician had already been reduced to twenty-two by the end of the Late Bronze Age" ("Ugaritic Alphabetic Cuneiform," 185). This is potentially an important benchmark for understanding the development of the linear alphabet, since all currently extant Iron I and later alphabetic inscriptions from the southern Levant exhibit the reduced sign inventory (even when they do not necessarily descend from Phoenician scribalism, e.g., Izbet Sartah sherd). That is, it appears that one (more) casualty of the Late Bronze cultural collapse was the larger alphabetic sign in-

ventories exhibited in early alphabetic inscriptions for much of the second millennium.

382. "What Was the Alphabet For?," 47; cf. *Invention of Hebrew*, 36–58.

383. There are allusions in eighteenth-century BCE Mari texts to scenes now preserved in the Ugaritic Baal Cycle, see Pardee, *Ugaritic Texts*, 26; Cf. van Soldt, "Babylonian Lexical," 187.

384. Esp. Schniedewind, *How the Bible Became a Book*, 61; cf. Parker, *Stories*, 8–9, 145, n. 15. It is perhaps worth noting that a significant downturn in climate (drought) occurred throughout the Levant (and Western Asia generally) roughly thirty-two hundred years ago (ca. 1200 BCE) and lasted for a prolonged period (ca. three hundred years or roughly till about 850 BCE), with cataclysmic consequences for societies in the region—this was the time of the general collapse of Late Bronze civilizations (such as that of ancient Ugarit; see most recently, D. Kaniewski et al., "Environmental Roots of the Late Bronze Age Crisis," *PLoS ONE* 8/8 (2013): e71004, http://journals.plos.org/plosone/article?id=10.1371/journal.pone.0071004 accessed February 13, 2015; D. Langgut, "Climate Changes during the Bronze and Iron Ages: Results of Palynological Studies in the Sea of Galilee and the Dead Sea," paper presented at annual meeting of the SBL, November 23, 2013; A. S. Issar and M. Zohar, *Climate Change: Environment and History of the Near East* [2d ed.; Berlin: Springer, 2007]; E. H. Cline, *1177 BC: The Year Civilization Collapsed* [Princeton University Press, 2014]). I do not mean to ascribe direct and facile correlations between climate change and scribal activity, but only to note that all presumptions about writing during the period will need to contend with the potential impact(s) of a severely degraded climate (among other pertinent social-historical factors), the evidence for which may in part inhere precisely in the lack of writing (or its survival on the margins in a "low-budget" form).

385. Doane makes an analogous point about the paucity of manuscript evidence for Anglo-Saxon poetry: "The facts of preservation suggest that Old English poetic texts never did exist in any great numbers, and for good reason—their natural mode of existence was in orality, with the result that they only got written down in rare and unusual (if now mostly irrecoverable) circumstances" ("Ethnography of Scribal Writing, " 425).

386. See Zumthor, "Text and the Voice," 67.

387. Cf. Cross, *Canaanite Myth and Hebrew Epic*, 112–13.

388. None of what the Bible holds in common with the local, religious, alphabetic literature of Ugarit requires writing to account for the commonality, though (ironically) the accident of writing (in both instances) is what has allowed generations of scholars to reveal this commonality. Obviously the medium (clay tablets) and script (alphabetic cuneiform) do not continue to be used for alphabetic writing in the Iron Age—the abrupt downturn in climate and its devastating impact on the Levant in particular is surely germane to any larger appreciation

of this fact (similarly, Linear B and Hittite cuneiform fail to survive the Late Bronze culture collapse). And neither running format (likely traceable ultimately to Egyptian models) nor word division (perhaps indigenous to the writing of West Semitic languages, but in any event antedating Ugarit, e.g., Nagila Sherd, Sinai 527, Grossman Seal, Sinai 363), both typical of Iron Age scribal practice for writing verse, requires mediation through Ugarit.

389. By way of comparison, A. Ford ("From Letters to Literature: Reading the 'Song Culture' of Classical Greece," in Yunis, *Written Texts*, 20), for example, presumes that some Greek songs must have been written down as early as their earliest singers, presumably to preserve the words (the melodies would have been transmitted orally since a written notation system for music only evolved later), otherwise it is hard to imagine how Hellenistic scholars had access to such an abundance of archaic Greek lyric (so also Herington, *Poetry into Drama*, 45). This is a period in Greek history (post-eighth century BCE) when material evidence for writing is extant, even if song manuscripts are lacking.

390. For example, it is difficult to see how poetic oracles from putative eighth-century prophets (as opposed to more generic lore or traditions about these prophets), given their express occasional and parochial natures, no matter how strongly engineered for oral delivery and aural reception, could have survived for centuries after the prophet's death outside of writing (see van der Toorn's illuminating discussion of three different accounts in the Mari letters of a single prophetic oracle, *Scribal Culture*, 112–14).

391. Early studies include P. Haupt, "Moses' Song of Triumph," *AJSL* 20 (1903–4), 149–72, and W. F. Albright, "The Earliest Forms of Hebrew Verse," *JPOS* 2 (1922), 69–86. Robertson's *Linguistic Evidence* is the classic post-Ugaritic study of this material. For a recent overview of the literature on the genral topic, cf. Smith, "Old Poetry," 197–205.

392. "Old Poetry," 203; cf. Smith, "What Is Prologue," 43–58; *Poetic Heroes*, esp. 211–33. Smith is equally (I believe rightly) critical as well of those who would date these "old poems" extremely late, e.g., fifth to third centuries BCE.

393. "What Is Prologue," 56; see Smith, "Old Poetry," 205. This is a position broadly consistent with that of G. Garbini ("Il cantico di Debora," *La Parola des Passato* 33 [1978], 5–31) and J. A. Soggin (*Judges: A Commentary* [trans. J. Bowden; OTL; Philadelphia: Westminster, 1987], 80–81, 93–94), for example.

394. For Smith's treatment of 2 Samuel 1:19–27, see *Poetic Heroes*, 267–83.

395. *Tablet of the Heart*, ch. 6.

396. Esp. Na'aman, "Sources and Composition," 23–25; Schniedewind, *How the Bible Became a Book*, 48–63; Byrne, "Refuge of Scribalism," 16–23; Sanders, *Invention of Hebrew*, 103–22.

397. Who is doing the writing, what is being written, where, and for what purpose are all critical issues that impinge on what kind of textuality is to be expected. Monumental inscriptions from a royal chancery, for example, are quite dif-

ferent in what they implicate about the nature of writing from that of day-to-day documentary texts, and neither may implicate anything necessarily about the textuality of poetic genres. As indicated at the outset of this chapter, orality, literacy, and textuality are not monolithic descriptors and should be expected to manifest themselves in particular cultural instantiations with a myriad of attendant differences.

398. Even Byrne and Sanders, for example, who have done much to provide on-the-ground (as it were) measures for expectations about alphabetic writing and its use(s) during this period, can imagine a few regional scribes writing in the standard linear alphabetic (Phoenician) script. So Sanders: "If David's court did keep records, Seriah (2 Sam 8:17), the sole scribe mentioned, may well have set them down on papyrus in the dignified Phoenician suitable to a tenth-century Levantine monarch" (*Invention of Hebrew*, 113; cf. 111; Byrne, "Refuge of Scribalism," 23). If anything the tenor of Byrne's comment on the narratives in 2 Samuel 8:16–18 and 20:23–26 is perhaps even more realistic: "Some have taken this to represent a larger bureaucracy (or worse still, an Egyptian derivative), but the text makes more sense at face value. David retains a scribe when scribes are curiosities. The narrative is less interested in the hint of a chancery (certainly an anachronism) than the accentuation of a status retainer fashionable for the time. These scribes were less administrators than hagiographers" (23).

399. "Old Poetry," 205 (emphasis added).

400. Discussions of these "old poems" often point to (putative) linguistic archaisms as a means of assigning to them a (relatively) high chronology (1000 BCE or earlier). As noted, Smith (building on recent discussions) has problematized both the assignment of such high dates and the very ability to be confident of what counts as archaic in the first place. What has not been accented as much in these discussions is that archaisms (of whatever antiquity) are broadly typical of oral verbal art generally (see the foregoing discussion)—ongoing performance preserves (and thus fossilizes) morphological, lexical, and syntactic elements (as well as nonlinguistic cultural references of many kinds), which otherwise fall out of the contemporary spoken dialect (Foley, "Word-Power," 285, 296, n. 14; cf. M. Parry, *The Making of Homeric Verse: The Collected Papers of Milman Parry* [ed. A. Parry; Oxford: Clarendon, 1971]). This is not to insist that the mere presence of a linguistic archaism is always indicative of oral performance—archaisms result generally from the fact of linguistic change—but only to note that for poems such as these where rootedness in oral tradition is suspected such a presence may be yet a further index of orality (despite unclarity as to the chronological significance of the archaism).

401. Cross, "Kinship and Covenant in Ancient Israel," in *From Epic to Canon*, 20; cf. *Canaanite Myth and Hebrew Epic*, 99–111.

402. Smith, "What Is Prologue," 57—the terminology is Smith's.

403. It is incredibly difficult to peer very far behind a traditional poem's first transcription, cf. Doane's comments on a putatively "original Beowulf" ("Ethnography of Scribal Writing," 434–35).

404. That the upsurge in alphabetic writing around the Levant at the beginning of
this period (late ninth century) corresponds more broadly with climatic melio-
ration is perhaps not entirely accidental.

405. One commonly identified characteristic of traditional verbal art is the uncommon nature of its language, the specialness (e.g., formally, lexically, rhythmically) that distinguishes it from the ordinary or everyday language out of which it
is made, see Doane, "Oral Texts," 77–78; Zumthor, "Text and the Voice," 86.

406. Esp. Greenstein, "Signs of Poetry Past."

407. On the thanksgiving song, see Gunkel and Begrich, *Introduction to Psalms*,
199–221—Gunkel even mentions the Zakkur stela himself (215), though J. Greenfield offers the most scrupulous description of Zakkur's use of the thanksgiving song, see "The Zakir Inscription and the Danklied," in S. Paul, M. Stone,
and A. Pinnick (ed.), *'Al Kanfei Yonah: Collected Studies of Jonas C. Greenfield on
Semitic Philology* (Leiden: Brill, 2001), I, 75–92.

408. See R. Reich, E. Shukron, and O. Lernau, "Recent Discoveries in the City of
David, Jerusalem," *IEJ* 57 (2007), 156–57, 161–63. As Sanders emphasizes,
"every excavated seal from the ninth- and tenth-century Levant is uninscribed"
(*Invention of Hebrew*, 108). Cf. O. Keel and A. Mazar, "Iron Age Seals and Seal
Impressions from Tel Rehov," *Eretz Israel* 28 (2009), 57*–69*.

409. Haran, "Book-Scrolls," 161–73.

410. Cf. A. R. Millard, "Epigraphic Notes, Aramaic and Hebrew," *PEQ* 110 (1978),
25; A. Lemaire, "Manuscrit, mur et rocher en épigraphie nord-ouest sémitiquè,"
in P. Brady and R. Laufer (ed.), *Le texte et son inscription* (Paris: Editions du
Centre national de la recherche scientifique, 1989), 38–39; "Les inscriptions
sur plâtre de Deir 'Alla et leur signification historique et culturele," in Hoftijzer
and van der Kooij, *Balaam Text*, 43; Weippert, "Balaam Text," 176–77. The practice is known from early Egyptian tomb inscriptions as well, cf. J. Cerny, *Paper
and Books in Ancient Egypt* (London: K. Lewias, 1952), 7.

411. J. Naveh, "A Paleographic Note on the Distribution of the Hebrew Script," *HTR*
61 (1968), 68–74; Niditch, *Oral World*, esp. 58–59; M. Coogan, "Literacy and
the Formation of Biblical Literature," in P. Williams and T. Hiebert (eds.),
*Realia Dei: Essays in Archaeology and Biblical Interpretation in Honor of Edward
F. Campbell, Jr. at His Retirement* (Atlanta: Scholars Press, 1999), 47–48;
Schniedewind, *How the Bible Became a Book*, 98–106; Sanders, "Writing and
Early Iron Age Israel," 106; cf. *Invention of Hebrew*, esp. ch. 4. There are a large
number of stamp seals and sealings or bullae (provenanced and nonprove-
nanced) from the period as well, indicative of the amount of writing on perish-
able materials that has been lost, see Avigad and Sass, *West Semitic Stamp Seals*.

412. So broadly, Greenstein, "Formation," 177; Schniedewind, *How the Bible Became a Book*, 84–90; and esp. van der Toorn, *Scribal Culture*, 173–204. The Deir 'Alla text (along with the notice in Lachish 3) provides positive indication that written prophecy is possible by the dates traditionally assigned to these prophets (cf. Sanders, *Invention of Hebrew*, 164–65).

413. Esp. Greenstein, "Formation," 151–78; cf. Na'aman, "Sources and Composition," 25; Schniedewind, *How the Bible Became a Book*, 64–164; van der Toorn, *Scribal Culture*, 143–72. There are scholars who imagine the "composition" of the Deuteronomistic history to have been an even more prolonged and complicated process, e.g., Person, *Deuteronomic History*.

414. Sanders, *Invention of Hebrew*, 166; see W. M. Schniedewind, "Aramaic, the Death of Written Hebrew, and Language Shift in the Persian Period," in S. L. Sanders (ed.), *Margins of Writing, Origins of Cultures* (Chicago: Oriental Institute of the University of Chicago, 2006), 137–47; D. Vanderhooft, "'el mĕdînâ ûmĕdînâ kiktābāh: Scribes and Scripts in Yehud and Achaemendi Transeuphratene," in O. Lipschitz, G. N. Knopers, and M. Oeming (eds.), *Judah and the Judeans in the Achaemenid Period: Negotiating Identity in an International Context* (Winona Lake, Ind.: Eisenbrauns, 2011), 529–44.

415. Psalms and Proverbs on internal criteria alone exhibit signs of having evolved out of a complex scribal process of compilation (cf. van der Toorn, *Scribal Culture*, 15–16, 118–19), and thus it would not be surprising to find earlier psalms and proverbs included in these collections (for the late linguistic aspects of some psalms, see A. Hurvitz, *The Transition Period in Biblical Hebrew: A Study in Post-Exilic Hebrew and Its Implications for the Dating of Psalms* [Jerusalem: Bialik, 1972] [in Hebrew]; for a generous estimate of possibly early psalms, see Carr, *Formation*, 386–402). Certainly the evidence from Qumran is suggestive of multiple psalms collections predating those currently extant from Qumran (parts of thirty-nine different scrolls dating roughly between 175 BCE and 70 CE) and differing (in various ways) from the MT-150 Psalter (for details, see P. W. Flint, *The Dead Sea Psalms Scrolls and the Book of Psalms* [Leiden: Brill, 1997]; cf. F. W. Dobbs-Allsopp, "The Poetry of Psalms," in W. Brown (ed.), *The Oxford Handbook on the Psalms* [Oxford: Oxford University Press, 2014], 79–98). Though there is debate over the precise dating of Job, too, that it is a post-sixth-century work is perhaps less controversial (see esp. A. Hurvitz, "The Date of the Prose-Tale of Job Linguistically Reconsidered," *HTR* 67 [1974], 17–34; Seow, *Job 1–21*, 25–26, 39–46).

416. See F. W. Dobbs-Allsopp, "Linguistic Evidence for the Date of Lamentations," *JANES* 26 (1998), 1–36; "Late Linguistic Features," 27–77.

417. Daniel, which is conventionally dated to the second century BCE, even includes snatches of poetry in Aramaic (e.g., 2:20–23; 3:33; 4:7–9, 11–14, 31–32; 6:27–28; 7:9–10, 13–14, 23–27), cf. J. C. Greenfield, "Early Aramaic Poetry," *JANES* 11 (1979), 45–51.

418. Schniedewind, *How the Bible Become a Book*, 149. Schniedewind (*How the Bible Became a Book*, 139–64; "Aramaic," 137–47; *Social History of Hebrew*, 126–37, 139–62) starkly and helpfully problematizes assumptions about the nature of Hebrew literary production especially from the late sixth through the fourth century, given the almost complete absence of extant writings (outside of the Bible) in Hebrew from this period. Preserved textuality here, too, requires an accounting. Nevertheless, it appears necessary to assume some inscription prior to Qumran (e.g., the stabilization of Pss 1–89 in the various Psalms scrolls at Qumran presumes the existence of earlier psalms collections; not all the texts preserved at Qumran originated there), and Schniedewind identifies the Aramaic chancellery as one possible site for such inscription (*Social History of Hebrew*, 155): "To be sure, Hebrew and Aramaic are closely related languages; and, theoretically, the skills of the Aramaic scribal chancellery would have been transferable to the copying, editing, and even composing of Hebrew texts. At the same time we must not forget that Hebrew came to be written in Aramaic script during this period, another sign of the role of the imperial scribal chancellery. The very letters that scholars came to label "Jewish script" are Aramaic, reflecting the trainng of scribes during the Persian period. The scribes of the Persian period were trained in the imperial language and tradition—not in Hebrew—and then these skills could have been transferred to the copying, editing, and (to a limited extent) composing of Hebrew literature."

419. It is at this point that the presence of Aramaisms in biblical books becomes remarkable, see A. Hurvitz, "The Chronological Significance of 'Aramaisms' in Biblical Hebrew," *IEJ* 18/4 (1968), 234–40.

420. Person, *Deuteronomic History*, 65; cf. Schniedewind, "Aramaic," 143–44; Sanders, *Invention of Hebrew*, 166; Carr, *Formation*. Certainly by Qumran, one might suppose with A. Lemaire (*Les écoles et la formation de la Bible dans l'ancien Israel* [OBO 38; Göttingen: Vändenhoeck und Ruprecht, 1981], 72–83), van der Toorn (*Scribal Culture*, 101–3), and others that scribal education is playing a (significant) part in the preservation and transmission of biblical writings—the specific means of written transmission will have been variable, as suggested by extant exemplars where the nature of transmission can be perceived.

421. The general effectiveness of literary criticism practiced on oral-derived poetry is not surprising. Oralists (e.g., Zumthor, Finnegan) often stress the linguistic sameness of oral and written verbal art and even the overlap in genres and techniques—especially since so much written verbal art was originally birthed in orality.

422. Doane, "Oral Texts," 79. Doane's notion of "interface" here is indebted to J. Goody (*The Interface between the Written and the Oral* [Cambridge: Cambridge University Press, 1987], 78–86) and his phrase "oral-residual texts" derived from W. Ong's broader idea of residual orality (as in *Orality and Literacy*, 11).

423. R. B. Coote, "Tradition, Oral, OT," in *IDBSup*, 917.

424. Cf. Charpin, *Reading and Writing in Babylon*, 41–42; Parkinson, *Reading Ancient Egyptian Poetry*, 31–40.

425. E.g., C. Serat, *Hebrew Manuscripts of the Middle Ages* (Cambridge: Cambridge University Press, 2002), 147–48. D. Boyarin, "Placing Reading in Ancient Israel and Medieval Europe," in *Sparks of the Logos* (Leiden: Brill, 2003), 59–88; van der Toorn, *Scribal Culture*, 12, 14; Doan and Giles, *Prophets, Performance, and Power*, 31; Miller, *Oral Tradition*, 110.

426. This is a reflection both of alphabetic writing's genealogical debt to Egyptian writing and of the syllable structure of West Semitic languages more generally, which require all syllables to start with a consonant (e.g., Cv, CvC). The supposed perfection of the alphabet by the Greeks through the addition of vowel letters (a kind of modification also widely attested in Levantine alphabetic writing) is nothing other than the necessary fine-tuning of a consonantal-based writing system for a language in which syllables may start with vowels. As R. Woodard observes, in such an environment "vowel representation would have been the *sine qua non* of writing" (*Greek Writing from Knossos to Homer: A Linguistic Interpretation of the Origin of the Greek Alphabet and the Continuity of Ancient Greek Literacy* [Oxford: Oxford University Press, 1997], 252). It seems likely that the extra *aleph* signs in the Ugaritic cuneiform alphabet were invented for writing languages in which syllables could begin with a vowel (e.g., Hurrian, Akkadian; see Pardee, "Ugaritic Alphabetic Cuneiform," 183).

427. I use the Tiberian vocalizations as a convenient means of distinguishing lexemes. The actual historical pronunciations would have been different (though uncertain), e.g., Tiberian *zeraʿ* < **zarʿ-* "seed"; Tiberian *zěrôaʿ* < **ziraʿ* "arm"; Tiberian *ʾārûr* <**ʾarûr* "cursed."

428. Cf. M. C. A. Macdonald, "Literacy in an Oral Environment," in C. Mee et al. (ed.), *Writing and Ancient Near Eastern Society: Papers in Honour of Alan R. Millard* (London: T. and T. Clark, 2005), 91. For details more generally, consult F. M. Cross and D. N. Freedman, *Early Hebrew Orthography: A Study of the Epigraphic Evidence* (New Haven: AOS, 1952); Z. Zevit, *Matres Lectionis in Ancient Hebrew Epigraphs* (Cambridge: ASOR, 1980); S. L Gogel, *A Grammar of Epigraphic Hebrew* (Atlanta: Scholars Press, 1998), 49–74.

429. This follows on the one hand from the example of all currently extant written poetic texts in West Semitic from the pre-Hellenistic Levant—the only two currently outstanding collections of Levantine poetry (the Ugaritic mythological texts and the proverbs of Ahiqar from Elephantine), the fragmentary and possibly poetic inscriptions from Kuntillet Ajrud (*KA* 4.2) and Deir ʿAlla (*KAI* 312), and the later Aramaic psalm text in Demotic script (papyrus Amherst 63, ca. third c. BCE)—and on the other hand from the usual Egyptian practice of writing papyrus rolls (whether verse or prose) in a running format. The latter may be underscored. On all current evidence, poetic texts (verse), like their prosaic counterparts, were written normatively in a running format—that Egyptian

practice was the principal model for writing on papyrus and leather at this time and in this region cannot be overemphasized. See Dobbs-Allsopp, "Space, Line," for details.

430. Dobbs-Allsopp, "Space, Line," 36–40 (with bibliography).

431. Cf. Macdonald, "Literacy in an Oral Environment," 90.

432. So also Carr, *Tablet of the Heart*, 5; cf. van der Toorn, *Scribal Culture*, 21–22.

433. "From Letters to Literature," 21; cf. Herington, *Poetry into Drama*, 44; in fact, the spareness (i.e., lack of metascript cues) of early writing generally meant that readers inevitably needed to bring an abundance of non/extratextual knowledge (e.g., content, melody) to bear on the reading of written texts, see F. G. Kenyon, *Books and Readers in Ancient Greece and Rome* (2d ed.; Oxford: Clarendon, 1951), 68–69; M. W. Green, "The Construction and Implementa- tion of the Cuneiform Writing System," *Visual Language* 15 (1981), 359–60; K. O'Brien O'Keeffe, *Visible Song: Transitional Literacy in Old English Verse* (Cambridge: Cambridge University Press, 1990), x–xi, 21; M. B. Parkes, *Pause and Effect: An Introduction to the History of Punctuation in the West* (Aldershot: Scolar Press, 1992), 10–11; R. Parkinson and S. Quirke, *Papyrus* (Austin: University of Texas, 1995), 46; P. Saenger, *Space between Words: The Origins of Silent Reading* (Stanford: Stanford University Press, 1997), 1–51. Parkes's examples of how readers of Latin negotiated the bare *scriptio continua* of written texts are also illuminating for imagining analogous ways in which readers of ancient Hebrew verse might have gone about negotiating nonspecially formatted manuscripts.

434. Parkes, *Pause and Effect*, 9, 11, 13–17, 18, 97–98; M. Irvine, *Making of Textual Culture: Grammatical and Literary Theory 350–1100* (Cambridge: Cambridge University Press, 2006), 69–72; O'Brien O'Keeffe, *Visible Song*, 3, 186–87; Zumthor, "Text and the Voice," 67; Pasternack, *Textuality of Old English Poetry*, 8–12, 21–28; Doane, "Ethnography of Scribal Writing," 431; cf. Kittay and Godzich, *Emergence of Prose*, 15.

435. Compare the rendering of NRSV, of which mine is a more literal and wooden adaptation: "The vision of all this has become for you like the words of a sealed document. If it is given to those who can read, with the command, 'Read this,' they say, 'We cannot, for it is sealed.' And if it is given to those who cannot read, saying, 'Read this,' they say, 'We cannot read'" (Isa 29:11–12).

436. Esp. J. L. Kugel, *The Idea of Biblical Poetry* (Baltimore: Johns Hopkins Univer- sity Press, 1981).

437. To the contrary, to suppose that the general corpus of biblical poetry as known since Lowth is something different altogether (and not poetry as currently un- derstood) requires at the very least sustained and ethnographically informed argumentation.

438. "Oral Texts," 83–87. Pasternack (*Textuality of Old English Poetry*, 2) uses "in- scribed verse" as a means of differentiating the kind of textuality evident in Old English poetic manuscripts from that of oral and printed (and now electronic)

compositions—"inscribed" because these texts "inherit significant elements of vocality from their oral forebears and yet address the reader from the pages of manuscripts."

439. Doane, "Oral Texts," 83.
440. See similarly Foley on Homeric manuscripts, "Word-Power," 291.
441. *Scribal Culture*, 14.
442. Olson, "From Utterance to Text," 263.

CHAPTER 5

1. *How to Read a Poem* (Oxford: Blackwell, 2007), 11; cf. C. Brooks, *The Well Wrought Urn* (New York: Harcourt Brace, 1942); F. Lentricchia and A. Dubois (eds.), *Close Reading: The Reader* (Durham, N.C.: Duke University Press, 2003). Thanks to Rolf Jacobson for first urging me to read this psalm.

2. E. L. Greenstein, "Aspects of Biblical Poetry," *Jewish Book Annual* 44 (1986–87), 42. The 1980s in particular witnessed a great amount of interest in scrutinizing key formal features (e.g., parallelism, meter, line structure) characteristic of biblical Hebrew verse, e.g., L. Alonso Schökel, *A Manual of Hebrew Poetics* (Subsidia biblica 11; Rome: Editrice Pontificio Istituto Biblico, 1988); R. Alter, *The Art of Biblical Poetry* (New York: Basic Books, 1985); A. Berlin, *The Dynamics of Biblical Parallelism* (Bloomington: Indiana University Press,1985); A. Cooper, "Biblical Poetics: A Linguistic Approach" (Ph.D. diss., Yale University, 1976); S. Geller, *Parallelism in Early Biblical Poetry* (Missoula: Scholars Press, 1979); E. Greenstein, "How Does Parallelism Mean?," in L. Nemoy (ed.), *A Sense of the Text: The Art of Language in the Study of Biblical Literature* (Jewish Quarterly Review Supplement; Winona Lake, Ind.: Eisenbrauns, 1983), 4–70; D. Grossberg, *Centripetal and Centrifugal Structures in Biblical Poetry* (SBLMS 39. Atlanta: Scholars Press, 1989); J. Kugel, *Idea of Biblical Poetry* (New Haven: Yale University Press, 1981); M. O'Connor, *Hebrew Verse Structure* (Winona Lake, Ind.: Eisenbrauns, 1980); D. Pardee, *Ugaritic and Hebrew Parallelism: A Trial Cut ('nt I and Proverbs 2)* (VTSup 39; Leiden: Brill, 1988); W. G. E. Watson, *Classical Hebrew Poetry: A Guide to Its Techniques* (London: T. and T. Clark, 2001 [1984]). So the desire for more attention to be paid to the biblical poems themselves and to the reading of these poems is understandable.

3. Cf. P. Zumthor, *Oral Poetry: An Introduction* (trans. K. Murphy-Judy; Minneapolis: University of Minnesota Press, 1990), 107.

4. This is to recognize, from the start, that the traditional psalm in view here is preserved in and known only as a written text. One of the peculiarities of written Hebrew from the beginning (in the "old Hebrew" script) is the presence of word division. "Words" in oral verbal art ignorant of writing, by contrast, are far more elastic, flowing continuously through space and time and consisting of chunks that can vary from the morphemic entities that we customarily

associate with the notion of a linguistic "word" to larger phraseological chunks (e.g., formulae, lines; cf. J. M. Foley, "Word-Power, Performance, and Tradition," *Journal of American Folklore* 105 [1992], 275–301).

5. Foley on the importance of context to traditional verbal art: "In short, we must make every effort to understand whatever can be understood of context (whether as a member of the participatory group present at a performance or as a latter-day, far-removed reader construing texts related in various significant ways to oral tradition)" ("Word-Power," 284).

6. Foley, "Word-Power," 276. This is W. J. Ong's "full existential contexts" (*Orality and Literacy: The Technologizing of the Word* [London: Routledge, 1982], 38).

7. Oral and oral-derived poems may be "read," too—indeed, must be read, decoded as Foley argues in *How to Read an Oral Poem* (Urbana: University of Illinois Press, 2002), esp. 77, 80.

8. *Die Psalmen* (5th ed.; Göttingen: Vändenhoeck und Ruprecht, 1968), 571.

9. There is still one other way of poetry in Psalm 133 that I do consciously try to map, namely, the way in which the words of ancient poetry are (necessarily) encountered materially in manuscripts (textually), and mostly nonpristinely at that, i.e., variation is the norm for scribal reproduction (as it is for oral performance). My comments on this topic are mostly kept to the notes. As it turns out, I am propounding a reading of Psalm 133 as preserved in MT. In my judgment, every case of variation attested by the witnesses is likely a variation from a text like the one preserved in MT—this as seen from the perspective of a traditional text-centered view of text criticism. This observation is not intended chiefly as warrant for preferring to read MT, but more as a datum for considering the readings preserved by MT and the other witnesses. That is, it is potentially relevant to note that a particular variation is likely in response to a perceived difficulty or problem or unfamiliarity in the received text, or just a performative variation. And no doubt, even in the short Psalm 133, to read the psalm in one of the versions other than MT, is to read a different poem, with different accents (see briefly below on 11QPs[a]). Here I recall A. N. Doane's idea that ancient scribes were cultural performers on par with singers of tales and songs and that their performances, though explicitly chirographic, were in many respects much closer to orally performed verbal art than to highly literary written compositions (see "The Ethnography of Scribal Writing and Anglo-Saxon Poetry: Scribe as Performer," *Oral Tradition* 9 [1994], 420–30). So in the notes I both register the fact of variation and offer an accounting of it. Sometimes the knowledge this generates will be put to work explicitly in behalf of the reading articulated in the body of the chapter. But whether acted on explicitly or not, I understand this material accounting of actual readings to be part and parcel of any close, slow reading of an ancient poem. Insofar as part of the way of this poetry is the messy materiality through which any encounter with it must pass, part of the way of reading it will involve negotiating the variation of attested material readings.

10. Over the course of this book I have tried to problematize the high literary form of "criticism" inherited from Lowth in light of its deployment to "read" what is now better understood as traditional verbal art in variable forms of emerging textuality. Oralists and folklorists are quick (and right) to worry about how sub-limated modes of explicitly literary cognition(s) on the part of contemporary critics can potentially block fuller appreciation of performative verbal art on its own terms (e.g., Foley, "Word-Power," 284–85). But there also is much overlap between oral and written poetry, in part because both are specifically language arts and because the latter emerges (at some point) developmentally out of the former. Still, in the matter of ancient poems only preserved in manuscripts phi-lology and its technology of recovery remains a vital tool for the critic no matter the nature (oral, written, or something in between) of the poem under analysis. Recovering knowledge about ancient context(s), whether literary or performa-tive in nature, is de facto managed only through a sifting of material remains. To the extent, then, that the closeness of Lowth's brand of "literary criticism" (as with more recent varieties, too) depends heavily on philology, as it must (see J. Turner, *Philology: The Forgotten Origins of the Modern Humanities* [Princeton: Princeton Univeristy, 2014], 156–62), its way of reading may be revealing even of poems that emerge out of (are rooted in) highly traditional and prominently oral cultures. That is, a special benefit of close reading is the habits of attending closely (philologically) to words and their contexts that this practice inculcates. And it is by necessity a kind of "decoding," too, which is how Foley glosses the reading of an oral (or oral-derived) poem.

11. In the various Hebrew manuscripts, the ending and/or beginning of the psalm is indicated through the use of space, i.e., spans of uninscribed text, and the superscriptions. In B19a (Leningrad Codex; fig. 42), the superscription (*šîr hammaʿălôt lĕdāwīd*) is set on its own manuscript line, right adjusted, followed by a large span of blank space (the VACAT). The first couplet is set on the next manuscript line, right adjusted. Psalm 134 is set in the same way, so that the page layout makes the psalm's integrity as a "poem" obvious. In the Aleppo Codex (fig. 43), where the ink is much faded, a fully blank manuscript line comes before and after each psalm (inclusive of the superscription)—again the poem's written integrity is well inscribed. And in 11QPsª (fig. 44) the first line of Psalm 133 is indented and space is left uninscribed after the last word, as in B19a. In other words, where Psalm 133 begins and ends is made (to varying de-grees) apparent in the various Hebrew manuscripts. Also in the Greek. For ex-ample, in Codex Sinaiticus (fig. 45), the superscription is set on two indented lines (continuations of lines are indented on the following manuscript line).

12. Lineation of biblical Hebrew poems always requires specification (see chap-ter 1). Which is to say that it is not a given. Two important sources of evidence for line structure in the Psalms come in the accents and page layout preserved in the various Masoretic manuscripts. In both Aleppo and B19a, normally each

manuscript line contains two poetic lines (or parts thereof) separated by a varying span of uninscribed text (space permitting). This ideal, of course, is not
always (ideally) realized. The blank space between the two lines of the first couplet is minimal (but noticeable) in both Aleppo and B19a as the scribes endeavor to get the complete couplet on one manuscript line (figs. 42–43). Spacing
between poetic lines is not typically shown in 11QPs^a—it is written chiefly in a
running format (fig. 44). However, there is a significant amount of uninscribed
space in this manuscript separating the end of the first poetic line of this psalm
from the beginning of the second—a significant juncture, too, in my reading of
the poem. Sinaiticus (and some other of the Greek uncials) lineate (fig. 45).
Here the couplet is taken as a whole—signaled by the use of indentation on the
following manuscript line containing the remainder of the couplet (*katoikein
adelphous epi to auto*).

13. The reading in MT is presupposed by 11QPs^a (*hnh*), Tg. (*h'*), and Vg. (*ecce*) as
    well. LXX reads *idou dē*, though often referring to added emphasis explicitly
    present in MT (e.g., *hinnê-nāʾ*, Judg 13:3, 1 Sam 9:6, 16:5, 2 Sam 14:21, 2 Kgs 4:9,
    Job 10:16; *hinnê ʾattâ*, 1 Sam 28:9, cf. Job 27:12; *rĕʾēh nāʾ*, 2 Sam 7:2; *kî hinnê*, Isa
    3:1), other times the emphasis implied represents LXX's interpretation, i.e.,
    there is no additional linguistic element in the immediate context in MT (e.g.,
    1 Sam 20:5; 28:21; 2 Kgs 5:11; Isa 22:17; 33:7; Ps 134:1), which seems to be the
    case here (and also in Ps 134:1). That is, there is no reason to think LXX was ac-
    tually reading a *Vorlage* with *hinnê-nāʾ* or the like. Syr. leaves out a corresponding
    literal gloss for *hinnê* altogether (also in Ps 134:1); as usual its chief aim is to give
    the semantic sense of the Hebrew as clearly as possible.

14. My punctuation and capitalization in the translation are minimal. My aim is to
    allow line and syntax to guide readers of English through the poem. Translation
    here is intended mostly as a rough gloss of the underlying Hebrew and should
    not be pressed too far as a precise construal of this song's Hebrew syntax. For
    example, as C. L. Seow has stressed to me (personal communication, February
    5, 2014), the syntax of the whole poem can be construed as a complete sentence.
    My minimally punctuated translation should not be taken to disagree with this
    assessment.

15. *Literary Theory: A Very Short Introduction* (Oxford: Oxford University Press,
    1997), 72.

16. For a good orientation to the force and syntax of both exclamatory *māh* and pre-
    sentative *hinnê* in biblical Hebrew, see *IBHS* sec. 18.3ff., 40.2.1a–c.

17. E. S. Gerstenberger, *Psalms, Part 2, and Lamentations* (FOTL 15; Grand Rapids:
    Eerdmans, 2001), 371.

18. Several of the versions are telling on this count as well. LXX underscores the
    hyperbole even further with its rendering of *hinnê* as *idou dē*—a double addition
    of sorts (i.e., compared to the Song passage). And the lack of an equivalent of
    hinnê in Syr. points up the hyperbole of MT of Psalm 133 from a different angle.

19. Akkadian *damqu* (lit. "to be good") is used similarly to indicate high aesthetic esteem (see I. Winters, "Aesthetics in Ancient Mesopotamian Art," in *CANE* IV, esp. 2573).

20. The poetic shaping of MT is also pointed up by the versions, which tend to prosaize in an effort to more clearly interpret the idiom, esp. Syr. *lḥ'* (pl.) *m' d'mryn 'yk ḥd'* (i.e., word order and syntax are changed to make explicit the construal on offer; Tg. is similar, ["for Zion and Jerusalem to dwell [*tmytb*] like [*k-*] brothers as one," though the word order of MT is retained) and LXX *all ē to katoikein adelphous epi to auto* (though not Vg.).

21. One of the defining (empirical) characteristics of biblical Hebrew verse is its tendency toward concision. This is evidenced by any number of phenomena, e.g., reduced syntactic frames, lack of temporal tracking, general paucity of the so-called prose particles, and the like. Of course, concision, like any other poetic phenomenon, may be played with as well. Here the compact nature of the line allows, among other things, for the addition of *gam*.

22. All of the couplets in the poem, as well as the closing triplet, are enjambed—that is, the syntax of the individual line continues on across line boundaries. For more details on enjambment in Hebrew poetry, see F. W. Dobbs-Allsopp, "The Enjambing Line in Lamentations: A Taxonomy (Part I)," *ZAW* 113/2 (2001), 219–39; "The Effects of Enjambment in Lamentations (Part 2)," *ZAW* 113/5 (2001), 370–85. For other examples in which an infinitive construct heads a phrase that functions as a subject, especially in verbless clauses, see *IBHS* sec. 36.2.1b.

23. T. Muraoka, *Emphatic Words and Structures in Biblical Hebrew* (Leiden: Brill, 1985), 143.

24. Cf. M. Dahood, *Psalms III* (AB 17A; Garden City: Doubleday, 1970), 251.

25. Cf. Muraoka, *Emphatic Words*, 143.

26. For details, see L. E. Stager, "The Archaeology of the Family in Ancient Israel," *BASOR* 260 (1985), 1–35; J. S. Holladay, "House, Israelite," in *ABD* 3, 308–18; "House: Syro-Palestinian Houses," in *OEANE* 3, 94–114; C. Meyers, "The Family in Early Israel," in L. Perdue et al. (eds.), *Families in Ancient Israel* (Louisville: Westminster John Knox, 1997), 1–47; D. Schloen, *The House of the Father as Fact and Symbol: Patrimonialism in Ugarit and the Ancient Near East* (Winona Lake, Ind.: Eisenbrauns, 2001); P. King and L. Stager, *Life in Biblical Israel* (Louisville: Westminster John Knox, 2001), esp. 36–40. Importantly, Schloen notes that "at certain stages of the household lifecycle, a theoretically joint household will be 'nuclear,' consisting only of a conjugal couple and their unmarried children, even though the full three-generation structure remains the ideal. Indeed, under preindustrial conditions, typical birth and mortality patterns ensure that a minority of all families will actually be 'joint' at any one time" (*House of the Father*, 108).

27. R. Westbrook, "The Law of Biblical Levirate," in *Property and the Family in Biblical Law* (JSOTSS 113; Sheffield: JSOT, 1991), 78; cf. D. Daub, "*Consortium* in Roman and Hebrew Law," *Juridical Review* 62 (1950), 71–91; Schloen, *House of the Father*, 149.

28. E.g., A. Weiser, *The Psalms* (OTL; Philadelphia: Westminster, 1962), 783; H.-J. Kraus, *Psalmen 60–150* (BK 15/2; Neukirchen-Vluyn: Neukirchener Verlag, 1978), 1068.

29. The manner of reference in each of these passages is different, as is their specific inflection. In Psalm 127 there is an awareness that the posterity of a man's house (v. 1) lay with his sons (v. 3), and yet the benefit of sons to the man that is extolled in vv. 4–5 has a pronounced this-worldly accent—all the better by which to confront the enemies at the gate. In Psalm 128 the familial image is more holistic, as wife and children are imagined sitting around the family table (v. 3). And in Qoheleth, it is the wife alone who is mentioned (9:9)—no doubt because future continuity is especially being deemphasized in the service of urging the enjoyment of life now, as one finds it in simple pleasures. (In Gilgamesh these same themes are in view, though wife and children are both explicitly mentioned.) By contrast the familial force of "brothers dwelling together" is decidedly horizontal, as opposed to the more vertical focus of these other passages—genealogies in the ancient world could give accent to either perspective (see R. Wilson, *Genealogy and History in the Biblical World* [New Haven: Yale University Press, 1977]).

30. For the prevalence of these other kinds of coresidence patterns in ancient Israel and Judah, see Meyers, "Family in Early Israel," 11–13; Schloen, *House of the Father*, 15–65.

31. Interestingly, Tg. construes the phrase most specifically as referring to two brothers dwelling together (Zion and Jerusalem!), which surely would have been the more common reality in antiquity (esp. Schloen, *House of the Father*, 150, n. 24). Of course, Aaron's mention a bit later in the poem makes one think of two other brothers, Moses and Aaron. And A. Berlin suggests that the image is to be understood as a call for the reunification of north and south ("On the Interpretation of Psalm 133," in E. Follis [ed.], *Directions in Biblical Hebrew Poetry* [Sheffield: JSOT, 1987], 142). The politics of the poem may also fall out more allusively, more tropologically, as *šēbet ʾaḥîm* plays on **šēbeṭ ʾaḥîm* (cf. *šēbeṭ ʾābîkā*, Num 18:2; *maṭṭê ʾābîhā*, Num 36:8) and the image (*šebet/*šēbeṭ ʾaḥîm*) tumbles down the surface of the poem along with the *yōrēd*ing oil and dew, until it reaches Zion, Judah's political capital, and "pools" there in Yahweh's "blessing" (*bĕrākâ* "blessing" playing on *bĕrēkâ* "pool"; the puns were pointed out to me by R. Van Leeuwen and the political implications of the imagery by C. L. Seow).

32. The language of the psalm as transmitted in MT is late (A. Hurvitz, *The Transition Period in Biblical Hebrew: A Study of Post-exilic Hebrew and its Implications for the Dating of Psalms* [in Hebrew] [Jerusalem: Bialik, 1972], esp. 156–60), suggesting a postexilic date. To what ideological end the poem's valuation of family (in whatever manifestation) would have been put in this period is hard to determine without detailed sociocultural information—it may well be, as Weiser contends (*Psalms*, 783), that the poem was intended to bolster the ancient family

norm at a time of its decline—though here, too, Berlin's reunification interpretation could make sense. Further, the language of this psalm (and of the psalms more generally) is open, and thus easily adaptable to the ever changing contexts of its auditors (see P. D. Miller, *Interpreting the Psalms* [Philadelphia: Fortress, 1986], 50–51).

33. LXX's gloss as *myron* "sweet oil" does not quite capture the grade distinction (see discussion further in this section), but it does nonetheless appear to get the extraordinary nature of the oil (the same rendering of *šemen ṭôb* is given in 2 Kgs 20:13 = Isa 39:2). In Qoheleth 7:1 LXX translates (perhaps) more literally, *elaion agathon*. Any in case, LXX should be construed here (in all likelihood) as supporting MT (along with 11QPsᵃ, Tg., and Vg.). The rendering in Syr., *mšḥ'*, again represents this translation's habit of leveling through all tropological density in favor of a (more) straightforward semantic rendering (cf. Tg.'s *kmšḥ ṭb*). Therefore, it, too, is unlikely to be witnessing to a *Vorlage* that varies from MT.

34. There is no need to emend by adding a *še-* in imitation of the two other occurrences of *šeyyōrēd* (so Gunkel, *Psalmen*, 572; Kraus, *Psalmen*, 1067) or to follow the minority of Masoretic manuscripts that add a definite article (see *BHS*), conforming to the clustering of definite articles in the couplet. Both strategies level MT in light of the broader context. LXX (*to katabainon*), Vg. (quod descendit), and Syr. (*dnḥt*) all similarly assimilate toward the other renderings of *šeyyōrēd* in the psalm. The reading in MT is reflected in 11QPsᵃ (*ywrd*) and Tg. (*nḥyt*). Further, while it is common in biblical Hebrew for the participle to be accompanied by a definite article when forming a relative clause, it is by no means syntactically necessary, "because the participle, as a verbal adjective, *by itself* can serve as a relative clause" (*IBHS* sec. 19.7b).

35. 11QPsᵃ reads *šyrd* in contradistinction to *ywrd* earlier and *šywrd* later. Of course, this could simply reflect a defective spelling of the participle (as in MT). However, the spelling in this scroll (and in the DSS more generally) is customarily full, opening up the possibility that scribe intends the perfective form of the verb here. On this reading, O. Keel ("Kultische Brüderlichkeit—Ps 133," *FZPhTh* 23 [1976], 69) suggests that 11QPsᵃ means to signal that it is taking the immediately preceding *zqn 'hrwn* as the subject and not the *šemen haṭṭôb*, which, like *ṭal*, governs a participle. However construed, the underlying Hebrew *Vorlage* is the same.

36. The Masoretes apparently vocalize as if from *middâ* "measure, measurement," for which the feminine plural is well attested (Num 13:32; 1 Kgs 7:9, 11; Jer 22:14; Ezek 40:24, 28, 29, 32, 33, 35; 41:17; 42:15; 43:13; 48:16). The reading would be something like: "the beard of Aaron which falls down according to [*'al-pî*; see Lev 27:8, 18; Num 26:56; Prov 22:6; Sir 13:24] its measures" (i.e., length, size, Num 13:32; 2 Sam 21:10; Isa 45:14; Jer 22:14; 2 Chron 3:3; more commonly in biblical Hebrew with *kě-*, e.g., 1 Kgs 7:9, 11; cf. Keel, "Ps 133," 71–73). Jastrow has no entry for a lexeme from *mdd* meaning "clothes" or the like (only Jewish Babylonian Aramaic *madda*)—though he does translate a paasage in Yeb. 76ᵇ with

reference to 1 Sam 17:38 *maddāyw kmiddātô* "his (Saul's) garments such as fitted his stature" (I, 732; cf. *ᵓyš špyr mddh* "a man whose stature is beautiful," *TAD* C1.1.95). In contrast, all the versions (LXX *ōan tou endymatos autou*, Tg. *ᵓymrᵓ dlbwšwy*, Syr. *br ṣwrᵓ dkwtynh*, Vg. oram vestimentorum eius) and also 11QPsᵃ and 11QPsᵇ (both read *mdyw*) construe as if from biblical Hebrew *mad* "garment" (Lev 6:3; Judg 3:16; 1 Sam 4:12; 17:38, 39; 18:4; 20:8; Ps 109:18) or *mādû / madweh* "garment" (2 Sam 10:4 = 1 Chron 19:4). The problem is that the lexeme in Hebrew is normally masculine, except for a single occurrence at Qumran (*mdt hdr* "robe of honor," 1QS 4.8). Ugaritic may also attest one instance of a feminine plural, *mdth* (CAT 4.182.55). MT is to be preferred (over the DSS readings) as the more difficult reading, though following the versions in construing the reference to be to a garment of some kind. This interpetation is supported by a number of considerations. One, there are the two other attested feminine forms at Qumran and in Ugaritic, the latter a plural. Two, if the Masoretes did not know a word for garment from the root *m-d-d*, then their construal as if a measure of some sort, as well as taking Aaron's beard as the antecedent, is sensible but no longer overly compelling. (The Masoretic accentuation, contra Dahood, *Psalms III*, 252, does not disambiguate the antecedent presumed to govern the relative clause.) Besides I know of only one late reference to a long beard in the ancient sources: R. Payne-Smith cites Syr *ᵓarrîq daqnāᵓ* "long bearded" as a translation of an Arabic original (Ibn S. Thes. sec. 3; s.v. *ᵓarrîq*), and none of the uses of *middâ* pointed out by Keel and others offer very precise parallels, mostly indicating a large person or structure. An allusion via a play on *middâ* to the stature of the individual, especially in light of the explicit naming of Aaron, and even possibly, given the iconographic evidence (see discussion of beard imagery in following section), to the fullness of the beard imagined (so Keel's "seiner ganzen Größe"), is entirely possible (so R. Van Leeuwen, personal communication, March 2008). Third, if the reference is to a garment, then there are good parallels to *pî* as indicating the collar or the neck opening of a garment (cf. all the versions): *kěpî kuttontî* "by the collar of my tunic" (Job 30:18), *kěpî taḥrāᵓ* "by the collar of a coat of mail" (Exod 28:32; 39:23), *ûpî hammě̆ᶜîl* "the opening of the robe" (Exod 39:23). Fourth, though perhaps incidentally, Aaron is himself fitted out with a "linen robe" (*middô bar*) in Leviticus 6:3. And the clincher is a passage in 1 Samuel 21 in which David, feigning madness, causes spittle to run down his beard: *wayyôred rîrô ᵓel-zěqānô* "and he causes spittle to run down his beard" (1 Sam 21:14; some Mss read *ᵓl* for *ᵓl*). That is, nowhere else do beards *yrd*. But to the contrary substances like "spittle," and thus presumably, potentially "oil," too, do *yrd* down upon and over the beard.

37. This is a late syntagma. Hurvitz (*Transition Period*, 156–58) points out that only here (two times) and in Haggai (Hag 2:1) and in Qoheleth (9:12; 10:15) does the syntagma *še* + participle appear in biblical Hebrew; otherwise it has the definite article (i.e., *h* + participle, cf. *IBHS* sec. 19.6; for the SBH construction with *y-r-d*,

see Deut 9:21; Josh 3:13; 2 Kgs 12:21; cf. Qoh 3:21; Neh 3:15). The *še* + participle construction is otherwise known in Rabbinic Hebrew (e.g., *t. Hag.* 2a; *Mek.* (226); *Sanh.* 7, 50b) and is also reflected in Targumic Aramaic (e.g., *Tg. Onq.* 2 Chron 18:7; see Hurvitz, *Transition Period*, 156–57). *Še-* is itself a typically late affix, substituting for and even replacing the relative particle *'ăšer* that dominates the early phases of the language (for discussion with earlier literature, see F. W. Dobbs-Allsopp, "Late Linguistic Features in the Song of Songs," in A. C. Hagedorn (ed.), *Perspectives on the Song of Songs—Perspektiven der Hoheliedauslegung* (BZAW; Berlin: de Gruyter), 46, 59–60.

38. The plural in MT is supported by LXX (*orē*), Tg. (*ṭwry*), and Vg. (*montana*). 11QPs^a (*hr*) and apparently Syr. (*ṭwr'*, without seyame), in contrast, read the singular. The latter reading is surely an assimilation to the standard phrase *har ṣiyyôn* "Mount Zion," elsewhere always in the singular (e.g., 2 Kgs 19:31; Isa 4:5; 8:18; 10:12; 24:23; 29:8; 31:4; Joel 3:5; Obad 17; Mic 4:7; Ps 48:3, 12; 74:2; 78:68; 125:1; Lam 5:18). The plural "mountains" is the more unique and difficult reading, and it is hard to imagine a scribe coming to it from a putative *Vorlage* with a singular. But the rendering in 11QPs^a and Syr. does point up a certain oddness to the phrasing of MT—perhaps indicating that something more or other than "Mount Zion" is intended here. The genitive construction involving "mountains" (in the plural) plus a geographical name is rather commonplace, e.g., "mountains of Ararat" (Gen 8:4), "mountains of Abarim" (Num 33:47), "mountains of Samaria" (Jer 31:5; Amos 3:9), "mountains of Israel" (Ezek 6:2, etc.), "mountains of Judah" (2 Chron 21:11). Hence, the reference may be taken rather straightforwardly (initially at any rate) as a reference to the "mountains of Zion," namely, the several hills on which Jerusalem is built (cf. Ps 87:1; 121:1; 125:2).

The reanalyzed form of the plural with the typical infixed-*a* plural of *qvtl* nouns (the standard plural of the *qvtl* pattern with geminate roots in biblical Hebrew is *qvllîm* in the absolute and *qvllê* in the construct, cf. J. Fox, *Semitic Noun Patterns* [HSS 52; Winona Lake, Ind.: Eisenbrauns, 2003], 136, 147, 153), though not indisputably diagnostic of LBH, becomes (more) prominent in LBH and later dialects of Hebrew. A general trend toward more prominence is to be observed diachronically in the Aramaic dialects as well. For details, see Dobbs-Allsopp, "Late Linguistic Features," 34–36.

39. All witnesses follow MT in reading "Zion." Yet a number of emendations are routinely pressed (*'iyyôn* "Ijon," *ṣiyyâ* "parched," *śiyyôn* [presumably for *śî'ōn*] "Sion"), since the notion of dew running down from Hermon to Zion is literally untenable. R. Alter (*The Book of Psalms* [New York: Norton, 2007], 463) is exemplary, pointing out that the reading "mountains of Zion" does not "make much sense because Mount Hermon is geographically removed from the Judean mountains around Jerusalem, and dew certainly does not travel in this fashion." But the realist assumptions of this logic do not necessarily hold. There is every reason to suspect that the poet means the image figuratively, similar to how

Zion in other passages is imagined as high and in the far north (Ps 48:3)—it neither has high peaks nor is located in the north—or in the Ugaritic Baal Cycle how the heavens can rain "oil" (*šmn*) and the wadis run with "honey" (*nbtm*) (CAT 1.6.III.6–7). On this view, all of the suggested emendations are assimilatory and have little appeal beside the only material reading attested.

40. The line structure represented here is basically that implied by the layout of B19a (fig. 42). The only difference is that in B19a there is no obvious extra space separating the fourth and fifth lines. But there is clearly a span of uninscribed text after *mdwtyw* in Aleppo (fig. 43), which otherwise is not as consistent in its use of spacing in this psalm (the first several lines in this block of material in particular are run together). LXX has three couplets, differently divided, plus the reference to Aaron's beard is set on its own manuscript line (in Sinaiticus: *ton pōgōna ton aarōn*, see fig. 45). By contrast, E. Zenger appears to follow the lineation (spacing) above all in Aleppo (though this is nowhere made explicit), see F.-L. Hossfeldt and E. Zenger, *Psalms 3* (Hermeneia; trans. L. Maloney; Minneapolis: Fortress, 2011), 469–70.

41. In B19a these participles straddle the various blank spaces that separate lines (cola)—even after *šeyyōrēd* in v. 2, which goes against the Masoretic accentuation (the spacing in *BHS* in this psalm generally reflects that of B19a, see fig. 42). This last bit is not an insignificant observation. Lineation for biblical poems always requires a positive construal, i.e., it is nowhere a given matter of fact. The Masoretic accentuation, like the spacing and columnar set of verse layout, is but one set of evidence for consideration. Here in B19a the two are at odds. The spacing of the Aleppo Codex is not the same—and the ink is very faded throughout this psalm (fig. 43).

42. The liquid imagery of the poem elicits the pun on *běrēkâ* "pool."

43. Berlin, "Psalm 133," 141, 145; cf. Keel, "Ps 133," 69.

44. The olive tree (*Olea Europeae*) is hardy and long-lived (capable of growing to an age of one thousand years or more). It thrives in the highlands and hill country of the Levant with its rocky and shallow soil (cf. Deut 32:13) and where there is just enough chill during the rainy season to cause the fruit to mature. See King and Stager, *Life in Biblical Israel*, 95; M. Zohary, *Plants in the Bible* (Cambridge: Cambridge University Press, 1982), 56–57; I. and W. Jacob, "Flora," in *ABD* 2, 807–8.

45. Related designations appear in Akkadian (*šamnu rēštu / rūštu, šamnu ṭābu*, see *CAD* Š/I, esp. 328) and Ugaritic (*šmn ṭb*, see CAT 4.780.8; 4.738.4). Both Heb. *rēʾšît* and *ṭôb* and their cognates in other Semitic languages are used throughout the ancient Near East to qualify superlatively various commodities, such as gold, grain, wines, oils, and the like.

46. King and Stager, *Life in Biblical Israel*, 96; cf. L. E. Stager, "The Finest Olive Oil in Samaria," *JSS* 28 (1983), 241–45.

47. "Psalm 133," 141; cf. Grossberg, *Centripetal and Centrifugal*, 28—the device is prominent in many of the Songs of Ascents.

48. The way that *ṭôb* plays across the surface of MT is spotlighted when comparing the translations of LXX (*kalon / myron*; cf. Vg.) and Syr. (*ṭb / mšḥ*), which forego any attempt to offer a literal rendering (for different reasons) of the "good oil" that might resonate with the poem's opening exclamation of "goodness"—contemporary English translations (e.g., NRSV, NJV) also obscure this play (but see Alter, *Psalms*, 463: "how good.../ Like goodly oil...").

49. Zumthor, *Oral Poetry*, 111.

50. *Life in Biblical Israel*, 96.

51. During Iron II, Ekron, for example, where some 114 olive presses were recovered by archeologists, appears to have an "industrial zone" dedicated to producing olive oil in amounts apparently greater than needed for local consumption (S. Gitin, "Ekron of the Philistines: Part II: Olive-Oil Suppliers to the World," *BAR* 16/2 [1990], 32–42; "Tell Miqne-Ekron in the 7th Century B.C.E.," in S. Gitin (ed.), *Recent Excavations in Israel* [Dubuque: Hunt, 1995], 61–79; "The Neo-Assyrian Empire and Its Western Periphery: The Levant, with a Focus on Philistine Ekron," in *Assyria 1995* [ed. S. Parpola and R. Whiting; Helsinki, 1997], 77–103; King and Stager, *Life in Biblical Israel*, 96; see Schloen, *House of the Father*, 141–47, for a slightly different understanding of the nature of oil production at Ekron). Though the function of the Samaria ostraca continues to be debated, they evidence, in admittedly smaller quantities, the regional transport of olive oil, presumably for uses other than that of a subsistence nature.

52. See the Egyptian tomb painting (ca. 1400 BCE) depicting a similar scene of joyous anointing in Hossfeld and Zenger, *Psalms 3*, Psalm 133, pl. I (on p. 480).

53. Labeled explicitly as *šemen rôqēaḥ* in Qoheleth 10:1 (cf. Ug. *šmn rqḥ*, CAT, 1.41.21; 1.148.21; 4.91.5; cf. 4.31.2; Aram. *rqḥ' zy mšḥ*, ATNS 45b.5), *šemen hammōr* in Est 2:12, and Aram. *mšḥ bšm* (*TAD* A2.2.12; 2.4.10–11; B3.3.5; *PAT* 259 ii.13, etc.; cf. Est 2:12; Song 1:3; 4:10).

54. A. Ohry and A. Levy, "Anointing with Oil—An Hygienic Procedure in the Bible and in the Talmud," *Koroth* 9 (1985), 174; Stager, "Finest Olive Oil," 245, n. 11; B. Porten, *Archives from Elephantine* (Berkeley: University of California Press, 1968), 91–92; cf. S. Pointer, *The Artifice of Beauty: A History and Practical Guide to Perfumes and Cosmetics* (Thrupp, Stroud, Gloucestershire: Sutton, 2005), 202–3.

55. Oil featured similarly in everyday life throughout the ancient Near East. The major difference came in the kind of oil that was featured; in Mesopotamia, it was mainly sesame seed oil and in Egypt, sesame seed (Egypt. *nḥ*) and castor (Egypt. *qɜqɜ*, cf. Heb. *qyqywn* in Jonah 4:6, or *tgm*, cf. Aram. *tqm* throughout the Elephantine documents) oil (see Porten, *Archives from Elephantine*, 91–93). Further, since olives could not be grown in either Mesopotamia or Egypt, olive oil was imported to both places, where it was coveted by the elites.

56. Several of the marriage contracts from Elephantine register oil—and even "olive oil" (*mšḥ zyt*)—as a part of the woman's dowry (e.g., *TAD* B.2.6.16; 3.3.5; 3.8.20).

57. For presses from Tell Beit Mirsim, for example, see: http://www.loc.gov/pictures/item/mpc2005001387/PP/, last accessed on May 1, 2015.

58. *House of the Father*, 140; cf. A. Mazar, *Archaeology of the Land of the Bible, 10,000–586 BCE* (New York: Doubleday, 1990), 489–91.

59. "Psalms at the Poetic Precipice," *HAR* 10 (1986), 356.

60. Oil is even used as an extravagant figure for rain (CAT 1.6.III.6–7; cf. Gen 27:28; 1 Kgs 17:14).

61. See Ohry and Levy, "Anointing with Oil," 174.

62. For a recent and provocative theoretical accounting of poetry's nonreferential ways of meaning, see M. K. Blasing, *Lyric Poetry: The Pain and the Pleasure of Words* (Princeton: Princeton University Press, 2007), esp. 3, 6–8, 10–13.

63. Another clear example of a run-on simile occurs in Song 5:12 ("His eyes are like doves / beside springs of water, / bathed in milk, / fitly set," NRSV). Here the second couplet is trading on either the whites of the beloved's eyes and figuring them or the dove imagery, in which case the run-on goes in an entirely new direction (as supposed, for example, by M. Fox, "Only 'like doves' belongs to the simile proper. The rest of the verse is an expansion of the picture of the doves and does not apply directly to the eyes" [*The Song of Songs and the Ancient Egyptian Love Songs* (Madison: University of Wisconsin Press, 1985), 147–48]). Such similes are especially prominent in classical Arabic poetry, where M. Sells ["Guises of the *Ghūl*: Dissembling Simile and Semantic Overflow in Classical Arabic *Nasīb*," in S. Steikevych (ed.), *Reorientations/ Arabic and Persian Poetry* (Bloomington: Indiana University Press, 1994), 130–64] dubs them "dissembling similes" because the new directions taken (and often extensively developed, to the point of completely overshadowing the original simile) prove vital to the poem's meaning, though this is far from apparent on the poem's surface.

64. E.g., Dahood, *Psalms III*, 252; D. T. Tsumura, "Sorites in Psalm 133:2–3a," *Bib* 61 (1980), 416–17.

65. E.g., Gunkel, *Psalmen*, 569; R. Kittel, *Die Psalmen* (Leipzig, 1922), 406; Weiser, *Psalms*, 783; W. G. E. Watson, "The Hidden Simile in Psalm 133," *Bib* 60 (1969), 108–9; Keel, "Ps 133," esp. 74–75; L. C. Allen, *Psalms 101–150* (Word; Waco: Word, 1983), 212. The plene reading of *šyrd* in 11QPs[a] is construable toward this end, see Keel, "Ps 133," 69.

66. A third option (so Kraus, *Psalmen*, 1067; *BHS*) is to delete the entire couplet as a later gloss. However, there is no textual support for such an excision and this kind of extended simile is well attested (see earlier and esp. n. 61).

67. Several scholars either emend the text by explicitly adding the preposition *kĕ-* "like" at the head of the couplet (e.g., Gunkel, *Psalmen*, 572; Kittel, *Psalmen*, 406; Weiser, *Psalms*, 783) or assume an ellipsis of the same (e.g., Watson, "Hidden Simile," 108–9).

68. *Leviticus 17–22* (AB3A; New York: Doubleday, 2000), 1691; cf. 1801–2. See, now, more generally, S. Niditch, *"My Brother Esau Is a Hairy Man": Hair and Identity in Ancient Israel* (Oxford: Oxford University Press, 2008), esp. 25–62.

69. "Sex, Rhetoric, and the Public Monument: The Alluring Body of Naram-Sin of Agade," in N. Kampen (ed.), *Sexuality in Ancient Art* (Cambridge: Cambridge University Press, 1996), 13.

70. "Ps 133," 74–75—my discussion draws principally on Keel at this point. He references a great many images in these two pages (many from J. A. Pritchard's *Ancient Near Eastern Pictures Relating to the Old Testament* [2d ed.; Princeton: Princeton University Press, 1969). The few images I have selected to offer in the figures are merely representative examples; if anything, thirty-plus years later, one could add significantly to the list furnished in Keel's notes.

71. Cf. G. Robins, *The Art of Ancient Egypt* (Cambridge, Mass.: Harvard University Press, 1997), ill. 107, 177, 233.

72. "Psalm 133," esp. 75; cf. Allen, *Psalms 101–150*, 212.

73. The physical layout of the Aleppo Codex (distinct from B19a) enhances further the feel of continuation (fig. 43)—there is no extra space between *zāqān* and *zĕqan*, and the two are the last words in the manuscript (columnar) line. The Masoretic accentuation also encourages the two to be taken together (contrast the punctuation in Syr., for example, which, if correct, would appear to separate the two).

74. "Psalm 133," 144.

75. LXX's neuter participle (*katabainon*) would appear to have the neuter noun *myron* "oil" specifically in view (Zenger in Hossfeld and Zenger, *Psalms 3*, 482).

76. Thus I see things the other way around from Allen (*Psalms 101–150*, 212), namely, that far from "the line" under this construal being "hardly viable poetically," it is precisely the poetics (namely syntax, word repetition, and the like) that makes this reading viable.

77. Similarly, Berlin, "Psalm 133," 144.

78. Most commentators do not fail to mention Aaron's consecration as high priest in connection with the oil running over head and beard in Psalm 133 (almost uniquely, Weiser [*Psalms*, 784] foregoes any such observation, keeping the focus of his comment on "the deliciously scented" oil's principal aesthetic significance). But if in fact this is what the psalmist "wishes to recall" (Dahood, *Psalms III*, 251), it is accomplished only through allusion, and at that not in any heavy-handed way. The language of oil *y-r-d*-ing over head and beard may well be compatible with that more specifically sacral anointing (though see Ezek 32:14), but it is not that language (see S. Paul, *Amos* [Hermeneia; Minneapolis: Fortress, 1991], 208) nor is it even close to the wording in the actual biblical accounts of Aaron's anointing (Exod 29:7; Lev 8:12). To put it slightly differently, the mention of Aaron (as with the mountains Hermon and Zion) is typically metonymic, as shown through the excruciating laconicism of the reference. That is, change the name—to David, Moses, Omri—and the tradition-laden associations that flood the poem change. Priestly anointing is surely one of those highly metonymic, extratextual associations that is achieved in attaching the

beard specifically to Aaron, but to focus this as some precise summing of the psalm's preserved wording is to fudge that wording, as noted, and to mistake traditional modes of making meaning for highly literate ones. Whatever more may be assumed about Psalm 133, it is composed specifically of "contexted" words that reach "beyond the confines of the individual performance or oral-derived text to a set of traditional ideas much larger and richer than any single performance or text" (Foley, "Word-Power," 281; cf. D. Hymes, "The Ethnography of Speaking," in T. Gladwin and W. Sturtevant (eds.), *Anthropology and Human Behavior* [Washington, D.C.: Anthropological Society of Washington, 1962], 13–53; Zumthor, *Oral Poetry*, 89).

79. D. Prinz, "The Role of Water Harvesting in Alleviating Water Scarcity in Arid Areas," keynote lecture, Proceedings, International Conference on Water Resources Management in Arid Regions, March 23–27, 2002, Kuwait Institute for Scientific Research, Kuwait (vol. III, 107–122); cf. "Water Harvesting—History, Techniques and Trends," *Zeitschrift für Bewässerungswirtschaft* 31/1 (1996), 64–105.

80. See "Palestine, Climate of," in *ABD* 5, 119–26.

81. See M. Mileta et al., "Comparison of Dew Yields in Four Mediterranean Sites: Similarities and Differences," in Proceedings of the Third International Conference on Fog, Fog Collection and Dew (2004); S. M. Berkowicz et al., "Urban Dew Collection under Semi-arid Conditions: Jerusalem," in Proceedings of the Third International Conference on Fog, Fog Collection and Dew (2004).

82. *Psalms III*, 251; cf. Tsumura, "Sorites," 416–17.

83. Translation by M. Smith in S. B. Parker (ed.), *Ugaritic Narrative Poetry* (WAW 9; Scholars Press, 1997), 109.

84. Here (and in v. 39) the Masoretes point as if from an original **qatall-* form (namely *ûmišmannê < *šamann-*), though the form with this root is not attested elsewhere in biblical Hebrew and has no known cognates. Dahood's instinct to read as if from the very common *šemen* "oil" makes good sense, especially in light of the Ugaritic parallels in phrasing (*Psalms III*, 251; cf. H. J. Zobel, "Der biblische Gebrauch von *šmn* im Ugaritischen un Hebräischen," *ZAW* 82 [1970], 209–16).

85. Contra Dahood (*Psalms III*, 251) and others who see the the "dew" and "oil" here as ciphers for rain; this is not so obviously the case in either the Ugaritic or biblical examples. This way of putting things, as if olive oil were a natural product from the earth without the need of human agency, is elliptical. The ellipsis, still apparent, is better glimpsed and more readily appreciated in phrases like *'ereṣ-zêt šemen* "land of olive oil, olives bearing oil" (Deut 8:8) and *wěšemen mēḥalmîš ṣûr* "oil from flinty rock" (Deut 32:13). That is, oil is of the earth only as it is processed by human hands. Interestingly, in reality dew is not the meteorological phenomenon supposed by the ancients.

86. G. A. Smith, *The Historical Geography of the Holy Land* (London, 1931), 65; cf. Weiser, *Psalms*, 784.

87. It is Hermon as boundary marker that Berlin seizes on in her suggestion that the poem's main interest lies in the unification of north and south—Hermon and Zion ("Psalm 133," 142, 145). However, one problem with the thesis is that Hermon itself is never really used elsewhere as a metonym for the north (Tg. Ps. construes the reference in Ps 89:13 as a metonym for the east, though the reading is likely motivated by the local context of the verse in the psalm) but more accurately mostly measures the northern extremities of ancient Israel. Sometimes the perspective even seems to be from the outside looking in (esp. Ps 42:7).

88. Cf. F.-L. Hossfeld and E. Zenger, *Psalms 2* (Hermeneia; Minneapolis: Fortress, 2005), 409. For the gods of the Lebanon more generally, see provisionally M. S. Smith, "The Problem of the God and His Manifestations: The Case of the Baals at Ugarit, with Implications for Yahweh of Various Locales," in Aaron Schart and Jutta Krispenz (ed.), *Die Stadt im Zwölfprophetenbuch* (BZAW 428; Berlin: de Gruyter, 2012), 205–50.

89. The insistence by so many (most recently, Alter, *Psalms*, 463) on a strictly mimetic or realistic sense here is unwarranted. Biblical poets often show off a capacity for imaging the world other than through realism (e.g., the deer–lover in the Song of Songs; the speaking-but-not-literally-through-speech-cosmos in Ps 19; conceptualizations of the deity).

90. For this motif and the Zion tradition more generally, see J. J. M. Roberts, "The Davidic Origin of the Zion Tradition" and "Zion in the Theology of the Davidic-Solomonic Empire," in *The Bible and the Ancient Near East: Collected Essays* (Winona Lake, Ind.: Eisenbrauns, 2002), 313–30 and 331–47; J. Levenson, "Zion Traditions," in *ABD* 6, 1098–1102.

91. See generally R. J. Clifford, *The Cosmic Mountain in Canaan and the Old Testament* (HSM 4: Cambridge, Mass.: Harvard University Press, 1972).

92. Some have stressed a connection with the Zion songs (e.g., Keel, "Ps 133," 77–78; Allen, *Psalms 101–150*, 214). However, such a connection (and its presumed cultic implications) is much more obvious in 11QPs^a and Syr. (and MT^{mss}) where *hr ṣywn* is read. Which is to say that the plural of MT troubles (at the very least) the cuing of the Zion tradition here. One implication of the plural, on my reading, is that the surrounding hills of Zion are placed most immediately in focus (cf. Ps 121:1; 125:2), with the Zion tradition itself being alluded to only secondarily and at a distance (cf. Ps 87:1). Put still differently, the reading of the singular phrase, which is otherwiase standard in the Zion songs, reads that tradition into this context far more explicitly than does the plural phrasing.

93. Berlin, "Psalm 133," 144. Berlin even suggests that "making a connection" between these verses "is unnecessary, if not harmful, to a correct understanding of the poem." In fact, one of the central aims of Berlin's interpretation of Psalm 133 is to maintain that "the two comparative particles (*k*) do not introduce two similes which relate back to 'dwelling in unity'" (144). Rather, she believes the two similes relate to each other, are equated, namely "like the good oil on the head...so

is the dew of Hermon." But the construction she cites in support of this construal (*k-...k-*, Joüon sec. 174i), whether in poetry or prose, inevitably involves the
sequence of particles in rather close proximity (esp. Isa 24:2; Ps 139:12), the
close juxtaposition itself effecting the sense of equation (e.g., "like father, like son"),
and often involves other linguistic cues in support of the construal (e.g., *ʾāz,
ʾattâ* in Josh 14:11; *kî...yaḥdāw yaḥălōkû* in 1 Sam 30:24). Neither is obviously
true of the similes in Psalm 133. Indeed, I think the scale (i.e., the comparisons
in question being separated by several couplets) in this instance works against
Berlin's suggestion. But in any case the syntactic profile of the whole is sufficiently indistinct as to warrant consideration of other possible construals.

94. *Psalms*, 784; cf. Zenger in Hossfeld and Zenger, *Psalms 3*, 472 ("vv. 2–3b...are
the pictorial half").

95. Spacing was used to divide words already in Aramaic from the seventh century
BCE on (e.g., *KAI* 233; *TAD* A1.1) and becomes the normative scribal practice
in most (biblical) manuscripts written in the so-called Jewish script recovered
from the Dead Sea and its environs, see E. Tov, *Scribal Practices and Approaches
Reflected in the Texts Found in the Judean Desert* (Leiden: Brill, 2004), 131; F. W.
Dobbs-Allsopp, "Space, Line, and the Written Biblical Poem in Texts from the
Judean Desert," in M. Lundberg et al. (ed.), *Puzzling Out the Past: Studies in
Northwest Semitic Languages and Literatures in Honor of Bruce Zuckerman*
(Leiden: Brill, 2012), 19–61.

96. The experience of temporality, "a sense of real-time unfolding," is a critical distinguishing characteristic of the poetic in general and nonnarrative, lyric poetry
in particular, especially aboriginally in actual performance—the elapse of time
makes no difference in the "silent" reading of narrative prose (cf. B. H. Smith,
Poetic Closure: A Study of How Poems End [Chicago: University of Chicago Press,
1968], 4; D. Attridge, *The Singularity of Literature* [London: Routledge, 204], 71).

97. "Examples of Wallace Stevens," in F. Lentricchia and A. Dubois (eds.), *Close
Reading: The Reader* (Durham: Duke, 2003), 116.

98. "Examples of Wallace Stevens," 116.

99. "Examples of Wallace Stevens," 116. Blackmur, of course, is writing expressly
about a highly literate poet. But traditional art (and poets) may also exhibit "creativity" and "inventiveness," albeit of a different kind, see M. C. Amodio,
Writing the Oral Tradition: Oral Poetics and Literate Culture in Medieval England
(Notre Dame: University of Notre Dame Press, 2004), 46–53.

100. Cf. Gunkel, *Psalmen*, 569. The lineation here again follows the spacing discernible in B19a. In Aleppo there is not a significant amount of space separating *ṣiwwâ* and *yhwh*. This line division has sometimes been questioned.
However, the fact of lineation itself is shown visually in the bicolumnar page
layout with interspersed spacing of MT (the combination of spacing and
column boundary is especially telling in Aleppo, fig. 43; in 11QPs^(a, b) the psalm

is written in a running format, fig. 44), and the resulting lengths of line are balanced (Dahood, *Psalms III*, 252) and comparable with those in the rest of the poem. Even the staging, i.e., in which subject and object make up a single line of their own, has good parallels (esp. Lam 2:1a).

101. 11QPs[a] reads the long form, *šmh*.

102. The rendering of *kî šām* as simply "there" follows the lead of NJV. This leaves ambiguous the question of whether to understand the force of *kî* here asseveratively or logically. As I indicate (in the body of the essay), I think both senses are to be heard. But any literal rendering of *kî* into English must favor one ("indeed, truly, verily") or the other ("because, for") construal.

103. *Ḥayyîm* is lacking in 11QPs[a]. LXX, Tg., and Syr. add a conjunction. Vg. and 11QPs[b] (as far as it is extant) follow MT. Of the two readings, the shorter and more syntactically challenging MT (and Vg.) is likely the more original reading. The addition of the conjunction eases, and thereby clarifies and interprets explicitly, the appositional construction of MT. (The addition of the conjunction earlier in v. 2 in Syr., namely *wʾ dqnʾ*, is also of this nature.) According to LXX, Tg., and Syr., Yahweh here commands two things: blessing *and* life. It is difficult to imagine the latter being simplified to an appositional construction, except through parablepsis (the *waw* being overlooked between the final *he* on *hbrkh* and the initial *het* from *ḥyym* (which are similar especially at Qumran, cf. P. Kyle McCarter, Jr., *Textual Criticism* [GBS; Philadelphia: Fortress, 1986], 46):

MT, Vg.	ʾt-hbrkh ḥyym	ʿd-hʿwlm
LXX, Tg., Syr.	ʾt-hbrkh wḥyym	ʿd-(h)ʿwlm
11QPs[a]	ʾt-hbrkh	ʿd- ʿwlm
11QPs[b]	ʾt-hbrkh ḥyym[	]lm

The absence of *ḥayyîm* in 11QPs[a] is more puzzling. There is no obvious mechanical explanation of the minus here. Though not precisely paralleled, the sentiment of blessing or being blessed forever is not uncommon in the Psalms in particular (e.g., 41:14; 45:3; 72:19; 89:53; 106:48; 113:5; 115:18; 145:1, 2, 21). The reading in 11QPs[a] could be explained as a simplification of MT or simply a performative alternative (not so much an "error" of any kind as a reperformance of a different kind), or even as D. N. Freedman (cited in Dahood, *Psalms III*, 253) suggests, an intentional omission that was theologically motivated, namely to get rid of any notion of an eternal life. But, in any case, of the two readings (MT and 11QPs[a]), it is hard to imagine the rationale for inserting *ḥayyîm* into a text like 11QPs[a]. Moreover, considerations of line length and of the sound patterns traced in the body of this chapter support the suspicion that the reading in MT is more likely to have given rise to a reading like that in 11QPs[a].

104. 11QPsᵃ and MTᵐˢˢ (Ken) read the common ʿd ʿwlm. The idiom with the definite article, as in MT, LXX (*heōs tou aiōnos*), and Tg. (ʿd ʿlm'; cf. Syr. ʿdm' l'lm), is the more difficult reading and is a feature of LBH (see Hurvitz, *Transition Period*, 158–59): outside of the four instances in the Psalms (28:9; 41:14; 106:48; 133:3), ʿd-hʿwlm occurs only in the books of Chronicles, Nehemiah, and Daniel; it is in contrast to the SBH idiom ʿd-ʿwlm; and the targums consistently translate the latter as ʿd ʿlm' (= Heb. ʿd-hʿwlm). Hurvitz gives the following example, which nicely points up the contrast:

2 Sam 7:16:	*wn'mn bytk wmmlktk*	ʿd ʿwlm
1 Chron 17:14:	*wh'mdtyhw bbyty wbmlkwty*	ʿd hʿwlm
Targum (to Samuel):	*wqym bytk wmlkwtk*	ʿd ʿlm'

11QPsᵃ (cf. 11QPsᵇ: *šlwm ʿl[yśrʾl]*) adds a line to the end of the poem not attested in MT or any of the other witnesses: *šlwm ʿl yśrʾl* lit. "Peace upon Israel." This addition, combined with other variations in 11QPsᵃ, significantly alters how this poem ends. The main upshot is to provide the blessing (*šlwm ʿl yśrʾl*) that Yahweh in 11QPsᵃ is understood to have commanded. The plus itself occurs elsewhere in Ps 125:5 and 128:6, where it also closes the respective poems, and thus looks suspiciously secondary in Psalm 133. Again it is difficult to imagine varying a text like 11QPsᵃ such that it would result in the verse attested in MT. (This is supported by the need to reconstruct *ḥyym* in 11QPsᵃ, which suggests the priority of MT.)

105. Further, it should be recalled that the lack of the so-called prose particles in biblical Hebrew poetry is largely a consequence of the compressed nature of the latter kind of discourse and the primordiality of the poetic tradtion more generally. There is no (metaphysical) reason why they should not appear in verse after the advent of written prose—and, in fact, they do quite commonly!—nor should their appearance be construed (invariably) as a sign of prose—though, perhaps, a prosaizing style is lent to the poetry, i.e., a style of verse showing an awareness of prose. Besides the Masoretes are not normally given to lineating prose, and prosaic glosses are not common in the Psalms (outside of the superscriptions).

106. On the notion of "terminal modification" as an especially commonplace means for signaling closure in poems, see Smith, *Poetic Closure*, esp. 28, 43–44.

107. Smith notices that poems often allude at the end to experiences (literary or nonliterary) that have associations with "termination, finality, repose or stability" (*Poetic Closure*, 175–76). The language of perpetuity (*ʿad-ʿôlām*, etc.) in the Hebrew Bible carries just these kinds of associations (esp. finality and permanence), and even a cursory reading of how psalms typically end reveals a conspicuous preference for this language in closing lines (e.g., Ps 5:12; 12:8; 15:5; 18:51; 28:9; 30:13; 41:14; 45:18; 48:15; 52:10–11; 61:9; 72:19; 79:13; 89:53;

100:5; 106:48; 111:10; 115:18; 117:2; 118:29; 121:8; 136:26; 138:8; 139:24; 145:21; 146:10).

108. So Keel, "Ps 133," 76 and n. 37; Allen, *Psalms 101–150*, 213. The question of asseverative *kî* has been thoroughly discussed of late. For bibliography, see Muraoka, *Emphatic Words*, 158–64; JM secs.164, 165a, e; *IBHS* sec. 39.3.4e. Muraoka's discussion is most judicious and his summary statement may be offered as a working premise for the consideration of individual cases of asseverative *kî* (164): "The etymologically deducible original demonstrative force of the particle *ki* was still alive alongside its later specializations, and this demonstrative function is the source of its occasional asseverative-emphatic use. It is used particularly when it appears in oath formulas, and closely related to that in the apodosis of conditional sentences. Beyond these uses, it may be used for the emphasizing purpose when directly fixed to the predicate, and that almost exclusively in poetic context." In his larger discussion, Muraoka also notes the use of asseverative *kî* in "a climatic construction" (e.g., Ps 77:12; Isa 32:13; *Emphatic Words*, 163). In all cases, of course, the discernment of emphasis is a consequence of contextual considerations. In Psalm 133 *kî šām*, which elsewhere is sometimes written with a *maqqaph* (i.e., *kî-šām*, e.g., Gen 11:9; 43:25; Num 11:34; 1 Sam 7:17; 22:22) emphasizing the words' close bond as a phrasal unit, directly precedes the predicate (*ṣiwwâ*) and, if not locally climatic (in Muraoka's sense), the closing triplet in Psalm 133 is certainly rhetorically prominent, even climatic. *Kî miššām* in Jeremiah 22:24 as a part of Yahweh's oath is emphatic ("even there…" NRSV), and *kî šām* in Hosea 9:15, Psalm 122:5, and Psalm 137:3 may be taken asseveratively—or at least the force of the particle is not so obviously or necessarily logical in these passages (cf. 2 Chron 20:26). *Hinnê-šām* (e.g., Ezek 8:4), *'ak-šām* (Isa 34:14, 15), and *gam-šām* (Ps 139:10) exemplify related types of asseverative markers.

109. Weiser, *Psalms*, 785; Dahood, *Psalms III*, 252; Berlin, "Psalm 133," 146; cf. *IBHS* secs. 38.4, 7–8, 39.3.4e. Syr. construes specifically in this way: *mṭl dtmn* "because there…"

110. The plainer sententiousness of the lines suits the causal or logical construal especially well, as the appeal of the explanation is enhanced by the apparent simplicity or straightforwardness with which it is made.

111. The writing in B19a runs on with no additional space (i.e., nothing more than normal space separating individual words) separating *ṣiyyôn* and *kî* (contrast Aleppo, fig. 43), lending itself, spatially, to being construed as a continuation of and therefore comment on the immediately preceding clause (fig. 42).

112. Dahood, *Psalms III*, 262; Keel, "Ps 133," 78–80; Weiser, *Psalms*, 785; Berlin, "Psalm 133," 146.

113. See Roberts, "Zion in the Theology of the Davidic-Solomonic Empire," 331–47.

114. Others, too, have noticed this tendency for *šām* to reference Zion/Jerusalem in a group of psalms (e.g., Allen, *Psalms 101–150*, 214). It is worth stressing here

that *šām* remains a deictic particle throughout and whatever more specific connotations accrue to it do so through iteration and deployment in specific discourses (such as in the Songs of Ascents).

115. In 11QPsᵃ Psalm 133 is followed immediately by Psalm 141, which also opens
on a note of blessing, namely *brwk yhwh*.

116. In Deuteronomy 28:8 the further specification of the commanded blessing is
effected analogously through prepositional phrases, namely "Yahweh will command upon you the blessing *in your barns* and *in all that you undertake*." That
this is not an obvious reading is perhaps suggested by the many witnesses and
versions that add the conjunctive *waw*, so that what is commanded is "the
blessing *and* life." Though it must be said that the latter is not entirely felicitous.
Why distinguish blessing from life? And nowhere else is "life" as such (i.e., in
these words) commanded by Yahweh. 11QPsᵃ lacks any mention of "life" at all,
meaning that readers of this text are forced to think back through the psalm for
a more particular understanding of "the blessing" here commanded.

117. Esp. J. J. Collins, *Daniel* (Hermeneia; Minneapolis: Fortress, 1993), 392, n. 212;
P. C. Craigie, *Psalms 1–50* (Word; Waco: Word, 1983), 191. Contra Dahood,
Psalms III, 253. Freedman (as cited in Dahood, *Psalms III*, 253) raises the possibility that *ḥyym* may have been omitted intentionally in 11QPsᵃ to avoid just
this connotation of eternal life.

118. The Karatepe inscription of Azatiwada (*KAI* 26) elaborates well the kind of
flourishing life (esp. ll. A i 1–21, ii 1–19) that the phrase "length of days" (l. A iii 5;
C iii 20) implies and that results from divine blessing (ll. Ai 1, iii 2; C iii 16).
The last rendition, written on the statue of Baal, fleshes out the general sense
behind the language of Psalm 133:3 (though the latter, of course, does not have
the king in view): "Now may Baal KRNTRYŠ bless (*wbrk*) Azatiwada with life
(*bḥym*) and health and mighty strength over every king; may Baal KRNTRYŠ
and all the gods of the city give Azatiwada length of days (*ʾrk ymm*) and multitude of years and good (*nʿmt*) prosperity" (*COS* II, 31).

119. *Psalms 1–50*, 191.

120. So, for example, in the Elephantine marriage contracts the *verba solemnia* that
establishes the marriage relationship includes language of perpetuity, usually
glossed as in *TAD*: "She is my wife and I am her husband *from this day and
forever*" (*mn ywmʾ znh wʿd ʾlm*, B2.6.4). And yet these same contracts go on to
speak to the eventuality of divorce, namely "tomorrow or the next day" (*mḥr ʾ[w]
ywm ḥrn*) should Miptahiah initiate divorce proceedings" (e.g., *TAD* B2.6.22ff.),
making the sense of *ʾlm*, as referencing some (at present) undeterminable
point in the future (even most literally "tomorrow or the next day"), quite clear.

121. Cf. Freedman as cited in Dahood, *Psalms III*, 253. In 11QPsᵃ, the lack of *ḥym* explodes the /-īm/ chain of MT. While the linking succession of /-ām/ sounds can
still be heard in the voiced wording of this manuscript, it is the thrice-repeated
/-ā/ in *śmḥ. ṣwh*, and *hbrkh* that answers most emphatically the doubled *mh* of v. 1.

122. Cf. Gunkel, *Psalmen*, 572; Weiser, *Psalms*, 785; Zenger in Hossfeld and Zenger, *Psalms 3*, 481–82.

123. See Schloen (*House of the Father*) on how the household metaphor shapes Israel's political imagination.

124. On the philosophical seriousness of this claim, see M. Wyschogrod, *The Body of Pain* (Northvale, N.J.: Jason Aronson, 1996), esp. 21–29, 58–70, 175–77.

125. "The Kerygma of the Yahwist," in W. Brueggemann (ed.), *The Vitality of Old Testament Traditions* (Atlanta: John Knox, 1975), 41–66.

126. *Literary Theory*, 75. Similarly, Frye notes that what is distinctively "lyrical" is the "union of sound and sense." (*Anatomy of Criticism* [Princeton: Princeton University Press, 1957], 272; Frye's additional notion of poetic creation as specifically "oracular," though but one way of conceptualizing the creative process, does flesh out quite vividly the lyrical fusion of "sound and sense": "an associative rhetorical process, most of it below the threshold of consciousness, a chaos of paronomasia, sound-links, ambiguous sense-links, and memory-links very like that of a dream," 271–72; cf. D. Levertov, *Light Up the Cave* [New York: New Directions, 1981], 29–45.) Levertov also stresses the importance of sound to the lyric poet: "All words are to some extent onomatopoeic" (60). And: "The primary impulse for me was always to make a structure out of words, words that *sounded* right. And I think that's a rather basic foundation of a poet's word" (78).

127. E.g., Berlin, "Psalm 133," 145.

128. The frame is itself fastened to the poem's body (ever so subtly) by the assonating play of sibilants and labials in *šebet* and *šemen* and sibilants and approximants in *ṣiyyôn* and *ṣiwwâ* (cf. Allen, *Psalms 101–150*, 215).

129. Cf. C. L. Seow, *Job 1–21* (Illuminations; Grand Rapids: Eerdmans, 2013), 362, 364.

130. Note the *šām / gam* play in the line-internal parallelism of Psalm 137:1: *šām yāšabnû gam bākînû*, which NRSV renders interestingly as "*there* we sat down and *there* we wept" (cf. ASV: "There we sat down, yea, we wept"). And *gam-šām* even occurs as a unit in several instances (Isa 23:12: 57:7; Ps 139:10). All four passages give further credence to the notion that the sound patterns noticed are intentionally deployed.

131. For a broad survey of the divine mountain in ancient Near Eastern thought, see R. Clifford, *The Cosmic Mountain in Canaan and the Old Testament* (Cambridge, Mass.: Harvard University Press, 1972). J. J. M. Roberts comments more explicitly on Zion as a site of blessing and well-being as a consequence of Yahweh's dwelling there in "Davidic Origin of the Zion Tradition" and "Zion in the Theology of the Davidic-Solomonic Empire," 313–30, 331–47).

132. Cf. Weiser, *Psalms*, 785.

133. There is a substantiality—a thingness—to blessings and cursings in antiquity as they were the tangible products (namely blessedness = deliverance from enemies, e.g., *Qom* 3.2) of speech acts (namely "I hereby bless you," *KA* 3.1.1–2;

Arad 16.2–3; cf. S. Sanders, "Performative Utterances and Divine Language in Ugaritic," *JNES* 63 [2004], 161–81, esp. 174). So in Leviticus 25:21 Yahweh's blessing, once commanded, takes on an agency such that it can be conceptualized as the subject of a transitive verb: "so that it (= blessing) will yield (lit. 'do,' *wě'āśāt*) a crop (*'et-hattěbû'â*) for three years."

134. For the idea of "retrospective patterning" in poetry, see esp. Smith, *Poetic Closure*, 10–14.

135. Gerstenberger (*Psalms, Part 2*, 372) recognizes something of this retrospective resonance of "blessing" in Psalm 133, even if I think it ultimately comes off quite differently from the way Gerstenberger supposes: "The inner logic of the psalm, therefore, runs counter to the sequence of the text [namely exclamation followed by similes and the concluding *kî* clause]. First, there is the blessing of Yahweh from Zion, then this blessing runs down to all who meet at the sanctuary, therefore they may be called 'happy' (although the standard expression of BEATITUDE, *'ašrê*, is missing; cf. [Ps] 1:1)." Weiser (*Psalms*, 785) is also alert to the prospective and retrospective play of this poem, the need to always "look both ways."

136. C. Altieri, "Tractatus Logico-Poeticus," *Critical Inquiry* 33 (2007), 537.

137. See the thoughts of M. Nussbaum on the medium of lyric verse and what it requires of readers in *The Fragility of Goodness* (Cambridge: Cambridge University Press, 1986), 67–70. See Altieri, "Tractatus Logico-Poeticus," 538.

138. Still another closing commonplace noticed by Smith (*Poetic Closure*, 182–86) is "unqualified assertion"—"an utterance apparently tends to sound particularly valid when it is delivered in the form of an unqualified assertion." The closing of Psalm 125 is also complex, involving alternative line groupings that are successively cued—the chiasm that shapes vv. 4–5b strands (and thereby emphasizes) the final benediction, while the resulting final shape of the stanza (couplet + triplet) echoes that of the opening stanza (vv. 1–2), enacting at the level of line structure an *inclusio* that checks and closes the poem.

139. "Ethnography of Scribal Writing," 423–25. For an example of a biblical scholar beginning to consider the possibility of "multiformity" as it impinges on traditional text critical issues, see R. F. Person, *The Deuteronomic History and the Books of Chronicles: Scribal Works in an Oral World* (Atlanta: SBL, 2010), esp. chs. 3–5.

140. So, according to Gerstenberger (*Psalms, Part 2*, 372), the "blissful state" of brothers dwelling together "could only be a consequence of blessings from above."

141. "Hearing from Books: The Rise of Fictionality in Old English Poetry," in A. N. Doane and C. B. Pasternack (eds.), *Vox Intexta: Orality and Textuality in the Middle Ages* (Madison: University of Wisconsin Press, 1991), 123.

142. Cf. K. Burke, "Symbolic Action in a Poem by Keats," in Lentricchia and DuBois, *Close Reading: The Reader*, 72–87, esp. 76.

Works Cited

Adorno, Theodor. "Lyric Poetry and Society." *Telos* 20 (1974): 56–71.

Ahituv, Shmuel. *Echoes from the Past: Hebrew and Cognate Inscriptions from the Biblical Period*. Jerusalem: Carta, 2008.

Ahituv, Shmuel, Esther Eshel, and Ze'ev Meshel. "The Inscriptions." Pages 73–142 in *Kuntillet 'Arud (Horvat Teman): An Iron Age II Religious Site on the Judah-Sinai Border*. Edited by Ze'ev Meshel. Jerusalem: Israel Exploration Society, 2012.

Aitken, Kenneth T. "Oral Formulaic Composition and Theme in the Aqhat Narrative." *Ugarit-Forschungen* 21 (1989): 1–16.

Aitken, Kenneth T. "Word Pairs and Tradition in an Ugaritic Tale." *Ugarit-Forschungen* 21 (1989): 17–38.

Albright, William F. "The Earliest Forms of Hebrew Verse." *Journal of the Palestine Oriental Society* 2 (1922): 69–86.

Alexander, P. S. *The Targum of Canticles. Translated, with a Critical Introduction Apparatus, and Notes*. Aramaic Bible 17A. Collegeville: Liturgical Press, 2003.

Allen, Gay Wilson. "Biblical Analogies for Walt Whitman's Prosody." *Revue Anglo-Americaine* 6 (1933): 490–507.

Allen, Gay Wilson. "Biblical Echoes in Whitman's Works." *American Literature* 6 (1934): 302–15.

Allen, Gay Wilson. *American Prosody*. New York: American Book, 1935.

Allen, Gay Wilson. *The New Walt Whitman Handbook*. New York: New York University Press, 1975.

Allen, Grant. *Physical Aesthetics*. New York: Appleton, 1877.

Allen, Leslie C. *Psalms 101–150*. Waco: Word Books, 1983.

Alonso Schökel, Luis. *A Manual of Hebrew Poetics*. Subsidia biblica 11; Rome: Editrice Pontificio Istituto Biblico, 1988.

Alter, Robert. *The Art of Biblical Narrative*. New York: Basic Books, 1981.

Alter, Robert. "How Convention Helps Us Read: The Case of the Bible's Annunciation Type-Scene." *Prooftexts* 3 (1983): 115–30.

Alter, Robert. *The Art of Biblical Poetry.* New York: Basic Books, 1985.

Alter, Robert. *The Pleasures of Reading in an Ideological Age.* New York: Norton, 1996.

Alter, Robert. *The Book of Psalms.* New York: Norton, 2007.

Altieri, Charles. "Motives in Metaphor: John Ashbery and the Modernist Long Poem." *Genre* 11/4 (1978): 653–87.

Altieri, Charles. "Taking Lyrics Literally: Teaching Poetry in a Prose Culture." *New Literary History* 32 (2001): 259–81.

Altieri, Charles. "Tractatus Logico-Poeticus." *Critical Inquiry* 33 (2007): 527–43.

Amit, Yairah. "Multi-purpose 'Leading Word' and the Problems of Its Usage." *Prooftexts* 9 (1989): 99–114.

Amodio, Mark. *Writing the Oral Tradition: Oral Poetics and Literate Culture in Medieval England.* Notre Dame: University of Notre Dame Press, 2004.

Andersen, Francis I., and David N. Freedman. *Amos.* Anchor Bible 24A. New York: Doubleday, 1989.

Anderson, W. S. "The Theory and Practice of Poetic Arrangement from Vergil to Ovid." Pages 44–65 in *Poems in Their Place: The Intertextuality and Order of Poetic Collections.* Edited by N. Fraistat. Chapel Hill: University of North Carolina Press, 1986.

Antomarini, Brunella. "The Acoustical Prehistory of Poetry." Translated by S. Stewart. *New Literary History* 35 (2004): 355–72.

Anttila, Raimo. "Philology and Etymology." Pages 323–34 in *Historical and Comparative Linguistics.* 2d rev. ed. Amsterdam: John Benjamins, 1989.

Attridge, Derek. *The Rhythms of English Poetry.* London: Longman, 1982.

Attridge, Derek. *Poetic Rhythm: An Introduction.* Cambridge: Cambridge University Press, 1995.

Attridge, Derek. *The Singularity of Literature.* London: Routledge, 2004.

Auden, Wystan Hugh. *The Dyer's Hand and Other Essays.* New York: Vintage, 1989.

Auerbach, Erich. *Mimesis: The Representation of Reality in Western Literature.* Princeton: Princeton University Press, 1953.

Avigad, Nahman, and Benjamin Sass. *Corpus of West Semitic Stamp Seals.* Jerusalem: Israel Academy of Sciences and Humanities, 1997.

Avishur, Yitzhak. "Addenda to the Expanded Colon in Ugaritic and Biblical Verse." *Ugarit-Forschungen* 4 (1972): 1–10.

Avishur, Yitzhak. *Stylistic Studies of Word Pairs in Biblical and Ancient Semitic Literatures.* Neukirchen-Vluyn: Neukirchener Verlag, 1984.

Baker, Aelred. "Parallelism: England's Contribution to Biblical Studies." *Catholic Biblical Quarterly* 35 (1973): 429–40.

Barfield, Owen. "Poetry, Verse and Prose." *New Statesman* 31 (1928): 793–94.

Barnes, Harry R. "Enjambement and Oral Composition." *Transactions of the American Philological Association* 109 (1979): 1–10.

Baroway, Israel. "The Bible as Poetry in the English Renaissance: An Introduction." *Journal of English and German Philology* 32 (1933): 447–80.

Baroway, Israel. "Tremellius, Sidney, and Biblical Verse." *Modern Language Notes* 49 (1934): 145–49.

Baroway, Israel. "The Hebrew Hexameter: A Study in Renaissance Sources and Interpretation." *English Literary History* 2 (1935): 66–91.

Baroway, Israel. "The Lyre of David: A Further Study of Renaissance Interpretation of Biblical Form." *English Literary History* 8 (1941): 119–42.

Baroway, Israel. "The Accentual Theory of Hebrew Prosody: A Further Study in Renaissance Interpretation of Biblical Form." *English Literary History* 17 (1950): 115–35.

Barry, Mary Martin. *An Analysis of the Prosodic Structure of Selected Poems of T. S. Eliot.* Rev. ed. Washington, D.C.: Catholic University Press, 1969.

Bartók, Béla, and Albert B. Lord. *Serbo-Croatian Folk Songs.* New York: Columbia University Press, 1951.

Bastianini, Guido, and Claudio Gallazzi, eds. *Posidippo di Pella Epigrammi (P.Mil. Vogl/ VIII 309).* 2 vols. Milan: LED, 2001.

Bauman, Richard. *Verbal Art as Performance.* Long Grove, Ill.: Waveland, 1977.

Bauman, Richard, and Charles Briggs. *Voices of Modernity: Language Ideologies and the Politics of Inequality.* Cambridge: Cambridge University Press, 2003.

Bäuml, Franz H. "Varieties and Consequences of Medieval Literacy and Illiteracy." *Speculum: A Journal of Medieval Studies* 55 (1980): 237–65.

Bäuml, Franz H. "Medieval Texts and the Two Theories of Oral-Formulaic Composition: A Proposal for a Third Theory." *New Literary History* 16 (1984): 51–66.

Beentjes, Pancratius C. *The Book of Ben Sira in Hebrew.* Leiden: Brill, 1997.

Berkowicz, S. M., et al. "Urban Dew Collection under Semi-arid Conditions: Jerusalem." In Proceedings of the Third International Conference on Fog, Fog Collection and Dew, 2004.

Berlin, Adele. "Motif and Creativity in Biblical Poetry." *Prooftexts* 3 (1983): 231–41.

Berlin, Adele. *The Dynamics of Biblical Parallelism.* Bloomington: Indiana University Press, 1985.

Berlin, Adele. "On the Interpretation of Psalm 133." Pages 141–47 in *Directions in Biblical Hebrew Poetry.* Edited by E. Follis. Sheffield: JSOT, 1987.

Berlin, Adele. *Biblical Poetry through Medieval Jewish Eyes.* Bloomington: Indiana University Press, 1991.

Bernstein, Charles. *Content's Dream: Essays 1975–1984.* Los Angeles: Sun and Moon, 1986.

Beyers, Chris. *A History of Free Verse.* Fayetteville: University of Arkansas Press, 2001.

Blackmur, R. P. "Examples of Wallace Stevens." Pages 111–35 in *Close Reading: The Reader.* Edited by F. Lentricchia and A. Dubois. Durham, N.C.: Duke University Press, 2003.

Blair, High. *Critical Dissertation on the Poems of Ossian, the Son of Fingal.* London: Garland, 1765.

Blasing, Mutlu. *Lyric Poetry: The Pain and the Pleasure of Words*. Princeton: Princeton University Press, 2007.

Blau, Joshua. *Phonology and Morphology of Biblical Hebrew*. Winona Lake, Ind.: Eisenbrauns, 2010.

Blayney, Benjamin. *Jeremiah and Lamentations*. 3d ed. London, 1836.

Booth, Wayne C. *The Company We Keep: An Ethics of Fiction*. Berkeley: University of California Press, 1988.

Borowski, Oded. *Every Living Thing: Daily Use of Animals in Ancient Israel*. Walnut Creek, Calif.: Altamira, 1998.

Bowie, E. "Lyric and Elegiac Poetry." Pages in *The Oxford History of the Classical World*. Edited by J. Boardman et al. Oxford: Oxford University Press, 1986.

Bowra, Cecil Maurice. *Greek Lyric Poetry: From Alcman to Simonides*. 2d ed. Oxford: Oxford University Press, 1961.

Boyarin, Daniel. "Placing Reading in Ancient Israel and Medieval Europe." Pages 59–88 in *Sparks of the Logos*. Leiden: Brill, 2003. Earlier as: Pages 10–37 in *Ethnography of Reading*. Edited by Jonathan Boyarin. Berkeley: University of California Press, 1993.

Boyd, Brian. *Why Lyrics Last: Evolution, Cognition, and Shakespeare's Sonnets*. Cambridge, Mass.: Harvard University Press, 2012.

Bradley, Sculley. "The Fundamental Metrical Principle in Whitman's Poetry." *American Literature* 10 (1939): 437–59.

Braun, Joachim. *Music in Ancient Israel/Palestine*. Translated by D. W. Stott. Grand Rapids: Eerdmans, 2002.

Brewster, S. *Lyric*. New York: Routledge, 2009.

Bright, William. " 'With One Lip, with Two Lips': Parallelism in Nahuatl." *Language* 66 (1990): 437–52.

Brooks, Cleanth. *The Well Wrought Urn*. New York: Harcourt Brace, 1942.

Brooks, Peter. *Reading for the Plot: Design and Intention in the Narrative*. New York: Knopf, 1984.

Brown, Donald E. "The Universal People." Pages 83–95 in *Evolution, Literature, and Film: A Reader*. Edited by B. Boyd, B., J. Carroll, and J. Gottschall. New York: Columbia University Press, 2010.

Buber, Martin. "The 'Leading Word' Device in the Narratives of the Torah." Pages 284–307 in *Darko shel miqra': 'iyunim bidfusey-signon batanakh*. Jerusalem: Bialik Institute, 1964.

Buber, Martin, and Franz Rosenzweig. *Scripture and Translation*. Translated by L. Rosenwald and E. Fox. Bloomington: Indiana University Press, 1994.

Bucke, Richard Maurice. *Walt Whitman*. Philadelphia: David McKay, 1883.

Budde, Karl. "Das hebräische Klagelied." *Zeitschrift für die alttestamentliche Wissenschaft* 2 (1882): 1–52.

Burke, Kenneth. *Counter-Statement*. 2d ed. Oxford: Oxford University Press, 2005 [1968].

Burke, Kenneth. *A Rhetoric of Motives.* Berkeley: University of California Press, 1969.

Burke, Kenneth. "Symbolic Action in a Poem by Keats." Pages 72–87 in *Close Reading.*

Burnshaw, Stanley, ed. *The Modern Hebrew Poem Itself.* New and updated ed. Detroit: Wayne State University Press, 2003.

Buss, Martin J. *Biblical Form Criticism in Its Context.* Journal for the Study of the Old Testament, Supp. Series 274. Sheffield: Sheffield Academic, 1998.

Byers, Prudence P. "A Formula for Poetic Intonation." *Poetics* 8 (1976): 367–80.

Byrne, Ryan. "The Refuge of Scribalism in Iron I Palestine." *BASOR* 345 (2007): 1–31.

Calame, Claude. *The Craft of Poetic Speech in Ancient Greece.* Ithaca: Cornell University Press, 1995.

Campbell, Lily Bess. *Divine Poetry and Drama in Sixteenth-Century England.* Berkeley: University of California Press, 1959.

Carmi, T. *The Penguin Book of Hebrew Verse.* New York: Penguin Books, 1982.

Carr, David M. *Writing on the Tablet of the Heart: Origins of Scripture and Literature.* Oxford: Oxford University Press, 2005.

Carr, David M. *The Formation of the Hebrew Bible: A New Reconstruction.* Oxford: Oxford University Press, 2011.

Carroll, Robert R. *Jeremiah: A Commentary.* Old Testament Library. Philadelphia: Westminster John Knox, 1986.

Casanowicz, I. M. *Paronomasia in the Old Testament.* Boston, 1894.

Cassuto, Umberto. *Biblical and Oriental Studies.* Vol. 2. *Bible and Ancient Oriental Texts.* Jerusalem: Magnes, 1975.

Cerny, J. *Paper and Books in Ancient Egypt.* London: K. Lewias, 1952.

Chafe, Wallace L. "Integration and Involvement in Speaking, Writing and Oral Literature." Pages in *Spoken and Written Language: Exploring Orality and Literacy.* Edited by D. Tannen; Norwood, N.J.: Ablex, 1982.

Chafe, Wallace L. "Linguistic Differences Produced by Differences between Speaking and Writing." Pages 105–23 in *Literacy, Language, and Learning.* Edited by David R. Olson et al. London: Cambridge University Press, 1985.

Charpin, D. *Reading and Writing in Babylon.* Translated by J. M. Todd. Cambridge, Mass.: Harvard University Press, 2010.

Chisholm, D. H. "Freie Rhythmen." Pages 427–28 in *NPEPP.*

Chisholm, D. H., and K. Bowers. "Freie Rhythmen." Pages in *PEPP.*

Chomsky, Noam. *The Minimalist Program.* Cambridge: MIT Press, 1995.

Clanchy, Michael T. "The Technology of Writing." Pages 114–44 in *From Memory to Written Record: England 1066–1307.* 2d ed. Oxford: Blackwell, 1993.

Clarke, Eric F. "Rhythm and Timing in Music." Pages 473–500 in *The Psychology of Music.* 2d ed. Edited by Diana Deutsch. San Diego: Academic, 1999.

Clayton, Martin R. L. "Free Rhythm: Ethnomusicology and the Study of Music without Metre." *Bulletin of the School of Oriental and African Studies* 59 (1996): 323–32.

Clifford, R. *The Cosmic Mountain in Canaan and the Old Testament.* HSM 4. Cambridge, Mass.: Harvard University Press, 1972.

Cline, Eric H. *1177 BC: The Year Civilization Collapsed.* Princeton: Princeton University Press, 2014.

Cohen, Matt. "Martin Tupper, Walt Whitman, and the Early Reviews of *Leaves of Grass.*" *Walt Whitman Quarterly Review* 16 (1998): 22–31.

Cole, Peter. *The Dream of the Poem.* Princeton: Princeton University Press, 2007.

Coleridge, Samuel T. "Shakespeare's Judgment Equal to His Genius." Pages 432–33 in *Selected Poetry and Prose of Samuel Taylor Coleridge.* Edited by Donald A. Stauffer. New York: Random House, 1951.

Collins, J. J. *Daniel.* Hermeneia. Minneapolis: Fortress, 1993.

Collins, Terrence. *Line-Forms in Hebrew Poetry: A Grammatical Approach to the Stylistic Study of the Hebrew Prophets.* Rome: Biblical Institute, 1978.

Condamin, Albert. *Le livre de Jérémie.* Paris, 1920.

Coogan, Michael. "Literacy and the Formation of Biblical Literature." Pages 47–61 in *Realia Dei: Essays in Archaeology and Biblical Interpretation in Honor of Edward F. Campbell, Jr. at His Retirement.* Edited by P. H. Williams, Jr., and T. Hiebert. Atlanta: Scholars Press, 1999.

Cooper, Alan. "Biblical Poetics: A Linguistic Approach." Ph.D. diss., Yale University, 1976.

Cooper, G. Burns. *Mysterious Music: Rhythm and Free Verse.* Stanford: Stanford University Press, 1998.

Cooper, G. Burns. "Free Verse." In *PEPP.*

Coote, Mary P. "Women's Songs in Serbo-Croatian." *Journal of American Folklore* 90 (1977): 331–38.

Coote, Mary P. "On the Composition of Women's Songs." *Oral Tradition* 7 (1992): 332–48.

Coote, Robert. "The Application of Oral Theory to Biblical Hebrew Literature." *Semeia* 5 (1976): 51–64.

Couey, J. Blake. "Amos vii 10–17 and Royal Attitudes toward Prophecy in the Ancient Near East." *VT* 58 (2008): 300–314.

Couey, J. Blake. "The Most Perfect Model of the Prophetic Poetry: Studies in the Poetry of First Isaiah." Ph.D. diss., Princeton Theological Seminary, 2009.

Cowley, A. E., and A. Neubauer. *The Original Hebrew of a Portion of Ecclesiasticus.* Oxford: Oxford University Press, 1897.

Craigie, P. C. *Psalms 1–50.* Word. Waco: Word, 1983.

Creach, Jerome. "Like a Tree Planted by the Temple Streams: The Portrait of the Righteous in Psalm 1:3." *Catholic Biblical Quarterly* 61 (1999): 34–46.

Cross, Frank Moore. "The Origin and Early Evolution of the Alphabet." *Eretz Israel* 8 [1967], 8–24.

Cross, Frank Moore. *Canaanite Myth and Hebrew Epic.* Cambridge, Mass.: Harvard University Press, 1972.

Cross, Frank Moore. "Prose and Poetry in the Mythic and Epic Texts from Ugarit." *Harvard Theological Review* 67 (1974): 1–15.

Cross, Frank Moore. *From Epic to Canon: History and Literature in Ancient Israel.* Baltimore: Johns Hopkins University Press, 1998.

Cross, Frank Moore. *Leaves from an Epigrapher's Notebook: Collected Papers in Hebrew and West Semitic Paleography and Epigraphy.* Winona Lake, Ind.: Eisenbrauns, 2003.

Cross, Frank Moore, and David Noel Freedman. *Early Hebrew Orthography: A Study of the Epigraphic Evidence.* New Haven: American Oriental Society, 1952.

Crown, Alan D. "Studies in Samaritan Scribal Practices and Manuscript History: III. Columnar Writing and the Samaritan Massora." *Bulletin of John Rylands Library* 1 (1984): 349–81.

Crüsemann, F. *Studien zur Formgeschichte von Hymnes und Danklied in Israel.* WMANT 32. Neukirchen-Vluyn: Neukirchener Verlag, 1969.

Culler, Jonathan. *Structural Poetics.* Ithaca: Cornell University Press, 1975.

Culler, Jonathan. *The Pursuit of Signs.* Ithaca: Cornell University Press, 1981.

Culler, Jonathan. "Reading Lyric." *Yale French Studies* 69 (1985): 98–106.

Culler, Jonathan. *Literary Theory: A Very Short Introduction.* Oxford: Oxford University Press, 1997.

Culler, Jonathan. "Why Lyric?" *Publications of the Modern Language Association* 123 (2008): 201–6.

Culler, Jonathan. "Lyric, History, and Genre." *New Literary History* 40/4 (2009): 879–99.

Culler, Jonathan. "Genre: Lyric." Paragraphs 21–60 in *The Work of Genre: Selected Essays from the English Institute.* Edited by R. Warhol. English Institute. 2011. Accessed March 5, 2015, http://quod.lib.umich.edu/cgi/t/text/text-idx?c=acls;idno =heb90055.0001.001.

Culley, Robert C. "An Approach to the Problem of Oral Tradition." *VT* 13 (1963): 113–25.

Culley, Robert C. *Oral Formulaic Language in the Biblical Psalms.* Toronto: University of Toronto Press, 1967.

Culley, Robert C. "Metrical Analysis of Classical Hebrew Poetry." Pages 12–28 in *Essays on the Ancient Semitic World.* Edited by J. Wevers and D. Redford. Toronto: University of Toronto Press, 1970.

Cureton, Richard. "Rhythm: A Multilevel Analysis." *Style* 19 (1985): 242–57.

Cureton, Richard. "A Definition of Rhythm." *Eidos* 3 (1987): 7–17.

Cureton, Richard. *Rhythmic Phrasing in English Verse.* London: Longman, 1992.

Curtius, Ernst R. *European Literature and the Latin Middle Ages.* London: Routledge and Kegan Paul, 1953.

Dahood, Mitchell. *Psalms III.* Anchor Bible 17A. Garden City: Doubleday, 1970.

Dahood, Mitchell. "Hebrew-Ugaritic Parallel Pairs." Pages 71–382 in *Ras Shamra Parallels.* Vol. 1. Edited by Loren Fisher. Rome: Pontificium institutum biblicum, 1972.

Dale, Amy M. "Stichos and Stanza." *Classical Quarterly* NS 13 (1963): 46–50.

Damásio, António. *Descartes' Error: Emotion, Reason, and the Human Brain.* New York: Quill, 1994.

Damásio, António. *The Feeling of What Happens.* San Diego: Harcourt, 1999.

Damrosch, David. *The Narrative Covenant: Transformations of Genre in the Growth of Biblical Literature.* Harper and Row, 1987.

Dantzig, Tobias. *Number: The Language of Science.* New York: Plume Penguin, 2007 (1930).

Darnell, John C., F. W. Dobbs-Allsopp, M. Lundberg, P. K. McCarter, and B. Zuckerman. *Two Early Alphabetic Inscriptions from the Wadi el-Ḥôl: New Evidence for the Origin of the Alphabet from the Western Desert of Egypt.* Annual of the American Schools of Oriental Research 59. Boston: American Schools of Oriental Research, 2005.

Daub, D. "*Consortium* in Roman and Hebrew Law." *Juridical Review* 62 (1950): 71–91.

Derrida, Jacques. *The Margins of Philosophy.* Translated by A. Bass. Chicago: University of Chicago Press, 1982.

Derrida, Jacques. *Acts of Literature.* London: Routledge, 1992.

Desain, Peter, and Luke Windsor. *Rhythm Perception and Production.* Lisse, Netherlands: Swets and Zeitlinger, 2000.

Dewey, John. *Art as Experience.* New York: Perigee, 1934.

Doan, William, and Terry Giles. *Prophets, Performance, and Power: Performance Criticism of the Hebrew Bible.* London: T. and T. Clark, 2005.

Doane, Alger N. "Oral Texts, Intertexts, and Intratexts: Editing Old English." Pages 75–113 in *Influence and Intertextuality in Literary History.* Edited by J. Clayton and E. Rothstein. Madison: University of Wisconsin Press, 1991.

Doane, Alger N. "The Ethnography of Scribal Writing and Anglo-Saxon Poetry: Scribe as Performer." *Oral Tradition* 9 (1994): 420–39.

Dobbs-Allsopp, F. W. *Weep, O Daughter of Zion: A Study of the City-Lament Genre in the Hebrew Bible.* BibOr 44. Rome: Editrice Pontificio Istituto Biblico, 1993.

Dobbs-Allsopp, F. W. "Linguistic Evidence for the Date of Lamentations." *Journal of the Ancient Near Eastern Society* 26 (1998): 1–36.

Dobbs-Allsopp, F. W. "Rethinking Historical Criticism." *Biblical Interpretation* 7 (1999): 235–71.

Dobbs-Allsopp, F. W. "Darwinism, Genre Theory, and City Laments." *JAOS* 120/4 (2000): 625–30.

Dobbs-Allsopp, F. W. "The Enjambing Line in Lamentations: A Taxonomy (Part I)." *Zeitschrift für die alttestamentliche Wissenschaft* 113/2 (2001): 219–39.

Dobbs-Allsopp, F. W. "The Effects of Enjambment in Lamentations (Part 2)." *Zeitschrift für die alttestamentliche Wissenschaft* 113/5 (2001): 370–85.

Dobbs-Allsopp, F. W. *Lamentations.* Interpretation: A Bible Commentary for Teaching and Preaching. Louisville: Westminster John Knox, 2002.

Dobbs-Allsopp, F. W. "The Delight of Beauty and Song 4:1–7." *Interpretation* 59 (July 2005): 260–77.

Dobbs-Allsopp, F. W. "Late Linguistic Features in the Song of Songs." Pages 27–77 in *Perspectives on the Song of Songs—Perspektiven der Hoheliedauslegung*. Edited by A. C. Hagedorn. Beihefte für Zeitschrift für die alttestamentliche Wissenschaft 346. Berlin: de Gruyter, 2005.

Dobbs-Allsopp, F. W. "Asia, Ancient Southwest: Scripts, Earliest." Pages 405–500 in vol. 1 of *Encyclopedia of Language and Linguistics*. 2d ed. Edited by K. Brown. Oxford: Elsevier, 2006.

Dobbs-Allsopp, F. W. "I Am Black *and* Beautiful: The Song, Cixous, and *Écriture Féminine*." Pages 128–40 in *Engaging the Bible in a Gendered World: An Introduction to Feminist Biblical Interpretation in Honor of Katharine Doob Sakenfeld*. Edited by C. Pressler and L. Day. Louisville: Westminster John Knox, 2006.

Dobbs-Allsopp, F. W. "Psalms and Lyric Verse." Pages 346–79 in *The Evolution of Rationality: Interdisciplinary Essays in Honor of J. Wentzel van Huyssteen*. Edited by F. L. Shults. Grand Rapids: Eerdmans, 2006.

Dobbs-Allsopp, F. W. "Psalm 133: A (Close) Reading." *Journal of Hebrew Scriptures* 8 (2008). Accessed, http://www.jhsonline.org/jhs-article.html (article_97.pdf).

Dobbs-Allsopp, F. W. "Acrostic: Ancient Near East and Hebrew Bible/Old Testament." In *Encyclopedia of the Bible and Its Reception*. Vol. 1. *A–Anic*. Edited by Dale Allison et al. Berlin: de Gruyter, 2009.

Dobbs-Allsopp, F. W. "Daughter Zion." Pages 125–34 in *Thus Says the LORD: Essays on the Former and Latter Prophets in Honor of Robert R. Wilson*. Edited by J. J. Ahn and S. L. Cook. LHBOTS 502. London: T. and T. Clark, 2009.

Dobbs-Allsopp, F. W. "Poetry, Hebrew." Pages 550–58 in *The New Interpreter's Dictionary of the Bible*. Vol. 4. *Me–R*. Edited by Doob Sakenfeld. Nashville: Abingdon, 2009.

Dobbs-Allsopp, F. W. "Song of Songs." Pages in *The New Interpreter's Dictionary of the Bible*. Vol. 5. *S–Z*. Edited by K. Doob Sakenfeld. Nashville: Abingdon, 2009.

Dobbs-Allsopp, F. W. "Song of Songs." Pages 375–86 in *New Interpreter's Bible One Volume Commentary*. Edited by B. Gaventa and D. Peterson. Nashville: Abingdon, 2010.

Dobbs-Allsopp, F. W. "The Art of Poetry in Jer 17:5–8." Paper presented at the annual meeting of the SBL. Chicago, November 20, 2012.

Dobbs-Allsopp, F. W. "Space, Line, and the Written Biblical Poem in Texts from the Judean Desert." Pages 19–61 in *Puzzling Out the Past: Studies in Northwest Semitic Languages and Literatures in Honor of Bruce Zuckerman*. Edited by M. Lundberg et al. Leiden: Brill, 2012.

Dobbs-Allsopp, F. W. "The Poetry of Psalms." Pages 79–98 in *The Oxford Handbook on the Psalms*. Edited by W. Brown. Oxford: Oxford University Press, 2014.

Dobbs-Allsopp, F. W. *Walt Whitman and the King James Bible: A Biblicist's Perspective*. In preparation.

Dobbs-Allsopp, F. W., and T. Linafelt. "The Rape of Zion in Lam 1:10." *ZAW* 113/1 (2001): 77–81.

Dobbs-Allsopp, F. W., et al. *Hebrew Inscriptions: Texts from the Biblical Period of the Monarchy with Concordance.* New Haven: Yale University Press, 2005.

Döller, Joh. *Rhythmus, Metrik und Strophik in der bibl.-hebr. Poesie.* Paderborn, 1899.

Donald, Merlin. *Origins of the Modern Mind and Three Stages in the Evolution of Culture and Cognition.* Cambridge, Mass.: Harvard University Press, 1991.

Draper, R. P. *Lyric Tragedy.* New York: St. Martin's, 1985.

Dresher, Bezalel Elan. "The Word in Tiberian Hebrew." Pages 95–111 in *The Nature of the Word: Essays in Honor of Paul Kiparsky.* Edited by K. C. Hanson and S. Inkelas. Cambridge, Mass.: MIT Press, 2009.

Driver, Samuel Rolles. *An Introduction to the Literature of the Old Testament.* Cleveland: 1892; reprint, Meridian, 1956.

Dubrow, Heather. *The Challenges of Orpheus: Lyric Poetry and Early Modern England.* Baltimore: Johns Hopkins University Press, 2008.

Eaglestone, Robert. *Ethical Criticism: Reading after Levinas.* Edinburgh: Edinburgh University Press, 1997.

Eagleton, Terry. *How to Read a Poem.* Oxford: Blackwell, 2007.

Ebeling, E. *Ein Hymnen-Katalog aus Assur.* Berlin, 1929.

Eliot, T. S. "The Borderline of Prose." *New Statesman* 9 (1917): 157–59.

Eissfeldt, Otto. *The Old Testament: An Introduction.* Translated by P. Ackroyd. New York: Harper and Row, 1965.

Erman, A. "Eine ägyptische Quelle der 'Spruch Salomos.'" *SPAW* (phil-hist. Kl. 15) (1924): 86–93.

Eskhult, M. "Verbal Syntax in Late Biblical Hebrew." Pages 84–93 in *Diggers at the Well.* Edited by T. Muraoka and J. F. Elwolde. Leiden: Brill, 2000.

Ewald, Heinrich. *Die Dichter des Alten Bundes.* Göttingen: Vändenhoeck und Ruprecht, 1866.

Exum, J. Cheryl. *Song of Songs.* Old Testament Library. Louisville: Westminster John Knox, 2005.

Fecht, Gerhard. "The Structural Principle of Ancient Egyptian Elevated Language." Pages 69–94 in *Verse in Ancient Near Eastern Prose.* Edited by J. C. de Moor and W. G. E. Watson. Alter Orient und Altes Testament 42. Neukirchen-Vluyn: Neukirchenener Verlag, 1993.

Fenoaltea, Doranne, and David Lee Rubin, eds. *The Ladder of High Designs: Structure and Interpretation of the French Lyric Sequence.* Charlottesville: University of Virginia Press, 1991.

Fineman, J. "Shakespeare's Sonnets' Perjured Eye." Pages 116–31 in *Lyric Poetry.* Edited by C. Hojek and P. Parker. Ithaca: Cornell University Press, 1985.

Finnegan, Ruth. *Oral Poetry: Its Nature, Significance, and Social Context.* Cambridge: Cambridge University Press, 1977.

Fisch, Harold. *Poetry with a Purpose.* Bloomington: Indiana University Press, 1988.

Flint, Peter, W. *The Dead Sea Psalms Scrolls and the Book of Psalms*. Leiden: Brill, 1997.

Flint, Peter W. "The Book of Canticles (Song of Songs) in the Dead Sea Scrolls." Pages 96–104 in *Perspectives on the Song of Songs—Perspektiven der Hoheliedausle-gung*. Edited by A. C. Hagedorn. Beihefte für Zeitschrift für die alttestamentliche Wissenschaft 346. Berlin: de Gruyter, 2005.

Fohrer, Georg. "Über den Kurzvers." *Zeitschrift für die Alttestamentliche Wissenschaft* 66 (1954): 199–236.

Fohrer, Georg. *Introduction to the Old Testament*. Translated by D. Green. Nashville: Abingdon, 1968.

Fokkelman, J. P. *Major Poems of the Hebrew Bible at the Interface of Prosody and Structural Analysis*. Vol. 3. *The Remaining 65 Psalms*. Studia semetica neerlandica. Assen: Van Gorcum, 2003.

Foley, John Miles. *Immanent Art: From Structure to Meaning in Traditional Oral Epic*. Bloomington: Indiana University Press, 1991.

Foley, John Miles. "Word-Power, Performance, and Tradition." *Journal of American Folklore* 105 (1992): 275–301.

Foley, John Miles. *How to Read an Oral Poem*. Urbana: University of Illinois Press, 2002.

Foley, John Miles, ed. *A Companion to Ancient Epic*. Malden: Blackwell, 2005.

Folsom, Ed. *Whitman Making Books Books Making Whitman: A Catalog and Commentary*. Iowa City: University of Iowa Press, 2005. Accessed March 5, 2015, www.whitmanarchive.org/criticism/current/anc.00150.html.

Ford, A. "From Letters to Literature: Reading the 'Song Culture' of Classical Greece." Pages 15–37 in *Written Texts and the Rise of Literate Culture in Ancient Greece*. Edited by H. Yunis. Cambridge: Cambridge University Press, 2003.

Foster, Benjamin R. *Before the Muses: An Anthology of Akkadian Literature*. Vols. 1–2. Bethesda: CDL Press, 1993.

Foster, Benjamin R. "Akkadian Literature." Pages 137–214 in *From an Antique Land: An Introduction to Ancient Near Eastern Literature*. Edited by C. Erhlich. Lanham, Md.: Rowman and Littlefield, 2009. [Kindle ed.]

Fowler, A. *Kinds of Literature*. Cambridge, Mass.: Harvard University Press, 1982.

Fowler, R. L. *The Nature of Early Greek Lyric: Three Preliminary Studies*. Toronto: University of Toronto, 1987.

Fox, Joshua. *Semitic Noun Patterns*. Harvard Semitic Studies 52. Winona Lake, Ind.: Eisenbrauns, 2003.

Fox, Michael V. *The Song of Songs and the Ancient Egyptian Love Songs*. Madison: University of Wisconsin Press, 1985.

Fox, Michael V. *Proverbs 10–31*. Anchor Bible 18B. New Haven: Yale University Press, 2009.

Fraisse, Paul. *The Psychology of Time*. Translated by J. Leith. Harper and Row, 1963.

Fraistat, N., ed. *Poems in Their Place: The Intertextuality and Order of Poetic Collections*. Chapel Hill: University of North Carolina Press, 1986.

Fränkel, H. *Early Greek Poetry and Philosophy.* Translated by M. Hadas and J. Willis. New York: Harcourt Brace Jovanovich, 1973.

Freedman, David Noel. "Counting Formulae in the Akkadian Epics." *Journal of the Ancient Near Eastern Society* 3 (1970–71): 65–81.

Freedman, David Noel. *Psalm 119: The Exaltation of Torah.* Winona Lake, Ind.: Eisenbrauns, 1999.

Friebert, Stuart, David Walker, and David Young, eds. *A Field Guide to Contemporary Poetry and Poetics.* New York: Longman, 1980.

Friedman, S. S. "Why Not Compare?" Pages 49–66 in *Comparison: Theories, Approaches, Uses.* Edited by R. Felski and S. S. Friedman. Baltimore: Johns Hopkins University Press, 2014.

Frigyesi, Judit. "Preliminary Thoughts toward the Study of Music without Clear Beat: The Example of 'Flowing Rhythm' in Jewish 'Nusah.'" *Asian Music* 24 (1993): 63.

Frost, Robert. *Collected Poems, Prose, and Plays.* New York: Library of America, 1995.

Frye, Northrup. *Anatomy of Criticism.* Princeton: Princeton University Press, 1957.

Frye, Northrup. "Approaching the Lyric." Pages 31–37 in *Lyric Poetry: Beyond New Criticism.* Edited by C. Hojek and P. Parker. Ithaca: Cornell University Press, 1985.

Fussell, Paul. *Poetic Meter and Poetic Form.* Rev. ed. New York, 1979.

Gamble, Harry. *Books and Readers in the Early Church.* New Haven: Yale University Press, 1997.

Garbini, Giovanni. "Il cantico di Debora." *La Parola des Passato* 33 (1978), 5–31.

Gardiner, John Hays. *The Bible as Literature.* New York, 1906.

Gardner, T. "Long Poem." In *PEPP.*

Garner, Robert Scott. "Studies in Early Greek Colometry: Traditional Techniques of Composition and Word Placement in Archaic Epic and Other Verse Forms." Ph.D. diss., Princeton University, 2003. Now published as *Traditional Elegy: The Interplay of Meter, Tradition, and Context in Early Greek Poetry.* Oxford: Oxford University Press, 2010.

Gaskill, H., ed. *Ossian Revisited.* Edinburgh: Edinburgh University Press, 1991.

Geller, Stephen A. *Parallelism in Early Biblical Poetry.* Missoula: Scholars Press, 1979.

Geller, Stephen A. "Theory and Method in the Study of Biblical Poetry." *JQR* 73 (1982): 65–77.

Geller, Stephen A. "The Dynamics of Parallel Verse: A Poetic Analysis of Deut 32:6–12," *HTR* 75 (1982): 35–56.

Geller, Stephen A. "The Language of Imagery in Psalm 114." Pages 179–94 in *Lingering over Words.* Edited by T. Abusch et al. HSS 37. Atlanta: Scholars Press, 1990.

Geller, Stephen A. "Hebrew Prosody and Poetics." Pages 509–11 in *NPEPP.*

Genette, Gérard. "The Dynamics of Parallel Verse: A Poetic Analysis of Deut 32:6–12." *Harvard Theological Review* 75 (1982): 35–56.

Genette, Gérard. *The Architext.* Berkeley: University of California Press, 1992.

Gentili, Bruno. *Poetry and Its Public in Ancient Greece: From Homer to the Fifth Century*. Translated by A. T. Cole. Baltimore: Johns Hopkins University Press, 1988.

Gerstenberger, E. S. *Psalms, Part 2, and Lamentations*. FOTL 15. Grand Rapids: Eerdmans, 2001.

Gertner, M. "The Masorah and the Levites." *VT* 10 (1960): 252–72.

Gesenius, Wilhelm. *Hebrew Grammar of Gesenius*. Edited by E. Roediger. Translated by M. Stuart. Andover, Mass.: Allen, Morrill, and Wardwell, 1846.

Gevirtz, Stanley. *Patterns in the Early Poetry of Israel*. Chicago: University of Chicago Press, 1963.

Ginsberg, H. L. "The Victory of the Land-God over the Sea God." *Journal of the Palestine Oriental Society* 15 (1935): 327–33.

Ginsberg, H. L. "The Rebellion and Death of Ba'lu." *Orientalia* NS 5 (1936): 161–98.

Ginsberg, H. L. "Ba'l and Anat." *Orientalia* NS 7 (1938): 1–11.

Ginsberg, H. L. "Ugaritic Studies and the Bible." *Biblical Archeologist* 8 (1945): 41–58.

Ginsberg, H. L., and B. Maisler. "Semitized Hurrians in Syria and Palestine." *Journal of the Palestine Oriental Society* 14 (1934): 243–67.

Gitin, S. "Ekron of the Philistines: Part II: Olive-Oil Suppliers to the World." *BAR* 16/2 (1990): 32–42.

Gitin, S. "The Neo-Assyrian Empire and Its Western Periphery: The Levant, with a Focus on Philistine Ekron." Pages 77–103 in *Assyria 1995*. Edited by S. Parpola and R. Whiting. Helsinki, 1997.

Gitin, S. "Tell Miqne-Ekron in the 7th Century B.C.E." Pages 61–79 in *Recent Excavations in Israel*. Edited by S. Gitin. Dubuque: Hunt, 1995.

Givón, Talmy. "The Drift from VSO to SVO in Biblical Hebrew: The Pragmatics of Tense-Aspect." Pages 184–254 in *Mechanisms of Syntactic Change*. Edited by C. N. Li. Austin: University of Texas Press, 1977.

Glück, Louise. *Proofs and Theories: Essays on Poetry*. Hopewell, N.J.: Ecco, 1994.

Gogel, Sandra L. *A Grammar of Epigraphic Hebrew*. Atlanta: Scholars Press, 1998.

Goody, Jack. *The Domestication of the Savage Mind*. Cambridge: Cambridge University Press, 1977.

Goody, Jack. *The Interface between the Written and the Oral*. Cambridge: Cambridge University Press, 1987.

Goody, Jack. *The Power of the Written Tradition*. Smithsonian Series in Ethnographic Inquiry. Washington, D.C.: Smithsonian Institution Press, 2000.

Goody, Jack, and Ian Watt. "The Consequences of Literacy." *Comparative Studies in Society and History* 5 (1963): 304–45.

Gordis, Robert. "Studies in the Relationship of Biblical and Rabbinic Hebrew." Pages 184–86 in *Louis Ginzberg Jubilee Volume*, vol. 1. New York: American Academy of Jewish Research, 1945.

Goshen-Gottstein, Moshe. "The Authenticity of the Aleppo Codex." *Textus* 1 (1960): 10–37.

Gottwald, Norman K. "Poetry, Hebrew." Pages 829–38 in *The Interpreter's Dictionary of the Bible*, vol. 3. Edited by G. A. Buttrick. New York: Abingdon Press, 1962.

Gray, Geroge B. *The Forms of Hebrew Poetry*. London: Hodder and Stoughton, 1915.

Green, Margaret W. "The Construction and Implementation of the Cuneiform Writing System." *Visual Language* 15 (1981): 345–72.

Greene, Roland. "Sir Philip Sidney's *Psalms*, the Sixteenth-Century Psalter, and the Nature of Lyric." *Studies in English Literature, 1500–1900* 30/1 (1990): 19–40.

Greene, Roland. *Post-Petrarchism: Origins and Innovations of the Western Lyric Sequence*. Princeton: Princeton University Press, 1991.

Greene, Roland. "Lyric Sequence." In *PEPP*.

Greenfield, Jonas C. *'Al Kanfei Yonah: Collected Studies of Jonas C. Greenfield on Semitic Philology*. Edited by Shalom Paul, Michael Stone, and Avital Pinnick. Leiden: Brill, 2001.

Greenstein, Edward L. "Two Variations of Grammatical Parallelism in Canaanite Poetry and Their Psycholinguistic Background." *Journal of the Ancient Near Eastern Society* 6 (1974): 87–105.

Greenstein, Edward L. "A Phoenician Inscription in Ugaritic Script?" *JANES* 8 (1976): 49–57.

Greenstein, Edward L. "One More Step on the Staircase." *Ugarit-Forschungen* 9 (1977): 77–86.

Greenstein, Edward L. "How Does Parallelism Mean?" Pages 41–70 in *A Sense of the Text: The Art of Language in the Study of Biblical Literature*. Edited by L. Nemoy. Jewish Quarterly Review Supplement. Winona Lake, Ind.: Eisenbrauns, 1983.

Greenstein, Edward L. "Aspects of Biblical Poetry." *Jewish Book Annual* 44 (1986–87): 33–42.

Greenstein, Edward L. "On the Genesis of Biblical Prose Narrative." *Prooftexts* 8 (1988): 347–54.

Greenstein, Edward L. "The Formation of the Biblical Narrative Corpus." *American Journal of Semitic Languages Review* 15 (1990): 151–78.

Greenstein, Edward L. "Wordplay, Hebrew." Pages 968–67 in *ABD* VI.

Greenstein, Edward L. "Direct Discourse and Parallelism." Pages 79–91 in *Discourse, Dialogue, and Debate in the Bible: Essays in Honor of Frank H. Polak*. Edited by A. Brenner-Idan. Sheffield: Sheffield Phoenix, 2014.

Greenstein, Edward L. Review of D. Pardee, *The Ugaritic Texts and the Origins of West Semitic Literary Composition*, *BASOR* 371 (2014): 215–18.

Greenstein, Edward L. "Signs of Poetry Past: Literariness in Pre-biblical Hebrew Literature." Unpublished manuscript.

Grenoble, Lenore, and John Kopper. *Essays in the Art and Theory of Translation*. Lewiston, Me.: Mellen, 1997.

Grier, Edward F., ed. *Notebooks and Unpublished Prose Manuscripts* 6 vols. New York: New York University Press, 1984.

Groneberg, B. "Searching for Akkadian Lyrics: From Old Babylonian to the 'Lieder-katalog,' KAR 158." *Journal of Cuneiform Studies* 55 (2003): 55–74.

Grossberg, Daniel. *Centripetal and Centrifugal Structures in Biblical Poetry.* Society of Biblical Literature Monograph Series 39. Atlanta: Scholars Press, 1989.

Grosser, Emmylou. "Perceptions and Expectations of the Biblical Hebrew Poetic Line: A Cognitive Poetics Approach to Lineation of David's Lament in 2 Samuel 1:19–27." Paper presented at the annual meeting of the SBL. Chicago, November 18, 2012.

Grosser, Emmylou. "The Poetic Line as Part and Whole: A Perception-Oriented Approach to Lineation of Poems in the Hebrew Bible." Ph.D. diss., Madison: University of Wisconsin, 2013.

Grossman, Allen. "Summa Lyrica: A Primer in the Commonplaces in Speculative Poetics." *Western Humanities Review* 44 (1990): 5–138.

Grossman, Allen, with Mark Halliday. *The Sighted Singer: Two Works on Poetry for Readers and Writers.* Baltimore: Johns Hopkins University Press, 1992.

Gruber, Mayer. "The Meaning of Biblical Parallelism: A Biblical Perspective." *Prooftexts* 13 (1993): 289–93.

Guillen, Claudio. *The Challenge of Comparative Literature.* Translated by C. Franzen. Cambridge, Mass.: Harvard University Press, 1993.

Gumbrecht, Hans Ulrich. *The Powers of Philology: Dynamics of Textual Scholarship.* Urbana: University of Illinois Press, 2003.

Gunkel, Hermann. *The Legends of Genesis.* Translated by W. H. Carruth. Chicago: Open Court, 1964 [1901].

Gunkel, Hermann. *Die Psalmen.* 5th ed. Göttingen: Vändenhoeck, 1968.

Gunkel, Hermann. *Twentieth Century Theology in the Making.* Edited by J. Pelikan. Translated by R. Wilson. New York: Harper and Row, 1969.

Gunkel, Hermann, and Joachim Begrich. *Introduction to Psalms: The Genres of the Religious Lyric of Israel.* Translated by J. D. Nogalski. Macon: Mercer University Press, 1998.

Gutzwiller, Kathryn J., ed. *The New Posidippus: A Hellenistic Poetry Book.* New York: Oxford University Press, 2005.

Halkin, Avraham Shelomoh, ed. *Kītāb al-Muḥāḍara wal-Mudhākara: Sefer ha-ʿIyyunim we-ha-Diyyunim (The Book of Discussion and Conversation).* Translated by Avraham Shelomoh Halkin; Jerusalem, 1975.

Hall, Frederick Wilson. *A Companion to Classical Texts.* Oxford: Clarendon, 1913.

Hamburger, Katie. *The Logic of Literature.* Bloomington: Indiana University Press, 1973.

Hamilton, Gordon J. "The Development of the Early Alphabet." Ph. D. diss., Harvard University, 1985.

Hamilton, Gordon J. "W. F. Albright and Early Alphabetic Epigraphy." *Near Eastern Archeology* 65 (2002): 35–42.

Hamilton, Gordon J. *The Origins of the West Semitic Alphabet in Egyptian Scripts.* Catholic Biblical Quarterly Monograph Series 40. Washington, D.C.: Catholic Biblical Association of America, 2006.

Hamilton, Gordon J. "Reconceptualizing the Periods of Early alphabetic Scripts." Pages 30–55 in *"An Eye for Form": Epigraphic Essays in Honor of Frank Moore Cross.* Edited by J. A. Hackett and W. Aufrecht. Winona Lake, Ind.: Eisenbrauns, 2014.

Hanson, K., and P. Kiparsky. "The Nature of Verse and Its Consequences for the Mixed Form." Pages 17–44 in *Prosimetrum: Cross-cultural Perspectives on Narrative in Prose and Verse.* Edited by J. Harris and K. Reichl. Cambridge: D. S. Brewer, 1997.

Haran, Menahem. "Mashal." Pages 548–53 in *Encyclopedia Biblica*, vol. 5. 9 vols. Jerusalem, 1968. [in Hebrew].

Haran, Menahem. "Book-Scrolls in Israel in Pre-exilic Times." *Journal of Jewish Studies* 33 (1982): 161–73.

Haran, Menahem. "Book-Scrolls at the Beginning of the Second Temple Period: The Transition from Papyrus to Skins." *Hebrew Union College Annual* 54 (1983): 111–22.

Haran, Menahem. "The Book of the Chronicles 'of the Kings of Judah' and 'of the Kings of Israel': What Sort of Books Were They?" *VT* 49 (1999): 159–60.

Harding, Denys W. *Words into Rhythm: English Speech Rhythm in Verse and Prose.* Cambridge: Cambridge University Press, 1976.

Hardy, Barbara. *The Advantage of Lyric: Essays on Feeling in Poetry.* Bloomington: Indiana University Press, 1977.

Harshav [Hrushovski], Benjamin. *Exploration in Poetics.* Stanford: Stanford University Press, 2007.

Hartman, Charles O. *Free Verse: An Essay on Prosody.* Evanston, Ill.: Northwestern University Press, 1980.

Haupt, Paul. "Moses' Song of Triumph." *American Journal of Semitic Languages and Literature* 20 (1903–4): 149–72.

Havelock, Eric A. *Preface to Plato.* Cambridge, Mass.: Harvard University Press, 1963.

Havelock, Eric A. *The Greek Concept of Justice: From Its Shadow in Homer to Its Substance in Plato.* Cambridge, Mass.: Harvard University Press, 1978.

Havelock, Eric A. *The Literate Revolution in Greece and Its Cultural Consequences.* Princeton Series of Collected Essays. Princeton: Princeton University Press, 1982.

Havelock, Eric A. *The Muse Learns to Write.* New Haven: Yale University Press, 1986.

Hayes, Bruce, and Margaret MacEachern. "Are There Lines in Folk Poetry." *UCLA Working Papers in Phonology* 1 (1996): 125–42.

Heaney, Seamus. *The Redress of Poetry.* New York: Farrar, Straus and Giroux, 1995.

Heaney, Seamus. *Beowulf: A New Verse Translation.* New York: Farrar, Straus and Giroux, 2000.

Hecker, Karl. *Untersuchungen zur akkadischen Epik.* Alter Orient und Altes Testament Vol. 8. Kevelaer: Neukirchener Verlag, 1974.

Heffelfinger, K. M. *"I Am Large, I Contain Multitudes": Lyric Cohesion and Conflict in Second Isaiah.* Leiden: Brill, 2011.

Hendel, Ron S. *The Epic of the Patriarch: The Jacob Cycle and the Narrative Traditions of Canaan and Israel.* Atlanta: Scholars Press, 1987.

Hepworth, Brian. *Robert Lowth.* Boston: Twayne, 1978.

Herder, Johann Gottfried. *The Spirit of Hebrew Poetry.* Translated by J. Marsh. Burlington: E. Smith, 1833.

Herington, John. *Poetry into Drama: Early Tragedy and the Greek Poetic Tradition.* Berkeley:University of California Press, 1985.

Hicks, R. Lansing. *"Delet* and *Megillah*: A Fresh Approach to Jeremiah XXXVI." *VT* 33 (1983): 46–66.

Higbie, Carolyn. *Meaning and Music: Enjambmen and Sentence Structure in the Iliad.* Oxford: Clarendon, 1990.

Hillers, Delbert R. "A Convention in Hebrew Literature: The Reaction to Bad News." *ZAW* 77 (1965): 86–90.

Hillers, Delbert R. "Observations on Syntax and Meter in Lamentations." Pages 265–70 in *A Light unto My Path: Old Testament Studies in Honor of Jacob M. Meyers.* Edited by H. N. Bream, R. D. Heim, and C. A. Moore. Philadelphia: Temple University Press, 1974.

Hillers, Delbert R. *Micah.* Hermeneia. Philadelphia: Fortress, 1984.

Hillers, Delbert R. "Analyzing the Abominable: Our Understanding of Canaanite Religion." *Jewish Quarterly Review* 75 (1985): 253–269.

Hillers, Delbert R. *Lamentations.* Anchor Bible 7A. 2d rev. ed. New York: Doubleday, 1992.

Hillers, Delbert R. *Poets before Homer: Collected Essays on Ancient Literature.* Edited by F. W. Dobbs-Allsopp. Winona Lake, Ind.: Eisenbrauns, 2015.

Hillers, Delbert R., and Marsh H. McCall. "Homeric Dictated Texts: A Reexamination of Some Near Eastern Evidence." *Harvard Studies in Classical Philology* 80 (1976): 19–23.

Hindus, Milton. *Walt Whitman.* New York: Routledge, 1997.

Hirsch, Edward. *How to Read a Poem.* New York: Harcourt Brace, 1999.

Hobbins, John F. "Meter in Ancient Hebrew Poetry: A History of Modern Research." 2005. ancienthebrewpoetry.typepad.com/ancient_hebrew_poetry/files/meter_in_ ancient_hebrew_poetry_a_history_of_modern_research.pdf, accessed February 19, 2015.

Hobbins, John F. "Regularities in Ancient Hebrew Verse: A New Descriptive Model." *Zeitschrift für die Alttestamentliche Wissenschaft* 119/4 (2007): 564–85.

Hoftijzer, J. and G. van der Kooij, eds. *The Balaam Text from Deir ʿAllā Re-Evaluated.* Leiden: Brill, 1991.

Hogan, Patrick C. *The Mind and Its Stories: Narrative Universals and Human Emotion.* Cambridge: Cambridge University Press, 2003.

Holder, Alan. *Rethinking Meter: A New Approach to the Verse Line.* Lewisburg: Bucknell University Press, 1995.

Holladay, J. S. "House, Israelite." Pages 308–18 in *ABD* 3.

Holladay, J. S. "House: Syro-Palestinian Houses." Pages 94–114 in *OEANE* 3.

Holladay, William L. *Jeremiah 2.* Minneapolis: Fortress, 1986.

Holladay, William L. "*Hebrew Verse Structure* Revisited (I): Which 'Words' Count?" *Journal of Biblical Literature* 118 (1999): 19–32.

Holladay, William L. "*Hebrew Verse Structure* Revisited (II): Conjoint Cola, and Further Suggestions." *Journal of Biblical Literature* 118 (1999): 401–16.

Holladay, William L. "Indications of Jeremiah's Psalter." *Journal of Biblical Literature* 121 (2002): 245–61.

Hollander, John. *Vision and Resonance: Two Senses of Poetic Form.* 2d ed. New York: Oxford University Press: 1975.

Hollander, John. *Rhyme's Reason: A Guide to English Verse.* Enlg. ed. New Haven: Yale University Press, 1989.

Holmstedt, Robert D. "The Typological Classification of the Hebrew of Genesis: Subject-Verb or Verb-Subject?" *Journal of Hellenistic Studies* 11 (2011): 1–39.

Holmstedt, Robert D. "Pro-drop." Pages 265–67 in *Encyclopedia of Hebrew Language and Linguistics*, vol. 3, *P–Z*. Edited by G. Khan; Boston: Brill, 2013.

Holscher, Rory, and Robert Schultz. "A Symposium on the Theory and Practice of the Line in Contemporary Poetry." *Epoch* 29 (winter 1980): 161–224.

Horowitz, Wayne, Takayoshi Oshima, and Seth L. Sanders. *Cuneiform in Canaan: Cuneiform Sources from the Land of Israel in Ancient Times.* Jerusalem: Israel Exploration Society, 2006.

Hošek, Chaviva, and Patricia Parker, eds. *Lyric Poetry: Beyond New Criticism.* Ithaca: Cornell University Press, 1985.

Hossfeld, Frank-Lothar, and Erich Zenger. *Psalms 2.* Hermeneia. Minneapolis: Fortress, 2005.

Hossfeld, Frank-Lothar, and Erich Zenger. *Psalms 3.* Hermeneia. Translated by L. Maloney. Minneapolis: Fortress, 2011.

Howard, Jr., D. M. "Recent Trends in Psalm Study." Pages 329–68 in *The Face of Old Testament Studies: A Survey of Contemporary Approaches.* Edited by D. W. Baker and B. T. Arnold. Grand Rapids: Baker Books, 1999.

Howe, E. A. *The Dramatic Monologue.* New York: Twayne, 1966.

Hrushovski [Harshav], B. "On Free Rhythms in Modern Poetry." Pages 173–90 in *Style in Language.* Edited by Thomas Sebeok. New York: Wiley, 1960.

Hrushovski [Harshav], B. "Prosody, Hebrew." In *EcyJud* (1971–72), 13: 1200–1203.

Hrushovski [Harshav], B. "Note on the Systems of Hebrew Versification." Pages 57–72 in *The Penguin Book of Hebrew Verse.* Edited by T. Carmi. New York: Penguin Books, 1982.

Huisman, Rosemary. *The Written Poem: Semiotic Conventions from Old to Modern English*. London: Cassell, 1998.

Hunter, Ian M. L. "Lengthy Verbatim Recall (LVR) and the Myth and Gift of Tape-Recorder Memory." Pages 425–40 in *Psychology in the 1990's*. Edited by Kirsti M. J. Lagerspetz and Pekka Niemi. Amsterdam: North Holland, 1984.

Hunter, Ian M. L. "Lengthy Verbatim Recall: The Role of Text." Pages 207–35 in *Psychology of Language*, vol. 1. Edited by A. Ellis. Hillsdale, N.J.: Erlbaum, 1985.

Huot, Sylvia. *From Song to Book*. Ithaca: Cornell University Press, 1987.

Hurvitz, Avi. "The Chronological Significance of 'Aramaisms' in Biblical Hebrew." *Israel Exploration Society* 18 (1968): 234–40.

Hurvitz, Avi. *The Transition Period in Biblical Hebrew: A Study in Post-exilic Hebrew and Its Implications for the Dating of Psalms*. Jerusalem: Bialik, 1972. [in Hebrew]

Hurvitz, Avi. "The Date of the Prose-Tale of Job Linguistically Reconsidered." *Harvard Theological Review* 67 (1974): 17–34.

Hutton, J. M. Review of D. Pardee, *The Ugaritic Texts and the Origins of West Semitic Literary Composition: The Schweich Lectures of the British Academy 2007*, *RBL* (August 2014).

Hymes, Dell. "The Ethnography of Speaking." Pages 13–53 in *Anthropology and Human Behavior*. Edited by T. Gladwin and W. Sturtevant. Washington, D.C.: Anthropological Society of Washington, 1962.

Hymes, Dell. *"In Vain I Tried to Tell You": Essays in Native American Ethnopoetics*. Philadelphia: University of Pennsylvania Press, 1981.

Hymes, Dell. "Warm Springs Sahaptin Narrative Analysis." Pages 62–102 in *Native American Discourse*. Edited by Joel Sherzer and Anthony C. Woodbury. Cambridge: Cambridge University Press, 1987.

Ifrah, G. *From One to Zero: A Universal History of Numbers*. Translated by L. Bair. New York: Viking Penguin, 1985.

Ifrah, G. *The Universal History of Numbers: From Prehistory to the Invention of the Computer*. Translated by D. Bellos, E. F. Harding, S. Wood, and I. Monk. New York: Wiley. 2000.

Isaacs, Elcanon. "The Origin and Nature of Parallelism." *American Journal of Semitic Languages and Literatures* 35 (1919): 113–27.

Iser, W. *The Act of Reading*. Baltimore: Johns Hopkins University Press, 1978.

Issar, Ari S., and Mattanyah Zohar. *Climate Change: Environment and History of the Near East*. 2d ed. Berlin: Springer, 2007.

Jabbour, Alan. "Memorial Transmission in Old English Poetry." *Chaucer Review* 3 (1969): 174–90.

Jackson, Virginia Walker. *Dickinson's Misery: A Theory of Lyric Reading*. Princeton: Princeton University Press, 2005.

Jacob, W. "Flora." In *ABD* 2.

Jacobson, Rolf. *"Many are Saying": The Function of Direct Discourse in the Hebrew Psalter*. London: T. and T. Clark, 2004.

Jahnow, H. *Das hebräische Leichenlied im Rahmen der Völkerdichtung.* BZAW 36. Giessen: A. Toppelmann, 1923.

Jakobson, Roman. *Verbal Art, Verbal Sign, Verbal Time.* Edited by K. Pomorska and S. Rudy. Minneapolis: University of Minnesota Press, 1985.

Jakobson, Roman. *Language in Literature.* Edited by K. Pomorska and S. Rudy. Cambridge, Mass.: Harvard University Press, 1987.

James, William. *Principles of Psychology.* 2 vols. New York: Holt, 1890.

Jeffreys, M. "Songs and Inscriptions: Brevity and the Idea of Lyric." *Texas Studies in Literature and Language* 36/2 (1994): 117–34.

Johnson, J. W. "Lyric." Pages 713–27 in *NPEPP*.

Johnson, Mark. *The Body in the Mind: The Bodily Basis of Meaning, Imagination, and Reason.* Chicago: University of Chicago Press, 1987.

Johnson, William A. *Bookrolls and Scribes in Oxyrhynchus.* Toronto: University of Toronto Press, 2004.

Johnson, W. Ralph. *The Idea of Lyric: Lyric Modes in Ancient and Modern Poetry.* Berkeley: University of California Press, 1982.

Jonson, Ben. *Poems of Ben Jonson.* Edited by G. B. Johnston. Cambridge, Mass.: Harvard University Press, 1955.

Josipovici, Gabriel. "The Rhythm Established: *Bereshit Bara.*" Pages 53–75 in *The Book of God: A Response to the Bible.* New Haven: Yale University Press, 1988.

Jourdain, Robert. *Music, the Brain, and Ecstasy.* New York: Harper Perennial, 1997.

Jousse, Marcel. *The Oral Style.* Translated by E. Sieneart and R. Whitaker. New York: Garland, 1990 [1925].

Jousse, Marcel. "Les Lois psycho-physiologiques du Style oral vivant et leur utilisation philologique." *L' Ethnographie* 23 (1931): 1–18.

Kafalenos, E. "Possibilities of Isochrony." Ph.D. diss., Washington University, 1974.

Kaniewski, David, et al. "Environmental Roots of the Late Bronze Age Crisis." *PLoS ONE* 8/8 (August 14, 2013): e71004. Accessed May 1, 2015; doi: 10.1371/journal.pone.0071004.

Kawashima, Robert. *Biblical Narrative and the Death of the Rhapsode.* Bloomington: Indiana University Press, 2004.

Kawashima, Robert. "Verbal Medium and Narrative Art in Homer and the Bible." *Philosophy and Literature* 28 (2004): 103–17.

Keel, Othmar. "Kultische Brüderlichkeit—Ps 133." *FZPhTh* 23 (1976): 68–80.

Keel, Othmar, and Amihai Mazar. "Iron Age Seals and Seal Impressions from Tel Rehov." *Eretz Israel* 28 (2009): 57–69.

Keller, Tsipi. *Poetry on the Edge: An Anthology of Contemporary Hebrew Poetry.* Albany: State University of New York Press, 2008.

Kennicott, Benjamin. *The Ten Annual Accounts of the Collation of Hebrew Mss of the Old Testament; Begun in 1760, and Compleated in 1769.* Oxford: Fletcher and Prince, 1770.

Kenyon, Frederic G. *The Poems of Bacchylides, from a Papyrus in the British Museum.* London, 1887.

Kenyon, Frederic G. *Books and Readers in Ancient Greece and Rome*. 2d ed. Oxford: Clarendon, 1951.

Khan, Geoffrey, ed. *The Encyclopedia of Hebrew Language and Linguistics*. 4 vols. Leiden: Brill, 2013.

Kilmer, A. D. "Music and Dance in Ancient Western Asia." Pages 2601–13 in *CANE* IV.

Kilmer, A. D., and R. L. Crocker, and R. R. Brown. *Sounds from Silence: Recent Discoveries in Ancient Near Eastern* Music. Berkeley: Bit Enki, 1976.

King, Philip, and Lawrence Stager. *Life in Biblical Israel*. Louisville: Westminster John Knox, 2001.

Kinzie, Mary. *A Poet's Guide to Poetry*. Chicago: University of Chicago Press, 1999.

Kiparsky, Paul. "Oral Poetry: Some Linguistic and Typological Considerations." Pages 73–106 in *Oral Literature and the Formula*. Edited by B. Stolz and R. Shannon. Ann Arbor: University of Michigan Press, 1976.

Kirk, Geoffrey Stephen. "Verse-Structure and Sentence-Structure in Homer." *Yale Classical Studies* 20 (1966): 105–52.

Kirk, Geoffrey Stephen. *Homer and the Oral Tradition*. Cambridge: Cambridge University Press, 1976.

Kittay, Jeffrey, and Wlad Godzich. *The Emergence of Prose: An Essay in Prosaics*. Minneapolis: University of Minnesota Press, 1987.

Kittel, Rudolf, ed. *Biblia hebraica*. Lipsiae: J. C. Hinrichs, 1905–.

Kittel, Rudolph. *Die Psalmen*. Leipzig, 1922.

Kochavi, Moshe. "An Ostracon of the Period of the Judges from ʿIzbet Ṣarṭah." *Tel Aviv* 4 (1977): 1–13.

Kohl, Katrin M. *Rhetoric, the Bible, and the Origins of Free Verse: The Early "Hymns" of Friedrich Gottlieb Klopstock*. Berlin: de Gruyter, 1990.

König, K. *Stilistik, Rhetorik, Poetik*. Leipzig, 1900.

Kraeling, Emil, ed. *The Brooklyn Museum Aramaic Papyri*. New Haven: Yale University Press, 1953.

Kraus, Hans-Joachim. *Klagelieder*. BK. 3d ed. Neukirchen-Vluyn: Neukirchener Verlag, 1968.

Kraus, Hans-Joachim. *Psalmen 60–150*. BK 15/2. Neukirchen-Vluyn: Neukirchener Verlag, 1978.

Kraus, Hans-Joachim. *Psalms 60–150: A Commentary*. Minneapolis: Augsburg, 1989.

Kraus, Hans-Joachim. *Psalms 1–59*. Translated by H. Oswald. Minneapolis: Fortress, 1993.

Kugel, James. *Idea of Biblical Poetry*. New Haven: Yale University Press, 1981.

Kurylowicz, Jerzy. *Studies in Semitic Grammar and Metrics*. London: Curzon Press, 1973.

Lakoff, George. *Women, Fire, and Dangerous Things: What Categories Reveal about the Mind*. Chicago: University of Chicago Press, 1987.

Lambert, Wilfred G. *Babylonian Wisdom Literature*. Oxford: Clarendon Press, 1960.

Landy, Francis. *Paradoxes of Paradise*. Sheffield: Almond, 1983.

Langer, Susanne. *Feeling and Form: A Theory of Art*. New York: Scribner, 1953.

Langgut, Dafna. "Climate Changes during the Bronze and Iron Ages: Results of Pal-ynological Studies in the Sea of Galilee and the Dead Sea." Paper presented at the annual meeting of the SBL. Baltimore, November 23, 2013.

Legaspi, M. C. *The Death of Scripture and the Rise of Biblical Studies*. Oxford: Oxford University Press, 2010.

Lehiste, Ilse. "Rhythm of Poetry, Rhythm of Prose." Pages 145–55 in *Phonetic Linguis-tics*. Edited by V. Fromkin. Orlando: Academic, 1985.

Lehiste, Ilse. "Speech Research: An Overview." Pages 98–107 in *Music, Language, Speech, and Brain*. Edited by J. Sundberg et al. Basingstoke: Macmillan, 1991.

Lemaire, André. *Les écoles et la formation de la Bible dans l'ancien Israel*. Orbis biblicus et orientalis 38. Göttingen: Vändenhoeck und Ruprecht, 1981.

Lemaire, André. "Manuscrit, mur et rocher en épigraphie nord-ouest sémitiquè." Pages 35–42 in *Le texte et son inscription*. Edited by Paul Brady and Roger Laufer. Paris: Editions du Centre national de la recherche scientifique, 1989.

Lemaire, André. "Les inscriptions sur plâtre de Deir ʿAlla et leur signification histo-rique et culturele." Pages 33–57 in *The Balaam Text from Deir ʿAllā Re-Evaluated*. Ed. J. Hoftijzer and G. van der Kooij. Leiden: Brill, 1991.

Lentricchia, Frank, and Andrew Dubois. *Close Reading: The Reader*. Durham: Duke University Press, 2003.

Leuchter, Mark. "Persian Imperial Mythology and the Levites: Implications for the Origins of Jewish Midrash." Unpublished manuscript. Paper presented to the Old Testament Research Colloquium, Princeton, NJ, on December 5, 2014.

Levenson, J. *Creation and the Persistence of Evil: The Jewish Drama of Divine Omnipo-tence*. Princeton: Princeton University Press, 1988.

Levertov, Denise. *The Poet in the World*. New York: New Directions, 1973.

Levertov, Denise. *Light Up the Cave*. New York: New Directions, 1981.

Lewalski, Barbara. *Milton's Brief Epic: The Genre, Meaning, and Art of Paradise Re-gained*. Providence: Brown University Press, 1966.

Lewalski, Barbara. *Protestant Poetics and the Seventeenth-Century Religious Lyric*. Princeton: Princeton University Press, 1979.

Lichtenstein, M. H. "Episodic Structure in the Ugaritic Keret Legend: Comparative Studies in Compositional Technique." Ph.D. diss., Columbia University, 1979.

Linafelt, Tod. "Private Poetry and Public Eloquence in 2 Samuel 1:17–27: Hearing and Overhearing David's Lament for Jonathan and Saul." *Journal of Religion* 88 (2008): 497–526.

Linafelt, Tod. "The Bible's Literary Merits." *Chronicle of Higher Education* 31 (April 10, 2009): B6–B9.

Linafelt, Tod. "On Biblical Style." *St. John Review* 54/1 (2012): 17–44.

Linafelt, Tod, and F. W. Dobbs-Allsopp. "Poetic Line Structure in Qoheleth 3:1." *VT* 60 (2010): 249–59.

Lindley, D. *Lyric*. London: Methuen, 1985.

Loewenstamm, Samuel E. "The Expanded Colon in Ugaritic and Biblical Verse." *JSS* 14 (1969): 176–96.

Livingstone, A. *Court Poetry and Literary Miscellanea*. SAA 3. Helsinki: Helsinki University Press, 1989.

Longenbach, James. *The Art of the Poetic Line*. St. Paul: Graywolf, 2008.

Longman, Tremper. "Form Criticism, Recent Developments in Genre Theory, and the Evangelical." *Westminster Theological Journal* 47 (1985): 46–67.

Lord, Albert B. "Homer and Huso III: Enjambement in Greek and Southslavic Heroic Song." *Transactions of the American Philological Association* 79 (1948): 113–24.

Lord, Albert B. *The Singer of Tales*. Cambridge, Mass.: Harvard University Press, 1960.

Lord, Albert B. "Formula and Non-narrative Theme in South Slavic Oral Epic and the OT." *Semeia* 5 (1976): 93–106.

Lord, Albert B. *Epic Singers and Oral Tradition*. Ithaca: Cornell University Press, 1991.

Lord, Albert B. *The Singer Resumes the Tale*. Edited by M. L. Lord. Ithaca: Cornell University Press, 1995.

Loretz, Oswald. "Die Analyse der ugaritischen und hebräischen Poesie mittels Stichometric und Konsonaenzählung." *Ugarit-Forschungen* 7 (1976): 265–69.

Lowth, R. *A Short Introduction to English Grammar*. London: J. Hughs, 1762.

Lowth, R. *De Sacra Poesi Hebraeorum Praelectiones Academicae Oxonii Habitae*. London: Clarendon, 1753. 3d ed. (1775) is reprinted in *Robert Lowth (1710–1787): The Major Works*. Edited by D. A. Reibel. London: Routledge, 1995.

Lowth, R. *Isaiah. A New Translation; with a Preliminary Dissertation, and Notes*. London: J. Nichols, 1778. Reprinted in *Robert Lowth (1710–1787): The Major Works*. London: Routledge, 1995.

Lowth, R. *Lectures on the Sacred Poetry of the Hebrews*. 2 vols. Translated by G. Gregory. London: J. Johnson, 1787. Reprinted in *Robert Lowth (1710–1787): The Major Works*. London: Routledge, 1995.

Macdonald, M. C. A. "Literacy in an Oral Environment." Pages 49–118 in *Writing and Ancient Near Eastern Society: Papers in Honour of Alan R. Millard*. Library of Hebrew Bible/Old Testament Studies 426. Edited by Christopher Mee et al. New York: T. and T. Clark, 2005.

Macpherson, James. *Fragments of Ancient Poetry, collected in the Highlands of Scotland, and translated from the Garlic or Erse language*. Edinburgh: G. Hamilton and J. Balfour, 1760.

Macpherson, James. *Fingal, an Ancient Epic Poem, in Six Books: together with several other poems*. London: T. Becket and P. A. De Hondt, 1762.

Macpherson, James. *The Works of Ossian, the Song of Fingal, in Two Volumes*. London: T. Becket and P. A. De Hondt, 1765.

Malinowski, Bronislaw. *Myth in Primitive Psychology*. London, 1926.

Man, Paul de. *The Resistance to Theory*. Minneapolis: University of Minnesota Press, 1986.

Marböck, Johannes. "קו—Eine Bezeichnung für das hebräische Metrum?" *VT* 20 (1970): 236–39.

Mazar, Amihai. *Archaeology of the Land of the Bible, 10,000–586 B.C.E.* New York: Doubleday, 1990.

Mazar, Amihai. "The Debate over the Chronology of the Iron Age in the Southern Levant." Pages 15–42 in *The Bible and Radiocarbon Dating: Archaeology, Text and Science.* Edited by Thomas E. Levy and Thomas Higham. London: Equinox, 2005.

McCarter, P. Kyle. *1 Samuel.* Anchor Bible 8. New York: Doubleday, 1980.

McCarter, P. Kyle. *2 Samuel.* Anchor Bible 9. New York: Doubleday, 1984.

McCarter, P. Kyke. *Textual Criticism.* GBS. Philadelphia: Fortress, 1986.

McCarter, P. Kyle. "Kuntillet ʿAjrud Plaster Wall Inscription (2.47D)." Page 173 in *The Context of Scripture: Monumental Inscriptions*, vol. 2. Edited by W. W. Hallo. Leiden: Brill, 2000.

McCarter, P. Kyle. "Paleographic Notes on the Tel Zayit Abecedary." Pages 45–60 in *Literate Culture and Tenth-Century Canaan: The Tel Zayit Abecedary in Context.* Edited by R. E. Tappy and P. K. McCarter. Winona Lake, Ind.: Eisenbrauns, 2008.

McCreesh, Thomas P. *Biblical Sound and Sense: Poetic Sound Patterns in Proverbs 10–29.* Journal for the Study of the Old Testament 128. Sheffield: Sheffield Academic, 1991.

McGann, Jerome J. *The Beauty of Inflections: Literary Investigations in Historical Method and Theory.* Oxford: Clarendon, 1985.

Meek, D. E. "The Gaelic Ballads of Scotland: Creativity and Adaptation." Pages 19–48 in *Ossian Revisited.*

Merwin, W. S. *The Moving Target: Poems.* New York: Atheneum, 1963.

Merwin, W. S. *Migration: New and Selected Poems.* Port Townsend, Wash.: Copper Canyon, 2005.

Meshel, Zeʾev. *Kuntillet ʿAjrud: A Religious Center from the Time of the Judaean Monarchy on the Border of Sinai.* Jerusalem: Israel Museum, 1978.

Metzger, B. M. *The Text of the New Testament.* 4th ed. Oxford: Oxford University Press, 2005 [1954].

Meyers, Carol. "The Family in Early Israel." Pages 1–47 in *Families in Ancient Israel.* Edited by L. Perdue et al. Louisville: Westminster John Knox, 1997.

Meyers, Carol, and M. O'Connor, eds. *The Word of the Lord Shall Go Forth: Essays in Honor of David Noel Freedman in Celebration of His Sixtieth Birthday.* Winona Lake, Ind.: Eisenbrauns, 1983.

Michaelis, Johann Heinrich, ed. *Biblia hebraica: ex aliqvot manvscriptis et complvribvs impressis codicibus; item masora tam edita, qvam manuscripta...recensita...; accedvnt loca Scriptvrae parallela...brevesqve adnotationes...* Halae Magdebvrgicae, Typis & sumtibus Orphanotrophei, 1720.

Michalowski, P. "Ancient Poetics." Pages 141–53 in *Mesopotamian Poetic Language: Sumerian and Akkadian.* Edited by M. Vogelzang and M. Vanstiphout. Groningen: STYX, 1996.

Mileta, M., et al. "Comparison of Dew Yields in Four Mediterranean Sites: Similarities and Differences." In Proceedings of the Third International Conference on Fog, Fog Collection and Dew, 2004.

Milgrom, J. *Leviticus 17–22.* AB3A. New York: Doubleday, 2000.

Millard, Alan R. "Epigraphic Notes, Aramaic and Hebrew." *Palestinian Exploration Quarterly* 110 (1978): 23–26.

Millard, Alan R. "In Praise of Ancient Scribes." *Biblical Archeologist* 45 (1982): 145–53.

Miller, C. L. *The Representation of Speech in Biblical Hebrew Narrative: A Linguistic Analysis.* HMS 55. Atlanta: Scholars Press, 1996.

Miller, George A. "The Magical Number Seven, Plus or Minus 2." *Psychology Review* 63 (1956): 81–97. Accessed March 5, 2015, www.musanim.com/miller1956/.

Miller, Matt. *Collage of Myself.* Lincoln: University of Nebraska Press, 2010.

Miller, Patrick D. *Sin and Judgement in the Prophets: A Stylistic and Theological Analysis.* Society of Biblical Literature Monograph Series 27. Chico: Scholars Press, 1982.

Miller, Patrick D. *Interpreting the Psalms.* Philadelphia: Fortress, 1986.

Miller, Patrick D. *They Cried to the LORD: The Form and Theology of Biblical Prayer.* Minneapolis: Fortress, 1994.

Miller, Paul A. *Lyric Texts and Lyric Consciousness.* London: Routledge, 1994.

Miller, Robert D., II. *Oral Tradition in Ancient Israel.* Eugene, Ore.: Cascade Books, 2011.

Miner, Earl. "On the Genesis and Development of Literary Systems: Part I." *Critical Inquiry* 5/2 (1978): 339–53.

Miner, Earl. "Some Issues for Study of Integrated Collections." Pages 18–43 in *Poems in Their Place: The Intertextuality and Order of Poetic Collections.* Edited by N. Fraistat. Chapel Hill: University of North Carolina Press, 1986.

Miner, Earl. *Comparative Poetics: An Intercultural Essay on Theories of Literature.* Princeton: Princeton University Press, 1990.

Miner, Earl. "Collections, Poetic." Pages 222–23 in *NPEPP.*

Miner, Earl. "Why Lyric?" Pages 3–15 in *The Renewal of Song: Renovation in Lyric Conception and Practice.* Edited by E. Miner and A. Dev. Calcutta: Seagull Books, 2000.

Mintz, A. "The Rhetoric of Lamentations and the Representation of Catastrophe." *Prooftexts* 2/1 (1982): 1–17.

Mintz, A. *Hurban: Responses to Catastrophe in Hebrew Literature.* New York: Columbia University Press, 1984.

Mintz, Ruth F. *Modern Hebrew Poetry: A Bilingual Edition.* 3d ed. Berkeley: University of California Press, 1982.

Mithen, Steven. *The Singing Neanderthals: The Origins of Music, Language, Mind, and Body.* Cambridge, Mass.: Harvard University Press, 2006.

Morris, David B. *The Religious Sublime: Christian Poetry and Critical Tradition in 18th-Century England.* Lexington: University of Kentucky Press, 1972.

Moulton, Richard G. *The Literary Study of the Bible*. London: Isbister, 1896.

Moulton, Richard G. *Modern Reader's Bible for Schools*. New York: Macmillan, 1922.

Mowinckel, Sigmund. *The Psalms in Israel's Worship*. 2 vols. New York: Abingdon Press, 1962.

Mowinckel, Sigmund. *The Spirit and the Word: Prophecy and Tradition in Ancient Israel*. Edited by K. C. Hanson. Minneapolis: Fortress Publishing, 2002.

Muraoka, T. *Emphatic Words and Structures in Biblical Hebrew*. Leiden: Brill, 1985.

Nagy, Gregory. "Formula and Meter." Pages 239–60 in *Oral Literature and the Formula*. Edited by B. A. Stolz and R. S. Shannon. Ann Arbor: University of Michigan Press, 1976.

Nagy, Gregory. *Pindar's Homer: The Lyric Possession of an Epic Past*. Baltimore: Johns Hopkins University Press, 1990.

Nagy, Gregory. "Reading Greek Poetry Aloud: Evidence from the Bacchylides Papyri." *Quaderni Urbinati di Cultura Classica* NS 64 (2000): 7–28.

Nagy, Gregory. "Lyric and Greek Myth." Pages 19–51 in *The Cambridge Companion to Greek Mythology*. Edited by R. D. Woodard. Cambridge: Cambridge University Press, 2007.

Naveh, Joseph. "A Paleographic Note on the Distribution of the Hebrew Script." *Harvard Theological Review* 61 (1968): 68–74.

Naveh, Joseph. *Early History of the Alphabet*. Jerusalem: Magnes, 1987.

Neely, C. T. "The Structure of English Renaissance Sonnet Sequences." *ELH* 45 (1978): 359–89.

Nettl, Bruno. *Music in Primitive Culture*. Cambridge, Mass.: Harvard University Press, 1956.

Newton, Adam. *Narrative Ethics*. Cambridge, Mass.: Harvard University Press, 1995.

Niditch, Susan. "The Composition of Isaiah 1." *Biblica* 61 (1980): 509–29.

Niditch, Susan. "Oral Register in the Biblical Libretto: Towards a Biblical Poetic." *Oral Tradition* 10 (1995): 347–408.

Niditch, Susan. *Oral World and Written World: Ancient Israelite Literature*. Louisville: Westminster John Knox, 1996.

Niditch, Susan. *"My Brother Esau Is a Hairy Man": Hair and Identity in Ancient Israel*. Oxford: Oxford University Press, 2008.

Nietzsche, Friedrich. *Daybreak: Thoughts on the Prejudices of Morality*. Translated by R. J. Hollingdale. Cambridge: Cambridge University Press, 1982.

Niles, John D. *Homo Narrans: The Poetics and Anthropology of Oral Literature*. Philadelphia: University of Pennsylvania Press, 2010.

Nissinen, Martti. "Love Lyrics of Nabû and Tašmetu: An Assyrian Song of Songs?" Pages 585–634 in *"Und Mose schrieb dieses Lied auf." Studien zum Alten Testament und zum Alten Orient*. Edited by M. Dietrich and I. Kottsieper. AOAT, 250. Münster: Ugarit- Verlag, 1998.

Nissinen, Martti. "Spoken, Written, Quoted, and Invented: Orality and Writtenness in Ancient Near Eastern Prophecy." Pages 235–72 in *Writings and Speech in*

Israelite and Ancient Near Eastern Prophecy. Edited by Ehud Ben Zvi and Michael Floyd. Atlanta: SBL, 2000.

Nissinen, Martti. "Akkadian Rituals and Poetry of Divine Love." Pages 93–136 in *Mythology and Mythologies: Methodological Approaches to Intercultural Influences*. Edited by R. M. Whiting. Helsinki: Neo-Assyrian Text Corpus Project, 2001.

Nissinen, Martti. "Song of Songs and Sacred Marriage." Pages 173–218 in *Sacred Marriages: The Divine-Human Sexual Metaphor from Sumer to Early Christianity*. Edited by M. Nissinen and R. Uro. Winona Lake, Ind.: Eisenbrauns, 2008.

Nissinen, Martti. "Akkadian Love Poetry and the Song of Songs: New Sources, New Perspectives." Unpublished manuscript. Paper presented at the annual meeting of the SBL, San Diego, November 23, 2014.

Nissinen, Martti, et al. *Prophets and Prophecy in the Ancient Near East*. Writings of the Ancient World. Atlanta: SBL, 2005.

Noegel, Scott, and Gary Rendsburg. *Solomon's Vineyard: Literary and Linguistic Studies in the Song of Songs*. Atlanta: SBL, 2009.

Norton, David. *A History of the English Bible as Literature*. Cambridge: Cambridge University Press, 2004.

Notopoulos, James A. "Parataxis in Homer: A New Approach to Homeric Literary Criticism." *Transactions and Proceedings of the American Philological Society* 80 (1949): 1–23.

Nussbaum, Martha C. *The Fragility of Goodness*. Cambridge: Cambridge University Press, 1986.

Nussbaum, Martha C. *Love's Knowledge*. Oxford: Oxford University Press, 1990.

Nussbaum, Martha C. *Upheavals of Thought: The Intelligence of Emotions*. Cambridge: Cambridge University Press, 2001.

O'Brien O'Keeffe, Katherine. *Visible Song: Transitional Literacy in Old English Verse*. Vol. 4. Cambridge Studies in Anglo-Saxon England 4. Cambridge: Cambridge University Press, 1990.

O'Connor, Michael Patrick. *Hebrew Verse Structure*. Winona Lake, Ind.: Eisenbrauns, 1997 [1980].

Ohry, A., and A. Levy. "Anointing with Oil—An Hygienic Procedure in the Bible and in the Talmud." *Koroth* 9 (1985): 173–76.

Oliver, Mary. *A Poetry Handbook*. New York: Harcourt Brace, 1994.

Olmo Lete, Gregorio del. *Mitos y leyendas de Canaán según la tradición de Ugarit*. Madrid: Cristiandad, 1981.

Olson, David R. "From Utterance to Text: The Bias of Language in Speech and Writing." *Harvard Educational Review* 47/3 (1977): 257–281.

Ong, Walter. *Orality and Literacy: The Technologizing of the Word*. London: Routledge, 1982.

Ong, Walter. "Writing Is a Technology That Restructures Thought." Pages 23–50 in *The Written Word: Literacy in Transition*. Edited by G. Bauman. Oxford: Clarendon, 1986.

Opland, Jeff. *Anglo-Saxon Oral Poetry: A Study of the Traditions.* New Haven: Yale University Press, 1980.

Opland, Jeff. *Xhosa Poets and Poetry.* Cape Town: New Africa Books, 1998.

Oppenheim, A. L. *Ancient Mesopotamia: Portrait of a Dead Civilization.* Rev. ed. Chicago: University of Chicago Press, 1977.

Pardee, Dennis. "Ugaritic and Hebrew Metrics." Pages 113–30 in *Ugarit in Retrospect: Fifty Years of Ugarit and Ugaritic.* Edited by Gordon D. Young. Winona Lake, Ind.: Eisenbrauns, 1981.

Pardee, Dennis. *Ugaritic and Hebrew Parallelism: A Trial Cut ('nt I and Proverbs 2).* VTSup 39. Leiden: Brill, 1988.

Pardee, Dennis. "Preliminary Presentation of a New Ugaritic Song to ʿAṯtart (RIH 98/02)." Pages 27–39 in *Ugarit at Seventy-Five.* Edited by K. L. Younger. Winona Lake, Ind.: Eisenbrauns, 2007.

Pardee, Dennis. "Ugaritic Alphabetic Cuneiform in the Context of Other Alphabetic Systems." Pages 181–200 in *Studies in Semitic and Afroasiatic Linguistics Presented to Gene B. Gragg.* Edited by C. L. Miller. Chicago: University of Chicago Press, 2007.

Pardee, Dennis. *The Ugaritic Texts and the Origins of West Semitic Literary Composition.* Oxford: Oxford University Press, 2012.

Parker, Simon. *The Pre-biblical Narrative Tradition: Essays on the Ugaritic Poems Keret and Aqhat.* Atlanta: Scholars Press, 1989.

Parker, Simon. *Stories in Scripture and Inscriptions: Comparative Studies on Narratives in Northwest Semitic Inscriptions and the Hebrew Bible.* New York: Oxford University Press, 1997.

Parker, Simon, ed. *Ugaritic Narrative Poetry.* WAW 9. Atlanta: Scholars Press, 1997.

Parkes, Malcolm B. *Pause and Effect: An Introduction to the History of Punctuation in the West.* Aldershot: Scholar Press, 1992.

Parkinson, Richard B. *Poetry and Culture in Middle Kingdom Egypt.* London: Continuum, 2002.

Parkinson, Richard B. *Reading Ancient Egyptian Poetry: Among Other Histories.* Oxford: Wiley, 2009.

Parkinson, Richard, and Stephen Quirke. *Papyrus.* Austin: University of Texas Press, 1995.

Parry, Milman. *The Making of Homeric Verse: The Collected Papers of Milman Parry.* Edited by Adam Parry. Oxford: Clarendon, 1971.

Pasternack, Carol B. *The Textuality of Old English Poetry.* Cambridge: Cambridge University Press, 1995.

Patterson, Lee. *Negotiating the Past: The Historical Understanding of Medieval Literature.* Madison: University of Wisconsin Press, 1987.

Paul, Shalom. *Amos.* Hermeneia. Minneapolis: Fortress, 1991.

Paul, Shalom. "The Return to Philology." Pages 231–44 in *The Past and Future of Medieval Studies.* Edited by J. Van Engen. South Bend: University of Notre Dame Press, 1994.

Penner, Jeremy, Ken Penner, and Cecilia Wassen, eds. *Prayer and Poetry in the Dead Sea Scrolls and Related Literature: Essays in Honor of Eileen Schuller on the Occasion of Her 65th Birthday.* Leiden: Brill, 2012.

Perloff, Marjorie. "The Linear Fallacy." *Georgia Review* 35 (1981): 855–69.

Perloff, Marjorie. "Lucent and Inescapable Rhythms: Metrical 'Choice' and Historical Formation." Pages 13–40 in *The Line in Postmodern Poetry.* Edited by R. Frank and H. Sayre. Urbana: University of Illinois Press, 1988.

Person, Raymond F. "The Ancient Israelite Scribe as Performer." *Journal of Biblical Literature* 117 (1998): 601–9.

Person, Raymond F. *The Deuteronomic School: History, Social Setting, and Literature.* Leiden: Brill, 2002.

Person, Raymond F. *The Deuteronomic History and the Books of Chronicles: Scribal Works in an Oral World.* Atlanta: SBL, 2010.

Petersen, David, and Kent Richards. *Interpreting Hebrew Poetry.* Minneapolis: Fortress, 1992.

Petitmengin, Claire. "Towards the Source of Thoughts: The Gestural and Transmodal Dimension of Lived Experience." *Journal of Consciousness Studies* 14 (2007): 54–82.

Pfeiffer, Rudolf. *History of Classical Scholarship.* Oxford: Clarendon, 1968.

Phillips, George S. "Literature. Leaves of Grass—by Walt Whitman." *New York Illustrated News* 2 (May 26, 1860): 43.

Pinker, Steven. *The Language Instinct: The New Science of Language and Mind.* Penguin Books, 1995.

Pinsky, Robert. *The Sounds of Poetry: A Brief Guide.* New York: Farrar, Straus and Giroux, 1998.

Pinsky, Robert. *Democracy, Culture and the Voice of Poetry.* Princeton: Princeton University Press, 2002.

Pioske, Daniel D. *David's Jerusalem: Between Memory and History.* London: Routledge, 2015.

Pointer, S. *The Artifice of Beauty: A History and Practical Guide to Perfumes and Cosmetics.* Thrupp, Stroud, Gloucestershire: Sutton, 2005.

Polak, Frank H. "Epic Formulae in Biblical Narrative and the Origins of Ancient Hebrew Prose." Pages 9–54 [in Hebrew] in *Studies in Judaica* Te'uda 7. Edited by M. A. Friedman. Tel Aviv: Tel Aviv University Press, 1991 [English summary pp. vii–viii].

Polak, Frank H. "Epic Formulas in Biblical Narrative: Frequency and Distribution." Pages 435–88 in *Actes du Second Colloque International "Bible et Informatique: Méthodes, Outils, Résultats" (Jérusalem 9–13 Juin 1988).* Edited by R. F. Poswick et al. Geneva: Slatkine, 1989.

Polak, Frank H. "The Oral and the Written: Syntax, Stylistics and the Development of Biblical Prose Narrative." *Journal of the Ancient Near Eastern Society* 26 (1998): 59–105.

Polak, Frank H. "Book, Scribe, and Bard: Oral Discourse and Written Text in Recent Biblical Scholarship." *Prooftexts* 31 (2011): 118–40.

Polak, Frank H. "Formulaic Style." Pages 906–11 in *Encyclopedia of Hebrew Language and Linguistics*, vol. 1, A–F. Edited by J. Khan. Leiden: Brill, 2013.

Polak, Frank H. "Orality: Biblical Hebrew." Pages 930–37 in *The Encyclopedia of Hebrew Language and Linguistics*, vol. 2, G–O. Edited by G. Khan. Leiden: Brill, 2013.

Pollock, Sheldon. "Future Philology? The Fate of a Soft Science in a Hard World." *Critical Inquiry* 35 (2009): 931–61.

Pope, Marvin H. "Number, Numbering, Numbers." In *IDB*, vol. K–Q, 561–67.

Porten, B. *Archives from Elephantine*. Berkeley: University of California Press, 1968.

Porter, James, ed. *"Special Issue*: James Macpherson and the Ossian Epic Debate." *Journal of American Folklore* 114/454 (2001).

Porter, James. "'Bring Me the Head of James Macpherson': The Execution of Ossian and the Wellsprings of Folkloristic Discourse." *Journal of American Folklore* 114/454 (2001): 396–435.

Porter, James I. *Nietzsche and the Philology of the Future*. Stanford: Stanford University Press, 2000.

Preminger, Alex, and T. V. F. Brogan, eds. *The New Princeton Encyclopedia of Poetry and Poetics*. Princeton: Princeton University Press, 1993.

Preston, Thomas R. "Biblical Criticism, Literature, and the Eighteenth-Century Reader." Pages 97–126 in *Books and Their Readers in Eighteenth-Century England*. Edited by I. Rivers. Leicester: Leicester University Press, 1982.

Price, Kenneth M. *Walt Whitman: The Contemporary Reviews*. Cambridge: Cambridge University Press, 1996.

Prinz, D. "Water Harvesting—History, Techniques and Trends." *Zeitschrift für Bewässerungswirtschaft* 31/1 (1996): 64–105.

Prinz, D. "The Role of Water Harvesting in Alleviating Water Scarcity in Arid Areas." Keynote Lecture, Proceedings, International Conference on Water Resources Management in Arid Regions. March 23–27, 2002, Kuwait Institute for Scientific Research, Kuwait. Vol. 3, 107–122.

Puech, E. "Origine de l'alphabet." *RB* 93 (1986): 161–213.

Race, W. H. "Melic." Page 755 in *NPEPP*.

Redford, D. "Scribe and Speaker." Pages 145–218 in *Writing and Speech in Israelite and Ancient Near Eastern Prophecy*. Edited by E. B. Zvi and M. H. Floyd. Atlanta: SBL, 2000.

Reibel, David A., ed. *Robert Lowth (1710–1787): The Major Works*. London: Routledge, 1995.

Reich, R., E. Shukron, and O. Lernau. "Recent Discoveries in the City of David, Jerusalem." *Israel Exploration Society* 57 (2007): 153–69.

Revell, E. J. "Pausal Forms and the Structure of Hebrew Poetry." *VT* 31 (1981): 186–99.

Reynolds, David S. *Walt Whitman's America*. New York: Vintage, 1995.

Reynolds, L. D., and N. G. Wilson. *Scribes and Scholars: A Guide to the Transmission of Greek and Latin Literature*. 3d ed. Oxford: Clarendon, 1991.

Roberts, J. J. M. *The Bible and the Ancient Near East: Collected Essays*. Winona Lake, Ind.: Eisenbrauns, 2002.

Robertson, A. E. "Word Dividers, Spot Markers and Clause Markers in Old Assyrian, Ugaritic, and Egyptian Texts: Sources for Understanding the Use of Red Ink Points in Two Akkadian Literary Texts, Adapa and Ereshkigal, Found in Egypt." Ph.D. diss., New York University, 1993.

Robertson, A. E. "Non-word Divider Use of the Small Vertical Wedge in *Yariḫ and Nikkal* and in an Akkadian Text Written in Alphabetic Cuneiform." Pages 89–109 in *Ki Baruch Hu*. Edited by R. Chazan, W. W. Hall, and L. Schiffman. Winona Lake, Ind.: Eisenbrauns, 1999.

Robertson, David A. *Linguistic Evidence in Dating Early Poetry*. Society of Biblical Literature Dissertation Series 3. Missoula, Mo.: Society of Biblical Literature, 1972.

Robins, G. *The Art of Ancient Egypt*. Cambridge, Mass.: Harvard University Press, 1997.

Robinson, Theodore Henry. *The Poetry of the Old Testament*. London: Duckworth, 1947.

Robinson, Theodore Henry. *Writing and Literacy in the World of Ancient Israel*. Atlanta: SBL, 2010.

Roche, T. L., Jr. *Petrarch and the English Sonnet Sequences*. New York: AMS, 1989.

Rosenthal, M. L. *The Poet's Art*. New York: Norton, 1987.

Rosenthal, M. L., and Sally Gall. *The Modern Poetic Sequence*. New York: Oxford University Press, 1983.

Roston, Murray. *Prophet and Poet: The Bible and the Growth of Romanticism*. Evanston, Ill.: Northwestern University Press, 1965.

Roth, Wolfgang M. W. "The Numerical Sequence x / x + 1 in the Old Testament." *VT* 12 (1962): 300–311.

Rubin, David. *Memory in Oral Traditions: The Cognitive Psychology of Epic, Ballads, and Counting-Out Rhymes*. New York: Oxford University Press, 1995.

Ryken, L. *The Literature of the Bible*. Grand Rapids: Zondervan, 1974.

Sachs, Curt. *Rhythm and Tempo: A Study in Music History*. New York: Norton, 1953.

Saenger, Paul. *Space between Words: The Origins of Silent Reading*. Stanford: Stanford University Press, 1997.

Said, Edward W. *Humanism and Democratic Criticism*. New York: Columbia University Press, 2004.

Sanders, James A. *The Psalms Scroll of Qumran Cave 11*. Oxford: Clarendon, 1965.

Sanders, Seth L. "What Was the Alphabet For? The Rise of Written Vernaculars and the Making of Israelite National Literature." *Maarav* 11 (2004): 25–56.

Sanders, Seth L. *The Invention of Hebrew*. Urbana: University of Illinois Press, 2009.

Sass, Benjamin. *The Genesis of the Alphabet and Its Development in the Second Millennium B.C.* AAT 13. Wiesbaden: Harrassowitz, 1988.

Sasson, Jack, ed. *Civilizations of the Ancient Near East*. 4 vols. New York: Scribner, 1995.

Sasson, Jack, ed. "Comparative Observations on the Near Eastern Epic Traditions." Pages 215–32 in *A Companion to Ancient Epic*. Edited by J. M. Foley. Malden: Blackwell, 2005.

Schaefer, Ursula. "Hearing from Books: The Rise of Fictionality in Old English Poetry." Pages 117–36 in *Vox Intexta: Orality and Textuality in the Middle Ages*. Edited by A. N. Doane and C. B. Pasternack. Madison: University of Wisconsin Press, 1991.

Schaff, P., ed. *Nicene and Post-Nicene Fathers, Series II*. Vol. 6. New York: Christian Literature Company, 1893.

Schechter, Solomon, and Charles Taylor. *The Wisdom of Ben Sira*. Cambridge: Cambridge University Press, 1899.

Schloen, D. *The House of the Father as Fact and Symbol: Patrimonialism in Ugarit and the Ancient Near East*. Winona Lake, Ind.: Eisenbrauns, 2001.

Schneider, M. "Primitive Music." Pages in *The New Oxford History of Music I, Ancient and Oriental Music*. Oxford: Oxford University Press, 1957.

Schniedewind, William. *How the Bible Became a Book*. Cambridge: Cambridge University Press, 2004.

Schniedewind, William. "Aramaic, the Death of Written Hebrew, and Language Shift in the Persian Period." Pages 137–47 in *Margins of Writing, Origins of Cultures*. Edited by S. L. Sanders. Chicago: Oriental Institute of the University of Chicago, 2006.

Schniedewind, William M. *A Social History of Hebrew: Its Origins through the Rabbinic Period*. New Haven: Yale University Press, 2013.

Scully, J. *Line Break: Poetry as Social Practice*. Willimantic: Curbstone, 2005 [1988].

Sefati, Yitschak. *Love Songs in Sumerian Literature: Critical Edition of the Dumuzi-Inanna Songs*. Ramat Gan: Bar-Ilan University Press, 1998.

Segert, Stanislav. "Die Schreibfehler in den ugaritischen literarischen Keilschrifttexten in Anschluss an das textkritische Hilfsbuch von Friedrich Delitzsch klassifiziert." Pages 193–212 in *Von Ugarit nach Qumran: Beiträge zur alttestamentlichen und altorientalischen Forschung*. Beihefte zur Zeitschrift für die alttestamentliche Wissenschaft 77. Edited by J. Hempel and L. Rost. Berlin: Töpelmann, 1958.

Sells, M. "Guises of the *Ghūl*: Dissembling Simile and Semantic Overflow in Classical Arabic *Nasīb*." Pages 130–64 in *Reorientations/Arabic and Persian Poetry*. Edited by S. Steikevych. Bloomington: Indiana University Press, 1994.

Seow, C. L. *Job 1–21*. Illuminations. Grand Rapids: Eerdmans, 2013.

Serat, C. *Hebrew Manuscripts of the Middle Ages*. Cambridge: Cambridge University Press, 2002.

Shapiro, Alan. *In Praise of the Impure: Poetry and the Ethical Imagination*. Evanston, Ill.: Northwestern University Press, 1993.

Sherzer, Joel. "Poetic Structuring of Kuna Discourse: The Line." Pages 371–90 in *Native American Discourse*. Edited by Joel Sherzer and Anthony C. Woodbury. Cambridge: Cambridge University Press, 1987.

Sherzer, Joel, and Anthony C. Woodbury, eds. *Native American Discourse*. Cambridge: Cambridge University Press, 1987.

Shuster, G. N. *The English Ode from Milton to Keats*. New York: Columbia University Press, 1940.

Sidney, Philip. "An Apologie for Poetrie." Pages 148–207 in *Elizabethan Critical Essays*. Edited by G. G. Smith. Oxford: Oxford University Press, 1904.

Sienaert, Edgar. "Marcel Jousse: The Oral Style and the Anthropology of Gesture." *Oral Tradition* 5 (1990): 91–106.

Sievers, Eduard. *Metrische Studien*. Leipzig: Teubner, 1901.

Sirat, Colette. *Hebrew Manuscripts of the Middle Ages*. Cambridge: Cambridge University Press, 2002.

Sjöberg, Å., and E. Bergman. *The Collection of Sumerian Temple Hymns*. Locust Valley, N.Y.: J. J. Augustin, 1969.

Skehan, Patrick W. "A Psalm Manuscript from Qumran (4QPs^b)." *Catholic Biblical Quarterly* 26 (1964): 313–22.

Skehan, Patrick W. *Studies in Israelite Poetry and Wisdom*. Catholic Biblical Quarterly Monograph Series 1. Washington, D.C.: Catholic Biblical Association of America, 1971.

Skehan, Patrick, W. E. Ulrich, and P. W. Flint. "Psalms." Pages 23–48 in *DJD* XVI. Oxford: Clarendon, 2001.

Smith, B. H. *Poetic Closure: A Study of How Poems End*. Chicago: University of Chicago Press, 1968.

Smith, G. A. *The Historical Geography of the Holy Land*. London, 1931.

Smith, Hallett. "English Metrical Psalms in the Sixteenth Century and Their Literary Significance." *Huntington Library Quarterly* 9 (1946): 249–71.

Smith, Mark S. "What Is Prologue Is Past: Composing Israelite Identity in Judges 5." Pages 43–58 in *Thus Says the Lord: Essays on the Former and Latter Prophets in Honor of Robert R. Wilson*. Edited by J. J. Ahn and S. L. Cook. Library Hebrew Bible/Old Testament Series 502. New York: T. and T. Clark, 2009.

Smith, Mark S. "The Problem of the God and His Manifestations: The Case of the Baals at Ugarit, with Implications for Yahweh of Various Locales." Pages 205–50 in *Die Stadt im Zwölfprophetenbuch*. Edited by Aaron Schart and Jutta Krispenz. BZAW 428. Berlin: de Gruyter, 2012.

Smith, Mark S. "Why Was 'Old Poetry' Used in Hebrew Narrative? Historical and Cultural Considerations about Judges 5." Pages 197–212 in *Puzzling Out the Past: Studies in Northwest Semitic Languages and Literatures in Honor of Bruce Zuckerman*. Edited by Marilyn Lundberg, Steven Fine, and Wayne T. Pitchard. Urbana: University of Illinois Press, 2012.

Smith, Mark S. *Poetic Heroes: The Literary Commemoration of Warriors and Warrior Culture in the Early Biblical World*. Grand Rapids: Eerdmans, 2014.

Smith, Mark S., and W. T. Pitard. *The Ugaritic Baal Cycle*. Vol. 2. Leiden: Brill, 2009.

Soden, Wolfram von. "Leistung und Grenze sumerischer und babylonischer Wissenschaft." Pages 411–64 in *Die Welt als Geschichte* 2. Edited by Hans E. Steir. Stuttgart: Kohlhammer, 1936.

Soggin, Jan A. *Judges: A Commentary.* Translated by J. Bowden. Old Testament Library. Philadelphia: Westminster John Knox, 1987.

Soldt, W. H. van. "Babylonian Lexical, Religious and Literary Texts and Scribal Education at Ugarit and Its Implications for the Alphabetic Literary Texts." Pages 171–212 in *Ugarit: Ein ostmediterranes Kulturzentrum in Alten Orient.* Edited by M. Dierich and O. Loretz. Muenster: Ugarit-Verlag, 1995.

Sontag, Susan. *Against Interpretation and Other Essays.* New York: Farrar, Straus and Giroux, 1966.

Spitzer, Leo. *Linguistics and Literary History.* Princeton: Princeton University Press, 1948.

Stager, Lawrence E. "The Finest Olive Oil in Samaria." *JSS* 28 (1983): 241–45.

Stager, Lawrence E. "The Archaeology of the Family in Ancient Israel." *BASOR* 260 (1985): 1–35.

Steiner, George. *After Babel: Aspects of Language and Translation.* Oxford: Oxford University Press, 1998.

Steiner, R. C. "The Aramaic Text in Demotic Script: The Liturgy of a New Year's Festival Imported from Bethel to Syenes by Exiles from Rash." *JAOS* 111/2 (1991): 362–63.

Stewart, Susan. *Poetry and the Fate of the Senses.* Chicago: University of Chicago Press, 2002.

Stock, Brian. *The Implications of Literacy.* Princeton: Princeton University Press, 1983.

Stovall, Floyd. *The Foreground of Leaves of Grass.* Charlottesville: University Press of Virginia, 1974.

Stuart, Douglas K. *Studies in Early Hebrew Meter.* Missoula: Scholars Press, 1976.

Stuart, Moses. *A Hebrew Chrestomathy.* Andover, Mass.: Codman Press, 1829.

Swete, Henry Barclay. *An Introduction to the Old Testament in Greek.* Rev ed. New York: Ktav, 1968.

Tappy, Ron E., and P. Kyle McCarter, Jr., eds. *Literate Culture and Tenth-Century Canaan: The Tel Zayit Abecedary in Context.* Winona Lake, Ind.: Eisenbrauns, 2008.

Tappy, Ron E., et al. "An Abecedary of the Mid-tenth Century B.C.E. from the Judaean Shephelah." *BASOR* 344 (2006): 5–46.

Tedlock, Dennis. "On the Translation of Style in Oral Narrative." *Journal of American Folklore* 84 (1971): 114–33.

Tedlock, Dennis. *Finding the Center: Narrative Poetry of the Zuni Indians.* New York: Dial, 1972.

Tedlock, Dennis. "Toward an Oral Poetics." *NLH* 8 (1977): 507–19.

Tedlock, Dennis. "Hearing a Voice in an Ancient Text: Quiche Maya Poetics in Performance." Pages 140–75 in *Native American Discourse.* Edited by Joel Sherzer and Anthony C. Woodbury. Cambridge: Cambridge University Press, 1987.

Thaut, Michael H. *Rhythm, Music, and the Brain.* New York: Routledge, 2005.

Thomas, Rosalind. *Oral Tradition and Written Record in Classical Athens.* Cambridge: Cambridge University Press, 1989.

Thomas, Rosalind. *Literacy and Orality in Ancient Greece.* Cambridge: Cambridge University Press, 1992.

Thomas, Rosalind. "Performance and Written Literature in Classical Greece: Envisaging Performance from Written Literature and Comparative Contexts." *Bulletin of the School of Oriental and African Studies* 66 (2003): 348–57.

Thomson, D. S. *The Gaelic Sources of Macpherson's Ossian.* Edinburgh: Edinburgh University Press, 1952.

Toorn, Karel van der. *Family Religion in Babylonia, Ugarit and Israel: Continuity and Changes in the Forms of Religious Life.* Leiden: Brill, 1996.

Toorn, Karel van der. "Cuneiform Documents from Syria-Palestine: Texts, Scribes, and Schools." *Zeitschrift des deutschen Palästina-Vereins* 116 (2000): 97–113.

Toorn, Karel van der. *Scribal Culture and the Making of the Hebrew Bible.* Cambridge, Mass.: Harvard University Press, 2007.

Tov, Emanuel. "Special Layout of Poetical Units in the Texts from the Judean Desert." Pages 115–28 in *Give Ear to My Words.* Edited by J. Dyk. Amsterdam: Societas Hebraica Amstelodamensis, 1996.

Tov, Emanuel. "Canticles." Pages 195–219 in *Qumran Cave 4/XI: Psalms to Chronicles.* Edited by E. C. Ulrich et al. DJD XVI. Oxford: Oxford University Press, 2000.

Tov, Emanuel. *Scribal Practices and Approaches Reflected in the Texts Found in the Judean Desert.* Vol. 54. Studies on the Texts of the Desert of Judah. Leiden: Brill, 2004.

Tov, Emanuel. "The Background of the Stichometric Arrangements of Poetry in the Judean Desert Scrolls." Pages 409–20 in *Prayer and Poetry in the Dead Sea Scrolls and Related Literature: Essays in Honor of Eileen Schuller on the Occasion of Her 65th Birthday.* Edited by K. Penner and C. Wassen. Leiden: Brill, 2012.

Treat, J. C. "Lost Keys: Text and Interpretation in Old Greek Song of Songs and Its Earliest Manuscript Witnesses." Ph.D. diss., University of Pennsylvania Press, 1996.

Trilling, Lionel. *The Liberal Imagination.* New York: Harcourt Brace Jovanovich, 1950.

Tsumura, D. T. "Sorites in Psalm 133:2–3a." *Bib* 61 (1980): 416–17.

Tsur, Reuven. *Poetic Rhythm: Structure and Performance—An Empirical Study in Cognitive Poetics.* Bern: Peter Lang, 1998.

Turner, Eric G. *Greek Papyri: An Introduction.* Princeton: Princeton University Press, 1968.

Turner, Eric G. *Greek Manuscripts of the Ancient World.* Princeton: Princeton University Press, 1971.

Turner, Eric G. *The Typology of the Early Codex.* Philadelphia: University of Pennsylvania, 1977.

Turner, Frederick, and Ernst Pöppel. "Neural Lyre: Poetic Meter, the Brain, and Time." Pages 61–105 in Turner, *Natural Classicism: Essays on Literature and Science.* New York: Paragon House, 1985.

Turner, Frederick, and Ernst Pöppel. "Metered Poetry, the Brain, and Time." Pages 71–90 in *Beauty and the Brain: Biological Aspects of Aesthetics.* Edited by I. Renchler et al. Basel: Birkhäuser, 1988.

Turner, James. *Philology: The Forgotten Origins of the Modern Humanities.* Princeton: Princeton University Press, 2014.

Ulrich, E., et al., eds. *Discoveries in the Judean Desert* XVI. Oxford: Clarendon, 2000.

Valéry, Paul. *The Art of Poetry.* Translated by D. Folliot. New York: Pantheon, 1958.

Vance, Donald R. *The Question of Meter in Biblical Hebrew Poetry.* Lewiston, Me.: Mellen, 2001.

Vanderhooft, David. "ʾel mĕdînâ ûmĕdînâ kiktābāh: Scribes and Scripts in Yehud and Achaemendi Transeuphratene." Pages 529–44 in *Judah and the Judeans in the Achaemenid Period: Negotiating Identity in an International Context.* Edited by O. Lipschitz, G. N. Knopers, and M. Oeming. Winona Lake, Ind.: Eisenbrauns, 2011.

Van Sickle, J. "The Book-Roll and Some Conventions of the Poetic Book." *Arethusa* 13 (1980): 5–42.

Vendler, Helen. *Soul Says.* Cambridge, Mass.: Harvard University Press, 1995.

Vendler, Helen. *Poets Thinking.* Cambridge, Mass.: Harvard University Press, 2004.

Vet, Thérèse de. "Parry in Paris: Structuralism, Historical Linguistics, and the Oral Theory." *Classical Antiquity* 24 (2005): 257–84.

Vogelzang, Mariana E., and H. L. J. Vanstiphout. *Mesopotamian Epic Literature: Oral or Aural?* Lewiston, Me.: Mellen, 1992.

Voigt, Ellen. *The Flexible Lyric.* Athens: University of Georgia, 1999.

Voigt, Ellen. *The Art of Syntax: Rhythm of Thought, Rhythm of Song.* Minneapolis: Graywolf, 2009.

Von Hallberg, Robert. *Lyric Powers.* Chicago: University of Chicago Press, 2008.

Wallaschek, Richard. *Primitive Music: An Inquiry into the Origins and Development of Music, Songs, Instruments, Dances, Pantomimes of Savafe Races.* London: Longmans, 1893.

Watkins, Calvert. "Observations on the 'Nestor's Cup' Inscription." *Harvard Studies in Classical Philology* 80 (1976): 25–40.

Watson, Wilfred G. E. "The Hidden Simile in Psalm 133." *Bib* 60 (1969): 108–9.

Watson, Wilfred G. E. "Lineation (Stichometry) in Ugaritic Verse." *Ugarit-Forschungen* 14 (1982): 311–12.

Watson, Wilfred G. E. *Classical Hebrew Poetry: A Guide to Its Techniques.* London: T. and T. Clark, 2001 [1984].

Watson, Wilfred G. E. *Traditional Techniques in Classical Hebrew Verse.* Journal for the Study of the Old Testament Supplement Series 170. Sheffield: Sheffield Academic, 1994.

Watson, Wilfred G. E. "Oral Traditional Lyric Poetry." Pages 22–68 in *The Singer Resumes the Tale*. Edited by M. L. Lord. Ithaca: Cornell University Press, 1995.

Watson, Wilfred G. E. "Ugaritic Poetry." Pages 165–92 in *Handbook of Ugaritic Studies*. Edited by W. G. E. Watson and N. Wyatt. Leiden: Brill, 1999.

Weber, Robert, and Roger Gryson, eds. *Biblia Sacra Vulgata*. Stuttgart: Deutsche Bibelgelleschaft, 1983.

Weiser, Artur. *The Old Testament: Its Formation and Development*. New York: Association, 1961.

Weiser, Artur. *The Psalms*. OTL. Philadelphia: Westminster, 1962.

Wellek, R. *Discriminations: Further Concepts of Criticism*. New Haven: Yale University Press, 1970.

Wellesz, Egon, ed. *The New Oxford History of Music I: "Ancient and Oriental Music."* Oxford: Oxford University Press, 1957.

Welsh, Andrew. *Roots of Lyric: Primitive Poetry and Modern Poetics*. Princeton: Princeton University Press, 1978.

Wertheimer, M. "Laws of Organization in Perceptual Forms." Pages 71–88 in *A Source Book of Gestalt Psychology*. Edited by Willis D. Ellis. London: Routledge and Kegan Paul, 1938.

Wesling, Donald. *The Scissors of Meter: Grammetrics and Reading*. Ann Arbor: University of Michigan Press, 1996.

West, Martin Litchfield. *Greek Metre*. Oxford: Clarendon, 1982.

West, Martin Litchfield. *Iambi et Elegi Graeci*. 2d ed. Oxford: Oxford University Press, 1989.

West, Martin Litchfield. *Ancient Greek Music*. Oxford: Clarendon Press, 1992.

West, Martin Litchfield. *Greek Lyric Poetry*. World Classics. Oxford: Oxford University Press, 1994.

West, Martin Litchfield. *The East Face of Helicon: West Asiatic Elements in Greek Poetry and Myth*. Oxford: Clarendon Press, 1997.

Westbrook, R. *Property and the Family in Biblical Law*. JSOTSS 113. Sheffield: JSOT, 1991.

Westenholtz, J. G. "Love Lyrics from the Ancient Near East." Pages 2471–84 in *CANE*, IV.

Whallon, William. "Formulaic Poetry in the Old Testament." *Comparative Literature* 15 (1963): 1–14.

Whitaker, R. E. "A Formulaic Analysis of Ugaritic Poetry." Ph.D. diss., Harvard University, 1969.

Whitman, Walt. "Blood-Money." *New York Daily Tribune*, supp. (March 22, 1850), 1.

Whitman, Walt. "The House of Friends." *New York Daily Tribune* (June 14, 1850), 3.

Whitman, Walt. "Resurgemus." *New York Daily Tribune* (June 21, 1850), 3.

Whitman, Walt. *Leaves of Grass*. Brooklyn, New York, 1855.

Whitman, Walt. "A Backward Glance o'er Travel'd Roads." In *November Boughs*. Philadelphia: David McKay, 1888, 12–13.

Whitman, Walt. *November Boughs*. Philadelphia: David McKay, 1888.

Whitman, Walt. *A Child's Reminiscence*. Edited by T. O. Mabbott and R. G. Silver. Seattle: University of Washington Press, 1930.

Whitman, Walt. *Daybooks and Notebooks*. Edited by W. H. White. 3 vols. New York: New York University Press, 1978.

Wilamowitz-Möllendorff, Ulrich von. *Der Timotheos-Papyrus: Gefunden bei Abusir am 1.2.1902*. Leipzig: J. C. Heinrichs, 1903.

Wildberger, Hans. *Isaiah 1–12*. Translated by T. H. Trapp. Minneapolis: Fortress, 1991.

Wilke, C. "Der aktuelle Bezug der Sammlung der sumerischer Tempelhymnen und ein Fragment eines Klagelieds." *ZA* 62 (1972): 35–61

Willet, Steven J. "Working Memory and Its Constraints on Colometry." *Quaderni Urbinati di Classica* NS 71 (2002): 7–19.

Willet, Steven J. "Reconsidering Reuven Tsur's *Poetic Rhythm: Structure and Performance—An Empirical Study in Cognitive Poetics*." *Journal of Pragmatics* 37 (2005): 497–503.

Williams, C. K. *On Whitman*. Princeton: Princeton University Press, 2010.

Wilson, G. H. *Editing of the Hebrew Psalter*. Chico: Scholars Press, 1985.

Wilson, R. *Genealogy and History in the Biblical World*. New Haven: Yale University Press, 1977.

Winter, I. J. "Sex, Rhetoric, and the Public Monument: The Alluring Body of Naram-Sin of Agade." Pages 85–108 *Sexuality in Ancient Art*. Edited by N. Kampen. Cambridge: Cambridge University Press, 1996.

Wither, George. *A Preparation to the Psalter*. London: Nicholas Okes, 1619.

Wolff, H. W. "The Kerygma of the Yahwist." Pages 41–66 in *The Vitality of Old Testament Traditions*. Edited by W. Brueggemann. Atlanta: John Knox, 1975.

Wood, James. *How Fiction Works*. New York: Farrar, Straus and Giroux, 2008.

Woodard, Roger. *Greek Writing from Knossos to Homer: A Linguistic Interpretation of the Origin of the Greek Alphabet and the Continuity of Ancient Greek Literacy*. Oxford: Oxford University Press, 1997.

Woodbury, Anthony C. "Rhetorical Structure in a Central Alaskan Yupik Eskimo Traditional Narrative." Pages 176–239 in *Native American Discourse*. Edited by Joel Sherzer and Anthony C. Woodbury. Cambridge: Cambridge University Press, 1987.

Wyschogrod, Michael. *The Body of Faith*. Northvale, N.J.: Jason Aronson, 1996.

Yadin, Yigael. *The Ben Sira Scroll from Masada*. Jerusalem: Israel Exploration Society, 1965.

Yeivin, Israel. *Introduction to the Tiberian Masorah*. Translated by E. J. Revel. Chico: Scholars Press, 1980.

Yoder, Perry B. "A-B Pairs and Oral Composition in Hebrew Poetry." *VT* 21 (1971): 470–89.

You, Haili. "Defining Rhythm: Aspects of an Anthropology of Rhythm." *Culture, Medicine and Psychiatry* 18 (1994): 361–84.

Younger, K. Lawson, Jr., ed. *Ugarit at Seventy-Five.* Winona Lake, Ind.: Eisenbrauns, 2007.

Yunis, Harvey, ed. *Written Texts and the Rise of Literate Culture in Ancient Greece.* Cambridge: Cambridge University Press, 2003.

Zakovitch, Yair. "Yes, There Was an Israelite Epic in the Biblical Period." *International Folklore Review* 8 (1991): 18–25.

Zakovitch, Yair. *Das Hohelied.* Freiburg: Herder, 2004.

Zevit, Ziony. *Matres Lectionis in Ancient Hebrew Epigraphs.* Cambridge: American Schools of Oriental Research, 1980.

Zevit, Ziony. "Psalms at the Poetic Precipice." *HAR* 10 (1986): 351–66.

Zim, Rivkah. *English Metrical Psalms: Poetry as Praise and Prayer, 1535–1601.* Cambridge: Cambridge University Press, 1987.

Zimmerli, W. *Ezekiel 2.* Hermeneia. Translated by J. D. Martin. Philadelphia: Fortress, 1983.

Zimmern, H. "Ein Zyklus altsumerischer Lieder auf die Haupttempel Babyloniens." *ZA* 5 (1930): 245–76.

Ziolkowski, Jan. *On Philology.* University Park: Pennsylvania State University Press, 1990.

Zohary, M. *Plants in the Bible.* Cambridge: Cambridge University Press, 1982.

Zumthor, Paul. "The Text and the Voice." *New Literary History* 16 (1984): 67–92.

Zumthor, Paul. *La lettre et la voix: De la "littérature" médiévale.* Vol. 44. Paris: Éditions du Seuil, 1987.

Zumthor, Paul. *Oral Poetry: An Introduction.* Minneapolis: University of Minnesota Press, 1990.

Zweig, Paul. *Walt Whitman: The Making of the Poet.* New York: Basic Books, 1984.

Selective Index of Authors, Primary Sources, and Subjects